Myanmar (Burma) since the 1988 Uprising

The **ISEAS – Yusof Ishak Institute** (formerly Institute of Southeast Asian Studies) is an autonomous organization established in 1968. It is a regional centre dedicated to the study of sociopolitical, security, and economic trends and developments in Southeast Asia and its wider geostrategic and economic environment. The Institute's research programmes are grouped under Regional Economic Studies (RES), Regional Strategic and Political Studies (RSPS), and Regional Social and Cultural Studies (RSCS). The Institute is also home to the ASEAN Studies Centre (ASC), the Singapore APEC Study Centre, and the Temasek History Research Centre (THRC).

ISEAS Publishing, an established academic press, has issued more than 2,000 books and journals. It is the largest scholarly publisher of research about Southeast Asia from within the region. ISEAS Publishing works with many other academic and trade publishers and distributors to disseminate important research and analyses from and about Southeast Asia to the rest of the world.

FOURTH EDITION

Myanmar (Burma) since the 1988 Uprising
A Select Bibliography

ANDREW SELTH

ISEAS YUSOF ISHAK INSTITUTE

First published in Singapore in 2022 by
ISEAS Publishing
30 Heng Mui Keng Terrace
Singapore 119614

Email: publish@iseas.edu.sg
Website: bookshop.iseas.edu.sg

All rights reserved. No part of this publication may be reproduced, stored in a retrieval system, or transmitted in any form or by any means, electronic, mechanical, photocopying, recording or otherwise, without the prior permission of the ISEAS – Yusof Ishak Institute.

© 2022 ISEAS – Yusof Ishak Institute, Singapore

The responsibility for facts and opinions in this publication rests exclusively with the author and his interpretations do not necessarily reflect the views or the policy of the publisher or its supporters.

ISEAS Library Cataloguing-in-Publication Data

Name(s): Selth, Andrew, 1951-, author.
Title: Myanmar (Burma) since the 1988 uprising : a select bibliography / by Andrew Selth.
Description: 4th edition. | Singapore : ISEAS-Yusof Ishak Institute, 2022.
Identifiers: ISBN 9789814951777 (paperback) | ISBN 9789814951784 (pdf)
Subjects: LCSH: Myanmar—History—1988-—Bibliography.
Classification: LCC DS530.65 S46 2022

Cover design by Lee Meng Hui
Photo courtesy of ISEAS Library, ISEAS – Yusof Ishak Institute
Typesetting by Stephen Logan
Printed in Singapore by Mainland Press Pte Ltd

Wisdom is in the literature.
    (Myanmar proverb)

Contents

Foreword by Distinguished
  Professor Emeritus David I.
  Steinberg *xi*
Preface to the Fourth Edition *xvii*
Preface to the Third Edition *xxvii*
Preface to the Second
  Edition *xxxvii*
Acknowledgements *xlvii*
List of Abbreviations *l*
Introduction 1
Protocols and Politics 30

THE BIBLIOGRAPHY
The Country and Its People 41
Guidebooks and Descriptions
  General 44
  Yangon (Rangoon) 46
  Mandalay 47
  Bagan (Pagan) 48
  Other Cities 48
Photography 50
Geography and Geology
  General 54
  Jade and Precious Stones 54

Environment and Natural History
  General 56
  Fauna 57
  Flora 59
Prehistory and Archaeology 61
Travellers' Accounts
  General 64
  Pre–Twentieth Century 64
  Twentieth and Twenty-First
    Centuries 66
History
  General 71
  Pre–Twentieth Century 73
  Twentieth and Twenty-First
    Centuries 77
The Second World War
  General 80
  The Fall of Burma 81
  The Land Campaign 82
  The Air War 85
  Naval and Other Maritime
    Operations 87
  Intelligence Organizations and
    Operations 87
  Prisoners of War and the Thailand–
    Burma Railway 88

Autobiographies, Biographies and
   Memoirs
   Colonial Era (1824–1947)   90
   Second World War (1939–45)   94
   *Post-Independence Period
      (1948–87)*   97
   *The Modern Period
      (1988–2021)*   99
Aung San Suu Kyi
   Works by Aung San Suu Kyi   102
   *Works about Aung San Suu
      Kyi*   103
Population and Ethnic Minorities
   Population   106
   Ethnic Minorities – General   108
   The Kayin (Karen)   110
   The Kachin   111
   The Shan   112
   The Mon   113
   *The Zo (Chin/Lushai/Mizo/Kuki)
      Group*   114
   The Naga   115
   The Kayah (Karenni)   115
   The Wa   116
   Other Ethnic Groups   116
The "Rohingya Question"
   Official Reports   119
   Other Publications   120
Languages
   General   126
   Dictionaries and Phrasebooks   127
   Instructional Works   128
Religions, Religious Communities
   and Religious Sites
   General   130
   Buddhism   130
   Islam   135
   Christianity   136
   *Other Faiths and Belief
      Systems*   137
Society, Education and Health
   Society   139
   Education   143
   Health   143
Women   145

Publishing and Mass Media   148
Narcotics   150
Migrants, Refugees and Displaced
   People
   General   153
   *Migrants and Migrant
      Workers*   154
   Refugees   155
   Displaced People   157
Human Rights
   General   159
   Political Prisoners   163
   Forced Labour   165
   Human Rights Yearbooks   165
Politics and Government
   Official Publications   167
   *The SLORC/SPDC Period
      (1988–2010)*   169
   *The Thein Sein Era
      (2011–15)*   176
   *The First NLD Administration
      (2016–20)*   179
   *The Second NLD Administration
      and State Administration Council
      (2021–)*   183
   *International Crisis Group
      Publications*   183
International Aid
   General   185
   Multilateral Aid   186
   Bilateral Aid   187
Foreign Relations
   General   188
   Multilateral Relations   190
   Bilateral Relations   192
Defence and National Security
   General   197
   *Specific Conflicts and Armed
      Groups*   201
   The Armed Forces   202
   Child Soldiers   204
   Landmines   205
   The Police Forces   205
   Intelligence Issues   206

Constitutions and Legal Issues
Constitutions 207
Legal Issues 209
Economy 211
Industry, Trade and Finance 217
Transport and
  Communications 221
Agriculture, Forestry and
  Fisheries 223
Literature
Criticism and Commentary 235
Myanmar (Burmese)
  Literature 226
Foreign Literature 230
Plays, Poetry and Songs 234
Graphic Books and Cartoon
  Collections 235
Culture, Arts and Crafts
General 237
The Visual Arts 239
The Plastic Arts 240
The Performing Arts 242
Sport, Recreation and Hobbies
Sport 244
Philately 244
Numismatics 246
Other Interests 246
Cuisine 247
Bibliographies and Research
  Guides 249

APPENDIX 1: Myanmar: A
  Reading Guide
Introduction 252
A Guide to Sources 253

APPENDIX 2: Maps and Charts
  of Myanmar 310
General 314
City Maps 315
Historical and Specialist
  Maps 316
Nautical Charts 317

APPENDIX 3: English
  Language Films about Myanmar
  (Burma) 322
Feature Films 323
Short Films and
  Documentaries 325

APPENDIX 4: Western
  Music with Burmese Themes,
  1824–1948 331
The Early Period (1824–89) 332
Kipling's "Mandalay" and After
  (1890–1939) 333
The War Years and After
  (1940–48) 341

Index of Names 345
About the Author 369

Foreword

The indefatigable Andrew Selth, fresh from his seemingly myriad major studies, chapters, research papers, intellectual excursions (see his Kipling and Western music piece),[1] blogs and op-eds,[2] has demonstrated once again his catholic knowledge and his capacity for care and detail related to Burma/Myanmar. This new edition of his bibliography, which should become an essential reference for those even minimally concerned with Burma/Myanmar, is path-breaking, and is a critical guide to those both figuratively and literally Burma bound, as were his earlier editions and his work on the state of Burmese studies.[3]

The publication of this fourth edition of the bibliography is especially timely. The state entered a new incarnation after the elections of 2015, following fifty years of direct and indirect military control, including its "civilianized" form from 2011. This process continued with the elections held in 2020 but has been interrupted by the February 2021 coup. Before the military takeover, foreign-imposed sanctions had largely been suspended or lifted, the iconic Nobel laureate Aung San Suu Kyi was an established part of public political life, international businesses were seeking Burmese opportunities, tourism had exploded, and violence continued in ethnic areas. It remains to be seen what now follows, but either way these and other developments will no doubt spur new publications, both ephemeral and more lasting, about aspects of Burma/Myanmar. Yet it is essential for those seriously concerned, and even those touristically inclined, to understand what has gone before if they are to comprehend the present, which is never written *de novo*. This bibliography, then, offers a Virgilian guide to Myanmar's recent past, and is an essential reference component for both the interested traveller and the dedicated student or specialist.

Burma/Myanmar formerly has been simplistically characterized as isolated and unknown. This may have been comparatively true for a quarter of a century following the coup of 1962, but has been inaccurate for the past few generations. In spite of direct rule by junta from 1988 under a regime that was noted worldwide for its repression and human rights violations, the state, known since 2011 as the Republic of the Union of Myanmar, attracted more academic and political interest than might have been imagined from a country previously insulated from much of the West. From the essentially isolationist policies of the Burma Socialist Programme Party (BSPP) under General Ne Win (1962–88), Myanmar (the name was changed in 1989) began to attract both international media attention and academic concern. In part, this was due to some changes in policy, such as the opening to foreign investment, but perhaps more importantly to the image of Nobel laureate Aung San Suu Kyi, who soon became the international icon of democracy, and whose example and appeal attracted many to enter the field of Burma studies and/or work on the Thai frontier among Burmese refugees. She personally seemed to exemplify the raised international concerns over human rights issues in that country. Her further leadership role in the elections of 2015 and 2020 and the positive expectations of the following government were juxtaposed by continuing violence and abuses in the country's northern reaches and in the militarization of communal conflict in the Rakhine State on the Bangladesh border. At the time of writing, she is once again under house arrest, at the mercy of a military regime.

This bibliography, then, reflects that new era—now past but quintessentially relevant to the present. Scholarship on Burma after the coup of 1962 essentially dried up, as few scholars were admitted for fieldwork, and then only in a few academic "safe" fields. Responsible professors could not advocate dissertation research on a country in which fieldwork was impossible. Tourism was discouraged and internal travel limited. With the quiet opening of Burma after the coup of 18 September 1988, and in spite of the bloody repression of the failed "people's revolution" earlier that spring and summer, growth in interest in Burma/Myanmar became evident.

This was reflected in both the human rights/democracy advocacy literature, which proliferated especially along the Thai border with Myanmar, and the stirring of disciplinary academic research and quiet fieldwork in-country. Scholars were allowed in, often with tourist visas. We now have a new generation of scholars and published scholarly works in all disciplines. Some reflect internal conditions; others compare, and draw lessons from, the Myanmar experience with other countries. Especially important have been the contributions of expatriate Burmese scholars who have markedly enhanced study of their country from perspectives that foreigners lack.

The importance of foreign scholarly research on Myanmar is especially salient if one understands the past stringent controls over research and publishing for those within the country. Until 1988, all internal research (even in science and medicine) by anyone employed by the state (which meant all academicians) was considered classified until presented at a state-sponsored research seminar and then formally approved for public dissemination. Since 1988, any research publications have had to meet the mercurial conditions of the official censorship board. History was reinterpreted and rewritten to emphasize the roles of the Myanmar military, and even when classic works were republished, their titles had to change "Burma" into "Myanmar", a name that was pursued with intense vigour. For example, *The Glass Palace Chronicle of the Kings of Burma* was published originally in 1923, but in 2008 was republished as *The Glass Palace Chronicle of the Kings of Myanmar*.[4] All publications had to list the military-sponsored state objectives.[5]

Burmese expatriates writing abroad, often with family in-country, often had to be circumspect in their analyses, and ardent critics of the regime sometimes neglected balanced reporting. Most books on Burma/Myanmar published abroad were legally banned from Myanmar, but increased travel and new technology enabled the surreptitious import and distribution of many. Now, works of all calibre and persuasion are available in the country's bookstores. With a decline in the easy capacity to read the English of academic treatises, a need for the translation of important works into Burmese has become evident as present trends since 2011 in relaxation of censorship continue. A number of seminal foreign studies have been translated—some under international copyright rules and others pirated.

Internal events have been the especial salience of foreign publications on Myanmar since 1988. These works have proliferated and have provided welcome analyses of internal dynamics and external relations. Conditions within Myanmar, however, resulted in the polarization of external opinions on whether to engage with, and if so how, the regime in Yangon and then Naypyidaw. Advocacy literature on all sides of the issue expanded, often based on anecdotal evidence, since few trustworthy statistics emanated from the government. And, as Professor Donald Emmerson once noted, "the plural of anecdote is not data".[6] Political liberalization has eased this gap, although Myanmar continues to invite strong opinions that often colour scholarship. The February 2021 coup will doubtless reinforce such trends.

Dr Selth, in his introduction, provides a fascinating and thorough account of the various previous attempts to engage in bibliographic work, and even specialists on Burma/Myanmar may not have been aware of some of these important contributions to the literature. His is also a service to the field. His professional background in the Foreign Service and security arena, as well as being an Australian, has demonstrated that personal history in this case is an asset, rather than a liability, in preparation of this bibliography. This has meant that Dr Selth has filled a lacuna often present in many bibliographies. As an Australian, his emphasis on works emanating from that country fills a void because, of all Western states, the Australian government and academic community has shown the most continuous and supportive roles in analysing Burma/Myanmar. The worldwide audience for serious study of that country needs to recognize this contribution.

There remain gaps needing analysis, and these are demonstrated by gaps in the bibliography, but as Burma/Myanmar continues to attract attention, they likely will be filled. In recent years, major studies of Myanmar's relations with China and the United States have appeared, but bilateral ties between Myanmar and Russia still need exploration, as do those between Burma and each or both of the Koreas.[7] A comprehensive study of Christianity in its sociopolitical setting is also needed. Dr Selth has wisely avoided including works in preparation on some of these issues, for the time disparities between research and publication may be extensive. Yet the increase in those enrolled in advanced programmes on Burma/Myanmar and those with experience in and on that country will no doubt begin the fill the void.

A corollary of the relative isolation of Burma/Myanmar, its notoriety in the narcotics literature, its strategic location, its long and porous border with Thailand, and its ostensible "exoticism" have all given rise to a variety of both serious literature and the pulp fiction inhabiting airport book kiosks. The last item may be dismissed, but the fiction field should not be ignored either by the serious scholar or the ardent traveller.

Dr Selth has expanded the section in the bibliography on the Rohingya (the Muslim community on the Bangladesh border), as their treatment at the hands of the Myanmar security forces in 2016 and 2017, and the question of their continuing safety, has prompted worldwide concerns. Their plight has also damaged the international reputations of the state and Aung San Suu Kyi, and resulted in an increased flow of publications.

Scholarship and analyses obviously need personal commitments, but they also need institutional bases. Although a variety of international academic institutions and some research organizations teach on and/or conduct research about Burma/Myanmar, their focus is usually Southeast Asia or Asia more broadly interpreted. There is a paucity of international educational institutions solely devoted to that country. There is one in the United States (Northern Illinois University), one in China (Yunnan National University), one in India (Manipur University), one in Thailand (Naresuan University) and two in Australia (the Australian National University and Melbourne University). The small number of such centres may limit future scholarship, and inadequate analyses could adversely affect policy choices. Universities also now tend to focus on disciplinary studies rather than on area research, which limits university employment opportunities for some Burmanically inclined. Two decades ago, a meeting on Burma/Myanmar attended by representatives of most ASEAN governments at that time needed to draw on Western specialists on that country because those in the ASEAN states had no such analytical capacity. That situation has begun to be rectified, but clearly the ASEAN states and their neighbours need to expand their sights.

Griffith University, the publisher of three earlier editions of this bibliography and Dr Selth's academic home since 2006, is to be congratulated for its interest in opening vistas on Burma/Myanmar. More than two decades ago, it sponsored a major international conference on Myanmar, attended in part by the Australian minister for foreign affairs and trade.[8] Since then, especially in the last decade, the steady stream of papers on public policy issues has added significantly to our understanding of that country and its relations with the region.

The serious student, the professional journalist, the potential investor, the policy advocate, and even the prospective traveller to Myanmar will welcome this publication. It is an important contribution to the burgeoning interest in Myanmar, and we are all once again, and in so many ways, in Dr Andrew Selth's debt.

> David I. Steinberg
> Distinguished Professor Emeritus of Asian Studies
> School of Foreign Service, Georgetown University
> Washington DC
> March 2021

Notes

1. Andrew Selth, *Burma, Kipling and Western Music: The Riff from Mandalay* (New York: Routledge, 2017).
2. Andrew Selth, *Interpreting Myanmar: A Decade of Analysis* (Canberra: Australian National University Press, 2020).
3. Andrew Selth, "Modern Burma Studies: A Survey of the Field", *Modern Asian Studies* 44, no. 2 (March 2010), pp. 401–40.
4. *The Glass Palace Chronicle of the Kings of Burma*, translated by Pe Maung Tin and G.H. Luce (London: Humphrey Milford [Oxford University Press], 1923); and *The Glass Palace Chronicle of the Kings of Myanmar*, translated by Pe Maung Tin and G.H. Luce (Yangon: Unity Publishing House, 2008).
5. There were four political objectives, four economic objectives and four social objectives. In addition, there were "Three Main National Causes", which were: "Non-disintegration of the Union, Non-disintegration of National Solidarity and Perpetuation of Sovereignty".
6. This comment was made at a workshop on Burma arranged by the Konrad Adenauer Foundation and held in Washington DC in October 2009.
7. See D.I. Steinberg and Hongwei Fan, *Modern China-Myanmar Relations: Dilemmas of Mutual Dependence* (Copenhagen: NIAS Press, 2012); and Kenton Clymer, *A Delicate Relationship: The United States and Burma/Myanmar since 1945* (Ithaca: Cornell University Press, 2015).
8. See "The Situation in Burma and Australia's Response", Opening Address by Senator the Hon. Gareth Evans QC, Minister for Foreign Affairs and Trade, to the International Seminar on Burma, Griffith University, Brisbane, 3 December 1992, http://www.gevans.org/speeches/old/1992/031292_fm_Burma.pdf.

Preface to the Fourth Edition

Thirty-five years ago, Myanmar (or Burma, as it was called back then) was little known and even less understood. It rarely featured in the international news media and few governments and international organizations devoted significant resources to monitoring its myriad problems. The small number of foreign scholars who studied and wrote about the country could only rely on a select audience for an appreciation of their published product.[1] All that changed in 1988, when a nationwide pro-democracy uprising in Myanmar demanded that the world pay it more attention. Almost overnight, there was a strong demand for articles and books that explained what was happening in the country, and why. A selection of such works was listed in the first edition of this bibliography, compiled in 2012, but since then the number of publications about Myanmar has grown exponentially. There are now hundreds, if not thousands, of foreign officials, scholars, journalists, students, tourists and others, both professionals and amateurs, writing about this fascinating but still deeply troubled Southeast Asian country.

As a result, there have been major changes to the publishing environment as it has related to Myanmar, both outside the country and inside it. Some of these developments were briefly noted in the prefaces written for the second and third editions of this bibliography, which were compiled in 2015 and 2018 respectively. Many of the trends identified in those works have evolved over the past few years as Myanmar has continued to undergo profound political, social and economic changes. The most recent development has been the military coup of 1 February 2021 and creation of a new State Administration Council (SAC) led by the Commander-in-Chief of Defence Services. For these and other reasons, not least several serious outbreaks of communal unrest and numerous examples of human rights abuses, Myanmar has remained the focus of international attention. Books, reports and other monographs about it (and of course articles of various kinds, although they are not included in this checklist) have continued to appear, mainly in the English-speaking world but elsewhere as well.

Among the many works published since the third edition of this bibliography was released, three genres in particular have dominated the academic and popular literature.

The first includes publications of all kinds about Myanmar's seemingly intractable problems, as the National League for Democracy (NLD), which first took office in 2016, struggled to give substance to the ambitious policies announced, and fulfil the bold promises made, by its leader, State Counsellor Aung San Suu Kyi.[2] There are now numerous works that attempt to describe Myanmar's complex challenges. Many recommend ways to overcome them, although few seem likely to be successful. The NLD's emphatic victory in the November 2020 elections and the subsequent military coup will doubtless prompt another spate of analysis and opinion. Also, to an even greater extent than before, studies of broader issues and aspects of the region are including references to Myanmar not only as a member of the Association of Southeast Asian Nations (ASEAN) but also as an important factor in its own right.[3]

Another category of publications that has made its mark since 2018 relates to the status and treatment given to the predominantly Muslim ethnic group known as the Rohingyas.[4] Pogroms against this group by Myanmar's security forces in 2012, 2016 and 2017 saw about three quarters of a million refugees flee to Bangladesh, to join about 250,000 Rohingyas already living in squalid camps there. As a result of these developments, there has been a flood of official reports, academic studies, commentaries, diatribes and other works about this community, their history and current plight. Out of the 120 books on the Goodreads' Burma/Myanmar list in early 2020, for example, a full quarter was on the Rohingyas.[5] Also, more than a dozen novels have been published since 2018 that focus on the "Rohingya question", in one way or another.[6] The human rights abuses associated with the pogroms also encouraged a range of works that examined related issues such as the political role of the armed forces (known as the *Tatmadaw*) in Myanmar and the Aung San Suu Kyi government's policies on broader ethnic and religious matters.

The third noteworthy trend since 2018 has been the continued production of books written by or aimed at foreign visitors to Myanmar (over four million in 2019) and foreigners who had taken up temporary residence.[7] These include tourist guides, phrase books, travelogues, memoirs and collections of photographs. Of the thirty most popular works about Myanmar sold on the Book Depository's website in 2020, for example, more than half fitted into this broad category.[8] Some of these works are rather shallow and peddle questionable notions about daily life in Myanmar, but others are well considered and shed fresh light on underappreciated aspects of the country and its people.[9] A few travellers have described visits to places rarely seen by tourists. Most collections of photographs focus on the usual clichéd subjects, but some have taken an original approach and a number demonstrate real artistic flair. There has also been a range of new maps produced, mainly to assist those visitors and armchair travellers who wish to orient themselves on paper or to stray from the beaten track.

Inside Myanmar, the book market has become more vibrant, sophisticated and better connected with the outside world.[10] There are now some 1,900 small book publishers in the country, although only a few dozen produce more than twenty titles a year. Some firms only release a couple of works annually.[11] In Yangon, there are now about twenty-five independent bookstores, with the number in other major population centres gradually increasing. Most sell at least a small number of books in foreign languages (usually English), which have proven quite popular.[12] Many of the small regional outlets that used to lend or rent books to the general public are now selling cheap editions to an expanding readership. (According to UNESCO, the adult literacy rate in Myanmar is now above seventy-five per cent).[13] There are also the ubiquitous and often surprisingly well-stocked street stalls in population centres like Yangon and Mandalay.[14] In 2019, an international firm specializing in discounted and remaindered books staged a book fair in Yangon that was well-attended.[15] The national telecommunications carrier MPT has launched an e-book service for local subscribers and it is now possible to buy books on memory sticks.[16]

On the downside, the demand for books in Myanmar still fluctuates strongly. Also, the market is subject to unexpected interventions from both local authorities and the national government. Despite undertakings by the NLD to relax various restrictions endured under the former military regime, there were some unwelcome signs of a return to the censorship and restrictions on freedom of speech that marked the bad old days.[17] If the freedoms permitted by the Thein Sein administration between 2012 and 2015 survive, despite the latest coup, including the ability to import books from abroad, the outlook for the reading public in Myanmar seems a reasonably positive one. That said, foreign authors and publishers continue to bemoan the lack of effective copyright laws in Myanmar and the publication of cheap pirate editions. Some unauthorized translations of foreign books have been so poorly executed, or possibly even deliberately distorted, that they have grossly misrepresented the original text, and thus the authors' views.[18] The artwork on the covers of some of these pirate editions has also been very misleading.[19]

All bibliographies are works in progress, and this one is no exception. It is the fourth edition of the book to be released. The first was published by the Griffith Asia Institute (GAI) at Griffith University in Australia, in 2012. Described as a "select bibliography", it listed 928 representative works that had been published in English, and in hard copy, since the abortive 1988 uprising. A second edition of the book, listing 1,318 titles, was produced by the GAI in 2015, and a third edition was released in 2018. By that time, the bibliography was much more comprehensive, listing 2,133 books, reports and other monographs, divided among thirty-five subject chapters and seventy-two sections. There were also three appendices. One appendix was an essay discussing a selection of books to read before going to Myanmar for the first time, another appendix listed feature and documentary films made about the country and a third offered an eclectic selection of maps available to scholars, tourists and armchair travellers. All three editions of the bibliography were made freely available online and a small number of each was printed in hard copy.

Not long after the third edition of the bibliography was released, a tentative decision was made not to produce a fourth. There were several reasons for this.

First, there was the problem that John Badgley once called "inflation in the quantity of publications".[20] The sheer number of works on Myanmar now being published made the task of keeping track of them all very difficult. It required a major effort to monitor publishers' catalogues, booksellers' websites, academic fora and other sources to keep abreast of all the new productions, assess their value and to choose titles that might be suitable for inclusion in the checklist. This problem was compounded by the large number of reports and other studies now being produced by government and non-government organizations of various kinds as the international community continued to examine Myanmar's myriad problems and, in many cases, recommend practical (and, in some cases, impractical) solutions.[21] This problem was not diminished by the fact that the bibliography was a select one only, did not aim to include everything in print about the country, and was in any case restricted to hard copies published in English.

Second, the range of subjects being covered by Myanmar-related publications has continued to expand, adding to the difficulty of monitoring the output of new materials. When the first edition of the bibliography was being compiled, most published works were written by a relatively small number of scholars in English-speaking countries who were mainly interested in broad topics like Myanmar's national politics, its economic problems and traditional society. There are still some notable gaps in the literature, but in recent years many have been filled.[22] There are now thousands of books, reports and monographs about different aspects of Myanmar, written or compiled by governments, multilateral institutions, activist organizations, scholars, journalists, tourists, travellers, and freelance authors of various kinds. Many of these new works are on subjects that, prior to 1988, had never been examined before, at least not in any depth. An increasing number stem from postgraduate studies and are highly specialized. Other works are currently in preparation or in press.[23]

Third, and perhaps most importantly, the quality of the publications about Myanmar now on the market is highly variable. There are many excellent studies that make major contributions to the literature and to current policy debates. Other works, including some intended for the mass market, are also deserving of praise. However, there are books available now that are of questionable value, in one way or another. Some purportedly serious studies do not meet the basic criteria used to judge scholarly works. Other books must be considered polemics advocating partisan views, or simply as political tracts.[24] Many memoirs written by foreigners about their time in Myanmar have been described as trite and self-indulgent, if not worse.[25] For example, as David Scott Mathieson has noted in characteristic fashion, Myanmar has produced "a minor canon of self-promotional reportage".[26] A number of foreign novels set in Myanmar barely qualify to be included in the definition of literature.[27]

All these issues added weight to the argument that an annotated bibliography, with short descriptions and judicious comments about each work listed, perhaps along the lines of Patricia Herbert's 1991 volume, would be more helpful to readers and researchers than another long checklist of titles.[28]

All that considered, it was decided to go ahead and produce a fourth edition of the bibliography, and to keep to the same broad format as before. This was largely in response to popular demand for an updated version, mainly from academic observers and professional pundits, but also from general readers and armchair travellers. Happily, the bibliography has also proven itself to be of value to students of Myanmar looking for a starting point for their research, or to follow up particular issues of interest. Feedback from the official community has also been positive. Given the book's growing size and coverage, however, it was felt that hard copy production and particularly international distribution of the new edition would be more easily managed by an established academic publishing house with wide experience in such matters. Hence, the baton has been passed from the Griffith Asia Institute to the ISEAS – Yusof Ishak Institute in Singapore.

This version of the bibliography follows the pattern established by the three earlier editions, with a few minor changes. Once again, it lists a selection of works on or about Myanmar published in English and in hard copy since the 1988 uprising, which marked the beginning of a new era in Myanmar history. The thinking behind the book's layout and particular choices made regarding its presentation is explained in the introduction. It has also been touched upon in the prefaces to the third and second editions, which have been reproduced in their entirety below. There are now 2,727 works listed. They have been written, edited, translated or compiled by over 2,000 people, whose names are listed in an index at the end of the book. These works have been organized into thirty-five chapters containing ninety-five discrete sections. There are now four appendices, the latest addition being a list of 184 musical works produced during the colonial era (1824–1948) which reference Myanmar in some way. This list first appeared in my 2017 book *Burma, Kipling and Western Music*, but a revised version is reproduced here for convenience.[29]

A number of other changes have been made to bring this edition up to date. The title has been amended to reflect modern practice, "Myanmar" now being widely accepted as the country's formal name. The introduction has been revised, mainly to include references to several bibliographers and bibliographical works that escaped mention in the first three editions. Also, David Steinberg has updated his foreword, and the acknowledgements page now better reflects all the suggestions and advice I have received since the first edition of the bibliography was released nearly a decade ago. This edition also includes a few titles that did not make the cut in earlier iterations. For example, it lists more self-published works and books by vanity publishers. Despite their various shortcomings, some make useful contributions to the field of Myanmar studies or fill gaps in the bibliography's broader coverage. Finally, the first three appendices have been revised and expanded. All these changes have been made in the interests of comprehensiveness, balance and the convenience of readers.

Anyone reading the book from start to finish will notice that, in a few places, notably the prefaces, there is a little repetition. However, this was an unavoidable result of republishing material that had been released over time. Also, a few references have been given in full more than once to permit readers to dip into the book without having to search for earlier notes giving the full details of particular works cited.

Canberra
March 2021

Notes

1. Andrew Selth, "Modern Burma Studies: A Survey of the Field", *Modern Asian Studies* 44, no. 2 (March 2010), pp. 401–40.
2. See, for example, Andrew Selth, *Be Careful What You Wish For: The National League for Democracy and Government in Myanmar*, Regional Outlook no. 56 (Brisbane: Griffith Asia Institute, Griffith University, 2017).
3. See, for example, Su Lin Lewis, *Cities in Motion: Urban Life and Cosmopolitanism in Southeast Asia, 1920–1940* (Cambridge: Cambridge University Press, 2018); and Ludovica Marchi [L.M.Balossi-Restelli], ed., *The European Union and Myanmar: Interactions via ASEAN* (London: Routledge, 2020).
4. For a concise explanation of the contested name "Rohingya", see Jacques P. Leider, "'Rohingya', Rakhaing and the Recent Outbreak of Violence

– A Note", *Bulletin of the Burma Studies Group*, nos. 89–90 (Spring/Fall 2012), pp. 9–11.
5. "Myanmar", Goodreads, https://www.goodreads.com/places/340-myanmar.
6. See Lucas Stewart, "14 Novels on the Rohingya Crisis", *Lucas Stewart*, 4 February 2020, https://sadaik.com/2020/02/04/14-novels-on-the-rohingya-crisis/.
7. Despite some reports, this number included all international arrivals, not just tourists. See "Myanmar Receives over 4 Mln Foreign Tourists in 2019", Xinhua, 29 January 2020, http://www.xinhuanet.com/english/2020–01/29/c_138741404.htm#:~:text=29%20(Xinhua)%20%2D%2D%20Myanmar%20received,in%20Myanmar%2C%20the%20ministry%20said.
8. "Myanmar: Most popular", Book Depository, https://www.bookdepository.com/search?searchTerm=myanmar&search=Find+book.
9. Some of these books are now available in digital form. See, for example, David Bockino, *Greetings from Myanmar: Exploring the Price of Progress in One of the Last Countries on Earth to Open for Business* (AmazonDigital Services, 2016), https://www.amazon.com/Greetings-Myanmar-Exploring-Progress-Countries-ebook/dp/B01GQU43PK.
10. On the local book scene, see for example Sebastian Strangio, "Reading Burma", *Los Angeles Review of Books*, 2 January 2017, http://www.sebastianstrangio.com/2017/01/02/reading-burma/.
11. Claudia Kaiser, "Book Publishing Market Overview: Myanmar's Challenges and Potential", *Publishing Perspectives*, 12 December 2016, https://publishingperspectives.com/2016/12/book-publishing-market-overview-myanmar/.
12. Mark Williams, "While Myanmar Bookstores Struggle, Street Bookstores and English-language Bookstores Thrive", Publishing Brief, *TNPS: The New Publishing Standard*, 15 December 2017, https://thenewpublishingstandard.com/while-myanmar-bookstores-struggle-street-bookstores-and-english-language-bookstores-thrive/. See also Zon Pann Pwint, "Super bookworm", *Myanmar Times*, 15 December 2017, https://www.mmtimes.com/news/super-bookworm.html.
13. "Myanmar", UNESCO, http://uis.unesco.org/country/MM. This is still a lower rate than in 1983. See "Myanmar Literacy Rate, 1983–2021", Macrotrends, https://www.macrotrends.net/countries/MMR/myanmar/literacy-rate.
14. David Scott Mathieson, "The Insouciance of the Downtown Rangoon Book Scene", *Tea Circle*, 17 September 2018, https://teacircleoxford.com/2018/09/17/the-insouciance-of-the-downtown-rangoon-book-scene/#more–3342.
15. Yuichi Nitta, "Affordable English-Language Bookseller Arrives in Myanmar", *Nikkei Asian Review*, 7 February 2019, https://asia.nikkei.com/Business/Business-Trends/Affordable-English-language-bookseller-arrives-in-Myanmar.

16. Mark Williams, "With an Online Population Bigger than the Netherlands, Myanmar Gets Its First National Ebook Store with Telco MPT", Publishing Brief, *TNPS: The New Publishing Standard*, 7 November 2018, https://thenewpublishingstandard.com/online-population-bigger-netherlands-myanmar-gets-first-national-ebook-store-telco-mpt/.
17. See, for example, Subir Bhaumik, "A Once Closed Space Opens in Myanmar", *Asia Times*, 19 November 2017, https://asiatimes.com/2017/11/closed-space-opens-myanmar/.
18. See, for example, Mandy Sadan, "Knowledge, Piracy and Academic Development in Myanmar (Part I)", *Tea Circle*, 30 November 2017, https://teacircleoxford.com/2017/11/30/knowledge-piracy-and-academic-development-in-myanmar-part-i/; and Mandy Sadan, "Knowledge, Piracy and Academic Development in Myanmar (Part II)", *Tea Circle*, 1 December 2017, https://teacircleoxford.com/2017/12/01/knowledge-piracy-and-academic-development-in-myanmar-part-ii/. Also relevant is Lucas Stuart, "Wendy Law Yone – Saving Face", *Times Literary Supplement*, 24 April 2018, https://sadaik.com/2018/04/24/wendy-law-yone-saving-face/.
19. An unauthorized translation of Andrew Selth's *Secrets and Power in Myanmar: Intelligence and the Fall of General Khin Nyunt* (Singapore: ISEAS – Yusof Ishak Institute, 2019) was published in Myanmar in 2020. It was sold with a lurid and sensationalist cover, which was completely at odds with the book's content and intended purpose.
20. John Badgley, review of Frank Trager, *Burma: A Selected and Annotated Bibliography* (New Haven: Human Relations Area Files Press, 1973), *American Political Science Review* 69, no. 3 (September 1975), p. 1093.
21. The majority of these works were posted online, but it was assumed that in most cases small numbers of hard copies were prepared and released to select audiences, thus making them eligible for inclusion in the bibliography.
22. One work that promises to fill a major gap is Edward Jarvis, *The Anglican Church in Burma: From Colonial Past to Global Future* (University Park: Pennsylvania State University Press, forthcoming).
23. See, for example, William George, *Ethnic Minorities and Myanmar's Future* (London: Zed Books, forthcoming); Kristina Simion, *Rule of Law Intermediaries: Brokering Influence in Myanmar* (Cambridge: Cambridge University Press, forthcoming); and Rohan Gunaratna et al. (eds), *The Rohingya Crisis* (London: World Scientific Europe, forthcoming). Security specialists are also awaiting the release of a comprehensive recognition guide that is being prepared by Miles Vining to assist in the identification of weapons and military equipment used in and around Myanmar.
24. The debate over the "Rohingya question" has thrown up several books that have been accused of bias, racism or in other ways inaccurate and unbalanced reporting. See, for example, Derek Tonkin, "A Detailed Examination of Misinformation in Dr Azeem Ibrahim's Book *The*

Rohingyas: Inside Myanmar's Hidden Genocide", 1 March 2017, http://www.networkmyanmar.org/ESW/Files/Detailed-Examination-Misinformation-Azeem-Ibrahim.pdf.

25. See, for example, "The Year of Living Degenerately", David Scott Mathieson's review of Peter Olszewski's *Land of a Thousand Eyes: The Subtle Pleasures of Everyday Life in Myanmar* (Sydney: Allen and Unwin, 2005), *The Irrawaddy*, June 2006, https://www2.irrawaddy.com/article.php?art_id=5824.
26. Mathieson describes "a slew of terrible books by faux adventurers" in "One Flew Over the Pigeon's Nest", *The Irrawaddy*, 11 May 2020, https://www.irrawaddy.com/culture/books/one-flew-pigeons-nest.html.
27. For one view, see "The Worst Novel Ever Written about Myanmar", *Late for Nowhere*, 3 February 2014, https://latefornowhere.wordpress.com/tag/worst-books-about-myanmar-burma/.
28. P.M. Herbert, *Burma* (Oxford: Clio Press, 1991).
29. Andrew Selth, *Burma, Kipling and Western Music: The Riff from Mandalay* (London: Routledge, 2017), pp. 230–39.

Preface to the Third Edition

Since the first version of this bibliography was released in 2012, the outpouring of books, reports and other publications about Burma (Myanmar) that was noted in earlier editions has continued. Indeed, over the past few years it seems to have picked up in both pace and range, although not always in quality. As one observer bluntly put it a few years ago, "There is a vast quantity of literature on Burma/Myanmar, some of it quite unreadable".[1] While many of these works have been posted online, and are only available in soft copy, most have been released in hard copy, and in English. Even if the print run was quite small, this has entitled them to a mention in this third and expanded edition. The newest works fall into a number of categories, which can easily be identified by comparing the contents pages above with those of earlier editions. Broadly speaking, they cover academic works, official reports, travelogues and tourist guides, books for the general reader, and older works that have been reprinted to meet a popular demand.

For example, the section on Burma's politics and government continues to grow apace, a result at least in part of the close attention being paid to the country's transition from a military dictatorship to a quasi-democratic administration. The advent of President Thein Sein's reformist government in 2011 and the election of a National League for Democracy (NLD) government in 2015 prompted a surge of publications on the country's rapidly changing political, economic and social landscape. There have also been several new books about Burma's once revered opposition leader, Aung San

Suu Kyi, who is now the country's de facto head of state.[2] Given her government's failure to meet unrealistically high popular expectations, and her dramatic fall from grace in the eyes of the international community (due mainly to her disappointing response to the so-called "Rohingya question"), it can be expected that more publications on the Nobel Peace laureate and her turbulent time in office will appear over the next few years.[3]

Also, as Burma has opened up to foreign aid and investment, there has been an increase in the number of reports by governments, international organizations and consultants interested in Burma's political reforms, economic growth and social development.[4] At the same time, a host of reports have been produced by human rights groups and bodies devoted to other causes, such as environmental protection. Most can be found online, but small numbers of hard copies have usually been produced for governments, donors and other interested parties. Many of these works provide useful summaries of past developments, current situations and future plans. They also enjoy the benefit of being published in a more timely fashion than many academic studies. That said, the increased access now available to Burma-watchers carries certain risks. Closer personal contacts with key players and a greater familiarity with local developments can result in deeper knowledge and more penetrating analyses of complex issues. However, they can also lead to narrower perspectives and a greater tendency towards personal bias.

There has been a marked increase in books written by, and for, foreign visitors to Burma, the number of which rose from some 310,000 in 2010 to nearly three million in 2017.[5] Once again, these works are a mixed bag, reflecting what Penny Edwards has called the "overnight expert syndrome", which has "fed a rapid demand for books on contemporary Myanmar".[6] One noteworthy trend has been the flood of travelogues and memoirs by tourists and temporary residents, on whom Burma has clearly made a strong impression. Many are rather shallow and descriptive, bringing to mind Rudyard Kipling's "Globe-trotter", "who 'does' kingdoms in days and writes books upon them in weeks".[7] In keeping with most memoirs—and current travel brochures—about Burma, they often emphasize nostalgic and romantic themes.[8] This trend is also seen in books of photographs, which tend to consist of clichéd shots of picturesque pagodas, smiling children and colourful ethnic minorities.[9] That said, there are also some notable collections of high quality images that record Burma's traditional culture, natural environment and colonial-era architecture, all of which are under threat.[10]

The number of English language novels about Burma is increasing. Once again, the quality is highly variable.[11] While there are some notable exceptions, the plots tend to be banal and rather predictable, with Burma serving simply as an exotic *locus dramaticus*. Another interesting development has been the publication of several graphic novels about Burma, including a number that look closely at the contemporary political scene. Most are high quality productions, with excellent illustrations, but not all have been listed in the bibliography as their texts are not in English.[12] There has also been an increase in the number of books about Burma intended for juvenile readers. They include introductions to Burma's geography and culture, and illustrated stories based on Burmese folk tales. There are also several short biographies of Aung San Suu Kyi that are aimed at children. Once again, this trend seems to reflect both the increased attention being paid to Burma in Western countries and the much larger number of people prompted to write about the place, for various reasons.

Also worthy of note is the increasing number of references to Burma, and even the inclusion of separate chapters about Burma, in broader studies of the region, and of particular subjects. There was a time when—books about insurgencies in Southeast Asia aside—such wide-ranging surveys usually ignored Burma or only referred to it in passing. For decades, there was neither the interest nor the expertise available to give it closer attention. Even standard textbooks about the region lacked significant Burma-related content.[13] This is no longer the case. For example, Anthony Reid's stimulating new history of Southeast Asia expertly folds critical aspects of Burma into his wider narrative of developments in the region.[14] There is a useful chapter about Burma in *Khaki Capital*, a recent study of the political economy of armed forces in Southeast Asia.[15] *The Everyday Political Economy of Southeast Asia*, published by Cambridge University Press in 2016, includes a chapter on trade union politics in Burma.[16]

As noted in earlier editions of this bibliography, there is a growing number of works written in English, or translated into English, by Burmese authors. Most major bookshops in Yangon now have a few shelves of memoirs, travel books and other works by local writers, doubtless encouraged by the influx of tourists, the easing of restrictions on freedom of expression and, probably, the increased availability of modern printing equipment. These books tend to be produced by boutique publishing houses, and in small numbers, but together they offer new and interesting perspectives on aspects of Burmese politics and history.[17] That said, the field is still quite narrow. One Western scholar visiting Burma wrote in 2015 that "I was surprised at how difficult it was to find translated contemporary literature by Burmese writers".[18] This echoed an earlier comment by the author Wendy Law-Yone, who noted in 2010 that "precious few [books in Burmese—novels especially] have been translated into English".[19] As the following checklist indicates, this situation is gradually improving, as local novelists, poets and artists gain wider recognition. One notable example of this trend is *Burma Storybook*, edited by Petr Lom and others.[20]

All these developments must be counted as positive contributions to the broad field of Burma studies, but another is a cause for concern. It used to be common practice for the personal libraries of major figures in Burma studies to be purchased by institutions. The British Library, Cornell University, the University of Heidelberg and the National Library of Australia, among others, acquired excellent collections of books, manuscripts and ephemera from former officials, academics and others with close connections to Burma.[21] Even before the country became fashionable in the West, there was a wish to preserve its scholarly and literary heritage. Albeit at a slower pace, this practice continued into the 1970s and 1980s. More recently, however, libraries, universities and research institutes seem to be increasingly reluctant to acquire hard copies of books, either to fill gaps in their collections or to keep them up to date. The reasons given for this attitude vary between institutions, but usually start with a lack of funds and insufficient shelf space. It would be a tragedy for Burma studies if existing collections were allowed to decline in value, or significant private libraries were broken up, simply because no institutions were willing or able to give them a home.[22]

This edition of the bibliography, like those published in 2012 and 2015, only lists books, reports and monographs that have been published in English and in hard copy since 1988. For other works, including e-books, online publications, articles and short items, readers will need to look elsewhere. As stated in earlier prefaces, Michael Charney's *Living Bibliography of Burma Studies* was not substantially updated after its 2004 iteration, and was formally closed down in 2012.²³ While in need of increased financial support, the *Online Burma/Myanmar Library* (OB/ML), begun by the Burma Peace Foundation in 2001, is still functioning, thanks to the efforts of the indefatigable David Arnott.²⁴ Its database is organized into more than ninety categories and 3,000 sub-categories. They guide readers to about 35,000 links to individual documents and more than 10,000 websites or multiple documents. These in turn give access to potentially millions of other Burma-related documents.²⁵ Needless to say, the OB/ML includes a great many works not listed here, notably those found only online.

This edition of the bibliography follows much the same pattern as the earlier two. There are, however, a number of changes.

The original title of the bibliography has been retained and, in all new and revised chapters, "Burma" rather than "Myanmar" has been used for the country's name. This does not reflect its formal title, or current usage, even by die-hard critics of the 1989 name change, such as Aung San Suu Kyi.²⁶ However, "Burma" has been retained for this edition, simply for consistency. All titles of books and reports have been cited as they were published, including the use of both "Rangoon" and its 1989 replacement, "Yangon". Some minor amendments have been made to the introduction, and David Steinberg has updated his foreword. The original acknowledgements page has been substantially revised to take account of contributions made by various Burma-watchers since the first edition of the bibliography was published six years ago. Also, a few individual entries carried forward from earlier editions have been amended. This has mainly been to correct errors and account for changed circumstances, such as the publication of new editions.

This is still a "select" bibliography in that it does not try to include all hard copy publications on Burma, or in all languages, but an effort has been made to make it more comprehensive. It now lists quite a number of works that, for various reasons, were left out of earlier editions. This is partly to provide a more rounded picture of Burma, but also to fill out some sections that readers felt were too thin. I have also relaxed my initial firm stance against reprints, books printed on demand and self-published works. The emphasis is still on original works produced by established publishing houses, governments and international organizations. However, an increasing number of older works on Burma are now being reprinted by reputable firms. To exclude them all would deprive readers of some useful sources on key subjects. The same consideration applies to self-published books and works printed on demand, some of which deserve a mention. Pirated copies of foreign works, reprinted in Burma, have not been included.[27]

There are now 2,133 works listed, compared with 928 in the first edition and 1,318 in the second edition. The much larger number has necessitated some structural changes. Instead of the twenty-nine chapters and forty-four sections found in the 2015 edition, there are now thirty-five chapters and seventy-two sections. For example, there are now separate chapters on the Second World War, Aung San Suu Kyi and the "Rohingya Question", to account for the greater number of titles now listed in those categories. The chapter on politics and government is still the longest, and has been divided chronologically. New sections have been created to cover works published when Burma was under the State Law and Order Restoration Council (SLORC) and its nominal successor, the State Peace and Development Council (SPDC), after the paradigm shift from direct military rule to President Thein Sein's "disciplined democracy" in 2011, and since the creation in 2016 of a semi-elected NLD administration under Aung San Suu Kyi. These categories are rather arbitrary in that they ignore the issues covered within each time frame, but it is hoped that such a device will help readers find particular works more easily. Sections have also been added to other chapters to make it easier for readers to find what they are looking for.

When I began this project in 2010, it was my intention personally to inspect, or at least to sight, every work listed in the bibliography, drawing on my own resources and those of the main libraries in Canberra and elsewhere. Given the large number of works cited in this latest edition, however, and the difficulty of accessing hard copies of every one, I have had to modify that aim. However, an effort has still been made to verify each entry, usually by cross-checking the details in more than one source. In the first edition, I was also determined to exclude works that were listed in publishers' catalogues and on the websites of the major booksellers but had not yet been published. That resolution was slightly relaxed in the second edition, as I was keen to include a number of important works that I was reliably informed were close to commercial release. I have taken a similar approach here, although a few books currently listed on major websites have not been included because of uncertainty over their publication dates.[28]

There are now three appendices. The first is a revised and updated essay on publications that readers may find helpful if they wish to become more familiar with specific aspects of Burma, or if they are going there for the first time. Once again, it is a personal selection and would profitably be read in conjunction with the recommendations of other Burma-watchers with particular areas of expertise.[29] The second appendix lists a range of maps and charts of Burma that are currently available either through commercial outlets or from other suppliers. If the websites of major booksellers are any guide, the demand for maps has grown significantly in recent years as more people have visited Burma, either for business or pleasure.[30] The third appendix lists a selection of feature movies and documentary films made about the country and released in English. Some have had a greater impact than others, but in their own ways they have all added to the romance, mystery and allure of a country that, until thirty years ago, was relatively unknown.[31] The extent to which they have added to a greater understanding of Burma's history, politics and culture, however, is debateable.

It is perhaps worth repeating that the main aim of this checklist is to provide academics, officials, students and members of the general public with an easily accessible list of works on Burma produced in hard copy, and in English, since the 1988 uprising. It includes a wide range of publications, covering many subjects, in an attempt to provide readers with the broadest choice possible. However, the inclusion of a particular work does not signify an endorsement of it or agreement with any of the opinions expressed in it. Once again, the watchwords of this checklist have been comprehensiveness and balance. No attempt has been made to exclude a work because of its perceived failure to meet criteria such as quality or political correctness. As Paul Duguid once remarked, albeit in a different context, an eclectic collection like this resembles "a church jumble-sale bookstall, where gems and duds are blessed alike by the vicar because all have been donated".[32] As always, it is for the reader to decide on the quality and value of each title.

Brisbane
May 2018

Notes

1. Richard Cockett, *Blood, Dreams and Gold: The Changing Face of Burma* (New Haven: Yale University Press, 2015), p. 259.
2. Under the terms of the 2008 constitution, she is unable to become president of the country. See Andrew Selth, *Aung San Suu Kyi and the*

Politics of Personality, Regional Outlook no. 55 (Brisbane: Griffith Asia Institute, Griffith University, 2017).

3. Already in the publishing pipeline are Hans-Bernd Zollner and Rodion Ebbighausen, *The Daughter: A Political Biography of Aung San Suu Kyi* (Chiang Mai: Silkworm Books, 2018); and Poppy Macpherson, *The Shadows of Myanmar: Aung San Suu Kyi and the Persecution of the Rohingya* (London: I.B. Taurus, forthcoming).

4. See, for example, "Myanmar Governance Discussion Paper Series", *The Asia Foundation*, https://asiafoundation.org/tag/myanmar-governance-discussion-paper-series; and "Myanmar: Publications and Documents", *Asian Development Bank*, https://www.adb.org/countries/myanmar/publications.

5. Htoo Thant, "Tourist Arrivals Rise 22pc in 8 Months", *Myanmar Times*, 10 October 2017, https://www.mmtimes.com/news/tourist-arrivals-rise-22pc-8-months.html.

6. Penny Edwards, "Truth to Power", *Mekong Review* 1, no. 4 (August–October 2016), p. 9.

7. Rudyard Kipling, *From Sea to Sea and Other Sketches: Letters of Travel* (New York: Doubleday, Page, 1909), p. 3.

8. For an interesting discussion of this phenomenon, see Debbie Lisle, *The Global Politics of Contemporary Travel Writing* (Cambridge: Cambridge University Press, 2006), pp. 204–7.

9. Steven Heller, "Isolated from the World for Sixty Years", *The Atlantic*, 6 April 2015, https://www.theatlantic.com/entertainment/archive/2015/04/a-rare-glimpse-into-burma/390567/.

10. See, for example, David Lazar, *Myanmar: Luminous Journey* (Bangkok: The author, 2016); and P.J. Heijmans, *Relics of Rangoon* (Yangon: Inya Media, 2016).

11. See Kyi May Kaung and John Feffer, "Out of Burma", *Foreign Policy in Focus*, 11 July 2007, http://fpif.org/out_of_burma/.

12. Most have been produced by French and Belgian publishers. For a brief discussion of this genre, see Andrew Selth, "Graphic Novels Chart Myanmar's History", *Nikkei Asian Review*, 1 April 2018, https://asia.nikkei.com/Life-Arts/Arts/Graphic-novels-chart-Myanmar-s-history?page=1.

13. For example, the six-man writing team responsible for the first edition of the joint volume *In Search of Southeast Asia: A Modern History* (Sydney: Allen and Unwin, 1971) did not include a Burma expert. This was rectified for the second (1987) edition by the recruitment of Robert H. Taylor.

14. Anthony Reid, *A History of Southeast Asia: Critical Crossroads* (Chichester: Wiley Blackwell, 2015).

15. Marco Bunte, "The Military-NLD Coalition in Myanmar: Military Guardianship and its Economic Foundations", in Paul Chambers and Napisa Waitoolkiat (eds.), *Khaki Capital: The Political Economy of the Military in Southeast Asia* (Copenhagen: NIAS Press, 2017).

16. Nicholas Henry, "Everyday Agents of Change: Trade Unions in Myanmar", in Juanita Elias and Lena Rethel (eds.), *The Everyday Political Economy of Southeast Asia* (Cambridge: Cambridge University Press, 2016).
17. See, for example, Thant Thaw Kaung, "Publication Trends in Myanmar and Reading Promotion Efforts", presentation given at the School of Culture, History and Language, College of Asia and the Pacific, Australian National University, Canberra, 28 February 2017.
18. Ellen Wiles, *Saffron Shadows and Salvaged Scripts: Literary Life in Myanmar under Censorship and in Transition* (New York: Columbia University Press, 2015), pp. 2–3.
19. "The Best Books on Her Own Burma", recommended by Wendy Law-Yone, *Five Books*, 1 December 2010, https://fivebooks.com/best-books/wendy-law-yone-on-her-own-burma/.
20. Petr Lom et al. (eds.), *Burma Storybook*, introduction by Emma Larkin, translations by Maung Tha Noe, Maung Day, Zeyar Lynn, Pandora, Kenneth Wong, Zaw Tun and Khun Cho, photographs by Dana Lixenberg (Amsterdam: ZINdoc: 2017). See also Melis Alemdar, "Petr Lom's 'Burma Storybook' Captures Poetry on Film", *TRT World*, 15 May 2017, https://www.trtworld.com/magazine/petr-lom-s-burma-storybook-captures-poetry-on-film-7035.
21. See, for example, Patricia Herbert, "The Making of a Collection: Burmese Manuscripts in the British Library", *British Library Journal* 15, no. 1 (Spring 1989), pp. 59–70, https://www.bl.uk/eblj/1989articles/pdf/article5.pdf; and Andrew Gosling, "Burma and Beyond", *National Library of Australia News*, October 1996, pp. 3–5, http://pandora.nla.gov.au/pan/131760/20120120–0944/www.nla.gov.au/pub/nlanews/1996/oct96/story–1.pdf.
22. For a brief discussion of this problem, see Andrew Selth, "The Wisdom in the Literature", *New Mandala*, 21 March 2017, http://www.newmandala.org/the-wisdom-in-the-literature/.
23. M.W. Charney, "The Bibliography of Burma (Myanmar) Research: The Secondary Literature (2004 Revision)", *SOAS Bulletin of Burma Research*, Bibliographic Supplement (Winter 2004), http://eprints.soas.ac.uk/6241/1/Bibliography_of_secondary_literature--2004.pdf.
24. "Online Burma/Myanmar Library", http://www.burmalibrary.org/. See also M.D. Alicias, "Online Burma/Myanmar Library: A Gateway to Burma/Myanmar", *Asian Politics and Policy* 4, no. 4 (October 2012), pp. 591–93.
25. The library is an invaluable resource but relies on donations to survive. Anyone wishing to assist can contact David Arnott by email at burmalibrary@gmail.com.
26. Questioned about the official name of the country soon after her party took office in 2016, Aung San Suu Kyi stated her continuing preference for the colonial-era term, but said that both "Burma" and "Myanmar" were acceptable. See Andrew Selth, "More Name Games in Burma/

Myanmar", *The Interpreter*, 10 August 2016, https://www.lowyinstitute.org/the-interpreter/more-name-games-burmamyanmar.

27. For an interesting discussion of this phenomenon, see Mandy Sadan, "Knowledge, Piracy and Academic Development in Myanmar (Part I)", *Tea Circle*, 30 November 2017, https://teacircleoxford.com/2017/11/30/knowledge-piracy-and-academic-development-in-myanmar-part-i/; and Mandy Sadan, "Knowledge, Piracy and Academic Development in Myanmar (Part II)", *Tea Circle*, 1 December 2017, https://teacircleoxford.com/2017/12/01/knowledge-piracy-and-academic-development-in-myanmar-part-ii/.

28. These include Sean Turnell, *Burma's Economic Renaissance* (Copenhagen: NIAS Press, forthcoming); Helen James, *Myanmar's Strategic Choices* (London: Routledge, forthcoming); Rohan Gunaratna et al., *The Rohingya Crisis* (London, World Scientific Europe, forthcoming); and Irene Slegt and Simon Long, *Myanmar: A Burmese People's Story* (London: Zed Books, forthcoming).

29. See for example, "The Best Books on Burma", recommended by Emma Larkin, *Five Books*, n.d., https://fivebooks.com/best-books/emma-larkin-on-burma/; "The Best Books on Understanding the Burmese Economy", recommended by Sean Turnell, *Five Books*, n.d., https://fivebooks.com/best-books/sean-turnell-burmese-economy/; and "The Best Books on Describing Burma", recommended by Sue Arnold, *Five Books*, n.d., https://fivebooks.com/best-books/sue-arnold-on-describing-burma/.

30. This subject is discussed in Andrew Selth, "Journeys without Maps in Myanmar", *New Mandala*, 12 September 2016, http://www.newmandala.org/journeys-without-maps-myanmar/.

31. Andrew Selth, "Burma, Hollywood and the Politics of Entertainment", *Continuum: Journal of Media and Cultural Studies* 23, no. 3 (June 2009), pp. 321–34; and Andrew Selth, "Burma-Watching on Film", *The Interpreter*, blog of the Lowy Institute, Sydney, 30 November 2010, http://www.lowyinterpreter.org/post/2010/11/30/Burma-watching-on-film.aspx.

32. Paul Duguid, "PG Tips", *Times Literary Supplement*, 11 June 2004, quoted in Stuart Kells, *The Library: A Catalogue of Wonders* (Melbourne: Text Publishing, 2017), pp. 270–71.

Preface to the Second Edition

A bibliography is never complete. No matter how conscientious the compiler there will always be gaps and scope for additions, particularly to select bibliographies. In this regard, Burma (renamed the Union of Myanmar in 1989, and given the formal title of the Republic of the Union of Myanmar in the 2008 constitution) is certainly no exception. Indeed, several developments over the past three years argue strongly for the preparation of an updated checklist of the English language literature on Burma.[1]

Since the first edition of this work was released in 2012, there has been an increasing flow of new, revised and reprinted publications about Burma. This activity has reflected the continued high level of interest in the country, not only in official and academic circles but also among the wider public. This interest is likely to be maintained in 2015, when Burma's hybrid civilian-military government is due to hold national elections, and in early 2016, when it will choose a new president. The outcome of these competitions will be critical to the future of President Thein Sein's ambitious reform programme, launched in 2011, and to Burma's relations with the wider world.

As this edition of the bibliography helps to demonstrate, most of the public (and scholarly) interest in Burma over the past few years has been related to the country's politics and economy, accounting for the large number of new works in those categories. This has included several edited works, with chapters provided by a range of noted Burma-watchers, covering such issues as the continuing political role of the armed forces, unresolved tensions with the ethnic minorities, the obstacles to further economic development and the growth of civil society. Also, the increased number of postgraduates working on Burma in Western countries has led to specialized studies on areas and issues that, until now, had rarely been subject to close examination.

Another factor has been the dramatic surge in foreign visitors to Burma, up from an estimated 310,000 in 2010 to more than three million in 2014.[2] Estimates for 2015 range as high as five million.[3] This has prompted the production of a large number of works that seem designed to cater mainly to tourists, businessmen and armchair travellers. They have included guide books, phrase books, cookery books, collections of photographs and personal accounts of visits to the country. There is also a trickle of novels that are set in Burma or have Burma-related themes. The quality of these works has tended to be highly variable but, in different ways and at different levels, they have helped fill niches in a market that still seems to be expanding.

Also, it is worth noting that many older books and monographs with Burma-related themes have been revised or reissued. There have long been a few firms (like the Bangkok-based White Lotus Press, established in 1972) that have specialized in reproducing out-of-print books on Burma. However, several other well-known publishers are now producing good quality, hard copy reprints of classic works. It is possible to find soft copies of many more online through the digital collections of major libraries, notably (since 1994) the Library of Congress and (since 1995) the British Library. Also helpful are large-scale collaborative repositories of digital content such as the Hathi Trust, which was formed in 2008.[4] These developments have made many rare books and other research materials much more accessible, helping to revive interest in Burma's history and culture, on which there are now some excellent studies.

Since 2012, a number of major gaps in the academic literature have been plugged, in part at least. For example, much closer attention has been given to legal issues in Burma, both during the colonial period and since 1948.[5] However, there are still some notable omissions, particularly in the area of Burma's foreign contacts. For example, there are still no definitive histories in English of Burma's relations with countries like the United States, Russia, Japan, the two Koreas or Australia. There is also a shortage of serious studies looking at Burma's role in the strategic competition between China and India, its membership of ASEAN since 1997, and its place in the wider environment of the Asia-Pacific. Some good work has been done recently on the place of Islam in Burma, but there is still no comprehensive or detailed overview of the development of Christianity.

There has been a revival of interest in foreign books within Burma itself.[6] Under the former military government a wide range of works were blacklisted (as were, of course, many publications in Burmese).[7] Often the reasons for these bans were not clear; one example being *Love and Sunshine in the East*, an obscure novel written in 1930 by Janet Aldis.[8] The intent behind other bans was more obvious, as in the case of Aung San Suu Kyi's three books on (among other things) modern Burmese politics and Bertil Lintner's graphic account of the 1988 uprising.[9] Under Thein Sein's more relaxed administration, however, English language versions of these and other banned books are being imported into Burma and are available from local bookshops and street vendors. For those Burmese with internet access, others can be read online. Since 2013, an international literary festival has been held in Burma, one feature of which has been the many formerly banned books openly displayed for sale.[10]

At the same time, there has been a revival in the translation of foreign books into the Burmese language. This has included some blacklisted books, notably copies of works by Aung San Suu Kyi. In 2012, a translation of George Orwell's seminal novel *Burmese Days*, which was also banned by the former military regime, even won a national literary award.[11] There are now Burmese versions of David Steinberg's popular primer *Burma/Myanmar: What Everyone Needs to Know* and Bertil Lintner's *Outrage: Burma's Struggle for Democracy*. Other foreign works that have been translated into Burmese and released in the country have included Robert Taylor's groundbreaking study *The State in Myanmar* and Wendy Law Yone's *Golden Parasol: A Daughter's Memoir of Burma* (all listed in this bibliography). Also on sale in Rangoon is a collection of broadcasts by the BBC's Burmese language service summarizing my own 2002 study *Burma's Armed Forces: Power without Glory*.

This is in addition, of course, to the bound photocopies and pirated versions of foreign language books that have long been a feature of Burma's literary scene.[12]

In recent years, there has also been a proliferation of books in English by Burmese authors and English language translations of Burmese works. The print runs may be small, but they too are having an impact on the local publishing scene. A representative sample has been included in this edition of the bibliography. While many of these publications seem to be aimed mainly at foreign visitors and foreign residents of Burma, they help represent a return to the lively literary and scholarly traditions that prevailed before General Ne Win's coup and the introduction of harsh censorship laws. Related to these developments has been the formation of several new literary associations in Burma, as various groups have taken advantage of the lifting of government restrictions in 2012.[13] The Myanmar Publishers and Booksellers Association, for example, holds Burma's largest annual book fair.

On the bibliographic front, there has also been some movement. The "Bibliography of Burma (Myanmar) Research", last produced by London University's School of Oriental and African Studies (SOAS) in 2004, is no longer being compiled, but work has continued on some other projects mentioned in the introduction to the first edition of this work. For example, the Heidelberg University bibliography now boasts electronic listings of articles and multi-author documents up to September 2012.[14] There have been several other checklists drawn up over the past three years, most of which have been posted online. They have tended to be subject-specific, to cater to the wider range of topics now being given attention by students and other researchers. For example, the University of California at Berkeley has compiled a list entitled "Myanmar: Women's Studies Bibliography".[15] An Australian researcher has drawn up a list of works in English about Burmese marionettes.[16] Most of the major studies of Burma published since 2012 have included extensive bibliographies.

In all these ways, the Burma literature scene is now a vibrant one, reflecting the dynamic state of modern Burma studies. There is every indication that, as the country continues to evolve and grow, so will the demand for fresh and original publications of all kinds.

Since the first edition of this bibliography appeared, Burma-watchers and others have alerted me to the existence of a number of works that they felt deserved inclusion. I have also been pointed in the direction of several major reports produced by think-tanks and international organizations. As this remains a select bibliography, and not an attempt to list every English-language publication about Burma released over the past twenty-seven years, I have not included them all. However, many suggestions have been taken up, helping to plug some gaps in the first edition and to fill out a few sections that were rather thin. This edition has also given me an opportunity to record more publications produced by Burma-related activist groups. Such works are often considered to be ephemera and omitted from checklists of this kind. However, they represent a major effort on the part of these organizations over the years and often provide information and views that are not readily available elsewhere.

To the 928 titles listed in the first edition of this bibliography, another 390 have been added. Most of these new works have been released over the past three years. As before, I have restricted myself to publications produced in English (or, in three cases, English and Burmese), and in hard copy, since the 1988 pro-democracy uprising.[17] Where there has been some doubt about whether or not a particular work was produced in hard copy, for example by an international organization with its own website, I have usually erred on the side of inclusion. This is because, in most cases, small numbers of hard copies were produced by these organizations for libraries and for presentation to select audiences, such as donors, journalists and government officials.

In order to make greater allowance for the latest publishing trends, I have slightly relaxed my earlier rule about books printed on demand. This has been to take account of the increasing number of academic theses and self-published works on Burma, some of which have made useful contributions to the field. Also, I have taken the risk of listing a small number of books that have not yet been formally released. They have been included because they are significant works that, as far as I have been able to determine from the authors and the publishers, are confidently expected to be released in 2015. Not to have included them would have detracted from the usefulness of this checklist over time and left gaps in areas that are currently subject to close attention. Once again, briefings, academic articles, chapters and short commentaries have not been listed, although a few examples are mentioned in the appendix.

This edition of the bibliography follows much the same format as the first. However, to help readers navigate their way through the many subjects covered in the checklist and to find particular works more easily, I have rearranged a few sections. I have also added a number of additional headings and subheadings. This has necessitated moving some titles from their original positions and giving them new reference numbers. As before, many of the books named could have been listed under more than one category. Inevitably, the placement of some titles will still strike a few readers as arbitrary, but that seemed preferable to duplicating entries or trying to include cumbersome cross references. Individual works can also be found by consulting the consolidated list of authors, editors, translators and photographers provided at the end of this book.

Some other parts of the first edition have been changed. David Steinberg has made a few amendments to his foreword to reflect developments since the original version appeared three years ago. A small number of editorial changes have been made to the introduction, and a few minor errors in the checklist have been corrected. The appendix has been substantially revised and updated to reflect the wider range of books now available to a newcomer to Burma (and Burma studies). It has also been expanded in response to the flood of tourists and short-term foreign residents who may be looking for some guidance on reading matter. As with all such exercises, the suggestions made in that essay reflect personal choices, and they are based mainly on my own reading. It has also benefited from helpful suggestions made by others in the field, but it should not in any way be considered authoritative.

At the risk of repeating myself, let me also briefly address a couple of comments made about the first edition of the bibliography.[18]

It is quite true that both the first edition and this one fail to represent the full range of modern Burma scholarship in that they do not include any works produced before 1988 (apart, that is, from modern reprints), in soft copy or written in languages other than English. Nor does it list any articles in academic journals or magazines. As explained in the introduction to the first edition, this reflects a deliberate decision to restrict the checklist to major works that are likely to be readily accessible to the majority of readers, in terms of both language and availability. It goes without saying that there is a large body of related works that do not fit into these categories. Despite their possible merits as sources on Burma, however, this checklist is not the place to look for them.

It is also acknowledged that the first edition listed at least one work that could be seen as racist in content.[19] Indeed, a few books cited below could be so described. Also, both editions of the bibliography include works that represent the propaganda of a repressive military government, as well as publications produced by a highly politicized activist community. No one could claim that all these works were accurate or balanced. A couple of other books named could be accused of being in poor taste, at least. As stated in the original introduction, however, I have listed titles that cover the full spectrum of opinion about Burma, not just those that express points of view I agree with or that are deemed by others to be politically acceptable. This reflects my firm conviction that only by being aware of all attitudes and opinions, both inside and outside Burma, can the "fiendishly complex" challenges facing modern Burma be fully understood.[20]

I am indebted to many people for helping me prepare a new version of this bibliography. As always, David Steinberg has been a great support. Contributions have also been made by several other Burma-watchers, among them John Brandon, Nick Cheesman, Melissa Crouch, Reneaud Egreteau, Nicholas Farrelly, Marie Lall, Jacques Leider, Stephen McCarthy, Lex Rieffel, Matthew Smith, Ashley South, Lindsay Stubbs, Robert Taylor, Sean Turnell and Trevor Wilson. I am grateful to them all for taking the time and trouble to help me with this project. The members and staff of the Griffith Asia Institute (GAI) have once again worked wonders to bring this work to its final stages. To those members of the GAI named in the original acknowledgements, I should like to add Russell Trood, Leong Liew, Natasha Vary, Belle Hammond and Vanessa Lau. The National Library of Australia and its staff constitute valuable resources for anyone interested in conducting research about Burma.

My wife Pattie has provided constant encouragement and support for this project, as she has done for so many others conducted over the past thirty-five years. I owe her much more than can be recorded here.

Brisbane
April 2015

Notes

1. Andrew Selth, "Burma/Myanmar: Bibliographic Trends", *New Mandala*, 16 February 2015, http://asiapacific.anu.edu.au/newmandala/2015/02/16/burmamyanmar-bibliographic-trends/.
2. San Yamin Aung, "Tourist Numbers Hit 3m in 2014: President", *The Irrawaddy*, 2 January 2015, http://www.irrawaddy.org/business/tourist-numbers-hit-3m-2014-president.html.
3. Interview with Tourist Police, Myanmar Police Force, Rangoon, March 2015.

4. Angelina Zaytsev, "14 Million Books and 6 Million Visitors: HathiTrust Growth and Usage in 2016", HathiTrust, February 2017, https://www.hathitrust.org/files/14MillionBooksand6MillionVisitors_1.pdf.
5. See, for example, Melissa Crouch and Tim Lindsey (eds.), *Law, Society and Transition in Myanmar* (Oxford: Hart, 2014); Nick Cheesman, *Opposing the Rule of Law: How Myanmar's Courts Make Law and Order* (Cambridge: Cambridge University Press, 2015); and Andrew Harding and Khin Khin Oo (eds.), *Constitutionalism and Legal Change in Myanmar* (Oxford: Hart, 2015).
6. Alisha Haridasani, "Myanmar Comes in from Cold with Bookish Revival", CNN, 10 November 2014, http://edition.cnn.com/2014/11/10/world/asia/myanmar-book-revival/.
7. See, for example, A.J. Allott, *Inked Over, Ripped Out: Burmese Storytellers and the Censors* (New York: PEN American Centre, 1993).
8. Janet Aldis, *Love and Sunshine in the East* (London: Herbert Joseph, 1930).
9. Aung San Suu Kyi, *Freedom from Fear and Other Writings*, edited with an introduction by Michael Aris (London: Penguin, 1995); Aung San Suu Kyi, *Letters from Burma*, introduction by Fergal Keane (London: Penguin, 1997); and Aung San Suu Kyi, *The Voice of Hope: Conversations with Alan Clements, with Contributions by U Kyi Maung and U Tin U* (New York: Seven Stories, 2008). See also Bertil Lintner, *Outrage: Burma's Struggle for Democracy* (London: White Lotus, 1990).
10. Sian Powell, "Festival Reflects Myanmar's Novel Freedoms", *The Australian*, 18 January 2013, http://www.theaustralian.com.au/arts/books/festival-reflects-myanmars-novel-freedoms/story-e6frg8nf-1226556087224.
11. Kyaw Phyo Tha, "Orwell's 'Burmese Days' Wins Govt Literary Award", *The Irrawaddy*, 19 November 2013, http://www.irrawaddy.org/culture/orwells-burmese-days-wins-govt-literary-award.html. See also George Orwell, *Burmese Days* (New York: Harper and Brothers, 1934).
12. Burma has not signed the 1886 Berne Convention for the Protection of Literary and Artistic Works, but it is a signatory to the World Trade Organisation's 1994 Agreement on Trade-Related Aspects of Intellectual Property Rights. Burma is also a member of the World Intellectual Property Organisation (WIPO). Despite the Copyright Act of 1911, promulgated in 1914, no formal copyright procedure has ever been instituted in Burma. In 2004, new copyright legislation began to be drafted based on a WIPO model, but it has still not entered into force.
13. Lucas Stewart, "Myanmar Literature Associations", *My Yangon*, no. 5 (January 2015), pp. 24–25.
14. S.M. Schwertner, "Burma/Myanmar Bibliographic Project", http://archiv.ub.uni-heidelberg.de/savifadok/2579/.

15. University of California Berkeley Library, "Myanmar: Women's Studies Bibliography", http://www.lib.berkeley.edu/SSEAL/SoutheastAsia/seaburm.html.
16. John Macallister, *Myanmar Marionettes (Burmese Puppets): A List of References in the English Language* (Glenbrook: The author, 1996).
17. The three multilingual books in question are *Constitution of the Republic of the Union of Myanmar (2008)* (Naypyidaw: Ministry of Information, 2008); Daw Khin Hnin Oo et al. (eds.), *Felicitations for U Thaw Kaung's 75th Birthday* (Yangon: Myanmar Book Centre, 2012); and Nick Cheesman and Htoo Kyaw Win (eds.), *Communal Violence in Myanmar* (Yangon: Myanmar Knowledge Society, 2015).
18. See, for example, David Gilbert, "Andrew Selth, 'Burma (Myanmar) since the 1988 Uprising: A Select Bibliography'", *Asian Studies Review* 38, no. 1 (March 2014), pp. 157–58. Also relevant is Nicholas Farrelly, "Andrew Selth's Burma Bibliography", *New Mandala*, 10 October 2012, http://asiapacific.anu.edu.au/newmandala/2012/10/10/andrew-selths-burma-bibiliography/.
19. One reviewer has singled out for criticism Maung Tha Hla, *Rohingya Hoax* (New York: Buddhist Rakhaing Cultural Association, 2009).
20. This description of Burma's problems was coined by Timothy Garton Ash in "Beauty and the Beast in Burma", *New York Review of Books*, 25 May 2000, http://www.nybooks.com/articles/2000/05/25/beauty-and-the-beast-in-burma/.

Acknowledgements

This bibliography—or, more properly, checklist—is in one sense a by-product of four and a half decades of collecting, reading and writing books, reports and sundry other publications about Myanmar (or Burma, as it was known when I was posted there as a fledgling diplomat in 1974). During this period I have incurred debts to many friends, colleagues and fellow Myanmar-watchers, both amateur and professional. A few key booksellers and fellow bibliophiles have kept me informed about new works, and helped me search for those that were out of print. Also, from time to time my personal library has benefited from gifts and bequests made by fellow travellers along the Burma Road. I owe them all my thanks. In compiling a work such as this, however, there are some people to whom special consideration is due.

Once again, I should like to record my gratitude to *Sayagyi* David Steinberg, formerly of Georgetown University. Not only has he provided an updated foreword to this fourth edition of the bibliography, but his advice, encouragement and practical support over the past quarter century has been invaluable. For their many contributions to this project, as it has grown and developed, I would also like to thank Nicholas Farrelly, now at the University of Tasmania, Nick Cheesman of the Australian National University (ANU), Sean Turnell of Macquarie University, John Brandon of the Asia Foundation, Sally Burdon of the Asia Bookroom and Thant Thaw Kaung of the Myanmar Book Centre.

For their help in this and other Myanmar-related projects undertaken since I made the Griffith Asia Institute (GAI) my academic home in 2006, mention must also be made of Caitlin Byrne, Michael Wesley, Andrew O'Neil, Russell Trood and Leong Liew, all directors (or acting directors) of the GAI. I also owe a debt to my fellow institute members, including Stephen McCarthy, Meegan Thorley, Kathy Bailey, Robyn White, Jill Moriarty, Natasha Vary, Christine Kowalski, Belle Hammond and Vanessa Lau. Meegan Thorley, Kathy Bailey and Jill Moriarty deserve special mentions for their administrative support and computing skills, and for shepherding earlier versions of the bibliography through the GAI and Griffith University production processes.

At the National Library of Australia (NLA) in Canberra, thanks are due to Amelia McKenzie and the staff of the Petherick Reading Room and the Asian Collections Reading Room for their interest in and help with this project since work began on it more than ten years ago. Brendan Whyte, the former Curator of Maps at the NLA, was generous with his time and expertise. I have also been assisted by the staff of the ANU's Menzies Library and the university's Coral Bell School of Asia Pacific Affairs, home of the Myanmar Research Centre.

Others who have contributed in various ways to this and past editions include (in alphabetical order) David Arnott, Lukas Birk, Michael Charney, Chit Win, Melissa Crouch, Gavin Douglas, Nic Dunlop, Renaud Egreteau, Zunetta Herbert, Richard Horsey, Larry Jagan, Nathalie Johnston, Marie Lall, Len Lambourne, Emma Larkin, David Lazar, Jacques Leider, Bertil Lintner, Joan Merenra, Edith Mirante, Lex Rieffel, Matthew Smith, Ashley South, Lucas Stewart, Lindsay Stubbs, Sun Myint, Robert Taylor, Ma Thanegi, Rhys Thompson, Derek Tonkin, Wim Vervest, Richard Warren, Evan Williams, Trevor Wilson and Garry Woodard. I owe them all my thanks.

As always, my greatest debt is to my wife, Pattie. Over the past forty years she has probably learned more about Myanmar and its books than she ever really cared to know. I owe her more than can be recorded here.

More than half a century ago, the renowned British academic librarian Alfred Johnson wrote that "the bibliographer's task is at once the most arduous and thankless form of scholarly endeavour".[1] I can happily record that, due in large part to those people and institutions named above, that has not been my experience.

Needless to say, any errors and omissions in this book are my responsibility alone.

Note

1. A.F. Johnson, "Review of Cecil Hobbs, *Southeast Asia: An Annotated Bibliography of Selected Reference Sources in Western Languages* (Washington DC: Orientalia Division, Library of Congress, 1964)", *Journal of Southeast Asian History* 6, no. 2 (September 1965), p. 145.

Abbreviations

AAF	Army Air Force
AAS	Association of Asian Studies
ABSDF	All Burma Students' Democratic Front
ADBI	Asian Development Bank Institute
AI	Amnesty International
AIIA	Australian Institute of International Affairs
ALTSEAN Burma	Alternative ASEAN Network on Burma
ANU	Australian National University
ASEAN	Association of Southeast Asian Nations
ASP	American Studies Program
BAFTA	British Academy of Film and Television Arts
BBC	British Broadcasting Corporation
BCP	Burma Communist Party
BESS	Basin Exploratory Scoping Study
BIMSTEC	Bangladesh-India-Myanmar-Sri Lanka-Thailand Economic Cooperation
BRS	Burma Research Society
BSPP	Burma Socialist Programme Party
C4ADS	Centre for Advanced Defence Studies
CBI	China Burma India (Theatre)

CDA	Collaborative for Development Action
CPB	Communist Party of Burma
CRPP	Committee Representing Peoples' Parliament
CRS	Congressional Research Service
CSIS	Centre for Strategic and International Studies
CSO	civil society organizations
DAB	Democratic Alliance of Burma
DFAT	Department of Foreign Affairs and Trade
DKBA	Democratic Karen Buddhist Army
DPS	Design Printing Services
ERIA	Economic Research Institute for ASEAN and East Asia
ExPP-ACT	Ex-Political Prisoners – Assistance, Counselling and Training
EU	European Union
FIDH	International Federation for Human Rights
GAI	Griffith Asia Institute
HPG	Humanitarian Policy Group
IAS	Institute of Asian Studies
IBAHRI	International Bar Association Human Rights Institute
ICAO	International Civil Aviation Organisation
ICC	International Criminal Court
ICG	International Crisis Group
ICVA	International Council of Voluntary Agencies
IDE	Institute for Developing Economies
IDP	internally displaced person
IIPS	Institute for International Policy Studies
IISS	International Institute for Strategic Studies
IMDb	International Movie Database
INGO	international non-governmental organization
IPCS	Institute of Peace and Conflict Studies
IRASEC	Institut de Recherche sur l'Asie du Sud-Est Contemporaine (Research Institute on Contemporary Southeast Asia)

ISEAS	ISEAS – Yusof Ishak Institute, formerly the Institute of Southeast Asian Studies
ISIS	Institute of Security and International Studies
ISJP	International Society for Japanese Philately
ISP-Myanmar	Institute for Strategy and Policy – Myanmar
JBRS	Journal of the Burma Research Society
LESC	Language Education and Social Cohesion
LGBT	lesbian, gay, bisexual, transgender
LORAN	long-range navigation
LSE	London School of Economics
MPT	Myanmar Posts and Telecommunications
MTA	Mong Tai Army
NBR	National Bureau of Asian Research
NGO	non-governmental organization
NIAS	Nordic Institute of Asian Studies
NIU	Northern Illinois University
NLD	National League for Democracy
NUS	National University of Singapore
OB/ML	Online Burma/Myanmar Library
ODA	official development assistance
OECD	Organisation for Economic Cooperation and Development
OHCHR	Office of the High Commissioner for Human Rights
OSS	Office of Strategic Services
PACSEA	Publications on Ancient Civilization in South East Asia
POW	prisoner of war
RACP	Royal Australasian College of Physicians
RAF	Royal Air Force
RCAF	Royal Canadian Air Force
RSC	Refugees Study Centre
SABREB	South Asia and Burma Retrospective Bibliography
SAC	State Administration Council

SASEC	South Asia Subregional Economic Cooperation
SEAC	South East Asia Command
SEAMEO	Southeast Asia Ministers of Education Organisation
SEASP	Southeast Asian Studies Program
SIIA	Swedish Institute of International Affairs
SLORC	State Law and Order Restoration Council
SOAS	School of Oriental and African Studies
SPDC	State Peace and Development Council
SSSNY	School for Shan State Nationalities Youth
STEDT	Sino-Tibetan Etymological Dictionary and Thesaurus
TRC	Tai Revolutionary Council
UCL	University College London
UG	Underground
UK	United Kingdom
UN	United Nations
UNDP	United Nations Development Programme
UNESCO	United Nations Educational, Scientific and Cultural Organisation
UNICEF	United Nations Children's Fund
UNLD	United Nationalities League for Democracy
UNODC	United Nations Office on Drugs and Crime
US	United States (of America)
USDA	Union Solidarity and Development Association
USDP	Union Solidarity and Development Party
USIM	Universiti Sains Islam Malaysia (Islamic Science University of Malaysia)
USIP	United States Institute of Peace
WHO	World Health Organization
WPF	World Peace Foundation
YMCA	Young Men's Christian Association
YSPS	Yangon School of Political Science
YWAM	Youth With A Mission

Introduction

Under the British colonial regime, and during the 1950s, there was a small but vibrant community of scholars in Myanmar, notably those associated with the Burma Research Society, which was founded in 1910. A number of major works were published by local figures, some in English or by foreign publishing houses. Also, the *Journal of the Burma Research Society* (JBRS), which began publication in 1911, was the outlet for over 1,300 peer-reviewed articles and commentaries, in both English and (mainly after Myanmar regained its independence from the British in 1948) the Burmese language.[1] In 1960, when the society celebrated its fiftieth anniversary, the society published two volumes of articles and papers read at a celebratory conference.[2] After the 1962 coup, the journal was permitted to continue publication but was closely monitored by the government. Both the Burma Research Society and the JBRS were closed down by General Ne Win in 1980. The baton was picked up to a certain extent by the officially sponsored Burma (later Myanmar) Historical Commission, which was created in 1955. However, until the advent of a more tolerant quasi-civilian government in 2011, academic research inside the country was still crippled by the lack of access to sources and other restrictions.[3]

Under Ne Win, Myanmar scholars were limited not only in what they could study but also in what they could write, and how they could publish their findings. For example, as David Steinberg has noted in the foreword to this book, all academic research results (even in science and medicine) were considered classified until they had been cleared for public release by the government.[4] Publications were carefully vetted for political correctness. One result of this demand for intellectual orthodoxy was a split between national and international research traditions. There was an effective division of Myanmar studies into what Hans-Bernd Zollner has described as "research from within" and "research from without".[5] "Research from within" tended to focus on Myanmar as a national entity (and then only within permitted bounds). Research conducted outside the country did not face such constraints, but was obliged by a lack of access to focus on aspects of Myanmar that could be examined relatively easily or, being deemed "safe" by the authorities, could gain a measure of official sponsorship. Such subjects included archeological discoveries, aspects of ancient civilizations, the traditional cultures of certain ethnic groups and Myanmar's Buddhist traditions.[6]

In any case, before the rise of a new democratic movement under Aung San Suu Kyi, Myanmar was neglected by the international academic community. The difficulty of gaining access to primary sources, and of reading them in local languages, tended to deter all but the most dedicated researchers. Also, from the time the armed forces (known as the Tatmadaw) first seized power in 1962, until they took back direct political control of the country in 1988, Myanmar retreated into economic isolation and strict neutrality in international affairs. "The imposed censorship of all media and imported books and materials was a comprehensive, if less than successful, attempt to isolate the population from politically modernising external influences".[7] Foreign residents were kept to a minimum and tourists were actively discouraged. Outsiders wishing to study the country were viewed with suspicion, either as potential challengers to the official version of Myanmar's history or as purveyors of "alien cultural influences".[8] Fieldwork was very difficult and access to reliable data almost impossible. Interviews with officials and even members of the general population were subject to draconian constraints. This inevitably had an impact on the production of academic publications.

There were a number of notable exceptions, but following the 1962 coup relatively few serious works were published in the major Western languages about Myanmar's history, politics, economy or contemporary society.[9] Occasionally, travel books featured a chapter or two on Myanmar, but they tended to deal only fleetingly with the state of the country and its people. From time to time, the international news media published stories about particular developments in Myanmar, but they tended to be short and lacked nuance. Also, they were not always very accurate or balanced. To understand the country's complex internal dynamics, expatriate Burmese and foreigners were obliged to read "the Rangoon tea leaves".[10] Widespread ignorance of the country meant that questionable claims were rarely challenged. Around the same time, global support for geographically defined "area studies" declined. Starved of funding and unable to conduct original research during the twenty-six years that General Ne Win ruled the country, many academics turned elsewhere for subjects to explore. Myanmar studies languished. As David Steinberg observed in 1981, for many years "contemporary Burma has been considered *terra incognita* by many scholars, journalists and development specialists".[11]

However, following the dramatic events of 1988, when nationwide pro-democracy demonstrations were crushed by the Tatmadaw, there was a remarkable resurgence of interest in Myanmar among officials and foreign scholars. A wide range of important studies has since appeared, offering "a variety of perspectives that reveal particular and sometimes contested perceptions of the Burmese past, present and future".[12] Also, over the past thirty years the struggle against military rule (in various forms) by both opposition political groups and the country's ethnic minorities has been the subject of hundreds of books, research papers and reports. Since 2016, the spotlight has fallen on the plight of the predominantly Muslim Rohingyas found in Myanmar's west. Close attention has been paid to Myanmar's defence policies and foreign relations, issues also highlighted by the February 2021 coup. New publications have been devoted to aspects of Myanmar's culture and society. There have also been important contributions to Myanmar studies in broader works covering subjects such as the involvement of armed forces in politics, the development problems of "failed" states, urban life in Southeast Asia, ethnic minorities in Southeast Asia and the re-emergence of Islam as a political force.[13]

This increased level of academic and official interest has been matched by a much greater awareness of Myanmar among the general populations of Western and regional countries, prompting the publication of numerous books designed largely for the mass market. These include travel guides, memoirs, collections of photographs, cookery books and novels. After a long hiatus, the Second World War's China-Burma-India (CBI) theatre has attracted renewed interest.[14] In 1998 alone, there were forty-four books published on this subject.[15] Between the 1988 uprising and the election of a National League for Democracy (NLD) government in 2015, there was a flood of political tracts, usually produced by Burmese exiles and activist groups of different kinds. Many took as their starting point the extended house arrest of NLD leader and Nobel Peace Prize winner Aung San Suu Kyi. Also, since 1988 think tanks like the International Crisis Group and United States Institute for Peace, and non-government organizations such as Amnesty International and Human Rights Watch, have commissioned detailed analyses on specific issues, albeit from quite different perspectives.[16] Most of these publications have been posted on the internet, but many have also been released in hard copy.

The military coup of 1 February 2021 has provided another spur to public interest in Myanmar and prompted numerous questions about the country, its institutions and its people. The level of international interest has reached a new peak. In these circumstances, the need for an updated bibliography or checklist of Myanmar-related publications, produced in English and hard copy since 1988, has become even more pressing.

Burma Bibliographies before 1988

Before 1988, Myanmar did not feature prominently in bibliographies or published source surveys. Reflecting the nature of the times, and the Victorian passion for taxonomy, a number of checklists and catalogues were produced during the colonial period, both by institutions in Britain and by the colonial administration. However, they tended to be rather specialized.[17] One listed the books and manuscripts (in Burmese and Pali) that were found in the royal library (and survived the vandalism that occurred) after Myanmar's monarchy was finally overthrown in 1885.[18] Other official publications, such as the gazetteers produced on the colony's twenty-six administrative districts, included reading lists, but these tended to be focused on the relevant geographical areas.[19] Myanmar also attracted its fair share of scholar-officials and missionaries who wrote articles and books, including reference lists, for public consumption. Examples included a list of works on Catholicism in Myanmar, published by two Roman Catholic priests in 1915, and a bibliography of Anglo-Burmese relations published in 1939 by the historian D.G.E. Hall.[20] During this early period, however, such bibliographical efforts were rare.

After the Second World War, which gave the country and surrounding region much higher public profiles in the West, Myanmar was mentioned in most bibliographies of South and Southeast Asia, including works produced by commercial publishing houses and official bodies.

In 1964, for example, Cecil Hobbs, the celebrated head of the Southern Asia Section of the Orientalia Division of the US Library of Congress, published *Southeast Asia: An Annotated Bibliography of Selected Reference Sources in Western Languages*, which included a chapter on Myanmar.[21] This was in fact a revised version of a bibliography published by the Library of Congress in 1952, itself an expanded version of a work produced by Hobbs in 1946.[22] Hobbs compiled several other bibliographies of Southeast Asia, most with sections on Myanmar.[23] Also worth mentioning in this regard is B.E. Moon's 1979 *Periodicals for South-East Asia Studies: A Union Catalogue of Holdings in British and Selected European Libraries*, and Patricia Herbert's chapter on Myanmar in J.D. Pearson's *South Asian Bibliography: A Handbook and Guide*.[24] Official publications around this time included a chapter on Myanmar in *Peninsula Southeast Asia: A Bibliographic Survey of Literature*, published in 1972 by the US Department of the Army.[25] In 1978, Thomas Willer published an index of references to Southeast Asian countries in British Parliamentary Papers between 1801 and 1973.[26]

To a greater or lesser degree, Myanmar also featured in specialized publications that focused on specific subject areas, such as Southeast Asian ethnic groups, languages and activities.[27] In 1963, for example, the American scholar Donn V. Hart published "Southeast Asia and Education: A Bibliographical Introduction", which devoted four pages to Myanmar and listed some rather obscure titles.[28] Hart also compiled a "Preliminary Checklist of Novels with a Burmese Background" and a "Draft Tribal List for Upper Burma". Bound copies of both can occasionally be found online and in private libraries, but it does not appear that either work was ever formally published.[29] A 1966 bibliographical guide to Christianity in Southeast Asia, produced by the Missionary Research Society and Yale University's Southeast Asian Studies Department, included a chapter on Myanmar.[30] In 1982, Fan Kok-sim compiled a bibliography about women in Southeast Asia that included numerous references to works on Myanmar.[31]

The most comprehensive list of works associated with Myanmar, however, was associated with an academic journal. From 1941 to 1991, the US-based Association of Asian Studies (AAS) published an annual bibliography of Asian studies as a supplement to its journal, the *Journal of Asian Studies* (and, before 1956, its predecessor the *Far Eastern Quarterly*).[32] These were occasionally supplemented by specialized reading lists compiled by scholars and librarians, such as Cecil Hobbs.[33] Generally speaking, the AAS lists were wide in scope but tended to favour the humanities and social sciences. These bibliographies typically included a list of monographs, journal articles and book chapters on Myanmar written in the main Western languages, sub-divided into broad categories such as history, biography, economics and politics. From 1991, the journal's bibliographies were made available to subscribers in electronic form, with online entries dating back to 1971. Cumulative printed volumes covering the period 1941–70 were produced in two separate multivolume sets, one in 1969–70 and the other in 1972–73.[34]

Such was the general lack of interest in Myanmar by Western scholars and officials that, prior to the 1988 uprising, there were relatively few bibliographies that looked at the country itself, in all its diversity.

There were, however, a few notable exceptions to this rule. They included works by the American scholar Frank Trager, who between 1956 and 1973 compiled four bibliographies through the Burma Research Project at New York University and the Human Relations Area Files at New Haven. Two were selected and annotated bibliographies that surveyed a wide range of subjects.[35] Another was a bibliography of the works of the British civil servant and celebrated Myanmar scholar John Furnivall.[36] It was initially planned to compile separate volumes on Chinese and Japanese language sources on Myanmar, but in the event these two projects were combined and only one volume was produced.[37] Trager and his research team also published a fifth volume, which detailed Myanmar's voting record at the United Nations (UN) and listed all the UN documents that made references to Myanmar. It was released in 1956 by the Institute of Pacific Relations.[38]

Three decades later, the Woodrow Wilson International Centre for Scholars in Washington DC published three bibliographical guides to coincide with an international conference on Myanmar studies being held in the US capital in 1986. Prepared in collaboration with the Library of Congress, one looked at scholarly resources, another listed international doctoral dissertations since 1898, and a third provided a selective guide to the periodical literature.[39] All three volumes made valuable contributions to the field. The Wilson Centre followed these works a year later with *Glimpses of the White Elephant: International Perspectives on the Study of Burma*, a special report based on the 1986 conference. It was edited by Ronald Morse and Helen Loerke and inter alia outlined the centre's bibliographical efforts.[40] The same year, Morse and Loerke edited *Burma: A Study Guide*, which drew three of the earlier reports together. It not only had nine discrete country sections but, harking back to the Centre's three bibliographies, also included selective guides to scholarly resources and the periodical literature.[41]

A number of other bibliographical works on Myanmar were produced during this period, and need to be included in a survey such as this.

In 1957, *A Select Bibliography for the Study of Buddhism in Burma in Western Languages* was published by the American scholar Richard Gard.[42] In 1961, John Davis compiled a bibliography of works relating to Myanmar's biology and natural history for the University of Florida.[43] In 1963, Annie Grimes of the US Weather Bureau produced *An Annotated Bibliography of Climate Maps of Burma*.[44] In 1972, James Scott published a bibliography that looked at land, peasants and politics in Myanmar and Thailand.[45] In 1975, William Tuchrello compiled his first list of source materials on Myanmar.[46] The following year, the Centre for East Asian Cultural Studies in Tokyo compiled a list of its microfilms about Myanmar.[47] In 1979, Michael Aung Thwin produced a short annotated guide to research tools on Myanmar for the University of Hawai'i.[48] A bibliography compiled in 1981 by Khin Thet Htar for the World Health Organization (WHO) covered the literature written in English relating to medicine, and allied subjects such as zoology and botany, in Myanmar from 1866 to 1980.[49] In 1985, a comprehensive guide to Myanmar studies in Japan was released by the Burma Studies Group in Tokyo.[50] In 1988, William Tuchrello published "A Survey of Selected Resources for the Study of Burma" in the journal *Crossroads*, published by Northern Illinois University (NIU).[51]

Another work that deserves mention here is Denise Bernot's multilingual and multivolume *Bibliographie Birmane*. The first instalment, published in 1968, was compiled from Myanmar-related items found in Paris libraries. While nominally covering the period

1950–60, it included numerous references outside that period.⁵² This work was prepared in part to update the Myanmar section of Henri Cordier's monumental *Bibliotheca Indosinica*.⁵³ It was also designed to supplement the section on "Burma and the Burmese" in the *Bibliography of the Peoples and Cultures of Mainland Southeast Asia*, compiled by John Embree and Lilian Dotson, and published by Yale University Press in 1950.⁵⁴ During the 1980s, Bernot and her colleagues at the National Centre for Scientific Research in Paris planned to produce two more volumes covering the period 1960–70. Four fascicules were to cover subjects and another four would alphabetically list works by author. It appears, however, that the project was never completed. Only four fascicules were ever published, two organized by subject and two organized by author.⁵⁵

Nor were British bibliographers idle. In 1969, Kenneth Whitbread published a catalogue of Burmese printed books in the India Office library.⁵⁶ It included books translated from Burmese into a European language (almost invariably English). Ten years later, Andrew Griffin of the India Office Library and Records produced a brief guide to sources for the study of Myanmar.⁵⁷ In 1982, the British Library Board approved a proposal to compile a "South Asia and Burma retrospective bibliography" (dubbed the SABREB). It was to be a comprehensive database that would eventually cover the entire subcontinent (including Afghanistan) and Myanmar from the introduction of printing technology in the sixteenth century up to 1900. Not only was it planned to draw on the British Library's own holdings but also on works held by institutions like the India Office Library, the School of Oriental and African Studies, the National Army Museum and the Royal Asiatic Society. Support was also to be sought from libraries and archives in relevant countries, including Myanmar.⁵⁸ The project was divided into three stages, but it appears that only a volume on stage one was produced in hard copy. It covered the period 1556–1800.⁵⁹

It should also be noted that, despite the relative dearth of books devoted to Myanmar before and after the Second World War, a number included lengthy bibliographies. One good example is Alleyne Ireland's 1907 report for the University of Chicago, *The Province of Burma*, which incorporated a twenty-five-page "Contribution to a Bibliography of Burma".⁶⁰ J.G. Scott's classic *Burma: A Handbook of Practical Information* included a "Classified List of Authorities".⁶¹ The second edition of John Christian's *Burma and the Japanese Invader*, published in 1945, had a comprehensive bibliography.⁶² Hugh Tinker's study *The Union of Burma*, first published in 1957 and updated three times, included a useful "Note on Printed Sources".⁶³

Before 1988, Myanmar had no national bibliography, although there were several lists of the old folding manuscripts known as *parabaiks*.⁶⁴ Perhaps the best-known list was one compiled by U Yan, a high court official under the last four Konbaung kings. After Myanmar regained its independence in 1948, lists of books published within the country "appeared only as registered in occasional issues of the government gazettes".⁶⁵ A guide to public documents, however, could usually be found in the *Catalogue of Books: Union Government Book Depot*, which was published annually.⁶⁶ Also, during the 1950s the Rangoon Hopkins Centre for Southeast Asian Studies at the University of Rangoon published two research guides. In 1953, Joseph Fisher produced a *Research Bibliography of Books, Documents, and Pamphlets on Burma* and Rose Calder compiled a guide to local library resources.⁶⁷ In 1961, the library of the Institute of Public Administration and Management in Yangon published a surprisingly long (sixty-six pages) bibliography of relevant works in English.⁶⁸ In 1966, Khin Thet Htar compiled a list of 709 titles on British Burma as part of her Diploma of Librarianship at the University of London.⁶⁹

Myanmar (Burma) Bibliographies since 1988

The 1988 pro-democracy uprising in Myanmar launched a major new phase in the country's national development. Over the next twenty or so years, it experienced a series of events that arguably changed its entire political, economic and social landscape. They also had a significant impact on the country's foreign relations and strategic environment. This transformation in Myanmar's internal and external circumstances was capped by the adoption of a new national constitution in 2008 and the stage-managed "election" in 2010 of a hybrid civilian-military parliament, which was ensconced in the newly built capital of Naypyidaw. In 2011, to the surprise of almost everyone, President Thein Sein and his pro-military government introduced a wide-ranging reform programme.⁷⁰ In 2015, the National League for Democracy, led by Aung San Suu Kyi, won a resounding victory in general elections, taking office the following year. The NLD won an even more emphatic victory in 2020, but in February 2021 the armed forces took back direct power in a military coup. They declared a state of emergency that would last at least one year.[71]

As a result of all these developments, Myanmar has attracted more international interest over the past thirty or so years than it probably has for any other period in its modern history. This level of attention is likely to continue for the foreseeable future as the country grapples with a wide array of seemingly intractable political, economic and social problems, and continues to be the focus of criticism in international fora because of its latest military takeover and its harsh policies towards its ethnic minorities, notably the Muslim Rohingyas.[72] The outpouring of publications—of almost every kind, and on almost every conceivable facet of Myanmar—seen in the years following the 1988 uprising has continued unabated. This has prompted the compilation of numerous bibliographies and checklists designed to bring the record up to date and to help fill gaps in the literature.[73] Some of these works warrant mention here.

In 1990, Patricia Herbert, then head of the Southeast Asia section in the British Library's Oriental and India Office Collections, and a Myanmar scholar in her own right, compiled a list of publications produced during the 1988 pro-democracy uprising in Myanmar and held by the British Library.[74] In 1991, she followed this up by publishing what was described as "the first and most fully annotated multi-disciplinary guide to English-language publications about Burma to appear in twenty years".[75] Altogether, it contained over 1,500 references in 850 numbered entries, listed under thirty subject headings. There were brief biographical notes on the authors of each work. Because of its comprehensiveness, extensive annotations and helpful layout, this book soon established itself as a standard reference work for scholars, librarians and booksellers interested in publications on Myanmar. A new edition is eagerly awaited by Myanmar-watchers.

From August 1992, the Burma Studies Group of the AAS, based since 1987 at Northern Illinois University in the United States, began printing lists of relevant publications in the *Bulletin of the Burma Studies Group*.[76] Initiated by the *Bulletin*'s then editor, reference librarian May Kyi Win, the project was described as "an attempt to bring together all current articles and books on Burma in English and other European languages".[77] The items listed were drawn from popular books and magazines as well as from publications designed for a more academic readership. Entries also covered ephemera such as conference papers, newsletters and even statements about Myanmar by government officials. One issue included a bibliography of maps of the country.[78] For a period, the *Bulletin* also published an annual bibliography on Myanmar.[79] Inevitably, there were gaps in these lists, as the effort to maintain them outstripped the resources of the Burma Studies Group. By 2002, the printed lists had been overtaken by more efficient and widely available electronic databases, but the *Bulletin* still occasionally has book reviews and other items about new publications.

Even before then, the staff of the Donn V. Hart Southeast Asia Collection, part of the Northern Illinois University Libraries group, had compiled a *Bibliography on Burma, 1988–1997*.[80] It was completed in June 1997, probably under the guidance of the collection's curator, May Kyi Win.[81] The bibliography included some material that had already been listed in the *Bulletin of the Burma Studies Group*, but it was above all an effort to provide students and specialists at NIU with a comprehensive reference to books, monographs, academic articles and news media reports that had been published during the decade following the 1988 pro-democracy uprising. Printed as an eighty-seven-page booklet on recycled computer paper by the NIU libraries, it does not appear ever to have been published commercially, or posted online. Occasionally, however, copies appear for sale on various websites.

From 2001, Michael Charney at London University's School of Oriental and African Studies periodically produced a detailed list of sources entitled "Bibliography of Burma (Myanmar) Research: The Secondary Literature". The full document was last updated in 2004, when it appeared online as a supplement to the twice-yearly *SOAS Bulletin of Burma Research*.[82] It was hoped that a new, updated version would be posted on the internet in 2012.[83] In the event, that did not happen, Charney ruling a line under the project that year. The SOAS compilation made no claims to completeness. Indeed, it was described as a "living" bibliography. It invited contributions from Myanmar-watchers and other scholars, and periodically published the details of new works online. The list of works became quite extensive, however, and ultimately ran to 264 pages. Importantly, it included references to journal articles and individual book chapters, categories of publication that were largely omitted from Pat Herbert's volume. Another SOAS publication worth mentioning in this context is Oliver B. Pollak's list of "Forgotten Scholarship on Burma". As he demonstrated, "The number of scholarly works concerning Burma in the quest for masters and doctorate degrees is prodigious."[84]

In addition, the library of the South Asia Institute at the University of Heidelberg has long been working on an ambitious bibliographic project, initially prompted by the acquisition of Frank Trager's extensive Myanmar collection in 1974. Additional titles have been found by investigating the holdings of major libraries and other institutions around the world. Since July 2005, four "pre-print" volumes have been produced, which list alphabetically and cite the locations of a large number of works on Myanmar, many published since 1988.[85] It seems to be envisaged that, when completed, this bibliography will consist of two major parts. The first will comprise eight volumes, covering monographs, periodicals and official publications on Myanmar in West European languages. The second part will cover articles in periodicals and "multi-author publications".[86] A date for the release of these works does not seem to have been set.

Since 1988, there have also been a number of specialized works in this vein. In 1993, for example, Alan Meech published an annotated bibliography of Myanmar philately that named 536 monographs and journal articles.[87] In 1998, Eugene Rasor produced a study of sources on the wartime CBI theatre, covering the period 1931–45.[88] The same year, Win Tint compiled an annotated bibliography of the works of pioneer Myanmar scholar Gordon Luce and a catalogue of books in his private library.[89] This was followed in 1999 by a "descriptive catalogue" and bibliography of works relating to the 1942–45 Burma campaign.[90] A list of Japanese sources on the campaign was published in Tokyo the following year.[91] In 2008, Mandy Sadan published a guide to colonial sources on Myanmar held in the India Office Records of the British Library. The guide was designed to provide a general introduction to sources for "the study of minority histories of Burma" during the period 1824–1948, but it also touched on works outside this frame of reference.[92] Another bibliography of the Burma campaign, listing 3,135 works, was published by Justin Corfield in 2015.[93]

From time to time, *The Journal of Burma Studies*, produced since 1997 by the Burma Studies Centre at Northern Illinois University, has published a number of specialist bibliographies. For example, in 1997 Sun Laichen compiled a detailed list of Chinese historical sources on Myanmar, which was released as a special edition of the journal.[94] In 2004, *The Journal of Burma Studies* published a bibliography by Pat Herbert of works written by the eminent Burmese scholar Pe Maung Tin, who had died in 1973.[95] In 2011, a similar honour was accorded to NIU emeritus professor F.K. Lehman (also known as F.K.L. U Chit Hlaing), who in a long academic career published more than sixty books and articles, many of them on Myanmar and related subejcts.[96]

Other lists can be found on the internet. The *Online Burma/ Myanmar Library*, launched in 2001 under the guidance of David Arnott, carries "classified and annotated links to more than 30,000 full-text documents on Burma/Myanmar".[97] It also has a section listing a number of bibliographies, library catalogues and checklists of works relating to Myanmar, and a separate page listing the publications of a number of individual Myanmar scholars.[98] A search of the World Wide Web reveals other works of this nature. In 2008, for example, Gandhimathy Durairaj from the library of the Institute of Southeast Asian Studies in Singapore compiled a "select list" of 723 sources on Myanmar's "Road to Democracy".[99] It covered books, journal articles and even audiovisual materials. The same year, annotated bibliographies of Myanmar's geology and hydrology were compiled by the US Army Corps of Engineers, probably in anticipation of US involvement in relief efforts after Cyclone Nargis devastated southern Myanmar.[100] Pamela Cross has posted a list of works on Myanmar's ethnic minorities and their textiles online, and the University of Bristol has compiled a checklist of publications related to Buddhist death rituals in Myanmar.[101]

Most secondary works on Myanmar published since 1988 have included lists of sources or suggestions for further reading, and in some cases these have been quite comprehensive. For example, Donald Seekins's 2017 *Historical Dictionary of Burma (Myanmar)* includes a comprehensive bibliography, divided into subjects.[102] Robert Taylor's revised study of *The State in Myanmar* also has an extensive bibliography of English and Burmese language sources, helpfully divided into pre-1988 and post-1988 sections.[103] Other good examples are Monique Skidmore's edited collection *Burma at the Turn of the 21st Century*, Chie Ikeya's *Refiguring Women, Colonialism, and Modernity in Burma*, Michael Leigh's *Conflict, Politics and Proselytism* and Roger Lee Huang's *The Paradox of Myanmar's Regime Change*.[104] The bibliography at the end of Mandy Sadan's *Being and Becoming Kachin* is twenty-six pages long.[105] Many other academic works contain similar aids to research. One unusual example in this genre is Jean-Marc Rastorfer's 1998 study of books reprinted—or photocopied for resale—in Myanmar itself.[106] Many of the works listed in his paper were originally published in English.

A valuable new bibliographical resource has been launched by the *Tea Circle* blog, which was established in November 2015, with the explanatory subtitle, "A Forum for New Perspectives on Burma/Myanmar". Based initially at Oxford University but now run by volunteers out of the University of Toronto, the objectives of *Tea Circle* were described as follows:

> It highlights analysis, research, opinions, book reviews, multimedia presentations and other types of submissions from a global audience of contributors. *Tea Circle* ... is particularly focused on creating opportunities for contributors from Myanmar.[107]

It is this last aim that seems to have prompted the compilation of a new list of publications.[108] Although it has the generic title "Bibliography of Burma Studies", this resource is devoted largely to publications on Myanmar by women and Myanmar scholars, who, most would agree, have so far been under-recognized in the field of Myanmar studies.[109] Contributors have been invited to add new material to the site.[110]

In Myanmar itself, the compilation of bibliographies has been a slow process, but it was given a boost in 1971 by the establishment of the Postgraduate Library Diploma Course at Rangoon Arts and Sciences University.[111] This prompted the production of several specialized subject bibliographies in English. A *Research Bibliography of Books, Documents, and Pamphlets on Burma* was published in 1972, but it appears simply to have been a revised version of Joseph Fisher's 1953 volume of the same name.[112] Since then, there have been efforts to compile more comprehensive lists, but none have been able to keep up with the dramatic surge in local publications that has occurred under the three quasi-civilian governments elected since 2010. A *Myanmar National Bibliography* is currently being compiled by the Myanmar National Library, to cover imprints since 1997. To date, however, no comprehensive bibliography of works published in Myanmar appears to have been produced in any major foreign language, although some helpful lists have been compiled, and commentaries on the literary scene provided, by private individuals.[113]

Content and Methodology

Inspired by all these projects, this bibliography aims to provide a readily accessible selection of books, reports and other monographs devoted to Myanmar, or with major components focused on Myanmar, that have been published, or in some cases republished, since the 1988 uprising. It is not intended to be exhaustive, either in its listings or in its coverage. As Heidelberg University's Siegfried Schwertner has written, "the collection of publications for a bibliography is a story that never ends, and a complete coverage cannot be achieved".[114] Also, as Alfred Johnson once wrote, "The compiler of a selective bibliography is always liable to criticism for faults of omission."[115] Even so, a conscious attempt has been made to include a wide range of publications representing all the main subject areas and political viewpoints. Broader works touching on Myanmar, or which include specific chapters on Myanmar, have not been listed, unless Myanmar has been specifically mentioned in the main title or subtitle. Also, with a small number of exceptions, entries have been restricted to works that have been produced in hard copy and released for sale or public distribution.[116]

The items listed have been restricted to those produced in whole or in part in the English language.[117] This is because both Myanmar studies and the wider public discourse on Myanmar since 1988 have been dominated by English speakers and English language publications, including on international websites. It is important to note, however, that there is also a rapidly growing body of work published in other languages, including of course Burmese, which reflect the high level of interest now being shown in Myanmar by scholars, activists, journalists and others in a wide range of countries around the world. Chinese, Japanese, French and German Myanmar-watchers, for example, have made notable contributions to the field, usually in their own languages.[118] There are also active circles of Myanmar-watchers in the Scandinavian countries. The Nordic Institute of Asian Studies (NIAS) in Copenhagen, for example, has published several well-regarded books about Myanmar.[119]

Where possible, an effort has been made to sight and verify each entry. This has become increasingly difficult as the checklist has grown, but many of those works not found in my own collection were personally inspected at the National Library of Australia or the Menzies Library of the Australian National University (ANU). Both have extensive holdings on Myanmar (in both English and Burmese). As far as possible, other works have been cross-checked using the resources of multiple booksellers. In a number of cases, I have contacted authors or publishers directly to confirm certain details. As a general rule, bibliographical "ghosts" and books listed by authors or publishers as "forthcoming" have not been included. These include works described in catalogues and advertised on retail websites but not yet released for sale.[120] Nor has any attempt been made to list all books described in catalogues and online as "printed on demand". Not only would this make the bibliography unwieldy but, certain e-books aside, such works tend either to be reproductions of books published prior to 1988 or unrefereed compilations of materials drawn from websites like Wikipedia.[121]

The categories into which the publications in this work have been divided broadly mirror those found in Pat Herbert's 1991 bibliography, which in turn follow established international library practice. Additional subheadings have been included in many places to help readers more easily find books and reports on subjects of particular interest. Where a publication could fit into more than one category—as is often the case—it has been listed once only, according to its dominant themes. If books have been given more than one title, as has sometimes occurred when a book published in Britain has been republished in the United States, or vice versa, usually only the title of the original version has been listed. For example, Zoya Phan's 2009 memoir *Little Daughter* was republished in the United States the following year as *Undaunted*.[122] Emma Larkin's 2010 book *Everything Is Broken* was released in the United States a year later under the title *No Bad News for the King*.[123] If a work does not include a specific place of publication, the country of publication is named, where that is known.

In this book, the name "Myanmar" has been used in preference to "Burma", except in specific cases where use of the old name seemed more appropriate. This has mainly been in references to the country before 1988, some formal titles, and direct quotations. Also, the preference for "Burma" demonstrated in the first three prefaces has been left unchanged. David Steinberg's foreword reflects his personal preferences. Publications have been cited exactly as they have appeared in print. Hence, in the checklist, the country is referred to both as "Burma" and "Myanmar". Similarly, the former national capital has been shown as both "Rangoon" and "Yangon" (the new name adopted in 1989), depending on the choice of the authors and the publishers. The descriptor "Burmese" has been retained both as an adjective and to describe the dominant language of the country.[124]

Although it raises its ugly head from time to time, strictly speaking there is no such word as "Myanmarese".[125] The vexed question of names is also discussed in the following chapter, on "Protocols and Politics".

Authors, editors, compilers, photographers and translators are listed under the names given on their books. Unless provided, no attempt has been made to identify pseudonyms, although these have long been common in the field of Myanmar studies.[126] Similarly, Burmese names are cited as they are given on the publications in question, although in some cases hyphens have been removed, for consistency. While strictly speaking this is not correct usage, it is hoped that this will help avoid any confusion arising from the fact that Burmese do not usually have first names and surnames, and many use honorifics or other identifiers as an integral part of their name. Thus, for example, Daw Than Han, Maung Aung Myoe and Ma Thanegi are cited as if the titles "Daw", "Maung" and "Ma" are part of their actual name.[127] The same principle has been applied to names like "Tekkatho" (University) Sein Ti, "Theippan" (Science) Maung Wa and "Pagan" (the place) U Khin Maung Gyi. Where first names are clearly given, however, as in Margaret Aung Thwin, Frankie Tun Tin or Ardeth Maung Thawnghmung, they have been recognized and listed as such.

Although the later editions of this bibliography have become more comprehensive, and thus more balanced in their listings, it is acknowledged that it still displays a slight geographical bias in that it cites a large number of works on Myanmar that have either been written by Australians or published in Australia. In large part, this reflects my own research base at the Griffith Asia Institute in Brisbane, and the holdings of the National Library of Australia and the ANU's Menzies Library, both situated in Canberra. No attempt has been made to correct this bias, as it does not distort the overall thrust of the checklist. Indeed, by including a number of works not cited in other bibliographies it helps to round out the list and demonstrates the increased attention that Myanmar has received over the past thirty or so years from Australians and Australian research centres.

No claims are made regarding the academic or literary merit of any of the works listed. As can be seen from even a cursory glance through the titles, they cover a very broad spectrum in terms of style, length, content and purpose. Indeed, given the highly politicized nature of the Myanmar-watching community over the past three decades, and the tendency of some observers to express moral judgements as readily as analytical views, it is perhaps also worth recording that the various personal and political positions represented by the publications in this checklist are noted without comment or wider implication. The bibliography is intended simply to draw attention to the wide range of books and reports on Myanmar that has appeared over the past thirty years or so. It is hoped that a work of this kind will help officials, scholars, students, travellers and others who might be looking for a readily available directory of contemporary sources, produced by a wide range of authors and institutions. As noted in successive prefaces, it is ultimately for the reader to decide on their quality and worth.

Indeed, a few works may be considered to have only slight links to Myanmar. I include in this category a couple of books on Burmese and Birman cats, whose actual ties to the country are rather slight. The links between Myanmar and so-called "Burmese glass" are even more tenuous.[128] Given its prominence in some countries as a pet (or a pest), I have also included a book or two on Burmese pythons. Following Patricia Herbert's lead, however, such works have been listed for completeness.[129] Similar thinking underpins the inclusion of Norval Morris's book *The Brothel Boy and Other Parables of the Law*, which uses George Orwell and Myanmar as a literary device to discuss broader points of British, Indian and Burmese customary law.[130] Also, the bibliography lists a number of novels that have appeared since 1988 and that are either set in Myanmar or in some way refer to developments there. While many are of dubious literary value, they have been included both for completeness and to give readers an idea of publishing trends as they relate to modern Myanmar.

The first appendix attempts to provide a comprehensive reading list for anyone intending to visit Myanmar for the first time, or who might wish to familiarize themselves with the country before undertaking more detailed studies. It was initially prepared for the Asia Bookroom in Canberra in 2006, but has been regularly updated to take account of various publications that have appeared since then. Like all such exercises, it represents a purely personal view and should not be considered as either authoritative or exhaustive. However, it is included in the hope that it may help provide an introduction of sorts to a dynamic and fascinating country of enormous complexity that is still little known and poorly understood. Also, the essay refers to a number of works that are not mentioned in this bibliography, either because they were published before 1988 or because they are journal articles or chapters in books. It can profitably be read in conjunction with other lists of books on Myanmar compiled by subject experts.[131]

In *Letters from Iceland*, the poet Louis MacNeice wrote of running away from "the excess of books".[132] This is not a frame of mind familiar to bibliographers, who happily embrace the growing number of publications on any chosen subject. Nor should it appeal to Myanmar-watchers, who, as even this "select" checklist attests, can now enjoy reading many works, of all kinds, published on the country over the past thirty years or so.

Notes

1. For the early years of the JBRS, see C.A. Boshier, *Mapping Cultural Nationalism: The Scholars of the Burma Research Society, 1910–1935* (Copenhagen: NIAS Press, 2018).
2. *Fiftieth Anniversary Publications*, 2 vols. (Rangoon: Burma Research Society, 1960 [vol. 2] and 1961 [vol. 1]).
3. See, for example, James Cemmell, *Academic Freedom International Study: Burma* (London: University and College Union, May 2009), https://www.ucu.org.uk/media/3422/Academic-Freedom-International-Study-Burma-chapter/pdf/acdemic_freedom_burma.pdf.
4. See also Andrew Selth, *Myanmar-Watching: Problems and Perspectives*, Regional Outlook no. 58 (Brisbane: Griffith Asia Institute, Griffith University, 2018), pp. 6–7.
5. Hans-Bernd Zollner, "Die langen Schatten der Politik – zum Stand der BirmaForschung" [The long shadow of politics – Research on Burma], *Internationales Asienforum: International Quarterly for Asian Studies* 39, nos. 1–2 (May 2008), pp. 55–79.
6. For example, Pam Gutman was granted special permission to conduct field research around Myohaung in 1972 and 1974. One result was Pamela Gutman, *Burma's Lost Kingdoms: Splendours of Arakan* (Sydney: Allen and Unwin, 2001). See also "A Conversation with Mikael Gravers: Research among the Karen, Past and Present", *The Irrawaddy*, 7 July 2017, https://www.irrawaddy.com/opinion/guest-column/a-conversation-withmikael-gravers-research-among-the-karen-past-and-present.html.
7. D.I. Steinberg, "Moving Myanmar: The Future of Military Prominence", *Kyoto Review of Southeast Asia*, no. 14 (September 2013), https://kyotoreview.org/issue-14/moving-myanmar-the-future-of-military-prominence/.
8. See, for example, Khin Nyunt, "Address to the 11th Myanmar Traditional Cultural Performing Arts Competitions", *New Light of*

Myanmar, 4 November 2003, http://www.myanmar.gov.mm/NLM-2003/enlm/Nov04 h2.html. See also Gustaaf Houtman, *Mental Culture in Burmese Crisis Politics: Aung San Suu Kyi and the National League for Democracy*, Institute for the Study of Languages and Cultures of Asia and Africa, Monograph no. 33 (Tokyo: Tokyo University of Foreign Studies, 1999), pp. 126–28.

9. Andrew Selth, "Modern Burma Studies: A Survey of the Field", *Modern Asian Studies* 44, no. 2 (March 2010), pp. 401–40. An earlier version of this article was posted online by the City University of Hong Kong's Southeast Asia Research Centre, as Andrew Selth, *Modern Burma Studies: A View from the Edge*, Southeast Asia Research Centre, Working Paper no. 96 (Hong Kong: City University of Hong Kong, 2007), http://www6.cityu.edu.hk/searc/Data/FileUpload/289/WP96_07_ASelth.pdf.

10. D.I. Steinberg, *Burma: The State of Myanmar* (Washington: Georgetown University Press, 2001), p. xxv.

11. D.I. Steinberg, *Burma's Road toward Development: Growth and Ideology under Military Rule* (Boulder, CO: Westview, 1981), p. 1.

12. Matrii Aung Thwin, "Introduction: Communities of Interpretation and the Construction of Modern Myanmar", *Journal of Southeast Asian Studies* 39, no. 2 (June 2008), p. 187.

13. See, for example, M.P. Callahan, "Burma: Soldiers as State Builders", in Muthiah Alagappa (ed.), *Coercion and Governance: The Declining Political Role of the Military in Asia* (Stanford: Stanford University Press, 2001), pp. 413–32; and Marco Bunte, "The NLD-Military Coalition in Myanmar: Military Guardianship and its Economic Foundations", in Paul Chambers and Napisa Waitoolkiat (eds.), *Khaki Capital: The Political Economy of the Military in Southeast Asia* (Copenhagen: NIAS Press, 2017), pp. 93–130.

14. All US forces in China, Burma and India were united in one command, referred to as the "CBI Theatre". This term has since gained popular currency. However, it was not one of the recognized theatres of the war, since it extended geographically across the boundaries of India Command and of the South-East Asia and China theatres. See Mountbatten of Burma, *Report to the Combined Chiefs of Staff by the Supreme Allied Commander, South-East Asia, 1943–1945* (New Delhi: The English Book Store, 1960), p. 7.

15. See, for example, Gordon Graham and Frank Cole (eds.), *Burma Campaign Memorial Library: A Collection of Books and Papers about the War in Burma 1942–1945* (London: School of Oriental and African Studies, 2001). Also of relevance is Gordon Graham and Jotika Khur-Yearn, "Browsing through a Treasure House: The Literature of the Burma Campaign", *SOAS Research Online*, 6 April 2011, http://eprints.soas.ac.uk/11668/.

16. See, for example, Bertil Lintner, *Why Burma's Peace Efforts Have Failed to End Its Internal Wars*, Peaceworks no. 169 (Washington DC: United States Institute of Peace, October 2020); and *Dashed Hopes: The*

Criminalisation of Peaceful Expression in Myanmar (New York: Human Rights Watch, 31 January 2019).

17. See, for example, L.D. Barnett, *A Catalogue of Burmese Books in the British Museum* (London: British Museum, 1913).
18. *Catalogue of Pali and Burmese Books and Manuscripts Belonging to the Library of the Late King of Burma and Found in the Palace at Mandalay in 1886* (Rangoon: Office of the Superintendent, Government Printing, 1910). Early European visitors described the large libraries of Myanmar's kings. See, for example, Anis Khurshid, "Library Development in Burma", *Journal of Library History* (1966–1972) 5, no. 4 (October 1970), p. 323.
19. The number of districts, and thus the number of gazetteers, varied over time. For details of all these works, see Henry Scholberg, *The District Gazetteers of British India: A Bibliography*, Bibliotheca Asiatica no. 3 (Zug: Inter Documentation Company, 1970), pp. 50–51 and 66–70.
20. See, for example, Henry Hosten and E. Luce, *Bibliotheca Catholica Birmana* (Rangoon: British Burma Press, 1915); and D.G.E. Hall, "Bibliography of Anglo-Burmese Relations", *International Committee of Historical Relations* 11 (October 1939), pp. 545–54.
21. Cecil Hobbs, *Southeast Asia: An Annotated Bibliography of Selected Reference Sources in Western Languages* (Washington DC: Orientalia Division, Library of Congress, 1964), pp. 25–41.
22. Cecil Hobbs, *Southeast Asia, 1935–45: A Selected List of Reference Books* (Washington DC: Orientalia Division, Library of Congress, 1946), pp. 1–17.
23. As a result of all these efforts, Hobbs was dubbed "the Dean of Southeast Asian bibliographers". See Cecil Hobbs, *Southeast Asia: A Bibliography of Writings, 1942–1978* (Carbondale: Centre for Vietnamese Studies, Southern Illinois University at Carbondale, 1980), p. i.
24. B.E. Moon, *Periodicals for South-East Asia Studies: A Union Catalogue of Holdings in British and Selected European Libraries* (London: Mansell, 1979), pp. 58–66; and Patricia Herbert, "Burma", in J.D. Pearson (ed.), *South Asian Bibliography: A Handbook and Guide* (Hassocks: Harvester Press, 1979), pp. 328–51.
25. "Burma", in *Peninsula Southeast Asia: A Bibliographic Survey of Literature* (Washington DC: Department of the Army, 1972), pp. 67–89.
26. T.F. Willer, *Southeast Asian References in the British Parliamentary Papers, 1801–1972/73: An Index*, Papers in International Studies, Southeast Asia Series no. 48 (Athens: Ohio University Centre for International Studies, 1978), pp. 16–41.
27. See, for example, F.E. Huffman, *Bibliography and Index of Mainland Southeast Asian Languages and Linguistics* (New Haven: Yale University Press, 1986); and Christian Bauer, *A Guide to Mon Studies* Centre of Southeast Asian Studies, Working Paper no. 32 (Clayton: Monash University, 1984), pp. 41–75.

28. D.V. Hart, "Southeast Asia and Education: A Bibliographical Introduction", *Silliman Journal* 10, no. 3 (3rd Quarter, 1963), pp. 241–71.
29. A copy of the "Draft Tribal List for Upper Burma" forms part of the Luce Collection, in the National Library of Australia.
30. G.H. Anderson (ed.), *Christianity in Southeast Asia: A Bibliographical Guide: An Annotated Bibliography of Selected References in Western Languages* (New York and New Haven: The Missionary Research Library and Yale University Southeast Asia Studies, 1966), pp. 18–23.
31. Kok-sim Fan, *Women in Southeast Asia: A Bibliography* (Boston: G.K. Hall, 1982). The bibliography was divided into subject chapters, but most carried a section on Myanmar-related publications.
32. The print version of the *Bibliography of Asian Studies* was available as a stand-alone title from 1969 to 1991, but before then was included as part of these journals.
33. See, for example, Cecil Hobbs, "Reading List on Burma", *Far Eastern Quarterly* 5, no. 1 (November 1945), pp. 60–66.
34. 'Burma', in Association for Asian Studies, *Cumulative Bibliography of Asian Studies, 1941–1965: Subject Bibliography*, 4 vols. (Boston: G.K. Hall, 1970), vol. 1, pp. 118–155; and "Burma", in Association for Asian Studies, *Cumulative Bibliography of Asian Studies, 1966–1970: Subject Bibliography*, 3 vols. (Boston: G.K. Hall, 1972), vol. 1, pp. 108–31. See also Association for Asian Studies, *Cumulative Bibliography of Asian Studies, 1941–1965: Author Bibliography*, 4 vols. (Boston: G.K. Hall, 1969).
35. F.N. Trager, J.N. Musgrave and Janet Welsh, *Annotated Bibliography of Burma* (New Haven: Burma Research Project, New York University, 1956); and F.N. Trager, *Burma: A Selected and Annotated Bibliography* (New Haven: Human Relations Area Files Press, 1973).
36. F.N. Trager, *Furnivall of Burma: An Annotated Bibliography of the Works of John S. Furnivall* (New Haven: Yale University Southeast Asian Studies, 1963).
37. F.N. Trager et al., *Japanese and Chinese Language Sources on Burma: An Annotated Bibliography* (New Haven: Burma Research Project, New York University, 1957).
38. F.N. Trager, Patricia Wohlgemuth and Lu-yu Kiang, *Burma's Role in the United Nations, 1948–1955* (New York: International Secretariat, Institute of Pacific Relations, 1956).
39. Anita Hibler and W.P. Tuchrello, *Burma: A Selective Guide to Scholarly Resources* (Washington DC: Asia Program, The Wilson Centre, and Asian Division, The Library of Congress, 1986); F.J. Shulman, *Burma: An Annotated Bibliographical Guide to International Doctoral Dissertation Research, 1898–1985* (Lanham: Asia Program, The Wilson Centre and University Press of America, 1986); and Anita Hibler and W.P. Tuchrello, *Burma: A Selective Guide to Periodical Literature, 1970–1986*

(Washington DC: Asia Program, The Woodrow Wilson International Centre for Scholars, 1986).
40. Ronald Morse and Helen Loerke (eds.), *Glimpses of the White Elephant: International Perspectives on the Study of Burma* (Washington DC: The Wilson Centre, 1987).
41. R.A. Morse (ed.), *Burma: A Study Guide* (Washington DC: The Wilson Centre, 1987).
42. R.A. Gard, *A Select Bibliography for the Study of Buddhism in Burma in Western Languages* (Los Angeles: Asia Foundation, 1957).
43. Davis, J.H., *Selected Bibliography: Burma and Adjacent Regions, Biology, Natural History* (Gainesville: University of Florida, 1961).
44. A.E. Grimes, *An Annotated Bibliography of Climate Maps of Burma* (Washington DC: US Weather Bureau, 1963).
45. J.C. Scott, *A Bibliography on Land, Peasants, and Politics for Burma and Thailand* (Madison: Land Tenure Centre, University of Wisconsin – Madison, 1972).
46. William Tuchrello, "Recent Articles on Burma, Chronologically Arranged" (Washington DC, 1976).
47. *List of Microfilms Deposited in the Centre for East Asian Cultural Studies, Part 8: Burma* (Tokyo: Centre for East Asian Cultural Studies, 1976).
48. Michael Aung Thwin, *Southeast Asian Research Tools: Burma*, Southeast Asia Paper no. 16, Part III (Honolulu: University of Hawai'i, 1979).
49. Khin Thet Htar, *Annotated Bibliography of Medical Literature on Burma (1866–1976), with Supplement up to 1980* (New Delhi: World Health Organisation, South-East Asia Regional Office, 1981).
50. *Burmese Studies in Japan, 1868–1985: Literary Guide and Bibliography*, edited by the Burma Studies Group (Tokyo: Burma Research Group, Tokyo University of Foreign Studies, 1985) (in Japanese and English).
51. William Tuchrello, "A Survey of Selected Resources for the Study of Burma", *Crossroads: An Interdisciplinary Journal of Southeast Asian Studies* 4, no. 1 (Fall 1988), pp. 128–51.
52. Denise Bernot, *Bibliographie Birmane, Annees 1950–1960* (Paris: Editions du Centre National de la Recherche Scientifique, 1968).
53. Henri Cordier, *Bibliotheca Indosinica: Dictionnaire Bibliographique des Ouvrages Relatifs a la Peninsule Indochinoise*, 4 vols. (Paris: L'Ecole Francais d'Extreme Orient/Leroux, 1912–15), vol. 1, columns 1–516.
54. "Burma and the Burmese", in J.F. Embree and L.O. Dotson, *Bibliography of the Peoples and Cultures of Mainland Southeast Asia* (New Haven: Yale University, Southeast Asia Studies, 1950), pp. 159–317.
55. Denise Bernot et al., *Bibliographie Birmane, Annees 1960–1970*, 4 vols. (Paris: Editions du Centre National de la Recherche Scientifique, 1982–4). The latter two fascicules, both dated 1984, covered authors from A to F and G to L. See also Denise Bernot et al., *Bibliographie Birmane – annees 1950–1960* (Paris: Editions du Centre National de la Recherche Scientifique, 1968).

56. Kenneth Whitbread, *Catalogue of Burmese Printed Books in the India Office Library* (London: Her Majesty's Stationery Office, 1969).
57. Andrew Griffin, *A Brief Guide to Sources for the Study of Burma in the India Office Records* (London: India Office Library and Records, 1979).
58. B.C. Bloomfield, "The South Asia and Burma Retrospective Bibliography", *Journal of the Royal Asiatic Society*, n.s., 115, no. 1 (January 1983), pp. 83–84.
59. Graham Shaw, *The South Asia and Burma Retrospective Bibliography (SABREB), Stage 1: 1556–1800* (London: The British Library Publishing Division, 1987). As the British conquest of Burma did not begin until 1824, there are few references to Burma in this volume. It was anticipated, however, that Burma would receive greater attention in the volumes covering stage 2 (1801–1862) and stage 3 (1868–1900).
60. Alleyne Ireland, *The Province of Burma: A Report Prepared on Behalf of the University of Chicago*, 2 vols. (Boston and New York: Houghton, Mifflin, 1907), vol. 2, pp. 973–1001.
61. J.G. Scott, *Burma: A Handbook of Practical Information* (London: Daniel O'Connor, 1921), pp. 519–27.
62. J.L. Christian, *Burma and the Japanese Invader* (Bombay: Thacker, 1945), pp. 390–408.
63. Hugh Tinker, *The Union of Burma: A Study of the First Years of Independence* (London: Oxford University Press, 1967), pp. 401–3.
64. See also Myaingkaing Myo Sa, *A Bibliographic Account of the Pitikas and Other Burmese Literature* (Rangoon, 1906) (in Burmese).
65. H.F. Conover, "The Bibliography of Newly Developing Areas", *Library Trends* 8, no. 2 (1959), p. 325.
66. *Catalogue of Books: Union Government Book Depot* (Rangoon: Superintendent of Government Printing and Stationary, annual). Some editions of this work listed "documents dating back to the mid-19th century". See H.F. Conover, *Current National Bibliographies* (Washington: Reference Department, The Library of Congress, 1955), p. i.
67. Joseph Fisher, *Research Bibliography of Books, Documents, and Pamphlets on Burma* (Rangoon: Rangoon Hopkins Centre for Southeast Asian Studies, University of Rangoon, 1953). See also R.E. Calder, *Guide to Library Resources in Rangoon* (Rangoon: Rangoon Hopkins Centre for Southeast Asian Studies, Rangoon University, 1958).
68. *A Selective Bibliography on Public Administration in Burma* (Rangoon: Institute of Public Administration and Management Library, Union of Burma, March 1961) (mimeograph).
69. Khin Thet Htar, *Select Bibliography of Books in English on British Burma, 1826–1948* (London: The author, 1966).
70. See, for example, *Reform in Myanmar: One Year On*, Asia Briefing no. 136 (Jakarta/Brussels: International Crisis Group, 11 April 2012). See also Andrew Selth, "Assessing Burma's Reform Program",

The Interpreter, 24 January 2012, http://www.lowyinterpreter.org/post/2012/01/24/Assessing-Burmas-reform-program.aspx.

71. Andrew Selth, "The Coup in Myanmar: What Do We Know?", *The Interpreter*, 3 February 2021, https://www.lowyinstitute.org/the-interpreter/coup-myanmar-what-do-we-know.

72. See, for example, "Myanmar's Genocide against Rohingya Not Over, Says Rights Group", *The Guardian*, 24 November 2020, https://www.theguardian.com/world/2020/nov/23/myanmar-is-still-committing-genocide-against-rohingya-says-rights-group.

73. A useful resource in this regard is H.C. Kemp, *Bibliographies on Southeast Asia* (Leiden: KITLV Press, 1998), pp. 982–85.

74. "List of Burmese Pro-democracy [August-September 1988] Publications in the British Library", *South-East Asia Library Group Newsletter* 34–35 (December 1990), pp. 25–38.

75. P.M. Herbert, *Burma* (Oxford: Clio Press, 1991), p. xv.

76. From its first issue in Spring 1973, the frequency of publication varied between one and four times a year. See Centre for Burma Studies, Northern Illinois University, *Bulletin of the Burma Studies Group*, https://www.niu.edu/clas/burma/publications/Bulletins/index.shtml

77. May Kyi Win, "Bibliography: Books and Articles on Burma", *Bulletin of the Burma Studies Group*, no. 59 (March 1997), p. 9.

78. "Bibliography of Maps of Burma", *Bulletin of the Burma Studies Group*, no. 71 (March 2003), pp. 17–29.

79. Richard Cooler, "May Kyi Win (1947–2002)", *Journal of Asian Studies* 61, no. 3 (August 2002), pp. 1139–40.

80. *Bibliography on Burma, 1988–1997* (De Kalb: Donn V. Hart Southeast Asia Collection, Northern Illinois University Libraries, 1997) (mimeograph).

81. Personal communication with NIU librarian, 12 January 2021.

82. M.W. Charney, "The Bibliography of Burma (Myanmar) Research: The Secondary Literature, 2004 Revision", *SOAS Bulletin of Burma Research*, Bibliographic Supplement (Winter 2004), http://eprints.soas.ac.uk/6241/1/Bibliography_of_secondary_literature--2004.pdf.

83. Personal communications with Michael Charney, 21 December 2011 and 25 April 2012.

84. O.B. Pollak, "Some Forgotten Scholarship on Burma: A Bibliographic Note", *SOAS Bulletin of Burma Research* 1, no. 2 (Autumn 2003), pp. 1–7. The list was published (with permission) by Michael Charney in 2003, but was actually compiled by Pollak about thirty years earlier.

85. S.M. Schwertner, *Burma/Myanmar Bibliographic Project: A Collection of Publications in West European Languages for Preparation a* [sic] *Burma/Myanmar Bibliography*, 4 vols. (Heidelberg: South Asia Institute, University of Heidelberg, 2005–8), http://crossasia-repository.ub.uni-heidelberg.de/254/.

86. 'Introduction', *Burma/Myanmar Bibliographic Project*, http://crossasia-repository.ub.uni-heidelberg.de/254/1/01_Intr_etc_.pdf.
87. Alan Meech, *An Annotated Bibliography of Burma Philately* (London: British Philatelic Trust, 1993).
88. E.L. Rasor, *The China-Burma-India Campaign, 1931–1945: Historiography and Annotated Bibliography* (Westport: Greenwood Press, 1998).
89. Win Tint, *An Annotated Bibliography of the Works of G.H. Luce and Catalogue of Books in His Library* (Meiktila: Meiktila University, 1998). Luce's library was purchased by the National Library of Australia in three stages, in 1980, 1985 and 1987. See "Guide to the Papers of Gordon Hannington Luce", National Library of Australia, https://nla.gov.au/nla.obj-247076022/findingaid.
90. Gordon Graham and Frank Cole, *Burma Campaign Memorial Library: A Collection of Books and Papers about the War in Burma, 1942–1945* (London: School of Oriental and African Studies, 1999). A second edition of this work was published in 2001. The first Japanese attacks against British Burma were launched in December 1941.
91. *A Bibliography of Japanese Books on the Burma Campaign: War in Burma 1942–1945* (Tokyo: All Burma Veterans Association of Japan, 2000).
92. Mandy Sadan, *A Guide to Colonial Sources on Burma: Ethnic & Minority Histories of Burma in the India Office Records, British Library* (Bangkok: Orchid Press, 2008), p. 1.
93. Justin Corfield, *The Burma Campaign, 1942–1945: A Bibliography* (Lara: Gentext Publications, 2015).
94. Sun Laichen, "Chinese Historical Sources on Burma: A Bibliography of Primary and Secondary Works", *Journal of Burma Studies* 2 (1997), pp. 1–116.
95. P.M. Herbert, "U Pe Maung Tin Bibliography", *Journal of Burma Studies* 9 (2004), pp. 130–76.
96. "Bibliography of F.K. Lehman's Published Works", *Journal of Burma Studies* 15, no. 1 (June 2011), pp. 59–67. Lehman died in 2016.
97. "Online Burma/Myanmar Library", http://www.ibiblio.org/obl/. See also David Arnott, "The Online Burma/Myanmar Library: A Brief Introduction", *Bulletin of the Burma Studies Group* (March–September 2002), pp. 19–21.
98. "Online Burma/Myanmar Library: Abstracts, Bibliographies, Scholarly Journals, Libraries, Institutes, Universities, Other Research Tools", http://www.burmalibrary.org/show.php?cat=794&lo=d&sl=0; and "Online Burma/Myanmar Library: Bibliographies and Online Documents of Individual Burma/Myanmar Scholars", http://www.burmalibrary.org/show.php?cat=1327&lo=d&sl=0.
99. *Myanmar: The Road to Democracy, a Select List*, ISEAS Library Bibliography Series no. 26 (Singapore: Institute of Southeast Asian Studies, May 2008), http://www.thebestfriend.org/wp-content/uploads/MyanmarTheRoadtoDemocracy.pdf.

100. R.L. Hadden, *The Geology of Burma (Myanmar): An Annotated Bibliography of Burma's Geology, Geography and Earth Science* (Alexandria: US Army Topographic Engineering Centre, September 2008), http://tec.army.mil/Burma/BurmaWater.pdf; and R.L. Hadden, *Myanmar (Burma): Water and Hydrology: A Bibliography* (Alexandria: US Army Topographic Engineering Centre, May 2008), http://www.tec.army.mil/Burma/Burma%20water.pdf.

101. "Myanmar (Burma) Bibliography", tribal textiles.info, http://www.tribaltextiles.info/bibliographies/Burma_books.htm ; and "Buddhist Death Rituals: Burma/Myanmar", University of Bristol, http://www.bristol.ac.uk/religion/buddhist-centre/projects/bdr/bibliography/burma.html.

102. D.M. Seekins, *Historical Dictionary of Burma (Myanmar)*, 2nd ed. (Lanham: Rowman and Littlefield, 2017), pp. 487–529. See also D.M. Seekins, *The A to Z of Burma (Myanmar)* (Lanham: Scarecrow Press, 2010), pp. 487–529.

103. R.H. Taylor, *The State in Myanmar* (London: Hurst, 2009), pp. 507–42. The first edition of Taylor's book was entitled *The State in Burma* (London: Hurst, 1987).

104. Monique Skidmore (ed.), *Burma at the Turn of the 21st Century* (Honolulu: University of Hawai'i Press, 2005), pp. 271–85; Chie Ikeya, *Refiguring Women, Colonialism, and Modernity in Burma* (Honolulu: University of Hawai'i Press, 2011), pp. 205–28; M.D. Leigh, *Conflict, Politics and Proselytism: Methodist Missionaries in Colonial and Postcolonial Upper Burma, 1887–1966* (Manchester: Manchester University Press, 2011), pp. 208–22; and RL. Huang, *The Paradox of Myanmar's Regime Change* (Abingdon: Routledge, 2020), pp. 156–89.

105. Mandy Sadan, *Being and Becoming Kachin: Histories beyond the State in the Borderworlds of Burma* (London: The British Academy, 2013), pp. 470–96.

106. Jean-Marc Rastorfer, "Reprints or Simple Photocopies? Current Trends in the Republishing Industry in Myanmar: With a Survey of All Books Reprinted by Photocopy Available in July and August 1997 and Some Locally Reprinted Books for Sale on Internet in September 1998", paper presented at the Burma Studies Conference held on 2–4 October 1998, Northern Illinois University De Kalb, USA (De Kalb: Northern Illinois University, 1998).

107. "About Tea Circle", https://teacircleoxford.com/about-us/.

108. "Bibliography of Burma Studies", *Tea Circle*, https://teacircleoxford.com/bibliography-of-burma-studies/.

109. Jenny Hedstrom, "Women Writing about Burma/Myanmar", *Tea Circle*, 9 September 2019, https://teacircleoxford.com/2019/09/09/3840/.

110. This bibliography is separate from the Myanmar Manuscript Digital Library housed at the University of Toronto Robarts Library. See Tony Scott, "New Open Access Database of Myanmar Manuscripts

and Textual Artefacts at the University of Toronto", *Tea Circle*, 1 April 2020, https://teacircleoxford.com/2020/04/01/new-open-access-database-of-myanmar-manuscripts-and-textual-artefacts-at-the-university-of-toronto/.

111. Thaw Kaung, "Bibliographies Compiled in Myanmar", in Pierre Pichard and Francois Robinne (eds.), *Etudes Birmanes: en homage a Denise Bernot* (Paris: Ecole Francais d'Extreme Orient, 1998), pp. 405–14.

112. *Research Bibliography of Books, Documents, and Pamphlets on Burma* (Rangoon: Union of Myanmar New Administrative System, 1972) (typescript).

113. The author and bibliophile Lucas Stewart, for example, keeps abreast of new publications and literary trends in Myanmar and often posts short articles about them on his blog. See Lucas Stewart, https://sadaik.com/.

114. Schwertner, *Burma/Myanmar Bibliographic Project*, vol. 1, p. vii.

115. Johnson, Review of Hobbs, *Southeast Asia: An Annotated Bibliography of Selected Reference Sources in Western Languages*, p. 147.

116. These exceptions include a number of reports by the Brussels-based International Crisis Group, which initially produced hard copies but later seems only to have posted soft copies on the internet. Many of the reports, academic papers and publications produced by advocacy groups and listed here can also be found on the internet.

117. In one case, for example, the book was published in France but contains several chapters written in English. A number of books contain both English and Burmese texts.

118. A useful reference in this regard is Uta Gartner, "Myanmar Studies: An Overview", in Georg Winterberger and Esther Tenberg (eds.), *Current Myanmar Studies: Aung San Suu Kyi, Muslims in Arakan, and Economic Insecurity* (Newcastle Upon Tyne: Cambridge Scholars, 2019), pp. 19–28.

119. More recent titles include H.M. Kyed (ed.), *Everyday Justice in Myanmar: Informal Resolutions and State Evasion in a Time of Contested Transition* (Copenhagen: NIAS Press, 2020); and C.A. Boshier, *Mapping Cultural Nationalism: The Scholars of the Burma Research Society, 1910–1935* (Copenhagen: NIAS Press, 2017).

120. A few exceptions were made where I was persuaded that publication was imminent. It should be noted, however, that there are several works listed in online catalogues or on publishers' websites that are no longer going to be published, or appear to have been postponed indefinitely. For example, Andrew Selth's book *Burma's Security: Myths, Mysteries and Misconceptions* is still listed on some websites, with a 2021 publication date. However, it was overtaken by events in 2011 and was shelved the following year.

121. A good example of the latter is Frederic P. Miller, Agnes F. Vandome and John McBrewster (eds.), *8888 Uprising* (Germany: Alphascript,

2010). This book is largely drawn from unrefereed Wikipedia entries. Its front cover carries a photograph of British policemen confronting a street demonstration, probably in the United Kingdom.

122. Zoya Phan and Damien Lewis, *Little Daughter: A Memoir of Survival in Burma and the West* (London: Simon and Schuster, 2009); and Zoya Phan and Damien Lewis, *Undaunted: My Struggle for Freedom and Survival in Burma* (New York: Free Press, 2010).

123. Emma Larkin, *Everything Is Broken: The Untold Story of Disaster under Burma's Military Regime* (London: Granta, 2010); and Emma Larkin, *No Bad News for the King: The True Story of Cyclone Nargis and Its Aftermath in Burma* (New York: Penguin, 2011).

124. The majority ethnic group is known as the *Bamar*, or Burmans.

125. See, for example, J.F., "Should you Say Myanmar or Burma?", *The Economist*, 20 December 2016, https://www.economist.com/the-economist-explains/2016/12/20/should-you-say-myanmar-or-burma.

126. See, for example, Andrew Selth, "Burma and the Politics of Names", *The Interpreter*, 12 July 2010, http://www.lowyinterpreter.org/post/2010/07/12/Burma-and-the-politics-of-names.aspx.

127. Other titles include Ko, Saw, Sai, Sao and Sayadaw. "Ko", "Maung" and "Ma", however, can also be integral parts of Burmese names, as in "Ko Ko Gyi", "Maung Maung" and "Ma Ma Lay".

128. Burmese Glass was first manufactured in 1885 by the Mount Washington Glass Company in the United States. It was so named by Queen Victoria because the colour of the glazes "reminded" her of a sunset in Myanmar (although she had never seen one). See Debbie and Randy Coe, *Fenton Burmese Glass* (Atglen: Schiffer, 2004).

129. Herbert, *Burma*, p. 39.

130. Norval Morris, *The Brothel Boy and Other Parables of the Law* (New York: Oxford University Press, 1994).

131. See, for example, the "FiveBooks Interviews" conducted by *The Browser* with several authors of works about Burma, https://fivebooks.com/best-books/bertil-lintner-on-burma/ (Bertil Lintner); https://fivebooks.com/best-books/emma-larkin-on-burma/ (Emma Larkin); https://fivebooks.com/best-books/sean-turnell-burmese-economy/ (Sean Turnell); and https://fivebooks.com/best-books/sue-arnold-on-describing-burma/ (Sue Arnold).

132. "Letter to Graham and Anne Shepard", in W.H. Auden and Louis MacNeice, *Letters from Iceland* (London: Faber and Faber, 1937), p. 34.

Protocols and Politics

Protocols

After Myanmar's armed forces crushed a nationwide pro-democracy uprising in September 1988, the country's official name (in English) was changed from its post-1974 form, the "Socialist Republic of the Union of Burma", back to the "Union of Burma", which had been adopted when Myanmar regained its independence from the United Kingdom in January 1948. In July 1989, the new military government changed the country's name once again, this time to the "Union of Myanmar", which had long been the vernacular version (in the literary register, at least). In the formal declaration of the country's independence, for example, it was called the Union of Burma in the English version and the Union of Myanmar (or "Myanma") in the Burmese version. In 2011, after formal promulgation of the 2008 national constitution, the country's official name was changed yet again, this time to the "Republic of the Union of Myanmar".

Also, in July 1989 a number of other place names were changed by the military government to conform more closely to their original pronunciation in the Burmese language. For example, Arakan State became Rakhine State and Tenasserim Division became Tanintharyi Division (later Tanintharyi Region). The Mergui Archipelago became the Myeik Archipelago, the Irrawaddy River became the Ayeyarwady River and the Salween River became the Thanlwin River. The city of Rangoon became Yangon, Moulmein became Mawlamyine, Akyab became Sittwe and Maymyo became Pyin Oo Lwin. The ethnolinguistic groups formerly known as the Burmans and the Karen are now called the Bamar and the Kayin.[1] The people of Kayah State are widely known as Karenni, the state's name until it was changed by the Burmese government in 1952.[2]

The new names were accepted by most countries, the United Nations and other major international organizations. A few governments, activist groups and news media outlets, however, still clung to "Burma" as the name of the country, apparently as a protest against the former military regime's refusal to put the question of a change to the people of Myanmar.[3] The old name was also believed to be the preference of then opposition leader Aung San Suu Kyi, who was held under house arrest by the military regime for periods totalling almost fifteen years.[4] Questioned about the official name of the country soon after her party took office in 2016, Aung San Suu Kyi stated her continuing preference for the colonial-era term "Burma" but said that both names were now acceptable.[5]

After the United Kingdom dispatched troops to the royal capital of Mandalay and completed its three-stage conquest of Burma (as it was then called) in December 1885, Yangon (then known as Rangoon) was confirmed as the administrative capital of the country. It remains the commercial capital, but in November 2005 the ruling military council formally designated the newly built city of Naypyidaw (or Nay Pyi Taw), 327 kilometres (203 miles) north of Yangon, as the seat of Myanmar's government.[6] The terms "Rangoon regime", "Yangon regime", or in some cases simply "Rangoon" or "Yangon", have often been used by authors and commentators as shorthand terms for the central government, including the military government that was created in 1962 and re-invented in 1974, 1988 and 1997. The government after 2005 is sometimes referred to as the "Naypyidaw regime", or "Naypyidaw", to reflect the administrative change that took place that year.

Another common term is *Tatmadaw*. It is usually translated as "royal force", but the honorific "daw" no longer refers to the monarchy. Since 1948, the name has been the vernacular term for Myanmar's tri-service (army, navy and air force) armed forces. In recent years, it has gained wide currency in English-language publications on Myanmar. Sometimes, the Tatmadaw is referred to simply as "the army", reflecting that service arm's overwhelming size and influence compared with the other two. While the term "Defence Services" usually refers only to the armed forces, it is sometimes used in a wider context to refer collectively to the armed forces, the Myanmar Police Force, the "people's militia" and sundry other state-endorsed paramilitary forces. On occasion, the Myanmar Fire Services Department and Myanmar Red Cross have also been included in this category. As the 2008 constitution decrees that "all the armed forces in the Union shall be under the command of the Defence Services", the formal title of the Tatmadaw's most senior officer is Commander-in-Chief of Defence Services.[7]

Over the years, some components of Myanmar's intelligence apparatus have changed their formal titles several times. The military intelligence organization, for example, has periodically been renamed, usually to coincide with structural changes in the armed forces. These adjustments have not always been known to, or recognized by, foreign observers. Also, Burmese language titles have been translated into English in different ways. The use of popular names has added another complication. For example, ever since 1948 the Tatmadaw's intelligence arm has been widely known as the Military Intelligence Service (MIS), or simply the "MI" ("em-eye"). Similarly, the Police Force's Special Intelligence Department (or, strictly translated, the "Information Police"), has long been known as Special Branch, or "SB". All this has meant that in the literature some agencies have been called by several different names, and not always accurately.[8]

All Burmese personal names are particular. Most people do not have surnames or forenames.[9] Names may be one to four syllables long, and are usually chosen depending on the day of the week that a child is born (which is why many people in Myanmar share the same names). Also, among the majority Bamar ethnic group, names are usually preceded by an honorific, such as "U", meaning "uncle", or "Daw", meaning "aunt". "U" can also form a part of a man's name, as in U Tin U. The titles "Maung", "Ko" ("brother") and "Ma" ("sister"), usually given to young men and women, are also found in personal names, as in Maung Maung Aye, Ko Ko Gyi and Ma Ma Lay. To all such rules, however, there are exceptions. Some of Myanmar's ethnic minorities, like the Kachin, have family or clan names, which are placed before their given names, as in cases like Maran Brang Seng, where "Maran" is the name of a clan.[10] Other ethnic minorities, like the Shan, Kachin, Karen and Chin, have their own systems of honorifics.

In Myanmar, names can be changed relatively easily, often without seeking official permission or registration. This situation is further complicated by the frequent use of nicknames and other sobriquets as identifiers, such as "Myanaung" (the town) U Tin, "Tekkatho" (university) Phone Naing, or "Guardian" (the magazine) Sein Win. Pen-names, *noms-de guerre* and pseudonyms also have a long history in Myanmar.[11] For example, the birth name of General Ne Win, who effectively ruled the country from 1962 to 1988, was Shu Maung. "Ne Win", which means "bright sun" in Burmese, was a *nom de guerre* he adopted in 1941, and retained after the war. Some Myanmar citizens were given or have adopted Western names, including those who attended Christian missionary schools in their youth. Others use only one part of their name for convenience, for example when travelling abroad or dealing with foreigners. It is not uncommon for an obituary to list more than one name by which the deceased was known.

Politics

At the risk of some repetition, it may also be helpful to sketch out recent political developments, and to note the changes in the names of some key institutions and positions.

The armed forces effectively ruled Myanmar for half a century, since Ne Win's coup in March 1962, when they formed a Revolutionary Council. From 1974 to 1988, they exercised power through an ostensibly elected "civilian" parliament (called the Pyitthu Hluttaw), dominated by the Burma Socialist Programme Party, the country's only legal political organization. On taking back direct control in September 1988, the armed forces created the State Law and Order Restoration Council (SLORC), which ruled by decree. In November 1997, apparently on the advice of an American public relations firm, the regime changed its name to the State Peace and Development Council (SPDC), but continued to rule through executive fiat.[12] In May 2008, the SPDC held a constitutional referendum, with predictable results.[13] This was followed by carefully managed elections on 7 November 2010. The resulting national parliament, consisting of 75 per cent elected officials and 25 per cent non-elected military officers, first met in January 2011. A new government was installed under President Thein Sein in March that year.

Continuing this process, by-elections were staged on 1 April 2012 to fill 48 seats left vacant after recently elected Members of Parliament had resigned to take up ministerial appointments or had died. The opposition National League for Democracy (NLD), which was re-registered for the elections in December 2011, claimed that fraud and rules violations were widespread, but the party still won 43 of the 45 seats available on the day. One successful candidate was the party's leader, Aung San Suu Kyi.

On 8 November 2015, a new general election was held that, by most accounts, was reasonably free and fair.[14] The NLD received about 65.6 per cent of all votes cast, while the pro-military Union Solidarity Development Party (USDP) received 27.5 per cent. Under Myanmar's "first past the post" electoral system, this gave the NLD 79.4 per cent of all the available seats.[15] It secured 255 in the 440-seat lower house (Pyitthu Hluttaw, or House of Representatives) and 135 in the 224-seat upper house (Amyotha Hluttaw, or House of Nationalities)—a total of 390 of the 491 seats contested at the Union level.[16] The armed forces are allocated 25 per cent of the seats in both houses, but this gave the NLD a clear majority in the combined Union Assembly (Pyidaungsu Hluttaw). As a result, it was able to elect a new president in 2016 and pass a law creating the position of State Counsellor for Aung San Suu Kyi (who under the 2008 constitution is unable to become president, as her two children are the citizens of foreign countries).[17]

The national charter clearly stated that the president "takes precedence over all other persons" in Myanmar. However, even before the elections, Aung San Suu Kyi had made it clear that she intended to be "above the president" and act as the country's de facto leader.[18] Under the NLD, the president acted essentially as a ceremonial head of state. For practical purposes, Aung San Su Kyi acted as head of the government, within the limits of the constitution, which ensures that considerable power is retained by the armed forces. This position was accepted by most other world leaders, as evidenced by her attendance at various ASEAN meetings and at the enthronement of the new Japanese emperor in October 2019. Aung San Su Kyi was also Myanmar's Minister for Foreign Affairs and, formally at least, attended some international meetings in this capacity.[19]

Another general election was held in November 2020, with an estimated voter turnout of more than 70 per cent. Despite "serious deficiencies in the legal framework" noted by neutral observers, voters were able "freely to express their wills".[20] The result was an even more emphatic victory for Aung San Suu Kyi and the NLD. The party won 258 seats (58.6 per cent) in the Pyitthu Hluttaw and

136 seats (61.6 per cent) in the Amyotha Hluttaw, or 83 per cent of the total.[21] Having secured more than 322 of the 476 elected seats, the NLD was able to form a government and choose a new president. The USDP suffered dramatic losses all around the country, garnering only 33 seats in both houses. The NLD also dominated the elections for the state and region assemblies, which were held at the same time. These results promised that, barring unforeseen eventualities, Aung San Suu Kyi and the NLD would remain in office for another five years.[22] Once again, they would govern in partnership with the armed forces, which, under the 2008 constitution, were allocated three ministries in addition to 25 per cent of all seats in both national and provincial assemblies.

On 1 February 2021, however, almost exactly a decade after the SPDC permitted the transition to a "disciplined democracy", those expectations were rudely dashed. Before the new parliament could meet that day, the armed forces unexpectedly declared a one-year state of emergency. They detained Aung San Suu Kyi and more than fifty other officials and activists. A military spokesman stated that the Tatmadaw had been forced to seize power because of the NLD's failure to acknowledge massive fraud in the November 2020 elections.[23] Few foreign observers believed that was the real reason, but, despite widespread speculation in the news media and online, the reasons for the takeover remained unknown.[24] To the people of Myanmar, however, one thing was clear. Once again, the country had an unelected military government, and faced an uncertain future.

Notes

1. "Writing Systems: Romanization, Government of the Union of Myanmar Notification 5/89", Eighth United Nations Conference on the Standardization of Geographical Names, Berlin, 27 August 2002, Doc. E/CONF.94/INF75, https://unstats.un.org/unsd/geoinfo/ungegn/docs/8th-uncsgn-docs/inf/8th_UNCSGN_econf.94_INF.75.pdf.
2. See "Karenni and Kayah: The Nature of Burma's Ethnic Problem over Two Names and the Path to Resolution", *Asia Peacebuilding Initiatives*, 5 February 2014, http://peacebuilding.asia/burmas-ethnic-problem-over-two-names-and-the-path-to-resolution/.
3. Andrew Selth and Adam Gallagher, "What's in a Name: Burma or Myanmar?", *The Olive Branch*, 21 June 2018, https://www.usip.org/blog/2018/06/whats-name-burma-or-myanmar.

4. Aung San Suu Kyi's incarceration occurred, with a number of breaks, between July 1989 and November 2010. She was detained once again in February 2021.
5. Andrew Selth, "More Name Games in Burma/Myanmar", *The Interpreter*, 10 August 2016, https://www.lowyinstitute.org/the-interpreter/more-name-games-burmamyanmar.
6. Occasionally, it is stated that Naypyidaw is 367 kilometres north of Yangon, but that calculation is based on the distance by road between the two cities.
7. *Constitution of the Republic of the Union of Myanmar* (Naypyidaw: Ministry of Information, 2008), chapter 7, clause 338.
8. This issue is discussed in Andrew Selth, *Secrets and Power in Myanmar: Intelligence and the Fall of General Khin Nyunt* (Singapore: ISEAS – Yusof Ishak Institute, 2019).
9. D.I. Steinberg, *Burma/Myanmar: What Everyone Needs to Know*, 2nd ed. (Oxford: Oxford University Press, 2013), pp. xix–xx.
10. "A Note on Burmese Names", in Thant Myint U, *The Hidden History of Burma: Race, Capitalism, and the Crisis of Democracy in the 21st Century* (New York: W.W. Norton, 2020), p. xii.
11. See Andrew Selth, "Burma and the Politics of Names", *The Interpreter*, 12 July 2010, https://archive.lowyinstitute.org/the-interpreter/burma-and-politics-names.
12. D.S. Mathieson, "The Burma Road to Nowhere: The Failure of the Developmental State in Myanmar", *Policy, Organisation and Society* 17, no. 7 (1999), p. 108. See also "A SLORC by Any Other Name", *Washington Post*, 6 March 1998, https://www.washingtonpost.com/archive/opinions/1998/03/06/a-slorc-by-any-other-name/84bdf222-1eb8-417c-97ee-032cd9535e91/.
13. The SPDC claimed that 92.48 per cent of eligible voters endorsed the new constitution. *Constitution of the Republic of the Union of Myanmar (2008)*, p. iv.
14. The Carter Centre, *Observing Myanmar's 2015 General Elections: Final Report* (Atlanta: Carter Centre, 2016), https://www.uec.gov.mm/show_data_content.php?name=209pdf&type=law&code=x&sno=8455&token=9ce69a1b8f9f0effbfeb662cab5728f5fbc183e9b61b04b06fc97ff71e62c7fc70510d5cc03e2cd38726c2d47dab9e8471cc95b390758055fbf40fa6fbe6e0cd.
15. Kyaw Kyaw, "Analysis of Myanmar's NLD Landslide", *New Mandala*, 1 May 2012, https://www.newmandala.org/analysis-of-myanmars-nld-landslide/.
16. *The Myanmar Elections: Results and Implications*, Asia Briefing no. 147 (Yangon/Brussels: International Crisis Group, 9 December 2015).
17. "Myanmar's 2015 Landmark Elections Explained", BBC News, 3 December 2015, https://www.bbc.com/news/world-asia-33547036.

18. *Constitution of the Republic of the Union of Myanmar (2008)*, chapter 3, clause 58. See also "Myanmar Election: Aung San Suu Kyi Will Be 'Above President'", BBC News, 5 November 2015, http://www.bbc.com/news/av/world-asia-34729691/myanmar-election-aung-san-suu-kyi-will-be-above-president.
19. When Aung San Suu Kyi represented Myanmar at the International Court of Justice in December 2019, to defend her country against charges of genocide, she did so in "a private capacity" as Myanmar's official agent, not as the de facto head of government or foreign minister. This posed a protocol and security dilemma for the Dutch authorities. Larry Jagan, "Suu Kyi Gears Up for Genocide Hearing", *Bangkok Post*, 2 December 2019, https://www.bangkokpost.com/opinion/opinion/1806409/suu-kyi-gears-up-for-genocide-hearing.
20. "Carter Centre Preliminary Statement on the 2020 Myanmar General Elections", The Carter Centre, 10 November 2020, https://www.cartercenter.org/news/pr/2020/myanmar-111020.html.
21. "Myanmar's 2020 General Election Results in Numbers", *The Irrawaddy*, 11 November 2020, https://www.irrawaddy.com/elections/myanmars-2020-general-election-results-numbers.html.
22. Tamas Wells, "Reading Myanmar's 2020 Elections", Election Watch, University of Melbourne, 28 October 2020, https://electionwatch.unimelb.edu.au/articles/reading-myanmars-2020-elections.
23. Sebastian Strangio, "Myanmar's Military Seizes Power in Early Morning Coup", *The Diplomat*, 1 February 2021, https://thediplomat.com/2021/02/myanmars-military-seizes-power-in-early-morning-coup/.
24. See, for example, Hannah Beech, "Democracy Hero? Military Foil? Myanmar's Leader Ends Up as Neither", *New York Times*, 1 February 2021, https://www.nytimes.com/2021/02/01/world/asia/myanmar-coup-aung-san-suu-kyi.html; and Andrew Selth, "The Coup in Myanmar: What Do We Know?", *The Interpreter*, 3 February 2021, https://www.lowyinstitute.org/the-interpreter/coup-myanmar-what-do-we-know.

The Bibliography

THE COUNTRY AND ITS PEOPLE

1. Casino, E.S., *Burma and the Burmese: A Historical Perspective* (Honolulu: University of Hawai'i, 1997)
2. Chandra, Puran, *Burma Past and Present: A Factbook* (Delhi: Forward Books, 2013)
3. Clancy, Tomas, *Countries of the World: Republic of the Union of Myanmar* (US: CreateSpace, 2012)
4. Cribbs, Gillian (ed.), *Back to Mandalay: Burmese Life, Past and Present* (New York: Abbeville Press, 1996)
5. Einspruch, Andrew, *Myanmar* (Melbourne: Heinemann, 2007)
6. Ferrars, Max, and Bertha Ferrars, *Burma*, reprint of 1901 edition (Bangkok: Ava House, 1996)
7. Gartner, Uta, and Jens Lorenz (eds.), *Tradition and Modernity in Myanmar: Proceedings of an International Conference Held in Berlin from May 7th to May 9th, 1993*, 2 volumes (Hamburg: LIT, 1994)
8. Gutman, Pamela, *Burma's Lost Kingdoms: Splendours of Arakan*, photographs by Zaw Min Yu (Bangkok: Orchid Press, 2001)
9. Hinchey, Jane, *Myanmar (Burma)* (French's Forest: Redback, 2019)
10. Hla Tun Aung, *Myanmar: The Study of Processes and Patterns* (Yangon: National Centre for Human Resources Development, Ministry of Education, 2003)
11. Horstmann, Ingrid, and Wolfgang Willaschek, *Glances – Beholden to Burma: A Journey of Discovery into the World of Myanmar* (Gnas: Weishaupt, 1999)
12. Kelly, R.G.T., *Burma*, reprint of 1933 edition (Abingdon: Routledge, 2009)
13. Khin Maung Nyunt, *Myanmar Superlatives* (Yangon: Unity, 2012)
14. Kraas, Frauke, Regine Spohner and Aye Aye Myint, *Socio-Economic Atlas of Myanmar* (Stuttgart: Franz Steiner, 2017)
15. Kraft, Heinrich, and M.M. Kraft, *Myanmar* (Bangkok: Supernova, 2000)
16. Kyi Kyi Hla, *A Myanmar Tapestry* (Yangon: Taw Win, 2004)
17. Ma Thanegi, *Burmese Traditions* (Yangon: Asia House, 2014)

18. Mackenzie, K.R.H., *Burmah and the Burmese*, reprint of 1853 edition (Charleston: BiblioLife, 2009)
19. Maung Kyaa Nyo, *Presenting Myanmar* (Yangon: Daw Shwe Eain, 2000)
20. *Myanmar* (Singapore: Times Editions, 2000)
21. *Myanmar: Facts and Figures* (Yangon: Ministry of Information, Union of Myanmar, 2000)
22. *Myanmar: Land of the Spirit* (Bangkok: Asia Books, 1996)
23. *Myanmar Statistical Yearbook 2019* (Nay Pyi Taw: Central Statistical Organisation, Ministry of Planning and Finance, Republic of the Union of Myanmar, 2019)
24. Nee, P.W., *Key Facts on Burma (Myanmar)* (Boston: The Internationalist Publishing Company, 2013)
25. Oh, Su-Ann (ed.), *Myanmar's Mountain and Maritime Borderscapes: Local Practices, Boundary-Making and Figured Worlds* (Singapore: ISEAS – Yusof Ishak Institute, 2016)
26. Pichard, Pierre, and Francois Robinne (eds.), *Etudes Birmanes: en homage a Denise Bernot*, in English and French (Paris: Ecole Francais d'Extreme Orient, 1998)
27. *Post Colonial Society and Culture in Southeast Asia: Proceedings of the Conference on Myanmar and Southeast Asian Studies, 16–18 December 1998*, 2 volumes (Yangon: Universities Historical Research Centre, 1999 [volume 1] and 2001 [volume 2])
28. Saitner, Gerard, and Bettina Winterfield, *Burma* (Munich: Bucher, 2001)
29. Saw Myat Yin, *Burma* (New York: Marshall Cavendish, 1990)
30. Seekins, D.M., *Historical Dictionary of Burma (Myanmar)*, 2nd edition (Lanham: Rowman and Littlefield, 2017)
31. Sell, Julie, *Whispers at the Pagoda: Portraits of Modern Burma* (Bangkok: Orchid Books, 1999)
32. Selth, Andrew, *Burma Watching: A Retrospective*, Regional Outlook no. 39 (Brisbane: Griffith Asia Institute, Griffith University, 2012)
33. Selth, Andrew, *Interpreting Myanmar: A Decade of Analysis* (Canberra: Australian National University Press, 2020)
34. Selth, Andrew, *Myanmar-Watching: Problems and Perspectives*, Regional Outlook no. 58 (Brisbane: Griffith Asia Institute, Griffith University, 2018)

35. *Seminar on Understanding Myanmar* (Yangon: Myanmar Institute of Strategic and International Studies, 2004)
36. Shippen, Mick, *Enchanting Myanmar* (Oxford: John Beaufoy, 2012)
37. Shway Yoe [J.G. Scott], *The Burman: His Life and Notions*, reprint of 1882 edition (Whiting Bay: Kiscadale, 1989)
38. Simpson, Adam, and Nicholas Farrelly, *Myanmar: Politics, Economy and Society* (Oxford: Routledge, 2021)
39. Simpson, Adam, Nicholas Farrelly and Ian Holliday (eds.), *Routledge Handbook of Contemporary Myanmar* (London: Routledge, 2018)
40. Skidmore, Monique (ed.), *Burma at the Turn of the Twenty-first Century* (Honolulu: University of Hawai'i Press, 2005)
41. Sochaczewski, P.S., *Curious Encounters of the Human Kind: Myanmar (Burma)* (Geneva: Explorer's Eye Press, 2015)
42. Steinberg, D.I., *Burma/Myanmar: What Everyone Needs to Know*, 2nd edition (New York: Oxford University Press, 2013)
43. Than Tun, *Essays on the History and Buddhism of Burma*, edited by Paul Strachan (Whiting Bay: Kiscadale, 1988)
44. Thu Ra Myint Maung, *The Golden Land of Myanmar* (Yangon: Khyap Sa Kha Pe, 2001)
45. Winterberger, Georg, and Esther Tenberg (eds.), *Current Myanmar Studies: Aung San Suu Kyi, Muslims in Arakan, and Economic Insecurity* (Newcastle Upon Tyne: Cambridge Scholars, 2019)
46. Wright, Arnold, et al. (eds.), *Twentieth Century Impressions of Burma: Its History, People, Commerce, Industries and Resources*, reprint of 1910 edition (Bangkok: White Lotus, 2015)
47. Yip, Dora, and Pauline Khng, *Welcome to Myanmar* (Singapore: Times Editions, 2001)
48. Zahler, Diane, *Than Shwe's Burma* (Minneapolis: Twenty-First Century Books, 2010)

GUIDEBOOKS AND DESCRIPTIONS

General

49. *101 Amazing Things to Do in Myanmar* (US: Independently published, 2018)
50. Abram, David, *Myanmar (Burma)*, revised edition (London: Dorling Kindersley, 2016)
51. *Admiralty Sailing Directions: Bay of Bengal Pilot, NP21*, 12th edition (Taunton: United Kingdom Hydrographic Office, 2013)
52. Barrett, Kenneth, *25 Walks in Myanmar: Exploring the Historic Landmarks of Myanmar* (US: Tuttle, 2017)
53. Bui, Hana, *When Global Meets Local: How Expatriates Can Succeed in Myanmar: A First-Time Guidebook* (Yangon: The author, 2019)
54. *Burma: The Alternative Guide* (London: Burma Action Group, 1995)
55. Cangi, E.C., *Faded Splendour, Golden Past: Urban Images of Burma* (Kuala Lumpur: Oxford University Press, 1997)
56. Chopra, P.N., and Prabha Chopra, *Monuments of the Raj: British Buildings in India, Myanmar, Pakistan, Bangladesh and Sri Lanka* (New Delhi: Aryan Books International, 1999)
57. Collins, Robert, and E.H. Sabido, *Black Hole with a Heart of Gold* (Bloomington: Xlibris, 2015)
58. Courtauld, Caroline, *Burma (Myanmar)* (Hong Kong: Odyssey, 1999)
59. Courtauld, Caroline, *Burma: Asia's Treasure Trove* (US: Passport Books, 1988)
60. Courtauld, Caroline, *Myanmar: Burma in Style: An Illustrated History and Guide* (Hong Kong: Odyssey, 2013)
61. Courtauld, Caroline, *Myanmar Today: Myanmar in Style: An Illustrated History and Guide* (Hong Kong: Myanmar Tourism Federation, 2013)
62. Courtauld, Caroline, *The Irrawaddy: Burma's Kingly Stream* (London: Sanctuary Retreats, 2014)
63. Davidson-Shaddox, Brenda, *Off the Beaten Path: Guide to Myanmar Shrines and Monuments* (Yangon: SST Tourism, 2003)
64. *Discovering Myanmar* (Yangon: Universities Historical Research Centre, 1999)

65. Edwardson, Morgan (ed.), *To Myanmar with Love: A Travel Guide for the Connoisseur* (San Francisco: ThingsAsian Press, 2009)
66. Eliot, Joshua, and Jane Bickersteth, *Myanmar (Burma) Handbook* (Bath: Footprint Handbooks, 1997)
67. *Fodor's Thailand: With Myanmar (Burma), Cambodia and Laos*, 14th edition (New York: Fodor's Travel, 2016)
68. *Forbidden Glimpses of Shan State: A Brief Alternative Guide*, 2nd edition (Chiang Mai: Shan Women's Action Network, 2010)
69. Greenwood, Nicholas, *Guide to Burma*, 2nd edition (Chalfont St Peter: Bradt Publications, 1995)
70. *Insight Guides: Myanmar*, 11th revised edition (London: Apa Publications, 2019)
71. Jotow, Elena, and Nicholas Ganz, *Burma: The Alternative Guide* (London: Thames and Hudson, 2009)
72. Khin Maung Nyunt, *Pilgrim's Guide to Yangon, Pagan, Mandalay and Bago* (Yangon: The author?, 1991)
73. Kollner, Helmut, and Axel Bruns, *Myanmar (Burma)* (Munich: Nelles, 1998)
74. Kraas, Frauke, Regine Spohner and Jorg Stadelbauer, *111 Places in Myanmar That You Shouldn't Miss*, translated by Tom Ashforth (Cologne: Emons, 2019)
75. Kyi Kyi May and Nicholas Nugent, *Myanmar (Burma)* (London: Kuperard, 2015)
76. Lyons, Keith, *Moon Myanmar* (Berkeley: Avalon Travel, 2017)
77. Ma Thanegi, *Inle Lake: Blue Sea in the Shan Hills* (Yangon: Asia House, 2005)
78. Ma Thanegi, *The Splendours of Myanmar* (Yangon: Asia House, 2005)
79. Mason, Mark, *Myanmar and Bangkok: Travel Guide* (US: CreateSpace, 2014)
80. Mehner, Martin, *Only in Myanmar! Twelve Unique Experiences in the Golden Country* (Norderstedt: Books on Demand, 2019)
81. Merchant, J.T., *Expatriate in Myanmar: A Guide for Newcomers* (Yangon: Myanmar Book Centre, 2014)
82. *Myanmar: An Illustrated Guide to the Country and its Wildlife* (Sevenoaks: Harrison Institute, 2002)
83. Richmond, Simon, et al., *Myanmar (Burma)*, 13th edition (Dublin: Lonely Planet Global, 2017)

84. Saw Myat Yin, *Culture Shock! Myanmar: A Survival Guide to Customs and Etiquette*, 4th edition (Singapore: Marshall Cavendish, 2013)
85. Scott, J.G., *Burma: A Handbook of Practical Information*, reprint of 1906 edition (Bangkok: Orchid Press, 1999)
86. Stevenson, John, and Barry Broman, *Irrawaddy: Benevolent River of Burma* (Singapore: Times Editions, 2004)
87. Strachan, Paul, *A Burma River Journey: A Handbook for Travellers* (Gartmore: Kiscadale, 1997)
88. Thaw Kaung, *Myanmar Wonderland: Places of Historical Interest and Scenic Beauty* (Yangon: Today Publishing House, 2013)
89. Thomas, Gavin, Stuart Butler and Tom Deas, *The Rough Guide to Myanmar (Burma)*, 2nd edition (London: Rough Guides, 2017)
90. *Welcome to the Sagaing Hills: The Abode of Holy Recluses* (Sagaing: Department of Research and Compilation, Sitagu International Buddhist Academy, 2009)
91. Win Pe, *Dos and Don'ts in Myanmar* (Bangkok: Book Promotion and Service Co., 1996)
92. *World Infopaedia: Myanmar* (New Delhi: Pragun Publications, 2007)

Yangon (Rangoon)

93. Bansal, Ben, and Elliott Fox, *Architectural Guide: Yangon*, photographs by Manuel Oka (Berlin: DOM, 2015)
94. Bayly, Christopher, *Rangoon (Yangon) 1939–49: The Death of a Colonial Metropolis*, Occasional Paper no. 3 (Cambridge: Centre of South Asian Studies, University of Cambridge, 2003)
95. Brac de la Perriere, Benedicte, *Eternal Rangoon: Contemporary Portrait of a Timeless City*, photographs by Thomas Renaut (Paris: Editions d'Indochine, 1999)
96. Coggan, Philip, *Journey through Yangon: A Pictorial Guide to the Green City of Grace*, photographs by Felix Hug (Singapore: Times Editions, 2005)
97. Golden, Steve, *Faces of Yangon* (Singapore: Talisman, 2020)
98. Heijmans, P.J., *Relics of Rangoon* (Yangon: Inya Media, 2016)
99. Henderson, Virginia, and Tim Webster, *Yangon Echoes: Inside Heritage Homes* (Bangkok: River Books, 2015)

100. Kraas, Frauke, Hartmut Gaese and Mi Mi Kyi (eds.), *Megacity Yangon: Transformation Processes and Modern Developments: Second German-Myanmar Workshop in Yangon, Myanmar, 2005* (Berlin: LIT, 2006)

101. Maung Khine Zaw, *Interesting Places of the Past in Yangon* (Yangon: Today Publishing House, 2015)

102. Morgan, Francis, *Vacation Goose Travel Guide, Yangon Myanmar Burma* (US: LLC-CreateSpace, 2017)

103. Percival, Bob, *Walking the Streets of Yangon: The People, Stories & Hidden Treasures of Downtown Cosmopolitan Yangon (Rangoon)* (Yangon: U Thein Myint, 2016)

104. Rhoden, T.F., *Yangon and Shwedagon Pagoda* (Durham: Other Places, 2014)

105. Rooney, Sarah, et al., *30 Heritage Buildings of Yangon: Inside the City that Captured Time* (Chicago: Association of Myanmar Architects and Serindia Publications, 2012)

106. Rush, Elizabeth, *Still Lifes from a Vanishing City: Essays and Photographs from Yangon*, foreword by Emma Larkin and afterword by Thant Thaw Kaung (San Francisco: Things Asian Press, 2015)

107. San Lin Tun and Keith Lyons, *Yangon Street Walker* (Yangon: Duwon Press/Muditar Books, 2018)

108. Singer, N.F., *Old Rangoon: City of the Shwedagon* (Gartmore: Kiscadale, 1995)

109. *Yangon: Green City of Grace* (Yangon: Yangon City Development Committee, 1999)

110. *Yangon: The Garden City* (Yangon: Yangon City Development Committee, 1995)

Mandalay

111. Duroiselle, Charles, *Guide to the Mandalay Palace*, reprint of 1931 edition (Singapore: Myanmar Rare Book Publications, 1999)

112. Moore, Elizabeth, *The Reconstruction of Mandalay Palace: An Interim Report on Aspects of Design* (London: School of Oriental and African Studies, 1993)

113. O'Connor, V.C.S., *Mandalay and Other Cities of the Past in Burma*, 2nd reprint of 1907 edition (Bangkok: White Lotus, 1996)

114. Saraya, Dhida, *Mandalay, the Capital City: The Center of the Universe* (Bangkok: Muang Boran, 1995)
115. Tainturier, Francois, *Mandalay and the Art of Building Cities in Burma* (Singapore: National University of Singapore Press, 2021)

Bagan (Pagan)

116. Aung Kyaing et al., *The Pagodas and Monuments of Bagan*, translated by Khin Maung Nyunt, 2 volumes (Yangon: Ministry of Information, 1995 [volume 1] and 1998 [volume 2])
117. Bautze-Picron, Claudine, *The Buddhist Murals of Pagan: Timeless Vistas of the Cosmos* (Bangkok: Orchid Press, 2003)
118. Broman, Barry, *Bagan: Temples and Monuments of Ancient Burma* (Bangkok: Book Promotion and Service Co., 2004)
119. Enriquez, C.M., *Pagan: Being the First Connected Account in English of the 11th Century Capital of Burma, with the History of a Few of its Most Important Pagodas*, reprint of 1914 edition (Charleston: BiblioLife, 2009)
120. Kyaw Lat, *Art and Architecture of Bagan, and Historical Background* (Yangon: Mudon Sarpay, 2010)
121. Ma Thanegi, *Bagan Mystique* (Yangon: Tanintaye Sarpay, 2011)
122. Sanda Khin, *Bagan Images of Mural Paintings* (Yangon: Asia Alin Sarpae, 2007)
123. Stadtner, D.M., with Michael Freeman, *Ancient Pagan: Buddhist Plain of Merit* (Bangkok: River Books, 2005)
124. Strachan, Paul, *Pagan: Art and Architecture of Old Burma* (Whiting Bay: Kiscadale, 1989)

Other Cities

125. Maung Aung Myoe, *The Road to Naypyidaw: Making Sense of the Myanmar Government's Decision to Move Its Capital*, Working Paper Series no. 79 (Singapore: Asian Research Institute, National University of Singapore, 2006)
126. Phone Kyaw, Thanegi and Tet Soe, *Guide to Bago: The Ancient Royal City of Hanthawaddy* (Yangon: Nyan Alin Books, 2016)
127. Preecharushh, Dulyapak, *Naypyidaw: The New Capital of Burma* (Bangkok: White Lotus, 2009)

128. Shwe Zan, *The Golden Mrauk-U: An Ancient Capital of Rakhine* (Yangon: Cho Tay Than Sar Pay, 1994)
129. Than Tun, *History of Pindaya: Town, Pagoda and Cave* (Yangon: Ah Thine Ah Wine Sarpay, 1998)
130. Tun Shwe Khine, *A Guide to Mrauk-U: An Ancient City of Rakhine, Myanmar*, photographs by Ko Tun Shaung (Sittway: U Tun Shwe, 1993)

PHOTOGRAPHY

131. Bader, Michael, et al., *100 Faces of Myanmar* (Heidelberg: Kehrer, 2013)
132. Becker, Reinhard, *Irrawaddy: Lifeline for Myanmar* (Bielefeld: Kerber, 2019)
133. Bieber, Joey, *Melting the Stars: An Exhibition of Photographs of the People of Burma* (London: Christies, 2001)
134. Bigg, P.J., *Burmese Gaze: Portraits from Burma 1988/2009* (Myanmar: Pansodan, 2015)
135. Birk, Lukas, *Burmese Photographers*, foreword by F.X. Augustin, essays by Nathalie Johnston and Christophe Loviny, and photographs by Har Si Yone et al. (Yangon: Goethe Institute, Myanmar, and The author, 2018)
136. Birk, Lukas (ed.), *Irene: A Burmese Icon* (Yangon: Fraglich Publishing and Myanmar Photo Archive, 2020)
137. Birk, Lukas (ed.), *One Year in Yangon 1978* (Yangon: Fraglich Publishing and Myanmar Photo Archive, 2018)
138. Birk, Lukas (ed.), *U Than Maung – The No.1 Amateur Photographer*, introduction by San Lin Tun (Yangon: Fraglich Publishing and Myanmar Photo Archive, 2019)
139. Birk, Lukas (ed.), *Yangon Fashion 1979: Fashion = Resistance* (Yangon: Fraglich Publishing and Myanmar Photo Archive, 2020)
140. Birk, Lukas, and Carmin Berchiolly, *Reproduced – Rethinking P.A. Klier and D.A. Ahuja* (Yangon: Fraglich Publishing and Myanmar Photo Archive, 2019)
141. Bo Bo Zaw, *Glimpses of Enchanting Myanmar: Myanmar Travel Photography* (Yangon?, 2009)
142. Brackenbury, Wade, *The Last Paradise on Earth: The Vanishing Peoples and Wilderness of Northern Burma* (Gold Beach: Flame of the Forest, 2005)
143. Briels, Edwin, *Yangon (Rangoon): The City I Live* (Yangon: Yone Kyi Chet Book House, 2004)
144. Broman, Barry, *Bagan: Temples and Monuments of Ancient Burma* (Reading: Paths International, 2003)
145. Broman, Barry, *Faces of Myanmar* (Bangkok: Book Promotion and Service Co., 2004)

146. Broman, Barry, *Myanmar: Serenity and Transition in Burma* (Reading: Paths International, 2004)
147. Broman, Barry, *Myanmar: The Land and Its People* (Singapore: Marshall Cavendish, 2013)
148. Buddee, Kim, *Once Was Burma: New Images from the Streets of Rangoon* (Roseville: Tour de Force Books, 2012)
149. Chan Chao, *Burma – Something Went Wrong: The Photographs of Chan Chao* (Tucson: Nazraeli Press, 2000)
150. Chan Chao, *Letter from PLF (Burma)* (Tucson: Nazraeli Press, 2001)
151. Constantine, Greg, *Exiled to Nowhere: Burma's Rohingya*, foreword by Emma Larkin (Thailand: The author, 2012)
152. Dell, Elizabeth (ed.), *Burma: Frontier Photographs, 1918–1935: The James Henry Green Collection* (London: Merrell, 2006)
153. Diamond, Jon, *Stilwell and the Chindits: The Allied Campaign in Northern Burma, 1943–1944: Rare Photographs from Wartime Archives* (Barnsley: Pen and Sword Books, 2014)
154. Dunlop, Nic, *Brave New Burma* (Stockport: Dewi Lewis, 2013)
155. Everarda, Ellis, *Burma: Encountering the Land of the Buddhas* (Gartmore: Kiscadale, 1994)
156. Falconer, John, et al., *Seven Days in Myanmar: A Portrait of Burma by 30 Great Photographers* (Singapore: Editions Didier Millet, 2014)
157. Falise, Thierry, *Burmese Shadows: Twenty-five Years Reporting on Life behind the Bamboo Curtain* (Alnwick: McNidder and Grace, 2012)
158. *Featured Collectives: Myanmar Photographers around the World* (Yangon: Crescent Moon, 2016)
159. Germaine, E.T., *Photos from Burma, 1937–1966: A Unique Collection of Over 140 Images*, revised edition (Ilford: Feedaread.com, 2017)
160. Gotoh, Masaharu, *The Country of Pagodas: Myanmar Burma* (Tokyo?: The author, 1998)
161. Heath, David, *Burma: An Enchanted Spirit* (US: The author, 2014)
162. Hillier, Geoffrey, and Francis Wade, *Daybreak in Myanmar* (Portland: Verve Photo Books, 2014)

163. Ho, Juh Lee, and Henry Kwoh, *Myanmar and Its People: People That Stay in Your Life Just for the Blink of an Eye, Unnoticed* (Singapore?: The authors, 2018)
164. Hurlimann, Martin, *Photographic Impressions of Burma, Siam, Cambodia, Yunnan, Champa, and Vietnam*, reprint of 1929 edition, translated by W.E.J. Tips (Bangkok: White Lotus, 2001)
165. Kayalar, Jim, *Burma Alight* (US: CreateSpace, 2017)
166. Kemp, Hans, and Tom Vater, *Burmese Light: Impressions of the Golden Land* (Hong Kong: Visionary World, 2013)
167. Lazar, David, *Myanmar: A Luminous Journey* (Bangkok: The author, 2016)
168. Ledergerber, R.A., *Burma: The Jewel of Asia: Impressions from Yangon* (San Francisco: The author and Blurb Inc., 2014)
169. Leonard, T.M., *Street 21* (San Francisco: Blurb, 2015)
170. Lu, Nan, *Prisons of North Burma* (Beijing?: China National Art Photograph Publishing House, 2015)
171. Mackay, James, *Abhaya: Burma's Fearlessness* (Bangkok: River Books, 2011)
172. MacLean, Joanna, *Portraits of Myanmar: A Celebration of Work, Play and Prayer* (Seattle: Marrowstone Press, 2017)
173. Maudy, Jacques, and Jimi Casaccia, *Yangon: A City to Rescue*, introduction by R.H. Taylor (Canberra: National Library of Australia, 2013)
174. Moe Min, *In Buddha's Land: Visions of Buddhist Myanmar* (Bangkok: Orchid Press, 2007)
175. Muecke, James, *Visions of Myanmar* (Adelaide: The author, 2005)
176. Neiser, Birgit, *Catching the Light: A Journey across Myanmar* (Bangkok: River Books, 2017)
177. Parkitny, J.U., *Blood Faces: Through the Lens: Chin Women of Myanmar* (Singapore: Flame of the Forest, 2007)
178. Polillo, Roberto, *Glances from Myanmar* (US?: The author, 2015)
179. Poncar, Jaroslav, *Burma: The Land That Time Forgot*, text by Emma Larkin (in German) (Mannheim: Edition Panaroma, 2007)
180. Poncar, Jaroslav, *Burma/Myanmar*, text by John Keay (in German) (Mannheim: Edition Panaroma, 2016)

181. Scalea, N.S., *Sights of Myanmar: The Golden City of Yangon* (US: Underline, 2018)
182. Scherman, Christine, and Birgit Neiser, *Golden Land: Burma/Myanmar – 100 Years* (Bangkok: White Lotus Press, 2014)
183. Schink, Hans-Christian, *Burma* (Bielefeld: Kerber, 2018)
184. Sein Myo Myint, Bagan Maung Maung and Ma Ohmer, *Myanmar Smiles* (Yangon, 2004)
185. Shaw, Scott, *Pagan, Burma: Shadows of the Stupa* (US: Buddha Rose Publications, 2012)
186. Shaw, Scott, *Rangoon and Mandalay: A Photographic Exploration* (US: Buddha Rose Publications, 2016)
187. Singer, N.F., *Burmah: A Photographic Journey, 1855–1925* (Gartmore: Kiscadale, 1993)
188. Stasinopoulou, Dimitra, *Burma's Plea* (Athens: Dimitra Stasinopoulou and Burma Campaign UK, 2011)
189. Stulberg, Scott, *Passage to Burma* (New York: Skyhorse, 2015)
190. Suga, Hiroshi, *The Golden Paradise of Myanmar* (Tokyo, 1997)
191. Swain, Anna, *Burma: Tiffin, Nuns and Tumeric* (Byron Bay: Shutter Books, 2016)
192. Taylor, Roger, and Crispin Branfoot, with Sarah Greenough and Malcolm Daniel, *Captain Linnaeus Tripe: Photographer of India and Burma, 1852–1860* (Munich: Prestel, 2014)
193. Tun Tin, Frankie, *Through Myanmar Eyes* (Singapore: Viscom Editions, 1997)
194. Voss, Peter, *Myanmar* (Petersburg: Michael Imhof, 2017)
195. Warner, Jeffrey, *Dignity amidst the Rubbish: Hour-by-Hour with a Burmese Migrant Community in Thailand* (Thailand: Compasio Relief and Development, 2014)
196. Willat, Felice, and Lark, *The Quiet Between: Song of Burma* (Topanga: Felice Willat Photography, 2009)
197. Yee, Jaffee, et al., *The Best of Myanmar: Golden Land of Hidden Gems* (Bangkok: Knowledge Media, 2017)

GEOGRAPHY AND GEOLOGY

General

198. *Atlas of Mineral Resources of the ESCAP Region: Geology and Mineral Resources of Myanmar* (New York: Economic and Social Commission for Asia and the Pacific, 2016)

199. Bannert, Dietrich, A.S. Lyen and Than Htay, *The Geology of the Indoburman Ranges in Myanmar* (Stuttgart: Schweizerbart Science, 2011)

200. Barber, A.J., Khin Zaw and M.J. Crow (eds.), *Myanmar: Geology, Resources and Tectonics*, Geological Society Memoir no. 48 (London: Geological Society Publishing House, 2018)

201. Duroiselle, Charles, *Notes on the Ancient Geography of Burma*, reprint of 1906 edition (New Delhi: SN Books World, 2015)

202. Hla Tun Aung, *Selected Articles in Geography* (Yangon: Unity, 2014)

203. Krishnan, M.S., *Geology of India and Burma*, 6th edition (New Delhi: CBS and Distributors, 2016)

204. Mitchell, Andrew, *Geological Belts, Plate Boundaries and Mineral Deposits in Myanmar* (US: Elsevier Science, 2017)

205. Morrison, Cameron, *A Geography of Burma: Standard*, reprint of 1921 edition (Charleston: Nabu Press, 2010)

206. Noetling [Notling], Fritz, *The Occurrence of Petroleum in Burma, and its Technical Exploitation*, reprint of 1897 edition (US: Sagwan Press, 2015)

207. Racey, Andrew, and M.F. Ridd, *Petroleum Geology of Myanmar*, Geological Society Memoir no. 45 (Bath: Geological Society, 2015)

208. Streissguth, Thomas, *Myanmar in Pictures*, Visual Geography Series (Minneapolis: Twenty-First Century Books, 2008)

Jade and Precious Stones

209. Clark, Carol, *Seeing Red: A View from inside the Ruby Trade* (Bangkok: White Lotus, 1999)

210. George, E.C.S., *Ruby Mines District*, reprint of 1962 edition (Bangkok: White Lotus, 2007)

211. Halford-Watkins, J.F., with R.W. Hughes, *The Book of Ruby and Sapphire* (US: RWH, 1997)

212. Iyer, L.A.N., *The Geology and Gem-Stones of the Mogok Stone Tract, Burma*, reprint of 1953 edition (Bangkok: White Lotus, 2007)
213. *Jade: Myanmar's "Big State Secret"* (London: Global Witness, 2015)
214. Nyan Thin, *Myanma Jade* (Mandalay: Mandalay Gem Association, 2002)
215. O'Connor, V.C.S., *Rubies of Mogok: Thabeit-Kyin, Capelan, Mogok*, reprints of 1904 and 1888 publications (Bangkok: White Lotus, 2008)
216. Samuels, S.K., *Burma Ruby: A History of Mogok's Rubies from Antiquity to the Present* (Tucson: SKS Enterprises, 2003)
217. Samuels, S.K., *Imperial Jade of Burma and Mutton-Fat Jade of India: Mining, Trade and Use from Antiquity to the Present* (Tucson: SKS Enterprises, 2014)
218. Themelis, Ted, *Gems and Mines of Mogok* (Bangkok: A&T, 2008)
219. Themelis, Ted, *Mogok: Valley of Rubies and Sapphires* (Bangkok: A&T, 2000)
220. Yavorskyy, V.Y., *Burma Gems* (Hong Kong: The author and Gemforest, 2018)

ENVIRONMENT AND NATURAL HISTORY

General

221. *Accessible Alternatives: Ethnic Communities' Contribution to Social Development and Environmental Conservation in Burma* (Chiang Mai: Burma Environmental Working Group, 2009)
222. Akimoto, Yuki (ed.), *The Salween Under Threat: Damming the Longest Free River in Southeast Asia* (Mae Sot: Salween Watch, Southeast Asia Rivers Network and the Centre for Social Development Studies, Chulalongkorn University, 2004)
223. *Burma's Environment: People, Problems, Policies* (Chiang Mai: The Burma Environmental Working Group, 2011)
224. *Country Environmental Analysis: A Road towards Sustainability, Peace and Prosperity: Synthesis Report* (Myanmar: World Bank Group, May 2019)
225. *Damming the Irrawaddy* (Chiang Mai: Kachin Development Networking Group, Kachin Environment Organisation, 2007)
226. *Diversity Degraded: Vulnerability of Cultural and Natural Diversity in Northern Karen State, Burma* (Chiang Mai: Karen Environmental and Social Action Network, 2005)
227. *Ecotourism Sites in Myanmar* (Naypyidaw: Forest Department, Ministry of Forestry, 2000)
228. Idd Idd Shwe Zin, *Status and Management of Tanintharyi Nature Reserve, Tenasserim in Myanmar* (Gottingen: Cuviller, 2017)
229. James, Jamie, *The Snake Charmer: A Life and Death in Pursuit of Knowledge* (New York: Hyperion, 2008)
230. Lasi Bawk Naw, *Biodiversity, Culture, Indigenous Knowledge: Nature and Wildlife Conservation Programmes in Kachin State, Myanmar: An Overview of Conservation Training in Kachin State between 1999 and 2003* (Myitkyina: YMCA, 2004)
231. McCoy, Cliff, *Turning Treasure into Tears: Mining, Dams, and Deforestation in Shwegyin Township, Pegu Division, Burma* (Chiang Mai: Earthrights International, January 2007)
232. Middleton, Carl, and Vanessa Lamb (eds.), *Knowing the Salween River: Resource Politics of a Contested Transboundary River* (Cham: Springer International, 2019)

233. *Myanmar's Next Great Transformation: Enclosing the Oceans and Our Aquatic Resources* (Amsterdam: Transnational Institute, March 2017)
234. Onishi, Shingo, *Natural Myanmar* (Bangkok: Tecpress Book, 2001)
235. *Our Forest, Our Life: Protected Areas in Tanintharyi Region Must Respect the Rights of Indigenous Peoples* (Myanmar: Conservation Alliance of Tanawthari, February 2018)
236. *Paradise Lost? The Suppression of Environmental Rights and Freedom of Expression in Burma* (London: Article 19, September 1994)
237. Rabinowitz, Alan, *Beyond the Last Village: A Journey of Discovery in Asia's Forbidden Wilderness* (Washington DC: Island Press, 2001)
238. Rabinowitz, Alan, *Life in the Valley of Death: The Fight to Save Tigers in a Land of Guns, Gold, and Greed* (Washington DC: Island Press, 2008)
239. Si Si Hla Bu and Paul Bates, *Myanmar: An Illustrated Guide to the Country and its Wildlife* (Yangon: Zoology Department, Yangon University, 2002)
240. Simpson, Adam, *Energy, Governance and Security in Thailand and Myanmar (Burma): A Critical Approach to Environmental Politics in the South* (Farnham: Ashgate, 2014)
241. *Tanawthari Landscape of Life: A Grassroots Alternative to Top-Down Conservation in Tanintharyi Region* (Myanmar: Conservation Alliance of Tanawthari, March 2020)
242. *Valley of Darkness: Gold Mining and Militarization in Burma's Hugawng Valley* (Chiang Mai: Kachin Development Networking Group, 2007)
243. Zin Mar Than, *Socio-Economic Development of Indawgyi Lake, Myanmar* (Stuttgart: Franz Steiner, 2017)

Fauna

244. Baker, E.C.S., *The Game-Birds of India, Burma and Ceylon*, 2 volumes, reprint of 1921 edition (Delhi: Pranava Books, 2020)
245. Day, Francis, *Report on the Freshwater Fish and Fisheries of India and Burma*, reprint of 1873 edition (Gottingen: Hansebooks, 2017)

246. De Vosjoli, Philippe, and Roger Klingenberg, *Burmese Pythons: Plus Reticulated Pythons and Related Species* (Santee: Advanced Vivarium Systems, 2005)

247. Dowling, H.G., and J.V. Jenner, *Snakes of Burma: Checklist of Reported Species and Bibliography*, Smithsonian Herpetological Information Service no. 76 (Washington DC: Smithsonian Institution, 1988)

248. Francis, C.M., *A Photographic Guide to Mammals of South-East Asia: Including Thailand, Malaysia, Singapore, Myanmar, Laos, Cambodia, Vietnam, Java, Sumatra, Bali and Borneo*, 3rd edition (London: New Holland, 2013)

249. Hume, Allan, and C.H.T. Marshall, *The Game Birds of India, Pakistan, Bangladesh, Burma & Sri Lanka (Including Bhutan, Nepal and Tibet)*, 3 volumes, incorporates 1879–81 editions (Lahore: Vanguard Books, 1995)

250. Kelsey-Wood, Dennis, *The Proper Care of Burmese Cats* (Neptune City: T.F.H., 1992)

251. Kyaw Nyunt Lwin and Khin Ma Ma Thwin, *Birds of Myanmar* (Chiang Mai: Silkworm Books, 2005)

252. Lydekker, Richard, *The Great and Small Game of India, Burma and Tibet*, reprint of 1900 edition (New Delhi: Asian Educational Services, 1996)

253. Murkett, Marvin, and Ben Team, *Burmese Pythons as Pets: Burmese Python Comprehensive Owner's Guide* (US: IMB, 2014)

254. Sein Tu, *Large Mammals of Myanmar* (Yangon: Innwa, 1998)

255. Shepherd, C.R., and Vincent Nijman, *Elephant and Ivory Trade in Myanmar* (Petaling Jaya: TRAFFIC Southeast Asia, 2008)

256. Shepherd, C.R., and Vincent Nijman, *The Wild Cat Trade in Myanmar* (Petaling Jaya: TRAFFIC Southeast Asia, 2011)

257. Smith, Vivienne, *The Birman Cat Worldwide (The Sacred Cat of Burma)* (Preston: The author, 1991)

258. Talbot, George, *The Fauna of British India, including Ceylon and Burma: Butterflies*, 2 volumes, reprint of 1939 and 1947 editions (New Delhi: Today and Tomorrow's Printers and Publishers, 2013)

259. Thet Zaw Naing, Robert Tizard and Geoffrey Davison, *A Naturalist's Guide to the Birds of Myanmar* (Oxford: John Beaufoy, 2021)

Environment and Natural History   59

260. Thorell, Tord, *Descriptive Catalogue of the Spiders of Burma, Based on the Collection Made by Eugene W. Oates and Preserved in the British Museum*, reprint of 1895 edition (Boston: Adamant Media, 2001)
261. Vella, Carolyn, and John McGonagle, *Burmese Cats* (Hauppauge: Barron's, 1995)
262. Win Maung and Win Ko Ko, *Turtles and Tortoises of Myanmar* (Yangon: San Yaung Shein Sarpay, 2002)
263. Zuo, D.L., and Rosie Ounsted (eds.), *The Status of Coastal Waterbirds and Wetlands in Southeast Asia: Results of Waterbird Surveys in Malaysia (2004–2006) and Thailand and Myanmar (2006)* (Wageningan: Wetlands International, 2007)

Flora

264. *A Disharmonious Trade: China and the Continued Destruction of Burma's Northern Frontier Forests* (London: Global Witness, 2009)
265. Clayton, Dudley, *Charles Parish – Plant Hunter and Botanical Artist in Burma* (London: Ray Society, 2017)
266. Collett, Henry, and W.B. Hemsley, *On a Collection of Plants from Upper Burma and the Shan States*, reprint of 1890 edition (Whitefish: Kessinger, 2014)
267. Kress, W.J., *The Weeping Goldsmith: Discoveries in the Secret Land of Myanmar* (New York: Abbeville Press, 2009)
268. Kress, W.J., R.A. DeFilipps, Ellen Farr and Yin Yin Kyi, *A Checklist of the Trees, Shrubs, Herbs and Climbers of Myanmar* (Washington DC: National Museum of Natural History, 2003)
269. Kurz, Sulpiz [Sulpice], *Forest Flora of British Burma*, 2 volumes, reprint of 1877 edition (Charleston: Nabu Press, 2011)
270. Kurzweil, Hubert, and Saw Lwin, *A Guide to Orchids of Myanmar* (Kota Kinabulu: Natural History Publications, 2014)
271. Kyaw Soe and Tin Myo Ngwe, *Medicinal Plants of Myanmar: Identification and Uses of Some 100 Commonly Used Species*, photographs by Htun Shaung (Yangon: Forest Resource Environment Development and Conservation Association and Pyi Zone, 2004)
272. *Medicinal Plants of Myanmar* (Yangon: Department of Traditional Medicine, 2002)

273. Nelson, E.C., *Shadow among Splendours: Lady Charlotte Wheeler-Cuffe's Adventures among the Flowers of Burma, 1897–1921* (Dublin: National Botanic Gardens of Ireland, 2013)
274. Nyan Tin, *Wild Orchids of Myanmar* (Yangon: Green Leaf, 2014)
275. Semwal, D.K. (ed.), *A Comprehensive Field Guide to Medicinal Plant Biodiversity of Myanmar and Mauritius* (New York: Nova Science, 2020)
276. Strettell, G.W., *The Ficus Elastica in Burma Proper, or a Narrative of My Journey in Search of It, Etc*, reprint of 1876 edition (London: British Library, 2011)
277. Tanaka, Norio, Yu Ito, Mu Mu Aung and Nobuyuki Tanaka, *A Field Guide to Aquatic Plants of Myanmar*, edited by Nobuyuki Tanaka (Kota Kinabalu: Natural History Publications (Borneo), 2019)
278. Tanaka, Yoshitaka, Nyan Htun and Tin Tin Yee, *Wild Orchids in Myanmar: Volume 1, Last Paradise of Wild Orchids* (Bangkok: Orchid Press, 2008)
279. Tanaka, Yoshitaka, Nyan Htun and Tin Tin Yee, *Wild Orchids in Myanmar: Volume 2, A Poem of Wild Orchids* (Bangkok: Orchid Press, 2008)
280. Tanaka, Yoshitaka, and Tin Tin Yee, *Wild Orchids in Myanmar: Volume 3, Shangri-La of Wild Orchids* (Bangkok: Orchid Press, 2008)

PREHISTORY AND ARCHAEOLOGY

281. *Architectural Drawings of Temples in Pagan* (Rangoon: Department of Higher Education, Ministry of Education, 1989)

282. Bautze-Picron, Claudine, and Than Tun, *Myanma Terracottas (Pottery in Myanma and Votive Tablets of Myanma)* (Yangon: Chit Sayar Sarpay, 2003)

283. De Terra, Hellmut, and H.L. Movius, *Research on Early Man in Burma, with Supplementary Reports upon the Pleistocene Vertebrates and Mollusks of the Region by E.H. Colbert and J. Bequaert, and Pleistocene Geology and Early Man in Java by Hellmut De Terra*, reprint of 1943 edition (New Delhi: Munshiram Manoharlal, 2005)

284. Green, Alexandra, and T.R. Blurton (eds.), *Burma: Art and Archeology* (London: British Museum Press, 2002)

285. *Inventory of Ancient Monuments in Bagan, Volume 1 (Monuments 1–150)* (Yangon: Department of Archeology, Ministry of Culture, 1998)

286. Ishizawa, Yoshiaki, and Yasushi Kono (eds.) (with the Organising Committee, Pagan Symposium), *Study on Pagan: Research Report* (Tokyo: Institute of Asian Cultures, Sophia University, 1989)

287. Khin Maung Nyunt et al., *The Pagodas and Monuments of Bagan*, 2 volumes (Yangon: Ministry of Information, 1995 [volume 1] and 1998 [volume 2])

288. Ko Myo (Arimaddana), *The Earliest Religious Buildings Discovered at the Ancient City of Wadee, Myanmar* (Yangon: Tun Foundation Bank Literary Committee, 2017)

289. Moore, E.H., *The Pyu Landscape: Collected Articles* (Naypyidaw: Ministry of Culture, Republic of the Union of Myanmar, 2012)

290. Myint Aung, *Revealing Myanmar's Past: An Anthology of Archaeological Articles* (Yangon: Tun Foundation Bank Literary Committee, 2012)

291. Nai Pan Hla, *Archaeological Aspects of Pyu Mon Myanmar* (Yangon: Thin Sapay, 2011)

292. Nan Hlaing, *Terracotta Votive Tablets of Thaton* (Mawlamyine: Bhadradevi Books, 2016)

293. Pichard, Pierre, *Inventory of Monuments at Pagan, Volume 1, Monuments 1–255* (Gartmore and Paris: Kiscadale and UNESCO, 1992)

294. Pichard, Pierre, *Inventory of Monuments at Pagan, Volume 2, Monuments 256–552* (Gartmore and Paris: Kiscadale and UNESCO, 1993)

295. Pichard, Pierre, *Inventory of Monuments at Pagan, Volume 3, Monuments 553–818* (Gartmore and Paris: Kiscadale and UNESCO, 1994)

296. Pichard, Pierre, *Inventory of Monuments at Pagan, Volume 4, Monuments 819–1136* (Gartmore and Paris: Kiscadale and UNESCO, 1994)

297. Pichard, Pierre, *Inventory of Monuments at Pagan, Volume 5, Monuments 1137–1439* (Gartmore and Paris: Kiscadale and UNESCO, 1995)

298. Pichard, Pierre, *Inventory of Monuments at Pagan, Volume 6, Monuments 1440–1736* (Gartmore and Paris: Kiscadale and UNESCO, 1996)

299. Pichard, Pierre, *Inventory of Monuments at Pagan, Volume 7, Monuments 1737–2064* (Paris: UNESCO and Ecole Francais d'Extreme Orient, 1999)

300. Pichard, Pierre, *Inventory of Monuments at Pagan, Volume 8, Monuments 2065–2834* (Paris: UNESCO and Ecole Francais d'Extreme Orient, 2001)

301. Pichard, Pierre, *The Pentagonal Monuments of Pagan* (Bangkok: White Lotus, 1991)

302. *Proceedings of the Workshop on Bronze Age Culture in Myanmar (Yangon, 7 January 1999)* (Yangon: Universities Historical Research Centre, 1999)

303. Stargardt, Janice, *The Ancient Pyu of Burma: Volume 1, Early Pyu Cities in a Man-Made Landscape* (Cambridge: PACSEA, 1990)

304. Stargardt, Janice, *Tracing Thought through Things: The Oldest Pali Texts and the Early Buddhist Archaeology of India and Burma*, The 7th Gonda Lecture (Amsterdam: Royal Netherlands Academy of Arts and Sciences, 2000)

305. *Sustainable Destination Plan for the Ancient Cities of Upper Myanmar: Mandalay, Amarapura, Innwa, Sagaing, Mingun (2016–2021)*, translated by Gavin Williams (Florence: Polistampa, 2016)

306. Tan, Terence, *Ancient Jewellery of Myanmar: From Prehistory to Pyu Period* (Yangon: Mudon Sar Pae, 2015)
307. Taw Sein Ko, *Archaeological Notes on Mandalay*, reprint of 1917 edition (New Delhi: Pranava, 2019)
308. Than Tun, *Myanma Terracottas: Pottery in Myanma and Votive Tablets of Myanmar* (Yangon: Khyit Saya Sape, 2003) (in English and Burmese)
309. Than Win, *Myanma Cultural Property: Ancient Ornament (Jewellery)* (Yangon: Department of Archaeology and National Museum, Ministry of Culture, 2014) (in English and Burmese)
310. Thein Win, *Beikthano: Summary of 2009–2010 Archaeological Excavations*, translated by E.H. Moore and Htwe Htwe Win, Nalanda-Sriwjaya Centre Archaeology Unit, Archaeology Report Series no. 4 (Singapore: ISEAS – Yusof Ishak Institute, August 2016)

TRAVELLERS' ACCOUNTS

General

311. Abbott, Gerry (ed.), *Inroads into Burma: A Travellers' Anthology* (Kuala Lumpur: Oxford University Press, 1997)
312. Abbott, Gerry (ed.), *There Before You: The Traveller's History of Burma* (Bangkok: Orchid Press, 1998)
313. Spain, Jack, *Retracing Marco Polo: A Tale of Modern Travelers Who Locate and Follow Marco Polo's Route to China and Burma* (Richmond: Gilgit Press, 2004)

Pre-Twentieth Century

314. Abreu, Robert, *Journal of a Tour through Pegu and Martaban Provinces in the Suite of Drs McClelland and Brandis*, reprint of 1858 edition (Bangkok: Orchid Press, 2001)
315. Alexander, J.E., *Travels from India to England Comprehending a Visit to the Burman Empire and a Journey through Persia, Asia Minor, European Turkey &c in the Years 1825–26*, reprint of 1827 edition (New Delhi: Munshiram Manoharlal, 2000)
316. An Officer, *A Thousand Miles up the Irrawaddy: Burmah Proper*, reprint of 1879 edition (New Delhi: Relnk Books, 2015)
317. Anderson, John, *Mandalay to Momien: A Narrative of the Two Expeditions to Western China of 1868 and 1875 under Colonel Edward B. Sladen and Colonel Horace Browne*, reprint of 1876 edition (Bangkok: White Lotus, 2009)
318. Bastian, Adolf, *A Journey in Burma (1861–1862)*, translated by W.E.J. Tips, edited by Christian Goodden, reprint of 1886 edition (Bangkok: White Lotus, 2004)
319. Bird, G.W., *Wanderings in Burma*, introduction by Guy Lubeigt, reprint of 1897 edition (Bangkok: White Lotus, 2003)
320. Burney, Henry, *The Journal of Henry Burney in the Capital of Burma, 1830–1832*, introduction by Nicholas Tarling, Resource Papers no. 5 (Auckland: New Zealand Asia Institute, University of Auckland, 1995)
321. Chaudoir, Georges, and Mr and Mrs Emile Jottrand, *Belgian Tourists in Burma, Siam, Vietnam and Cambodia*, translated by W.E.J. Tips (Bangkok: White Lotus, 2011)

322. Cox, Hiram, *Journal of a Residence in the Burmhan Empire, and More Particularly at the Court of Amarapoorah*, reprint of 1821 edition, edited by H.C.M. Cox, British Library Historical Print Edition (Charleston: British Library, 2011)

323. Crawfurd, John, *Journal of an Embassy from the Governor General of India to the Court of Ava in the Year 1827*, reprint of 1829 edition (Cambridge: Cambridge University Press, 2012)

324. Ehlers, O.E., *On Horseback through Indochina*, 3 volumes, reprint of 1901 edition, translated by W.E.J. Tips (Bangkok: White Lotus, 2001 [volume 2] and 2002 [volumes 1 and 3])

325. Gordon, C.A., *Our Trip to Burmah, with Notes on that Country*, reprint of 1875 edition (Bangkok: Orchid Press, 2002)

326. Gouger, Henry, *Two Years Imprisonment in Burma (1824–26): A Personal Narrative of Henry Gouger*, reprint of 1860 edition (Bangkok: White Lotus, 2003)

327. Grant, Colesworthy, *Rough Pencillings of a Rough Trip to Rangoon in 1846*, reprint of 1853 edition (Bangkok: White Orchid Press, 1995)

328. Katherine, Sister, *Towards the Land of the Rising Sun: Or, Four Years in Burma*, reprint of 1900 edition (London: Forgotten Books, 2019)

329. Khazeni, Arash, *The City and the Wilderness: Indo-Persian Encounters in Southeast Asia* (Oakland: University of California Press, 2020)

330. Lefevre-Pontalis, Pierre, *Travels in Upper Laos and on the Borders of Yunnan and Burma (The Pavie Mission Indochina Papers [1879–1895], Volume 5)*, reprint of 1902 edition, translated by W.E.J. Tips (Bangkok: White Lotus, 2000)

331. Lycett, Andrew (ed.), *Kipling Abroad: Traffics and Discoveries from Burma to Brazil* (London: I.B. Taurus, 2010)

332. MacGregor, John, *Through the Buffer State: Travels in Borneo, Siam, Cambodia, Malaya and Burma*, reprint of 1896 edition, introduction by W.E.J. Tips (Bangkok: White Lotus, 1994)

333. Malcom, Howard, *Travels in the Burma Empire*, reprint of 1840 edition (Bangkok: Ava House, 1997)

334. Massieu, Isabelle, *Around Southeast Asia in 1897: A Frenchwoman's Observations in Vietnam, Cambodia, Thailand, Burma and Laos*, translated by W.E.J. Tips (Bangkok: White Lotus, 2013)

335. Morrison, G.E., *An Australian in China: Being the Narrative of a Quiet Journey across China to Burma*, reprint of 1895 edition (Hong Kong: China Economic Review Publishing, 2009)

336. O'Connor, V.C.S., *The Silken East: A Record of Life and Travel in Burma*, reprint of 1928 edition (Gartmore: Kiscadale, 1993)

337. Oertel, F.O., *Note on a Tour in Burma in March and April 1892*, reprint of 1892 edition (Bangkok: White Orchid Press, 1995)

338. Roux, Emile, *Searching for the Sources of the Irrawaddy: With Prince Henri d'Orleans from Hanoi to Calcutta Overland, 1895–1896*, reprint of 1897 edition, translation and introduction by Walter E.J. Tips (Bangkok: White Lotus, 1999)

339. Symes, William, *An Account of an Embassy to the Kingdom of Ava in the Year 1795* (New Delhi: Asian Educational Services, 2007)

340. Wheeler, J.T., *Journal of a Voyage up the Irrawaddy to Mandalay and Bhamo*, reprint of 1871 edition (Bangkok: White Orchid Press, 1996)

341. Younghusband, G.J., *Eighteen Hundred Miles on a Burmese Tat through Burmah, Siam and the Eastern Shan States*, reprint of 1888 edition (New Delhi: Asian Educational Services, 1995)

342. Younghusband, G.J., *The Trans-Salwin State of Kiang Tung*, reprint of 1888 edition (Chiang Mai: Silkworm Books, 2005)

Twentieth and Twenty-first Centuries

343. Allardice, Rory, *Rory's Myanmar (Burmese) Journal* (Charleston: The author and CreateSpace, 2015)

344. Bakshi, Akhil, *The Road to Freedom: Travels through Singapore, Malaysia, Burma and India in the Footsteps of the Indian National Army* (New Delhi: Odyssey Books, 1998)

345. Benfield, Andy, *The Wrong Way Round: How Not to Travel to Burma by Motorcycle* (Lake Wales: Road Dog Publications, 2019)

346. Caldicott, Alistair, *Is This Burma?* (Raleigh: The author and Lulu Press, 2010)

347. Chevrillon, Andre, *Among the Burmese in 1902: French Impressions of a Buddhist Country*, reprint of 1902 and 1905 editions, translated by W.E.J. Tips (Bangkok: White Lotus, 2014)

348. Childers, J.S., *Bangkok to Bali, Burma and Bombay: The Mysteries of the Oriental Souls*, reprint of 1932 edition (Pakthongchai: ThaiSunset, 2010)

349. Damrong Rajanubhab, *Journey through Burma in 1936*, translated by Kennon Breazeale (Bangkok: River Books, 1991)

350. De Lajonquiere, Lunet, *Siam and the Siamese: Travels in Thailand and Burma in 1904*, reprint of 1906 edition (Bangkok: White Lotus, 2001)

351. De Vries, Clare, *Of Cats and Kings* (London: Bloomsbury, 2002)

352. Dutta, Abhijit, *Myanmar in the World: Journeys through a Changing Burma* (New Delhi: Aleph Book Company, 2018)

353. Eimer, David, *A Savage Dreamland: Journeys in Burma* (London: Bloomsbury, 2019)

354. Fable, James, *In Search of Myanmar: Travels through a Changing Land*, illustrated by Chuu Wai Nyein (London: The author, 2019)

355. Fetherling, George, *Three Pagodas Pass: A Roundabout Journey to Burma* (Bangkok: Asia Books, 2003)

356. Forsyth, Patrick, *Beguiling Burma: Awe and Wonder on the Road to Mandalay* (Great Yarmouth: Rethink Press, 2012)

357. Ghosh, Amitav, *Dancing in Cambodia, At Large in Burma* (Delhi: Ravi Dayal, 1998)

358. Goodden, Christian, *Three Pagodas: A Journey down the Thai-Burmese Border*, revised edition (Halesworth: Jungle Books, 2002)

359. Hasinoff, E.L., *Confluences: An American Expedition to Northern Burma, 1935* (New Haven: Bard Graduate Centre and Yale University Press, 2013)

360. Ivanoff, Jacques, and Thierry Lejard, in collaboration with Luca and Gabriella Gansser, *A Journey through the Mergui Archipelago* (Bangkok: White Lotus, 2002)

361. Johnston, R.F., *From Peking to Mandalay: A Journey from North China to Burma through Tibetan Ssuch'uan and Yunnan*, reprint of 1908 edition (Cambridge: Cambridge University Press, 2012)

362. Kingdon-Ward, Frank, *Burma's Icy Mountains*, reprint of 1949 edition (Bangkok: Orchid Press, 2006)

363. Kingdon-Ward, Frank, *In Farthest Burma: The Record of an Arduous Journey of Exploration and Research through the Unknown Frontier Territory of Burma and Tibet*, reprint of 1921 edition (Bangkok: Orchid Press, 2005)

364. Kingdon-Ward, Frank, *Return to the Irrawaddy*, reprint of 1956 edition (Bangkok: Orchid Press, 2019)
365. Larkin, Emma, *Secret Histories: Finding George Orwell in a Burmese Teashop* (London: John Murray, 2004)
366. Laube, Lydia, *From Burma to Myanmar: On the Road to Mandalay* (Adelaide: Wakefield Press, 2015)
367. Lazarus, Leo, *Myanmar in Moments* (Port Adelaide: Ginninderra Press, 2020)
368. Lintner, Bertil, *Land of Jade*, 2nd edition (Bangkok: Orchid Press, 1996)
369. Ma Thanegi, *Defiled on the Ayeyarwaddy* (San Francisco: ThingsAsian Press, 2011)
370. Ma Thanegi, *The Native Tourist: In Search of Turtle Eggs*, reprint of 2000 edition (Chiang Mai: Silkworm Books, 2004)
371. MacLean, Rory, *Under the Dragon: Travels in a Betrayed Land* (London: HarperCollins, 1998)
372. Marshall, Andrew, *The Trouser People: Burma in the Shadows of the Empire*, 2nd edition (Bangkok: River Books, 2012)
373. Mirante, Edith, *Burmese Looking Glass: A Human Rights Adventure and a Jungle Revolution* (New York: Grove Press, 1993)
374. Mirante, Edith, *Down the Rat Hole: Adventures Underground on Burma's Frontiers* (Bangkok: Orchid Press, 2005)
375. Paragu, *The Bagan Warfarer*, translated by Kyi Kyi Hla (Yangon: Seikku Cho Cho, 2013)
376. Schramm-Evans, Zoe, *Dark Ruby: Travels in a Troubled Land* (London: Pandora, 1997)
377. Sims, Matt, *Burma: A Journey across Time* (Charleston: The author and CreateSpace, 2015)
378. Stanley, Tracy, and Les Stanley, *Soft Nut Bike Tour of Burma* (Brisbane: The authors, 2020)
379. Strachan, Paul, *Mandalay: Travels from the Golden City* (Gartmore: Kiscadale, 1994)
380. Strachan, Paul, *The Pandaw Story: On the Rivers of Burma and Beyond* (Kenmore: Irrawaddy Flotilla Company and Kiscadale, 2015)
381. Syrota, Timothy, *Welcome to Burma: and Enjoy the Totalitarian Experience* (Bangkok: Orchid Press, 2001)

382. Van Tibes, Ken, *Spirits and Wonders: Following Orwell in Burma* (Norderstedt: Books on Demand, 2018)

383. Wurlitzer, Rudolph, *Hard Travel to Sacred Places* (Boston: Shambhala Publications, 1994)

HISTORY

General

384. Aung Thwin, Michael, and Matrii Aung Thwin, *A History of Myanmar since Ancient Times: Traditions and Transformations*, 2nd edition (London: Reaktion Books, 2013)
385. Becka, Jan, *Historical Dictionary of Myanmar*, Asian Historical Dictionaries no. 15 (Metuchen: Scarecrow Press, 1995)
386. Bhattacharya, Swapna, *The Rakhine State (Arakan) of Myanmar: Interrogating History, Culture and Conflict* (New Delhi: Manohar, 2015)
387. Charney, M.W., *A History of Modern Burma* (Cambridge: Cambridge University Press, 2009)
388. Cockett, Richard, *Blood, Dreams and Gold: The Changing Face of Burma* (New Haven: Yale University Press, 2015)
389. *Comparative Studies in Literature and History of Thailand and Myanmar*, IAS Monograph no. 52 (Bangkok: Institute of Asian Studies, Chulalongkorn University, and Universities Historical Research Centre, Yangon, 1997)
390. *Cruel and Vicious Repression of Myanmar Peoples by Imperialists and Fascists and the True Story about the Plunder of the Royal Jewels* (Yangon: News and Periodicals Enterprise, Ministry of Information, 1991)
391. Delphin, Tin Tin, *Burma's Path to Democracy: The Military, Aung San Suu Kyi and the Rohingya* (New York: Algora, 2020)
392. Egerton, Wilbraham, *An Illustrated Handbook of Indian Arms and Those of Nepal, Burma, Thailand and Malaya*, reprint of 1880 edition (Bangkok: White Orchid Press, 1986)
393. Forbes, C.J.F.S., *British Burma and Its People: Being Sketches of Native Manners, Customs and Religions*, reprint of 1878 edition (Washington DC: Westphalia, 2019)
394. Ghosh, Lipi, *Burma: Myth of French Intrigue* (Calcutta: Naya Udyog, 1994)
395. Ghosh, Parumal, *Brave Men of the Hills: Resistance and Rebellion in Burma, 1825–1932* (London: Hurst, 2000)
396. Gommans, Jos, and Jacques Leider (eds.), *The Maritime Frontier of Burma* (Leiden: KITLV Press, 2002)

397. Greenwood, Nicholas (ed.), *Shades of Gold and Green: Anecdotes of Colonial Burmah, 1886–1948* (New Delhi: Asian Educational Services, 1998)
398. Khin Maung Nyunt, *Selected Writings of Dr Khin Maung Nyunt* (Yangon: Myanmar Historical Commission, 2004)
399. Khin Maung Nyunt, *The Historic Bells of Yangon* (Yangon: Department of Historical Research and National Library, Yangon University, 2016)
400. Metro, Rosalie, and Aung Khine, *Histories of Burma: A Source-Based Approach to Myanmar's History* (Yangon: Mote Oo Education, 2013)
401. Midwood, Jimmy, *The Burmah Oil Society: A History* (UK: Burmah Oil Society, 2005)
402. *Myanmar Two Millennia: Proceedings of the Myanmar Two Millennia Conference, 15–17 December 1999*, 4 volumes (Yangon: Universities Historical Research Centre, 2000)
403. Myo Myint, *Collected Essays on Myanmar History and Culture* (Yangon: Department for the Promotion and Propagation of the Sasana, 2010)
404. Ni Ni Myint, *Selected Writings of Ni Ni Myint* (Yangon: Myanmar Historical Commission, 2004)
405. Pradhan, M.V., *Burma, Dhamma and Democracy*, foreword by Daw Than Than Nu (Bombay: Mayflower, 1994)
406. Seekins, D.M., *State and Society in Modern Rangoon* (London: Routledge, 2011)
407. Selth, Andrew, *Burma, Kipling and Western Music: The Riff from Mandalay* (New York: Routledge, 2017)
408. Selth, Andrew, *Colonial Burma and Popular Western Culture: An Exploratory Survey*, Working Paper no. 197 (Hong Kong: Southeast Asian Research Centre, City University of Hong Kong, 2020)
409. Selth, Andrew, *Making Myanmar: Colonial Burma and Popular Western Culture*, Research Paper, revised edition (Brisbane: Griffith Asia Institute, Griffith University, 2020)
410. *Short History of Myanmar's Independence Struggle* (Yangon: Defence Services Museum and Historical Research Institute, 2001)

411. Stuart, John, *Burma through the Centuries: Being a Short Account of the Leading Races of Burma, of Their Origin, and of Their Struggles for Supremacy throughout Past Centuries; Also of the three Burmese Wars and of the Annexation of the Country by the British Government*, reprint of 1909 edition (London: Routledge, 2018)

412. *Studies in Myanma History, Volume 1* (Yangon: Innwa, 1999)

413. Than Tun, *A Modern History of Myanmar (1752–1948)* (Yangon: Myonywe Sarpay, 2010)

414. Than Tun (ed.), *The Royal Orders of Burma, A.D. 1598–1885*, 10 volumes (Kyoto: The Centre for Southeast Asian Studies, Kyoto University, 1983 [volume 1] to 1990 [volume 10]) (in English and Burmese)

415. Thant Myint U, *The Making of Modern Burma* (Cambridge: Cambridge University Press, 2001)

416. Thant Myint U, *The River of Lost Footsteps: Histories of Burma* (New York: Farrer, Straus and Giroux, 2006)

417. Thaw Kaung, *Aspects of Myanmar History and Culture* (Yangon: Loka Ahlinn, 2010)

418. Thaw Kaung, *Selected Writings of U Thaw Kaung* (Yangon: Myanmar Historical Commission, 2004)

419. Thet Tun, *Selected Writings of Retired Ambassador U Thet Tun* (Yangon: Myanmar Historical Commission, 2004)

420. Topich, W.J., and K.A. Leitich, *The History of Myanmar* (Santa Barbara: Greenwood, 2013)

421. *Traditions in Current Perspective: Proceedings of the Conference on Myanmar and Southeast Asian Studies, 15–17 November 1995* (Yangon: Universities Historical Research Centre, 1996)

422. Tun Aung Chain, *Broken Glass: Pieces of Myanmar History* (Yangon: SEAMEO Regional Centre for History and Tradition, 2004)

423. Tun Aung Chain, *Flowing Waters: Dipping into Myanmar History* (Yangon: Myanmar Knowledge Society, 2013)

424. Tun Aung Chain, *Selected Writings of Tun Aung Chain* (Yangon: Myanmar Historical Commission, 2004)

425. Walker, Andrew, *The Legend of the Golden Boat: Regulation, Trade and Traders in the Borderlands of Laos, Thailand, China and Burma* (Honolulu: University of Hawai'i Press, 1999)

426. Webb, Paul, *The Peacock's Children: The Struggle for Freedom in Burma, 1885–Present* (Bangkok: Orchid Press, 2009)

427. Yunus, Mohammed, *A History of Arakan: Past and Present* (Chittagong: University of Chittagong, 1994)

Pre–Twentieth Century

428. Allott, Anna, *The End of the First Anglo-Burmese War: The Burmese Chronicle Account of How the 1826 Treaty of Yandabo Was Negotiated* (Bangkok: Chulalongkorn University Press, 1994)
429. Aung Thwin, M.A., *Irrigation in the Heartland of Burma: Foundations of the Pre-Colonial Burmese State*, Occasional Paper no. 15 (DeKalb: Centre for Southeast Asian Studies, Northern Illinois University, 1990)
430. Aung Thwin, M.A., *Myanmar in the Fifteenth Century: A Tale of Two Kingdoms* (Honolulu: University of Hawai'i Press, 2017)
431. Aung Thwin, M.A., *Myth and History in the Historiography of Early Burma: Paradigms, Primary Sources and Prejudices*, Monograph in International Studies, Southeast Asia Series no. 102 (Athens: Centre for International Studies, Ohio University, 1998)
432. Aung Thwin, M.A., *The Mists of Ramanna: The Legend That Was Lower Burma* (Honolulu: University of Hawai'i Press, 2005)
433. Aung Thwin, Matrii, *The Return of the Galon King: History, Law, and Rebellion in Colonial Burma* (Athens: Ohio University, 2011)
434. Bagshawe, L.E., *The Kinwun Min-Gyi's London Diary* (Bangkok: Orchid Press, 2006)
435. Bhone Tint Kyaw, *The Ancient History of Pyu-Byammar before Anawrahtar* (Yangon: Kant Kaw Wut Yee, 2015) (in English and Burmese)
436. Bigandet, P.A., *An Outline of the History of the Catholic Burmese Mission from the Year 1720 to 1857*, reprint of 1887 edition (Bangkok: White Orchid Press, 1996)
437. Blackburn, T.R., *A Sadistic Scholar: Captain Latter's War* (New Delhi: APH Publishing, 2002)
438. Blackburn, T.R., *An Ill-Conditioned Cad: Mr Moylan of "The Times"* (New Delhi: APH Publishing, 2002)
439. Blackburn, T.R., *Burma and the Enemy Within* (New Delhi: APH Publishing, 2006)
440. Blackburn, T.R., *Executions by the Half-Dozen: The Pacification of Burma* (New Delhi: APH Publishing, 2008)

441. Blackburn, T.R., *The British Humiliation of Burma* (Bangkok: Orchid Press, 2000)
442. Blackburn, T.R., *The British Lion and the Burmese Tiger: Campbell and Maha Bandula* (New Delhi: APH Publishing, 2002)
443. Blackburn, T.R., *The Defeat of Amarapura: The Second Anglo-Burmese War of 1852* (New Delhi: APH Publishing, 2009)
444. Blackburn, T.R., *The Defeat of Ava: The First Anglo-Burmese War, 1824–26* (New Delhi: APH Publishing, 2009)
445. Blackburn, T.R., *The Defeat of Mandalay: The Third Anglo-Burmese War of 1885* (New Delhi: APH Publishing, 2010)
446. Bowers, Alexander, *Report on the Practicability of Re-opening the Trade Route, between Burma and Western China*, reprint of 1869 edition (Paderborn: Salzwasser, 2020)
447. Charney, M.W., *Powerful Learning: Buddhist Literati and the Throne in Burma's Last Dynasty, 1752–1885* (Ann Arbor: University of Michigan, 2006)
448. Chattopadhyay, Basudeb, et al., *Dissent and Consensus: Protest in Pre-industrial Societies (India, Burma and Russia)* (Calcutta: K.P. Bagchi, 1989)
449. Cobden, Richard, *How Wars Are Got Up in India: The Origin of the Burmese War*, reprint of 1853 edition (Delhi: S.N. Books World, 2015)
450. Damrong Rajanubhab, *Our Wars with the Burmese: Hostilities between Siamese and Burmese When Ayutthaya Was the Capital of Siam* (Bangkok: White Lotus, 2001)
451. Dibiasio, Jame, *Who Killed the King of Bagan?* (Singapore: Penguin Random House, 2021)
452. Dijk, W.O., *Seventeenth-Century Burma and the Dutch East India Company, 1634–1680* (Singapore: Singapore University Press, 2006)
453. Fortescue, J.W., *Sir John Fortescue's Thunder in the East: The British Army during the First and Second Burma Wars* (London: Leonaur, 2015)
454. *Frontier and Overseas Expeditions from India, Compiled in the Intelligence Branch, Division of the Chief of Staff, Army Headquarters, India, Volume V, Burma* (Uckfield: Naval and Military Press, 2006)

History 75

455. Furnivall, J.S, *The Fashioning of Leviathan: The Beginnings of British Rule in Burma*, edited by Gehan Wijeyewardene (Canberra: Department of Anthropology, Australian National University, 1991)

456. Geary, Grattan, *Burma after the Conquest, Viewed in Its Political, Social and Commercial Aspects from Mandalay*, reprint of 1886 edition (Marston Gate: Elibron Classics, 2005)

457. Godwin, Henry, *The Burmese War: Letters and Papers Written in 1852–53*, reprint of 1854 edition (Uckfield: Naval and Military Press, 2004)

458. Goh, Geok Yian, *The Wheel-Turner and His House: Kinship in a Buddhist Ecumene* (De Kalb: Northern Illinois University Press, 2015)

459. Goh, Geok Yian, J.N. Miksic and Michael Aung-Thwin (eds.), *Bagan and the World: Early Myanmar and its Global Connections* (Singapore: ISEAS – Yusof Ishak Institute, 2017)

460. Grabowsky, Volker, and Andrew Turton, *The Gold and Silver Road of Trade and Friendship: The McLeod and Richardson Diplomatic Missions to Tai States in 1837* (Chiang Mai: Silkworm Books, 2003)

461. Halton, Elaine, *Lord of the Celestial Elephant* (London: The author, 1999)

462. Hla Thein, *Myanmar and the Europeans (1878–1885)* (Yangon: Tun Foundation Bank Literary Committee, 2010)

463. Htun Yee (ed.), *Collection of Sayin (Various Lists on Myanmar Affairs in the Kon-baung Period) (AD 1752–1885)*, 4 volumes (Toyohashi: Aichi University, 2003)

464. Koenig, W.J., *The Burmese Polity, 1752–1819: Politics, Administration, and Social Organization in the Early Kon-baung Period*, Michigan Papers on South and Southeast Asia no. 34 (Ann Arbor: Centre for South and Southeast Asian Studies, University of Michigan, 1990)

465. Kyaw Kyaw Hlaing, *A Study of the Leadership Skills of Ancient Myanmar Monarchs: (The First Myanmar Propre)*, translated by Sun Thit Aung (Yangon: The author and U Kyaw Hin, 2015)

466. Laurie, W.F.B., *Our Burmese Wars and Relations with Burma, Being an Abstract of Military and Political Operations, 1824–25–26, and 1852–53*, reprint of 1880 edition (Uckfield: Naval and Military Press, 2005)

467. Laurie, W.F.B., *The Second Burmese War: A Narrative of the Operations at Rangoon, in 1852*, reprint of 1853 edition (Bangkok: Orchid Press, 2002)
468. Mahe de la Bourdonnais, A., *A French Engineer in Burma and Siam (1880): With a Discussion on the Kra Canal Controversy*, reprint of 1886 edition, translated by W.E.J. Tips (Bangkok: White Lotus, 2014)
469. Moore, E.H., *Early Landscapes of Myanmar* (Bangkok: River Books, 2007)
470. Myo Myint, *War and Tactics in Traditional Myanmar: A Study of Two Eighteenth Century Texts* (Yangon: Tun Foundation, 2012)
471. Newland, A.G.E., *Sketches on the Chin Hills*, reprint of 1894 edition (Gurgaon: Vintage Books, 1993)
472. Phayre, A.P., *History of Burma: Including Burma Proper, Pegu, Taungu, Tennasserim, and Arakan. From the Earliest Time to the End of the First War with British India*, reprint of 1883 edition (Bangkok: Orchid Press, 1998)
473. Richell, J.L., *Disease and Demography in Colonial Burma* (Singapore: Singapore University Press, 2006)
474. Ryley, J.H., *Ralph Fitch: England's Pioneer to India and Burma* (New Delhi: Asian Educational Services, 1998)
475. Saha, Jonathan, *Law, Disorder and the Colonial State: Corruption in Burma c1900* (Houndmills: Palgrave Macmillan, 2013)
476. Singer, N.F., *The Sorcerer-King and the "Great Abortion" at Mingun* (New Delhi: APH Publishing, 2004)
477. Singer, N.F., *Vaishali and the Indianization of Arakan* (New Delhi: APH Publishing, 2008)
478. Smith, J.S.F., *The Chiang Tung Wars: War and Politics in Mid–19th Century Siam and Burma* (Bangkok: Institute of Asian Studies, Chulalongkorn University, 2013)
479. Soe Thuzar Myint, *The Portrayal of the Battle of Ayuttiyah in Myanmar Literature*, edited by Sunait Chutintaranond and Chris Baker (Bangkok: Institute of Asian Studies, Chulalongkorn University, 2011)
480. *The Glass Palace Chronicle of the Kings of Myanmar*, translated by Pe Maung Tin and G.H. Luce (Yangon: Unity, 2008)
481. *The Myanmar Royal Regalia and Royal Household Articles Displayed at the National Museum* (Rangoon: Ministry of Culture, Department of Cultural Institute, National Museum, 2001)

482. *The Padaeng Chronicle and the Jengtung State Chronicle Translated*, translated by Sao Saimong Mangrai, Michigan Papers on South and Southeast Asia no. 52 (Ann Arbor: Centres for South and Southeast Asian Studies, University of Michigan, 2002)

483. Tin, *The Royal Administration of Burma*, translated by L.E. Bagshawe (Bangkok: Ava House, 2001)

Twentieth and Twenty-first Centuries

484. Aung Chin Win Aung, *Burma and the Last Days of General Ne Win* (Indianapolis: Yoma, 1996)

485. Aye Kyaw, *The Voice of Young Burma*, Southeast Asia Program Series no. 12 (Ithaca: Cornell University, 1993)

486. Bose, S.C., *In Burmese Prisons: Correspondence May 1923–July 1926*, edited by Sisir K. Bose (Kolkata: Netaji Research Bureau, 2009)

487. Boshier, C.A., *Mapping Cultural Nationalism: The Scholars of the Burma Research Society, 1910–1935* (Copenhagen: NIAS Press, 2017)

488. Brockman, Andy, and Tracy Spaight, *The Buried Spitfires of Burma: A "Fake" History* (Cheltenham: The History Press, 2020)

489. *Burma: The 18 September 1988 Military Takeover and its Aftermath*, AI Index 16/00/88 (London: Amnesty International, December 1988)

490. Hla Oo, *Burma in Limbo: Book One: Rich Colony to Dictatorship* (Raleigh: The author and Lulu Press, 2011)

491. Keck, S.L., *British Burma in the New Century, 1895–1918* (Basingstoke: Palgrave Macmillan, 2015)

492. Khin Let Ya, *Burma's Fate: Vision and Struggles for Independence, Unity and Development* (Yangon: Zunn Pwint, 2019)

493. Khin Yi, *The Dobama Movement in Burma (1930–1938)*, 2 volumes (Ithaca: Southeast Asia Program, Cornell University, 1988)

494. Kin Oung, *Eliminate the Elite: Assassination of Burma's General Aung San and His Six Cabinet Colleagues*, 3rd edition (Sydney: The author, 2011)

495. Kin Oung, *Who Killed Aung San?*, 2nd edition (Bangkok: White Lotus, 1996)

496. Leigh, M.D., *The Collapse of British Rule in Burma: The Civilian Evacuation and Independence* (London: Bloomsbury Academic, 2018)

497. Maung Maung, *Grim War against the KMT*, reprint of 1953 edition (Yangon: Seikku Cho, 2013)

498. Mya Doung Nyo, *The Thirty Comrades* (Yangon: News and Periodicals Enterprise, 1992)

499. Myoma Lwin [Myomalwin], *Dha-Byet-See: The Gun That Saved Rangoon* (Woodstock: The author and Writers World, 2011)

500. Nakanishi, Yoshihiro, *Strong Soldiers, Failed Revolution: The State and Military in Burma, 1962–88* (Singapore: NUS Press, in association with Kyoto University Press, 2013)

501. Naw, Angelene, *Aung San and the Struggle for Burmese Independence* (Chiang Mai: Silkworm Books, 2001)

502. Pe Kin, *Pinlon: An Inside Story* (Yangon: News and Periodicals Enterprise, Government of the Union of Myanmar, 1994)

503. Rajshekhar, *Myanmar's Nationalist Movement (1906–1948) and India* (New Delhi: South Asian Publishers, 2006)

504. *Reports on British Prison-Camps in India and Burma: Visited by the International Red Cross Committee in February, March, and April, 1917*, reprint of 1918 edition (Washington DC: Westphalia Press, 2020)

505. Selth, Andrew, *Australia's Relations with Colonial Burma, 1886–1947*, Working Paper no. 89 (Clayton: Centre of Southeast Asian Studies, Monash University, 1994)

506. Selth, Andrew, *Death of a Hero: The U Thant Disturbances in Burma, December 1974*, 3rd edition, Research Paper (Brisbane: Griffith Asia Institute, Griffith University, 2018)

507. Shah, Sudha, *The King in Exile: The Fall of the Royal Family of Burma* (New Delhi: HarperCollins, 2012)

508. Silverstein, Josef (ed.), *The Political Legacy of Aung San*, Southeast Asia Program Series no. 11, revised edition with an introductory essay (Ithaca: Cornell University, 1993)

509. Singh, Balwant, *Independence and Democracy in Burma, 1945–1952: The Turbulent Years*, Michigan Papers on South and Southeast Asia no. 40 (Ann Arbor: Centre for South and Southeast Asian Studies, University of Michigan, 1993)

510. Singh, K.B.N., *Freedom Struggle in Burma* (Patna: Janaki Prakashan, 1989)

511. Singh, T.S., *The Endless Kabaw Valley (British Created Vicious Cycle of Manipur, Burma and India)* (New Delhi: Qills Ink, 2014)
512. Tucker, Shelby, *Burma: The Curse of Independence* (London: Pluto Press, 2001)
513. Wessendorf, Larah, *The Era of General Ne Win: A Biographical Approach of His Military and Political Career Considering Burmese Traditions of Political Succession* (Berlin: Regiospectra, 2012)
514. Zollner, Hans-Bernd, *The Beast and the Beauty: The History of the Conflict between the Military and Aung San Suu Kyi in Myanmar, 1988–2011, Set in a Global Context* (Berlin: Regiospectra, 2012)

THE SECOND WORLD WAR

General

515. Bond, Brian, and Kyoichi Tachikawa, *British and Japanese Military Leadership in the Far Eastern War, 1941–1945* (London: Frank Cass, 2004)

516. Callahan, R.A., and Daniel Marston, *The 1945 Burma Campaign and the Transformation of the British Indian Army* (Lawrence: University Press of Kansas, 2021)

517. Dunlop, Graham, *Military Economics, Culture and Logistics in the Burma Campaign, 1942–1945* (London: Pickering and Chatto, 2009)

518. Fischer, Edward, *The Chancy War: Winning in China, Burma, and India in World War Two* (New York: Orion Books, 1991)

519. Hantzis, S.J., *Rails of War: Supplying the Americans and Their Allies in China-Burma-India* (Dulles: Potomac Books, 2017)

520. Hengshoon, Harry, *Green Hell: Unconventional Warfare in the CBI* (Huntington Beach: B&L Lithograph, 2000)

521. Jaffe, Sally, and Lucy Jaffe, *Chinthe Women: Women's Auxiliary Service Burma, 1942–1946* (Chipping Norton: The authors, 2002)

522. Joshi, K.D., *Burma War Narratives: Fresh Reinterpretation* (New Delhi: Akansha, 2013)

523. Jowett, Philip, *Japan's Asian Allies, 1941–45*, illustrated by Stephen Walsh (New York: Osprey, 2020)

524. Jowett, Philip, *The Battle for Burma, 1942–1945* (Barnsley: Pen and Sword Books, 2021)

525. Kirby, S.W., *The War against Japan*, 5 volumes, reprints of 1957 [volume 1] to 1969 [volume 5] editions (London: Her Majesty's Stationery Office, London, 2004)

526. Lyman, Robert, *Among the Headhunters: An Extraordinary World War II Story of Survival in the Burmese Jungle* (Boston: Da Capo Press, 2016)

527. Mason, H.A., R.A. Bergeron and J.A. Renfrow, *Operation Thursday: Birth of the Air Commandos* (Miami: University Press of the Pacific, 2004)

528. Mori, Takato, *"Co-Prosperity" or "Commonwealth"? Japan, Britain and Burma, 1940–1945* (Saarbrucken: VDM Verlag Dr Müller, 2009)

529. Morris, D.G., *Beyond the Irrawaddy and the Salween: RAF Special Duty Missions in the South East Asia Theatre of War, 1944–45* (Gardenvale: Mostly Unsung, 1996)

530. Nunneley, John (ed.), *Tales from the Burma Campaign 1942–1945* (Petersham: Burma Campaign Fellowship Group, 1998)

531. Ritter, J.T., *Stilwell and Mountbatten in Burma: Allies at War, 1943–1944* (Denton: University of North Texas Press, 2017)

532. Sinclair, W.B., *Confusion beyond Imagination*, 10 volumes (Coeur d'Alene: J.F. Whitley, 1986 [volume 1] to 1991 [volume 10])

533. *The US Army Campaigns of World War II: India-Burma* (Washington DC: US Government Printing Office, 1992)

534. Thompson, Julian, *The Imperial War Museum Book of the War in Burma, 1942–1945* (London: Sidgwick and Jackson, 2002)

535. Warren, Alan, *Burma 1942: The Road from Rangoon to Mandalay* (London: Continuum International, 2011)

536. Webster, Donovan, *The Burma Road: The Epic Story of the China-Burma-India Theatre in World War II* (New York: Farrar, Straus and Giroux, 2003)

537. Y'Blood, W.T., *Air Commandos against Japan: Allied Special Operations in World War II Burma* (Annapolis: Naval Institute Press, 2008)

The Fall of Burma

538. Enriquez, C.M., *Burma Invaded 1942*, edited by M.P. Stanford (Charleston: The author and CreateSpace, 2013)

539. Foucar, E.C.V., *First Burma Campaign: The Japanese Conquest of 1942*, compiled and introduced by John Grehan (Barnsley: Frontline Books, 2020)

540. Germaine, E.T., *Stories of Survival in Burma WW2* (Ilford: Feedaread.com, 2020)

541. Goodall, Felicity, *Exodus Burma: The British Escape through the Jungles of Death 1942* (Stroud: Spellmount, 2011)

542. Grant, I.L., and Kazuo Tamayama, *Burma 1942: The Japanese Invasion – Both Sides Tell the Story of a Savage Jungle War* (Chichester: Zampi Press, 1999)

543. Grehan, John, and Martin Mace (eds.), *The Fall of Burma, 1941–1943* (Barnsley: Pen and Sword Books, 2015)

544. Leigh, M.D., *The Evacuation of Civilians from Burma: Analysing the 1942 Colonial Disaster* (London: Bloomsbury, 2014)

545. Woods, Philip, *Reporting the Retreat: War Correspondents in Burma, 1942* (London: Hurst, 2016)

The Land Campaign

546. Astor, Gerald, *The Jungle War: Mavericks, Marauders, and Madmen in the China-Burma-India Theatre of World War II* (Hoboken: John Wiley and Sons, 2004)

547. Bowen, C.G., *West African Way: The Story of the Burma Campaigns, 1943–1945, 5th Bn Gold Coast Regt., 81 West African Division* (Uckfield: Naval and Military Press, 2014)

548. Carruthers, Bob (ed.), *Merrill's Marauders: The Road to Burma: The Illustrated Edition* (Stratford Upon Avon: Coda Books, 2013)

549. Chinnery, Philip, *Wingate's Lost Brigade: The First Chindit Operation 1943* (Barnsley: Pen and Sword Books, 2010)

550. Colvin, John, *Not Ordinary Men: The Battle of Kohima Reassessed* (London: Leo Cooper, 1997)

551. Davies, Philip, *Lost Warriors: Seagrim and Pagani of Burma: The Last Great Untold Story of WWII* (Croxley Green: Atlantic, 2017)

552. Diamond, Jon, *Burma Road, 1943–44: Stilwell's Assault on Myitkyina* (Oxford: Osprey, 2016)

553. Diamond, Jon, *Chindit versus Japanese Infantryman, 1943–44* (Oxford: Osprey, 2015)

554. Evans, Charles, *A Doctor in XIVth Army: Burma, 1944–1945* (London: Leo Cooper, 1998)

555. Farquharson, R.H., *For Your Tomorrow: Canadians and the Burma Campaign, 1941–1945* (Toronto: Trafford, 2004)

556. Fergusson, Bernard, *The Battle for Burma: Wild Green Earth*, reprint of 1946 edition (Barnsley: Pen and Sword Books, 2016)

557. Fitzpatrick, Gerald, *Chinese Save Brits – In Burma (Battle of Yenangyaung)* (York: Fitzpatrick, 2013)

558. Fitzpatrick, Gerald, *No Mandalay, No Maymyo (79 Survive): Unique Episodes in British History* (Lewes: The Book Guild, 2002)

559. Fowler, William, *We Gave Our Today: Burma 1941–1945* (London: Weidenfeld and Nicolson, 2009)

560. Freer, A.F., *Nunshigum: On the Road to Mandalay* (Edinburgh: Pentland Press, 1995)
561. Gabbett, Michael, *The Bastards of Burma: Merrill's Marauders and the Mars Task Force Revisited* (Albuquerque: Desert Dreams, 1989)
562. Grant, I.L., *Burma: The Turning Point* (London: Leo Cooper, 2003)
563. Grehan, John, and Martin Mace (eds.), *The Battle of Burma, 1943–1945: From Kohima and Imphal through to Victory* (Barnsley: Pen and Sword Books, 2015)
564. Hamilton, J.A.L., *War Bush: 81 (West African) Division in Burma, 1943–1945* (Norwich: Michael Russell, 2001)
565. Hickey, Michael, *The Unforgettable Army: Slim's XIVth Army in Burma* (Staplehurst: Spellmount, 1998)
566. Higgs, Colin, *Wingate's Men: The Chindit Operations: Special Forces in Burma* (Barnsley: Frontline Books, 2019)
567. Hill, John, *China Dragons: A Rifle Company at War, Burma 1944–45* (London: Blandford Press, 1991)
568. Hill, John, *Slim's Burma Boys* (Chalford: Spellmount, 2007)
569. Holland, James, *Burma '44: The Battle That Turned Britain's War in the East* (London: Bantam Press, 2016)
570. Hopkins, J.E.T., *Spearhead: A Complete History of Merrill's Marauder Rangers* (Baltimore: Galahad Press, 1999)
571. Igbino, John, *Spidermen: Nigerian Chindits and Wingate's Operation Thursday, Burma 1943–1944* (UK: AuthorHouse UK, 2018)
572. Isaac, A.H., *Behind Enemy Lines: Burma 1944* (Salisbury: Baskerville Press, 2014)
573. Katoch, H.S., *Imphal 1944: The Japanese Invasion of India* (New York: Osprey, 2018)
574. Katoch, H.S., *The Battlefields of Imphal: The Second World War and North East India* (London: Routledge, 2018)
575. Keane, Fergal, *Road of Bones: The Siege of Kohima 1944: The Epic Story of the Last Great Stand of Empire* (London: HarperPress, 2011)
576. Latimer, Jon, *Burma: The Forgotten War* (London: John Murray, 2004)

577. Luto, James, *Fighting with the Fourteenth Army in Burma: Original War Summaries of the Battle against Japan, 1943–1945* (Barnsley: Pen and Sword Books, 2013)

578. Lyman, Robert, *Japan's Last Bid for Victory: The Invasion of India, 1944* (Barnsley: Pen and Sword Books, 2011)

579. Lyman, Robert, *Slim, Master of War: Burma and the Birth of Modern Warfare* (London: Constable, 2004)

580. Manwaring, Randle, *On the Road to Mandalay* (Barnsley: Pen and Sword Books, 2006)

581. Marston, D.P., *Phoenix from the Ashes: The Indian Army in the Burma Campaign* (Westport: Praeger, 2003)

582. McLynn, Frank, *The Burma Campaign: Disaster into Triumph, 1942–45* (London: Bodley Head, 2010)

583. Moreman, Tim, *Chindit 1942–45*, Warrior no. 136 (Oxford: Osprey, 2009)

584. Moremon, John, *Burma and India, 1941–1945: Australians in the Pacific War* (Canberra: Department of Veterans Affairs, 2006)

585. Mororama, Kohei, Kobayashi Kurisaki and Yukata Kurisaki, *Victory into Defeat: Japan's Disastrous Road to Burma (Myanmar) and India*, translated by Myanma Athan Kyaw Oo, Hasio Tanabe and Tin Hlaing (Yangon: Thu Ri Ya, 2007)

586. Mylne, B.H. (ed.), *An Account of the Operations in Burma Carried Out by Probyn's Horse during February, March and April 1945* (Uckfield: Naval and Military Press, 2015)

587. Nemoto, Kei (ed.), *Reconsidering the Japanese Military Occupation in Burma (1942–45)* (Tokyo: Research Institute for Languages and Cultures of Asia and Africa, Tokyo University of Foreign Studies, 2007)

588. Nesbit, R.C., *The Battle for Burma: An Illustrated History* (Barnsley: Pen and Sword Books, 2009)

589. Noonan, William, *Lost Legion: Mission 204 and the Reluctant Dragon* (Sydney: Allen and Unwin, 1990)

590. Nunneley, John, and Kazuo Tamayama, *Tales by Japanese Soldiers of the Burma Campaign, 1942–1945* (London: Cassell, 2000)

591. Pearson, Michael, *End Game Burma: Slim's Masterstroke, Meiktila 1945* (Barnsley: Pen and Sword Books, 2010)

592. Prefer, N.N., *Vinegar Joe's War: Stilwell's Campaigns for Burma* (Novato: Presidio, 2000)

593. Randle, John, *Battle Tales from Burma* (London: Pen and Sword Books, 2004)
594. Redding, Tony, *War in the Wilderness: The Chindits in Burma, 1943–1944* (Stroud: Spellmount, 2011)
595. Shephard, Alastair, *Crossing the Irrrawaddy: The Allied Offensive to Retake Burma 1945* (Auckland: Rara Avis, 2016)
596. Towill, Bill, *A Chindit's Chronicle* (Lincoln: Author's Choice Press, 2000)
597. Wax, Andrew, *Born in the Jungles of Burma: Behind Enemy Lines in the China-Burma-India Theater of Operations* (Newcastle Upon Tyne: Cambridge Scholars, 2010)
598. Young, E.M., *Meiktila 1945: The Battle to Liberate Burma* (Wellingborough: Osprey, 2004)
599. Young, E.M., *Merrill's Marauders* (Oxford: Osprey, 2009)

The Air War

600. Brown, A.S., *Silently into the Midst of Things: 177 Squadron Royal Air Force in Burma, 1943–1945 – History and Personal Narratives* (Victoria: Trafford, 2001)
601. Daughtery, L.J., *The Allied Resupply Effort in the China-Burma-India Theatre during World War II* (Jefferson: McFarland, 2008)
602. Diebold, William, *Hell Is So Green: Search and Rescue over the Hump in World War II* (Guilford: Lyons Press, 2012)
603. Ethell, Jeff, and Don Downie, *Flying the Hump: In Original World War II Colour* (Osceola: Motorbooks International, 1995)
604. Evans, Bryn, *Air Battle for Burma: Allied Pilots' Fight for Supremacy* (Barnsley: Pen and Sword Books, 2016)
605. Findon, Angus, with Mark Hillier, *Thunderbolts over Burma: A Pilot's War against the Japanese in 1945 and the Battle of Sittang Bend* (Barnsley: Pen and Sword Books, 2020)
606. Ford, Daniel, *Flying Tigers: Claire Chennault and his American Volunteers, 1941–1942* (New York: HarperCollins and Smithsonian Books, 2007)
607. Franks, Norman, *Hurricanes over the Arakan* (Sparkford: Patrick Stephens, 1989)
608. Franks, Norman, *RAF Fighter Pilots over Burma* (Barnsley: Pen and Sword Books, 2014)

609. Franks, Norman, *Spitfires over the Arakan* (London: William Kimber, 1988)
610. Gordon, J.W., *Wings from Burma to the Himalayas* (Prescott: Wolfe, 1992)
611. Greenlaw, Olga, *The Lady and the Tigers: The Story of the Remarkable Woman Who Served with the Flying Tigers in Burma and China, 1941–1942* (US: CreateSpace, 2011)
612. Gwynne-Timothy, J.R.W., *Burma Liberators: RCAF in SEAC*, 2 volumes (Toronto: Next Level Press, 1991)
613. Isby, David, *C–47/R4D Skytrain Units of the Pacific and CBI* (Oxford: Osprey, 2007)
614. King, W.C., *Building for Victory: World War II in China, Burma, and India and the 1875th Engineer Aviation Battalion* (Lanham: Taylor Trade Publishing, 2004)
615. Kirkness, Bill, and Matt Poole, *RAF Liberators over Burma: Flying with 519 Squadron* (Stroud: Fonthill Media, 2017)
616. Kitley, Alan, *Take Mary to the Pictures: A Fighter Pilot in Burma, 1941–1945* (Congleton: Coston, 2003)
617. Kleiner, S.M., *The Flying Tigers: The Untold Story of the American Pilots Who Waged a Secret War against Japan* (New York: Penguin, 2019)
618. Kozlovsky, J., *Twin Dragons: P–38 Lightnings over Burma* (Charleston: The author and CreateSpace, 2014)
619. Pearson, Michael, *The Burma Air Campaign, December 1941– August 1945* (Barnsley: Pen and Sword Books, 2006)
620. Preston-Hough, Peter, *Commanding Far Eastern Skies: A Critical Analysis of the Royal Air Force Superiority Campaign in India, Burma and Malaya 1941–1945*, Wolverhampton Military Studies no. 9 (Solihull: Helion, 2015)
621. Sansome, R.S., *The Bamboo Workshop: The History of the RAF Repair and Salvage Units India/Burma 1941–1946* (Braunton: Merlin Books, 1995)
622. School of Advanced Air and Space Studies, *Slim Chance: The Pivotal Role of Air Mobility in the Burma Campaign* (US: CreateSpace, 2014)
623. Shores, C.F., *Air War for Burma: The Allied Air Forces Fight Back in South-East Asia, 1942–1945* (London: Grub Street, 2005)
624. Shores, C.F., with Brian Cull and Yasuho Isawa, *Bloody Shambles*, 2 volumes (London: Grub Street, 1992 [volume 1] and 1993 [volume 2])

625. Stanaway, John, *Mustang and Thunderbolt Aces of the Pacific and CBI* (London: Osprey, 1999)
626. Sutcliffe, D.H., *Airborne over Burma* (Upton Upon Severn: The author, 1988)
627. Thomas, Andrew, *Spitfire Aces of Burma and the Pacific* (Oxford: Osprey, 2009)
628. Underbrink, Robert, *Somewhere We Will Find You: Search and Rescue Operations in the CBI, 1942–1945*, 2nd edition (London: Merriam Press, 2013)
629. Warwick, N.W.M., *Constant Vigilance: The RAF Regiment in the Burma Campaign* (Barnsley: Pen and Sword Aviation, 2007)
630. Watkins, R.A., *Battle Colours: Insignia and Aircraft Markings of the US Army Air Forces in World War II, Volume VI, China/Burma/India and Western Pacific Theatre of Operations* (Atglen: Schiffer, 2017)
631. *Wings of the Phoenix: The Official Story of the Air War in Burma*, reprint of 1949 edition prepared by the United Kingdom Air Ministry and Central Office for Information (Honolulu: University Press of the Pacific, 2005)
632. Young, E.M., *B–24 Liberator Units of the CBI* (New York: Osprey, 2011)

Naval and Other Maritime Operations

633. Banks, Arthur, *Wings of the Dawning: The Battle for the Indian Ocean, 1939–1945* (Upton-upon-Severn: Malvern Publishing, 1999)
634. Boyd, Andrew, *The Royal Navy in Eastern Waters: Linchpin of Victory, 1935–1942* (Singapore: NUS Press, 2017).
635. Clancy, John, *The Most Dangerous Moment of the War: Japan's Attack on the Indian Ocean, 1942* (Havertown: Casemate, 2017)
636. Haining, Peter, *The Banzai Hunters: The Small Boat Operations That Defeated the Japanese, 1944–5* (London: Robson Books, 2006)

Intelligence Organizations and Operations

637. Conant, Jennet, *A Covert Affair* (New York: Simon and Schuster, 2011)

638. Duckett, Richard, *The Special Operations Executive in Burma: Jungle Warfare and Intelligence Gathering in World War II* (London: I.B. Taurus, 2018)

639. Dunlop, Richard, *Behind Japanese Lines: With the OSS in Burma*, reprint of 1979 edition (New York: Skyhorse, 2014)

640. Mains, A.A., *Field Security: Very Ordinary Intelligence* (Chippenham: Picton, 1992)

641. O'Brien, Terence, *The Moonlight War: The Story of Clandestine Operations in South East Asia, 1944–45*, reprint of 1987 edition (London: Arrow Books, 1989)

642. Sacquety, T.J., *The OSS in Burma: Jungle War against the Japanese* (Lawrence: University Press of Kansas, 2013)

643. Thomas, G.J., *Eyes for the Phoenix: Allied Aerial Photo-Reconnaissance Operations, South-East Asia 1941–1945* (Aldershot: Hikoki Publications, 2002)

644. Todd, Ann, *OSS Operation Black Mail: One Woman's Covert War against the Imperial Japanese Army* (Annapolis: Naval Institute Press, 2017)

Prisoners of War and the Thailand–Burma Railway

645. Atcherley, Harold, *Prisoner of Japan: A Personal War Diary – Singapore, Siam and Burma, 1941–1945* (Cirencester: Memoirs Publishing, 2015)

646. Boyd, John, and Gary Garth, *Tenko! Rangoon Jail: The Amazing Story of Sgt John Boyd's Survival as a POW in a Notorious Japanese Prison Camp* (Paducah: Turner, 1996)

647. Chalker, Jack, *Burma Railway Artist: An Artist at War in Singapore, Thailand and Burma, 1942–45* (Barnsley: Pen and Sword Books, 1994)

648. Coubrough, C.R.L., *Memories of a Perpetual Second Lieutenant* (York: Wilton 65, 1999)

649. Davey, Mary, *Back to Burma: For the Love of John* (Croydon: Rathgar Press, 1995)

650. Denis, Gavin, *Quiet Jungle, Angry Sea: My Escapes from the Japanese* (Oxford: Lennard, 1989)

651. Futamatsu, Yoshihiko, *Across the Three Pagodas Pass: The Story of the Thai–Burma Railway*, translated by Ewart Escritt and edited by P.N. Davies (Folkestone: Renaissance Books, 2013)

652. Gill, Geoff, and Meg Parkes, *Burma Railway Medicine: Disease, Death and Survival on the Thai–Burma Railway, 1942–1945*: (Lancaster: Palatine Books, 2017)

653. Hall, L.G., *The Blue Haze: Incorporating the History of "A" Force, Groups 3 & 5, Burma–Thai Railway, 1942–1943* (Kenthurst: Kangaroo Press, 1996)

654. Heagney, Brenda, et al., *The Long Days of Slavery: Fellows and Members of the RACP Who Were Prisoners of War in South East Asia* (Sydney: Royal Australasian College of Physicians, 1996)

655. Hudson, Lionel, *The Rats of Rangoon*, reprint of 1987 edition (London: Leo Cooper, 1988)

656. Jeynes, Jacqueline, *Before Hiroshima: Forgotten Prisoners of War in Japan, Burma and the Far East*, 2nd revised edition (Llanarth: Pen Coed, 2016)

657. Kinvig, Clifford, *River Kwai Railway: The Story of the Burma–Siam Railway* (London: Brassey's [UK], 1992)

658. Kratoska, P.H. (ed.), *The Thailand–Burma Railway, 1942–1946: Documents and Selected Writings*, 6 volumes (London: Routledge, 2006)

659. La Forte, R.S., and R.E. Marcello (eds.), *Building the Death Railway: The Ordeal of American POWs in Burma, 1942–1945* (Lanham: Rowman and Littlefield, 1993)

660. Moremon, John, *Australians on the Burma–Thailand Railway, 1942–43* (Canberra: Department of Veterans Affairs, 2003)

661. Newland, Jean, *Guests of the Emperor: Allied POWs of WWII in Rangoon Burma* (Bloomington: AuthorHouse, 2012)

662. Sareen, T.R., *Building the Siam–Burma Railway during World War II (A Documentary Study)* (New Delhi: Kalpaz Publications, 2005)

663. Stibbe, P.G., *Return via Rangoon: A Young Chindit Survives the Jungle and Japanese Captivity*, 2nd revised edition (London: Leo Cooper, 1994)

664. Tamayama, Kazuo, *Railwaymen in the War: Tales by Japanese Railway Soldiers in Burma and Thailand 1941–47* (London: Palgrave Macmillan, 2005)

665. Tate, William, *Surviving the Japanese Onslaught: An RAF PoW in Burma* (Barnsley: Pen and Sword Books, 2016)

AUTOBIOGRAPHIES, BIOGRAPHIES AND MEMOIRS

Colonial Era (1824–1947)

666. *A Dog's Life in Burma, Told by the Dog*, reprint of 1909 edition (Ithaca: Cornell University Library, 2014)

667. Adams, Nel, *My Vanished World: The True Story of a Shan Princess* (Frodsham: Horseshoe, 2000)

668. Ainsworth, Leopold, *A Merchant Venturer among the Sea Gypsies: Being a Pioneer's Account of Life on an Island in the Mergui Archipelago*, reprint of 1930 edition (Bangkok: White Lotus, 2000)

669. Anderson, Joseph, *Sound Advance! Experiences of an Officer of HM 50th Regiment in Australia, Burma and during the Gwalior War, in India* (Driffield: Leonaur, 2007)

670. Baird-Murray, Maureen, *A World Overturned: A Burmese Childhood, 1933–47* (London: Constable, 1997)

671. Baker, Richard, *Burma Post: A Personal Story of Air Mails and Other Activities in the Burma Campaign, 1944–1945* (Worthing: Churchman, 1989)

672. Bates, A.B., *For All Time: The Story of Ann Judson* (Birmingham: New Hope, 1998)

673. Bayne, Nicholas, *Burma and Tudor History: The Life and Work of Charles Bayne, 1860–1947* (Bideford: Edward Gaskell, 2008)

674. Bierman, John, and Colin Smith, *Fire in the Night: Wingate of Burma, Ethiopia and Zion* (London: Pan, 2001)

675. Butler, John, *With the Madras European Regiment in Burma: The Experiences of an Officer of the Honourable East India Company's Army during the First Anglo-Burmese War, 1824–1826, with A Brief History of the Army of the Honourable East India Company by G.F. MacMunn*, reprint of 1911 edition (London: Leonaur, 2007)

676. Campagnac, C.H., *The Autobiography of a Wanderer in England and Burma* (Raleigh: Sandra L. Carney and Lulu Enterprises, 2011)

677. Crain, Carolyn, *Boy from Burma* (Tacoma: Pilgrim Spirit Communications, 2019)

678. Donnison, David, *Last of the Guardians: A Story of Burma, Britain and a Family* (Newtown: Superscript, 2005)

679. Doveton, F.B., *Reminiscences of the Burmese War in 1824–5–6*, reprint of 1852 edition (Cambridge: Cambridge University Press, 2012)

680. Easton, D.S., *Long Ago, Far Away: The Burma Diaries of Doris Sarah Easton*, compiled by M. Sylvia Morris (London: Minerva Press, 1994)

681. Ellis, Beth, *An English Girl's First Impressions of Burmah*, reprint of 1899 edition (Bangkok: White Orchid, 1997)

682. Evans, E.P., *Blessed Paolo Manna: Missionary Trail-Blazer, Founder of the Missionary Union of the Clergy* (Eluru: Pontifical Institute for Foreign Missions, 2001?)

683. Evans, E.P., *Father Clemente Vismara – Patriarch of Burma (1897–1988)* (Canberra: The author, n.d.)

684. Fowells, Gavin, *From the Dogs of War to a Brave New World and Back Again – Burma '47* (London: The author, 2000)

685. Freeman, J.H., *An Oriental Land of the Free: Mission Work among the Laos of Siam, Burma, China & Indochina*, reprint of 1910 edition (Bedford: Applewood Books, 2009)

686. Germaine, E.T., *Distant and Dangerous Days in Burma and China: With Letters, a Diary and Historic Photographs* (Leamington Spa: Anona Publications, 2013)

687. Germaine, E.T., *Lives in Burma and China, 1927–1951, with True Stories of Escapes from Civil Wars and WW2, and Many Old Photographs* (Ilford: Feedaread.com, 2017)

688. Goff, S. Le M., *A Tinkling of Bells* (UK: The author, 2006)

689. Hare, W.F., *Memoirs: Burma Independence, 1947–1948* (Myanmar: Pekhon University Press, 1998)

690. Hellings, David, *A Civil Servant in Burma: A Memoir of Harold Arrowsmith Brown* (London: The author, 1997)

691. James, Sharon, *Ann Judson: A Missionary Life for Burma* (Welwyn Garden City: Evangelical Press, 2016)

692. Johnson, R.G., *On the Back Road to Mandalay* (Fairfax: Xulon, 2007)

693. Kin Thida Oung, *A Twentieth Century Burmese Matriarch: A Biography*, foreword by Melford Spiro, revised edition (Morrisville: Lulu.com and the author, 2009)

694. Kin Thida Oung, *The Road from Mandalay* (San Marino: Lulu.com and the author, 2019)

695. Kyaw Ma Ma Lay, *A Man Like Him: Portrait of the Burmese Journalist, Journal Kyaw U Chit Maung*, translated by Ma Thanegi (Ithaca: Southeast Asia Program, Cornell University, 2008)

696. Listowel, Earl of, *Memoirs: Burma Independence 1947–1948* (Pekhon: Pekhon UniversityPress, 1998)

697. Macdonald, Denise, *Ma Ma Hta: Burmese Headwoman* (Carlisle: OM, 2001)

698. Maung Maung, *Aung San of Burma*, reprint of 1962 edition (Yangon: Unity, 2015)

699. Midwood, Jimmy (ed.), *Chinthe Tales: Reminiscences by Members of the Burmah Oil Society* (UK: Burmah Oil Society, 1994)

700. Mole, Robert, *The Temple Bells Are Calling: A Personal Record of the Last Years of British Rule in Burma* (Durham: Pentland Books, 2001)

701. Molloy, Sylvia, *Burma Bride* (Letchworth: Molloy Publications, 1995)

702. Morse, Gertrude, *The Dogs May Bark, but the Caravan Moves On* (Joplin: College Press, 1998)

703. Orwell, George [Eric Blair], *Shooting an Elephant and Other Essays*, includes a reprint of 1936 title essay, introduction by Jeremy Paxman (London: Penguin Books, 2009)

704. P-B, E.M., *A Year on the Irrawaddy*, reprint of 1911 edition (Bangkok: White Lotus, 1998)

705. Paske, C.T., *Myanma: A Retrospect of Life and Travel in Lower Burmah*, reprint of 1893 edition (Charleston: BiblioLife, 2009)

706. Robertson, Joan, *Maymyo – More Far: A Walk out of Burma, 1942* (Banbury: Norman Hudson, 1999)

707. Robinson, H.R., *A Modern De Quincy: Autobiography of an Opium Addict*, reprint of 1942 edition (Bangkok: Orchid Press, 2004)

708. Rorke, Grace, *A Child in Burma* (Lancaster: Scotforth Books, 2002)

709. Royle, Trevor, *Orde Wingate: A Man of Genius, 1903–1944* (Barnsley: Pen and Sword Books, 2010)

710. Samaranayake, J.F., *Rangoon Journalist* (Honolulu: The author, 2010)

711. Sao Khemawadee Mangrai, *Burma My Mother – And Why I Had to Leave* (Sydney: Sydney School of Arts and Humanities, 2014)
712. Sloggett, Diane, *Angels of Burma* (Edinburgh: Pentland Press, 2000)
713. Snodgrass, J.J., *War beyond the Dragon Pagoda: A Personal Narrative of the First Anglo-Burmese War 1824–1826*, reprint of 1827 edition (Driffield: Leonaur, 2007)
714. Spencer, Lynette (ed.), *We Won the War but Lost the Peace* (London: The author, 2017)
715. Stevens, S.W., *A Half-Century in Burma: A Memorial Sketch of Edward Abiel Stevens*, reprint of 1897 edition (New Delhi: SN Books World, 2015)
716. Stuart, A.W., *Lives of the Three Mrs Judsons* (Gloucester: Dodo Press, 2009)
717. Swift, J.W., *Hattie: A Woman's Mission to Burma* (San Geronimo: Half Meadow Press, 2003)
718. Tekkatho Sein Tin, with Kan Nyunt Sein, *Thakin Ba Sein and Burma's Struggle for Independence* (Saarbrucken: VDM Verlag Dr Müller, 2011)
719. Tinsa Maw-Naing and Han, Y.M.V., *A Burmese Heart* (US: Y.M.V. Han, 2015)
720. Titcomb, J.H., *Personal Recollections of British Burma and its Church Mission Work in 1878–79*, reprint of 1880 edition (Delhi: Facsimile Publisher, 2016)
721. Tooze, G.H., *The Life and Letters of Emily Chubbuck Judson*, 7 volumes (Georgia: Mercer University Press, 2009 [volume 1] to 2013 [volume 7])
722. Turner, Alicia, Lawrence Cox and Brian Bocking, *The Irish Buddhist: The Forgotten Monk Who Faced Down the British Empire* (New York: Oxford University Press, 2020)
723. *U Pe Maung Tin: A Tribute* (Yangon: Universities Historical Research Centre, 1999)
724. Upfill, M.S.D., *An American in Burma, 1930–1942* (Tempe: Arizona State University, 1999)
725. Wai Wai Myaing, *A Journey in Time: Family Memoirs (Burma, 1914–1948)* (New York: iUniverse, 2005)
726. Whitehead, John, *Thangliena: The Life of T.H. Lewin* (Gartmore: Kiscadale, 1992)

727. Win, Junior, *A Memory of my Grandparents*, preface by Khin Maung Win (Yangon: Yan Aung Book Publishing House, 2015)

728. Windon, Deanna, *Gentle Moon: The Story of Molly Lee* (Midland: Search for Truth Publications, 2016)

729. Windsor, Neville, *Burma: Land of my Dreams* (Sidcup: Jasmine Publications, 1994)

Second World War (1939–45)

730. Ausland, J.E., *The Last Kilometer and Other War Stories*, edited by J.C. Ausland (Oslo: Land Productions, 1994)

731. Baines, Frank, *Chindit Affair: A Memoir of the War in Burma*, edited by Brian Mooney (Barnesly: Pen and Sword Military, 2011)

732. Bates, R.F., *Memories of Military Service (A Teenager in Burma)* (Bloomington: Authorhouse/1st Books, 2004)

733. Benegal, R.S., *Burma to Japan with Azad Hind: A War Memoir, 1941–1945* (New Delhi: Lancer, 2009)

734. Brookes, Stephen, *Through the Jungle of Death: A Boy's Escape from Wartime Burma* (London: John Murray, 2000)

735. Campagnac-Carney, Sandra, *Burma: Memories of WWII* (Raleigh: Blue Mist Publications, 2010)

736. Chaikin, R.B., *To My Memory Sing: A Memoir Based on Letters and Poems from Sol Chick Chaikin, an American Soldier in China-Burma-India during World War II* (Monroe: Library Research Associates, 1997)

737. Croke, V.C., *Elephant Company: The Inspiring Story of an Unlikely Hero and the Animals Who Helped Him Save Lives in World War II* (New York: Random House, 2014)

738. Devereux, Brian, *Escape to Pagan* (Oxford: Casemate, 2016)

739. Dudley, Ronald, *The Road to Rangoon and Back* (Abertillery: Old Bakehouse Publications, 2007)

740. Ellis, Jean, *Goodbye Burma* (Bath: Charlcombe Books, 2017)

741. Enriquez, C.M., *Brewing Storm 1939–1941* (US: Margaret P. Stanford, 2013)

742. Ezdani, Y.V. (ed.), *New Songs of the Survivors: The Exodus of Indians from Burma*, foreword by Amitav Ghosh (New Delhi: Speaking Tiger Books, 2015)

743. Ezdani, Y.V. (ed.), *Songs of the Survivors* (Goa: Goa 1556, 2007)
744. Fenton, James, *The Forgotten Army: A Burma Soldier's Story in Letters, Photographs, and Sketches* (Stroud: Fonthill, 2012)
745. Fraser, G.M., *Quartered Safe Out Here: A Recollection of the War in Burma with a New Epilogue: Fifty Years On*, revised edition (London: HarperCollins, 2000)
746. *From Burma with Love: Fifteen Months of World War II Letters between Irwin and Mary Reiss*, compiled by S.W. Reiss (Bloomington: AuthorHouse, 2011)
747. Gilmore, Scott, *A Connecticut Yankee in the 8th Gurkha Rifles: A Burma Memoir* (Washington DC: Brassey's, 1995)
748. Goode, F.C., *No Surrender in Burma: Operations behind Japanese Lines, Captivity and Torture* (Barnsley: Pen and Sword Books, 2014)
749. Hedley, J.D.H., *Jungle Fighter: Infantry Officer, Chindit and SOE Agent in Burma, 1941–1945* (Brighton: Tom Donovan, 1996)
750. Hilsman, Roger, *American Guerrilla: My War behind Japanese Lines* (Washington DC: Brassey's, 1990)
751. Humphreys, Roy, *To Stop a Rising Sun: Reminiscences of Wartime in India and Burma* (Thrupp: Sutton, 1999)
752. James, R.R., *The Road from Mandalay: A Journey in the Shadow of the East* (Milton Keynes: AuthorHouse, 2007)
753. Kelly, Desmond, *Kelly's Burma Campaign: Letters from the Chin Hills* (London: Tiddim Press, 2003)
754. Kilvington, Maude, *Burma and Beyond: The True Story of a Family Devastated by War* (Chichester: Crosswave, 2010)
755. King-Clark, Rex, *Forward from Kohima: A Burma Diary, November 1944–May 1945* (Knutsford: Fleur De Lys, 2003)
756. Koerner, B.I., *Now the Hell Will Start: One Soldier's Flight from the Greatest Manhunt of World War II* (New York: Penguin Press, 2008)
757. Lewin, Ronald, *Slim: The Standardbearer*, reprint of 1976 edition (Barnsley: Pen and Sword Books, 1990)
758. Lockhart-Mure, E.J., *Front Line and Fortitude: Memoirs of a Wasbie with the "Forgotten Army"* (Leicester: Troubador, 2019)
759. Looker, Bob, *The Long Walk Home* (UK: Looker Publications, 2015)

760. Martin, Andrew, *Flight by Elephant: The Untold Story of World War Two's Most Daring Jungle Rescue* (London: Fourth Estate, 2013)
761. McPhedran, Colin, *White Butterflies* (Canberra: Pandanus Books, 2002)
762. Miller, Russell, *Uncle Bill: The Authorised Biography of Field Marshall Viscount Slim* (London: Weidenfeld and Nicolson, 2013)
763. Peek, I.D., *One Fourteenth of an Elephant* (Sydney: Macmillan, 2003)
764. Phillips, Barnaby, *Another Man's War: The Story of a Burma Boy in Britain's Forgotten African Army* (London: Oneworld, 2014)
765. Pickford, S.C., *Destination Rangoon* (Denbigh: Gee and Son, 1989)
766. Richards, Rowley, *A Doctor's War* (Sydney: HarperCollins, 2005)
767. Rooney, David, *Mad Mike: A Life of Michael Calvert* (London: Leo Cooper, 1997)
768. Rooney, David, *Stilwell the Patriot: Vinegar Joe, the Brits and Chiang Kai-Shek* (New York: Skyhorse, 2016)
769. Sharpe, Philip, *To Be a Chindit* (Lewes: The Book Guild, 1995)
770. Spill, G.H., and Nick Spill, *Reluctant Q: A Quartermaster's Tale of Survival in the Burma Jungle in WWII* (US: Midnight over Miami Beach, 2014)
771. Stephenson, Charles, *Boyhood Trials Shape the Chindit: Living through the War in Burma*, edited by Trophy D'Souza (Charleston: The author and CreateSpace, 2014)
772. Stilwell, J.W., *The Stilwell Papers*, edited by Theodore White, preface by Eric Larrabee, reprint of 1948 edition (Boston: Da Capo Press, 1991)
773. Street, Robert, *A Brummie in Burma* (Grantham: Barny Books, 1997)
774. Tanner, R.E.S., and D.A. Tanner, *Burma 1942: Memories of a Retreat: The Diary of Ralph Tanner, 2nd Battalion the King's Own Yorkshire Light Infantry* (Stroud: The History Press, 2009)
775. Theippan Maung Wa [U Sein Tin], *Wartime in Burma: A Diary, January to June 1942*, translated by L.E. Bagshawe and A.J. Allott, Ohio University Research in International Studies, Southeast Asia Series no. 120 (Athens: Ohio University Press, 2009)

776. Tinsley, Terence, *Stick and String* (London: Buckland Publications, 1992)

777. Verlander, Harry, *My War in SOE* (Bromley: Independent Books, 2010)

778. Wunna Kyaw Tin Dr Myint Swe, *The Japanese Era Rangoon General Hospital: Memoir of a Wartime Physician*, translated by Zarny Tun (Yangon: Myanmar Book Centre, 2014)

Post-Independence Period (1948–87)

779. Abbott, Gerry, *Back to Mandalay: An Inside View of Burma* (Bromley: Impact Books, 1990)

780. Abbott, Gerry, *From Bow to Burma* (Ely: Melrose Books, 2017)

781. Allmark, C.V., *Letters from Burma* (Lynwood: UsForOz Publications, 2004)

782. Allmark, C.V., *Rebel of Burma: The Autobiography of Constance Veronica Allmark* (Lynwood: UsForOz Publications, 2004)

783. Aung Aung Taik, *Visions of Shwedagon* (Bangkok: White Lotus, 1989)

784. Aye Saung, *Burman in the Back Row: An Autobiography* (Hong Kong: Asia 2000, 1989)

785. Brooke-Wavell, Derek (ed.), *Lines from a Shining Land* (Caversham: The Britain-Burma Society, 1998)

786. Broughton, M.D., *East Meets West: A Memoir* (UK: The author, 2021)

787. Carter, Anne, *Bewitched by Burma: A Unique Insight into Burma's Complex Past* (Kibworth Beauchamp: Matador, 2012)

788. Chao Tzang Yawnghwe, *The Shan of Burma: Memoirs of a Shan Exile*, reprint of 1987 edition (Singapore: Institute of Southeast Asian Studies, 2010)

789. Chen, Fu Hua, *Between East and West: Life on the Burma Road, the Tibet Highway, the Ho Chi Minh Trail and in the United States* (Niwot: University Press of Colorado, 1996)

790. Chu, Winston, *Reborn: Journeys from the Abyss* (Mustang: Tate Publishing, 2015)

791. Crozier, L.A., *Mawchi: Mining, War and Insurgency in Burma*, Australians in Asia Series no. 11 (Brisbane: Centre for the Study of Australia-Asia Relations, Griffith University, 1994)

792. Eather, C.E.J., *We Flew in Burma* (Surfers Paradise: Chingchic, 1993)
793. Elliott, Patricia, *The White Umbrella* (Bangkok: Post Books, 1999)
794. Helfrich, P.Z., *Dinosaur in the Garden: Memoirs of Burma (1940–1966)* (US: CreateSpace, 2016)
795. Hidalgo, C.P., *Five Years in a Forgotten Land: A Burmese Notebook* (Quezon City: University of the Philippines Press, 1996)
796. Hla Oo, *The Scourge of Burma and Four Short Stories* (Raleigh: The author and Lulu Press, 2010)
797. K., *Myanmar in My Lifetime* (Yangon: Today Publishing House, 2013)
798. Kyi May Kaung, *A Time to Write: Not Just about Burma: A Memoir* (US: CreateSpace, 2016)
799. Kyi May Kaung (ed.), *Let it Fly with the Flowers: Essays about the Institute of Economics, Rangoon, Burma* (US: CreateSpace, 2015)
800. Kyi Win Sein, Malcolm, *Me and the Generals of the Revolutionary Council: Memoirs of Turbulent Times in Myanmar* (Whitley Bay: UK Book Publishing, 2015)
801. Kyi Win Sein, Malcolm, *Revolutionary Council to Military Dictatorship* (Whitley Bay: UK Book Publishing, 2018)
802. Law-Yone, Wendy, *Golden Parasol: A Daughter's Memoir of Burma* (London: Chatto and Windus, 2013)
803. O'Brien, Harriet, *Forgotten Land: A Rediscovery of Burma* (London: Michael Joseph, 1991)
804. O'Hara, Randolph, *Fragments from the Past* (Bangkok: Orchid Press, 2008)
805. Raschid, B.M., *The Invisible Patriot: Reminiscences of Burma's Freedom Movement* (Charleston: The author and CreateSpace, 2015)
806. Rustam, M.S., *Myanmar: Seeing is Believing*, edited by Hon Ah Fah (Yangon: IT Myanmar Business Magazine, 2002) (in English and Burmese)
807. Sao Sanda, *The Moon Princess: Memories of the Shan States* (Bangkok: River Books, 2008)
808. Sargent, Inge, *Twilight over Burma: My Life as a Shan Princess* (Chiang Mai: Silkworm Books, 1994)

809. Taylor, R.H., *General Ne Win: A Political Biography* (Singapore: Institute of Southeast Asian Studies, 2015)
810. Taylor, R.H. (ed.), *Dr Maung Maung: Gentleman, Scholar, Patriot* (Singapore: Institute of Southeast Asian Studies, 2008)
811. Thaung, *A Journalist, a General and an Army in Burma* (Bangkok: White Lotus, 1995)
812. Thet Tun, *Waves of Influence* (Yangon: Thin Sapay, 2011)
813. Tin Maung Aye, *It Started in Phyu...: A Childhood Memoir from World War Two in Burma and the Journey Forward* (Yangon: Myanmar Book Centre, 2013)
814. Tun Tin, J.K., *Luck's a Fortune* (Adelaide: Peacock Press, 2017)
815. Wai Wai Myaing, *Of Roots and Wings: A Memoir* (Bloomington: iUniverse, 2015)
816. Wong, Kenneth, *A Prayer for Burma* (Santa Monica: Santa Monica Press, 2003)
817. Yang Li, *The House of Yang: Guardians of an Unknown Frontier* (Sydney: Bookpress, 1997)
818. Zan, Saw Spencer, *Life's Journey in Faith: Burma, from Riches to Rags* (Bloomington: Author House, 2007)

The Modern Period (1988–2021)

819. Armour-Hileman, Victoria, *Singing to the Dead: A Missioner's Life among Refugees from Burma* (Athens: University of Georgia Press, 2002)
820. Ball, Joseph (ed.), *Come Rain or Shine: A Personal Account of Burma, the 2007 Uprising and Cyclone Nargis* (Chiang Mai: Mizzima News Agency, 2008)
821. Broman, Barry, *Risk Taker, Spy Maker: Tales of a CIA Case Officer* (US: Casemate, 2020)
822. Connelly, Karen, *Burmese Lessons: A True Love Story* (Toronto: Random House, 2009)
823. Connew, Bruce, *On the Way to an Ambush* (Wellington: Victoria University Press, 1999)
824. Dada, Feroze, *Children of the Revolution* (Croydon: Filament, 2014)
825. Daw Khin Hnin Oo et al. (eds.), *Felicitations for U Thaw Kaung's 75th Birthday* (Yangon: Myanmar Book Centre, 2012) (in English and Burmese)

826. Gregory-Smith, Judyth, *Myanmar: A Memoir of Loss and Recovery* (London: The author and Lulu Press, 2012)
827. Hsu, Douglas, *Never Say Die: The Story of David Yone Mo and the Myanmar Young Crusaders* (US: Advancing Native Missions, 2009)
828. Htet Aung Kyaw, *Far from Home: 20 Years in Exile: The Life and Views of a Burmese Rebel and Journalist* (Chiang Mai: Irrawaddy Publishing Group, 2008)
829. Johnson, B.K., *The Shan: Refugees without a Camp: An English Teacher in Thailand and Burma* (Paramus: Trinity Matrix, 2009)
830. Khoo Thwe, Pascal, *From the Land of Green Ghosts: A Burmese Odyssey* (London: HarperCollins, 2002)
831. Kyaw Win, *My Conscience: An Exile's Memoir of Burma* (Eugene: Resource Publications, 2016)
832. Kyaw Zwa Moe, *The Cell, Exile and the New Burma: A Political Education amid the Unfinished Journey toward Democracy* (Yangon: New Myanmar Publishing House, 2018)
833. Lenarcik, Marek, *Burma Lost and Found: Three Years Living My Dream Job in the Travel Industry in Rangoon and Beyond* (Charleston: The author and CreateSpace, 2014)
834. Lyons, Keith, et al., *Opening Up Hidden Burma: Journeys with – and without – Author Dr Bob Percival* (Yangon: Duwon Books, 2018)
835. Ma Thanegi, *Nor Iron Bars a Cage* (San Francisco: ThingsAsian Press, 2013)
836. Ma Thida, *Prisoner of Conscience: My Steps through Insein* (Chiang Mai: Silkworm Books, 2016)
837. MacLean, Joanna, *Two Eggs and a Lemon: My Four Years in Myanmar* (Seattle: Marrowstsone, 2016)
838. Mawdsley, James, *The Heart Must Break: The Fight for Democracy and Truth in Burma* (London: Century, 2001)
839. Moe Aye, *Ten Years On: The Life and Views of a Burmese Student Political Prisoner* (Bangkok: Louise Southalan, 1999)
840. Nang Zing La, *Life in Burma Military Prisons: Memoir of a Pro-democracy Advocate* (Pittsburgh: Rose Dog Books, 2005)
841. Olszewski, Peter, *Land of a Thousand Eyes: The Subtle Pleasures of Everyday Life in Myanmar* (Sydney: Allen and Unwin, 2005)

842. Phan, Zoya, with Damien Lewis, *Little Daughter: A Memoir of Survival in Burma and the West* (London: Simon and Schuster, 2009)

843. Pickrem, Paul, *No Easy Road: A Burmese Political Prisoner's Story: The Life of Thiha Yarzar*, 2nd edition (Ottawa and Mae Sot: Canadian Friends of Burma, ExPP-ACT and The Best Friend Library, 2011)

844. Robinette, M.A., *Myanmar Gold* (Harrisburg: Foundations of Grace Publishing, 2020)

845. Rogers, Benedict, *From Burma to Rome: A Journey into the Catholic Church*, preface by Charles Maung Bo (Leominster: Gracewing, 2015)

846. Rogers, Benedict, *Than Shwe: Unmasking Burma's Tyrant* (Chiang Mai: Silkworm Books, 2010)

847. Russell, Rosalind, *Burma's Spring: Real Lives in Turbulent Times* (London: Thistle, 2014)

848. Sterken, R.E., *Teaching Barefoot in Burma: Insights and Stories from a Fulbright Year in Burma* (Yangon: YSPS Press, 2016)

849. Tucker, Shelby, *Among Insurgents: Walking through Burma* (London: Radcliffe Press, 2000)

850. Ullathorne, Feraya, *Beatnik Artist from Burma: Weaving a tapestry of my life* (UK: The author, 2019)

851. Wakeman, Carolyn, and San San Tin, *No Time for Dreams: Living in Burma under Military Rule*, introduction by Emma Larkin (Lanham: Rowman and Littlefield, 2009)

852. Welch, Larry, *School Days in Burma: Stories from the Heart* (Bloomington: Trafford, 2014)

853. Wilson, Trevor, *Eyewitness to Early Reform in Myanmar*, Asian Studies Series, Monograph no. 7 (Canberra: Australian National University Press, 2016)

854. Zakreski, Ron, *On a Short Leash: Detained in Burma* (Canada: The author, 2012)

AUNG SAN SUU KYI

Works by Aung San Suu Kyi

855. Aung San Suu Kyi, *Aung San of Burma: A Biographical Portrait by His Daughter* (Edinburgh: Kiscadale, 1990)

856. Aung San Suu Kyi, *Burma and India: Some Aspects of Intellectual Life under Colonialism* (Shimla: Indian Institute of Advanced Study, 1990)

857. Aung San Suu Kyi, *Democratic Transition in Myanmar: Challenges and the Way Forward*, The 43rd Singapore Lecture, 21 August 2018 (Singapore: ISEAS – Yusof Ishak Institute, 2018)

858. Aung San Suu Kyi, *Freedom from Fear and Other Writings*, 2nd edition, edited with an introduction by Michael Aris (London: Penguin, 1995)

859. Aung San Suu Kyi, *Letters from Burma*, introduction by Fergal Keane (London: Penguin, 1997)

860. Aung San Suu Kyi, *The Voice of Hope: Conversations with Alan Clements, with contributions by U Kyi Maung and U Tin U*, 2nd edition (New York: Seven Stories, 2008)

861. Aung San Suu Kyi, *Towards a True Refuge: Eighth Joyce Pearce Memorial Lecture, Delivered by Dr Michael Aris on 19 May 1993, with an Introduction by Sir Claus Moser and a Response by Peter Carey* (Oxford: Refugee Studies Programme, Queen Elizabeth House, with Perpetua Press, 1993)

862. *Aung San Suu Kyi Quotes* (US: Providence Books, 2010)

863. *Images of Mother Loved by the People: Daw Aung San Suu Kyi's World Famous Speeches and Historic Words*, translated by Nay Win San, photographs by Kyaw Soe Naing (Yangon: Book Street, 2003)

864. *Quotes by Aung San Suu Kyi*, compiled by Lilith Regan (US?: The author, 2020)

865. Zollner, Hans-Bernd (ed.), *Daw Su's 25 Dialogues with the People, 1995–1996*, translated by Ko Ko Thett and Frankie Tun (Yangon: Kantkawwutyee, 2014) (in English and Burmese)

866. Zollner, Hans-Bernd (ed.), *Talks over the Gate: Aung San Suu Kyi's Dialogues with the People, 1995 and 1996*, translated by Ko Ko Thett and Frankie Tun (Hamburg: AberaVerlag, 2014)

Works about Aung San Suu Kyi

867. Aung Htoo, *Engaging Politics in Myanmar: A Study of Aung San Suu Kyi and Martin Luther King Jr in Light of Walter Wink's Political Theology* (Carlisle: Langham, 2020)

868. Aung Zaw, *The Face of Resistance: Aung San Suu Kyi and Burma's Fight for Freedom* (Chiang Mai: Silkworm Books, 2014)

869. Bengtsson, Jesper, *Aung San Suu Kyi: A Biography* (London: Fourth Estate, 2011)

870. Bjorklund, Ruth, *Aung San Suu Kyi* (New York: Cavendish Square, 2013)

871. Burling, Alexis, *Aung San Suu Kyi: Burmese Politician and Activist for Democracy* (New York: Rosen, 2018)

872. Drummond, Allan, *Aung San Suu Kyi: The Burma Lady* (Mentone: Green Barrow, 2015)

873. Gearon, Liam, *A Noble Life: Story of Aung San Suu Kyi* (London: Religious and Moral Education Press, 2004)

874. Geok, A.C., *Aung San Suu Kyi: Towards a New Freedom* (Sydney: Prentice Hall, 1998)

875. Hasday, J.L., *Aung San Suu Kyi: Activist for Democracy in Myanmar* (New York: Chelsea House, 2007)

876. Johnson, Amy, *Aung San Suu Kyi, A Treatise: Sonnets for a Modern Trailblazer* (Bloomington: Authorhouse, 2011)

877. Kanbawza Win, *Daw Aung San Suu Kyi, the Nobel Laureate: A Burmese Perspective* (Bangkok: CPDSK Publications, 1992)

878. La Bella, Laura, *Aung San Suu Kyi: Myanmar's Freedom Fighter* (New York: Rosen Publishing Group, 2014)

879. Ling, Bettina, *Aung San Suu Kyi: Standing Up for Democracy in Burma* (New York: Feminist Press, 1999)

880. Lintner, Bertil, *Aung San Suu Kyi and Burma's Struggle for Democracy* (Chiang Mai: Silkworm Books, 2011)

881. Lintner, Bertil, *Aung San Suu Kyi and Burma's Unfinished Renaissance*, Working Paper no. 64 (Clayton: Centre of Southeast Asian Studies, Monash University, 1990)

882. Loviny, Christophe, *Aung San Suu Kyi: A Portrait in Words and Pictures* (Melbourne: Hardie Grant, 2013)

883. Lubina, Michal, *A Political Biography of Aung San Suu Kyi: A Hybrid Politician* (London: Routledge, 2021)

884. Lubina, Michal, *The Moral Democracy: The Political Thought of Aung San Suu Kyi* (Warsaw: Scholar, 2019)
885. Moe Lin [Pho Lay], *Up Close: Two Decades of Close Encounters with Aung San Suu Kyi* (Yangon: MCM Books, 2013)
886. Nemoto, Kei, and M.I. Minamida, *Aung San Suu Kyi and Contemporary Burma* (Osaka: Kansai Institute of Asia-Pacific Studies, 1996)
887. Noah, *Aung San Suu Kyi: The Face of the Buddhist Beast* (US: Kim, 2018)
888. O'Keefe, Sherry, *Champion of Freedom: Aung San Suu Kyi* (Greensboro: Morgan Reynolds, 2011)
889. Oishi, Mikio, *Aung San Suu Kyi's Struggle: Its Principles and Strategy* (Penang: Just World Trust, 1997)
890. Parenteau, John, *Prisoner for Peace: Aung San Suu Kyi and Burma's Struggle for Democracy* (Greensboro: Morgan Reynolds, 1994)
891. Pederson, Rena, *The Burma Spring: Aung San Suu Kyi and the New Struggle for the Soul of a Nation* (New York: Pegasus, 2015)
892. Popham, Peter, *The Lady and the Generals: Aung San Suu Kyi and Burma's Struggle for Freedom* (London: Rider Books, 2016)
893. Popham, Peter, *The Lady and the Peacock: The Life of Aung San Suu Kyi* (London: Rider Books, 2011)
894. Rose, Simon, *Aung San Suu Kyi* (New York: AV2 by Weigl, 2011)
895. Sayar Mya (MOFA) [Mya Tun], *Daw Aung San Suu Kyi: World's Number One Democracy Icon* (Raleigh: Lulu Enterprises, 2017)
896. Selth, Andrew, *Aung San Suu Kyi and the Politics of Personality*, Regional Outlook no. 55 (Brisbane: Griffith Asia Institute, Griffith University, 2017)
897. Sherman, Patrice, *Aung San Suu Kyi: Peaceful Resistance to the Burmese Military Junta* (New York: Cavendish, 2018)
898. Shwe Lu Maung, *Is Suu Kyi a Racist?* (US: Shahnawaz Khan, 2014)
899. Stewart, Whitney, et al., *Aung San Suu Kyi: Fearless Voice of Burma*, 2nd edition (New York: iUniverse, 2008)
900. Thomas, William, *Aung San Suu Kyi* (Milwaukee: Gareth Stevens, 2004)

901. Victor, Barbara, *The Lady: Aung San Suu Kyi: Nobel Laureate and Burma's Prisoner*, 2nd edition (York: Faber, 2002)

902. Wintle, Justin, *Perfect Hostage: A Life of Aung San Suu Kyi* (London: Hutchinson, 2007)

903. Yerande, V.L., *Aung San Suu Kyi's Struggle for Democracy* (Kanpur: Chandralok Prakashan, 2007)

904. Zeiger, Stacy, *Profiles of Resilience: Aung San Suu Kyi* (US: Createspace, 2014)

905. Zollner, Hans-Bernd, and Rodion Ebbighausen, *The Daughter: A Political Biography of Aung San Suu Kyi* (Chiang Mai: Silkworm Books, 2018)

POPULATION AND ETHNIC MINORITIES

Population

906. *Census Atlas Myanmar: The 2014 Myanmar Population and Housing Census* (Nay Pyi Taw: Ministry of Labour, Immigration and Population, 2017)

907. *Counting the Costs: Myanmar's Problematic Census*, Asia Briefing no. 144 (Yangon/Brussels: International Crisis Group, 15 May 2014)

908. *Ethnicity without Meaning, Data without Context: The 2014 Census, Identity and Citizenship in Burma/Myanmar*, Burma Policy Briefing no. 13 (Amsterdam: Transnational Institute, February 2014)

909. Hutton, J.S., *Census of India 1931: With Complete Survey of Tribal Life and System*, introduction by K.S. Singh, 3 volumes, reprint of 1933 edition (New Delhi: Gyan Books, 2012)

910. Khin Maung, M.I., *Estimates of Burma's Mortality, Age Structure, and Fertility, 1973–83*, Papers of the East-West Population Institute no. 116 (Honolulu: East-West Centre, 1990)

911. Lahpai Shawng Htoi, *Taing-Yinn Tharr and the Acts of the Apostles: A Lens for Anti-Colonial Existence in Burma*, edited by Adam L. Brackin (US: The author, 2020)

912. *Myanmar Population Changes and Fertility Survey: Preliminary Report 1992* (Yangon: Immigration and Manpower Department, Ministry of Home Affairs, Government of the Union of Myanmar, 1992)

913. *Population Changes and Fertility Survey 1991* (Yangon: Immigration and Population Department, 1995)

914. *The 2014 Population and Housing Census of Myanmar: Questions and Answers about Myanmar's Census* (Naypyitaw and Geneva: Ministry of Immigration and Population and United Nations Population Fund, 2014)

915. *The Population and Housing Census of Myanmar, 2014: Findings of the Census Observation Mission: An Overview* (Naypyitaw and Geneva: Ministry of Immigration and Population and United Nations Population Fund, 2014)

916. *The Republic of the Union of Myanmar: Census Observation Mission Report, 2014 Population and Housing Census* (New York: United Nations Population Fund, 2014)

917. *The Republic of the Union of Myanmar: Population and Housing Census of Myanmar, 2014: Provisional Results*, Census Report Volume 1 (Naypyitaw: Ministry of Immigration and Population, August 2014)

918. *The Republic of the Union of Myanmar: The 2014 Myanmar Population and Housing Census: Highlights of the Main Results*, Census Report Volume 2-A (Naypyitaw: Ministry of Immigration and Population, May 2015)

919. *The Republic of the Union of Myanmar: The 2014 Population and Housing Census: The Union Report*, Census Report Volume 2 (Naypyitaw: Ministry of Immigration and Population, May 2015)

920. *The Republic of the Union of Myanmar: The 2014 Population and Housing Census: The Union Report: Occupation and Industry*, Census Report Volume 2-B (Naypyitaw: Ministry of Immigration and Population, March 2016)

921. *The Republic of the Union of Myanmar: The 2014 Population and Housing Census: The Union Report: Religion*, Census Report Volume 2-C (Naypyitaw: Ministry of Labour, Immigration and Population, July 2016)

922. *The Republic of the Union of Myanmar: The 2014 Population and Housing Census: Thematic Report on Fertility and Nuptiality*, Census Report Volume 4-A (Naypyitaw: Ministry of Labour, Immigration and Population, September 2016)

923. *The Republic of the Union of Myanmar: The 2014 Population and Housing Census: Thematic Report on Maternal Mortality*, Census Report Volume 4-C (Naypyitaw: Ministry of Labour, Immigration and Population, September 2016)

924. *The Republic of the Union of Myanmar: The 2014 Population and Housing Census: Thematic Report on Migration and Urbanization*, Census Report Volume 4-D (Naypyitaw: Ministry of Labour, Immigration and Population, December 2016)

925. *The Republic of the Union of Myanmar: The 2014 Population and Housing Census: Thematic Report on Mortality*, Census Report Volume 4-B (Naypyitaw: Ministry of Labour, Immigration and Population, September 2016)

926. *The Republic of the Union of Myanmar: The 2014 Population and Housing Census: Thematic Report on Population Dynamics*, Census Report Volume 4-E (Naypyitaw: Ministry of Labour, Immigration and Population, December 2016)

Ethnic Minorities – General

927. *Burma: Extrajudicial Execution and Torture of Members of Ethnic Minorities*, AI Index ASA 16/05/88 (London: Amnesty International, May 1988)
928. Callahan, M.P., *Political Authority in Burma's Ethnic Minority States: Devolution, Occupation, and Coexistence*, Policy Studies no. 31 (Washington DC: East-West Centre, 2007)
929. Clarke, S.L., Seng Aung Sein Myint and Zabra Yu Siwa, *Re-examining Ethnic Identity in Myanmar* (Siem Reap: Centre for Peace and Conflict Studies, 2019)
930. Diran, R.K., *The Vanishing Tribes of Burma* (London: Weidenfeld and Nicolson, 1997)
931. *Elections for Ethnic Equality? A Snapshot of Ethnic Perspectives on the 2015 Elections* (Thailand?: Burma Partnership, 2015)
932. *Ethnic Groups in Burma: Development, Democracy and Human Rights* (London: Anti-Slavery International, 1994)
933. Fryer, Frederic, *Tribes on the Frontier of Burma*, reprint of 1907 edition (New Delhi: Gyan, 2018)
934. Gravers, Mikael (ed.), *Exploring Ethnic Diversity in Burma* (Copenhagen: Nordic Institute of Asian Studies, 2007)
935. Howard, David, *Ten Southeast Asian Tribes from Five Countries: Thailand, Burma, Vietnam, Laos, Philippines* (San Francisco: Last Gasp of San Francisco, 2008)
936. *Identity Crisis: Ethnicity and Conflict in Myanmar*, Asia Report no. 312 (Brussels/Yangon: International Crisis Group, 28 August 2020)
937. Jolliffe, Kim, *Ethnic Armed Conflict and Territorial Administration in Myanmar* (Yangon: The Asia Foundation, July 2015)
938. Jolliffe, Kim, *Ethnic Conflict and Social Services in Myanmar's Contested Regions* (Yangon: The Asia Foundation, 2014)
939. *Listening to Voices from Inside: Ethnic People Speak* (Siem Reap: Centre for Peace and Conflict Studies, June 2010)
940. Matthews, Bruce, *Ethnic and Religious Diversity: Myanmar's Unfolding Nemesis*, ISEAS Working Papers, Visiting Researchers Series no. 3 (Singapore: Institute of Southeast Asian Studies, 2001)
941. McCartan, Brian, and Kim Jolliffe, *Ethnic Armed Actors and Justice Provision in Myanmar* (Yangon: Asia Foundation, 2016)

942. *Measures Taken for Development of Border Areas and National Races, 1989–1992* (Yangon: Ministry of Border Areas and National Races Development, 1993)

943. *Myanmar: Ethnic Minorities: Targets of Repression*, AI Index ASA 16/014/2001 (London: Amnesty International, June 2001)

944. *Myanmar: Human Rights Violations against Ethnic Minorities*, AI Index ASA 16/038/1996 (London: Amnesty International, August 1996)

945. *Myanmar Backgrounder: Ethnic Minority Politics*, Asia Report no. 52 (Bangkok/Brussels: International Crisis Group, 7 May 2003)

946. Min Naing, *National Ethnic Groups of Myanmar*, translated by Hpone Thant (Yangon: Swiftwinds, 2000)

947. Sakhong, L.H., *In Defence of Identity: The Ethnic Nationalities' Struggle for Democracy, Human Rights, and Federalism in Burma: A Collection of Writings and Speeches, 2001–2010* (Bangkok: Orchid Press, 2010)

948. Smith, Martin, *Burma (Myanmar): The Time for Change* (London: Minority Rights Group International, 2002)

949. Smith, Martin, *State of Strife: The Dynamics of Ethnic Conflict in Burma*, Policy Studies no. 36 (Washington DC: East-West Centre, 2007)

950. Smith, Martin, with Annie Allsebrook, *Ethnic Groups in Burma: Development, Democracy and Human Rights* (London: Anti-Slavery International, 1994)

951. South, Ashley, *Ethnic Politics in Burma: States of Conflict*, 2nd edition (London: Routledge, 2010)

952. Stepan, Alfred, *Multi-Nationalism, Democracy and "Asymmetrical Federalism" (with Some Tentative Comparative Reflections on Burma)*, Technical Advisory Network of Burma, Working Paper no. 2/02 (Washington DC: The Burma Fund, 2002)

953. Taylor, R.H., *Refighting Old Battles, Compounding Misconceptions: The Politics of Ethnicity in Myanmar Today*, ISEAS Perspective no. 12 (Singapore: Institute of Southeast Asian Studies, 2015)

954. Thawnghmung, A.M., *Beyond Armed Resistance: Ethnonational Politics in Burma (Myanmar)*, Policy Studies no. 62 (Honolulu: East-West Centre, 2011)

955. Thornton, Phil, *Restless Souls: Rebels, Refugees, Medics and Misfits on the Thai-Burma Border* (Bangkok: Asia Books, 2006)
956. Walaiporn Tantikanangkul and Ashley Pritchard (eds.), *Politics of Autonomy and Sustainability in Myanmar: Change for New Hope ... New Life?* (Singapore: Springer International, 2016)
957. Wunna Kyaw Tin and Artist Hla Myint Swe, *Homeland: Traditional Culture and Customs of Myanmar Ethnics*, translated by Kyaw Swe (Singapore: Spirit Asia, 2014)
958. Wunna Kyaw Tin and Artist Hla Myint Swe, *Paragon: Exotic Cultural Heritage Beauties of Myanmar* (Singapore: Spirit Asia, 2011)

The Kayin (Karen)

959. A Resident of Kayin State, *Whither KNU?* (Yangon: News and Periodicals Enterprise, Ministry of Information, 1995)
960. Bleming, T.J., *War in Karen Country: Armed Struggle for a Free and Independent Karen State in Southeast Asia* (New York: iUniverse, 2007)
961. Bunker, Alonzo, *Soo Thah: A Tale of the Making of the Karen Nation*, reprint of 1902 edition (Gloucester: Dodo Press, 2009)
962. Coomar, P.C., M.K. Raha and Sudip Bhui, *Tradition and Transformation in an Immigrant Island Society (The Karen of Andaman Islands)* (Delhi: Abhijeet Publications 2009)
963. Delang, C.O., *Living at the Edge of Thai Society: The Karen in the Highlands of Northern Thailand* (London: Routledge, 2010)
964. Falla, Jonathan, *True Love and Bartholomew: Rebels on the Burmese Border* (Cambridge: Cambridge University Press, 1991)
965. Fong, Jack, *Revolution as Development: The Karen Self-Determination Struggle against Ethnocracy (1949–2004)* (Boca Raton: Universal, 2008)
966. Hayami, Yoko, *Between Hills and Plains: Power and Practice in Socio-religious Dynamics among Karen* (Kyoto: Kyoto University Press, 2004)
967. Hinton, Elizabeth, *Oldest Brother's Story: Tales of the Pwo Karen* (Chiang Mai: Silkworm Books, 1999)
968. Jolliffe, Kim, *Ceasefires, Governance and Development: The Karen National Union in Times of Change* (Yangon: Asia Foundation, December 2016)

969. Jolliffe, Pia, *Learning, Migration and Intergenerational Relations: The Karen and the Gift of Education* (Basingstoke: Palgrave Macmillan, 2016)
970. Marshall, H.I., *The Karen People of Burma: A Study in Anthropology and Ethnology*, reprint of 1922 edition (Bangkok: White Lotus, 1997)
971. Pedersen, Daniel, *Secret Genocide: Voices of the Karen of Burma* (Dunboyne: Maverick House, 2011)
972. Rajah, Ananda, *Remaining Karen: A Study of Cultural Reproduction and the Maintenance of Identity* (Canberra: ANU Press, 2008)
973. Rogers, Benedict, *A Land without Evil: Stopping the Genocide of Burma's Karen People* (Oxford: Monarch Books, 2004)
974. San C. Po, *Burma and the Karens*, reprint of 1928 edition (Bangkok: White Lotus, 2001)
975. Saw Ralph and Naw Sheera, *Fifty Years in the Karen Revolution in Burma: The Soldier and the Teacher*, edited by Stephanie Olinga-Shannon, introduction by Martin Smith (Ithaca: Southeast Asia Program, Cornell University, 2019)
976. Thawnghmung, A.M., *The Karen Revolution in Burma: Diverse Voices, Uncertain Ends*, Policy Studies no. 45 (Washington DC: East-West Centre, 2008)
977. Thawnghmung, A.M., *The "Other" Karen in Myanmar: Ethnic Minorities and the Struggle without Arms* (Lanham: Lexington Books, 2012)
978. Tucker, Mike, *The Long Patrol: With Karen Guerrillas in Burma* (Bangkok: Asia Books, 2003)
979. *Village Agency: Rural Rights and Resistance in a Militarized Karen State* (Thailand: Karen Human Rights Group, 2008)

The Kachin

980. Armstrong, R.M., *The Kachins of Burma* (Bloomington: Eastern Press, 1997)
981. Dean, Karin, *The Kachin Tackling the Territorial Trap: A Nation Divided by the Sino-Myanmar Boundary* (Saarbrucken: VDM Verlag Dr Müller, 2010)
982. Enriquez, C.M., *In Quest of Greatness*, reprint of 1951 edition with additional material, edited by C.C. Naw Ja (Myitkyina: Kachin Veterans Committee, 2003)

983. Gilhodes, A., *The Kachin: Religion and Customs* (Bangkok: White Lotus, 1996)
984. Hanson, Ola, *The Kachins: Their Customs and Traditions*, reprint of 1913 edition (Cambridge: Cambridge University Press, 2012)
985. *Isolated in Yunnan: Kachin Refugees from Burma in China's Yunnan Province* (New York: Human Rights Watch, 2012)
986. Leach, E.R., *Political Systems of Highland Burma: A Study of Kachin Social Structure*, reprint of 1954 edition (London: Athlone Press, 2008)
987. Lintner, Bertil, *The Kachin: Lords of Burma's Northern Frontier* (Chiang Mai: Teak House, 1997)
988. Min Thu, Z., *The Kachins (Their Unique Traditions and Customary Laws)* (Myitkyina?: The author, 2015)
989. Robinne, Francois, and Mandy Sadan (eds.), *Social Dynamics in the Highlands of Southeast Asia: Reconsidering "Political Systems of Highland Burma" by E.R. Leach* (Leiden: Brill, 2007)
990. Sadan, Mandy, *Being and Becoming Kachin: Histories beyond the State in the Borderworlds of Burma* (Oxford: The British Academy and Oxford University Press, 2013)
991. Sadan, Mandy (ed.), *War and Peace in the Borderlands of Myanmar: The Kachin Ceasefire, 1994–2011* (Copenhagen: NIAS Press, 2016)
992. Visser, L.J., *Building Relationships across Divides: Peace and Conflict Analysis of Kachin State* (Siem Reap: Centre for Peace and Conflict Studies, 2016)

The Shan

993. Aye, Henri-Andre, *The Shan Conundrum in Burma*, revised edition (North Charleston: Booksurge, 2010)
994. Cochrane, W.W., *The Shans*, reprint of 1915 edition (US: HardPress, 2013)
995. Conway, Susan, *The Shan: Culture, Arts and Crafts* (Bangkok: River Books, 2006)
996. Czarnecki, Amanda (ed.), *Letters from Shan State, by the Students of the School for Shan State Nationalities Youth – Seventh Training* (Chiang Mai: School for Shan State Nationalities Youth, 2007)

997. Eberhardt, Nancy, *Imagining the Course of Life: Self-Transformation in a Shan Buddhist Community* (Chiang Mai: Silkworm Books, 2007)

998. Ferguson, J.M., *Repossessing Shanland: Myanmar, Thailand, and a Nation-State Deferred* (Madison: University of Wisconsin Press, 2021)

999. Kantar, Sally (ed.), *Plants That Grew in the Fire: Portraits of Young Activists from Shan State, by the Students of SSSNY's 10th Social Justice Education Program* (Chiang Mai: School for Shan State Nationalities Youth, 2011)

1000. Milne, Leslie, *Shans at Home: Burma's Shan States in the Early 1900s*, reprint of 1910 edition (Bangkok: White Lotus, 2001)

1001. Prakai Nonthawasi, *Changes in Northern Thailand and the Shan States, 1886–1940*, Southeast Asian Studies Program, Comparative Research Award, Report no. 1 (Singapore: Institute of Southeast Asian Studies, 1988)

1002. Rato, Montira, and Khanidtha Kanthavichai (eds.), *Shan and Beyond: Essays on Shan Archaeology, Anthropology, History, Politics, Religion and Human Rights* (Bangkok: Institute of Asian Studies, Chulalongkorn University, 2011)

1003. Sai Aung Tun, *History of the Shan State from its Origins to 1962* (Chiang Mai: Silkworm Books, 2009)

1004. Sai Kam Mong, *The History and Development of the Shan Scripts* (Chiang Mai: Silkworm Books, 2004)

1005. Tannenbaum, Nicola, *Who Can Compete against the World? Power-Projection and Buddhism in Shan Worldview* (Ann Arbor: Association for Asian Studies, 1995)

1006. Thitiwut Boonyawongwiwat, *The Ethno-narcotic Politics of the Shan People: Fighting with Drugs, Fighting for the Nation on the Thai-Burmese Border* (Lanham: Lexington Books, 2018)

1007. Yawnghwe, Samara, *Maintaining the Union of Burma 1946–1962: The Role of the Ethnic Nationalities in a Shan Perspective* (Bangkok: Institute of Asian Studies, Chulalongkorn University, 2013)

The Mon

1008. Guillon, Emmanuel, *The Mons: A Civilization of Southeast Asia* (Bangkok: Siam Society, 1999)

1009. Halliday, Robert, *The Mons of Burma and Thailand: Volume 1, The Talaings*, reprint of 1917 edition (Bangkok: White Lotus, 1999)

1010. Halliday, Robert, *The Mons of Burma and Thailand: Volume 2, Selected Articles* (Bangkok: White Lotus, 2000)

1011. McCormick, Patrick, Mathias Jenny and Chris Baker (eds.), *The Mon over Two Millenia: Monuments, Manuscripts, Movements* (Bangkok: Institute of Asian Studies, Chulalongkorn University, 2011)

The Zo (Chin/Lushai/Mizo/Kuki) Group

1012. East, E.H., *Burma Manuscript*, edited by Tim Marsh (Yangon: C. Thang Za Tuan, 1996?)

1013. Ghosh, S.K., *Epic as History: Diffusion of Ramkatha from Chin Hills to Lushai Hills* (Delhi: BR, 2011)

1014. Gin Khan Thang, T., and Paoneikhai Suantak, *Tributary Hill Polity: Chiefs and Overlords in Northern Chin Hills, c.1800–1948* (New Delhi: Mittal Publications, 2015)

1015. Head, W.R., *Handbook on the Haka Chin Customs*, reprint of 1917 edition (US: Hardpress, 2012)

1016. Khiangte, Laltluangliana, *Tribal Culture, Folklore and Literature (Mizos of India, Bangladesh and Myanmar)* (New Delhi: Mittal Publications, 2013)

1017. Khup Chin Pau, S., *A Northern Chin Tradition: Architecture, History, Life, Death and Feasting in Sukte-Kamhau* (Oxford: Sean Kingston, 2011)

1018. Khup Za Go, *Zo Chronicles: A Documentary Study of History and Culture of the Kuki-Chin-Lushai Tribe* (New Delhi: Mittal, 2008)

1019. Pum Khan Pau, *Indo-Burma Frontier and the Making of the Chin Hills: Empire and Resistance* (London: Routledge, 2020)

1020. Rizvi, S.H.M., and Shibani Roy, *Kuki Chin Tribes of Mizoram and Manipur* (Delhi: BR, 2006)

1021. Sakhong, L.H., *In Search of Chin Identity: A Study in Religion, Politics and Ethnic Identity in Burma* (Copenhagen: NIAS Press, 2003)

1022. Sakhong, L.H., *Religion and Politics among the Chin People in Burma (1896–1949)* (Uppsala: Uppsala University, 2000)

1023. Strait, C.U., *The Chin People: A Selective History and Anthropology of the Chin People* (US: Xlibris, 2014)

1024. Suantak, Joseph, *Chin+Kuki+Zo: Genesis and Exodus: Unravelling the Mystified Lost Past of the Unidentified Proto-Sino-Tibeto-Burman Family* (New Delhi: Akansha, 2012)

1025. Vervest, Wim, *The Lost Dictionary: A History of the Chin People, the Newland Family and the American Baptist Chin Mission*, edited by C.M. Jordan (Fremantle: Vivid, 2014)

1026. *"We Are Like Forgotten People": The Chin People of Burma: Unsafe in Burma, Unprotected in India* (New York: Human Rights Watch, 2009)

The Naga

1027. Aosenba, *The Naga Resistance Movement: Prospects of Peace and Armed Conflict* (New Delhi: Regency Publications, 2001)

1028. Bon, Olk, *Culture Change among the Naga Tribes of Myanmar: The Former Headhunters Seek to Modernize* (Chiang Mai: The author, March 2019)

1029. Draguet, Michel, *Naga: Awe-Inspiring Beauty* (New Haven: Yale University Press, 2018)

1030. Drouyer, I.A., and Rene Drouyer, *The Nagas: Memories of Headhunters, Indo-Burmese Borderland*, photographs by Rene Drouyer, volume 1 (Bangkok: White Lotus, 2016)

1031. Ma Thanegi, *Naga: A Celebration of Identity*, photographs by Barry Broman (Bangkok: Ava Books, 2011)

1032. Saul, J.D., *The Naga of Burma: Their Festivals, Customs and Way of Life* (Bangkok: Orchid Press, 2005)

1033. Stirn, Aglaja, and Peter Van Ham, *The Hidden World of the Naga: Living Traditions in Northeast India and Burma* (Munich: Prestel, 2003)

1034. Welman, Frans, and Ngathingkhui Jagoi, *Naga Culture: Free against the Odds* (New Delhi: Dev Publishers and Distributors, 2012)

The Kayah (Karenni)

1035. Chapman, Dean, *Karenni: The Forgotten War of a Nation Besieged* (London: Dewi Lewis, 1998)

1036. *Dammed by Burma's Generals: The Karenni Experience with Hydropower Development, From Lawpita to the Salween* (Mae Hong Son: Karenni Development Research Group, 2006)

1037. *History of Karenni Leadership and Karenni Documents: Documents from the Website* (Pekhon: Pekhon University Press, 2013)

1038. Kramer, Tom, Oliver Russell and Martin Smith, *From War to Peace in Kayah (Karenni) State: A Land at the Crossroads in Myanmar* (Amsterdam: Transnational Institute, July 2018)

1039. *Military Confiscation of Karenni Ancestral Land in Karenni State, Burma* (Nai Soi: Karenni Social Development Centre, June 2016)

1040. Rastorfer, Jean-Marc, *On the Development of Kayah and Kayan National Identity: A Study and Bibliography* (Bangkok: Southeast Asian Publishing House, 1994)

The Wa

1041. Kramer, Tom, *The United Wa State Party: Narco-Army or Ethnic Nationalist Party?*, Policy Studies no. 38 (Washington DC: East-West Centre, 2007)

1042. Lintner, Bertil, *The Wa of Myanmar and China's Quest for Global Dominance* (Chiang Mai: Silkworm Books, 2021)

1043. Tin Yee, *The Socio-economic Life of the Wah National* (Yangon: Ministry of Education, 2002)

1044. Young, H.M., *Burma Headhunters: The History and Culture of the Ancient Wa, a Mountain Tribal People*, compiled and edited by D.Y. Chase (US: Xlibris, 2014)

Other Ethnic Groups

1045. Bahadur, Mutua, *Manipuri Costumes through Ages (India, Bangladesh and Myanmar)* (Imphal: Mutua Museum, 2011)

1046. Barua, S.N., *Tribes of Indo-Burma Border: A Socio-cultural History of the Inhabitants of the Patkai Range* (Delhi: Mittal Publications, 1991)

1047. Bollepally, Sudhakshana, *Emigration of Andhras to Burma: A Historical Survey* (New Delhi: Research India Press, 2017)

1048. Christensen, Russ, and Sann Kyaw, *The Pa-O: Rebels and Refugees* (Chiang Mai: Silkworm Books, 2006)

1049. Farrelly, Nicholas, and Stephanie Olinga-Shannon, *Establishing Contemporary Chinese Life in Myanmar*, Trends in Southeast Asia, 2015 no. 15 (Singapore: Institute of Southeast Asian Studies, 2015)

1050. Forbes, Andrew, and David Henley, *The Haw: Traders of the Golden Triangle* (Bangkok: Teak House, 1997)

1051. Goodman, Jim, *The Akha: Guardians of The Forest* (Bangkok: Amarin Printing and Publishing, 1997)

1052. Hpone Thant, *The Yinn: Still Proud in Their Culture*, photographs by Kyaw Kyaw Win (Yangon: The author, 2012)

1053. Ivanoff, Jacques, *The Moken Boat: Symbolic Technology*, translated by Francine Nicolle (Bangkok: White Lotus Press, 1999)

1054. Jhala, A.D., *An Endangered History: Indigeneity, Religion, and Politics on the Borders of India, Burma, and Bangladesh* (New Delhi: Oxford University Press, 2019)

1055. Lisupha, *Life behind the Backdrop of Kachin State: Suffering of a Tribe Neglected by the World Communities* (Charleston: The author and CreateSpace, 2014)

1056. Loffler, L.G., *Ethnographic Notes on the Mru and Khumi of the Chittagong and Arakan Hill Tracts: A Contribution to Our Knowledge of South and Southeast Asian Indigenous Peoples Mainly Based on Field Research in the Southern Chittagong Hill Tracts* (Cambridge: Harvard University Press, 2012)

1057. Maung Tha Hla, *The Rakhaing* (New York: Buddhist Rakhaing Cultural Association, 2004)

1058. Milne, Leslie, *The Home of an Eastern Clan: A Study of the Palaungs of the Shan States*, reprint of 1924 edition (Bangkok: White Lotus, 2004)

1059. Myint Myint Kyu, *Spaces of Exception: Shifting Strategies of the Kokang Chinese along the Myanmar/China Border* (Chiang Mai: Chiang Mai University Press, 2018)

1060. Roberts, J.L., *Mapping Chinese Rangoon: Place and Nation among the Sino-Burmese* (Seattle: University of Washington Press, 2016)

1061. Sai Kham Mong, *Kokang and Kachin in the Shan State (1945–1960)* (Bangkok: Institute of Asian Studies, Chulalongkorn University, 2005)

1062. *Stateless at Sea: The Moken of Burma and Thailand* (New York: Human Rights Watch, 2015)

1063. Wolleng, Angelee, *The Politics of Identity and Settlement of Manipuri in Myanmar* (New Delhi: Ruby Press, 2017)

1064. Yi, Li, *Yunnanese Chinese in Myanmar: Past and Present*, Trends in Southeast Asia, 2015 no. 12 (Singapore: Institute of Southeast Asian Studies, 2015)

1065. Zack, Michele, *The Lisu: Far from the Ruler* (Boulder: University Press of Colorado, 2017)

THE "ROHINGYA QUESTION"

Official Reports

1066. *Bangladesh and Burma: The Rohingya Crisis*, House of Commons, International Development Committee, Second Report of Session 2017–19 (London: House of Commons, Parliament of the United Kingdom, January 2018)

1067. *Burma's Brutal Campaign against the Rohingya*, Hearing before the Subcommittee on Asia and the Pacific of the Committee on Foreign Affairs, House of Representatives, US Congress, 27 September 2017 (Washington DC: US Government Publishing Office, 2017)

1068. *Burma's Challenge: Democracy, Human Rights, Peace and the Plight of the Rohingya*, Statement by Daniel R. Russel, Assistant Secretary, Bureau of East Asian and Pacific Affairs, US Department of State, before the Subcommittee on Asia and the Pacific of the Committee on Foreign Affairs, House of Representatives, US Congress (US: CreateSpace, 2016)

1069. *Detailed Findings of the Independent International Fact-Finding Mission on Myanmar*, A/HRC/42/CRP.5 (Geneva: UN Human Rights Council, 16 September 2019)

1070. *Documentation of Atrocities in Northern Rakhine State* (Washington DC: Bureau of Democracy, Human Rights and Labor, US Department of State, August 2018)

1071. Martin, M.F., Rhoda Margesson and Bruce Vaughn, *The Rohingya Crises in Bangladesh and Burma*, CRS Report (Washington DC: Congressional Research Service, 8 November 2017)

1072. *Rakhine State: A Snapshot of Myanmar's Current Efforts for Peace and Reconciliation* (Nay Pyi Taw: The Republic of the Union of Myanmar, Ministry of Foreign Affairs, 8 January 2020)

1073. *Report of OHCHR Mission to Bangladesh: Interviews with Rohingyas Fleeing from Myanmar since 9 October 2016*, Flash Report (New York: United Nations Human Rights, Office of the High Commissioner, 3 February 2017)

1074. *Report of the Detailed Findings of the Independent International Fact-Finding Mission on Myanmar*, A/HRC/39/CRP.2 (Geneva: UN Human Rights Council, 17 September 2018)

1075. *Report of the Independent International Fact-Finding Mission on Myanmar*, A/HRC/42/50 (New York: United Nations General Assembly, 8 August 2019)

1076. *Sentenced to a Slow Demise: The Plight of Myanmar's Rohingya Minority*, Report of the Standing Committee on Foreign Affairs and International Development, Subcommittee on International Human Rights, 42nd Parliament, First Session (Ottawa: House of Commons, Parliament of Canada, June 2016)

1077. *Situation of Human Rights of Rohingya Muslims and Other Minorities in Myanmar: Report of the United Nations High Commissioner for Human Rights*, General Assembly A/HRC/32/18 (New York: United Nations, 29 June 2016)

Other Publications

1078. Adams, Simon, *"If Not Now, When?": The Responsibility to Protect, the Fate of the Rohingya and the Future of Human Rights* (New York: Global Centre for the Responsibility to Protect, 2019)

1079. Ahmed, Imtiaz (ed.), *The Plight of the Stateless Rohingyas: Responses of the State, Society and the International Community* (Dhaka: University Press Ltd., 2010)

1080. Ahmed, Kawser, and Helal Mohiudden, *The Rohingya Crisis: Analyses, Responses, and Peacebuilding Avenues* (Lanham: Lexington Books, 2020)

1081. *"All of My Body Was Pain": Sexual Violence against Rohingya Women and Girls in Burma* (New York: Human Rights Watch, November 2017)

1082. *"All You Can Do Is Pray": Crimes against Humanity and Ethnic Cleansing of Rohingya Muslims in Burma's Arakan State* (New York: Human Rights Watch, 2013)

1083. *"An Open Prison without End": Myanmar's Mass Detention of Rohingya in Rakhine State* (New York: Human Rights Watch, 8 October 2020)

1084. Ansel, Sophie, et al., *Stateless Rohingya ... Running on Empty*, photographs by Suthep Kritsanavarin, Wutinun Jantori and Gary Morrison (Chiang Mai: Burma Concern, Regional Centre for Social Science and Sustainable Development, Chiang Mai University, and Asian Resource Foundation, 2013)

1085. Aron, Gabrielle, *Reshaping Engagement: Perspectives on Conflict Sensitivity in Rakhine State* (Cambridge: CDA Collaborative Learning Projects, May 2016)

1086. Bahar, Abid, *Burma's Missing Dots: The Emerging Face of Genocide: Essays on Chauvinistic Nationalism and Genocide in Burma, with the Popular Novel Rohingyama* (New Jersey: Xlibris, 2010)

1087. *Bangladesh-Myanmar: The Danger of Forced Repatriation*, Asia Briefing no. 153 (Yangon/Brussels: International Crisis Group, 12 November 2018)

1088. Bari, M.A., *The Rohingya Crisis: A People Facing Extinction* (Markfield: Kube, 2018)

1089. Berlatsky, Noah (ed.), *Genocide and Persecution: Burma* (Farmington Hills: Greenhaven Press, 2015)

1090. Bin Ali, Asif, and Sabbir Ahmed (eds.), *Burmese Nationalism: Rohingya Crisis and Contemporary Politics* (Dhaka: Borno Prokash, 2019)

1091. *Building Resilience to Communal Violence: Lessons from Rakhine State* (Yangon: Centre for Diversity and National Harmony, September 2017)

1092. Chaudhury, S.B.R., and Ranabir Samaddar (eds.), *The Rohingya in South Asia: People without a State* (London: Routledge, 2018)

1093. *Crimes against Humanity in Western Burma: The Situation of the Rohingyas* (Galway: Irish Centre for Human Rights, National University of Ireland, 2010)

1094. Dapice, David, *A Fatal Distraction from Federalism: Religious Conflict in Rakhine*, Occasional Paper (Cambridge: Ash Centre for Democratic Governance and Innovation, Harvard Kennedy School, 2015)

1095. *"Everywhere is Trouble": An Update on the Situation of the Rohingya Refugees in Thailand, Malaysia and Indonesia* (Bangkok: Fortify Rights, 2016)

1096. Farzana, K.F., *Memories of Burmese Rohingya Refugees: Contested Identity and Belonging* (New York: Palgrave Macmillan, 2017)

1097. Galache, C.S., *The Burmese Labyrinth: A History of the Rohingya Tragedy* (London: Verso Books, 2020)

1098. Green, Penny, Thomas MacManus and Alicia de la Cour Venning, *Countdown to Annihilation: Genocide in Myanmar* (London: International State Crime Initiative, 2015)

1099. Green, Penny, Thomas MacManus and Alicia de la Cour Venning, *Genocide Achieved, Genocide Continues: Myanmar's Annihilation of the Rohingya* (London: International State Crime Initiative, 2018)

1100. Habib, Mohshin, et al., *Forced Migration of Rohingya: The Untold Experience* (Ottawa: Ontario International Development Agency, 2018)

1101. Habiburahman, with Sophie Ansel, *First, They Erased Our Name: A Rohingya Speaks*, translated by Andrea Reece (Melbourne: Scribe, 2019)

1102. Hargrave, Karen, et al., *The Rohingya Response in Bangladesh and the Global Compact on Refugees: Lessons, Challenges and Opportunities*, HPG Working Paper (London: Humanitarian Policy Group, April 2020)

1103. Holt, J.C., *Myanmar's Buddhist-Muslim Crisis: Rohingya, Arakanese, and Burmese Narratives of Siege and Fear* (Honolulu: University of Hawai'i Press, 2019)

1104. Ibrahim, Azeem, *The Rohingyas: Inside Myanmar's Hidden Genocide*, revised edition (London: Hurst, 2018)

1105. Karim, Abdul, *The Rohingyas: A Short Account of Their History and Culture* (Chittagong: Arakan Historical Society, 2000)

1106. Karim, M.A., *Genocide and Geopolitics of the Rohingya Crisis* (New York: Nova Science, 2020)

1107. Khin Maung Saw, *Arakan: A Neglected Land and a Voiceless People*, 2nd edition (Yangon: Kha Yee Phaw Publication House, 2016)

1108. Khin Maung Saw, *Behind the Mask: The Truth behind the Name "Rohingya"* (Yangon: Taunggyi Publishing House, 2016)

1109. Kyi May Kaung, *The Rohingya Genocide in Burma 2012–2017: Activists' Handy Handbook* (US: Words Sounds and Images, 2017)

1110. Lee, Ronan, *Myanmar's Rohingya Genocide: Identity, History and Hate Speech* (London: I.B. Taurus, 2021)

1111. *Living in Limbo: Burmese Rohingyas in Malaysia* (New York: Human Rights Watch, 2000)

1112. Maung Tha Hla, *Rohingya Hoax* (New York: Buddhist Rakhaing Cultural Association, 2009)

1113. Maung Zarni and Natalie Brinham, *Essays on Myanmar's Genocide of Rohingyas (2012–2018)* (Dhaka: Refugee and Migratory Movements Research Unit, 2019)

1114. *Myanmar: "Caged without a Roof": Apartheid in Myanmar's Rakhine State*, AI Index ASA 16/7484/2017 (London: Amnesty International, November 2017)

1115. *Myanmar: Questions and Answers on Human Rights Law in Rakhine State*, Briefing Note (Geneva: International Commission of Jurists, November 2017)

1116. *Myanmar: "My World Is Finished": Rohingya Targeted in Crimes against Humanity in Myanmar*, AI Index ASA 16/7288/2017 (London: Amnesty International, October 2017)

1117. *Myanmar: Remaking Rakhine State*, AI Index ASA 16/8018/2018 (London: Amnesty International, March 2018)

1118. *Myanmar: "We Are at Breaking Point" – Rohingya: Persecuted in Myanmar, Neglected in Bangladesh*, AI Index ASA 16/5362/2016 (London: Amnesty International, December 2016)

1119. *Myanmar's Rohingya Crisis Enters a Dangerous New Phase*, Asia Report no. 292 (Yangon/Brussels: International Crisis Group, 7 December 2017)

1120. Othman, Zarina, M.M. Haque and Bakri Mat, *Rohingya Suvivors: Regional Security Implication of Gender Based Violence* (Negeri Sembilan: USIM Press, 2019)

1121. *Perilous Plight: Burma's Rohingya Take to the Seas* (New York: Human Rights Watch, 2009)

1122. *Persecution of the Rohingya Muslims: Is Genocide Occurring in Myanmar's Rakhine State? A Legal Analysis* (New Haven and Bangkok: Yale Law School and Fortify Rights, 2015)

1123. *Rape by Command: Sexual Violence as a Weapon against the Rohingya* (Chittagong: Kaladan Press Network, February 2018)

1124. Rodger, Ellen, *A Refugee's Journey from Myanmar* (New York: Crabtree, 2017)

1125. Rodger, Ellen, *Hoping for a Home after Myanmar* (New York: Crabtree, 2018)

1126. Saddiqui, Habib, *The Forgotten Rohingya: Their Struggle for Human Rights in Burma* (US: The author, 2008)

1127. Selth, Andrew, *Myanmar's Armed Forces and the Rohingya Crisis*, Peaceworks no. 140 (Washington DC: United States Institute of Peace, August 2018)

1128. Shaw Zan and Aye Chan, *Influx Viruses: The Illegal Muslims in Arakan* (New York: Arakanese in United States, 2005)

1129. Shwe Lu Maung, *The Rakhine State Violence: Volume One: The Rakhaing Revolution* (US: Shahnawaz Khan, 2014)

1130. Shwe Lu Maung, *The Rakhine State Violence: Volume Two: The Rohingya* (US: Shahnawaz Khan, 2014)

1131. Sidasathian, Chutima, *Rohingya: The Persecution of a People in Southeast Asia* (US: CreateSpace, 2012)

1132. Smith, Matthew, and Taylor Landis, *Policies of Persecution: Ending Abusive State Policies against Rohingya Muslims in Myanmar* (Bangkok: Fortify Rights, 2014)

1133. Swazo, N.K., et al., *The Rohingya Crisis: A Moral, Ethnographic, and Policy Assessment* (London: Routledge, 2021)

1134. *"The Government Could Have Stopped This": Sectarian Violence and Ensuing Abuses in Burma's Arakan State* (New York: Human Rights Watch, 2012)

1135. *The Long Haul ahead for Myanmar's Rohingya Refugee Crisis*, Asia Report no. 296 (Yangon/Brussels: International Crisis Group, 16 May 2018)

1136. *The Rohingya Muslims: Ending a Cycle of Exodus?* (New York: Human Rights Watch, 1996)

1137. *The Torture in My Mind: The Right to Mental Health for Rohingya Survivors of Genocide in Myanmar and Bangladesh* (Bangkok: Fortify Rights, December 2020)

1138. *"They Gave Them Long Swords": Preparations for Genocide and Crimes against Humanity against Rohingya Muslims in Rakhine State, Myanmar* (Bangkok: Fortify Rights, July 2018)

1139. *"They Tried to Kill Us All": Atrocity Crimes against Rohingya Muslims in Rakhine State, Myanmar* (Washington DC: Simon-Skjodt Centre for the Prevention of Genocide, United States Holocaust Memorial Museum, and Fortify Rights, 2017)

1140. *"Tools of Genocide": National Verification Cards and the Denial of Citizenship of Rohingya Muslims in Myanmar* (Belfast, Bangkok and Geneva: Fortify Rights, September 2019)

1141. Uddin, Nasir, *The Rohingya: An Ethnography of "Subhuman" Life* (New Delhi: Oxford University Press, 2020)

1142. Ware, Anthony, and Costas Laoutides, *Myanmar's "Rohingya" Conflict* (London: C. Hurst, 2018)

1143. *"We Will Destroy Everything": Military Responsibility for Crimes against Humanity in Rakhine State, Myanmar*, AI Index ASA 16/8630/2018 (London: Amnesty International, 2018)

1144. Zaw Min Htut, *Human Rights Abuses and Discrimination on Rohingyas* (Tokyo: Burmese Rohingya Association in Japan, 2003)

LANGUAGES

General

1145. Bradley, David (ed.), *Studies in Burmese Languages*, Papers in Southeast Asian Linguistics no. 13 (Canberra: Research School of Pacific and Asian Studies, Australian National University, 1995)

1146. Button, Christopher, *Proto Northern Chin*, STEDT Monograph no. 10 (Berkeley: Department of Linquistics, University of California, 2011)

1147. Grierson, G.A., *Linguistic Survey of India: Volume 3, Tibeto-Burman Family: Part 3, Specimens of the Kuki-Chin, and Burma Groups*, reprint of 1928 edition (Delhi: Kalpaz Publications, 2017)

1148. Hill, N.W., *The Historical Phonology of Tibetan, Burmese and Chinese* (Cambridge: Cambridge University Press, 2019)

1149. Jenny, Mathias, *A Short Introduction to Mon Language* (Sangkhlaburi: The Mon Culture and Literature Survival Project, 2001)

1150. Kirkpatrick, Robert (ed.), *English Language Teaching in Thailand and Myanmar* (Bangkok: Shinawatra International University, 2011)

1151. LaPolla, R.J., and Dory Poa, *Rawang Texts*, Languages of the World/Text Collections no. 18 (Munich: Lincom Europa, 2001)

1152. Luzoe, *Myanmar Newspaper Reader* (Kensington: Dunwoody Press, 1996)

1153. Miyake, Marc, *The Pyu Language of Ancient Burma* (Berlin: De Gruyter, 2021)

1154. *Myanmar Country Report: Language Education and Social Cohesion (LESC) Initiative* (Thailand: UNICEF East Asia and Pacific Regional Office, 2016)

1155. Romeo, Nicoletta, *Aspect in Burmese: Meaning and Function* (Amsterdam: John Benjamins, 2008)

1156. Sandamuni, U., *Origin and Development of Arakanese Script* (Kolkata: Mahabodhi Book Agency, 2016)

1157. Solnit, David, *Eastern Kayah Li: Grammar, Text, Glossary* (Honolulu: University of Hawai'i Press, 1997)

1158. Watkins, Justin, *The Phonetics of Wa: Experimental Phonestics, Phonology, Orthography and Sociolinguistics*, Pacific Linguistics 531 (Canberra: Research School of Pacific and Asian Studies, Australian National University, 2002)

1159. Watkins, Justin (ed.), *Studies in Burmese Linguistics* (Canberra: Research School of Pacific and Asian Studies, Australian National University, 2005)

1160. Yu, Defen, *Aspects of Lisu Phonology and Grammar: A language of Southeast Asia*, Pacific Linguistics 588 (Canberra: Research School of Pacific and Asian Studies, Australian National University, 2007)

Dictionaries and Phrasebooks

1161. A Zun Mo, *Essential Burmese Phrasebook and Dictionary* (North Clarendon: Tuttle, 2020)

1162. Ba Han, *The University English-Myanmar Dictionary* (Rangoon: Win Literature, 1996)

1163. Bradley, David, and Vicky Bowman, *Burmese Phrasebook*, 3rd edition (Hawthorn: Lonely Planet, 2001)

1164. Bowman, Vicky, *Burmese* (Hawthorn: Lonely Planet, 2008)

1165. *Burmese Phrasebook and Dictionary*, 6th edition (Dublin: Lonely Planet, 2020)

1166. *Burmese Phrase Book and Dictionary*, 2nd revised edition (London: Berlitz, 2019)

1167. Cunningham, Nancy, *Mini Burmese Dictionary* (Boston: Tuttle, 2020)

1168. Gonzales, Jessy, *English Burmese Topical Dictionary* (US: The author, 2020)

1169. Hough, G.H., *An Anglo-Burmese Dictionary*, reprint of 1845 edition (US: BiblioLife, 2008)

1170. Ma Tin Cho Mar and Bi Bi, Noorjahan, *Myanmar Phrase Book: A Quick and Effective Way to Learn Myanmar Conversation* (Subang Jaya: Pelanduk Publications, 2011)

1171. Myanmar Language Commission, *Myanmar-English Dictionary* (Springfield: Dunwoody Press, 1997)

1172. Nolan, Stephen, and Nyi Nyi Lwin, *Pocket Burmese Dictionary* (Singapore: Periplus, 2009)

1173. Okell, John, and Anna Allott, *Burmese/Myanmar Dictionary of Grammatical Forms* (Richmond: Curzon, 2001)

1174. Sun Associates, *Practical Myanmar* (Bangkok: Book Promotion and Service Ltd., 1995)

1175. Rhoden, T.F., *Karen Language Phrasebook: Basics of Sgaw Dialect* (Bangkok: White Lotus, 2015)

1176. *Southeast Asian Phrasebook: 9 Languages: Burmese, Chinese, Filipino, Indonesian, Khmer, Lao, Malay, Thai, Vietnamese* (Peterborough: Thomas Cook, 2006)

1177. Taranov, Andrey, *Burmese Vocabulary for English Speakers* (Hong Kong: T&P Books, 2019)

1178. Taranov, Andrey, *Phrasebook – Burmese; The Most Important Phrases* (Hong Kong: T&P Books, 2021)

1179. The Paw Family and Betsy Wrisley (eds.), *English–Sgaw Karen Dictionary* (US: Bevans Books, 2008)

1180. Van Breugel, Seino, *A Dictionary of Atong: A Tibeto-Burman Language of Northeast India and Bangladesh* (Berlin: De Gruyter Mouton, 2021)

1181. Watkins, Justin, *Dictionary of Wa, with Translations into English, Burmese and Chinese*, 2 volumes (Leiden: Brill, 2013)

1182. Wong, Kenneth, *Survival Burmese: Phrasebook and Dictionary* (North Clarendon: Tuttle, 2018)

1183. Zafari, N.M.K., *Zafari's English to Rohingya Dictionary: An Easy Guide to the Rohingya Language* (Germany: SPS, 2020)

Instructional Works

1184. Cushing, J.N., *Grammatical Sketch of the Kakhyen Language* (Munich: LINCOM, 2018)

1185. Fraser, J.O., *Handbook of the Lisu Language*, reprint of 1922 edition (US: Franklin Classics Trade Press, 2018)

1186. Hertz, H.F., *A Practical Handbook of the Kachin or Chingpaw Language, Containing the Grammatical Principals and Peculiarities of the Language, Colloquial Exercises, and a Vocabulary, with an Appendix on Kachin Customs, Laws and Religion*, reprint of 1902 edition (Delhi: Relnk Books, 2017)

1187. Jenny, Mathias, and San San Hnin Tun, *Burmese: A Comprehensive Grammar* (London: Routledge, 2016)

1188. Josi, C.V., *A Manual of Pali: Being a Graduated Course of Pali for Beginners* (Whitefish: Literary Licensing, 2012)

1189. Judson, Adoniram, *A Grammar of the Burmese Language*, reprint of 1888 edition (Munich: Lincom, 2012)

1190. Latter, Thomas, *A Grammar of the Language of Burmah*, reprint of 1845 edition (New Delhi: Asian Educational Services, 1991)

1191. Nai Pan Hla, *An Introduction to Mon Language* (Kyoto: The Centre for Southeast Asian Studies, 1989)

1192. Nakaji Nay Win, *Mayanmar Language: 101 Burmese Verbs* (US: Preceptor Language Guides, 2015)

1193. Okell, John, *Burmese by Ear or Essential Myanmar* (London: Sussex Publications, 2002)

1194. Okell, John, *First Steps in Burmese* (London: School of Oriental and African Studies, 1989)

1195. Okell, John, Saw Tun and Khin Mya Swe, *Burmese (Myanmar): An Introduction to the Literary Style* (DeKalb: Northern Illinois University Press, 2010)

1196. Okell, John, Saw Tun and Khin Mya Swe, *Burmese (Myanmar): An Introduction to the Script* (DeKalb: Northern Illinois University Press, 2010)

1197. Okell, John, Saw Tun and Khin Mya Swe, *Burmese (Myanmar): Book 1: An Introduction to the Spoken Language* (DeKalb: Northern Illinois University Press, 2010)

1198. Okell, John, Saw Tun and Khin Mya Swe, *Burmese (Myanmar): Book 2: An Introduction to the Spoken Language* (DeKalb: Northern Illinois University Press, 2010)

1199. Rhoden, T.F., *Making Out in Burmese* (North Clarendon: Tuttle, 2010)

1200. San San Hnin Tun, with Patrick McCormick, *Colloquial Burmese: The Complete Course for Beginners* (London: Routledge, 2015)

1201. So-Hartmann, Helga, *Descriptive Grammar of Daai Chin*, STEDT Monograph no. 7 (Berkeley: Department of Linquistics, University of California, 2009)

1202. Thuzar Winn and Detlef Eckert, *Burmese: A Gateway to an Intriguing Language* (US: CreateSpace, 2015)

RELIGIONS, RELIGIOUS COMMUNITIES AND RELIGIOUS SITES

General

1203. Khin Maung Yee Khawsiama, *Towards a "Ludu" Theology: A Critical Evaluation of "Minjung" Theology and its Implication for a Theological Response to the "Dukkha" (Suffering) of People in Myanmar (Burma)* (Pieterlen: Peter Lang AG, 2013)

1204. Ling, S.N., *The Meeting of Christianity and Buddhism in Burma: Its Past, Present, and Future Perspectives* (Tokyo: International Christian University, 1998)

1205. McKay, Melyn, *The Religious Landscape in Myanmar's Rakhine State*, Peaceworks no. 149 (Washington DC: United States Institute of Peace, August 2019)

1206. Nyi Nyi Kyaw, *Freedom of Religion, the Role of the State and Interreligious Relations in Myanmar* (Colombo: International Centre for Ethnic Studies & Equitas – International Centre for Human Rights Education, 2018)

1207. Nyi Nyi Kyaw, *Interreligious Conflict and the Politics of Interfaith Dialogue in Myanmar*, Trends in Southeast Asia, 2019 no. 10 (Singapore: ISEAS – Yusof Ishak Institute, 2019)

1208. Stadtner, D.M., *Sacred Sites of Burma: Myth and Folklore in an Evolving Spiritual Realm* (Bangkok: River Books, 2011)

1209. Teasdale, Malcolm, *Religion, Spirituality and the Way of Life in the Himalayas: Nepal, Bhutan, Tibet, Myanmar* (US: CreateSpace, 2016)

1210. *The Great Temples of India, Ceylon, and Burma*, reprint of 1904 edition (New Delhi: Asian Educational Services, 1999)

1211. Wade, Francis, *Myanmar's Enemy Within: Buddhist Violence and the Making of a Muslim "Other"* (London: Zed Books, 2017)

Buddhism

1212. Ashin Jagaralankara, *Dynamics of Socially Engaged Buddhism in Myanmar* (Delhi: Eastern Book Linkers, 2017)

1213. Ashon Nyanuttara, *A Study of Buddhism in Arakan* (US: Oo Thein Maung, 2014)

1214. Bautze-Picron, Claudine, *The Bejewelled Buddha: From India to Burma. New Considerations* (New Delhi: Sanctum Books and the Centre for Archeological Studies and Training, 2010)
1215. Bigandet, P.A., *The Life or Legend of Gaudama: The Buddha of the Burmese*, Trubner's Oriental Series, 2 volumes, reprint of 1880 edition (London: Routledge, 2001)
1216. Bischoff, Roger, *Buddhism in Myanmar: A Short History*, The Wheel Publication no. 399/401 (Kandy: Buddhist Publication Society, 1995)
1217. Bogle, J.E., *Buddhist Cosmology: The Study of a Burmese Manuscript* (Chiang Mai: Silkworm Books, 2016)
1218. Brac de la Perriere, Benedicte, Guillaume Rozenberg and Alicia Turner (eds.), *Champions of Buddhism: Weikza Cults in Contemporary Burma* (Singapore: NUS Press, 2014)
1219. Braun, Erik, *The Birth of Insight: Meditation, Modern Buddhism, and the Burmese Monk Ledi Sayadaw* (Chicago: University of Chicago Press, 2013)
1220. Carbine, J.A., *Sons of the Buddha: Continuities and Ruptures in a Burmese Monastic Tradition* (Berlin: De Gruyter, 2011)
1221. Chew, Anne-May, *The Cave-Temples of Po Win Taung, Central Burma: Architecture, Sculpture and Murals* (Bangkok: White Lotus, 2005)
1222. Christel, Pascal, *Splendour of Buddhism in Burma: A Journey to the Golden Land* (Singapore: Partridge, 2020)
1223. Clements, Alan, and Fergus Harlow, *Wisdom for the World and Mindful Advice to My Nation, The Requisites for Reconciliation: Venerable Sayadaw U Pandita of Burma in Conversation with Alan Clements* (New York: Buddha Sasana Foundation, 2019)
1224. Das, Asha, *The Chronicle of Burma Cha-Kesadhatuvamsa (A Short-Story of the Six Hair Elements of the Buddha)* (Delhi: Pratibha Prakashan, 1994)
1225. De Thabrew, W.V., *Buddhist Monuments and Temples of Myanmar and Thailand* (US: Authorhouse, 2014)
1226. Di Crocco, V.M., *Footprints of the Buddhas of This Era in Thailand and the Indian Subcontinent, Sri Lanka, Myanmar* (Bangkok: Siam Society, 2004)
1227. Finger, H.W., *Dhammayangyi: The Pyramid by the Irrawaddy: The Biography of a Temple, its People and the Kingdom of Pagan* (Bangkok: Orchid Press, 2004)

1228. Grandjean, Jean-Pierre, *Buddhas of Burma* (Boston: Shambala, 2002)

1229. Haldhar, S.M., *Buddhism in Myanmar and Thailand* (New Delhi: OM Publications, 2005)

1230. Hazra, K.L., *Buddhism and Pali Literature of Myanmar* (Delhi: Buddhist World Press, 2015)

1231. Herbert, P.M., *The Life of the Buddha* (London: British Library, 1993)

1232. Hla Myint Swe, *Buddham, Dhammam, Samghan: Buddhist Faith in Myanmar* (Singapore: Spirit Asia, 2009)

1233. Htun Tin Htun, *Shwedagon Pagoda Great Wonder and (5) Articles Relating to Mind-Centred Teaching* (Yangon: Myin Gyan Printing House, 2015)

1234. Jordt, Ingrid, *Burma's Mass Lay Meditation Movement: Buddhism and the Cultural Construction of Power* (Athens: Ohio University Press, 2007)

1235. Kawanami, Hiroko, *Renunciation and Empowerment of Buddhist Nuns in Myanmar-Burma: Building a Community of Female Faithful* (Leiden: Brill, 2013)

1236. Keeler, Ward, *The Traffic in Hierarchy: Masculinity and Its Others in Buddhist Burma* (Honolulu: University of Hawai'i Press, 2017)

1237. Khammai Dhammasami, *Buddhism, Education and Politics in Burma and Thailand: From the Seventeenth Century to the Present* (London: Bloomsbury, 2018)

1238. King, W.L., *A Thousand Lives Away: Buddhism in Contemporary Burma*, reprint of 1964 edition (Berkeley: Asian Humanities Press, 1990)

1239. Kirichenko, Alexey, Cristophe Munier-Gaillard and Minbu Aung Kyaing, *The Life of the Buddha: Burmese Murals from the Late 16th to the Late 18th Centuries* (Bangkok: River Books, 2021)

1240. Lall, Vikram, *The Golden Lands: Cambodia, Indonesia, Laos, Myanmar, Thailand & Vietnam* (New York: Abbeville Press, 2014)

1241. Ledi Sayadaw, *The Manual of Insight and the Noble Eightfold Path and Its Factors Explained* (Onalaska: Pariyatti Press, 2017)

1242. Ledi Sayadaw, *The Requisites of Enlightenment* (Onalaska: Pariyatti Press, 2013)

1243. Lehr, Peter, *Militant Buddhism: The Rise of Religious Violence in Sri Lanka, Myanmar and Thailand* (Cham: Palgrave Macmillan, 2019)

1244. Ma Thanegi, *Shwedagon Mystique* (Yangon: Asia House, 2007)

1245. Mahasi Sayadaw, *The Fundamentals of Insight: Discourse on Meditation Practice*, translated by Maung Tha Noe (Bangkok: Buddhadhamma Foundation, 2001).

1246. Man-kri Mahasirijajeya-su, *Catalogue of the Pitaka and Other Texts in Pali, Pali-Burmese and Burmese*, translated by Peter Nyunt (Bristol: Pali Text Society, 2012)

1247. Matthews, Bruce (ed.), *Religion, Culture and Political Economy in Burma*, Research Monograph no. 3 (Vancouver: Centre for Southeast Asian Research, University of British Columbia, 1993)

1248. Min Yu Wai, *Life of Buddha and His Teachings*, illustrated by U Sein, translated by Daw Khin Thein (Yangon: Innwa Publishing House, 2008) (in English and Burmese)

2149. Moore, Elizabeth, Hansjorg Mayer and Win Pe, *Shwedagon: Golden Pagoda of Myanmar* (London: Thames and Hudson, 1999)

1250. Myint Aung, et al. (eds.), *Shwedagon: Symbol of Strength and Serenity* (Yangon: Yangon City Development Committee, 1997)

1251. Naidu, S.K., *Buddhism in Myanmar* (New Delhi: Mohit Publications, 2008)

1252. Pal, Pratapaditya, and Julia Meech-Pekarik, *Buddhist Book Illuminations* (New York: Ravi Kumar, 1988)

1253. Patton, T.N., *The Buddha's Wizards: Magic, Protection and Healing in Burmese Buddhism* (New York: Columbia University Press, 2018)

1254. Ray, Niharranjan, *An Introduction to the Study of Theravada Buddhism in Burma*, reprint of 1946 edition (Bangkok: Orchid Press, 2002)

1255. Ray, Niharranjan, *Sanskrit Buddhism in Burma*, reprint of 1936 edition (Bangkok: Orchid Press, 2002)

1256. Rozenberg, Guillaume, *Renunciation and Power: The Quest for Sainthood in Contemporary Burma*, translated by J.L. Hackett, Monograph no. 59 (New Haven: Yale Southeast Asia Studies, 2010)

1257. Rozenberg, Guillaume, *The Immortals: Faces of the Incredible in Buddhist Burma*, translated by Ward Keeler (Honolulu: University of Hawai'i Press, 2015)

1258. Saibaba, V.V.S., *Theravada Buddhist Devotionalism in Ceylon, Burma and Thailand* (New Delhi: DK Printworld, 2005)

1259. Sao Htun Hmat Win, *The Initiation of Novicehood and the Ordination of Monkhood in Burmese Buddhist Culture* (Bangkok: White Lotus, 1996)

1260. Schober, Juliane, *Modern Buddhist Conjunctures in Myanmar: Cultural Narratives, Colonial Legacies, and Civil Society* (Honolulu: University of Hawai'i Press, 2011)

1261. *Selected Suttas*, 3 volumes (Sagaing: Department of Research and Compilation, Sitagu International Buddhist Academy, 2004 [volume 1] to 2006 [volume 3])

1262. Shwe Lu Maung, *The "Prima Materia" of Myanmar Buddhist Culture: Laukathara of Rakhine Thu Mrat* (US: Shahnawaz Khan, 2016)

1263. Slater, R.L., *Paradox and Nirvana: A Study of Religious Ultimates with Special Reference to Burmese Buddhism*, reprint of 1951 edition (Whitefish: Literary Licensing, 2011)

1264. Somkiart Lopetcharat, *Myanmar Buddha: The Image and Its History* (Bangkok: Siam International Books, 2007)

1265. Soni, Sujata, *Evolution of Stupas in Burma: Pagan Period: 11th to 13th centuries A.D.* (Delhi: Motilal Banarsidass, 1991)

1266. Stargardt, Janice, and Michael Willis (eds.), *Relics and Relic Worship in Early Buddhism: India, Afghanistan, Sri Lanka and Burma* (London: British Museum Press, 2018)

1267. Teich, Anne (ed.), *Blooming in the Desert: Favourite Teachings of the Wildflower Monk Taungpulu Sayadaw* (Berkeley: North Atlantic Books, 1996)

1268. Than Tun, *Buddhist Art and Architecture with Special Reference to Myanma* (Yangon: Monywe, 2002)

1269. Tun Aung Chain and Thein Hlaing, *Shwedagon* (Yangon: Universities Press, 1996)

1270. Tun Shwe Khine, *A Guide to Mahamuni* (Yangon: Tun Hla Kyaw Sarpay, 1996)

1271. Turner, Alicia, *Saving Buddhism: The Impermanence of Religion in Colonial Burma* (Honolulu: University of Hawai'i Press, 2014)

1272. Walton, M.J., *Buddhism, Politics and Political Thought in Myanmar* (Cambridge: Cambridge University Press, 2017)
1273. Walton, M.J., and Susan Hayward, *Contesting Buddhist Narratives: Democratization, Nationalism, and Communal Violence in Myanmar* (Honolulu: East-West Centre, 2014)

Islam

1274. Berlie, J.A., *The Burmanization of Myanmar's Muslims* (Bangkok: White Lotus, 2008)
1275. Crouch, Melissa (ed.), *Islam and the State in Myanmar: Muslim-Buddhist Relations and the Politics of Belonging* (New Delhi: Oxford University Press, 2016)
1276. Maung Maung Ta, *Myanmar and the Shiah Muslims in Myanmar* (Yangon: The author, 2004)
1277. *Persecution of Muslims in Burma* (London: Burma Human Rights Network, 2017)
1278. *Report on the Situation for Muslims in Burma* (Chiang Mai: Images Asia, 1997)
1279. Selth, Andrew, *Burma's Muslims: Terrorists or Terrorised?*, Canberra Papers on Strategy and Defence no. 150 (Canberra: Strategic and Defence Studies Centre, Australian National University, 2003)
1280. Shwe Lu Maung, *The Price of Silence: Muslim-Buddhist War of Bangladesh and Myanmar – A Social Darwinist's Analysis* (Columbia: DewDrop Arts and Technology, 2005)
1281. Ten Veen, R.C., *Myanmar's Muslims: The Oppressed of the Oppressed* (Wembley: Islamic Human Rights Commission, 2005)
1282. *The Dark Side of Transition: Violence against Muslims in Myanmar*, Asia Report no. 251 (Brussels: International Crisis Group, 1 October 2013)
1283. Yegar, Moshe, *Between Integration and Secession: The Muslim Communities of the Southern Philippines, Southern Thailand and Western Burma/Myanmar* (Lanham: Lexington, 2002)
1284. Yusuf, C.F., et al., *The Dynamics of Islam: Philippines, Myanmar and Thailand* (Jakarta: Centre for Research and Development of Religious Lectures and Corpus Agency of Research, Development, Education and Training, Ministry of Religious Affairs, 2015)

Christianity

1285. Benge, Janet, and Geoff Benge, *Adoniram Judson: Bound for Burma* (Seattle: YWAM, 2001)

1286. Byar Bowh Si, Oliver, *God in Burma: Civil Society and Public Theology in Myanmar* (Milwaukee: The author and CreateSpace, 2014)

1287. *Burmese-Myanmar Bible (Burmese Edition)* (New York: American Bible Society, 2000)

1288. Carson, L.H., *Pioneer Trails, Trials and Triumphs: The Story of Arthur and Laura Carson and the Chin People*, reprint of 1927 edition (Harrisburg: Foundations of Grace Publishing, 2020)

1289. *Centenary Jubilee St Mary's Cathedral, Yangon, Myanmar, 1911–2011* (Yangon: St Mary's Cathedral, 2011)

1290. Chaney, E.N., and Jeannie Lockerbie, *In Judson's Footsteps: National Christian Workers in Burma Today are the Result of the Work of American Missionaries of Yesterday* (Harrisburg: American Baptists for World Evangelism, 2001)

1291. *Chin Church History* (Falam: Zomi Theological College, 2007)

1292. Cung Lian Hup (ed.), *Thinking about Christianity and the Chins in Myanmar* (Yangon: The editor, 1999)

1293. Duesing, J.G. (ed.), *Adoniram Judson: A Bicentennial Appreciation of the Pioneer American Missionary* (Nashville: B&H Publishing, 2012)

1294. Evans, E.P., *Faithful unto Death: The Trials of Catholic Missionaries Killed in Burma* (Canberra: The author, 1998)

1295. Houghton, A.T., *Tailum Jan: Christian Widow in the Wild Mountains of Upper Burma*, reprint of 1930 edition (London: Crosslinks, 2014)

1296. Ismara, Clemente, and E.P. Evans, *Father Stephen Wong: First Native Martyr of Burma* (Canberra: The authors and German Mission, 2006)

1297. Johnson, R.G., *History of the American Baptist Chin Mission: A History of the Introduction of Christianity into the Chin Hills of Burma by Missionaries of the American Baptist Foreign Mission Society during the Years 1899 to 1966*, 2 volumes (Valley Forge: The author, 1988)

1298. Khaw Tailo, *Church History: Early Church History*, Myanmar (US: Blessed Hope, 2013)

1299. Khin Maung Phone Ko, *When Mountains Melted: The Hidden History of the First Myanmar Empire, 1044–1287 AD* (Singapore: Partridge, 2018)

1300. Leigh, M.D., *Conflict, Politics and Proselytism: Methodist Missionaries in Colonial and Postcolonial Upper Burma, 1887–1966* (Manchester: Manchester University Press, 2011)

1301. Mason, Francis, *The Karen Apostle: or, Memoir of Ko Thah-Byu, the First Karen Convert*, reprint of 1843 edition, edited by H.J. Ripley (Gloucester: Dodo Press, 2009)

1302. Nichols, Alan, *Dancing with Angels: The Life Story of Stephen Than, Archbishop of Myanmar* (Moreland: Acorn Press, 2015)

1303. Saw Maung Doe, *Discipling the Church: A Study of Christian Education in the Anglican Church of Myanmar* (Oxford: Regnum Books, 2016)

1304. *Short History of the Cathedral of the Holy Trinity (Yangon), Compiled by the Rev. N.K. Anderson, MA, and Published in the Rangoon Gazette, Dated January 7th, 1930, Reprinted in 2010, with Additional Notes by the Vicar, Revd. Reginald Bennett and Cathedral Council*, 3rd edition (Yangon: Cathedral of the Holy Trinity, 2010)

1305. Thein Nyunt, Peter, *Missions amidst Pagodas: Contextual Communication of the Gospel in the Burmese Buddhist Context* (Carlisle: Langham Monographs, 2014)

1306. Tin Tin Aye and Jack McElroy, *Adoniram Judson's Soul Winning Secrets Revealed: An Inspiring Look at the Tools Used by "Jesus Christ's Man" in Burma* (Shirley: McElroy, 2013)

1307. Yates, Timothy, *Pioneer Missionary, Evangelical Statesman: A Life of A T (Tim) Houghton* (Milton Keynes: AuthorHouse, 2011)

Other Faiths and Belief Systems

1308. Allen, M.P., Zachary Drucker and Eli Coleman, *Transcendents: Spirit Mediums in Burma and Thailand* (Durham: Daylight Books, 2017)

1309. Brac de la Perriere, Benedicte, and Cristophe Munier-Gaillard, *Bobogyi: A Burmese Spiritual Figure*, preface by D.M. Stadtner (Bangkok: River Books, 2019)

1310. Cernea, R.F., *Almost Englishmen: Baghdadi Jews in British Burma* (Lanham: Lexington Books, 2007)

1311. Conway, Susan, *Tai Magic: Arts of the Supernatural in the Shan States and Lan Na* (Bangkok: River Books, 2014)

1312. De Bont, Hein, *Meeting Mystics in Myanmar* (Ulvenhout: The author, 2017)

1313. Ma Thanegi, *Nats: Spirits of Fortune and Fear*, photographs by Barry Broman (Bangkok: Ava Books, 2011)

1314. Ray, Niharranjan, *Brahmanical Gods in Burma: A Chapter of Indian Art and Iconography*, reprint of 1932 edition (Bangkok: Orchid Press, 2001)

1315. Sprague, Sydney, *A Year with the Bahais in India and Burma*, reprint of 1908 edition (Charleston: Nabu Press, 2011)

1316. Temple, R.C., *The Thirty-seven Nats: A Phase of Spirit Worship Prevailing in Burma*, reprint of 1906 edition (London: Kiscadale, 1991)

SOCIETY, EDUCATION AND HEALTH

Society

1317. *Active Citizens under Political Wraps: Experiences from Myanmar/Burma and Vietnam* (Chiang Mai: Heinrich Boell Foundation, 2006)

1318. Bello, Walden, *Paradigm Trap: The Development Establishment's Embrace of Myanmar and How to Break Loose* (Amsterdam: Transnational Institute, 2018)

1319. *Burma: Children's Rights and the Rule of Law* (New York: Human Rights Watch, 1997)

1320. Burma Centre Netherlands and Transnational Institute (eds.), *Strengthening Civil Society in Burma: Possibilities and Dilemmas for International NGOs* (Chiang Mai: Silkworm Books, 1999)

1321. Byar Bowh Si, Oliver, *Solidarity and Civil Society: An Answer to Dictatorship in Burma* (Milwaukee: The author, 2011)

1322. Carpenter, E.A., *Precious Children of Myanmar: Giving Voice to Destitute Children of the World* (Abbotsford: Aneko Press, 2020)

1323. Chang, Wen-Chin, and Eric Tagliacozzo (eds.), *Burmese Lives: Ordinary Life Stories under the Burmese Regime* (Oxford: Oxford University Press, 2014)

1324. Chua, L.J., *The Politics of Love in Myanmar: LGBT Mobilization and Human Rights as a Way of Life* (Stanford: Stanford University Press, 2018)

1325. *Civil Society in Myanmar's New Democracy: Conference Report* (Yangon: World Learning Myanmar, September 2017)

1326. Fink, Christina, *Living Silence in Burma: Surviving under Military Rule*, 2nd edition (Chiang Mai: Silkworm Books, 2009)

1327. Griffiths, M.P., *Community Welfare Organisations in Rural Myanmar: Precarity and Parahita* (London: Routledge, 2020)

1328. Hanjabam, S.S., Sapam Dilipkumar and Ningthoujam Rameshchandra, *Child Trafficking in the Indo-Myanmar Region* (New Delhi: Concept, 2020)

1329. Heidel, Brian, *The Growth of Civil Society in Myanmar* (Bangalore: Books for Change, 2006)

1330. Hornig, Laura, *Money and Metta: Economy and Morality in Urban Buddhist Myanmar* (Munster: LIT, 2021)

1331. Hudson-Rodd, Nancy, and Myo Nyunt, *Land Rights Policy for Future Burma*, Working Paper no. 1/00 (Washington DC: Technical Advisory Network of Burma, The Burma Fund, 2000)

1332. Hudson-Rodd, Nancy, and Sein Htay, *Arbitrary Confiscation of Farmers' Land by the State Peace and Development Council (SPDC) Military Regime in Burma* (Washington DC: National Coalition Government of the Union of Burma, 2008)

1333. *"I Want to Help My Own People": State Control and Civil Society in Burma after Cyclone Nargis* (New York: Human Rights Watch, 2010)

1334. *Insight into Urban Well-Being in Myanmar: The 2018 City Life Survey: Summary Report* (Yangon: Asia Foundation, 2019)

1335. Jacob, Cecilia, *Child Security in Asia: The Impact of Armed Conflict in Cambodia and Myanmar* (Abingdon: Routledge, 2014)

1336. James, Helen, *Governance and Civil Society in Myanmar: Education, Health and Environment* (London: RoutledgeCurzon, 2005)

1337. Kawanami, Hiroko, *The Culture of Giving in Myanmar: Buddhist Offerings, Reciprocity and Interdependence* (London: Bloomsbury Academic, 2020)

1338. Khin Maung Nyunt, *Myanmar Traditional Monthly Festivals* (Yangon: Innwa Publishing House, 2005)

1339. Khin Myo Chit, *Flowers and Festivals Round the Myanmar Year*, 2nd edition (Yangon: Sarpaylawka, 2002)

1340. Kosem, Samak (ed.), *Border Twists and Burma Trajectories: Perceptions, Reforms, and Adaptations* (Chiang Mai: Centre for ASEAN Studies, Chiang Mai University, 2016)

1341. Kraas, Frauke, Mi Mi Kyi and Win Maung (eds.), *Sustainability in Myanmar* (Zurich: LIT, 2016)

1342. La Ring, et al., *Nonviolent Action in Myanmar: Challenges and Lessons for Civil Society and Donors*, Special Report no. 483 (Washington DC: United States Institute of Peace, September 2020)

1343. Lall, Marie, et al., *Citizenship in Myanmar: Contemporary Debates and Challenges in Light of the Reform Process* (Yangon and Bangkok: Myanmar Egress and Friedrich Naumann Stiftung, 2014)

1344. *Listening to Voices from Inside: Myanmar Civil Society's Response to Cyclone Nargis* (Phnom Penh: Centre for Peace and Conflict Studies, 2009)

1345. Ma Thanegi, *Thanakha: Nature's Gift to Myanmar*, photographs by Barry Broman (Bangkok: Ava Books, 2011)

1346. Ma Tint Sein, *Government Policy and the Village in Burma, 1886–1941*, reprint of 1960 edition (US: Open Dissertation Press, 2017)

1347. McCarthy, Stephen, *Civil Society in Burma: From Military Rule to "Disciplined Democracy"*, Regional Outlook no. 37 (Brisbane: Griffith Asia Institute, Griffith University, 2012)

1348. McCarthy, Stephen, *Land Tenure Security and Policy Tensions in Myanmar (Burma)*, Asia Pacific Issues no. 127 (Honolulu: East-West Centre, October 2016)

1349. Mullen, Matthew, *Pathways That Changed Myanmar* (London: Zed Books, 2016)

1350. Mya Than Tint, *On the Road to Mandalay: Tales of Ordinary People* (Bangkok: White Orchid, 1996)

1351. *Myanmar: The Role of Civil Society*, Asia Report no. 27 (Bangkok/Brussels: International Crisis Group, 6 December 2001)

1352. *Myanmar 2014: Civic Knowledge and Values in a Changing Society: Summary Report* (San Francisco: The Asia Foundation, 2014)

1353. *Myanmar Living Conditions Survey 2017, Key Indicators Report* (Nay Pyi Taw and Yangon: Ministry of Planning and Finance, Republic of the Union of Myanmar, UNDP and World Bank, 2018)

1354. *Next Generation: Myanmar* (London: British Council, May 2019)

1355. *Next Steps: Myanmar* (London: British Council, October 2020)

1356. *No More Denial: Children Affected by Armed Conflict in Myanmar (Burma)* (New York: Watchlist on Children and Armed Conflict, 2009)

1357. Noack, Georg, *Local Traditions, Global Modernities: Dress, Identity and the Creation of Public Self-Images in Contemporary Urban Myanmar* (Berlin: RegioSpectra, 2011)

1358. *Post Colonial Society and Culture in Southeast Asia: Proceedings of the Conference on Myanmar and Southeast Asian Studies, 16–18 December 1998*, 2 volumes (Yangon: Universities Historical Research Centre, 1999 [volume 1] and 2001 [volume 2])

1359. Pritchard, Bill, et al., *Livelihoods and Food Security in Rural Myanmar: Survey Findings* (Sydney: University of Sydney, 2017)

1360. *Situation Analysis of Children in Myanmar*, 2nd edition (Naypyitaw: Ministry of National Planning and Economic Development and UNICEF, 2012)

1361. South, Ashley, and Liliana Demartini, *Towards a Tipping Point? Climate Change, Disaster Risk Reduction and Resilience in Southeast Myanmar* (Yangon: ActionAid Myanmar, 2020)

1362. South, Ashley, and Marie Lall (eds.), *Citizenship in Myanmar: Ways of Being in and from Burma* (Singapore: ISEAS – Yusof Ishak Institute and Chiang Mai University Press, 2017)

1363. *Sticks and Stones: Hate Speech Narratives and Facilitators in Myanmar* (Washington DC: C4ADS (Centre for Advanced Defence Studies), 2016)

1364. *This is Not Who We Are: Listening to Communities Affected by Communal Violence in Myanmar* (Siem Reap: Centre for Peace and Conflict Studies, 2015)

1365. Tower, Jason, and Priscilla Clapp, *Myanmar's Casino Cities: The Role of China and Transnational Criminal Networks*, Special Report no. 471 (Washington DC: United States Institute of Peace, July 2020)

1366. Winter, Michael, and Mya Nandar Thin, *The Provision of Public Goods and Services in Urban Areas in Myanmar: Planning and Budgeting by Development Affairs Organizations and Departments* (Yangon: The Asia Foundation and Renaissance Institute, December 2016)

1367. Wyler, L.S., *Burma and Transnational Crime* (Washington DC: Congressional Research Service, 21 January 2010)

1368. Yamahata, Chosein, D.M. Seekins and Makiko Takeda (eds.), *Social Transformations in India, Myanmar and Thailand: Volume 1: Social, Political and Ecological Perspectives* (Singapore: Springer, 2021)

Education

1369. *Education in Myanmar* (Yangon: Ministry of Education, Government of the Union of Myanmar, 1999)
1370. *Enhancing Regional and International Collaboration* (Yangon: Ministry of Education, 2003)
1371. Jolliffe, Kim, and E.S. Mears, *Strength in Diversity: Towards Universal Education in Myanmar's Ethnic Areas* (Yangon: Asia Foundation, October 2016)
1372. Lall, Marie, *Myanmar's Education Reforms: A Pathway to Social Justice?* (London: UCL Press, 2020)
1373. Lall, Marie, et al., *Teachers' Voice: What Education Reforms Does Myanmar Need?* (Yangon and Bangkok: Myanmar Egress and Friedrich Naumann Stiftung, 2013)
1374. Maber, E.J.T., and M.T.A. Lopes Cardozo (eds.), *Sustainable Peacebuilding and Social Justice in Times of Transition: Findings on the Role of Education in Myanmar* (Cham: Springer International, 2019)
1375. South, Ashley, and Marie Lall, *Schooling and Conflict: Ethnic Education and Mother Tongue-based Teaching in Myanmar* (Yangon: Asia Foundation, February 2016)
1376. *Sustainable Development in Education Sector and Health Sector* (Yangon: Printing and Publishing Enterprise, Ministry of Information, 2005)

Health

1377. Allden, Kathleen, and Nancy Murakami (eds.), *Trauma and Recovery on War's Border: A Guide for Global Health Workers*, foreword by Cynthia Maung (Hanover: Dartmouth College Press, 2015)
1378. Aung Than Batu, *The Growth and Development of Medical Research in Myanmar (1886–1986)* (Yangon: Myanmar Academy of Medical Science, 2003)
1379. Brancati, Emanuele, et al., *Coping with COVID–19: Protecting Lives, Employment, and Incomes in Myanmar* (London: International Growth Centre, London School of Economics, October 2020)
1380. Davis, Bill, and Kim Jolliffe, *Achieving Health Equity in Contested Areas of Southeast Myanmar*, Policy Dialogue Brief Series no. 12 (Yangon: Asia Foundation, July 2016)

1381. Ko Ko, Kyaw Lwin and U Thaung, *Conquest of Scourges in Myanmar* (Yangon: Myanmar Academy of Medical Science, 2002)

1382. Minoletti, Paul, and Aung Hein, *Coronavirus Policy Response Needs and Options for Myanmar*, Policy Report (London: International Growth Centre, April 2020)

1383. *Myanmar: The HIV/AIDS Crisis*, Asia Briefing no. 15 (Bangkok/Brussels: International Crisis Group, 2 April 2002)

1384. Myanmar: *Update on HIV/AIDS Policy*, Asia Briefing no. 34 (Yangon/Brussels: International Crisis Group, 16 December 2004)

1385. Naono, Atsuko, *State of Vaccination: The Fight against Smallpox in Colonial Burma* (Hyderabad: Orient Blackswan and the Wellcome Trust Centre for the History of Medicine at University College London, 2009)

1386. Naw May Oo, *The New Constitution and the Future of Public Health in Burma*, Technical Advisory Network of Burma, Working Paper no. 8 (Washington DC: The Burma Fund, December 2003)

1387. Pyone Mjinzu Lwin, *The Role of General Practitioners in the Myanmar Healthcare System: A Study of Private Clinics in Yangon Region, Myanmar* (Chiang Mai: Regional Centre for Social Science and Sustainable Development, Chiang Mai University, 2016)

1388. Smith, Martin, *Fatal Silence? Freedom of Expression and the Right to Health in Burma* (London: Article 19, 1996)

1389. *The Gathering Storm: Infectious Diseases and Human Rights in Burma* (Berkeley: Human Rights Centre, University of California, and Centre for Public Health and Human Rights, Johns Hopkins Bloomberg School of Public Health, July 2007)

1390. *The Republic of the Union of Myanmar: Health System Review* (Manila: World Health Organization, 2015)

1391. Watkins, Gary, *Outside Our Hearts: Heroic Stories from the Leprosy Hospital in Myanmar* (Nashville: T4T Press, 2018)

1392. Win Aung and Aye Kyaw, *Hand Book of the Biochemical Norms of Myanmar* (Yangon: Department of Medical Research, 1999)

WOMEN

1393. *A Modern Form of Slavery: Trafficking of Burmese Women and Girls into Brothels in Thailand* (New York: Human Rights Watch, 1993)

1394. *A Situation Analysis of Children and Women in Myanmar* (Rangoon: United Nations Children's Fund, 1990)

1395. Apple, Betsy, and Veronika Martin, *No Safe Place: Burma's Army and the Rape of Ethnic Women* (Washington DC: Refugees International, 2003)

1396. Apple, Betsy, *School for Rape: The Burmese Military and Sexual Violence* (Bangkok: Earthrights International, 1998)

1397. *Behind the Silence: Violence against Women and their Resilience: Myanmar*, Research Report (Yangon: Gender Equality Network, February 2015)

1398. *Burma – More Women's Voices* (Bangkok: Alternative ASEAN Network on Burma, 2000)

1399. *Burma: Voices of Women in the Struggle* (Bangkok: Alternative ASEAN Network on Burma, 1998)

1400. *Burma – Women's Voices for Freedom* (Bangkok: Alternative ASEAN Network on Burma, 2005)

1401. *Burma – Women's Voices for Peace* (Bangkok: Alternative ASEAN Network on Burma, 2010)

1402. *Burma – Women's Voices Together* (Bangkok: Alternative ASEAN Network on Burma, 2003)

1403. Caouette, Therese, et al., *Sexuality, Reproductive Health and Violence: Experiences of Migrants from Burma in Thailand* (Nakhonprathom: Mahidol University, 2000)

1404. *Censored Gender: Women's Right to Freedom of Expression and Information in Myanmar* (London: Article 19, 2015)

1405. *Dignity in the Shadow of Oppression: The Abuse and Agency of Karen Women under Militarization* (Thailand: Karen Human Rights Group, November 2006)

1406. *Driven Away: Trafficking of Kachin Women on the China-Burma Border* (Chiang Mai: Kachin Women's Association Thailand, 2005)

1407. *Estimating Trafficking of Myanmar Women for Forced Marriage and Childbearing in China* (Washington DC: Johns Hopkins Bloomberg School of Public Health, December 2018)

1408. *"Give Us a Baby and We'll Let You Go": Trafficking of Kachin "Brides" from Myanmar to China* (New York: Human Rights Watch, 21 March 2019)

1409. Harriden, Jessica, *The Authority of Influence: Women and Power in Burmese History* (Copenhagen: NIAS Press, 2012)

1410. Ho, T.C., *Romancing Human Rights: Gender, Intimacy, and Power between Burma and the West* (Honolulu: University of Hawai'i Press, 2015)

1411. Ikeya, Chie, *Refiguring Women, Colonialism, and Modernity in Burma* (Honolulu: University of Hawai'i Press, 2011)

1412. Kolas, Ashild (ed.), *Women, Peace and Security in Myanmar: Between Feminism and Ethnopolitics* (London: Routledge, 2019)

1413. Mason, E.B., *Tounghoo Women*, reprint of 1860 edition (Gloucester: Dodo Press, 2009)

1414. *"Migrating with Hope": Burmese Women Working in Thailand and the Sex Industry* (Chiang Mai: Images Asia, 1997)

1415. Minoletti, Paul, *Women's Participation in the Subnational Governance of Myanmar* (Yangon: The Asia Foundation, 2014)

1416. Ni Ni Myint, *The Status of Myanmar Women* (Yangon: Kitakyushu Forum on Asian Women, Japan, and Universities Historical Research Centre, 2002)

1417. *No Women, No Peace: Gender Equality, Conflict and Peace in Myanmar*, Myanmar Policy Briefing no. 18 (Amsterdam: Transnational Institute, January 2016)

1418. O'Kane, Mary, *Borderlands and Women: Transversal Political Agency on the Burma-Thailand Border*, Working Paper no. 126 (Clayton: Centre of Southeast Asian Studies, Monash University, 2005)

1419. O'Shannassy, Teresa, *Burma's Excluded Majority: Women, Dictatorship and the Democracy Movement* (London: Catholic Institute for International Relations, 2000)

1420. *Poisoned Flowers: The Impact of Spiraling Drug Addiction on Palaung Women in Burma* (Mae Sot: Palaung Women's Association, 2006)

1421. Rigby, Jennifer, *The Other Ladies of Myanmar* (Singapore: ISEAS – Yusof Ishak Institute, 2018)

1422. Salerno, Carin, *The World of Women – Myanmar*, photographs by Guiseppe Salerno (US: Odyssey Books and Maps, 2017)

1423. Sengupta, Nilanjana, *The Female Voice of Myanmar: Khin Myo Chit to Aung San Suu Kyi* (New Delhi: Cambridge University Press, 2015)

1424. *Sexual and Gender-Based Violence in Myanmar and the Gendered Impact of its Ethnic Conflicts*, A/HRC/42/CRP.4 (Geneva: United Nations Human Rights Council, 9–27 September 2019)

1425. Shwe Shwe Sein Latt et al., *Women's Political Participation in Myanmar: Experiences of Women Parliamentarians 2011–2016* (Yangon: The Asia Foundation, April 2017)

1426. *State of Terror: The Ongoing Rape, Murder, Torture and Forced Labour Suffered by Women Living under the Burmese Military Regime in Karen State* (Mae Sariang: Karen Women's Organization, 2007)

1427. *Stronger Together: A Twenty-Year Journey of Activism* (Chiang Mai: Shan Women's Action Network, March 2019)

1428. Takeda, Makiko, *Women, Children and Social Transformation in Myanmar* (Singapore: Springer, 2019)

1429. Tharaphi Than, *Women in Modern Burma* (London: Routledge, 2014)

1430. Tinzar Lwyn, *The Mission: Colonial Discourse on Gender and the Politics of Burma*, Working Paper no. 3 (Canberra: Gender Relations Project, Australian National University, 1994)

1431. Tun Thwin, *Burma: Role of Women in Socio-political Change* (Ann Arbor: University of Michigan, 1992)

1432. Urbano, Mia and Tony Dickinson, *Women and the Economy in Myanmar: An Assessment of DFAT's Private Sector Development Programs* (Canberra: Department of Foreign Affairs and Trade, January 2016)

1433. *Unsafe State: State-Sanctioned Sexual Violence against Chin Women in Burma* (New Delhi?: Women's League of Chinland, March 2007)

1434. *Walking amongst Sharp Knives: The Unsung Courage of Karen Women Village Chiefs in Conflict Areas of Eastern Burma* (Mae Sariang: Karen Women Organization, 2010)

1435. Win May, *Status of Women in Myanmar* (Yangon: The author, 1995)

PUBLISHING AND MASS MEDIA

1436. *Assessment of Media Development in Myanmar* (Bangkok and Copenhagen: UNESCO and International Media Support, 2016)

1437. Brooten, Lisa, J.M. McElhone and Gayathry Venkiteswaran (eds.), *Myanmar Media in Transition: Legacies, Challenges and Change* (Singapore: ISEAS – Yusof Ishak Institute, 2019)

1438. Danitz, Tiffany, et al., *Networking Dissent: Cyber Activists Use the Internet to Promote Democracy in Burma* (Washington DC: United States Institute of Peace, 2000)

1439. Dolan, Theo and Stephen Gray, *Media and Conflict in Myanmar: Opportunities for Media to Advance Peace*, Peaceworks no. 92 (Washington DC: United States Institute of Peace, 2014)

1440. Harris, Mike, *Burma: Freedom of Expression in Transition* (London: Index on Censorship, July 2013)

1441. *Hate Speech: A Study of Print, Movies, Songs and Social Media in Myanmar* (Yangon: PEN Myanmar, 2016)

1442. *Internet Filtering in Burma in 2006–2007: A Country Study* (Toronto, Cambridge and Ottawa: OpenNet Initiative, 2007)

1443. Ismail, Benjamin, *Burmese Media Spring* (Paris: Reporters Without Borders, 2012)

1444. Iyer, Venkat, *Acts of Oppression: Censorship and the Law in Burma* (London: Article 19, 1999)

1445. Jacobson, A.S., et al., *Gender in the Myanmar Media Landscape: First Study: Yangon and Beyond* (Stockholm: Fojo Institute, 2013)

1446. Kumar, Manish, *Media in an Authoritarian State: A Study of Myanmar* (New Delhi: Atlantic Publishers and Distributors, 2014)

1447. Kyaw Thu, *The Impact of Censorship on the Development of the Private Press Industry in Myanmar/Burma*, Reuters Institute Fellowship Paper (Oxford: Reuters Institute for the Study of Journalism, University of Oxford, 2012)

1448. *Myanmar: Caught between State Censorship and Self-Censorship: Prosecution and Intimidation of Media Workers in Myanmar*, AI Index ASA 16/1743/2015 (London: Amnesty International, June 2015)

1449. Ohnmar Nyunt, *Challenges to Press Freedom of Private News Media in Myanmar*, Consortium of Development Studies in Southeast Asia Series no. 9 (Chiang Mai: Regional Centre for Social Science, Chiang Mai University, 2018)

1450. Smith, Martin, *State of Fear: Censorship in Burma (Myanmar)* (London: Article 19, 1991)

1451. Soe Lynn Htwe, *The Role of Ethnic Media in the "New Myanmar"*, Research Report no. 6 (Chiang Mai: Regional Centre for Social Science and Sustainable Development, Chiang Mai University, 2017)

1452. *Unfinished Freedom: A Blueprint for the Future of Free Expression in Myanmar* (New York: PEN American Centre, 2015)

NARCOTICS

1453. *A Failing Grade: Burma's Drug Eradication Efforts* (Bangkok: ALTSEAN Burma, 2004)
1454. *Addressing Drug Problems in Myanmar: 5 Key Interventions That Can Make a Difference* (Myanmar: Drug Policy Advocacy Group Myanmar, February 2017)
1455. Ball, Desmond, *Burma and Drugs: The Regime's Complicity in the Global Drug Trade*, Working Paper no. 336 (Canberra: Strategic and Defence Studies Centre, Australian National University, 1999)
1456. Boucaud, Andre, and Louis Boucaud, *Burma's Golden Triangle: On the Trail of the Opium Warlords*, revised edition (Hong Kong: Asia 2000, 1992)
1457. Chin, Ko-lin, *The Golden Triangle: Inside Southeast Asia's Drug Trade* (Ithaca: Cornell University Press, 2009)
1458. Chin, Ko-lin, and S.X. Zhang, *The Chinese Connection: Cross-Border Drug Trafficking between Myanmar and China: Final Report to the United States Department of Justice* (Washington DC: National Institute of Justice?, 2007)
1459. Chin, Ko-lin, and S.X. Zhang, *The Chinese Heroin Trade: Cross-Border Drug Trafficking in Southeast Asia and Beyond* (New York: New York University Press, 2015)
1460. Chouvy, P.A., and Joel Meissonnier, *Yaa Baa: Production, Traffic and Consumption of Methamphetamine in Mainland Southeast Asia* (Singapore: Singapore University Press, 2004)
1461. Felber, Ron, *The Hunt for Khun Sa: Drug Lord of the Golden Triangle* (Walterville: Trine Day, 2011)
1462. *General Khun Sa: His Life and Speeches* (Shan State: Department of Information, the Government of Tai Revolutionary Council [TRC], August 1989)
1463. Gibson, R.M., and Wenhua Chen, *The Secret Army: Chiang Kai-shek and the Drug Warlords of the Golden Triangle* (Singapore: John Wiley and Sons [Asia], 2011)
1464. Jelsma, Martin, and Tom Kramer, *Downward Spiral: Banning Opium in Afghanistan and Burma*, Drugs and Conflict Debate Papers no. 12 (Amsterdam: Transnational Institute, 2005)

1465. Jelsma, Martin, Tom Kramer and Pietje Vervest, *Drugs and Conflict in Burma (Myanmar): Dilemmas for Policy Responses*, Drugs and Conflict Debate Papers no. 9 (Amsterdam: Transnational Institute, 2003)

1466. Jelsma, Martin, Tom Kramer and Pietje Vervest (eds.), *Trouble in the Triangle: Opium and Conflict in Burma* (Chiang Mai: Silkworm Books, 2005)

1467. Jensema, Ernestien, and Nang Pann Ei Kham, *"Found in the Dark": The Impact of Drug Law Enforcement Practices in Myanmar*, Drug Policy Briefing no. 47 (Amsterdam: Transnational Institute, September 2016)

1468. Kramer, Tom, *The Current State of Counternarcotics Policy and Drug Reform Debates in Myanmar* (Washington DC: Brookings Institution, 2015)

1469. Kramer, Tom, et al., *Bouncing Back: Relapse in the Golden Triangle* (Amsterdam: Transnational Institute, 2014)

1470. Kramer, Tom, and Kevin Woods, *Financing Dispossession: China's Opium Substitution Programme in Northern Burma* (Amsterdam: Transnational Institute, 2012)

1471. Kramer, Tom, Martin Jelsma and Tom Blickman, *Withdrawal Symptoms in the Golden Triangle: A Drugs Market in Disarray* (Amsterdam: Transnational Institute, 2009)

1472. Lintner, Bertil, *Cross-Border Drug Trade in the Golden Triangle (S.E. Asia)*, Territory Briefing no. 1 (Durham: International Boundaries Research Unit, Boundaries Research Press, 1991)

1473. Lintner, Bertil, *The Politics of the Drug Trade in Burma*, Occasional Paper no. 33 (Nedlands: Indian Ocean Centre for Peace Studies, University of Western Australia, 1993)

1474. Lintner, Bertil, and Michael Black, *Merchants of Madness: The Methamphetamine Explosion in the Golden Triangle* (Chiang Mai: Silkworm Books, 2009)

1475. McCoy, A.W., *The Politics of Heroin: CIA Complicity in the Global Drug Trade*, 2nd revised version of 1972 edition (Chicago: Lawrence Hill, 2003)

1476. *Naypyidaw's Drug Addiction: The Burma Army's Strategic Use of the Drug Trade In the Golden Triangle and Its Impact on the Lahu* (Chiang Mai: Lahu National Development Association, 2016)

1477. Pho Shoke, *Why Did U Khun Sa's MTA Exchange Arms for Peace?* (Yangon: Meik Kaung Press, 1999)

1478. Renard, R.D., *The Burmese Connection: Illegal Drugs and the Making of the Golden Triangle* (Boulder: Lynne Rienner, 1996)
1479. Takano, Hideyuki, *The Shore beyond Good and Evil: A Report from Inside Burma's Opium Kingdom* (Reno: Kotan, 2002)
1480. *The Truth That Cannot Be Concealed and Selected Articles* (Yangon: Central Committee for Drug Abuse Control, 2003)
1481. *The War on Drugs: Myanmar's Efforts for the Eradication of Narcotic Drugs* (Yangon: Central Committee for Drug Abuse Control, 1999)
1482. Wright, Ashley, *Opium and Empire in Southeast Asia: Regulating Consumption in British Burma* (Houndmills: Palgrave Macmillan, 2014)

MIGRANTS, REFUGEES AND DISPLACED PEOPLE

General

1483. *10 Years of IOM in Myanmar (2005–2014)* (Geneva: International Organisation for Migration, 2015)

1484. *"Fleeing My Whole Life": Older People's Experience of Conflict and Displacement in Myanmar*, AI Index ASA 16/0446/2019 (London: Amnesty International, 2019)

1485. Guzel, M.S., *Solving Statelessness in Myanmar* (London: Lulu.com, 2020)

1486. Humphries, Richard, *Frontier Mosaic: Voices of Burma from the Lands in Between* (Bangkok: Orchid Press, 2007)

1487. Johnson, Pamela, *Though I Run through the Valley: A Persecuted Family Rescues Over a Thousand Children in Myanmar* (Milton Keynes: Authentic Media, 2020)

1488. Jolliffe, Kim, *Ceasefires and Durable Solutions in Myanmar: A Lessons Learned Review*; and South, Ashley, *Commentary: IDPs and Refugees in the Current Myanmar Peace Process*, Research Paper no. 271 (Geneva: United Nations High Commissioner for Refugees, 2014)

1489. Lemere, Maggie, and Zoe West (eds.), *Nowhere to be Home: Narratives from Survivors of Burma's Military Regime* (San Francisco: Voice of Witness, 2011)

1490. *Lives on the Line: Voices for Change from the Thailand-Burma Border* (Thailand: Burma Link, 2016)

1491. Maung, Cynthia, and Suzanne Belton, *Working Our Way Back Home: Fertility and Pregnancy Loss on the Thai-Burmese Border* (Mae Sot: Mae Tao Clinic, 2005)

1492. *No Safety in Burma, No Sanctuary in Thailand* (New York: Human Rights Watch, 1997)

1493. Sharples, Rachel, *Spaces of Solidarity: Karen Activism in the Thai-Burma Borderlands* (Oxford: Berghahn Books, 2020)

1494. *"Sold Like Fish": Crimes against Humanity, Mass Graves, and Human Trafficking from Myanmar and Bangladesh to Malaysia from 2012 to 2015* (Bangkok: Fortify Rights, March 2019)

1495. South, Ashley, *Burma: The Changing Nature of Displacement Crises*, RSC Working Paper no. 39 (Oxford: Refugee Studies Centre, 2007)

1496. South, Ashley, *Displacement and Dispossession: Forced Migration and Land Rights in Burma* (Geneva: Centre on Housing Rights and Evictions, 2007)

1497. South, Ashley, and Kim Jolliffe, *Forced Migration and the Myanmar Peace Process*, New Issues in Refugee Research, Research Paper no. 274 (Geneva: United Nations High Commission for Refugees, February 2015)

1498. Webb, Paul, *Escape from Burma: Asylum Seekers and a Thai Response*, Occasional Paper Series no. 2 (Darwin: Centre for Southeast Asian Studies, Northern Territory University, 1993)

Migrants and Migrant Workers

1499. Amporn Jirattikorn, *Managing Migration in Myanmar and Thailand: Economic Reforms, Policies, Practices and Challenges*, Trends in Southeast Asia, 2015 no. 9 (Singapore: Institute of Southeast Asian Studies, 2015)

1500. Caouette, T.M., and M.E. Pack, *Pushing Past the Definitions: Migration from Burma to Thailand* (Washington DC: Refugees International and Open Society Institute, December 2002)

1501. Chang, Wen-Chin, *Beyond Borders: Stories of Yunnanese Chinese Migrants of Burma* (Ithaca: Cornell University Press, 2014)

1502. *Feeling Small in Another Person's Country: The Situation of Burmese Migrant Children in Mae Sot, Thailand* (Mae Sot?: Committee for the Protection and Promotion of Child Rights [Burma], 2009)

1503. Huguet, J.W., and Sureeporn Punpuing, *International Migration in Thailand* (Bangkok: International Organisation for Migration, 2005)

1504. Khin Soe Kyi, *Social Relationships of Myanmar Migrant Workers in Malaysia: An Ethnographic Study*, Research Report no. 8 (Chiang Mai: Regional Centre for Social Science, Chiang Mai University, 2018)

1505. Lee, Tang Lay, *Statelessness, Human Rights and Gender: Irregular Migrant Workers from Burma in Thailand* (Leiden: Martinus Nijhoff, 2005)

1506. Lehane, Leigh, *Illness, Poverty, and Abuse of Migrants on the Thai-Burma Border: The Vulnerability of a Displaced People* (New York: Edwin Mellen Press, 2014)

Migrants, Refugees and Displaced People   155

1507. *Myanmar's Cross-Border Migrant Workers and the COVID–19 Pandemic: Their Life Stories and the Social Structures Shaping Them* (Amsterdam: Transnational Institute, and others, November 2020)
1508. Ndegwa, David, *Migrants from Myanmar and Risks Faced Abroad: A Desk Study* (Geneva: International Organisation for Migration, 2016)
1509. Pearson, Ruth, and Kyoko Kusakabe, *Thailand's Hidden Workforce: Burmese Migrant Women Factory Workers* (London: Zed, 2012)
1510. Pim Koetsawang, *In Search of Sunlight: Burmese Migrant Workers in Thailand* (Bangkok: Orchid Press, 2001)
1511. Robertson, P.S. (ed.), *Helpless before and after the Wave: The Plight of Burmese Migrant Workers in the Andaman Tsunami* (Bangkok: Thai Action Committee for Democracy in Burma, 2007)
1512. Stahr, Erica, *Australia's Burmese* (Melbourne: The author, 2002)
1513. Wagner, Alex, *Futureface: A Family Mystery, an Epic Quest, and the Secret to Belonging* (New York: One World, 2018)

Refugees

1514. *A Question of Security: A Retrospective on Cross-Border Attacks on Thailand's Refugee and Civilian Communities along the Burmese Border since 1995* (Chiang Mai: Images Asia and Borderline Video, 1998)
1515. *A Sustainable Policy for Rohingya Refugees in Bangladesh*, Asia Report no. 303 (Yangon/Brussels: International Crisis Group, 27 December 2019)
1516. *"Bangladesh Is Not My Country": The Plight of Rohingya Refugees from Myanmar* (New York: Human Rights Watch, August 2018)
1517. Barron, Sandy (ed.), *Between Worlds: Twenty Years on the Border*, photographs by Masaru Gotu (Bangkok: Thailand Burma Border Consortium, 2004)
1518. Barron, Sandy (ed.), *Nine Thousand Nights: Refugees from Burma: A Peoples' Scrapbook* (Bangkok: Thailand Burma Border Consortium, 2010)
1519. Berg, Erika, *Forced to Flee: Visual Stories by Refugee Youth from Burma* (US?: Visions for Peace, 2015)

1520. *Burmese Refugees in Bangladesh: Still No Durable Solution* (New York: Human Rights Watch, 2000)
1521. Dudley, S.H., *Materialising Exile: Material Culture and Embodied Experience among Karenni Refugees in Thailand* (Oxford: Berghahn, 2010)
1522. *From Burma to Thailand: Refugee Flows and US Policy* (Washington DC: Congressional Research Service, 21 November 2003)
1523. Goudeau, Jessica, *After the Last Border: Two Families and the Story of Refuge in America* (New York: Viking, 2020)
1524. Gumaer, Oddny, *Displaced Reflections: Refugees and Displaced People from Burma Shed Light on Life, Love and Faith*, photographs by Brent Madison (Albuquerque: Partners Publishing House, 2007)
1525. Lang, H.J., *Fear and Sanctuary: Burmese Refugees in Thailand* (Ithaca: Southeast Asia Program, Cornell University, 2002)
1526. Lang, H.J., *The Repatriation Predicament of Burmese Refugees in Thailand: A Preliminary Analysis*, New Issues in Refugee Research, Working Paper no. 46 (Geneva: United Nations High Commission for Refugees, 2001)
1527. Mate, Rituraj, *Rohingya Refugee Crisis and Indian Perspective* (US: The author, 2020)
1528. McConnachie, Kirsten, *Governing Refugees: Justice, Order and Legal Pluralism* (London: Routledge, 2014)
1529. *Out of Sight, Out of Mind: Thai Policy towards Burmese Refugees and Migrants* (New York: Human Rights Watch, 2004)
1530. *People of Burma in Melbourne: Perspectives of a Refugee Community* (Dandenong: South Eastern Region Migrant Resource Centre, May 2011)
1531. *Preliminary Findings and Conclusions on the Material Support for Terrorism Bar as Applied to the Overseas Resettlement of Refugees from Burma* (Cambridge: Harvard Law School, 2006)
1532. *Refugees from Myanmar: A Study by the International Commission of Jurists* (Geneva: International Commission of Jurists, 1992)
1533. *Repatriation of Burmese Refugees from Thailand and Bangladesh: A Briefing Paper*, Research Information Series no. 8 (Canberra: Australian Council for Overseas Aid, 1996)

1534. Rhoden, T.F., and T.L.S. Rhoden (eds.), *Burmese Refugees: Letters from the Thai-Burma Border* (US?: Digital Lycanthrope, 2011)

1535. Roof, Lisa, and M.B. McVee, *The Experiences of Refugee Youth from Burma in an American High School: Countering Deficit-Based Narratives through Student Voice* (New York: Routledge, 2021)

1536. *Shan Refugees: Dispelling the Myths* (Chiang Mai: Shan Women's Action Network, September 2003)

1537. Spurlock, Michael, *All Saints: The Surprising True Story of How Refugees from Burma Brought Life to a Dying Church* (Ada: Baker Publishing Group, 2017)

1538. Stokle, Tony, *The Revolution Is Only a Tea-Shop Away: A Family's Odyssey through Thailand and Burma in Search of Justice, Peace and Democracy for the People of Burma* (UK: The author, 2021)

1539. *Subversive Hope: Accounts of Transformation from the Jungles, Refugee Camps & Frontiers of Burma* (Beaverton: Good Catch, 2014)

1540. Supang Chantavanich and Aungkana Kamonpech, *Refugee and Return: Displacement along the Thai-Myanmar Border* (Cham: Springer International, 2016)

Displaced People

1541. Bamforth, Vicky, Steven Lanjouw and Graham Mortimer, *Conflict and Displacement in Karenni: The Need for Considered Responses* (Chiang Mai: Burma Ethnic Research Group, 2000)

1542. Duffield, Mark, *On the Edge of "No Man's Land": Chronic Emergency in Myanmar*, Working Paper no. 01–08 (School of Sociology, Politics and International Studies, University of Bristol, 2008)

1543. *Flight, Hunger and Survival: Repression and Displacement in the Villages of Papun and Nyaunglebin Districts* (Thailand: Karen Human Rights Group, 2001)

1544. *Forgotten Victims of a Hidden War: Internally Displaced Karen in Burma* (Chiang Mai: Burma Ethnic Research Group and Friedrich Naumann Foundation, 1998)

1545. Harkins, Benjamin, and Supang Chantavanich, *The Resettlement of Displaced Persons on the Thai-Myanmar Border* (Cham: Springer International, 2013)

1546. *Invisible Lives: The Untold Story of Displacement Cycle in Burma* (Thailand?: Human Rights Foundation of Monland, Burma Link and Burma Partnership, 2016)

1547. Mason, Jana, *No Way Out, No Way In: The Crisis of Internal Displacement in Burma* (Washington DC: United States Committee for Refugees, April 2000)

1548. *There Is No One Who Does Not Miss Home: A Report on Protracted Displacement Due to Armed Conflict in Myanmar* (Mae Sot?: Progressive Voice and others, June 2019)

1549. *"They Came and Destroyed Our Village Again": The Plight of Internally Displaced Persons in Karen State* (New York: Human Rights Watch, 2005)

1550. *Unsettling Moves: The Wa Forced Resettlement Program in Eastern Shan State* (Chiang Mai: Lahu National Development Organisation, 2002)

1551. *"Untold Miseries": Wartime Abuses and Forced Displacement in Burma's Kachin State* (New York: Human Rights Watch, 2012)

HUMAN RIGHTS

General

1552. *A Report on Human Rights and the Lack of Progress Towards Democracy in Burma (Myanmar)*, Joint Standing Committee on Foreign Affairs, Defence and Trade of the Parliament of Australia (Canberra: Australian Government Publishing Service, 1995)

1553. *A Swamp Full of Lilies: Human Rights Violations Committed by Units/Personnel of Burma's Army, 1992–1993* (New Jersey: Project Maje, 1994)

1554. Bugher, Matthew, et al., *Midnight Intrusions: Ending Guest Registration and Household Inspections in Myanmar* (Bangkok: Fortify Rights, 2015)

1555. *"Caught in the Middle": Abuses against Civilians amid Conflict in Myanmar's Northern Shan State*, AI Index ASA 16/1142/2019 (London: Amnesty International, 2019)

1556. Cemmell, James, *Academic Freedom International Study: Burma, Colombia, Israel, Palestine, Zimbabwe* (London: University and College Union and Education International, 2009)

1557. *Conflicting Realities: Reform, Repression and Human Rights in Burma: Report of the Standing Committee on Foreign Affairs and International Development, Subcommittee on International Human Rights, 41st Parliament, June 2013* (Ottawa: House of Commons, Parliament of Canada, 2013)

1558. *Crackdown at Letpadan: Excessive Force and Violations of the Rights to Freedom of Expression in Letpadan, Bago Region, Myanmar* (Bangkok and Cambridge: Fortify Rights and Harvard Law School International Human Rights Clinic, October 2015)

1559. *Crimes in Burma: A Report by the International Human Rights Clinic at Harvard Law School* (Cambridge: Harvard Law School, 2009)

1560. Delang, C.O. (ed.), *Suffering in Silence: The Human Rights Nightmare of the Karen People of Burma* (Parkland: Universal, 2000)

1561. *Development by Decree: The Politics of Poverty and Control in Karen State* (Thailand: Karen Human Rights Group, 2007)

1562. *Dispossessed: Forced Relocation and Extra-judicial Killings in Shan State* (Chiang Mai: Shan Human Rights Foundation, 1998)

1563. Doherty, Faith, and Nyein Han, *Burma: Human Lives for Natural Resources, Oil and Natural Gas* (Bangkok: Southeast Asian Information Network, All Burma Students Democratic Front, 1994)

1564. Erikson, Brian, *Crimes in Northern Burma: Results from a Fact Finding Mission to Kachin State, November 2011* (Oslo: Partners Relief and Development, 2011)

1565. Goldston, J.A., *Human Rights in Burma (Myanmar)* (New York: Human Rights Watch/Asia, 1990)

1566. Greer, Jed, and Tyler Giannini, *Valued Less Than a Milk Tin: Discrimination against Ethnic Minorities in Burma by the Ruling Military Regime* (Washington DC: Earthrights International, 2001)

1567. Horton, Guy, *Dying Alive: An Investigation and Legal Assessment of Human Rights Violations Inflicted in Burma, with Particular Reference to the Internally Displaced, Eastern Peoples* (Chiang Mai: Images Asia, 2005)

1568. *"I Want to Help My Own People": State Control and Civil Society in Burma after Cyclone Nargis* (New York: Human Rights Watch, 2010)

1569. *"I Will Not Surrender": The Criminalization of Human Rights Defenders and Activists in Myanmar*, AI Index ASA 16/2041/2020 (London: Amnesty International, 2020)

1570. Lahkdhir, Linda, *Dashed Hopes: The Criminalization of Peaceful Expression in Myanmar* (New York: Human Rights Watch, 2019)

1571. Lahkdhir, Linda, *"They Can Arrest You at Any Time": The Criminalization of Peaceful Expression in Burma* (New York: Human Rights Watch, 2016)

1572. *Legal Memorandum: War Crimes and Crimes against Humanity in Eastern Myanmar* (Cambridge: Harvard Law School, 2014)

1573. Liddell, Zunetta, *Burma: Children's Rights and the Rule of Law* (New York: Human Rights Watch, 1997)

1574. *Living Ghosts: The Spiraling Repression of the Karenni Population under the Burmese Military Junta*, Burma Issues (Bangkok: Peace Way Foundation, March 2008)

1575. Martin, Michael, *Burmese Security Forces and Personnel Implicated in Serious Human Rights Abuses and Accountability Options* (Washington DC: Congressional Research Service, 5 March 2019)

1576. *Myanmar: A Challenge for the International Community*, AI Index ASA 16/028/1997 (London: Amnesty International, September 1997)

1577. *Myanmar: "All the Civilians Suffer": Conflict, Displacement, and Abuse in Northern Myanmar*, AI Index ASA 16/6429/17 (London: Amnesty International, June 2017)

1578. *Myanmar: Amnesty International Briefing*, AI Index ASA 16/09/90 (London: Amnesty International, November 1990)

1579. *Myanmar: Atrocities in the Shan State*, AI Index ASA 16/005/1998 (London: Amnesty International, April 1998)

1580. *Myanmar – Exodus from the Shan State*, AI Index ASA 16/011/2000 (London: Amnesty International, July 2000)

1581. *Myanmar: Human Rights after Seven Years of Military Rule*, AI Index ASA 16/023/1995 (London: Amnesty International, October 1995)

1582. *Myanmar: No Law at All: Human Rights Violations under Military Rule*, AI Index ASA 16/011/1992 (New York: Amnesty International, September 1992)

1583. *Myanmar: The Institution of Torture*, AI Index ASA 16/024/2000 (London: Amnesty International, December 2000)

1584. *Myanmar (Burma): Continued Killings and Ill-Treatment of Minority Peoples*, AI Index ASA 16/005/1991 (London: Amnesty International, July 1991)

1585. *No Stone Unturned: Q&A on Accountability for Crimes in Myanmar* (Paris and Bangkok: FIDH and ALTSEAN Burma, September 2018)

1586. *"Our Demands Are for All Students": Violations of Students' Rights in Mandalay, Myanmar* (Bangkok: Fortify Rights, March 2020)

1587. *Policy Memorandum: Preventing Indiscriminate Attacks and Wilful Killings of Civilians by the Myanmar Military* (Cambridge: Harvard Law School, 2014)

1588. Rajkumar, Brajananda, *Human Rights in Myanmar* (New Delhi: Rajesh Publications, 2012)

1589. *Responsible Investment in Myanmar: The Human Rights Dimension*, Occasional Paper no. 1 (London: Institute for Human Rights and Business, September 2012)

1590. *Same Impunity, Same Patterns* (Chiang Mai: Women's League of Burma, 2014)

1591. Smith, Matthew, et al., *"I Thought They Would Kill Me": Ending Wartime Torture in Northern Myanmar* (Bangkok: Fortify Rights, 2014)

1592. *Summary Injustice: Military Tribunals in Burma (Myanmar)* (New York: Lawyers Committee for Human Rights, 1991)

1593. *Supporting Human Rights in Myanmar: Why the U.S. Should Maintain Existing Sanctions Authority* (Bangkok: Fortify Rights, 2016)

1594. *The Repression of Ethnic Minority Activists in Myanmar*, AI Index ASA 16/001/2010 (London: Amnesty International, February 2010)

1595. *"Threats to Our Existence": Persecution of Ethnic Chin Christians in Burma* (Nepean: Chin Human Rights Organisation, September 2012)

1596. *To Stand and Be Counted: The Suppression of Burma's Members of Parliament* (Bangkok: Documentation and Research Centre, All Burma Students' Democratic Front, 1998)

1597. Todd, David, *Dirty Clothes – Dirty System: How Burma's Military Dictatorship Uses Profits from the Garment Industry to Bankroll Oppression* (Ottawa: Canadian Friends of Burma, 1996)

1598. *Trained to Torture: Systematic War Crimes by the Burma Army in Ta'ang Areas of Northern Shan State (March 2011 – March 2016)* (Mae Sot?: Ta'ang Women's Organisaton, 2016?)

1599. *Truce or Transition? Trends in Human Rights Abuse and Local Response in Southeast Myanmar since the 2012 Ceasefire* (Thailand: Karen Human Rights Group, 2014)

1600. *Union of Myanmar (Burma): Human Rights Violations against Muslims in the Rakhine (Arakan) State*, AI Index ASA 16/006/1992 (London: Amnesty International, April 1992)

1601. *Uprooting the Shan* (Chiang Mai: Shan Human Rights Foundation, 1996)

1602. *Voice of the Hungry Nation: The People's Tribunal on Food Scarcity and Militarization in Burma, October 1999* (Hong Kong: Asian Human Rights Commission, 1999)

1603. Yamahata, Chosein, Sueo Sudo and Takashi Matsugi (eds.), *Rights and Security in India, Myanmar and Thailand* (Singapore: Palgrave Macmillan, 2020)

Political Prisoners

1604. *"After Release I Had to Restart My Life from the Beginning". The Experiences of Ex-political Prisoners in Burma and Challenges to Reintegration* (Thailand: Assistance Association for Political Prisoners and Former Political Prisoner Society, 2016)

1605. *Burma: A Land Where Buddhist Monks Are Disrobed and Detained in Dungeons* (Mae Sot: Assistance Association for Political Prisoners [Burma], November 2004)

1606. *Burma's Prisons and Labour Camps: Silent Killing Fields* (Mae Sot: Assistance Association for Political Prisoners [Burma], 2009)

1607. *Eight Seconds of Silence: The Death of Democracy Activists behind Bars* (Mae Sot: Assistance Association for Political Prisoners [Burma], 2006)

1608. Martin, Michael, *Burma's Political Prisoners and U.S. Policy* (Washington DC: Congressional Research Service, January 2021)

1609. Martin, Michael, *Burma's Political Prisoners and U.S. Sanctions* (Washington DC: Congressional Research Service, December 2013)

1610. Mathieson, David, *Burma's Forgotten Prisoners* (New York: Human Rights Watch, 2009)

1611. *Myanmar (Burma): Prisoners of Conscience: A Chronicle of Developments since September 1988*, AI Index ASA 16/23/89 (London: Amnesty International, November 1989)

1612. *Myanmar: "In the National Interest": Prisoners of Conscience, Torture, Summary Trials under Martial Law*, AI Index ASA 16/010/1990 (London: Amnesty International, November 1990)

1613. *Myanmar: Prisoners of Political Repression*, AI Index ASA 16/006/2001 (London: Amnesty International, April 2001)

1614. *Pleading Not Guilty in Insein: A Special Report on the Summary Trial of 22 Political Prisoners in Burma's Infamous Insein Prison* (Bangkok: All Burma Students Deomocratic Front, 1997)

1615. *Prison Conditions in Burma and the Potential for Prison Reform* (Mae Sot: Assistance Association for Political Prisoners [Burma], 2016)

1616. *Spirit for Survival* (Mae Sot: Assistance Association for Political Prisoners (Burma), 2001)

1617. *The Darkness We See: Torture in Burma's Interrogation Centres and Prisons* (Mae Sot: Assistance Association for Political Prisoners [Burma], 2005)

1618. *The Role of Political Prisoners in the National Reconciliation Process* (Mae Sot: Assistance Association for Political Prisoners [Burma], 2010)

1619. *The Ten Year Fight for Burma's Political Prisoners: A History of the Assistance Association for Political Prisoners (Burma): The First Decade, 23 March 2000 – 23 March 2010* (Mae Sot: Assistance Association for Political Prisoners [Burma], 2010)

1620. *Tortured Voices: Personal Accounts of Burma's Interrogation Centres* (Bangkok: All Burma Students Democratic Front, 1998)

1621. *Uncounted: Political Prisoners in Burma's Ethnic Areas: A Special Report* (Bangkok: Peace Way Foundation, Burma Issues and ALTSEAN Burma, 2003)

1622. *Union of Myanmar (Burma): Arrests and Trials of Political Prisoners, January – July 1991*, AI Index ASA 16/010/1991 (New York: Amnesty International, December 1991)

1623. Weerwag, Nola, *Dog Cells, Torture and Glue: A Case Study of Solitary Confinement in Burma* (Saarbrucken: Lambert Academic, 2017)

1624. Win Naing Oo, *Cries from Insein: A Report on Conditions for Political Prisoners in Burma's Infamous Insein Prison* (Bangkok: All Burma Students Democratic Front, 1996)

1625. Win Naing Oo, *Human Rights Abuse in Burmese Prisons* (Sydney: Australian Council for Overseas Aid, December 1996)

1626. *Women Political Prisoners in Burma* (Chiang Mai and Mae Sot: Burmese Women's Union and Assistance Association for Political Prisoners (Burma), 2004)

Forced Labour

1627. *A Legal Review of National Laws and Regulations Related to Child Labour in Myanmar in Light of International Laws and Standards* (Geneva: International Labour Organisation, 2015)

1628. *Dead Men Walking: Convict Porters on the Front Lines in Eastern Burma* (New York: Human Rights Watch, 2011)

1629. *From Prison to Frontline: Portering for SPDC Troops during the Offensive in Eastern Karen State, Burma, September–October 2003*, Special Report (Bangkok: Peace Way Foundation, Burma Issues, 2005)

1630. *From Prison to Front Line: Analysis of Convict Porter Testimony 2009–2011* (Thailand: Karen Human Rights Group, 2011)

1631. Horsey, Richard, *Ending Forced Labour in Myanmar: Engaging a Pariah Regime* (London: Routledge, 2011)

1632. *"If We Don't Have Time to Take Care of Our Fields, the Rice Will Die": A Report on Forced Labour in Burma* (Washington DC: Earthrights International, 2005)

1633. *Less Than Human: Convict Porters in the 2005–2006 Northern Karen State Offensive* (Thailand: Karen Human Rights Group, 22 August 2006)

1634. *Slave Labour in Burma: An Examination of the SLORC's Forced Labour Policies*, Research Information Series no. 9 (Canberra: Australian Council for Overseas Aid, 1996)

1635. *Ye-Tavoy Railway Construction: Report on Forced Labour in the Mon State and Tenasserim Division in Burma* (US: National Coalition Government of the Union of Burma, 1994)

Human Rights Yearbooks

1636. *Human Rights Yearbook 1994: Burma* (Bangkok: Human Rights Documentation Unit, National Coalition Government of the Union of Burma, 1995)

1637. *Human Rights Yearbook 1995: Burma* (Bangkok: Human Rights Documentation Unit, National Coalition Government of the Union of Burma, 1996)

1638. *Human Rights Yearbook 1996: Burma* (Bangkok: Human Rights Documentation Unit, National Coalition Government of the Union of Burma, 1997)

1639. *Human Rights Yearbook 1997–98: Burma* (Bangkok: Human Rights Documentation Unit, National Coalition Government of the Union of Burma, 1998)

1640. *Human Rights Yearbook 1998–99: Burma* (Bangkok: Human Rights Documentation Unit, National Coalition Government of the Union of Burma, 1999)

1641. *Human Rights Yearbook 1999–2000: Burma* (Bangkok: Human Rights Documentation Unit, National Coalition Government of the Union of Burma, 2000)

1642. *Human Rights Yearbook 2000: Burma* (Bangkok: Human Rights Documentation Unit, National Coalition Government of the Union of Burma, 2001)

1643. *Human Rights Yearbook 2001–02: Burma* (Nonthaburi: Human Rights Documentation Unit, National Coalition Government of the Union of Burma, 2002)

1644. *Human Rights Yearbook 2002–03: Burma* (Nonthaburi: Human Rights Documentation Unit, National Coalition Government of the Union of Burma, 2003)

1645. *Human Rights Yearbook 2003–04: Burma* (Nonthaburi: Human Rights Documentation Unit, National Coalition Government of the Union of Burma, 2004)

1646. *Human Rights Yearbook 2004: Burma* (Nonthaburi: Human Rights Documentation Unit, National Coalition Government of the Union of Burma, 2005)

1647. *Human Rights Yearbook 2005: Burma* (Nonthaburi: Human Rights Documentation Unit, National Coalition Government of the Union of Burma, 2006)

1648. *Human Rights Yearbook 2006: Burma* (Nonthaburi: Human Rights Documentation Unit, National Coalition Government of the Union of Burma, 2007)

1649. *Human Rights Yearbook 2007: Burma* (Mae Sot: Human Rights Documentation Unit, National Coalition Government of the Union of Burma, 2008)

1650. *Human Rights Yearbook 2008: Burma* (Mae Sot: Human Rights Documentation Unit, National Coalition Government of the Union of Burma, 2009)

POLITICS AND GOVERNMENT

Official Publications

1651. *Burma Communist Party's Conspiracy to Take Over State Power* (Yangon: News and Periodicals Enterprise, Ministry of Information, 1989)

1652. *Burma's Saffron Revolution: Hearing before the Subcommittee on East Asian and Pacific Affairs of the Committee on Foreign Relations, United States Senate, 110th Congress, First Session, October 3, 2007* (Washington DC: US Government Printing Office, 2008)

1653. *Crazy, Bogus Hluttaw and Selected Articles* (Yangon: News and Periodicals Enterprise, Ministry of Information, 1998)

1654. *Daw Suu Kyi, NLD Party and Our Ray of Hope and Selected Articles* (Yangon: Ministry of Information, 2003)

1655. *Democracy and Development in Burma*, International Development Committee, Ninth Report of Session 2013–14 (London: House of Commons, UK Parliament, 2014)

1656. *Discipline-Flourishing Democracy and Selected Articles* (Yangon: News and Periodicals Enterprise, Ministry of Information, 1999)

1657. Hill, Cameron, *Burma: Domestic Reforms and International Responses*, Background Note (Canberra: Department of the Parliamentary Library, Parliament of Australia, 2012)

1658. *Historic Records of Endeavours Made by the State Law and Order Restoration Council (from 1 April 1995 to 14 November 1997)* (Yangon: News and Periodicals Enterprises, Ministry of Information, July 1999)

1659. Hla Min, *Political Situation of Myanmar and its Role in the Region*, 26th edition (Yangon: Office of Strategic Studies, 2000)

1660. Hluttaw Brochure Working Group, *Hluttaw: Brochure* (Nay Pyi Taw: The Republic of the Union of Myanmar Hluttaw, 2017)

1661. *Hluttaw Cannot Be Convened Forcibly and Selected Articles* (Yangon: News and Periodicals Enterprise, Ministry of Information, 1998)

1662. *Magnificent Myanmar (1988–2003)* (Rangoon: Ministry of Information, 2004?)

1663. Min Maung Maung, *The Tatmadaw and Its Leadership Role in National Politics* (Yangon: News and Periodicals Enterprise, Ministry of Information, 1993)

1664. Minye Kaungbon, *Our Three Main National Causes* (Yangon: News and Periodicals Enterprise, Ministry of Information, 1994)

1665. Mya Win, *Tatmadaw's Traditional Role in National Politics* (Yangon: News and Periodicals Enterprise, Ministry of Information, 1999)

1666. *Myanmar Politics and the Tatmadaw (Part 1)* (Naypyidaw: Directorate of Public Relations and Psychological Warfare, July 2018)

1667. Myint Kyi and Angiline Naw (eds.), *Myanmar Politics, 1958–1962*, volume 2, translated by Hla Thein (Yangon: Myanmar Historical Commission, 2007)

1668. Nawrahta, *Destiny of the Nation* (Yangon: News and Periodicals Enterprise, 1995)

1669. *Points to Heed about Their Plot to Convene Hluttaw and Selected Articles* (Yangon: News and Periodicals Enterprise, 1999)

1670. San Yein and Myint Kyi (eds.), *Myanmar Politics, 1958–1962*, volume 1, translated by Thet Tun (Yangon: Myanmar Historical Commission, 2006)

1671. *Scheming and Activities of the Burma Communist Party Politburo to Seize State Power* (Yangon: News and Periodicals Enterprise, Ministry of Information, 1989?)

1672. *Seminar on Understanding Myanmar* (Yangon: Myanmar Institute of Strategic and International Studies, 2004)

1673. *Skyful of Lies; BBC, VOA: Their Broadcasts and Rebuttals to Disinformation* (Yangon: News and Periodicals Enterprise, Ministry of Information, 1990)

1674. *The Conspiracy of Treasonous Minions within the Myanmar Naing-ngan and Traitorous Cohorts Abroad* (Yangon: News and Periodicals Enterprise, Ministry of Information, 1989)

1675. *The Working People's Daily, Collected Articles*, 16 volumes? (Yangon: News and Periodicals Enterprise, Ministry of Information, 1989–1991)

1676. *Time to Go Home and Selected Articles* (Yangon: News and Periodicals Enterprise, Ministry of Information, 1998)

1677. *Union of Myanmar, State Law and Order Restoration Council, Information Committee, Press Conferences*, 4 volumes? (Yangon: News and Periodicals Enterprise, Ministry of Information, 1989–1990)

1678. *Web of Conspiracy: Complicated Stories of Treacherous Machinations and Intrigues of BCP UG, DAB, and Some NLD Leaders, to Seize State Power* (Yangon: News and Periodicals Enterprise, Ministry of Information, 1991)

1679. *Will Tell All That Is True, Barring None, and Special Articles* (Yangon: New Light of Myanmar, 2002)

1680. Yan Nan Aye, *Endeavours of the Myanmar Armed Forces Government for National Reconciliation* (Yangon: State Peace and Development Council, 2000)

The SLORC/SPDC Period (1988–2010)

1681. Andrieux, Aurelie, Diana Sarosi and Yeshua Puangsuwan, *Speaking Truth to Power: The Methods of Nonviolent Struggle in Burma*, Nonviolence in Asia Series no. 2 (Bangkok: Nonviolence International, 2005)

1682. Aung Chin Win Aung, *O Burma!* (Indianapolis: Yoma, 2000)

1683. Badgley, J.H., and Aye Kyaw, *Red Peacocks: Commentaries on Burmese Socialist Nationalism* (New Delhi: Readworthy, 2009)

1684. Blum, Franziska, Friederike Trotier and Hans-Bernd Zollner (eds.), *In Their Own Voice: "Democracy" as Perceived in Burma/Myanmar, 1921–2010*, Working Paper no. 14 (Passau: University of Passau, 2010)

1685. Brandon, J.J. (ed.), *Burma/Myanmar towards the Twenty-first Century: Dynamics of Continuity and Change* (Bangkok: Chulalongkorn University, 1997)

1686. *Bullets in the Alms Bowl: An Analysis of the Brutal SPDC Suppression of the 2007 Saffron Revolution* (Mae Sot: National Coalition Government of the Union of Burma, Human Rights Documentation Unit, March 2008)

1687. *Burma: Country in Crisis* (New York: Open Society Institute, 1998)

1688. *Burma: Time for Change: Report of an Independent Task Force Sponsored by the Council on Foreign Relations* (New York: Council on Foreign Relations, 2003)

1689. *Burma's 2010 Elections: A Comprehensive Report* (New York: Burma Fund UN Office, 2011)

1690. *Burma's 2010 Elections: Implications of the New Constitution and Election Laws* (Washington DC: Congressional Research Service, 4 June 2010)

1691. Carey, Peter, *From Burma to Myanmar: Military Rule and the Struggle for Democracy* (London: Research Institute for the Study of Conflict and Terrorism, 1997)

1692. Carey, Peter (ed.), *Burma: The Challenge of Change in a Divided Society* (Houndsmills: Macmillan, 1997)

1693. *Censorship Prevails: Political Deadlock and Economic Transition in Burma* (London: Article 19, 1995)

1694. Chao Tzang Yawnghwe, *Military Regimes: Nature, Structures, Power Dynamics, and Political Transition*, Working Paper no. 2/00 (Washington DC: Technical Advisory Network of Burma, The Burma Fund, 2000)

1695. Chao Tzang Yawnghwe and L.H. Sakhong (eds.), *The New Panglong Initiative: Rebuilding the Union of Burma* (Chiang Mai: UNLD Press, 2004)

1696. Cheesman, Nick, Monique Skidmore and Trevor Wilson (eds.), *Ruling Myanmar: From Cyclone Nargis to National Elections* (Singapore: Institute of Southeast Asian Studies, 2010)

1697. Clapp, Priscilla, *Building Democracy in Burma*, Working Paper no. 2 (Washington DC: United States Institute of Peace, 24 July 2007)

1698. Clements, Alan, *Burma: The Next Killing Fields?* (Berkeley: Odonian Press, 1992)

1699. Clements, Alan, and Leslie Kean, *Burma's Revolution of the Spirit: The Struggle for Democratic Freedom and Dignity* (New York: Aperture, 1994)

1700. *Crackdown: Repression of the 2007 Popular Protests in Burma* (New York: Human Rights Watch, 2007)

1701. *Daw Aung San Suu Kyi, the SLORC and Initiatives for Burma's Future: Seminar Proceedings*, Research Information Series no. 7 (Canberra: Australian Council for Overseas Aid, 1996)

1702. Dittmer, Lowell (ed.), *Burma or Myanmar? The Struggle for National Identity* (New Jersey: World Scientific, 2010)

1703. Donkers, Jan, and Minka Nijhuis (eds.), *Burma behind the Mask*, translated by P.J. Van de Paverd (Amsterdam: Burma Centrum Nederland, 1996)

1704. Ebashi, Masahiko, *Myanmar: Recent Trends and Challenges* (Tokyo: Sasakawa Peace Foundation, 2006)
1705. Fleischmann, Klaus (ed.), *Documents on Communism in Burma, 1945–1977* (Hamburg: Mitteilungen des Instituts fur Asienkunde, 1989)
1706. Ganesan, N., and Kyaw Yin Hlaing (eds.), *Myanmar: State, Society and Ethnicity* (Singapore: Institute of Southeast Asian Studies, 2007)
1707. Gravers, Mikael, *Nationalism as Political Paranoia in Burma: An Essay on the Historical Practice of Power*, NIAS Report no. 11 (Copenhagen: Nordic Institute of Asian Studies, 1993)
1708. Grover, Verinder (ed.), *Myanmar: Government and Politics* (New Delhi: Deep and Deep, 2000)
1709. Houtman, Gustaaf, *Human Origins, Myanmafication and "Disciplined" Burmese Democracy* (Myanmar: Pekhon University Press, 2000)
1710. Houtman, Gustaaf, *Mental Culture in Burmese Crisis Politics: Aung San Suu Kyi and the National League for Democracy* (Tokyo: Tokyo University of Foreign Studies, 1999)
1711. Kanbawza Win, *Impunity Inconceivable*, Working Paper no. 1/02 (Washington DC: Technical Advisory Network of Burma, The Burma Fund, 2002)
1712. Keeler, Ward, *Fighting for Democracy on a Heap of Jewels*, Working Paper no. 102 (Clayton: Centre of Southeast Asian Studies, Monash University, 1997)
1713. Kyaw Yin Hlaing, *The State of the Pro-democracy Movement in Authoritarian Burma*, Working Paper no. 11 (Washington DC: East West Centre, December 2007)
1714. Kyaw Yin Hlaing, R.H. Taylor and Tin Maung Maung Than (eds.), *Myanmar: Beyond Politics to Societal Imperatives* (Singapore: Institute of Southeast Asian Studies, 2005)
1715. Larkin, Emma, *Everything is Broken: The Untold Story of Disaster under Burma's Military Rule* (London: Granta, 2010)
1716. Len, Christopher, and Johan Alvin, *Burma/Myanmar's Ailments: Searching for the Right Remedy*, Silk Road Paper (Washington DC: Silk Road Studies Program, Central Asia-Caucasus Institute, Johns Hopkins University, March 2007)
1717. Leone, Faye, and Tyler Giannini, *Traditions of Conflict Resolution in Burma* (Washington DC: Earthrights International, 2005)

1718. *Letters to a Dictator: Official Correspondence from NLD Chairman U Aung Shwe to the SLORC's Senior General Than Shwe from December 1995 to March 1997* (Bangkok: All Burma Students Democratic Front, 1997)

1719. Levenstein, S.L. (ed.), *Finding Dollars, Sense, and Legitimacy in Burma* (Washington DC: Woodrow Wilson International Centre for Scholars, 2010)

1720. Li, Chenyang, and Wilhelm Hoffmeister (eds.), *Myanmar: Prospect for Change* (Singapore: Konrad Adenauer Foundation, Yunnan University and Select, 2010)

1721. Lintner, Bertil, *Burma in Revolt: Opium and Insurgency since 1948*, 2nd edition (Chiang Mai: Silkworm Books, 1999)

1722. Lintner, Bertil, *Outrage: Burma's Struggle for Democracy* (London: White Lotus, 1990)

1723. Lintner, Bertil, *The Rise and Fall of the Communist Party of Burma (CPB)* (Ithaca: Southeast Asia Program, Cornell University, 1990)

1724. *Managing Democratic Transition in Burma: Learning Lessons from Abroad* (Washington DC: The Burma Fund, 2002)

1725. Mathieson, D.S., and R.J. May (eds.), *The Illusion of Progress: The Political Economy of Reform in Burma/Myanmar* (Adelaide: Crawford House, 2004)

1726. Maung Maung, *The 1988 Uprising in Burma*, Monograph no. 49 (New Haven: Yale Southeast Asia Studies, Yale University, 1999)

1727. McCarthy, Stephen, *From Coup d'Etat to "Disciplined Democracy": The Burmese Regime's Claims to Legitimacy*, Regional Outlook no. 23 (Brisbane: Griffith Asia Institute, Griffith University, 2010)

1728. McCarthy, Stephen, *Losing My Religion? Protest and Political Legitimacy in Burma*, Regional Outlook no. 18 (Brisbane: Griffith Asia Institute, Griffith University, 2008)

1729. McCarthy, Stephen, *The Political Theory of Tyranny in Singapore and Burma* (London: Routledge, 2006)

1730. Metraux, D.A., and Khin Oo (eds.), *Burma's Modern Tragedy* (Lewiston: Edwin Mellen Press, 2005)

1731. Pedersen, M.B., et al., *Democracy and Discontent: The 2010 Elections in Myanmar*, AIIA Policy Commentary no. 9 (Canberra: Australian Institute of International Affairs, 2010)

1732. Pedersen, M.B., Emily Rudland and R.J. May (eds.), *Burma-Myanmar: Strong Regime, Weak State?* (Bathurst: Crawford House, 2000)

1733. *Policy Vision of the Committee Representing Peoples' Parliament (CRPP) on the Reconstruction of Burma* (Washington DC: National Coalition Government of the Union of Burma, 2007)

1734. Rieffel, Lex (ed.), *Myanmar/Burma: Inside Challenges, Outside Interests* (Washington DC: Brookings Institution Press and Konrad Adenauer Foundation, 2010)

1735. Rotberg, R.I. (ed.), *Burma: Prospects for a Democratic Future* (Washington DC: Brookings Institution Press, 1998)

1736. Sakhong, Run Pen, *Understanding Peacebuilding in the Context of Burma* (Chiang Mai: UNLD Press, 2004)

1737. Saw Myat Sandy [Sandy Minsat], *Problems of Democratic Transitions in Multi-ethnic States: Comparison between the Former Yugoslavia and Present Days Myanmar* (Stuttgart: Ibedim-Verlag, 2009)

1738. Schneebaum, S.M., et al., *Post-election Myanmar: A Popular Mandate Withheld* (Washington DC: International Human Rights Law Group, 1990)

1739. Seekins, D.M., *The Disorder in Order: The Army-State in Burma since 1962* (Bangkok: White Lotus, 2002)

1740. Sharp, Gene, *From Dictatorship to Democracy: A Conceptual Framework for Liberation* (London: Profile Books, 2012)

1741. Shwe Lu Maung, *Burma: Nationalism and Ideology: An Analysis of Society, Culture and Politics* (Dhaka: University Press Ltd., 1989)

1742. Silverstein, Josef (ed.), *Independent Burma at Forty Years: Six Assessments* (Ithaca: Southeast Asia Program, Cornell University, 1989)

1743. Silverstein, Josef, *Two Papers on Burma*, Discussion Paper Series no. 17 (Canberra: Department of Political and Social Change, Australian National University, 1996)

1744. Singh, L.S., *Movement for Democracy in Myanmar* (New Delhi: Akansha, 2006)

1745. Skidmore, Monique, *Karaoke Fascism: Burma and the Politics of Fear* (Philadelphia: University of Pennsylvania Press, 2004)

1746. Skidmore, Monique, and Trevor Wilson (eds.), *Dictatorship, Disorder and Decline in Myanmar* (Canberra: ANU Press, 2008)

1747. Skidmore, Monique, and Trevor Wilson (eds.), *Myanmar: The State, Community and Environment* (Canberra: ANU Press and Asia Pacific Press, 2007)

1748. Smith, Martin, *Burma: Insurgency and the Politics of Ethnicity*, 2nd edition (London: Zed Books, 1999)

1749. Soe Myint, *Burma File: A Question of Democracy* (Singapore: Marshall Cavendish Academic, 2004)

1750. South, Ashley, *Civil Society in Burma: The Development of Democracy amidst Conflict*, Policy Studies no. 51 (Washington DC: East-West Centre, 2008)

1751. Steinberg, D.I., *Burma: Prospects for Political and Economic Reconstruction*, WPF Reports no. 15 (Cambridge: World Peace Foundation, 1997)

1752. Steinberg, D.I., *Burma: The State of Myanmar* (Washington DC: Georgetown University Press, 2001)

1753. Steinberg, D.I., *Crisis in Burma: Stasis and Change in a Political Economy in Turmoil*, ISIS Paper no. 5 (Bangkok: Institute of Security and International Studies, Chulalongkorn University, 1989)

1754. Steinberg, D.I., *Myanmar: The Anomalies of Politics and Economics*, Working Paper no. 5 (San Francisco: The Asia Foundation, November 1997)

1755. Steinberg, D.I., *The Future of Burma: Crisis and Choice in Myanmar*, Asian Agenda Report no. 14 (Lanham: Asia Society and University Press of America, 1990)

1756. Steinberg, D.I., *Turmoil in Burma: Contested Legitimacies in Myanmar* (Norwalk: EastBridge, 2006)

1757. Taylor, R.H., *The State in Myanmar*, 2nd edition (London: Hurst, 2009)

1758. Taylor, R.H. (ed.), *Burma: Political Economy under Military Rule* (London: Hurst, 2001)

1759. Thawnghmung, A.M., *Behind the Teak Curtain: Authoritarianism, Agricultural Policies and Political Legitimacy in Rural Burma/Myanmar* (London: Kegan Paul, 2004)

1760. *The Crisis in Burma: An Agenda for the United Nations Security Council?* (Washington DC: National Coalition Government of the Union of Burma and The Burma Fund, October 2003)

1761. *The Free Burma Coalition Manual: How You Can Help Burma's Struggle for Freedom* (Madison: Free Burma Coalition, 1997)

1762. *The Resistance of the Monks: Buddhism and Activism in Burma* (New York: Human Rights Watch, December 2009)

1763. *The White Shirts: How the USDA Will Become the New Face of Burma's Dictatorship* (Mae Sariang: Network for Democracy and Development, 2006)

1764. *Threat to the Peace: A Call for the UN Security Council to Act in Burma* (Washington DC: DLA Piper Rudnick Gray Cary, 2005)

1765. Tin Maung Maung Than, *Myanmar: The Dilemma of Stalled Reforms* (Singapore: Institute of Southeast Asian Studies, 2000)

1766. Toe Zaw Latt, *Politics of Reconciliation in Burma*, Working Paper no. 9 (Washington DC: Technical Advisory Network of Burma, The Burma Fund, 2005)

1767. Tomar, Ravi, *Burma since 1988: The Politics of Dictatorship*, Background Paper no. 30 (Canberra: Department of the Parliamentary Library, Parliament of the Commonwealth of Australia, 1992)

1768. *Towards Democracy in Burma* (Washington DC: Institute for Asian Democracy, 1992)

1769. *Voices of '88: Burma's Struggle for Democracy* (New York: Open Society Institute, 1998)

1770. Weller, Marc (ed.), *Democracy and Politics in Burma: A Collection of Documents* (Manerplaw: National Coalition Government of the Union of Burma, 1993)

1771. Wilson, Trevor (ed.), *Myanmar's Long Road to National Reconciliation* (Singapore: Institute of Southeast Asian Studies and Asia-Pacific Press, 2006)

1772. Yhome, K., *Myanmar: Can the Generals Resist Change?* (New Delhi: Rupa, 2008)

1773. Zaw Oo (ed.), *Managing Democratic Transition in Burma: Learning Lessons from Abroad: Proceedings of International Conference sponsored by The Ford Foundation and The Burma Fund* (Washington DC: The Burma Fund, 2002)

1774. Zaw Oo (ed.), *Shaping Concepts for Democratic Transition in Burma: Policies for Socially Responsible Development* (Washington DC: The Burma Fund, 2002)

1775. Zaw Oo and Win Min, *Assessing Burma's Ceasefire Accords*, Policy Studies no. 39 (Washington DC: East-West Centre, 2007)

1776. Zollner, Hans-Bernd, *Neither Saffron nor Revolution: A Commentated and Documented Chronology of the Monks' Demonstrations in Myanmar in 2007 and their Background*, Sudostasien Working Paper no. 36 (Berlin: Department of Southeast Asian Studies, Humboldt University, 2009)

The Thein Sein Era (2011–15)

1777. Aye Myint, Oscar, and Swan Tha Khin, *Change for Burma, Change for World* (US: The authors, 2015)

1778. Batcheler, Richard, et al., *State and Region Governments in Myanmar*, new edition (Yangon: Asia Foundation, October 2018)

1779. Blum, Franziska, *Teaching Democracy: The Program and Practice of Aung San Suu Kyi's Concept of People's Education* (Berlin: RegioSpectra, 2011)

1780. Chalk, Peter, *On the Path of Change: Political, Economic and Social Challenges for Myanmar*, Special Report (Canberra: Australian Strategic Policy Institute, December 2013)

1781. Cheesman, Nick, and Htoo Kyaw Win (eds.), *Communal Violence in Myanmar* (Yangon: Myanmar Knowledge Society, 2015)

1782. Cheesman, Nick, Nicholas Farrelly and Trevor Wilson (eds.), *Debating Democratization in Myanmar* (Singapore: Institute of Southeast Asian Studies, 2014)

1783. Cheesman, Nick, Monique Skidmore and Trevor Wilson (eds.), *Myanmar's Transition: Openings, Obstacles and Opportunities* (Singapore: Institute of Southeast Asian Studies, 2012)

1784. Clapp, Priscilla, *Burma's Long Road to Democracy*, Special Report no. 193 (Washington DC: United States Institute of Peace, November 2007)

1785. Clapp, Priscilla, *Myanmar: Anatomy of a Political Transition*, Special Report no. 369 (Washington DC: United States Institute of Peace, April 2015)

1786. Clapp, Priscilla, and Suzanne DiMaggio, *Advancing Myanmar's Transition: A Way Forward for U.S. Policy* (New York: Asia Society, 16 February 2012)

1787. Clapp, Priscilla, and Suzanne DiMaggio, *Sustaining Myanmar's Transition: Ten Critical Challenges* (New York: Asia Society, 24 June 2013)

1788. Dale, J.G., *Free Burma: Transnational Legal Action and Corporate Accountability* (Minneapolis: University of Minnesota Press, 2011)

1789. Desaine, Lois, *The Politics of Silence: Myanmar NGOs' Ethnic, Religious and Political Agenda*, Occasional Paper no. 17 (Bangkok: Research Institute on Contemporary Southeast Asia, 2011)

1790. *Economics of Peace and Conflict* (Chiang Mai: Myanmar Peace Monitor and Burma News International, September 2013)

1791. Egreteau, Renaud, *Retired Military Officers in Myanmar's Parliament: An Emerging Legislative Force?*, Trends in Southeast Asia, 2015 no. 17 (Singapore: Institute of Southeast Asian Studies, 2015)

1792. Ferdinand, Peter, *Governance in Pacific Asia: Political Economy and Development from Japan to Burma* (New York: Continuum, 2012)

1793. Frankovic, K.A., et al., *From Novelty to Normalcy: Polling in Myanmar's Democratic Transition* (New York: Open Society Foundations, 2015)

1794. Gravers, Mikael, and Flemming Ytzen (eds.), *Burma/Myanmar – Where Now?* (Copenhagen: NIAS Press, 2014)

1795. Hohmeyer, Ursula, *Burma in Transition: But Buddha is Never in a Hurry*, translated by Roger Powell (Munich: Books on Demand, 2014)

1796. Holliday, Ian, *Burma Redux: Global Justice and the Quest for Political Reform in Myanmar* (Hong Kong: Hong Kong University Press, 2011)

1797. Hook, David, Tin Maung Than and K.N.B. Ninh, *Conceptualizing Public Sector Reform in Myanmar* (Yangon: Asia Foundation, 2015)

1798. Katsiaficas, George, *Asia's Unknown Uprisings, Volume 2: People Power in the Philippines, Burma, Tibet, China, Taiwan, Bangladesh, Nepal, Thailand, and Indonesia, 1947–2009* (Oakland: PM Press, 2013)

1799. Kipgen, Nehginpao, *Democracy Movement in Myanmar: Problems and Challenges* (New Delhi: Ruby Press, 2015)

1800. Kironska, Kristina, *The Electoral System of Myanmar* (Riga: Lambert Academic, 2013)

1801. Koh Kim Seng, *Misunderstood Myanmar: An Introspective Study of a Southeast Asian State in Transition* (Singapore: Humanities Press, 2011)

1802. Kramer, Tom, *Ending 50 Years of Military Rule? Prospects for Peace, Democracy and Development in Burma* (Oslo: Norwegian Peacebuilding Resource Centre, 2012)

1803. Kyaw Win, Mya Han and Thein Hlaing (eds.), *Myanmar Politics, 1958–1962*, volume 3, translated by Hla Shain (Yangon: Myanmar Historical Commission, 2011)

1804. Kyaw Yin Hlaing (ed.), *Prisms on the Golden Pagoda: Perspectives on National Reconciliation in Myanmar* (Singapore: NUS Press, 2014)

1805. Kyi Pyar Chit Saw and Matthew Arnold, *Administering the State in Myanmar: An Overview of the General Administration Department* (Yangon: The Asia Foundation, 2014)

1806. Lall, Marie, et al., *Myanmar's Ethnic Parties and the 2015 Elections* (Yangon: International Management Group, 2015) (in English and Burmese)

1807. Martin, M.F., *Burma's 2015 Parliamentary Elections: Issues for Congress* (Washington DC: Congressional Research Service, 28 March 2016)

1808. Martin, M.F., *Burma's April Parliamentary By-elections* (Washington DC: Congressional Research Service, 28 March 2012)

1809. Min Zin, *Wave or Eddy? "Analysis of Burma's Transition"* (Yangon: Open Minded Media Group, 2016) (in English and Burmese)

1810. Mya Han and Thein Hlaing (eds.), *Myanmar Politics, 1958–1962*, volume 4, translated by Sai Aung Tin (Yangon: Myanmar Historical Commission, 2011)

1811. *Nation Building in Myanmar*, 2nd edition (Yangon: Myanmar Egress and The Myanmar Peace Centre, 2014)

1812. Nixon, Hamish, et al., *State and Region Governments in Myanmar* (Yangon: Asia Foundation, 2013)

1813. On Kin, *Cruising down the Irrawaddy and Other Writings*, edited by Zali Win (Yangon: Myanmar Book Centre, 2015)

1814. Rogers, Benedict, *Burma: A Nation at the Crossroads*, revised edition (London: Rider, 2015)

1815. Schrank, Delphine, *The Rebel of Rangoon: A Tale of Defiance and Deliverance in Burma* (New York: Nation Books, 2015)

1816. South, Ashley, *Local to Global Protection in Burma (Myanmar), Sudan, South Sudan and Zimbabwe*, Humanitarian Practice Network Paper no. 72 (London: Overseas Development Institute, 2012)

1817. South, Ashley, *Prospects for Peace in Myanmar: Opportunities and Threats* (Oslo: Peace Research Institute, 2012)

1818. Steinberg, D.I. (ed.), *Myanmar: The Dynamics of an Evolving Polity* (Boulder: Lynne Rienner, 2014)

1819. *Struggle for Peace: The 25 Year Journey of the ABSDF* (Siem Reap: Centre for Peace and Conflict Studies, 2014)

1820. Taylor, R.H., *The Armed Forces in Myanmar Politics: A Terminating Role?* Trends in Southeast Asia, 2015 no. 2 (Singapore: Institute of Southeast Asian Studies, 2015)

1821. *The Parliaments of Myanmar: Pyithu Hluttaw (House of Representatives), Amyotha Hluttaw (House of Nationalities)* (Yangon: MCM Books, 2013)

1822. Trivedi, Sonu, *Transition from Authoritarianism to Democracy: A Comparative Study of Indonesia and Myanmar* (New Delhi: Atlantic Publishers and Distributors, 2015)

1823. Winward, John, and Zai Chi Oo (eds.), *November (8) Diary: The Narratives of the Historic Election Day Portrayed by Writers, Journalists, Observers and Commoners Based on Their Experience* (Yangon: PEN Myanmar, 2015)

1824. Ye Htut, *Myanmar's Political Transition and Lost Opportunities (2010–2016)* (Singapore: ISEAS – Yusof Ishak Institute, 2019)

The First NLD Administration (2016–20)

1825. *A Year in Transition: Assessing Democracy in Myanmar*, Special Report no. 186 (New Delhi: Institute of Peace and Conflict Studies, March 2017)

1826. Aung Aung, *Emerging Political Configurations in the Run-up to the 2020 Myanmar Elections*, Trends in Southeast Asia, 2019 no. 1 (Singapore: ISEAS – Yusof Ishak Institute, 2019)

1827. Bhattacharyya, Harihar, *Federalism in Asia: India, Pakistan, Malaysia, Nepal and Myanmar*, 2nd edition (London: Routledge, 2020)

1828. Breen, M.G., et al., *Deliberative Polling on Federalism in Myanmar: Report* (Melbourne: School of Social and Political Sciences, University of Melbourne, November 2018)

1829. Breen, M.G., *The Road to Federalism in Nepal, Myanmar and Sri Lanka: Finding the Middle Ground* (London: Routledge, 2018)

1830. Callahan, Mary, with Myo Zaw Oo, *Myanmar's 2020 Elections and Conflict Dynamics*, Peaceworks no. 146 (Washington DC: United States Institute of Peace, April 2019)

1831. Cannon, J.W., *The Rise of Democratic Student Movements in Thailand and Burma* (US: Open Dissertation Press, 2017)

1832. Chambers, Justine, Charlotte Galloway and Jonathan Liljeblad (eds.), *Living with Myanmar* (Singapore: ISEAS – Yusof Ishak Institute, 2020)

1833. Chambers, Justine, Gerard McCarthy, Nicholas Farrelly and Chit Win (eds.), *Myanmar Transformed? People, Places and Politics* (Singapore: ISEAS – Yusof Ishak Institute, 2018)

1834. Cheesman, Nick (ed.), *Interpreting Communal Violence in Myanmar* (London: Routledge, 2018)

1835. Cheesman, Nick, and Nicholas Farrelly (eds.), *Conflict in Myanmar: War, Politics, Religion* (Singapore: ISEAS – Yusof Ishak Institute, 2016)

1836. Clapp, Priscilla, *Securing a Democratic Future for Myanmar*, Council Special Report no. 75 (New York: Council on Foreign Relations, March 2016)

1837. Clements, Alan, and Fergus Harlow, *Burma's Voices of Freedom: In Conversation with Alan Clements: An Ongoing Struggle for Democracy*, 4 volumes (New York: World Dharma Publications, 2020)

1838. David, Roman, and Ian Holliday, *Liberalism and Democracy in Myanmar* (Oxford: Oxford University Press, 2018)

1839. *Deciphering Myanmar's Peace Process: A Reference Guide 2016* (Chiang Mai: Burma News International, 2017)

1840. Dey, Amrita (ed.), *Myanmar: Democratization, Foreign Policy and Elections* (New Delhi: Pentagon Press, 2016)

1841. Dukalskis, Alexander, *The Authoritarian Public Sphere: Legitimation and Autocratic Power in North Korea, Burma, and China* (London: Routledge, 2017)

1842. Egreteau, Renaud, *Caretaking Democratization: The Military and Political Change in Myanmar* (London: Hurst, 2016)

1843. Egreteau, Renaud, *Parliamentary Development in Myanmar: An Overview of the Union Parliament 2011–2016* (Yangon: Asia Foundation, May 2017)

1844. Egreteau, Renaud, *The Emergence of Pork-Barrel Politics in Parliamentary Myanmar*, Trends in Southeast Asia, 2017 no. 4 (Singapore: ISEAS – Yusof Ishak Institute, 2017)

1845. Egreteau, Renaud, and François Robinne (eds.), *Metamorphosis: Studies in Social and Political Change in Myanmar* (Singapore: NUS Press and IRASEC, 2016)

1846. Huang, R.L., *The Paradox of Myanmar's Regime Change* (London: Routledge, 2020)

1847. Kipgen, Nehginpao, *Democratisation of Myanmar* (New Delhi: Routledge, 2016)

1848. Kipgen, Nehginpao, *Myanmar: A Political History* (New Delhi: Oxford University Press, 2016)

1849. Kyaw Sein and Nicholas Farrelly, *Myanmar's Evolving Relations: The NLD in Government*, Asia Paper (Stockholm: Institute for Security and Development Policy, 2016)

1850. Lall, Marie, *Understanding Reform in Myanmar: People and Society in the Wake of Military Rule* (London: Hurst, 2016)

1851. Lin Htet Aung, *The Peace Process and Civil-Military Relations during the NLD Administration's First Year*, Trends in Southeast Asia, 2017 no. 13 (Singapore: ISEAS – Yusof Ishak Institute, 2017)

1852. Maung Zarni, *Myanmar's "Enemy of the State" Speaks: Irreverent Essays and Interviews* (Petaling Jaya: Strategic Information and Research Development Centre, 2019)

1853. O'Doherty, Mark, *The Legacy of Aung San Suu Kyi and Myanmar's Military Dictatorship – A Military State Facilitating Ethnic Cleansing, Islamophobia and Disregard for Human Rights* (US: Crystal Grove Books, 2017)

1854. *Observing Myanmar's 2015 General Elections: Final Report* (Atlanta: The Carter Centre, 2016)

1855. Oh, Su-Ann, *Making Sense of the Election Results in Myanmar's Rakhine and Shan States*, Trends in Southeast Asia, 2016 no. 1 (Singapore: ISEAS – Yusof Ishak Institute, 2016)

1856. Pavin Chachavalpongpun, Elliott Prasse-Freeman and Patrick Strefford (eds.), *Unraveling Myanmar's Transition: Progress, Retrenchment, and Ambiguity amidst Liberalisation* (Singapore and Kyoto: National University of Singapore Press and Kyoto University Press, 2020)

1857. Rotkin, K.A., *The Murder of U Ko Ni: IBAHRI Trial Observation Highlights Fair Trial Concerns in Myanmar* (London: International Bar Association Human Rights Institute, 2019)

1858. Sai Wansai, *Tracking the Transition: The Path from Quasi-civilian Rule to Fully Fledged Democracy* (Yangon: Mizzima Media Group, 2017)

1859. Sayar Mya (MOFA) [Mya Tun], *The Fighting Peacock and a Nation in Transition* (Singapore: Partridge, 2018)

1860. Selth, Andrew, *All Going According to Plan? The Armed Forces and Government in Myanmar*, Regional Outlook no. 54 (Brisbane: Griffith Asia Institute, Griffith University, 2017)

1861. Selth, Andrew, *Be Careful What You Wish For: The National League for Democracy and Government in Myanmar*, Regional Outlook no. 56 (Brisbane: Griffith Asia Institute, Griffith University, 2017)

1862. Soe Thane, *Myanmar's Transformation and U Thein Sein: An Insider's Account* (Yangon: Tun Foundation Literature Committee, 2017)

1863. Stokke, Kristian, Roman Vakulchuk and Indra Overland, *Myanmar: A Political Economy Analysis* (Oslo: Norwegian Institute of International Affairs, 2018)

1864. Su Mon Thant, *Party Mergers in Myanmar: A New Development*, Trends in Southeast Asia, 2020 no. 8 (Singapore: ISEAS – Yusof Ishak Institute, 2020)

1865. Su Mon Thazin Aung and Matthew Arnold, *Managing Change: Executive Policy Making in Myanmar* (Yangon: Asia Foundation, May 2018)

1866. Taylor, R.H., *Can Myanmar's NLD Government Undo the Gordian Knot of Federalism and Ethnicity?* Trends in Southeast Asia, 2016 no. 3 (Singapore: ISEAS – Yusof Ishak Institute, 2016)

1867. Thant Myint U, *The Hidden History of Burma: Race, Capitalism, and the Crisis of Democracy in the 21st Century* (New York: W.W. Norton, 2020)

1868. Thura U Shwe Mann, *The Lady, I and Affairs of State* (Yangon: U Thein Htway, 2018)

1869. Trivedi, Sonu, *Democratisation in Myanmar: Progress and Prospects* (New Delhi: Gyan, 2018)

1870. Welsh, Bridget, et al., *Myanmar: Grappling with Transition: 2019 Asian Barometer Survey Report* (Petaling Jaya: Strategic Information and Research Centre, 2020)

1871. Woodier, J.R., *The Military in Politics in Thailand and Burma: A Strategic Withdrawal?*, reprint of 1995 edition (US: Open Dissertation Press, 2017)

The Second NLD Administration and State Administration Council (2021–)

1872. O'Doherty, Mark, *Healing Myanmar – Restoring Rule of Law, Justice and Democracy in the Republic of the Union of Myanmar* (US: Lulu Press, 2021)

1873. Wells, Tamas, *Narrating Democracy in Myanmar: The Struggle between Activists, Democratic Leaders and Aid Workers* (Amsterdam: Amsterdam University Press, 2021)

International Crisis Group Publications

1874. *Buddhism and State Power in Myanmar*, Asia Report no. 290 (Yangon/Brussels: International Crisis Group, 5 September 2017)

1875. *Building Critical Mass for Peace in Myanmar*, Asia Report no. 287 (Yangon/Brussels: International Crisis Group, 29 June 2017)

1876. *Burma/Myanmar: After the Crackdown*, Asia Report no. 144 (Brussels: International Crisis Group, 31 January 2008)

1877. *Burma/Myanmar: How Strong is the Military Regime?*, Asia Report no. 11 (Bangkok/Brussels: International Crisis Group, 21 December 2001)

1878. *Myanmar: A New Peace Initiative*, Asia Report no. 214 (Brussels: International Crisis Group, 30 November 2011)

1879. *Myanmar: Major Reform Underway*, Asia Briefing no. 127 (Jakarta/Brussels: International Crisis Group, 22 September 2011)

1880. *Myanmar: Storm Clouds on the Horizon*, Asia Report no. 238 (Brussels: International Crisis Group, 12 November 2012)

1881. *Myanmar: The Military Regime's View of the World*, Asia Report no. 28 (Bangkok/Brussels: International Crisis Group, 7 December 2001)

1882. *Myanmar: The Politics of Rakhine State*, Asia Report no. 261 (Brussels: International Crisis Group, 22 October 2014)

1883. *Myanmar: Towards the Elections*, Asia Report no. 174 (Brussels: International Crisis Group, 20 August 2009)

1884. *Myanmar's Electoral Landscape*, Asia Report no. 266 (Yangon/Brussels: International Crisis Group, 28 April 2015)

1885. *Myanmar's New Government: Finding Its Feet?*, Asia Report no. 282 (Yangon/Brussels: International Crisis Group, 29 July 2016)

1886. *Myanmar's Peace Process: A Nationwide Ceasefire Remains Elusive*, Asia Briefing no. 146 (Yangon/Brussels: International Crisis Group, 16 September 2015)

1887. *Myanmar's Peace Process: Getting to a Political Dialogue*, Asia Briefing no. 149 (Yangon/Brussels: International Crisis Group, 19 October 2016)

1888. *Myanmar's Post-election Landscape*, Asia Briefing no. 118 (Yangon/Brussels: International Crisis Group, 7 Match 2011)

1889. *Not a Rubber Stamp: Myanmar's Legislature in a Time of Transition*, Asia Briefing no. 142 (Yangon/Brussels: International Crisis Group, 13 December 2013)

1890. *Reform in Myanmar: One Year On*, Asia Briefing no. 136 (Yangon/Brussels: International Crisis Group, 11 April 2012)

1891. *Responding to the Myanmar Coup*, Asia Briefing no. 166 (Yangon/Brussels: International Crisis Group, 16 February 2021)

1892. *The Myanmar Elections*, Asia Briefing no. 105 (Yangon/Bangkok/Brussels: International Crisis Group, 27 May 2010)

1893. *The Myanmar Elections: Results and Implications*, Asia Briefing no. 147 (Yangon/Brussels: International Crisis Group, 9 December 2015)

INTERNATIONAL AID

General

1894. *Burma/Myanmar after Nargis: Time to Normalise Aid Relations*, Asia Report no. 161 (Brussels: International Crisis Group, 20 October 2008)

1895. Carr, Thomas, *Supporting the Transition: Understanding Aid to Myanmar since 2011* (Yangon: Asia Foundation, February 2018)

1896. Currie, Kelley, *Burma in the Balance: The Role of Foreign Assistance in Supporting Burma's Democratic Transition* (Arlington: Project 2049 Institute, 2012)

1897. Decobert, Anne, *The Politics of Aid to Burma: A Humanitarian Struggle on the Thai-Burmese Border* (London: Routledge, 2016)

1898. *Development, Environment and Human Rights in Burma/Myanmar – Examining the Impacts of ODA and Investment*, Public Symposium Report (Tokyo: Mekong Watch, Japan, 2001)

1899. *Guide to International Assistance to Myanmar* (Naypyidaw: Foreign Economic Relations Department, Ministry of National Planning and Economic Development, Republic of the Union of Myanmar, July 2014)

1900. *Humanitarian Assistance to Burma* (New York: Burma UN Service Office and The Burma Fund, 2003)

1901. Khin Maung Nyunt, *Foreign Loans and Aid in the Economic Development of Burma, 1974/75 to 1985/86*, Institute of Asian Studies Monograph no. 46 (Bangkok: Chulalongkorn University, 1990)

1902. Ko Lwin, *Cyclone Nargis Relief Assistance: Preliminary Research Study on Government, International and Local Response to Cyclone Nargis in Myanmar (May 2008)* (Saarbrucken: Lambert Academic, 2010)

1903. Leake, J.E., *Cyclone Nargis, Myanmar: Risk Reduction in Natural Resource Management* (Adelaide: Institute for International Development, in association with Thaksin University Press, 2013)

1904. *Myanmar: Aid to the Border Areas*, Asia Report no. 82 (Yangon/Brussels: International Crisis Group, 9 September 2004)

1905. *Myanmar: New Threats to Humanitarian Aid*, Asia Briefing no. 58 (Yangon/Brussels: International Crisis Group, 8 December 2006)

1906. *Myanmar: The Politics of Humanitarian Aid*, Asia Report no. 32 (Bangkok/Brussels: International Crisis Group, 2 April 2002)

1907. Pavin Chachavalpongpun and Moe Thuzar, *Myanmar: Life after Nargis* (Singapore: ASEAN Secretariat and Institute of Southeast Asian Studies, 2009)

1908. *Post-Nargis Recovery and Preparedness Plan: A Report Prepared by the Tripartite Core Group Composed of Representatives of the Government of the Union of Myanmar, the Association of Southeast Asian Nations and the United Nations with the Support of the Humanitarian and Development Community* (Yangon?: Tripartite Core Group, December 2008)

1909. Rieffel, Lex, and J.W. Fox, *Too Much, Too Soon? The Dilemma of Foreign Aid to Myanmar/Burma* (Arlington: Nathan Associates, 2013)

1910. Ware, Anthony, *Context-Sensitive Development: How International NGOs Operate in Myanmar* (Sterling: Kumarian Pres, 2012)

Multilateral Aid

1911. *A Bridge to Recovery: ASEAN's Response to Cyclone Nargis* (Jakarta: ASEAN Secretariat, 2009)

1912. *A Humanitarian Call: The ASEAN Response to Cyclone Nargis* (Jakarta: ASEAN Secretariat, 2010)

1913. *EU Assistance to Myanmar/Burma*, Special Report no. 4 (Luxenbourg: European Court of Auditors, European Union, 2018)

1914. Rollason, Russell, et al., *ICVA Mission to Burma: Report* (Canberra: International Council of Voluntary Agencies, 1993)

1915. Saha, S.R., *Working through Ambiguity: International NGOs in Myanmar* (Cambridge: Hauser Centre for Nonprofit Organisations, Harvard University, September 2011)

1916. Soe Saing, *United Nations Technical Aid in Burma: A Short Survey* (Singapore: Institute of Southeast Asian Studies, 1990)

1917. *The Role of NGOs in Burma: Report by the Policy and Research Department of World Vision* (Milton Keynes: World Vision, 1995)

1918. *"They Block Everything": Avoidable Deprivations in Humanitarian Aid to Ethnic Civilians Displaced by War in Kachin State, Myanmar* (Bangkok: Fortify Rights, 2018)

Bilateral Aid

1919. *Burma: The Silent Emergency: The Report of a Conference Held in Sydney on 28 May 1993, Convened by the Burma NGO Forum and the Australian Council for Overseas Aid* (Canberra: Australian Council for Overseas Aid, 1993)

1920. Hirono, Ryokichi, *Evaluation of Grant Assistance for Japanese NGO Projects*, Third Party Evaluation Report 2019 (Tokyo: International Development Centre of Japan and Ministry of Foreign Affairs of Japan, March 2020)

1921. Premjai Vungsiriphisal et al. (eds.), *Humanitarian Assistance for Displaced Persons from Myanmar: Royal Thai Government Policy and Donor, INGO, NGO and UN Delivery* (Cham: Springer International, 2014)

1922. *Review of Australia's Humanitarian Assistance to Myanmar: Evaluation Report* (Canberra: Department of Foreign Affairs and Trade, Australian Government, December 2017)

1923. San San Khine, *A Study on South Korea's Aid Policy towards Myanmar* (Riga: Lambert Academic, 2019)

1924. *Strategy for Development Cooperation with Myanmar, 2018–2022* (Stockholm: Ministry of Foreign Affairs, Government Offices of Sweden, 2018)

1925. Watanabe, Chika, *Becoming One: Religion, Development, and Environmentalism in a Japanese NGO in Myanmar* (Honolulu: University of Hawai'i Press, 2019)

FOREIGN RELATIONS

General

1926. Anguelov, Nikolay, et al., *Economic Sanctions vs Soft Power: Lessons from North Korea, Myanmar and the Middle East* (New York: Palgrave Macmillan, 2015)

1927. Basu, Rimli, *The 2011 Myanmar Spring: Implications for India and China* (Germany: Lambert Academic, 2012)

1928. Bray, John, *Burma: The Politics of Constructive Engagement*, Discussion Paper no. 58 (London: Royal Institute of International Affairs, 1995)

1929. Caballero-Anthony, Mely, et al., *Myanmar's Growing Regional Role*, NBR Special Report no. 45 (Seattle: National Bureau of Asian Research, March 2014)

1930. *Challenges to Democratization in Burma: Perspectives on Multilateral and Bilateral Responses* (Stockholm: International Institute for Democracy and Electoral Assistance, 2001)

1931. *Current Realities and Future Possibilities in Burma/Myanmar: Perspectives from Asia* (New York: Asia Society, March 2010)

1932. Dey, Babul (ed.), *The Twenty First Century India-Myanmar Relations* (Kolkata: Institute of Social and Cultural Studies, 2017)

1933. Egreteau, Renaud, and Larry Jagan, *Back to the Old Habits: Isolationism or the Self-preservation of Burma's Military Regime*, Occasional Paper no. 7 (Bangkok: Institute of Research on Contemporary Southeast Asia, 2008)

1934. Egreteau, Renaud, and Larry Jagan, *Soldiers and Diplomacy in Burma: Understanding the Foreign Relations of the Burmese Praetorian State* (Singapore: NUS Press, 2013)

1935. Foley, Matthew, *The Cold War and National Assertion in Southeast Asia: Britain, the United States and Burma, 1948–1962* (London: Routledge, 2010)

1936. Frost, Frank, *Burma/Myanmar: Internal Issues and Regional and International Responses*, Background Note 2009–10 (Canberra: Parliamentary Library, Parliament of the Commonwealth of Australia, 2009)

1937. Guo, Xiaolin, and Johan Alvin, *Engaging with the Issue of Myanmar: A New Perspective*, Policy Paper (Stockholm: Institute for Security and Development Policy, October 2007)

1938. Haacke, Jurgen, *Myanmar's Foreign Policy: Domestic Influences and International Implications*, Adelphi Paper no. 381 (London: International Institute for Strategic Studies, 2006)

1939. Haacke, Jurgen, *Myanmar's Foreign Policy under President U Thein Sein: Non-aligned and Diversified*, Trends in Southeast Asia, 2016 no. 4 (Singapore: ISEAS – Yusof Ishak Institute, 2016)

1940. Hla Min, *The Way I See It: Myanmar and its Evolving Global Role, 1988–2012* (Yangon: MCM Books, 2013)

1941. James, Helen, *Security and Sustainable Development in Myanmar* (Abingdon: Routledge, 2006)

1942. Joint Forces Staff College [Heinold, P.A.], *Burma: Strategic Backwater or Strategic Fulcrum? US Choices in the Bay of Bengal* (Charleston: The author and CreateSpace, 2014)

1943. Jones, Lee, *Societies Under Siege: Exploring How International Economic Sanctions (Do Not) Work* (Oxford: Oxford University Press, 2015)

1944. Kanbawza Win, *Constructive Engagement in the Burmese Context* (Bangkok: CPDSK Publications, 1995)

1945. Lagerkvist, Johan (ed.), *Between Isolation and Internationalization: The State of Burma*, SIIA Papers no. 4 (Stockholm: Swedish Institute of International Affairs, 2008)

1946. Lewis, Su Lin, *Soft Power and Civil Society in Myanmar: A Historical Case Study*, Cultural Relations Collection (London: British Council, 2020)

1947. Li, Chenyang, Chaw Chaw Sein and Xianghui Zhu (eds.), *Myanmar: Reintegrating into the International Community* (Singapore: World Scientific, 2016)

1948. Liang, Chi-shad, *Burma's Foreign Relations: Neutralism in Theory and Practice* (New York: Praeger, 1990)

1949. Lyall, E.E., D.I. Steinberg and Michael McDevitt (eds.), *Strategic Rivalries on the Bay of Bengal: The Burma/Myanmar Nexus*, Conference Report (Washington DC: CNA Corporation, 2001)

1950. Mahmood, Rohana, and Hans-Joachim Esderts, *Myanmar and the Wider Southeast Asia: Proceedings of the International Seminar on ASEAN and the Wider Southeast Asia, Kuala Lumpur, July 11–13, 1990* (Kuala Lumpur: Institute of Strategic and International Studies, 1991)

1951. *History and Activities* (Yangon: Ministry of Foreign Affairs, 2005)

1952. Mitchell, Derek, Chris Milligan and Jessica Davey, *Implementing a Unified Approach to Fragility: Lessons Learned from Burma*, Fragility Study Group, Policy Brief no. 6 (Washington DC: Carnegie Endowment for International Peace, Centre for a New American Security and United States Institute of Peace, October 2016)

1953. *Myanmar: Sanctions, Engagement or Another Way Forward?*, Asia Report no. 78 (Yangon/Brussels: International Crisis Group, 26 April 2004)

1954. Nair, Deepak, *Learning Diplomacy: Cambodia, Laos, Myanmar and Vietnam Diplomats in ASEAN*, Trends in Southeast Asia, 2016 no. 14 (Singapore: ISEAS – Yusof Ishak Institute, 2016)

1955. Pedersen, M.B., *Promoting Human Rights in Burma: A Critique of Western Sanctions Policy* (Lanham: Rowman and Littlefield, 2008)

1956. Roycee, A.T. (ed.), *Burma in Turmoil* (New York: Nova Science, 2008)

1957. Singh, M.P., *Myanmar and its Strategic Dilemmas* (New Delhi: Pentagon Press, 2018)

1958. *The State Visits: The Milestones in History* (Yangon: Ministry of Information, 2003)

1959. Thant Myint U, *Where China Meets India: Burma and the New Crossroads of Asia* (London: Faber and Faber, 2011)

1960. *The United States and Japan: Assisting Myanmar's Development* (Washington DC: Sasakawa Peace Foundation USA, 2015)

1961. Tiwari, A.K., Kyi Thein and P.K. Raju, *Glitter N Gold: Positioning Myanmar in a Globalized World* (New Delhi: Ocean Books P.L., 2005)

Multilateral Relations

1962. Bachoe, Ralph, and Debbie Stothard (eds.), *From Consensus to Controversy: ASEAN's Relationship with Burma's SLORC* (Bangkok: Alternative ASEAN Network on Burma, 1997)

1963. Daw Than Han, *Common Vision: Burma's Regional Outlook*, Occasional Paper (Washington DC: Institute for the Study of Diplomacy, Edmund A. Walsh School of Foreign Service, Georgetown University, 1988)

1964. Devi, T.N. (ed.), *India and Bay of Bengal Community, the BIMSTEC Experiment: Bangladesh-India-Myanmar-Sri Lanka-Thailand Economic Cooperation* (New Delhi: Gyan, 2007)

1965. Htike, M.T., *Challenges ahead on Burma's Road to ICC: Universal Jurisdiction versus National Sovereignty and Other Issues* (US: The author and CreateSpace, 2009)

1966. Magnusson, Anna, and M.B. Pedersen, *A Good Office? Twenty Years of UN Mediation in Myanmar* (New York: International Peace Institute, 2012)

1967. Marchi, Ludovica, [Balossi-Restelli, L.M.] (ed.), *The European Union and Myanmar: Interactions via ASEAN* (London: Routledge, 2020)

1968. McCarthy, Stephen, *Beyond Naypyidaw: Burma and the ASEAN Way to Human Rights*, Regional Outlook no. 20 (Brisbane: Griffith Asia Institute, Griffith University, 2009)

1969. McCarthy, Stephen, *The Black Sheep of the Family: How Burma Defines its Foreign Relations with ASEAN*, Regional Outlook no. 7 (Brisbane: Griffith Asia Institute, Griffith University, 2006)

1970. Mya Than, *Myanmar in ASEAN: Regional Cooperation Experience* (Singapore: Institute of Southeast Asian Studies, 2005)

1971. *Myanmar and Cambodia in a New ASEAN: Dilemmas and Opportunities* (Tokyo: Research Institute for Peace and Security, 2000)

1972. *Myanmar, Cambodia and the Asian Crisis: Challenges of ASEAN Membership* (Tokyo: Research Institute for Peace and Security, 1999)

1973. *Quality of Partnership: Myanmar, ASEAN and the World Community* (Singapore: Asia Dialogue Society, 2003)

1974. Roberts, Christopher, *ASEAN's Myanmar Crisis: Challenges to the Pursuit of a Security Community* (Singapore: Institute of Southeast Asian Studies, 2010)

1975. Sanchez-Cacicedo, Amaia, *Building States, Building Peace: Global and Regional Involvement in Sri Lanka and Myanmar* (Houndmills: Palgrave Macmillan, 2014)

1976. Taneja, Nisha, D.K. Das and Samridhi Bimal (eds.), *Sub-Regional Cooperation between India, Myanmar and Bangladesh* (New Delhi: Academic Foundation, 2018)

1977. *The New ASEANs: Vietnam, Burma, Cambodia and Laos* (Canberra: East Asia Analytical Unit, Department of Foreign Affairs and Trade, 1997)

Bilateral Relations

1978. Abrahamian, Andray, *North Korea and Myanmar: Divergent Paths* (Jefferson: McFarland, 2018)
1979. Arunatilaka, Ahungalle, and Praneeth Abhayasundara, *Golden Links: Myanmar-Sri Lanka, Eternal Cultural and Religious Relations between Two Theravada Buddhist Countries* (Colombo: Godage and Bros., 1999)
1980. Badgley, J.H. (ed.), *Reconciling Burma/Myanmar: Essays on US Relations with Burma*, NBR Analysis, volume 15, no. 1, March 2004 (Seattle: National Bureau of Asian Research, 2004)
1981. Banerjee, Dipankar, *Myanmar and Northeast India* (New Delhi: Delhi Policy Group, 1997)
1982. Banerjee, Reshmi, *Land Conflicts across Frontiers: Contested Spaces in Myanmar and North East India* (Chennai: Notion Press, 2018)
1983. Bhatia, R.K., Vijay Sakhuja and Vikash Ranjan (eds.), *Change in Myanmar* (New Delhi: Shipra Publications and Indian Council of World Affairs, 2014)
1984. Bhatia, Rajiv, *India-Myanmar Relations: Changing Contours* (New Delhi: Routledge, 2015)
1985. Bhattacharya, Swapna, *India-Myanmar Relations, 1886–1948* (Kolkata: K.P. Bagchi, 2007)
1986. *China's Engagement in Myanmar: From Malacca Dilemma to Transition Dilemma*, Myanmar Policy Briefing no. 19 (Amsterdam: Transnational Institute, July 2016)
1987. *China's Myanmar Dilemma*, Asia Report no. 177 (Brussels: International Crisis Group, 14 September 2009)
1988. *China's Myanmar Strategy: Elections, Ethnic Politics and Economics*, Asia Briefing no. 112 (Beijing/Jakarta/Brussels: International Crisis Group, 21 September 2010)
1989. *China's Role in Myanmar's Internal Conflicts*, USIP Senior Study Group Final Report (Washington DC: United States Institute of Peace, 2018)

1990. Clymer, Kenton, *A Delicate Relationship: The United States and Burma/Myanmar since 1945* (Ithaca: Cornell University Press, 2015)
1991. Cole, B.E., et al., *From Pariah to Partner: The US Integrated Reform Mission in Burma, 2009–2015* (Washington DC: United States Institute of Peace, 2017)
1992. *Commerce and Conflict: Navigating Myanmar's China Relationship*, Report no. 305 (Yangon/Brussels: International Crisis Group, 30 March 2020)
1993. *Current Realities and Future Possibilities in Burma/Myanmar: Options for U.S. Policy*, Asia Society Task Force Report (New York: Asia Society, March 2010)
1994. Egreteau, Renaud, *Wooing the Generals: India's New Burma Policy* (Delhi: Author's Press, 2003)
1995. *For Whom Does the US Impose Economic Sanctions on Myanmar? and Other Articles* (Yangon: Ministry of Information, December 2004)
1996. Ghosh, Lipi (ed.), *India-Myanmar Relations: Historical Links to Contemporary Convergences* (New Delhi: Paragon International, 2016)
1997. Gordon, J.F., and Leonard Dixon (eds.), *Burma (Myanmar): Developments and United States's Interests* (New York: Nova, 2012)
1998. Haacke, Jurgen, *Myanmar and the United States: Prospects for a Limited Security Partnership* (Sydney: The United States Studies Centre, University of Sydney, 2015)
1999. Haksar, Nandita, *Rogue Agent: How India's Military Intelligence Betrayed the Burmese Resistance* (New Delhi: Penguin, 2009)
2000. Hanjabam, S.S., et al., *Manipur Myanmar Connections: An Indic Perspective* (New Delhi: Concept, 2021)
2001. Heinemann, T.S., *Weaponising US Economic Engagement in Burma: Operationalising US National Security Economics* (US: The author, January 2018)
2002. Hiebert, Murray, *Whither U.S. Myanmar Policy after the Rohingya Crisis?*, CSIS Southeast Asia Program (Washington DC: Centre for Strategic and International Studies, 2018)
2003. Kanbawza Win, *Comparative Study of the Two Military Juntas (Thailand and Burma)* (Bangkok: CPDSK Publications, 1994)

2004. Kuok, Lynn, *Promoting Peace in Myanmar: U.S. Interests and Role* (Washington DC: Centre for Strategic and International Studies, 2014)

2005. Lintner, Bertil, *The People's Republic of China and Burma: Not Only Pauk-Phaw* (Arlington: Project 2049 Institute, 9 May 2017)

2006. Malik, Preet, *My Myanmar Years: A Diplomat's Account of India's Relations with the Region* (New Delhi: Sage, 2016)

2007. Martin, Michael, *U.S. Restrictions on Relations with Burma*, 6th edition (Washington DC: Congressional Research Service, 22 May 2017)

2008. Martin, Michael, *U.S. Sanctions on Burma* (Washington DC: Congressional Research Service, 19 October 2012)

2009. Maung Aung Myoe, *In the Name of Pauk-Phaw: Myanmar's China Policy since 1948* (Singapore: Institute of Southeast Asian Studies, 2011)

2010. Maung Aung Myoe, *Neither Friend nor Foe: Myanmar's Relations with Thailand since 1988: A View from Yangon*, Monograph no. 1 (Singapore: Institute of Defence and Strategic Studies, Nanyang Technological University, 2002)

2011. Maung Swe Thet, *From Ayeyarwaddy to Chao Phraya* (Yangon: Sein Nyet Chan Thar, 2016)

2012. Niksch, L.A., *Burma-US Relations* (Washington DC: Congressional Research Service, 2 June 2008)

2013. Parker, E.H., *Burma: With Special Reference to Her Relations with China*, reprint of 1893 edition (Delhi: Facsimile Publisher, 2016)

2014. Pavin Chachavalpongpun, *A Plastic Nation: The Curse of Thainess in Thai-Burmese Relations* (Lanham: University Press of America, 2005)

2015. Peng, Nian, *International Pressures, Strategic Preference, and Myanmar's China Policy since 1988* (Singapore: Springer, 2021)

2016. Powell, M.D. (ed.), *Burma: Human Rights, Political Reform Efforts and US Sanctions* (New York: Nova Science, 2013)

2017. Pradhan, S.K., *New Dimensions in Indo-Burmese Relations* (New Delhi: Rajat Publications, 2000)

2018. Saikia, Pahi, and A.B. Ray Chaudhury (eds.), *India and Myanmar Borderlands: Ethnicity, Security and Connectivity* (London: Routledge, 2020)

2019. Seekins, D.M., *Burma and Japan since 1940: From "Co-prosperity" to "Quiet Dialogue"* (Copenhagen: NIAS Press, 2007)

2020. Selth, Andrew, *Burma and North Korea: Conventional Allies or Nuclear Partners?*, Regional Outlook no. 22 (Brisbane: Griffith Asia Institute, Griffith University, 2009)

2021. Selth, Andrew, *Burma's China Connection and the Indian Ocean Region*, Working Paper no. 377 (Canberra: Strategic and Defence Studies Centre, Australian National University, 2003)

2022. Selth, Andrew, *Burma's North Korean Gambit: A Challenge to Regional Security?*, Canberra Papers on Strategy and Defence no. 154 (Canberra: Strategic and Defence Studies Centre, Australian National University, 2004)

2023. Selth, Andrew, *United States Relations with Burma: From Hostility to Hope*, Regional Outlook no. 36 (Brisbane: Griffith Asia Institute, Griffith University, 2012)

2024. Shrestha, H.L., *Nepal-Myanmar Relations* (Kathmandu: Janamaitri Prakashan, 2010)

2025. Steinberg, D.I., and Hongwei Fan, *Modern China-Myanmar Relations: Dilemmas of Mutual Dependence* (Copenhagen: NIAS Press, 2012)

2026. Stromberg, B.E. (ed.), *Bangladesh and Burma: Background and Issues* (New York: Nova Science, 2011)

2027. Sunait Chutintaranond and Than Tun, *On Both Sides of the Tenasserim Range: History of Siamese-Burmese Relations*, Asian Studies Monographs no. 50 (Bangkok: Chulalongkorn University, 1995)

2028. Tea, Billy, *China-Myanmar Relations* (Saarbrucken: Lambert Academic, 2010)

2029. Tea, Billy, *China and Myanmar: Strategic Interests, Strategies and the Road Ahead*, IPCS Research Papers, no. 26 (New Delhi: Institute of Peace and Conflict Studies, September 2010)

2030. Wilasinee Sittisomboon, *The United States Reengagement with Myanmar*, ASP Working Paper no. 1/2013 (Bangkok: Institute of Security and International Studies, Chulalongkorn University, 2013)

2031. Woodard, Garry, *Human Rights in Australian Foreign Policy: With Special Reference to Cambodia, Burma and China*, Occasional Paper no. 6 (Melbourne: Australian Institute of International Affairs and Deakin University, 1991)

2032. Yun Sun, *China and Myanmar's Peace Process*, Special Report no. 401 (Washington DC: United States Institute of Peace, March 2017)

2033. Yun Sun, *Myanmar in US-China Relations*, Issues Brief no. 3 (Washington DC: Stimson Centre, June 2014)

DEFENCE AND NATIONAL SECURITY

General

2034. *Abuse under Orders: The SPDC and DKBA Armies through the Eyes of Their Soldiers* (Thailand: Karen Human Rights Group, 2001)

2035. Aung Naing Oo, *Lessons Learned from Myanmar's Peace Process* (Siem Reap: Centre for Peace and Conflict Studies, 2018)

2036. Aung Naing Oo, *Pathway to Peace: An Insider's Account of the Myanmar Peace Process* (Yangon: Mizzima Media Group, 2016)

2037. Ball, Desmond, and Hazel Lang, *Factionalism and the Ethnic Insurgent Organisations*, Working Paper no. 356 (Canberra: Strategic and Defence Studies Centre, Australian National University, 2001)

2038. Brenner, David, *Rebel Politics: A Political Sociology of Armed Struggle in Myanmar's Borderlands*, Southeast Asia Program Publications (Ithaca: Cornell University Press, 2019)

2039. Brenner, David, *The Development-Insecurity Nexus: Geo-economic Transformations and Violence in Myanmar*, Working Paper no. 1/2017 (London: LSE Global South Unit, London School of Economics and Political Science, 2017)

2040. Buchanan, John, *Militias in Myanmar* (Yangon: Asia Foundation, 2016)

2041. Buchanan, John, *Security Integration Efforts in Myanmar (1945–2010): A Historical Overview*, ISP-Myanmar Briefing Paper (New Haven: Institute for Strategy and Policy – Myanmar, Yale University, February 2019)

2042. Burke, Adam, et al., *The Contested Areas of Myanmar: Subnational Conflict, Aid, and Development* (Yangon: Asia Foundation, 2017)

2043. Callahan, M.P., *Making Enemies: War and State Building in Burma* (Ithaca: Cornell University Press, 2003)

2044. Campagnac, R.G.A., and S.L. Campagnac-Carney, *Burma's Son* (Raleigh: Blue Mist Publications, 2020)

2045. Clarke, S.L., *The Soldier, above All Others, Prays for Peace: An Analysis of the Myanmar Armed Forces in an Era of Transition* (Siem Reap: Centre for Peace and Conflict Studies, 2016)

2046. Fredholm, Michael, *Burma: Ethnicity and Insurgency* (Westport: Praeger, 1993)

2047. Fung, Wai-Ming Terry, *Military Professionalization and Intervention in Thailand and Burma, 1945–1980*, reprint of 1993 edition (US: Open Dissertation Press, 2017)

2048. Guo, Xiaolin, *Myanmar/Burma: Challenges and Perspectives* (Stockholm: Institute for Security and Development Policy, 2008)

2049. Haseman, John, *Burma's Myriad National Security Challenges: The Historical Background and Contemporary Events*, Working Paper no. 50 (Canberra: Australian Defence Studies Centre, 1997)

2050. Hendrickson, Dylan, with Kim Jolliffe, *Security Integration in Conflict-Affected Societies: Considerations for Myanmar* (London: Saferworld, August 2018)

2051. *Indian Helicopters for Myanmar: Making a Mockery of Embargoes?*, AI Index ASA 20/014/2007 (London: Amnesty International UK and Saferworld, July 2007)

2052. *Insignia of Gurkha Units in India and Burma (Para-military, Military Police, Frontier Force and War-Raised Units) up to 1948*, reprint of 2006 edition (Winchester: The Gurkha Museum, 2011)

2053. Jolliffe, Kim, *Democratising Myanmar's Security Sector: Enduring Legacies and a Long Road Ahead* (London: Saferworld, November 2019)

2054. Jolliffe, Kim, John Bainbridge and Ivan Campbell, *Security Integration in Myanmar: Past Experiences and Future Visions* (London: Saferworld, May 2017)

2055. Keenan, Paul, *By Force of Arms: Armed Ethnic Groups in Burma* (New Delhi: Vij Books, 2013)

2056. Kramer, Tom, *Neither War nor Peace: The Future of the Ceasefire Agreements in Burma* (Amsterdam: Transnational Institute, 2009)

2057. Lintner, Bertil, *Why Burma's Peace Efforts Have Failed to End Its Internal Wars*, Peaceworks no. 169 (Washington DC: United States Institute of Peace, October 2020)

2058. *Listening to Voices: Myanmar's Foot Soldiers Speak* (Siem Reap: Centre for Peace and Conflict Studies, 2014)

2059. *Listening to Voices: Perspectives from the Tatmadaw's Rank and File* (Siem Reap: Centre for Peace and Conflict Studies, 2015)

Defence and National Security

2060. Maung Aung Myoe, *Military Doctrine and Strategy in Myanmar: A Historical Perspective*, Working Paper no. 339 (Canberra: Strategic and Defence Studies Centre, Australian National University, 1999)
2061. McCarthy, Gerard, *Military Capitalism in Myanmar: Examining the Origins, Continuities and Evolution of "Khaki Capital"*, Trends in Southeast Asia, 2019 no. 6 (Singapore: ISEAS – Yusof Ishak Institute, 2019)
2062. *Military Ltd: The Company Financing Human Rights Abuses in Myanmar*, AI Index ASA 16/2969/2020 (London: Amnesty International, 2020)
2063. Min Zaw Oo, *Understanding Myanmar's Peace Process: Ceasefire Agreements* (Bern: Swisspeace, 2014)
2064. Montesano, M.J., Terence Chong and Prajak Kongkirati (eds.), *Praetorians, Profiteers or Professionals? Studies on the Militaries of Myanmar and Thailand* (Singapore: ISEAS – Yusof Ishak Institute, 2020)
2065. *Myanmar: Army, National Security and Defence Policy Handbook* (Washington DC: International Business Publications, 2007)
2066. *Myanmar: Army Weapon Systems Handbook: Strategic Information* (Washington DC: International Business Publications, 2015)
2067. *Myanmar: Lack of Security in Counter-insurgency Areas*, AI Index ASA 16/007/2002 (London: Amnesty International, July 2002)
2068. *Myanmar's Military: Back to the Barracks?*, Asia Briefing no. 143 (Yangon/Brussels: International Crisis Group, 22 April 2014)
2069. Ott, M.C., *Burma: A Strategic Perspective* (Washington DC: Institute for National Strategic Studies, National Defence University, 1996)
2070. *Perspectives on the Myanmar Peace Process, 2011–2015* (Basel: Swiss Peace Foundation, 2016)
2071. Raghavan, V.R. (ed.), *Internal Conflicts in Myanmar: Transnational Consequences* (New Delhi: Vij Books, 2011)
2072. *Rebooting Myanmar's Stalled Peace Process*, Asia Report no. 308 (Yangon/Brussels: International Crisis Group, 19 June 2020)
2073. Santoro, David, *Myanmar: A Nonproliferation Success Story*, Special Report (Canberra: Australian Strategic Policy Institute, March 2017)

2074. Selth, Andrew, *"Assisting the Defence of Australia": Australian Defence Contacts with Burma, 1945–1987*, Working Paper no. 218 (Canberra: Strategic and Defence Studies Centre, Australian National University, 1990)

2075. Selth, Andrew, *Burma: A Strategic Perspective*, Working Paper no. 13 (San Francisco: Asia Foundation, 2001)

2076. Selth, Andrew, *Burma and Nuclear Proliferation: Policies and Perceptions*, Regional Outlook no. 12 (Brisbane: Griffith Asia Institute, Griffith University, 2007)

2077. Selth, Andrew, *Burma and the Threat of Invasion: Regime Fantasy or Strategic Reality?*, Regional Outlook no. 17 (Brisbane: Griffith Asia Institute, Griffith University, 2008)

2078. Selth, Andrew, *Burma and Weapons of Mass Destruction*, Working Paper no. 334 (Canberra: Strategic and Defence Studies Centre, Australian National University, 1999)

2079. Selth, Andrew, *Burma and Weapons of Mass Destruction: Not If, But Why, How and What*, Regional Outlook no. 34 (Brisbane: Griffith Asia Institute, Griffith University, 2011)

2080. Selth, Andrew, *Burma's Arms Procurement Programme*, Working Paper no. 289 (Canberra: Strategic and Defence Studies Centre, Australian National University, 1995)

2081. Selth, Andrew, *Burma's Defence Expenditure and Arms Industries*, Working Paper no. 309 (Canberra: Strategic and Defence Studies Centre, Australian National University, 1997)

2082. Selth, Andrew, *Burma's Secret Military Partners*, Canberra Papers on Strategy and Defence no. 136 (Canberra: Strategic and Defence Studies Centre, Australian National University, 2000)

2083. Selth, Andrew, *Burma's Security Forces: Performing, Reforming or Transforming?* Regional Outlook no. 45 (Brisbane: Griffith Asia Institute, Griffith University, 2013)

2084. Selth, Andrew, *Chinese Military Bases in Burma: The Explosion of a Myth*, Regional Outlook no. 10 (Brisbane: Griffith Asia Institute, Griffith University, 2007)

2085. Selth, Andrew, *Civil-Military Relations in Burma: Portents, Predictions and Possibilities*, Regional Outlook no. 25 (Brisbane: Griffith Asia Institute, Griffith University, 2010)

2086. Singh, T.H., *Terrorism in Indo-Myanmar Region* (New Delhi: Akansha, 2016)

2087. Stein, P.T., *The Role of the Military in Myanmar's Political Economy* (US: Progressive Management Publications, 2016)

2088. Steinberg, D.I., *The Military in Myanmar: Longevity and Future Roles?*, Astor Visiting Lecture 2015 (Oxford: University of Oxford, 2015)

2089. Streit, Cornelius, *The Problem of Ethnic Insurgencies and Its Impact on State Building in Myanmar* (Norderstedt: GRIN, 2013)

2090. *The Economic Interests of the Myanmar Military*, Report of the Independent International Fact-Finding Mission on Myanmar, A/HRC/42CRP.3 (Geneva: United Nations Human Rights Council, 12 September 2019)

2091. *The Role of CSOs in the Myanmar Peace Process* (Yangon: Enlightened Myanmar Research Foundation, 2019)

Specific Conflicts and Armed Groups

2092. *A New Dimension of Violence in Myanmar's Rakhine State*, Asia Briefing no. 154 (Yangon/Brussels: International Crisis Group, 24 January 2019)

2093. *A Tentative Peace in Myanmar's Kachin Conflict*, Asia Briefing no. 140 (Yangon/Brussels: International Crisis Group, 12 June 2013)

2094. *All Quiet on the Western Front? The Situation in Chin State and Sagaing Division, Burma* (Chiang Mai: Images Asia, 1998)

2095. *An Avoidable War: Politics and Armed Conflict in Myanmar's Rakhine State*, Asia Report no. 307 (Yangon/Brussels: International Crisis Group, 9 June 2020)

2096. Ball, Desmond, *Security Developments in the Thailand-Burma Borderlands*, Working Paper no. 9 (Sydney: Australian Mekong Resource Centre, University of Sydney, October 2003)

2097. *Final Report of Inquiry Commission on Sectarian Violence in Rakhine State* (Naypyitaw: Republic of the Union of Myanmar, 8 July 2013)

2098. *Fire and Ice: Conflict and Drugs in Myanmar's Shan State*, Asia Report no. 299 (Yangon/Brussels: International Crisis Group, 8 January 2019)

2099. Lintner, Bertil, *The United Wa State Army and Burma's Peace Process*, Peaceworks no. 147 (Washington DC: United States Institute of Peace, April 2019)

2100. MacDonald, Martin, *Kawthoolei Dreams, Malaria Nights: Burma's Civil War* (Bangkok: White Lotus, 1999)

2101. Mathieson, D.S., *The Arakan Army in Myanmar: Deadly Conflict Rises in Rakhine State*, Special Report no. 486 (Washington DC: United States Institute of Peace, November 2020)

2102. McClelland, Mac, *For Us Surrender is Out of the Question: A Story from Burma's Never-Ending war* (Berkeley: Soft Skull, 2010)

2103. *Myanmar: A New Muslim Insurgency in Rakhine State*, Asia Report no. 283 (Yangon/Brussels: International Crisis Group, 15 December 2016)

2104. Smith, Martin, *Arakan (Rakhine State): A Land in Conflict on Myanmar's Western Frontier* (Amsterdam: Transnational Institute, December 2019)

2105. South, Ashley, *Burma's Longest War: Anatomy of the Karen Conflict* (Amsterdam: Transnational Institute, Burma Centre Netherlands, 2011)

2106. South, Ashley, *Mon Nationalism and Civil War in Burma*, 2nd edition (London: RoutledgeCurzon, 2005)

2107. South, Ashley, with Malin Perhult and Nils Carstensen, *Conflict and Survival: Self-Protection in South-east Burma*, Asia Program Paper ASP PP 2010/04 (London: Chatham House, 2010)

2108. *Towards a Peaceful, Fair and Prosperous Future for the People of Rakhine: Final Report of the Advisory Commission on Rakhine State* (Naypyidaw: Advisory Commission on Rakhine State, August 2017)

The Armed Forces

2109. A Tatmadaw Researcher, *A Concise History of Myanmar and the Tatmadaw's Role 1948–1988*, 2 volumes (Yangon: Ministry of Education, 1989 [volume 1] and 1991 [volume 2])

2110. Ball, Desmond, *How the Tatmadaw Talks: The Burmese Army's Radio Systems*, Working Paper no. 388 (Canberra: Strategic and Defence Studies Centre, Australian National University, 2004)

2111. *Brief History of the Myanmar Army* (Yangon: Defence Services Museum and Historical Research Institute, 1999)

2112. Heath, Ian, *Armies of the Nineteenth Century: Asia, Volume 4, Burma and Indochina* (Nottingham: Foundry Books, 2003)

2113. Maung Aung Myoe, *Building the Tatmadaw: Myanmar Armed Forces since 1948* (Singapore: Institute of Southeast Asian Studies, 2009)

2114. Maung Aung Myoe, *Building the Tatmadaw: The Organisational Development of the Armed Forces in Myanmar, 1948–98*, Working Paper no. 327 (Canberra: Strategic and Defence Studies Centre, Australian National University, 1998)

2115. Maung Aung Myoe, *Officer Education and Leadership Training in the Tatmadaw: A Survey*, Working Paper no. 346 (Canberra: Strategic and Defence Studies Centre, Australian National University, 1999)

2116. Maung Aung Myoe, *The Tatmadaw in Myanmar since 1988: An Interim Assessment*, Working Paper no. 342 (Canberra: Strategic and Defence Studies Centre, Australian National University, 1999)

2117. *Myanmar: The Future of the Armed Forces*, Asia Briefing (Bangkok/Brussels: International Crisis Group, 27 September 2002)

2118. *Myanmar Air Force* (Yangon: Ministry of Defence, 1997)

2119. Myomalwin [Myoma Lwin], *The Navy I Love* (Singapore: Partridge Publishing Singapore, 2016)

2120. Selth, Andrew, *Burma's Armed Forces: Looking down the Barrel*, Regional Outlook no. 21 (Brisbane: Griffith Asia Institute, Griffith University, 2009)

2121. Selth, Andrew, *Burma's Armed Forces: Power without Glory* (Norwalk: EastBridge, 2002)

2122. Selth, Andrew, *Burma's Armed Forces under Civilian Rule: A Return to the Past?*, Working Paper no. 2/01 (Washington DC: Technical Advisory Network of Burma, The Burma Fund, 2001)

2123. Selth, Andrew, *Burma's Order of Battle: An Interim Assessment*, Working Paper no. 351 (Canberra: Strategic and Defence Studies Centre, Australian National University, 2000)

2124. Selth, Andrew, *"Strong, Fully Efficient and Modern": Myanmar's New Look Armed Forces*, Regional Outlook no. 49 (Brisbane: Griffith Asia Institute, Griffith University, 2015)

2125. Selth, Andrew, *The Burma Air Force*, Working Paper no. 315 (Canberra: Strategic and Defence Studies Centre, Australian National University, 1997)

2126. Selth, Andrew, *The Burma Navy*, Working Paper no. 313 (Canberra: Strategic and Defence Studies Centre, Australian National University, 1997)

2127. Selth, Andrew, *The Burmese Armed Forces Next Century: Continuity or Change?*, Working Paper no. 338 (Canberra: Strategic and Defence Studies Centre, Australian National University, 1999)

2128. Selth, Andrew, *Transforming the Tatmadaw: The Burmese Armed Forces since 1988*, Canberra Papers on Strategy and Defence no. 113 (Canberra: Strategic and Defence Studies Centre, Australian National University, 1996)

Child Soldiers

2129. *A Dangerous Refuge: Ongoing Child Recruitment by the Kachin Independence Army* (London: Child Soldiers International, 2015)

2130. *Chance for Change: Ending the Recruitment and Use of Child Soldiers in Myanmar* (London: Child Soldiers International, 2013)

2131. Chen, Kai, *Comparative Study of Child Soldiering on Myanmar-China Border: Evolutions, Challenges and Countermeasures* (Singapore: Springer International, 2014)

2132. Malindog, A.R., *Children Playing War Games in Burma* (Riga: Lambert Academic, 2013)

2133. *"My Gun Was as Tall as Me": Child Soldiers in Burma* (New York: Human Rights Watch, 2002)

2134. *No Childhood at All: Child Soldiers in Burma* (Chiang Mai: Images Asia, 1997)

2135. *Sold to be Soldiers: The Recruitment and Use of Child Soldiers in Burma* (New York: Human Rights Watch, 2007)

2136. *Under the Radar: Ongoing Recruitment and Use of Children by the Myanmar Army* (London: Child Soldiers International, 2015)

Landmines

2137. *Humanitarian Impact of Landmines in Burma/Myanmar* (Geneva: Geneva Call and DCA Mine Action, 2011)

2138. *Impact of Landmines in Burma, 2002* (Bangkok: Nonviolence International, 2002)

2139. Oh, Su-Ann, and Veena Nair, *Landmines in Myanmar: No Solution in Sight*, Perspective 2016 no. 54 (Singapore: ISEAS – Yusof Ishak Institute, 29 September 2016)

2140. Selth, Andrew, *Landmines in Burma: The Military Dimension*, Working Paper no. 352 (Canberra: Strategic and Defence Studies Centre, Australian National University, 2000)

2141. Steinemann, Gabriela, *Landmine Victim Assistance, Peace Process, and Mine Action Effectiveness in Kayin State and on the Thai-Myanmar Border* (Bangkok: Institute of Asian Studies, Chulalongkorn University, 2017)

2142. *Uncertain Ground: Landmines in Eastern Burma* (Thailand: Karen Human Rights Group, 2012)

The Police Forces

2143. Hanwong, L.H., *Policing in Colonial Burma* (Chiang Mai: Centre for ASEAN Studies, Chiang Mai University, 2015)

2144. *Myanmar Police Force* (Yangon: Ministry of Home Affairs, 2005)

2145. Selth, Andrew, *Burma's Police Forces: Continuities and Contradictions*, Regional Outlook no. 32 (Brisbane: Griffith Asia Institute, Griffith University, 2011)

2146. Selth, Andrew, *Police Reform in Burma (Myanmar): Aims, Obstacles and Outcomes*, Regional Outlook no. 44 (Brisbane: Griffith Asia Institute, Griffith University, 2013)

2147. Thura Aung and Win Win May, *Public Trust in the Myanmar Police Force: Exploring the Influencing Factors*, edited by Radka Antalikova (Yangon: Peace Leadership and Research Institute, Thabyay Education Foundation, and Friedrich-Ebert-Stiftung, 2019)

Intelligence Issues

2148. Ball, Desmond, *Burma's Military Secrets: Signals Intelligence (SIGINT) from the Second World War to Civil War and Cyber Warfare* (Bangkok: White Lotus, 1998)
2149. Selth, Andrew, *Burma's Intelligence Apparatus*, Working Paper no. 308 (Canberra: Strategic and Defence Studies Centre, Australian National University, 1997)
2150. Selth, Andrew, *Secrets and Power in Myanmar: Intelligence and the Fall of General Khin Nyunt* (Singapore: ISEAS – Yusof Ishak Institute, 2019)

CONSTITUTIONS AND LEGAL ISSUES

Constitutions

2151. *Constitution of the Republic of the Union of Myanmar (2008)* (Naypyidaw: Ministry of Information, 2008) (in English and Burmese)

2152. *Constitutional Seminar Record: Analysis of SLORC's National Convention* (Bangkok: Burma Lawyer's Council, 1995)

2153. Crouch, Melissa, *The Constitution of Myanmar: A Contextual Analysis* (Oxford: Hart, 2019)

2154. *Fundamental Principles and Detailed Basic Principles Adopted by the National Convention in Drafting the State Constitution* (Yangon: Printing and Publishing Enterprise, Ministry of Information, September 2007) (in English and Burmese)

2155. Harding, Andrew (ed.), with Khin Khin Oo, *Constitutionalism and Legal Change in Myanmar* (Oxford: Hart, 2017)

2156. *Impunity Prolonged: Burma and its 2008 Constitution* (New York: International Centre for Transitional Justice, 2009)

2157. *The 1947 Constitution and the Nationalities*, 2 volumes (Yangon: Universities Historical Research Centre, 1999)

2158. *Vote to Nowhere: The May 2008 Constitutional Referendum in Burma* (New York: Human Rights Watch, 2008)

Legal Issues

2159. Aung Than Tun, *Myanmar Laws Digest* (Yangon: Innwa, 2000)

2160. Aye Kyaw, *On the Birth of Modern Family Law in Burma and Thailand*, Southeast Asian Studies Program (SEASP), Teaching and Research Exchange Fellowships, Report no. 4 (Singapore: Institute of Southeast Asian Studies, 1990)

2161. *Burma: Beyond the Law* (London: Article 19, 1996)

2162. Cheesman, Nick, *Opposing the Rule of Law: How Myanmar's Courts Make Law and Order* (Cambridge: Cambridge University Press, 2015)

2163. *Citizenship and Human Rights in Myanmar: Why Law Reform is Urgent and Possible: A Legal Briefing* (Geneva: International Commission of Jurists, June 2019)

2164. Crouch, Melissa (ed.), *The Business of Transition: Law Reform, Development and Economics in Myanmar* (Cambridge: Cambridge University Press, 2017)
2165. Crouch, Melissa, and Tim Lindsey (eds.), *Law, Society and Transition in Myanmar* (Oxford: Hart, 2014)
2166. *Eleven Mon Dhammasat Texts*, collected and translated by Nai Pan Hla, in collaboration with Ryuji Okudaira (Tokyo: Centre for East Asian Cultural Studies for UNESCO, 1992)
2167. *English-Myanmar Law Dictionary* (Rangoon, 2002) (in English and Burmese)
2168. Felbab-Brown, Vanda, *Enabling War and Peace: Drugs, Logs, Gems and Wildlife in Thailand and Burma*, East Asia Policy Paper no. 7 (Washington DC: Brookings Institution, December 2015)
2169. Felbab-Brown, Vanda, *Myanmar Maneuvers: How to Break Political-Criminal Alliances in Contexts of Transition*, Crime-Conflict Nexus Series no. 9 (Tokyo: United Nations Centre for Policy Research, United Nations University, April 2017)
2170. Forchhammer, Emil, *The Jardine Prize: An Essay on the Sources and Development of Burmese Law from the Era of the First Introduction of the Indian Law to the Time of the British Occupation of Pegu*, reprint of 1885 edition (Charleston: Nabu Press, 2010)
2171. Gutter, P., and B.K. Sen, *Burma's State Protection Law: An Analysis of the Broadest Law in the World* (Mae Sot: Burma Lawyer's Council, 2001)
2172. Huxley, Andrew (ed.), *Thai Law, Buddhist Law: Essays on the Legal History of Thailand, Laos and Burma* (Bangkok: White Orchid, 1996)
2173. *Improving Access to Justice through Community Based Dispute Resolution (CBDR) for Housing, Land and Property Disputes in Myanmar* (Geneva: Displacement Solutions and Norwegian Refugee Council, October 2018)
2174. International Tribunal for the Law of the Sea, *Pleadings, Minutes of Public Sittings and Documents 2012: Dispute Concerning Delimitation of the Maritime Boundary between Bangladesh and Myanmar, in the Bay of Bengal*, 2 volumes (Leiden: Martinus Nijhoff, 2014)
2175. Khan, M.A., *The Burmese Way: To Where? Report of a Mission to Myanmar (Burma)* (Geneva: International Commission of Jurists, 1991)

2176. Kyed, H.M. (ed.), *Everyday Justice in Myanmar: Informal Resolutions and State Evasion in a Time of Contested Transition* (Copenhagen: NIAS Press, 2020)

2177. Kyed, H.M., and A.M. Thawnghmung, *The Significance of Everyday Access to Justice in Myanmar's Transition to Democracy*, Trends in Southeast Asia, 2019 no. 9 (Singapore: ISEAS – Yusof Ishak Institute, 2019)

2178. Lammerts, D.C., *Buddhist Law in Burma: A History of Dhammasattha Texts and Jurisprudence, 1250–1850* (Honolulu: University of Hawai'i Press, 2018)

2179. *Land Acquisition Law and Practice in Myanmar: Overview, Gap Analysis with IFC PS1 & PS5 and Scope of Due Diligence Recommendations* (Geneva: Displacement Solutions, May 2015)

2180. *Land Grabbing as an Internationally Wrongful Act: A Legal Roadmap for Ending Land Grabbing and Housing, Land and Property Rights Abuses, Crimes and Impunity in Myanmar* (Geneva: Displacement Solutions, October 2019)

2181. Lutter, H.M., *A Manual of Buddhist Law: Being Sparks' Code of Burmese Law with Notes of All the Rulings on Points of Buddhist Law*, reprint of 1887 edition (New Delhi: Gyan Books, 2019)

2182. Morris, Norval, *The Brothel Boy and Other Parables of the Law* (New York: Oxford University Press, 1994)

2183. *Myanmar: Justice on Trial*, AI Index ASA 16/019/2003 (London: Amnesty International, July 2003)

2184. *Myanmar: Travesties of Justice: Continued Misuse of the Legal System*, AI Index ASA 16/029/2005 (London: Amnesty International, December 2005)

2185. *Myanmar's Plural Justice System*, Policy Brief 2 (Yangon: MyJustice, November 2016)

2186. Okudaira, Ryuji, *Kingship and Law in the Early Konbaung Period of Myanmar (1752–1819): A Study of the Manugye Dhammathat – An Eighteenth Century Major Law Book* (Tokyo: Mekong, 2018)

2187. Simion, Kristina, *Rule of Law Intermediaries: Brokering Influence in Myanmar* (Cambridge: Cambridge University Press, 2021)

2188. Stevens, Jake, *Myanmar Criminal Defence Practice Manual*, edited by U Hla Ko (Taunggyi: International Bridges to Justice, 2018)

2189. Thaing Htun, *A Digest of Myanmar Rulings (Civil) (1948–1969)* (Yangon: The author, 2013)

2190. *The Abridged Law Manual for Sub-Inspectors of Police Burma Issued under the Authority of the Inspector-General of Police, Burma*, reprint of 1926 edition (Farmington Hills: Gale, 2014)

2191. *The Child Law: Rules Related to the Child Law* (Rangoon: Ministry of Social Welfare, Relief and Resettlement, 2002) (in English and Burmese)

2192. *The English-Myanmar Law Dictionary*, revised edition (Yangon, 2015)

2193. *The Rule of Law in Myanmar: Challenges and Prospects* (London: International Bar Association, 2012)

2194. *Towards a Healthier Legal Environment: A Review of Myanmar's Drug Laws* (Amsterdam: Transnational Institute, February 2015)

2195. *Understandings of Justice in Myanmar*, Policy Brief 1 (Yangon: MyJustice, November 2016)

ECONOMY

2196. Abonyi, David, and Masato Abe, *What the ASEAN Economic Community Will Mean for Businesses: A Look at the Case of Myanmar* (Bangkok: UN Economic and Social Commission for Asia and the Pacific, 2016)

2197. Adas, Michael, *The Burma Delta: Economic Development and Social Change on an Asian Rice Frontier, 1852–1941*, reissue of 1974 edition (Madison: University of Wisconsin Press, 2011)

2198. Amakawa, Naoko (ed.), *Industrialization in Late-Developing ASEAN Countries: Cambodia, Laos, Myanmar and Vietnam* (Singapore: NUS Press, 2010)

2199. Aung Tun Thet, *Burmese Entrepreneurship: Creative Response in the Colonial Economy* (Stuttgart: Franz Steiner, 1989)

2200. Bauer, Andrew, Paul Shortell and Lorenzo Delesgues, *Sharing the Wealth: A Roadmap for Distributing Myanmar's Natural Resource Revenues* (London: Natural Resource Governance Institute, 2016)

2201. Bello, Walden, *Paradigm Trap: The Development Establishment's Embrace of Myanmar and How to Break Loose* (Yangon/Amsterdam: Transnational Institute, 2018)

2202. Bhattacharya, Andindya, and Tania Bhattacharya, *ASEAN-India Gas Cooperation: Redefining India's "Look East" Policy with Myanmar*, ERIA Discussion Paper 2014–19 (Jakarta: Economic Research Institute for ASEAN and East Asia, 2014)

2203. Bissinger, Jared, *Myanmar's Economic Governance Actors* (Yangon: Asia Foundation, September 2019)

2204. Blank, Jonah, Shira Efron and Katya Migacheva, *"The Project May Serve the Nation – But What About Us Who Live Here?": Villagers' Views of the Dawei Special Economic Zone, an Internationally Funded Infrastructure Project in Myanmar* (Santa Monica: RAND Corporation, 2019)

2205. Bourdier, Frederic, et al., *From Padi States to Commercial States: Reflections on Identity and the Social Construction Space in the Borderlands of Cambodia, Vietnam, Thailand and Myanmar* (Amsterdam: Amsterdam University Press, 2015)

2206. Brown, Ian, *Burma's Economy in the Twentieth Century* (Cambridge: Cambridge University Press, 2013)

2207. Buchanan, John, Tom Kramer and Kevin Woods, *Developing Disparity: Regional Investment in Burma's Borderlands* (Amsterdam: Transnational Institute and Burma Centre Netherlands, 2013)

2208. Chhor, Heang, et al., *Myanmar's Moment: Unique Opportunities, Major Challenges* (Singapore?: McKinsey Global Institute, 2013)

2209. *China in Burma: The Increasing Investment of Chinese Multinational Corporations in Burma's Hydropower, Oil and Natural Gas, and Mining Sectors* (Washington DC: Earthrights International, 2008)

2210. *Chronicle of National Development: Comparison between Period preceding 1988 and After (up to 31–12–2005)* (Yangon: Ministry of Information, 2006)

2211. Clapp, Priscilla, *The Intersection of Investment and Conflict in Myanmar*, Special Report no. 463 (Washington DC: United States Institute of Peace, February 2020)

2212. Dana, L.P., *When Economies Change Paths: Models of Transition in China, the Central Asian Republics, Myanmar and the Nations of Former Indochine Francais* (New Jersey: World Scientific, 2002)

2213. Foran, Tira, et al., *At the Heart of Myanmar: Exploring Futures of the Ayeyarwady River System. Ayeyarwady Basin Exploratory Scoping Study (BESS), Final Report* (Australia: CSIRO, January 2019)

2214. Fujita, Koichi, Fumiharu Mieno and Ikuko Okamoto (eds.), *The Economic Transition in Myanmar after 1988: Market Economy versus State Control* (Singapore: NUS Press and Kyoto University Press, 2009)

2215. *Globalisation and Development Strategy in Myanmar toward ASEAN Economic Integration: Summary Report of ERIA Capacity Building Program* (Jakarta: Economic Research Institute for ASEAN and East Asia, 2012)

2216. *Growth amidst Uncertainty*, Myanmar Economic Monitor (Yangon: World Bank Group, May 2018)

2217. *Guns, Cronies and Crops: How Military, Political and Business Cronies Conspired to Grab Land in Myanmar* (London: Global Witness, 2015)

2218. *Human Resource Development and Nation Building in Myanmar* (Yangon: Office of Strategic Studies, Ministry of Defence, 1998)

2219. Kanayama, Hisahiro, *Expectations and Reality: The Economic & Political Transition of Vietnam & Myanmar*, IIPS Policy Paper no. 138E (Tokyo: Institute for International Policy Studies, February 1995)

2220. Khin Maung, M.I., *The Myanmar Labour Force: Growth and Change, 1973–1983* (Singapore: Institute of Southeast Asian Studies, 1997)

2221. Khin Maung Kyi, et al., *Economic Development of Burma: A Vision and a Strategy* (Singapore: Singapore University Press, 2000)

2222. Kudo, Toshihiro, Satoru Kumagai and So Umezaki, *Making Myanmar the Star Growth Performer in ASEAN in the Next Decade: A Proposal of Five Growth Strategies*, ERIA Discussion Paper 2013–19 (Jakarta: Economic Research Institute for ASEAN and East Asia, 2013)

2223. Kushnir, Ivan, *Economy of Myanmar* (US: The author, 2019)

2224. Larkin, Stuart, *Establishing Infrastructure Projects: Priorities for Myanmar's Industrial Development — Part I: The Role of the Private Sector*, Trends in Southeast Asia, 2014 no. 9 (Singapore: Institute of Southeast Asian Studies, 2014)

2225. Larkin, Stuart, *Establishing Infrastructure Projects: Priorities for Myanmar's Industrial Development — Part II: The Role of the State*, Trends in Southeast Asia, 2014 no. 10 (Singapore: Institute of Southeast Asian Studies, 2014)

2226. Mya Maung, *The Burma Road to Capitalism* (Westport: Praeger, 1998)

2227. Mya Maung, *The Burma Road to Poverty* (New York: Praeger, 1991)

2228. Mya Maung, *The Burmese Approach to Development: Economic Growth without Democratization*, East-West Centre Working Paper, Economics and Politics Series no. 7 (Honolulu: East-West Centre, 1995)

2229. Mya Maung, *Totalitarianism in Burma: Prospects for Economic Development* (New York: Paragon House, 1992)

2230. Mya Than and J.L.H. Tan (eds.), *Myanmar Dilemmas and Options: The Challenge of Economic Transition in the 1990s* (Singapore: Institute of Southeast Asian Studies, 1990)

2231. *Myanmar: Energy Assessment, Strategy and Road Map* (Manila: Asian Development Bank, 2016)

2232. *Myanmar – Policies for Sustaining Economic Reform*, Report no. 14062-BA (Washington DC: Country Operations Division, World Bank, 16 October 1995)

2233. *Myanmar: The Politics of Economic Reform*, Asia Report no. 231 (Brussels: International Crisis Group, 27 July 2012)

2234. *Myanmar in Transition: Opportunities and Challenges* (Mandaluyong City: Asian Development Bank, 2012)

2235. *Myanmar Trade and Investment Strategy: Paper Presented to the Government and People of Myanmar* (Canberra and Yangon: East Asian Bureau of Economic Research and Myanmar Development Resource Institute, 2015)

2236. Myat Thein, *Economic Development of Myanmar* (Singapore: Institute of Southeast Asian Studies, 2004)

2237. Nurhasim, Moch. (ed.), *Practices of Military Business: Experiences from Indonesia, Burma, Philippines and South Korea* (Jakarta: The Ridep Institute, 2005)

2238. Odaka, Konosuke (ed.), *The Myanmar Economy: Its Past, Present and Prospects* (Tokyo: Springer International, 2016)

2239. *OECD Development Pathways: Multi-dimensional Review of Myanmar*, 3 volumes (Paris: Organisation for Economic Cooperation and Development, 2020)

2240. Oh, Su-Ann, and Philip Andrews-Speed, *Chinese Investment and Myanmar's Shifting Political Landscape*, Trends in Southeast Asia, 2015 no. 16 (Singapore: Institute of Southeast Asian Studies, 2015)

2241. Okamoto, Ikuko, *Economic Disparity in Rural Myanmar: Transformation under Market Liberalization* (Singapore: NUS Press, 2008)

2242. *Opportunities and Pitfalls: Preparing for Burma's Economic Transition* (New York: Open Society Institute, 2006)

2243. Otto, Silke-Susann, et al., *Sustaining Economic Momentum in Myanmar* (Yangon: McKinsey, October 2018)

2244. Perry, P.J., *Myanmar (Burma) since 1962: The Failure of Development* (Aldershot: Ashgate, 2007)

2245. Puusaag, Kamile, David Abonyi and Masato Abe, *Business and Development in Myanmar: A Policy Handbook for Private Sector Development*, Studies in Trade and Investment no. 82 (Bangkok: UN Economic and Social Commission for Asia and the Pacific, 2015)

2246. Rana, P.B., and Naved Hamid, *From Centrally Planned to Market Economies: The Asian Approach, Volume 3: Lao PDR, Myanmar and Viet Nam* (Hong Kong: Oxford University Press, 1996)

2247. *Ready, Aim, Sanction: A Special Report* (Bangkok: ALTSEAN Burma, 2003)

2248. *Resilience amidst Risk*, Myanmar Economic Monitor (Yangon: World Bank Group, December 2019)

2249. Rieffel, Lex, *The Economy of Burma/Myanmar on the Eve of the 2010 Elections*, Special Report no. 241 (Washington DC: United States Institute of Peace, May 2010)

2250. Rieffel, Lex, *The Myanmar Economy: Tough Choices* (Washington DC: Brookings Institution, September 2012)

2251. Saito, Teruko, and Kin Kiong Lee, *Statistics on the Burmese Economy: The 19th and 20th Centuries*, Data Paper Series no. 7 (Singapore: Institute of Southeast Asian Studies, 1999)

2252. *SASEC Vision – Myanmar* (Manila: South Asia Subregional Economic Cooperation Program, Asian Development Bank, 2018)

2253. Soans, Aaron, and Masato Abe, *Bribery, Corruption and Bureaucratic Hassle: Evidence from Myanmar*, ARTNet Working Paper no. 512 (Bangkok: Economic and Social Commission for Asia and the Pacific, 2015)

2254. Steinberg, D.I., *Burma's Road toward Development: Growth and Ideology under Military Rule*, reprint of 1981 edition (London: Routledge, 2020)

2255. Sulistiyanto, Priyambudi, *Thailand, Indonesia and Burma in Comparative Perspective* (Aldershot: Ashgate, 2002)

2256. *Supply and Command: Natural Gas in Western Burma Set to Entrench Military Rule* (Mae Sot: Shwe Gas Movement, 2006)

2257. *Symposium on Socio-economic Factors Contributing to National Consolidation* (Yangon: Office of Strategic Studies, Ministry of Defence, 1997)

2258. Tay, S.S.C., *Shadows across the Golden Land: Myanmar's Opening, Foreign Influence and Investment* (Singapore: World Scientific, 2021)

2259. Thawnghmung, A.M., *Everyday Economic Survival in Myanmar* (Madison: The University of Wisconsin Press, 2019)

2260. Thet Aung Lynn and Mari Oye, *Natural Resources and Subnational Governments in Myanmar* (Yangon: The Asia Foundation, 2014)

2261. Tin Maung Maung Than, *State Dominance in Myanmar: The Political Economy of Industrialisation* (Singapore: Institute of Southeast Asian Studies, 2007)

2262. Tin Maung Maung Than, *The Political Economy of Burma's (Myanmar's) Development Failure, 1948–1988* (Singapore: Institute of Southeast Asian Studies, 1999)

2263. *Tourism Sector Assessment, Strategy and Roadmap for Cambodia, Lao People's Democratic Republic, Myanmar and Vietnam (2016–2018)* (Manila: Asian Development Bank, 2017)

2264. Tyn Myint-U, *Developing Myanmar: Towards a Knowledge-Based Economy* (Deer Park: Linus Publications, 2010)

2265. Van Schendel, Willem, *Three Deltas: Accumulation and Poverty in Rural Burma, Bengal and South India* (Thousand Oaks: Sage Publications, 1991)

2266. Von Hauff, Michael, *Economic and Social Development in Burma/Myanmar: The Relevance of Reforms* (Marburg: Metropolis-Verl, 2007)

2267. Woods, K.M., *The Conflict Resource Economy and Pathways to Peace in Burma*, Peaceworks no. 144 (Washington DC: United States Institute of Peace, November 2018)

INDUSTRY, TRADE AND FINANCE

2268. Augustin, Andreas, *The Strand, Yangon* (Vienna: The Most Famous Hotels in the World, 2013)

2269. Bezbaruah, M.P., *Indo-Myanmar Cross-Border Trade: A Passage to Asian Prosperity or a Dead End?* (Saarbrucken: VDM Verlag Dr Müller 2010)

2270. Bhasin, Balbir, *Business and Investment Opportunities in Emerging Myanmar* (New York: Business Expert Press, 2014)

2271. Combs, Daniel, *Until the World Shatters: Truth, Lies and the Looting of Myanmar* (New York: Melville House, 2021)

2272. Corley, T.A.B., *A History of the Burmah Oil Company, 1924–66*, volume 2 (London: William Heinemann, 1988)

2273. Das, Gurudas, and R.K. Purkayastha (eds.), *Border Trade: North-East India and Neighbouring Countries* (New Delhi: Akansha, 2000)

2274. Das, Gurudas, N.B. Singh and C.J. Thomas (eds.), *Indo-Myanmar Border Trade: Status, Problems and Potentials* (New Delhi: Akansha, 2005)

2275. De, Prabir, and Ajitava Raychaudhuri (eds.), *Myanmar's Integration with the World: Challenges and Policy Options* (Singapore: Springer, 2017)

2276. *"Doing Business in Myanmar" under the Myanmar Companies Act: Provisions Relative to a Foreign Company*, 2nd edition (Yangon: Government of the Union of Myanmar, Ministry of Trade, 1990)

2277. Freeman, N.J., *Whither Myanmar's Garment Sector?*, Trends in Southeast Asia, 2019 no. 7 (Singapore: ISEAS – Yusof Ishak Institute, 2019)

2278. *Guide to Foreign Investment in Myanmar*, Parts 1 and 2 (Yangon: Union of Myanmar Foreign Investment Commission, 1990)

2279. *Investing in Myanmar* (Yangon: Union of Myanmar Investment Commission, 1995)

2280. Khin Maung Nyunt, *Market Research of Principal Exports and Imports of Burma with Special Reference to Thailand (1970/71 to 1985/86)*, Institute of Asian Studies Monograph no. 40 (Bangkok: Chulalongkorn University, 1988)

2281. Khundrakpam, Padmabati, *Experiences of Manipur and Indo-Myanmar Border Trade: A Relook* (New Delhi: Akansha, 2016)

2282. Kiryu, Minoru (ed.), *Industrial Development and Reforms in Myanmar: ASEAN and Japanese Perspectives* (Bangkok: White Lotus Press, 1999)

2283. Kubo, Koji, *Myanmar's Foreign Exchange Market: Controls, Reforms, and Informal Market* (Singapore: Springer, 2018)

2284. Longmuir, M.V., *Oil in Burma: The Extraction of 'Earth-Oil' to 1914* (Bangkok: White Lotus, 2001)

2285. Longmuir, M.V., *The Money Trail: Burmese Currencies in Crisis, 1937–1947* (DeKalb: Centre for Southeast Asian Studies, Northern Illinois University, 2002)

2286. Mya Than, *Myanmar's External Trade: An Overview in the Southeast Asian Context* (Singapore: Institute of Southeast Asian Studies, 1992)

2287. Mya Than and Myat Thein (eds.), *Financial Resources for Development in Myanmar: Lessons from Asia* (Singapore: Institute of Southeast Asian Studies, 2000)

2288. *Myanmar: Open for Business? Corporate Crime and Abuses at Myanmar Copper Mine*, AI Index ASA 16/0003/2015 (London: Amnesty International, February 2015)

2289. Nichols, J.P., *Puk Time: Stories and Business Lessons on How to Make it Happen in Myanmar* (Hong Kong: Asia Business Books, 2013)

2290. Nixon, Hamish, and Cindy Joelene, *Fiscal Decentralization in Myanmar: Towards a Roadmap for Reform* (Yangon: The Asia Foundation, 2014)

2291. *OECD Investment Policy Reviews: Myanmar 2020* (Paris: Organisation for Economic Cooperation and Development, 2013–2015)

2292. O'Kane, Michael, *Doing Business in Myanmar* (Santa Monica: Andalus, 2018)

2293. Pagan U Khin Maung Gyi, *Memoirs of the Oil Industry in Burma, 905 AD – 1980 AD: Technological, Structural, Social Aspects Coupled with Contemporary Historical, Economics and Cultural Backgrounds* (Rangoon: The author, 1989)

2294. *Public Financial Management Systems – Myanmar: Key Elements from a Financial Management Perspective* (Manila: Asian Development Bank, May 2020)

2295. Sai Seng Sai, *An Industrial Policy of Myanmar under East Asian Economic Integration: Policy Implications for Myanmar* (Saarbrucken: Lambert Academic, 2017)

2296. Sim, H.C.M., *Myanmar on My Mind: A Guide to Living and Doing Business in Myanmar* (Singapore: Times Books, 2001)
2297. Soans, Aaron, and Masato Abe, *Myanmar Business Survey: Data Analysis and Policy Implications* (Bangkok: United Nations Economic and Social Commission for Asia and the Pacific, and the Mekong Institute, 2015)
2298. Tan, Teck Meng, et al., *Business Opportunities in Myanmar* (Singapore: Nanyang Technological University and Prentice Hall, 1996)
2299. Taneja, Nisha, D.K. Das and Samridhi Bimal (eds.), *Sub-regional Cooperation between India, Myanmar and Bangladesh: Trade, Investment and Connectivity* (New Delhi: Academic Foundation, 2018)
2300. Than Nyun and Dalchoong Kim, *Myanmar-Korea Economic Cooperation* (Seoul: Institute of East and West Studies, Yonsei University, 1992)
2301. Thein Swe and Paul Chambers, *Cashing In across the Golden Triangle: Thailand's Northern Border Trade with China, Laos, and Myanmar* (Chiang Mai: Mekong Press, 2011)
2302. *Total Denial: A Report on the Yadana Pipeline Project in Burma* (Washington DC?: Earth Rights International and Southeast Asian Information Network, 1996)
2303. Turnell, Sean, *A Proposal for a Currency Board in a Democratic Burma*, Macquarie Economics Research Paper no. 6/1999 (Sydney: Department of Economics, Macquarie University, August 1999)
2304. Turnell, Sean, *Central Banking at the Periphery of the British Empire: Colonial Burma, 1886–1937*, Macquarie Economics Research Paper no. 11/2005 (Sydney: Department of Economics, Macquarie University, July 2005)
2305. Turnell, Sean, *Fiery Dragons: Banks, Moneylenders and Microfinance in Burma* (Copenhagen: NIAS Press, 2009)
2306. Turnell, Sean, *Reforming the Banking System in Burma: A Survey of the Problems and Possibilities*, Technical Advisory Network of Burma, Working Paper no. 7 (Washington DC: The Burma Fund, 2002)
2307. Turnell, Sean, *The Chettiars in Burma*, Macquarie Economics Research Paper no. 12/2005 (Sydney: Department of Economics, Macquarie University, July 2005)

2308. Turnell, Sean, *The Rise and Fall of Cooperative Credit in Colonial Burma*, Macquarie Economics Research Paper no. 9/2005 (Sydney: Department of Economics, Macquarie University, June 2005)

2309. Vickery, Alison, *Rent Extraction by Burma's Military Regime: A Link between State Ownership, Military Expenditure and Human Rights Abuses*, Macquarie Economics Research Paper no. 1/1999 (Sydney: Department of Economics, Macquarie University, January 1999)

2310. Wong, Yvonne, *Money Matters in Myanmar: Banking and Finance Law and Practice* (Sydney: Lexus Nexus, 2016)

TRANSPORT AND COMMUNICATIONS

2311. Charney, M.W., *Imperial Military Transportation in British Asia: Burma 1941–1942* (London: Bloomsbury Academic, 2019)

2312. Florento, Hector, and M.I. Corpuz, *Myanmar: The Key Link between South Asia and Southeast Asia*, ADBI Working Paper no. 506 (Tokyo: Asian Development Bank Institute, December 2014)

2313. Haws, Duncan, *Merchant Fleets: British India S.N. Co.* (Pembroke: TCL Publications, 1988)

2314. Haws, Duncan, *Merchant Fleets: The Burma Boats: Henderson and Bibby* (Pembroke: TCL Publications, 1996)

2315. Heimburger, D.J., *Garratt Locomotives* (US: Heimburger House, 2013)

2316. *Infrastructure in Myanmar* (Yangon: KPMG Advisory [Myanmar], 2013)

2317. McIntyre-Brown, Arabella, *Time and Tide: 200 Years of the Bibby Line Group, 1807–2007* (Liverpool: Capsica, 2007)

2318. *Myanmar ICT Sector-Wide Impact Assessment* (Yangon, London and Copenhagen: Myanmar Centre for Responsible Business, Institute for Human Rights and Business, and Danish Institute for Human Rights, 2015)

2319. *Myanmar: Transport Sector Initial Assessment* (Manila: Asian Development Bank: 2012)

2320. *Myanmar Transport Sector Policy Note: Railways* (Manila: Asian Development Bank, 2016)

2321. *Myanmar Transport Sector Policy Note: River Transport* (Manila: Asian Development Bank, 2016)

2322. *Myanmar Transport Sector Policy Note: Rural Roads and Access* (Manila: Asian Development Bank, 2016)

2323. *Myanmar Transport Sector Policy Note: Trunk Roads* (Manila: Asian Development Bank, 2016)

2324. *Myanmar Transport Sector Policy Note: Urban Transport* (Manila: Asian Development Bank, 2016)

2325. Nam, Kee-Yung, M.R Cham and P.R. Halili, *Developing Myanmar's Information and Communication Technology Sector towards Inclusive Growth*, ADB Economics Working Paper no. 462 (Manila: Asian Development Bank, November 2015)

2326. Rastorfer, Jean-Marc, *By Rail to Loikaw? Paper Presented at Colloquium on Burma Studies, Northern Illinois University, Centre for Burma Studies, 1 November 1992* (San Marino: Editrice Hoya, 1994)

2327. *Reforming Telecommunications in Burma: Human Rights and Responsible Investment in Mobile and the Internet* (New York: Human Rights Watch, 2013)

2328. Sechler, R.P., *Electric Traction in the Burmese Capital: A History of the Rangoon Electric Tramway and Supply Company Limited* (Cypress: The author, 2000)

2329. Strachan, Paul, *Pandaw: The Irrawaddy Flotilla Company and the Rivers of Burma* (Kenmore: Kiscadale, 2003)

2330. Watson, Nigel, *The Bibby Line 1807–1990: A Story of Wars, Booms and Slumps* (London: James and James, 1990)

AGRICULTURE, FORESTRY AND FISHERIES

2331. *A Choice for China: Ending the Destruction of Burma's Northern Frontier Forests* (Washington DC: Global Witness, 2005)

2332. *A Conflict of Interests: The Uncertain Future of Burma's Forests* (London: Global Witness, October 2003)

2333. Brown, Ian, *A Colonial Economy in Crisis: Burma's Rice Cultivators and the World Depression of the 1930s* (London: RoutledgeCurzon, 2005)

2334. Brunner, Jake, Kirk Talbott and Chantal Elkin, *Logging Burma's Frontier Forests: Resources and the Regime* (Washington DC: World Resources Institute, 1998)

2335. Bryant, R.L., *The Political Ecology of Forestry in Burma* (London: Hurst, 1997)

2336. Day, Francis, *Report on the Sea Fish and Fisheries of India and Burma*, reprint of 1873 edition (US: Hardpress, 2013)

2337. Durrenberger, E.P., and Nicola Tannenbaum, *Analytical Perspectives on Shan Agriculture and Village Economics*, Yale Center for International and Area Studies, Monograph Series no. 37 (New Haven: Yale University, 1990)

2338. Fujita, Koichi, and Ikuko Okamoto, *Agricultural Policies and Development of Myanmar's Agricultural Sector* (Tokyo: Institute of Developing Economies, Japan External Trade Organization, 2006)

2339. *Guns, Cronies and Crops: How Military, Political and Business Cronies Conspired to Grab Land in Myanmar* (London: Global Witness, March 2015)

2340. Khin Maung Soe et al., *Myanmar Inland Fisheries and Aquaculture: A Decade in Review* (Canberra: Australian Centre for International Agricultural Research, 2020)

2341. Khin Maung Soe, *Trends of Development of Myanmar Fisheries: With References to Japanese Experiences*, Visiting Research Fellow Monograph Series no. 433 (Tokyo: Institute of Developing Economies, Japan External Trade Organization, February 2008)

2342. Khin Win, *A Century of Rice Improvement in Burma* (Manila: International Rice Research Institute, 1991)

2343. Nay Myo Aung, *Agricultural Efficiency of Rice Farmers in Myanmar: A Case Study in Selected Areas*, IDE Discussion Paper no. 306 (Tokyo: Institute for Developing Economies, Japan External Trade Organisation, September 2011)

2344. Nyein Set Lin, *Sesame in Myanmar*, translated by U Tin Maung (Nay Pyi Taw: Department of Agricultural Planning, Ministry of Agriculture and Irrigation, 2007?)

2345. San Thein, *Agro-based Industries in Myanmar: The Long Road to Industrialisation*, Visiting Research Fellow Monograph Series no. 414 (Tokyo: Institute of Developing Economies, Japan External Trade Organisation, March 2006)

2346. Tin Htut Oo, *Myanmar* (Los Banos: Southeast Asian Regional Centre for Graduate Study and Research in Agriculture, 2006)

2347. Wai, Wing-Kun Henry, *Rice Economy of Burma and Thailand: A Comparative Study* (US: Open Dissertation Press, 2017)

LITERATURE

Criticism and Commentary

2348. Allott, Anna, *Inked Over, Ripped Out: Burmese Storytellers and the Censors* (New York: PEN American Centre, 1993)

2349. Ampika Rattanapitak (ed.), *A Collection of Papers on Myanmar Language and Literature* (Chiang Mai: Myanmar Centre, Chiang Mai University, 2017)

2350. d'Hubert, Thibaut, *In the Shade of the Golden Palace: Alaol and Middle Bengali Poetics in Arakan* (Oxford: Oxford University Press, 2018)

2351. Herbert, P.M., *The Art of the Painted Book in Burma* (Gartmore: Kiscadale, 1994)

2352. Institute of Asian Studies, Chulalongkorn University, Bangkok, and Universities Historical Research Centre, Yangon, *Comparative Studies on Literature and History of Thailand and Myanmar*, IAS Monographs no. 52 (Bangkok: Institute of Asian Studies, October 1997)

2353. Kanwar, Amar, *The Torn First Pages* (Cologne: Verlag der Buchhandlung Walther Konig, 2008)

2354. Khin Maung Nyunt, *An Outline History of Myanmar Literature (Pagan Period to Kon-Baung Period)*, revised edition (Yangon: Printing and Publishing Enterprise, Ministry of Information, 1999)

2355. Mayo, I.F., *Old Stories and Sayings from India, Ceylon, Burma, and the Near East*, reprint of 1912 edition (Washington DC: Westphalia Press, 2019)

2356. Myint Zan, *Selected Essays on International Law, Philosophy, Science and Literature* (Yangon: Nay Myo Sarpatheda Literary House, 2012)

2357. Myo Thant, *Biographical Dictionary of Twentieth Century Myanmar Writers* (Yangon: Myanmar Book Centre, 2017)

2358. Rooney, D.F. (ed.), *The Thiri Rama: Finding Ramayana in Myanmar* (London: Routledge, 2017)

2359. Sendker, Jan-Philipp, *The Long Path to Wisdom: Tales from Burma*, translated by Lisa Liesener and Kevin Wiliarty (Edinburgh: Polygon, 2018)

2360. Smyth, David (ed.), *The Canon in Southeast Asian Literatures: Literatures of Burma, Cambodia, Indonesia, Laos, Malaysia, the Philippines, Thailand and Vietnam* (Richmond: Curzon, 2000)

2361. Soe Marlar Lwin, *Narrative Structures in Burmese Folk Tales* (New York: Cambria Press, 2010)

2362. Stewart, Lucas, *The People Elsewhere: Unbound Journeys with the Storytellers of Myanmar* (Hawthorn: Penguin Australia, 2016)

2363. Thaw Kaung, *From the Librarian's Window: Views of Library and Manuscript Studies and Myanmar Literature* (Yangon: Myanmar Book Centre, 2008)

2364. Wiles, Ellen, *Saffron Shadows and Salvaged Scripts: Literary Life in Myanmar under Censorship and in Transition* (New York: Columbia University Press, 2015)

2365. Zollner, Hans-Bernd (ed.), *Material on Three Books on "World War and Burma"*, Working Paper no. 10:8 (Passau: Universitat Passau, 2008)

2366. Zollner, Hans-Bernd (ed.), *Material on Three Novels: Ba Thoung, "Pantha Ma Sa U" and "Oil", Dagon Taya, "May"*, Working Paper no. 10:19 (Passau: Universitat Passau, 2010)

2367. Zollner, Hans-Bernd (ed.), *The Nagani Book Club – An Introduction*, Working Paper no. 10:1 (Passau: Universitat Passau, 2006)

Myanmar (Burmese) Literature

2368. Abbott, Gerry, and Khin Thant Han, *The Folk Tales of Burma: An Introduction* (Leiden: Brill, 2000)

2369. Ai Pun, *49 Lahu Stories*, translated by Angela Pun and P.W. Lewis (Bangkok: White Lotus, 2002)

2370. Ashin Yevata, *Revolution of the Monks* (France?: The author, 2015)

2371. Aung Thin, Michelle, *Crossing the Farak River* (Toronto: Annik Press, 2020)

2372. Aung Thin, Michelle, *Hasina: Through My Eyes*, edited by Lyn White (Sydney: Allen and Unwin, 2019)

2373. *Burmese Manuscripts*, compiled by Heinz Bechert, Daw Khin Khin Su and Daw Tin Tin Myint, assisted by Heinz Braun and Anne Peters, 4 volumes (Stuttgart: Franz Steiner, 1978–1996)

2374. *Collecting the Water While It Rains: Fiction, Poetry and Memoir from Myanmar* (Yangon: International Friendship Group, 2016)
2375. Fielding-Hall, H., *Burmese Palace Tales*, reprint of 1900 edition (Bangkok: White Lotus, 1997)
2376. Froese, Deborah, *The Wise Washerman: A Folktale from Burma*, illustrated by Wang Kui (New York: Hyperion, 1996)
2377. Gray, James, *Ancient Proverbs and Maxims from Burmese Sources: Or the Niti Literature of Burma*, reprint of 1886 edition (London: Routledge, 2001)
2378. Gurung, Madhu, *Burmese Folktales: Stories from Forgotten Kingdoms* (Delhi: Scholastic India, 2012)
2379. Hla Gyaw, James, *Maung Yin Maung and Ma Me Ma*, translated by Tun Aung Chain (Yangon: MKS, 2014)
2380. Hla Thamein, *Myanmar Idioms* (Yangon, 2005)
2381. Ivanoff, Jacques, *Rings of Coral: Moken Folktales*, translated by Francine Nicolle (Bangkok: White Lotus Press, 2001)
2382. Journal Kyaw Ma Ma Lay, *Blood Bond*, translated by Than Than Win (Honolulu: Centre for Southeast Asian Studies, University of Hawai'i, 2004)
2383. Kantar, Sally (ed.), *The Dog Holding the Moon in His Mouth and Other Folk Tales from Shan State, by the Students of SSSNY's 9th Social Justice Education Program* (Chiang Mai: School for Shan State Nationalities Youth, 2009)
2384. Khet Mar, *Night Birds and Other Stories*, translated by Maung Maung Myint (Pittsburgh: Sampsonia Way, 2014)
2385. Khin Hnin Yu, *Stories from Her Heart*, translated by Ma Thanegi (Yangon: Lettwe Baw Books, 2009)
2386. Khin Swe Oo, *Beloved Country*, reprint of 1961 edition, translated by Aung Myo Min (Naypyitaw: Min Myo Aung Sarpay, 2015)
2387. Ko Ko Thett, *The Burden of Being Burmese* (Brookline: Zephyr Press, 2015)
2388. Krajanek, S.I., *Don't Make a Sign on the Boat: Stories from Burma* (US: CreateSpace, 2014)
2389. Kyaw Maung Maung Nyunt, *Oh! Ayeyarwady* (Yangon: Thwe Thwe Than, 2004)

2390. Kyawt Maung Maung Nyunt, *Careless Talk and Other Memories of a Myanmar Village* (Yangon: Thwe Thwe Than, 2000)

2391. Kyawt Maung Maung Nyunt, *Myanmar Thoughts* (Yangon: Thwe Thwe Than, 2003)

2392. Law-Yone, Wendy, *Irrawaddy Tango* (New York: Alfred Knopf, 1993)

2393. Law-Yone, Wendy, *The Coffin Tree*, reprint of 1983 edition (Evanston: Northwestern University Press, 2003)

2394. Law-Yone, Wendy, *The Road to Wanting* (London: Chatto and Windus, 2010)

2395. Ledgard, Edna, *The Snake Prince and Other Stories: Burmese Folk Tales* (New York: Interlink, 2007)

2396. Lu Zoe [San Lwin], *Myanmar Proverbs* (Bangkok: Ava House, 1996)

2397. Ludu U Hla, *The Caged Ones*, illustrated by U Wa Thone (London: Orchid Press, 2006)

2398. Ma Ma Lay, *Not Out of Hate: A Novel of Burma*, translated by Margaret Aung Thwin, Ohio University Monographs in International Studies, Southeast Asia Series no. 88 (Athens: Ohio University, 1991)

2399. Maung Htin Aung, *Burmese Monk's Tales*, reprint of 1966 edition (Onalaska: Pariyatti Press, 2016)

2400. Maung Swe Tint, *Being Eaten Alive on a Cool, Pleasant Winter's Morning*, translated by Nance Cunningham (Yangon: Pansodan, 2012)

2401. Moe, Julien, *Beyond Burma* (US: CreateSpace, 2017)

2402. Mon Mon Myat (ed.), *Heartless Forest: An Anthology of Burmese Women Writers*, translated by Nance Cunningham (Yangon: Pansodan Books, 2013)

2403. Myint Swe, James, *Cannon Soldiers of Burma* (Canada: The author, 2014)

2404. *Naga and Pa-O Folktales* (Yangon: Educational Endowment, 2016)

2405. Nu Nu Yi, *Smile as They Bow*, translated by Alfred Birnbaum and Thi Thi Aye (New York: Hyperion, 2008)

2406. Prabhakar, C.P. (ed.), *Selected Burmese Short Stories* (New Delhi: Irrawaddy Publications, 1998)

2407. Pruitt, William (ed.), *Illustrations of Myanmar: Manuscript Treasures of the Musee Guimet* (Chiang Mai: Silkworm Books, 2019)

2408. Pu Loi Hom, *Shan Legends* (Yangon: Myanmar Book Centre, 2014)

2409. Rahman, R.R., *The Unexpected Friend: A Rohingya Children's Story* (US: Guba, 2020)

2410. Sai Wai Lwin Moe, *Golden Boy and Other Stories from Burma* (Bangkok: White Lotus, 2001)

2411. San Lin Tun, *Reading a George Orwell Novel in a Myanmar Teashop and Other Essays* (Myanmar: The author, 2016)

2412. San Shwe Baw, *Enslaved by English* (Yangon: Pann Wei Wei Sarpay, 2013)

2413. *Selected Myanmar Short Stories*, translated by Ma Thanegi (Yangon: Unity, 2009)

2414. *Shan Folklore Stories from the Hill and Water Country of Burma*, compiled by W.C. Griggs (US: Abela, 2015)

2415. *Shan Thammasat Manuscripts*, collected and translated with an introduction by Sai Kam Mong (Tokyo: Mekong, 2012)

2416. Spencer, Lynette (ed.), *Folk and Fairy Tales from Burma (Myanmar)* (Sandhurst: Abela, 2014)

2417. Stewart, Lucas, and Alfred Birnbaum (eds.), *Hidden Words, Hidden Worlds: Contemporary Short Stories from Myanmar* (London: British Council, 2017)

2418. Suragamika, *The Roadmap* (Chiang Mai: Silkworm Books, 2011)

2419. *Shan Manuscripts, Part 1*, compiled and edited by B.J. Terwiel with the assistance of Chaichuen Khamdaengyodtai (Stuttgart: Franz Steiner, 2003)

2420. *The Journey of the Kayah People*, illustrated by Lat Swan Htan (Yangon: Banyan Tree Reading Centre, 2014)

2421. Thein Pe Myint, *Sweet and Sour: Burmese Short Stories*, translated by Usha Narayanan (New Delhi: Sterling, 1999)

2422. Thet Tun, *The Contemporary Myanmar and Selected Writings of Retired Ambassador U Thet Tun* (Yangon: IT Myanmar Business Magazine, 2002) (in English and Burmese)

2423. Troughton, Joanna, *Make-Believe Tales: A Folk Tale from Burma* (New York: Bedrick, 1991)

2424. *Voices from the Jungle: Burmese Youth in Translation* (Tokyo: Centre for Christian Response to Asian Issues, 1989)

2425. Yang, Bo, *The Alien Realm*, translation of the 1961 edition by J.J. Yu (London: Janus, 1996)

2426. Zaw Gyi and Alan Nichols (eds.), *The Words Cry Out: New Writing by Burmese in Exile* (Prahran: Australia-Burma Support Group [Prahran] 1984)

Foreign Literature

2427. Abrahamson, K.L., *A Death in Passing* (Vancouver: Twisted Root, 2017)

2428. Abrahamson, K.L., *Death by Effigy* (UK: Guardbridge Books, 2017)

2429. Abrahamson, K.L., *Death in Umber* (Vancouver: Twisted Root, 2018)

2430. Adirex, Paul, *Until the Karma Ends: A Plot to Destroy Burma* (Bangkok: Aries Books, 1996)

2431. Aebi, Ernst, *A Short Stint in Burma: A Thriller* (Lincoln: iUniverse, 2005)

2432. Anderson, Liz, *Under Running Laughter: Burma – The Hidden Heart* (Leicester: Matador, 2009)

2433. Archer, Geoffrey, *The Burma Legacy* (London: Century, 2002)

2434. Aung Thin, Michelle, *The Monsoon Bride* (Melbourne: Text, 2011)

2435. Baillie, Allan, *Rebel*, illustrated by Di Wu (New York: Ticknor and Fields, 1994)

2436. Bandele, Biyi, *Burma Boy* (Lagos: Farafina, 2007)

2437. Bandele, Biyi, *The King's Rifle* (New York: Harper Paperbacks, 2009)

2438. Barden, Stanley, *Burma Ruby* (Penzance: United Writers Publications, 1997)

2439. Barden, Stanley, *The Golden Rock of Kyaik-Tiyo* (Penzance: United Writers Publications, 1997)

2440. Block, Lawrence, *Tanner on Ice* (New York: Harper, 1998)

2441. Bower, Robin, *Beyond Home: A Daughter's Journey* (US: RB, 2014)

2442. Brandsma, David, *The Silent Screams from Myanmar* (Netherlands?: ClusterEffect, 2013)

2443. Browne, Peter, *The Irrawaddy: River of Evil* (Buddina: Joshua Books, 2008)
2444. Carter, Nick [Canon, Jack], *Killmaster 240: Rangoon Man* (New York: Jove, 1988)
2445. Chapman, Alison, *The Burmese Spy Adventure Book* (London: Austin Macauley, 2018)
2446. Connelly, Karen, *The Lizard Cage* (London: Harvill, 2007)
2447. Craig, Charmaine, *Miss Burma* (New York: Grove Press, 2017)
2448. Cruickshanks, Lucy, *The Road to Rangoon* (London: Heron Books, 2015)
2449. Dahlberg, Keith, *Flame Tree: A Novel of Modern Burma* (Bangkok: Orchid Press, 2004)
2450. Davidson, Toni, *My Gun Was as Tall as Me* (Glasgow: Freight Books, 2012)
2451. De Hetrick, A.F.V., *The True Adventures of Brodie the Burmese Dog*, illustrated by Jenny Lyn Young (US: Trafford, 2014)
2452. Denaro, Jason, *A Passage to Burma* (Lakewood: Avid Readers, 2008)
2453. Denham, A.V., *Unintended Consequences* (London: Robert Hale, 2007)
2454. Freer, A.F., *Nemesis from Burma: The Bamboo Murders* (Durham: Pentland Press, 2000)
2455. Gaynor, Maurice, *Dark Moon over Burma* (Bloomington: AuthorHouse, 2018)
2456. Ghosh, Amitav, *The Glass Palace* (London: HarperCollins, 2000)
2457. Greenberg, Cynthia, *Burmese Jade: A Mystery* (London: The author and Lulu Press, 2012)
2458. Hantover, Jeffrey, *The Jewel Trader of Pegu* (New York: William Morrow, 2008)
2459. Harvey, Caroline [Joanna Trollope], *City of Gems* (London: Corgi, 1999)
2460. Hughes, Robert, *Mandalay Memories: Musings on Myanmar* (Bangkok: Mark Standen, 2003)
2461. Kasai, Yasuyuki, *Dragon of the Mangroves* (New York: iUniverse, 2006)
2462. Kenmore, F.J., *Southeast of Mandalay* (New York: Pinnacle, 1990)

2463. King, Dedie, *I See the Sun in Myanmar (Burma)*, illustrations by Judith Inglese (Hardwick: Satya House, 2013)
2464. Kline, O.A., *Tam, Son of the Tiger* (US: Pulpville Press, 2009)
2465. Laskin, P.M., *Why No Goodbye?* (Fredonia: Leapfrog Press, 2019)
2466. Lawrence, Eugene, *The Lacquered Curtain of Burma* (New Delhi: Niyogi Books, 2019)
2467. Le Roy, Patricia, *The Glass Palace Chronicle* (London: Piatkus, 2000)
2468. Leonard, Raymond, *Mandalay: A Ruby for the Queen* (US: CreateSpace, 2012)
2469. Lovett, Anne, *Rubies from Burma* (US: The author, 2016)
2470. Manieri, R.A., *The Myanmar Maneuver* (US: Authorhouse, 2006)
2471. Mason, David, *The Piano Tuner* (New York: Alfred Knopf, 2002)
2472. Metro, Rosalie, *Have Fun in Burma* (Dekalb: Northern Illinois University Press, 2018)
2473. Moore, C.G., *Missing in Rangoon: A Vincent Calvino P.I. Novel* (Bangkok: Heaven Lake Press, 2013)
2474. Moore, H.C., *Britons at Bay: The Adventures of Two Midshipmen in the Second Burmese War*, reprint of 1900 edition (Ithaca: Cornell University Library, 2009)
2475. Morrissey, Di, *The Golden Land* (Sydney: Macmillan, 2012)
2476. Nugent-Smith, Jerome, *Bo-Gyi* (Brighton: Burmah Publishing, 1995)
2477. Nugent-Smith, Jerome, *The Burma Conspiracy* (Brighton: Burmah Publishing, 1995)
2478. O'Brien, Alex, *Midnight in Burma* (Bangkok: Asia Books, 2001)
2479. O'Hara, Randolph, *Letters from a Burmese Grandfather* (Bangkok: Orchid Press, 2013)
2480. O'Hara, Randolph, *Memories from Afar* (Bangkok: Orchid Press, 2007)
2481. O'Hara, Randolph, *The Homecoming* (Bangkok: Orchid Press, 2005)
2482. O'Hara, Randolph, *The Lion and the Peacock* (Bangkok: Orchid Press, 2014)

Literature   **233**

2483. Orwell, George [Eric Blair], *Burmese Days*, reprint of 1934 edition, introduction by Emma Larkin and a note on the text by Peter Davison (London: Penguin, 2009)
2484. Perkins, Mitali, *Bamboo People: A Novel* (Watertown: Charlesbridge, 2010)
2485. Price, E.H., *Burma Guns*, reprint of 1940 version (Bloomington: Black Dog Books, 2004)
2486. Reeman, Douglas, *A Dawn Like Thunder* (London: Arrow Books, 2007)
2487. Richter, Jill, *The Burmese Sister* (Morrisville: The author and Lulu Press, 2017)
2488. Samuels, S.K., *Rangoon 1941: A Novel Based on True Events* (Tucson: SKS Enterprises, 2012)
2489. Sendker, Jan-Philipp, *A Well-Tempered Heart*, translated by Kevin Wiliarty (New York: Others Press, 2013)
2490. Sendker, Jan-Philipp, *The Art of Hearing Heartbeats*, translated by Kevin Wiliarty (Edinburgh: Polygon, 2013)
2491. Shanle, Leland, *Project Seven Alpha: American Airlines in Burma 1942* (Barnsley: Pen and Sword Books, 2009)
2492. Sharma, Prem, *Escape from Burma* (Charlottesville: Bookwrights, 2007)
2493. Sharma, Prem, *Mandalay's Child* (Charlottesville: Bookwrights Press, 1999)
2494. Smith, Roland, *Elephant Run* (New York: Hyperion, 2007)
2495. Strait, F.T., *Chin Boy* (US: Xlibris, 2014)
2496. Sweeney, John, *Elephant Moon* (Ferndown: Silvertail Books, 2014)
2497. Takeyama, Michio, *Harp of Burma*, reprint of 1966 edition, translated by Howard Hibbett (Boston: Tuttle, 1997).
2498. Tan, Amy, *Saving Fish from Drowning* (London: Fourth Estate, 2005)
2499. Thomas, Craig, *Slipping into Shadow* (London: Warner Books, 1999)
2500. Timmons, W.V., *Burma Tiger* (Charleston: The author and CreateSpace, 2010)
2501. Van Loon, Karel, *The Invisible Ones*, translated by David Colmer (London: Maia, 2006)
2502. Vaughn, Dennis, *The Longboat* (Aspen: Denlin Press, 2018)

2503. Vroman, B.F., *Linger Not at Chebar: A Novel of Love and War in Burma* (San Jose: Author's Choice Press, 2001)

2504. Whiting, Charles [Leo Kessler], *Sabres in the Sun* (London: Century, 1991)

2505. Wiggins, Marianne, *John Dollar* (London: Penguin, 1989)

2506. Wray, M.R., *Kites and Dragons: Stories of China, Japan and Burma for 7–9 Year Olds*, reprint of 1944 edition (Alcester: Read Books, 2010)

2507. Young, Gordon, *The Wind Will Yet Sing* (US: Xlibris, 2010)

Plays, Poetry and Songs

2508. Aung Chin Win Aung, *The Burma Cry* (Indianapolis: Yoma, 1996)

2509. *Bones Will Crow: 15 Contemporary Burmese Poets*, edited and translated by Ko Ko Thett and James Byrne (Todmorden: Arc Publications, 2012)

2510. Byrne, James, and Shehzar Doja (eds.), *I Am a Rohingya: Poetry from the Camps and Beyond* (UK: Arc Publications, 2019)

2511. Child, Kenneth, *No Poppies in the Jungle: War Poetry and Drawings, Burma 1942–45* (Bognor Regis: Woodfield, 2004)

2512. Cordingley, Arthur (ed.), *Scorn Not Our Tears* (Carnforth: Savant Institute, 1990)

2213. Knight, Si, *Wait as You Move On: Portraits and Poems of Myanmar* (US: The author, 2020)

2514. Law, David, *Ballads for Aung San: A Collection of Songs and Poems about the Struggle in Burma for Freedom, Democracy and Human Rights* (Chicago: Burma Freedom Writer, 1994)

2515. *Memorable Poems from the Era of Myanmar Kings*, translated by Lokethar (Yangon: U Kyaw Win, 2019)

2516. Lom, Petr, et al. (eds.), *Burma Storybook*, introduction by Emma Larkin, translations by Maung Tha Noe, Maung Day, Zeyar Lynn, Pandora, Kenneth Wong, Zaw Tun and Khun Cho, photographs by Dana Lixenberg (Amsterdam: ZINdoc: 2017)

2517. Mizuha, Akazu, and Mimic, *Aung San Suu Kyi: The Fighting Peacock*, Super Nobel Prize Story, vol. 2, translation of 1994 edition (Bangkok: Negibose Thailand, 2008)

2518. Oolay [Poole, M.C.C.], *Ballads of Burma*, reprint of 1912 edition (Bangkok: Orchid Press, 2000)

2519. *Poems of Mya Kabyar, Tin Nwan Lwin & Khaing Mar Kyaw Zaw*, translated and introduced by Violet Cho and David Gilbert (Sydney: Vagabond Press, 2014)

2520. Satoko, Hiwa, *Biruma*, translated by J.W. Carpenter (Japan: Yamaguchi City, 2003)

2521. Shannon, Richard, *The Lady of Burma: The Story of Aung San Suu Kyi* (London: Oberon Books, 2007)

2522. Shepherd, Elizabeth, *Poems of Life* (Yangon: IT Myanmar Business Magazine, 2002) (in English and Burmese)

2523. Slater, Guy, *Eastern Star* (London: Oberon Books, 2018)

2524. Symns, J.M., *Horace in Burma*, reprint of 1910 edition (Bangkok: White Orchid Press, 1997)

2525. Williams, H.E. (ed.), *The Stars: Anthology of Poems Collected and Compiled for The Burma Star Association by the Boston and North Cambridgeshire Branch* (Boston: Richard Kay, 1990)

2526. Winther, Barbara, *Plays from Asian Tales*, vol. 1 *(India, Burma/Thailand, Vietnam)* (US: Players Press, 2004)

2527. Woods, Joseph, *Monsoon Diary* (Dublin: Dedalus, 2018)

Graphic Books and Cartoon Collections

2528. Ansel, Sophie, *Burmese Moons*, illustrations by Sam Garcia, translated by Jeremy Melloul (San Diego: IDW, 2019)

2529. Corey, Daniel, *The Lazarus Tree* (*Moriarty*, volume 2), illustrated by Anthony Diecidue (Fullerton: Image Comics, 2012)

2530. Delisle, Guy, *Burma Chronicles* (Montreal: Drawn and Quarterly, 2008)

2531. Francq, Philippe, and Jean Van Hamme, *Largo Winch: The Hour of the Tiger*, translated by Luke Spear (Ashford: Cinebook, 2009)

2532. Harn Lay, *Defiant Humour* (Chiang Mai: The Irrawaddy, 2006)

2533. Harn Lay, *Defiant Humour 2* (Chiang Mai: The Irrawaddy, 2011)

2534. Harn Lay, *Defiant Humour: The Best of Harn Lay's Political Cartoons from The Irrawaddy*, 2nd edition (Yangon: U Thaung Win, 2016)
2535. Haupeur, J.H., *Hot Nights in Rangoon* (Seattle: Fantagraphics, 1997)
2536. Kelly, Claire, *The Caged Bird*, illustrations by Mike Rooth (Oxford: Oxford University Press, 2009)
2537. Thirault, Philippe, et al., *Mandalay* (Los Angeles: Humanoids Inc., 2015)
2538. Wagner, John, and Mike Western, *Darkie's Mob: The Secret War of Joe Darkie* (London: Titan Books, 2011)

CULTURE, ARTS AND CRAFTS

General

2539. Artist Hla Myint Swe, *Splendour Land: Traditional Culture and Customs of Myanmar Kinfolk* (Singapore: Spirit Asia, 2010)

2540. Bhattacharya, A.K., *The Arts and Crafts of Myanmar: The Indian Museum Collection* (Kolkata: Indian Museum, 2006)

2541. Blackburn, T.R., *A Report on the Location of Burmese Artefacts in Museums*, Kiscadale Asia Research Series no. 2 (Gartmore: Kiscadale, 1994)

2542. Chase, Jackie, *World Cultures: Burma* (Lady Lake: Adventure Travel Press, 2014)

2543. Dumarcay, Jacques, and Michael Smithies, *Cultural Sites of Burma, Thailand and Cambodia* (Oxford: Oxford University Press, 1995)

2544. Falconer, John, et al., *Burmese Design and Architecture* (Hong Kong: Periplus, 2000)

2545. Falconer, John, et al., *Myanmar Style: Art, Architecture and Design of Burma* (London: Thames and Hudson, 1998)

2546. Fraser-Lu, Sylvia, *Burmese Crafts: Past and Present* (Kuala Lumpur: Oxford University Press, 1994)

2547. Fraser-Lu, Sylvia, *Splendour in Wood: The Buddhist Monasteries of Burma* (Bangkok: Orchid Press, 2001)

2548. Gear, Donald, and Joan Gear, *An Ancient Bird-Shaped Weight System from Lan Na and Burma* (Chiang Mai: Silkworm Books, 2002)

2549. Gear, Donald, and Joan Gear, *Earth to Heaven: The Royal Animal-Shaped Weights of the Burmese Empires*, revised edition (Chiang Mai: Silkworm Books, 2000)

2550. *Gender Awareness in Myanmar's Film Industry* (Yangon: Enlightened Myanmar Research Foundation, 2018)

2551. Green, Alexandra (ed.), *Eclectic Collecting: Art from Burma in the Denison Museum* (Singapore: National University of Singapore Press, 2008)

2552. K, *Myanmar Culture*, 2nd edition (Yangon: Today Publishing House, 2006)

2553. Karnath, Lorie, *Architecture in Burma: Moments in Time* (Ostfildern: Hatje Cantz, 2013)

2554. Khin Maung Nyunt, *A Pot-Pourri of Myanmar Culture* (Yangon: Yoke Pyaung, 2016)

2555. Khin Maung Nyunt, *Radio Talks on Myanmar Culture* (Yangon: Printing and Publishing Enterprise, 2006)

2556. Khin Myo Chit, *Cultural Heritage and Other Articles* (Yangon: U Kyaw Oo Parami Sarpay, 2015)

2557. Khin Myo Chit and Paw Oo Thet, *Festivals and Flowers of the Twelve Burmese Seasons* (Bangkok: Orchid Press, 2002)

2558. Ma Thanegi, *Gold Leaf and Terra-cotta: Burmese Crafts throughout History* (San Francisco: ThingsAsian Press, 2017)

2559. Ma Thanegi and Barry Broman, *Myanmar Architecture: Cities of Gold* (Singapore: Times Editions, 2005)

2560. McGill, Forrest, and M.L. Pattaratorn Chirapravati, *Emerald Cities: Arts of Siam and Burma, 1775–1950* (San Francisco: Asian Art Museum of San Francisco, 2009)

2561. Moilanen, Irene, and S.S. Ozhegov, *Mirrored in Wood: Burmese Art and Architecture* (Bangkok: White Lotus, 1999)

2562. Mornin, Edward, and Lorna Mornin, *Understanding Buddhist Art in Thailand, Cambodia, Laos and Myanmar* (US: CreateSpace, 2014)

2563. Murphy, S.A., et al. (eds.), *Cities and Kings: Ancient Treasures from Myanmar* (Honolulu: University of Hawai'i Press, 2016)

2564. Myat Min Hlaing, *Myanmar Traditional Festivals* (Yangon: Cho Tay Tan Sarpay, 2000)

2565. Rawson, Philip, *The Art of Southeast Asia: Cambodia, Vietnam, Thailand, Laos, Burma, Java, Bali* (London: Thames and Hudson, 1990)

2566. Scherman, Lucian, and Christine Scherman, *Textiles, Crafts and Customs of Burma's Women World*, reprint of 1922 edition, translated by W.E.J. Tips, biographies by Wolfgang Stein (Bangkok: White Lotus, 2014)

2567. Soe, Meiji, *Culture and Beyond: Myanmar*, 3rd edition (Yangon: Sarpay Beikman, 2017)

2568. Than Htun (Shwebo), *The Hindu-Buddhist Impact on Myanmar Culture* (Myanmar: The author, 2005)

2569. Toru, Ohno, *A Study of the Burmese Rama Story: With an English Translation from a Duplicate Printing of the Original Palm Leaf Manuscript Written in Burmese Language in 1233 Year of Burmese Era (1871 AD)* (Osaka: Osaka University of Foerign Studies, 1999)

2570. Toru, Ohno, *Burmese Ramayana* (Delhi: BR Publishing, 2000)

2571. Willis, R.J., and Greg Herman, *Burmese Weights and Other Animal-Shaped Weights* (Melbourne: Hintha Books, 2019)

The Visual Arts

2572. Artist Hla Myint Swe, *Myanmar National Tribes: Pen Sketches of Artist Hla Myint Swe* (Yangon: Daw Khin Myo Than, 2008)

2573. Aung Min, *Myanmar Contemporary Art 1*, translated by Maung Day, edited by Aung Myint, Mrat Lunn Htwann and Nathalie Johnston (Yangon: Myanmar Art Resource Centre and Archive [MARCA] and theart.com, 2017)

2574. Aye Myint, *Burmese Design through Drawings*, translated by U Thanoe (Bangkok: Silpakorn University, 1993)

2575. Fraser-Lu, Sylvia, and D.M. Stadtner (eds.), *Buddhist Art of Myanmar* (New Haven: Asia Society Museum and Yale University Press, 2015)

2576. Hasson, Haskia, *Ancient Buddhist Art from Burma* (Bangkok: White Lotus, 1993)

2577. Hla Tin Htun, *Old Myanmar Paintings in the Collection of U Win* (Bangkok: Thavibu Gallery, 2006)

2578. Khin Let Ya, *Paintings of Bo Let Ya* (Yangon: Zun Pwint, 2012)

2579. Khin Mya Zin, *Myanmar Women Artists*, translated by Pann Hmone Wai (Yangon: Ye Aung Sarpay, 2009)

2580. Khin Zaw Latt, *Seeing into Portraits* (Yangon: KZL Art Studio and Gallery, 2016)

2581. Ma Thanegi, *Paw Oo Thet (1936–1993): His Life and Creativity* (Yangon: Swiftwinds, 2004)

2582. Ma Thanegi and Sonny Nyein, *This Is Kin Maung Yin* (Yangon: Thin Sarpay, 2010)

2583. Ma Thanegi et al., *Myanmar Painting: From Worship to Self-Imaging* (Ho Chi Minh City: Education Publishing House, 2006)

2584. Middelborg, Jorn (ed.), *U Lun Gywe: A Master Painter from Myanmar* (Bangkok: Thavibu Gallery, 2005)

2585. Min Wae Aung, *Min Wae Aung: Golden Heritage 1989–2010* (Hong Kong: Asia Fine Art, 2010)

2586. Munier, Christophe, and Myint Aung, *Burmese Buddhist Murals: Volume 1, Epigraphic Corpus of the Powin Taung Caves* (Bangkok: White Lotus, 2007)

2587. Naziree, Shireen (ed.), *Aung Kyaw Htet: Myanmar Inspirations* (Bangkok: Thavibu Gallery, 2007)

2588. Naziree, Shireen (ed.), *U Lun Gywe – A Master Painter from Myanmar* (Bangkok: Thavibu Gallery, 2005)

2589. Ranard, Andrew, *Burmese Painting: A Linear and Lateral History* (Chiang Mai: Silkworm Books, 2009)

2590. Rao, V.K., *Buddhist Art of Pagan*, 2 volumes (New Delhi: Agam Kala Prakashan, 2011)

2591. Shwe Sin Aye, *The Identity of Artist Shwe Sin Aye and Unconscious Imageries*, translated by Cho Ara (Republic of Korea?: The author, 2016)

2592. Stadtner, D.M. (ed.), *The Art of Burma: New Studies* (Mumbai: Marg, 1999)

2593. Than Tun and Aye Myint, *Ancient Myanmar Designs* (Bangkok: iGroup Press, 2011)

2594. Thomann, Th.H., *Pagan and Burma in 1899: A Millenium of Buddhist Temple Art*, reprint of 1923 edition, translated by W.E.J. Tips (Bangkok: White Lotus Press, 2014)

2595. Wunna Kyaw Tin and Artist Hla Myint Swe, *Myanmar Brethren: Compilation and Pen Sketches by Wunna Kyaw Tin and Artist Hla Myint Swe*, translated by Kyaw Swe (Singapore: Spirit Asia, 2014)

The Plastic Arts

2596. Cooler, R.M., *The Karen Frog Drums of Burma: Type, Iconography, Manufacture and Use* (Leiden: E.J. Brill, 1995)

2597. Dell, Elizabeth, and Sandra Dudley (eds.), *Textiles from Burma: Featuring the James Henry Green Collection* (London: Philip Wilson, 2003)

2598. Fink, Jella, *Voices of Weavers: Textile Cultures, Craftsmanship, and Identity in Contemporary Myanmar* (Munster: Waxmann, 2020)

2599. Fraser, D.W., and B.G. Fraser, *Mantles of Merit: Chin Textiles from Myanmar, India and Bangladesh* (Bangkok: River Books, 2005)

2600. Fraser-Lu, Sylvia, *Burmese Lacquerware*, 2nd edition (Bangkok: Orchid Press, 2000)

2601. Fraser-Lu, Sylvia, *Textiles in Burman Culture* (Chiang Mai: Silkworm Books, 2020)

2602. Honda, Hiromu, and Noriki Shimazu, *The Beauty of Fired Clay: Ceramics from Burma, Cambodia, Laos, and Thailand*, introduction by D.F. Rooney (Oxford: Oxford University Press, 1997)

2603. Howard, M.C., *Textiles of the Highland Peoples of Burma*, 2 volumes (Bangkok: White Lotus, 2005)

2604. Howard, M.C., *Textiles of the Hill Tribes of Burma* (Bangkok: White Lotus, 1999)

2605. Isaacs, Ralph, *Sazigyo: Burmese Manuscript Binding Tapes: Woven Miniatures of Buddhist Art* (Chiang Mai: Silkworm Books, 2014)

2606. Isaacs, Ralph, and T.R. Blurton, *Visions from the Golden Land: Burma and the Art of Lacquer* (London: British Museum Press, 2000)

2607. Koretsky, Elaine, and Donna Koretsky, *The Goldbeaters of Mandalay: An Account of Hand Papermaking in Burma Today* (Brookline: Carriage House Press, 1991)

2608. Kunlabutr, Punvasa, *Burmese Court Textiles: Luntaya-acheiq* (Bangkok: H.P. Ahrens, 2005)

2609. Ma Thanegi, *Bagan Lacquerware* (Yangon: Asia House, 2013)

2610. Novak, Tibor, *Burmese Gold Plate Inscribed with a Section of the Pali Canon*, Treasures from Southeast Asia in the Zelnik Collection 1, edited by Zsuzsanna Renner, translated by M.J. Webb (Budapest: Hungarian Southeast Asian Research Institute, 2013)

2611. Owens, D.C., *Burmese Silver Art: Masterpieces Illuminating Buddhist, Hindu and Mythological Stories of Purpose and Wisdom* (Singapore: Marshall Cavendish International [Asia], 2020)

2612. Pratt, H.S., *Monograph on Ivory Carving in Burma*, reprint of 1901 edition (Whitefish: Kessinger, 2010)

2613. Shaw, J.C., *Introducing Thai Ceramics: Also Burmese and Khmer*, 2nd edition (Bangkok: DK Bookhouse, 1988)

2614. Sumitr Pitiphat, *Ceramics from the Thai-Burma Border* (Bangkok: Thai Khadi Research Institute, Thammasat University, 2003)

2615. Than Htun (Dedaye), *Lacquerware Journeys: The Untold Story of Burmese Lacquer* (Bangkok: River Books, 2013)

2616. Tin Myaing Thein, *Old and New Tapestries of Mandalay* (Oxford: Oxford University Press, 2000)

2617. Wilkinson, W.R.T., *Indian Silver, 1858–1947: Silver from the Indian Sub-continent and Burma Made by Local Craftsmen in Western Forms* (London: The author, 1999)

The Performing Arts

2618. Anderson, Vincent, *The Burmese Theater*, reprint of 1921 edition (New Delhi: Gyan Books, 2019)

2619. Bruns, A.R.H., *Burmese Puppetry* (Bangkok: White Lotus, 2006)

2620. Ehrlich, Daniel, *Backstage Mandalay: The Netherworld of the Burmese Performing Arts* (Bangkok: River Books, Bangkok)

2621. Inoue, Sayuri, *The Formation of Genre in Burmese Classical Songs* (Osaka: Osaka University Press, 2014)

2622. Khin Khin Si, *The Aspects of Myanmar Orchestra* (Saarbrucken: Lambert Academic, 2019)

2623. Ma Ma Naing, *The Wiles of the Dancing Strings*, translated by Naing Ye Kyaw (Yangon: Panmyo Tayar Book House, 2013)

2624. Ma Thanegi, *The Illusion of Life* (Bangkok: White Orchid Press, 1994)

2625. MacLachlan, Heather, *Burma's Pop Music Industry: Creators, Distributors, Censors* (Rochester NY: University of Rochester Press, 2011)

2626. Rodrigues, Yves, *Nat-Pwe: Burma's Supernatural Sub-culture*, translated by Roser Flotats, photographs by Yves Rodrigues and Paul Strachan (Glasgow: Kiscadale, 1995)

2627. Singer, N.F., *Burmese Dance and Theatre* (Kuala Lumpur: Oxford University Press, 1995)

2628. Singer, N.F., *Burmese Puppets* (Singapore: Oxford University Press, 1992)

2629. Stewart, J.A., *The Burmese Stage*, reprint of 1939 edition (US: Hardpress, 2013)

2630. Tekkatho Maung Thu Hlaing, *Myanma Traditional Orchestra Instruments* (Yangon: U Tin Ohn and Moe Min Sapay, 1993) (in English and Burmese)

2631. Williamson, M.C., *The Burmese Harp: Its Classical Music, Tunings and Modes* (DeKalb: Northern Illinois University, 2000)

2632. Ye Dway, *Myanmar Dance and Drama* (Yangon: Today Publishing House, 2014)

2633. Ye Dway, *Stories from the Myanmar Classical Theatre* (Myanmar: The author, 2015)

SPORT, RECREATION AND HOBBIES

Sport

2634. Allan, David, Jeremy Skaggs and Jason Tran (eds.), *Southeast Asian Martial Arts: Cambodia, Myanmar, Thailand, Vietnam* (US: Via Media, 2017)

2635. Bradley, John, *A Narrative of Travel and Sport in Burmah, Siam, and the Malay Peninsula*, reprint of 1876 edition (Norderstedt: Hansebooks, 2016)

2636. Jackson, Jack, *Diving in the Indian Ocean* (New York: Rizzoli, 1999)

2637. Macdonald, A. St.J., *Circumventing the Mahseer and Other Sporting Fish in India and Burma*, reprint of 1948 edition (Dehra Dun: Natraj, 1992)

2638. Pekin Pyan Win Ko, *Facts about Myanmar Traditional Chinlone Game and Correct Methods of Chinlone Playing*, translated by Naing Thit and San Lin Tun (Yangon: U Win Cho, 2013)

2639. Pollok, F.T., *Sport in British Burmah, Assam, and the Cassyah and Jyntiah Hills*, reprint of 1879 edition (US: Palala Press, 2015)

2640. Pollock, F.T., and W.S. Thom, *Wild Sports of Burma and Assam*, reprint of 1900 edition (Charleston: Nabu Press, 2010)

2641. Rebac, Zoran, *Traditional Burmese Boxing: Ancient and Modern Methods from Burma's Training Camps* (Boulder: Paladin, 2003)

2642. Thorn, Philip, and Philip Bailey (compilers), *European Cricketers in India, Ceylon and Burma* (Nottingham: Association of Cricket Statisticians and Historians, 1998)

Philately

2643. Davis, Gerald, and Alan Meech, *A Catalogue of Telegraph and Revenue Stamps for Burma and Myanmar* (Edmonton: Burma Philatelic Study Circle, 1998)

2644. Herman, H.S., *The Japanese Military Burma–Thailand Railroad, 1942–1945*, ISJP Monograph no. 13 (Schaumberg: International Society for Japanese Philately, August 2000)

2645. Kyaw Myint Maung, *A Short History of Myanmar Stamps (1937–1947)* (Yangon: Stamp Knowledge Series, 2007)

SPORT, RECREATION AND HOBBIES

Sport

2634. Allan, David, Jeremy Skaggs and Jason Tran (eds.), *Southeast Asian Martial Arts: Cambodia, Myanmar, Thailand, Vietnam* (US: Via Media, 2017)

2635. Bradley, John, *A Narrative of Travel and Sport in Burmah, Siam, and the Malay Peninsula*, reprint of 1876 edition (Norderstedt: Hansebooks, 2016)

2636. Jackson, Jack, *Diving in the Indian Ocean* (New York: Rizzoli, 1999)

2637. Macdonald, A. St.J., *Circumventing the Mahseer and Other Sporting Fish in India and Burma*, reprint of 1948 edition (Dehra Dun: Natraj, 1992)

2638. Pekin Pyan Win Ko, *Facts about Myanmar Traditional Chinlone Game and Correct Methods of Chinlone Playing*, translated by Naing Thit and San Lin Tun (Yangon: U Win Cho, 2013)

2639. Pollok, F.T., *Sport in British Burmah, Assam, and the Cassyah and Jyntiah Hills*, reprint of 1879 edition (US: Palala Press, 2015)

2640. Pollock, F.T., and W.S. Thom, *Wild Sports of Burma and Assam*, reprint of 1900 edition (Charleston: Nabu Press, 2010)

2641. Rebac, Zoran, *Traditional Burmese Boxing: Ancient and Modern Methods from Burma's Training Camps* (Boulder: Paladin, 2003)

2642. Thorn, Philip, and Philip Bailey (compilers), *European Cricketers in India, Ceylon and Burma* (Nottingham: Association of Cricket Statisticians and Historians, 1998)

Philately

2643. Davis, Gerald, and Alan Meech, *A Catalogue of Telegraph and Revenue Stamps for Burma and Myanmar* (Edmonton: Burma Philatelic Study Circle, 1998)

2644. Herman, H.S., *The Japanese Military Burma–Thailand Railroad, 1942–1945*, ISJP Monograph no. 13 (Schaumberg: International Society for Japanese Philately, August 2000)

2645. Kyaw Myint Maung, *A Short History of Myanmar Stamps (1937–1947)* (Yangon: Stamp Knowledge Series, 2007)

2631. Williamson, M.C., *The Burmese Harp: Its Classical Music, Tunings and Modes* (DeKalb: Northern Illinois University, 2000)
2632. Ye Dway, *Myanmar Dance and Drama* (Yangon: Today Publishing House, 2014)
2633. Ye Dway, *Stories from the Myanmar Classical Theatre* (Myanmar: The author, 2015)

Sport, Recreation and Hobbies 245

2646. Lang, Derek, *British India Postal Stationery: An Illustrated History and Listing of Postal Stationery Issued in India up to Independence in 1947* (Bristol: Stuart Rossiter Trust Fund, 1997)

2647. Malcolm, Donald, *Detective Story – Or How the Mail Got from Burma to Athens in October 1932* (Paisley: The author, January 1990)

2648. Maung Maung Lin, *Stamps of Myanmar* (Yangon: Yone Kyi Chat, 2002)

2649. Min Sun Min, *Stamps of Burma: A Historical Record through 1988* (Chiang Mai: Mekong Press, 2007)

2650. *Myanma Postage Stamps* (Yangon: Myanma Posts and Telecommunications, 2006)

2651. *Myanma Postage Stamps, 1965–1985* (Yangon: Myanma Posts and Telecommunications, 1986?)

2652. Proud, E.B., *The Postal History of Burma* (Heathfield: Proud-Bailey, 2002)

2653. Singer, Peter (ed.), *Japanese Occupation Issues: The British Colonies, 1942–1945* (Clovis: Moon Tree, 1997)

2654. Song, James, *Burma: The Stamps and Postal History under the Reign of the Three British Kings 1901–1947, Part 1 and Part 2, Airmail in Burma* (Singapore: James Song Philatelics, 2020)

2655. *Stanley Gibbons Commonwealth Stamp Catalogue: Bangladesh, Burma, Pakistan and Sri Lanka*, 3rd edition (London: Stanley Gibbons, 2015)

2656. *Stanley Gibbons Stamp Catalogue: Part 21: South East Asia (including Bhutan, Cambodia, Indonesia, Laos, Myanmar, Nepal, Philippines, Thailand and Vietnam)*, 5th edition (London: Stanley Gibbons, 2012)

2657. Tett, David, *A Postal History of the Prisoners of War and Civilian Internees in East Asia During the Second World War, Volume 3, Burma, Thailand and Indochina, 1942–1946: The Railway, The River and The Bridge* (Wheathampstead: BFA, 2005)

2658. Warren, Richard, *The Postal Stationery of Burma and Myanmar, 1948–97* (Bilston: White Elephant Press, 1998)

2659. Zwillinger, Steven, *Burmese Cachets: A Catalog of Burmese Illustrated Envelopes, 1937–1947* (Silver Spring: The author, 2002)

Numismatics

2660. Mahlo, Dietrich, *The Early Coins of Myanmar (Burma): Messengers from the Past, First Millenium AD* (Bangkok: White Lotus, 2012)

2661. Mitchiner, Michael, *The Land of Water: Coinage and History of Bangladesh and Later Arakan, circa 300 BC to the Present Day* (London: Hawkins Publications, 2000)

2662. Than Htun (Dedaye), *Auspicious Symbols and Ancient Coins of Myanmar* (Selangor: Ava House, 2007)

2663. Valentine, W.H., *The Copper Coins of India, Including Bangladesh, Burma, Nepal and Pakistan* (Delhi: Low Price Publications, 2002)

Other Interests

2664. Coe, Debbie, and Randy Coe, *Fenton Burmese Glass* (Atglen: Schiffer, 2004)

2665. Hoey Middleton, S.E., *Intaglios, Cameos, Rings and Related Objects from Burma and Java: The White Collection and a Further Small Private Collection*, photographs by Robert Wilkins (Oxford: BAR Publishing, 2005)

2666. Lewis, S.D.W., *The Three Burma Awards: The Story of the Creation, Design, Manufacture and Awards of the Burma Police Medal, Order of Burma and the Burma Gallantry Medal* (Cheltenham: The author, 2019)

2667. Belcher, J.J., *Bagan Myanmar: Colouring Book for Adults Relaxation* (US: Createspace, 2017)

2668. Khan, Omar, *Postcards from the Raj* (Ahmedabad: Mapin, 2018)

2669. Maung Maung Lwin [Sit-Tu-Yin], *How to Play Myanmar Traditional Chess* (Yangon: Ma Khin Mya, 2011)

2670. Young, M.G., *The Best Ever Book of Burmese Jokes* (New York: Dolyttle and Seamore, 2012)

CUISINE

2671. Anderson, Bridget, and Stephen Anderson, *Burma: Food, Family and Conflict* (Valencia: Makhin Markets SL, 2018)

2672. Aung Aung Taik, *Under the Golden Pagoda: The Best of Burmese Cooking* (San Francisco: Chronicle Books, 1993)

2673. Bingham, Page, *A Taste of Shan: A Culinary and Photographic Expedition through the Shan Province of Northern Myanmar* (Singapore: Marshall Cavendish, 2009)

2674. Boundy, Anthony, *Bountiful Burmese Recipes: A Complete Cookbook of Tasty Asian Dish Ideas* (US: The author, 2019)

2675. *Burmese Cuisine* (Eastbourne: Burmese Doctor's Association, UK, 2000)

2676. Carmack, Robert, and Morrison Polkinghorne, *The Burma Cookbook: Recipes from the Land of a Million Pagodas, from Rangoon Burma to Yangon Myanmar* (Bangkok: River Books, 2014)

2677. Chan, Susan, *Flavours of Burma/Myanmar* (New York: Hippocrene Books, 2003)

2678. Chung, Amy, and Emily Chung, *The Rangoon Sisters: Recipes from Our Burmese Family Kitchen* (London: Ebury, 2020)

2679. Daw Ena Win, *Burma Cook Book* (Myanmar: U Tin Ong, 2010)

2680. Duguid, Naomi, *Burma: Rivers of Flavour* (New York: Workman, 2012)

2681. Gallardo, Juan, *Delicious Myanmar: Discover Myanmar through its People and Food* (Spain?: The author and JETLAUNCH, 2014)

2682. Gill, Mohana, *Myanmar: Cuisine, Culture and Customs* (Singapore: Marshall Cavendish International [Asia], 2014)

2683. Howes, E.B., *The Modern Salad: Innovative New American and International Recipes Inspired by Burma's Iconic Tea Leaf Salad* (Berkeley: Ulysses Press, 2016)

2684. Koh, Bryan, *0451 Mornings Are for Mont Hin Gar: Burmese Food Stories* (Singapore: Xochpilli Press, 2015)

2685. Ma Thanegi, *An Introduction to Myanmar Cuisine* (Yangon: Yone Kyi Chet Sarpay, 2004)

2686. Ma Thanegi, *Ginger Salad and Water Wafers: Recipes from Myanmar*, photographs by Tiffany Wan (San Francisco: ThingsAsian Press, 2013)

2687. Marks, Copeland, and Aung Thein, *The Burmese Kitchen*, reprint of 1987 edition (New York: Evans, 1994)

2688. Mi Mi Aye, *Mandalay: Recipes and Tales from a Burmese Kitchen* (London: Bloomsbury, 2019)

2689. Myint Myint Soe, *My Burmese Cookbook*, 3 volumes (US: Authorhouse, 2014 [parts 1 and 2] and 2016 [part 3])

2690. Nan San San Aye, *Cooking with Love Myanmar Style*, translated by Ma Thanegi (Myanmar: Seikku Cho Cho, 2016)

2691. Ray, Valeria, *Collection of the Most Authenic Flavours of Burma: Burmese Cookbook with the Finest Recipes* (US: The author, 2019)

2692. Robert, Claudia Saw Lwin, et al., *The Food of Myanmar: Authentic Recipes from the Land of the Golden Pagodas*, 2nd edition (Boston: Tuttle, 2014)

2693. Shirr, Ohnmar, *Bamar Snacks*, 2 volumes (Yangon: Domestic Group Publishing House, 2011)

2694. Solomon, Charmaine, *The Complete Asian Cookbook: Thailand, Vietnam, Cambodia, Laos and Burma* (Melbourne: Hardie Grant Books, 2014)

2695. Tan, Desmond, and Kate Leahy, *Burma Superstar: Addictive Recipes from the Crossroads of Southeast Asia* (Berkeley: Ten Speed Press, 2017)

2696. Tin Cho Chaw, *Hsa*ba: Burmese Cookbook* (London: Grassblades, 2008)

BIBLIOGRAPHIES AND RESEARCH GUIDES

2697. *A Bibliography of Japanese Books on the Burma Campaign: War in Burma 1942–1945* (Tokyo: All Burma Veterans Association of Japan, 2000)

2698. Avicenna, Milo, *Aung San Suu Kyi: A Selective Bibliography of Dissertations and Theses* (US: The author and CreateSpace, 2017)

2699. Barnett, L.D., *A Catalogue of the Burmese Books in the British Museum*, reprint of 1913 edition (US: Forgotten Books, 2016)

2700. *Bibliography on Burma, 1988–1997* (De Kalb: Donn V. Hart Southeast Asia Collection, Northern Illinois University Libraries, 19 June 1997)

2701. Corfield, Justin, *The Burma Campaign, 1942–1945: A Bibliography* (Lara: Gentext Publications, 2015)

2702. *Doing Research in Myanmar: Country Report* (Yangon and New Delhi: Centre for Economic and Social Development, and The Global Development Network, June 2020)

2703. Graham, Gordon, and Frank Cole (eds.), *Burma Campaign Memorial Library: A Collection of Books and Papers about the War in Burma 1942–1945*, 2nd edition (London: School of Oriental and African Studies, 2001)

2704. *Guide to Universities' Central Library* (Rangoon: Union of Myanmar, Ministry of Education, Department of Higher Education, Universities Central Library, 1999)

2705. Hadden, R.L., *The Geology of Burma (Myanmar): An Annotated Bibliography of Burma's Geology, Geography and Earth Science* (Alexandria: US Army Corps of Engineers, 2008)

2706. Herbert, P.M., *Burma*, World Bibliographical Series, Volume 132 (Oxford: Clio Press, 1991)

2707. Khin Mar Mar, *Guide to the Archival Sources of the British Administration Period, 1826–1948: Myanmar* (Yangon: National Archives Department, Ministry of National Planning and Economic Development, 2003)

2708. Kratz, E.U. (ed.), *Southeast Asian Languages and Literatures: A Bibliographic Guide to Burmese, Cambodian, Indonesian, Javanese, Malay, Minangkabau, Thai, and Vietnamese* (London: I.B. Taurus, 1996)

2709. Macallister, John, *Myanmar Marionettes (Burmese Puppets): A List of References in the English Language* (Glenbrook: The author, 1996)

2710. Manson, Ken, *A Bibliography of Karenic Linguistics* (Chiang Mai: Department of Linguistics, Payap University, January 2004)

2711. Mayerchak, P.M., *Scholars' Guide to Washington, D.C., for Southeast Asian Studies: Brunei, Burma, Cambodia, Indonesia, Laos, Malaysia, Philippines, Singapore, Thailand, and Vietnam*, reprint of 1983 edition (Washington DC: Woodrow Wilson Centre Press, 1991)

2712. Meech, Alan, *An Annotated Bibliography of Burma Philately* (London: British Philatelic Trust, 1993)

2713. Moe Myint, *List of Books from the Library of U Moe Myint, 2008, with Pictures and Descriptions* (Yangon: The author, 2008)

2714. Nyunt, Peter, *A Descriptive Catalogue of Burmese Manuscripts in the Fragile Palm Leaves Collection* (Bangkok: Fragile Palm Leaves Foundation, Lumbini International Research Institute, 2014)

2715. Oldham, R.D., *A Bibliography of Indian Geology: Being a List of Books and Papers, Relating to the Geology of British India and Adjoining Countries, Published Previous to the End of A.D. 1887*, reprint of 1888 edition (Cambridge: Cambridge University Press, 2013)

2716. Pruitt, William, and Roger Bischoff, *Catalogue of the Burmese-Pali and Burmese Manuscripts in the Library of the Wellcome Institute for the History of Medicine* (London: Wellcome Institute, 1998)

2717. Pruitt, William, Y. Ousaka and S. Kasamatsu, *The Catalogue of Manuscripts in the U Pho Thi Library, Thaton, Myanmar* (Bristol: Pali Text Society, 2019)

2718. Rasor, E.L., *The China-Burma-India Campaign, 1931–1945: Historiography and Annotated Bibliography* (Westport: Greenwood Press, 1998)

2719. Rastorfer, Jean-Marc, *Reprints or Simple Photocopies? Current Trends in the Republishing Industry in Myanmar: With a Survey of All Books Reprinted by Photocopy Available in July and August 1997 and Some Locally Reprinted Books for Sale on Internet in September 1998*, Paper presented at the Burma Studies Conference held on 2–4 October 1998, Northern Illinois University De Kalb, USA (De Kalb: Northern Illinois University, 1998)

2720. Sadan, Mandy, *A Guide to Colonial Sources on Burma: Ethnic and Minority Histories of Burma in the India Office Records, British Library* (Bangkok: Orchid Press, 2008)

2721. Schwertner, S.M., *Burma/Myanmar Bibliographic Project: A Collection of Publications in West European Languages for Preparation a* [sic] *Burma/Myanmar Bibliography*, 4 volumes (Heidelberg: South Asia Institute, University of Heidelberg, 2005–8)

2722. *Selected Bibliographies on Labour and Industrial Relations in Burma, Indonesia, Korea, Malaya, Singapore, Thailand*, reprint of 1962 edition (New Delhi: Relnk Books, 2017)

2723. Selth, Andrew, *Burma (Myanmar) since the 1988 Uprising: A Select Bibliography*, 3rd edition, foreword by David Steinberg (Brisbane: Griffith Asia Institute, Griffith University, 2018)

2724. Selth, Andrew, *Myanmar (Burma): A Reading Guide*, Research Paper (Brisbane: Griffith Asia Institute, Griffith University, 2021)

2725. Tin Naing Win, *Myanmar Historical Cartography: Parabaik Maps and Other Map Sources: A Post-doctoral Research Work Done by the Support of the Korea Foundation for Advanced Studies, Seoul, Korea* (Saarbrucken: Lambert Academic, 2018)

2726. Win Tint, *An Annotated Bibliography of the Works of G.H. Luce and Catalogue of Books in His Library* (Meiktila: Meiktila University, 1998)

2727. Win Tint, *Selected Bibliographical Guide to Scholastic Works of Archaeologists in Myanmar* (Meiktila: Meiktila University, 2001)

APPENDIX 1
Myanmar: A Reading Guide

Introduction

In 2006, the Asia Bookroom in Canberra posted a list of books, monographs and other works about Myanmar, written in English, on its website. This was partly to advertise its wares, but also in the hope that such a list would help those intending to visit Myanmar for the first time or who wished to familiarize themselves with particular aspects of the country before pursuing more in-depth studies. Over the next five years, as opportunity permitted, this list was updated and expanded, not only to reflect the much larger number of books, reports and other monographs being published on Myanmar, but also to cater to the widening range of Myanmar-related subjects in which the bookshop's customers had expressed an interest. After 2012, successive versions of the list were published as appendices to the first three editions of this select bibliography, with brief annotations to assist readers in making their choices. The most recent iteration of the list follows below.[1]

As noted in the introduction to this book, the guide is not meant to be either authoritative or exhaustive, although an attempt has been made to cover all the main subject areas in one way or another. Some shorter and more specialized studies have been included, but the essay focuses mainly on books and monographs that help provide a broad introduction to the country and its people and are likely to be readily available from good bookshops and libraries. Most can also be found on the websites of major online booksellers.

Anyone wishing to delve more deeply into any of the subjects touched upon below or who wants to pursue particular interests is encouraged also to consult the more detailed and scholarly works listed in this bibliography, as well as the burgeoning literature on Myanmar found in academic and professional journals. There are also a number of specialist websites that list additional sources.[2] The latter are often the best source of information on rapidly evolving issues, but they need to be approached with caution. As with other subjects of popular interest, the internet has become a platform for a great deal of inaccurate and tendentious material on contemporary Myanmar.

It is possible to find other lists of recommended books online. A few have been compiled by experienced Myanmar-watchers, such as Bertil Lintner, Emma Larkin, Wendy Law-Yone and Sean Turnell. They are useful in highlighting some key sources. However, as often required by their hosts, most tend to focus on more recent works and popular titles that are likely to appeal to the tourist and armchair traveller. Needless to say, all such lists, including this one, constitute personal choices and reflect the reading habits, experiences, professional backgrounds and, in a few cases, the commercial interests of those compiling them.[3] In my own case, I confess that I have included a few favourites in this essay simply because I should like others to enjoy reading them as much as I did. It also mentions a few obscure or forgotten works about Myanmar that I feel deserve to be better remembered.[4]

The appendix broadly follows the structure of the bibliography, within an overarching chronological framework. However, there are a few variations where some minor adjustments helped the discussion to flow more easily. The paragraph looking at works on jade and gemstones, for example, logically follows the paragraphs on economic matters, not those relating to Myanmar's geography and geology (which in any case are not discussed in any detail).

A Guide to Sources

Over the past thirty years or so, a large number of "coffee table" books about Myanmar have appeared as foreigners have enjoyed greater access to the country and the market for pictorial works has grown. Many contain technically proficient but rather clichéd photographs of the country's spectacular scenery and colourful population. One work notable for its distinguished contributors, however, is *Myanmar: Land of the Spirit*.[5] Also worth looking at is *7 Days in Myanmar: A Portrait of Burma by 30 Great Photographers* by John Falconer et al.[6] David Lazar's *Myanmar: A Luminous Journey* provides a sensitive portrayal of the country and its people by a young Australian photographer.[7] A more specialized but lavishly illustrated volume describing sites in Myanmar that are not well known is Ma Thanegi and Barry Broman's *Myanmar Architecture: Cities of Gold*.[8] For some stunning black and white photographs, accompanied by an insightful commentary, see Nic Dunlop's *Brave New Burma*.[9] For an unusual but revealing glimpse of contemporary Rangoon, *Still Lifes from a Vanishing City* by Elizabeth Rush is strongly recommended.[10] A more comprehensive tour of the city, with photos of places off the beaten tourist track, is given in *Relics of Rangoon* by P.J. Heijmans.[11]

There are also a few books for sale that reproduce old photographs of Myanmar. Most of these pictures were taken during the British colonial period, but are well worth a look, not just out of historical interest but also for their artistic flair and technical proficiency. Three books in this category that stand out are *Captain Linnaeus Tripe: Photographer of India and Burma, 1852–1860*; *Burmah: A Photographic Journey, 1855–1925* by Noel Singer, and *Burma: Frontier Photographs 1918–1935*, edited by Elizabeth Dell.[12] In this regard, it is also worth noting that the Myanmar Photo Archive has recently produced four publications that preserve and present to modern audiences a range of images taken by Burmese photographers late last century.[13] They are designed both to inform and amuse.

After being ignored, or shunned, by the tourist industry for decades, foreign interest in Myanmar exploded after the introduction of a "disciplined democracy" in 2011. There is now a wide range of travel guides available. Caroline Courtauld's *Myanmar: Burma in Style: An Illustrated History and Guide* provides an easy introduction.[14] This can be read alongside her album *The Irrawaddy: Burma's Kingly Stream*.[15] The most informative and practical work in English is probably still *Myanmar (Burma)* by Simon Richmond et al. in the ubiquitous Lonely Planet series.[16] However, the *Myanmar (Burma)* Insight Guide is easier to read and has more colour illustrations.[17] Other travellers swear by *The Rough Guide to Myanmar (Burma)* by Gavin Thomas, Stuart Butler and Tom Deas, which is quite comprehensive.[18] A different approach is taken in Morgan Edwardson's *To Myanmar with Love: A Travel Guide for the Connoisseur*.[19] It is organized by themes rather than by destinations. Although it is now showing its age, a useful reference book for those wishing to look up some basic facts and figures is the revised version of Donald Seekins's *Historical Dictionary of Burma (Myanmar)*.[20]

Win Pe's *Dos and Don'ts in Myanmar* provides foreign visitors with a simple guide to the customs and culture of the Burmese people.[21] A more recent publication in this genre is Saw Myat Yin's *Culture Shock! Myanmar: A Survival Guide to Customs and Etiquette*.[22] Inevitably, perhaps, both books tend to focus on the social practices of the Burman, or *Bamar*, ethnic majority. In their defence, however, these customs are now widespread in Myanmar and can be safely observed by foreign visitors wherever they go. Although now rather dated, one expatriate businessman's view is given in H.C.M. Sim's *Myanmar On My Mind: A Guide to Living and Doing Business in Myanmar*.[23] More recent is Michael O'Kane's *Doing Business in Myanmar*.[24] The latest offering in this genre is Hana Bui's *When Global Meets Local: How Expatriates Can Succeed in Myanmar*. It is notable for the fact that it is based on a survey of over a hundred expatriates in Myanmar and fifty local professionals.[25] It needs to be remembered, however, that the commercial scene in Myanmar is constantly evolving and can change unexpectedly. No one yet knows what business conditions will be like in the aftermath of the February 2021 coup.

Having four tones, a unique script and multiple social variations, Burmese is a notoriously difficult language to learn, but the Lonely Planet's *Burmese Phrasebook and Dictionary* has been compiled by three experts and can help those wishing to acquire some basic words and phrases.[26] A much more comprehensive and professional approach has been taken by the noted British linguist John Okell in his four-volume work *Burmese (Myanmar)*. In more than 1,200 pages of text and thirty-four cassette tapes, it not only covers the spoken language but also looks at the script and literary style.[27] For anyone wanting to pursue this subject further, Mary Callahan has an interesting chapter on "Language Policy in Modern Burma" in *Fighting Words: Language Policy and Ethnic Relations in Asia*, edited by M.E. Brown and Sumit Ganguly.[28] It is worth comparing this work with Kyaw Yin Hlaing's "The Politics of Language Policy in Myanmar: Imagining Togetherness, Practising Difference" in *Language, Nation and Development in Southeast Asia*, edited by Lee Hock Guan and Leo Suryadinata.[29]

For many years, it was difficult for foreign archeologists to conduct fieldwork in Myanmar, and the published works of local researchers were hard to come by. This situation is gradually changing. An easy introduction to the subject is *Cultural Sites of Burma, Thailand and Cambodia* by Jacques Dumarcay and Michael Smithies.[30] Elizabeth Moore has written a scholarly yet entertaining and well-illustrated survey of the *Early Landscapes of Myanmar*.[31] Donald Stadtner has looked more closely at one celebrated site in *Ancient Pagan: Buddhist Plain of Merit*.[32] This can be profitably read in conjunction with *The Buddhist Murals of Pagan* by Claudine Bautze-Picron.[33] Pam Gutman has published a number of works about ancient Arakan (Rakhine), including the sumptuous *Burma's Lost Kingdoms: Splendours of Arakan*.[34] Local scholar Myint Aung has offered views on a range of archeological finds in Myanmar in his anthology *Revealing Myanmar's Past*.[35] The former military regime's efforts to use archeology for propaganda purposes are discussed in an amusing 1999 article by Gustaaf Houtman.[36]

About two thirds of Myanmar's population still live in rural towns and villages, but the country is facing the challenges of rapid and largely unplanned urbanization. A first-time visitor to the country would benefit from reading E.C. Cangi's *Faded Splendour, Golden Past: Urban Images of Burma*.[37] It gives short histories of the former capitals of Rangoon (Yangon), Mandalay and Pagan (Bagan). Old Yangon is succinctly described by Sarah Rooney in *30 Heritage Buildings of Yangon: Inside the City That Captured Time*.[38] It serves as a guide to anyone wishing to explore Yangon's wonderful but sadly neglected colonial architecture, a subject also covered by Virginia Henderson and Tim Webster in *Yangon Echoes: Inside Heritage Homes*.[39] Bob Percival's *Walking the Streets of Yangon: The People, Stories & Hidden Treasures of Downtown Cosmopolitan Yangon (Rangoon)* helps those wishing to see city life close up.[40] A good introduction to Mandalay is Dhida Saraya's *Mandalay: The Capital City, The Centre of the Universe*.[41] On Pagan, Michael Aung-Thwin's *Pagan: The Origins of Modern Burma* offers some interesting views.[42] Also of interest in this regard is Uta Gartner's "Nay Pyi Taw—The Reality and Myths of Capitals in Myanmar" in *Southeast Asian Historiography: Unravelling the Myths*, edited by Volker Grabowsky.[43]

Michael Charney offers a concise and accessible introduction to Myanmar's recent past in *A History of Modern Burma*.[44] Another historical overview worth reading is Thant Myint U's *The Making of*

Modern Burma.⁴⁵ The same author examines the past twenty years more closely in his most recent major work, *The Hidden History of Burma*.⁴⁶ Despite a few surprising lapses, Richard Cockett provides a very readable survey of the modern period in *Blood, Dreams and Gold: The Changing Face of Burma*.⁴⁷ A different approach was taken by Michael Aung Thwin and Matrii Aung Thwin in *A History of Myanmar since Ancient Times*.⁴⁸ In a bold and at times provocative study, they emphasize local sources and fresh interpretations of historical trends and events. For the earlier historical period, one of the best introductions is the chapter about the formation of Myanmar in the first volume of Victor Lieberman's *Strange Parallels: Southeast Asia in Global Context, c.800–1830*.⁴⁹ Also worth consulting is Michael Aung Thwin's *Myth and History in the Historiography of Early Burma*.⁵⁰ Jame Dibiasio's surprisingly chatty book *Who Killed the King of Bagan?* can best be described as "fictionalized history".⁵¹

The writings of early European visitors to Myanmar are a rich source of material, able to both inform and amuse. In 2004, the *SOAS Bulletin of Burma Research* helpfully reproduced extracts from the works of several explorers, traders and missionaries who recorded their experiences and views of the country between the thirteenth and nineteenth centuries.⁵² Most of these early contacts were summarized by Daniel Hall in *Europe and Burma*.⁵³ The Dutch experience in the seventeenth century has been examined in detail by Wil Dijk.⁵⁴ While a little repetitive at times, Arash Khazeni's description of Indo-Persian encounters with Myanmar offers a new perspective.⁵⁵ For anyone wishing to investigate early British interventions in Myanmar, comprehensive reports were produced by several envoys to the Burmese court. Foremost among them were Michael Symes (who was sent on missions in 1795 and 1802), John Crawfurd (in 1827) and Henry Yule (in 1855).⁵⁶ They described Myanmar as they saw it at the time, but of equal interest to modern readers are their reactions to the new and unusual phenomena they encountered. Another important work on Britain's early dealings with Myanmar is *The Pacification of Burma* by Charles Crosthwaite, the Chief Commissioner of the province between 1887 and 1890.⁵⁷

While a little hard to find, a local account of Myanmar's resistance to conquest and colonial occupation can be found in Ni Ni Myint's *Burma's Struggle against British Imperialism (1885–1895)*.⁵⁸ The same broad theme is picked up in Maung Maung's more detailed treatment of the subject, titled *Burmese Nationalist Movements, 1940–1948*.⁵⁹ Another local perspective on the nationalist struggle and its aftermath can be found in Tekkatho Sein Tin's *Thakin Ba Sein and Burma's Struggle for Independence*.[60] For developments during the 1930s, when Burma's modern nationalist movement began to take shape and become organized, the standard text is Khin Yi's *The Dobama Movement in Burma (1930–1938)*.[61] It is complemented well by Aye Kyaw's *The Voice of Young Burma*, published by Cornell University's Southeast Asia Program.[62] Pulling many of these strands together into a cogent narrative is *Aung San and the Struggle for Burmese Independence* by Angeline Naw.[63] An unapologetically sympathetic look at this subject by a foreign scholar is Paul Webb's *The Peacock's Children: The Struggle for Freedom in Burma, 1885–Present*.[64]

Looking at Burmese history from a different viewpoint is *Inroads into Burma: A Travellers' Anthology*, edited by Gerry Abbott.[65] It contains extracts from the writings of more than forty foreign observers of Myanmar from the fifteenth to the twentieth century. Also very useful in this regard is Helen Trager's *Burma through Alien Eyes: Missionary Views of the Burmese in the Nineteenth Century*.[66] One notable Western visitor to Myanmar during the 1890s was V.C.S. (Scott) O'Connor, who vividly recorded his impressions in *The Silken East: A Record of Life and Travel in Burma*.[67] Another British visitor with an interesting worldview was George Bird, who wrote his comprehensive book *Wanderings in Burma* "for those who have occasion to visit the country".[68] For a lighter survey of Myanmar during much the same period, see Mrs Ernest Hart's *Picturesque Burma: Past and Present*.[69] Another intrepid female traveller was Geraldine Mitton, who wrote an entertaining account of *A Bachelor Girl in Burma*.[70] An interesting sidelight on life in colonial Myanmar is provided by the chapter on Maymyo (now known as Pyin Oo Lwin) in Barbara Cossette's *The Great Hill Stations of Asia*.[71]

Rudyard Kipling spent only three days in Myanmar, in 1889. He never visited Mandalay, the city with which he is most often associated, through his "Barrack Room Ballad" of that name.[72] Even so, there is a large body of literature and music that trades on his imagined knowledge of the country. There are even bars named after him in tourist hotels in Yangon and Mandalay. Those wishing to learn more about Kipling's links to Myanmar might start by reading his own account of the 1889 visit, in *From Sea to Sea and Other Sketches: Letters of Travel*, or by consulting the edited volume by Andrew Lycett on *Kipling Abroad: Traffics and Discoveries: From*

Burma to Brazil.⁷³ In 1981, a useful discussion of "Kipling's Burma" appeared in *The Kipling Journal*.⁷⁴ In 1984, the journal *Asian Affairs* published an entertaining literary and historical review, also titled "Kipling's Burma".⁷⁵ On the ballad itself, its many musical settings and continuing connections to Myanmar in literature, art and the movies, see Andrew Selth's *Kipling, "Mandalay" and Burma in the Popular Imagination*, published by the City University of Hong Kong's Southeast Asia Research Centre.⁷⁶ The role of Kipling's ballad and Western music in shaping popular perceptions of colonial Myanmar was examined in Selth's later book *Burma, Kipling and Western Music: The Riff From Mandalay*.⁷⁷

There are many fascinating memoirs of the colonial period (1824–1948), written by civil servants, soldiers, missionaries and travellers. A good example is H.T. White's *A Civil Servant in Burma*.⁷⁸ Also very enjoyable are the works of Maurice Collis, who was in Myanmar from 1912 to 1934. Among other books, Collis wrote *Trials in Burma*, *Lords of the Sunset* and *Into Hidden Burma*.⁷⁹ One of the most entertaining and elegantly written memoirs available is *The Changing of Kings: Memories of Burma, 1934–1949* by Leslie Glass.⁸⁰ A rare Thai perspective is offered in Damrong Rajanubhab's *Journey through Burma in 1936*.⁸¹ An unusual take on this period is Carol Boshier's *Mapping Cultural Nationalism: The Scholars of the Burma Research Society, 1910–1935*.⁸² Two other books that offer personal views of Myanmar in the early twentieth century are David Donnison's *Last of the Guardians: A Story of Burma, Britain and a Family* and C.H. Campagnac's *The Autobiography of a Wanderer in England and Burma*.⁸³ For an engaging biography of the British forester J.H.Williams, author of *Elephant Bill* and other well-known works, see V.C. Croke's *Elephant Company*.⁸⁴

One aspect of the European experience in colonial Myanmar that was paid considerable attention by British and American publishers during the nineteenth and early twentieth centuries, but has been largely neglected since, is the role of Christian missionaries. Myanmar history buffs are still waiting for a comprehensive and erudite overview of their activities, but anyone interested in this subject could start with two early works, *Christian Missions in Burma* by W.C.B. Purser and *An Outline of the History of the Catholic Burmese Mission* by Paul Bigandet.⁸⁵ More modern, albeit specialized, studies include *Conflict, Politics and Proselytism: Methodist Missionaries in Colonial and Postcolonial Upper Burma, 1887–1966* by Michael Leigh and *Adoniram Judson: A Bicentennial Appreciation of the Pioneer American Missionary*, edited by J.G. Duesing.[86] The dramatic impact of Christian teachings on the Karen ethnic minority is discussed in J.R. Case's *An Unpredictable Gospel: American Evangelicals and World Christianity, 1812–1920*.[87] It is not easy to find a copy, but Wim Vervest gives a detailed account of the American Baptist Chin mission and a pioneering missionary family in *The Lost Dictionary*.[88]

After a period of neglect, several popular histories of Myanmar during the Second World War have appeared in recent years, including Jon Latimer's *Burma: The Forgotten War* and Frank McLynn's *The Burma Campaign: Disaster into Triumph, 1942–45*.[89] Julian Thompson has published a valuable collection of interviews with veterans.[90] The standard reference work, however, remains Louis Allen's *Burma: The Longest War, 1941–45*.[91] For a first-hand account of the Burma campaign by its most celebrated participant, a reader cannot go past William Slim's epic *Defeat into Victory*.[92] Another outstanding memoir, this time from a foot soldier's point of view, is George MacDonald Fraser's *Quartered Safe Out Here: A Recollection of the War in Burma*.[93] Two newer books that look at specific aspects of the war, and are worth reading, are *Lost Warriors* by Philip Davies and *The Special Operations Executive in Burma* by Richard Duckett.[94] An overview of the air war can be found in Michael Pearson's *The Burma Air Campaign*.[95] Andrew Boyd provides a good introduction to naval operations in the period leading up to the Japanese invasion in *The Royal Navy in Eastern Waters*.[96] Two quirky but original perspectives on the war are provided by Robert Lyman's *Among the Headhunters* and Brendan Koerner's *Now The Hell Will Start*.[97]

Still of interest, despite their age, are two works that describe Japan's relations with the Burmese nationalist movement led by Aung San in the period leading up to the war. One is Izumiya Tatsuro's *The Minami Organ*, first published in 1967.[98] The other is Won Z. Yoon's *Japan's Scheme for the Liberation of Burma*, released by Ohio University in 1973.[99] Both draw heavily on Japanese documents and the memories of Japanese personnel involved. The broader Japanese experience during the war is captured well by John Nunneley and Kazuo Tamayama in *Tales by Japanese Soldiers of the Burma Campaign, 1942–1945*.[100] Another Japanese view is offered by *Victory into Defeat*, which has been translated into English by a group of Burmese scholars.[101] Although it was published more than fifty years ago, still relevant is Yuji Aida's *Prisoner of the British:*

A Japanese Soldier's Experiences in Burma.[102] Anyone wishing to pursue this aspect of the war can also consult T.R. Sareen's *Japanese Prisoners of War in India, 1942–46*.[103] For a compelling fictional look at the war, and the basis of an award-winning 1956 film, see Michio Takeyama's *Harp of Burma*.[104]

Myanmar's own perspectives on the war have been captured in a number of interesting and readable books. For example, the country's president during the conflict gave his view of events in Ba Maw's *Breakthrough in Burma: Memoirs of a Revolution, 1939–1946*.[105] This account complements two classics in this category; namely, Khin Myo Chit's *Three Years under the Japs* and U Nu's *Burma under the Japanese*.[106] Another account of the period is found in Robert Taylor's translation of Thein Pe Myint's book *Wartime Traveller*, which was published under the title *Marxism and Resistance in Burma, 1942–1945*.[107] Also worth tracking down and reading, if possible, are English translations of two other Burmese books about the war. One is *Wartime in Burma: A Diary, January to June 1942* by Theippan Maung Wa (U Sein Tin).[108] The other is *A Man Like Him: Portrait of the Burmese Journalist, Journal Kyaw U Chit Maung* by Kyaw Ma Ma Lay.[109] Both works help correct the rather distorted picture painted by conventional Western histories, which not surprisingly tend to focus on the Allied campaign and tense US-British relations during this period.[110]

Dozens of books have been published about the infamous Burma–Thai railway. Most memoirs, however, have been written by former Allied prisoners of war (POW) based in Thailand, and do not refer specifically to conditions working on the line in Myanmar. Two notable exceptions, giving perspectives from both sides, are *A Doctor's War* by Rowley Richards and *Railwaymen in the War: Tales by Japanese Railway Soldiers in Burma and Thailand 1941–47* by Kazuo Tamayama.[111] An original view of the lives of the Allied prisoners is given in S.A. Eldredge's *Captive Audiences/Captive Performers: Music and Theatre as Strategies for Survival on the Thailand–Burma Railway, 1942–1945*.[112] The dreadful plight of the thousands of Asian (including Burmese) labourers conscripted by the Japanese to work on the railway is spelt out in volume four of a monumental six-volume study by Paul Kratoska entitled *The Thailand–Burma Railway, 1942–1946: Documents and Selected Writings*.[113] This subject is also covered in Kratoska's edited study of Asian labourers under the Japanese.[114] For a picture of life as an Allied POW in Rangoon's Central Gaol, see Lionel Hudson's *The*

Rats of Rangoon.[115] Also of interest in this regard is Jean Newland's *Guests of the Emperor.*[116]

Post-war developments in Myanmar, and events after the country regained its independence from Great Britain in 1948, are covered by the rather idiosyncratic memoirs of U Nu, the country's first democratically elected prime minister, in *U Nu – Saturday's Son.*[117] Michael Leigh also discusses the "post-war mess" in *The Collapse of British Rule in Burma.*[118] Kin Oung offers a personal view on the vexed question *Who Killed Aung San?*[119] For a more scholarly account of the circumstances surrounding the assassination of Myanmar's independence hero in 1947, see Robert Taylor's article "Politics in Late Colonial Burma: The Case of U Saw", in the journal *Modern Asian Studies.*[120] Ba U, who was Myanmar's president from 1952 to 1957, wrote one of the first autobiographies to be written by a senior Burmese figure, in *My Burma*. It was described at the time as "intimate, detailed, introspective, honest, generally humorous", and for that is of considerable interest, but it contains little discussion of public issues.[121] By far the best study of the early development of the Burmese armed forces and their critical political role during this period is Mary Callahan's *Making Enemies: War and State Building in Burma.*[122] A Burmese soldier's memories of the time are recorded in *Burma's Son.*[123]

In 1983 and 1984, Hugh Tinker edited two massive volumes of official documents on colonial Myanmar's constitutional relations with Britain, titled *Burma: The Struggle for Independence, 1944–1948.*[124] It is hardly the kind of work that one sits down and reads from cover to cover, but it contains an excellent introduction and a useful chronology of events. It is also well worth dipping into the documents themselves for candid and sometimes surprising revelations about particular personalities and developments in the immediate post-war period. Lucian Pye's 1962 study *Politics, Personality, and Nation Building*, on the thorny issue of Myanmar's "national identity", still manages to stir controversy but is worth a glance, at least.[125] On the same broad subject, see Andrew Selth's "Geoffrey Gorer and the Study of Burma's 'Personality'" in *The Journal of Burma Studies.*[126] First published in 1973, Ernst Schumacher's revolutionary study *Small is Beautiful* made numerous references to Myanmar, which, following a visit there in 1955, he felt represented a decentralized, human-scale society that was to be emulated.[127] Also worth reading on the post-independence era is Thant Myint U's *The River of Lost Footsteps: Histories of Burma.*[128]

The period from General Ne Win's military *coup d'etat* in 1962 to the 1988 pro-democracy uprising has been examined in several books, of widely varying quality. One essential text is Robert Taylor's *General Ne Win: A Political Biography*.[129] This book followed Taylor's ground-breaking study *The State in Myanmar*.[130] A rare look inside military circles is provided by Kyi Win Sein in *Me and the Generals of the Revolutionary Council*.[131] Two classic American studies covering the socialist period are Josef Silverstein's *Burma: Military Rule and the Politics of Stagnation* and David Steinberg's *Burma's Road toward Development: Growth and Ideology under Military Rule*.[132] Another excellent source of information, statistics and insights on the Ne Win era is Yoshihiro Nakanishi's *Strong Soldiers, Failed Revolution: The State and Military in Burma, 1962–88*.[133] Two sweeping yet detailed studies of modern Myanmar, describing the seizure of power by the armed forces in 1962 and its dire consequences for the country, are Martin Smith's *Burma: Insurgency and the Politics of Ethnicity* and Bertil Lintner's *Burma in Revolt: Opium and Insurgency since 1948*.[134] Both are essential reading.

There is no definitive history of the nationwide pro-democracy uprising that wracked Burma in 1988. The best-known account, written shortly after the events described and based largely on interviews with eye-witnesses, is Bertil Lintner's *Outrage: Burma's Struggle for Democracy*.[135] A radically different version of events is given by one of the country's presidents at the time, in Maung Maung's *The 1988 Uprising in Burma*, published by Yale University in 1999.[136] These two accounts and one other are usefully compared in Hans-Bernd Zollner's "Behind the Smoke of 'Myth' and 'Counter-Myth': Contours of What Happened in Burma in 1988" in *Southeast Asian Historiography*, edited by Volker Grabowsky.[137] Also relevant in this regard are two moving prison memoirs: Ma Thanegi's *Nor Iron Bars a Cage*, and Ma Thida's *Prisoner of Conscience: My Steps through Insein*.[138] On political prisoners more generally, there are some excellent studies by international organizations like Amnesty International and Human Rights Watch, but for a more personal perspective see for example *The Darkness We See: Torture in Burma's Interrogation Centres and Prisons*, published in 2005 by the Assistance Association for Political Prisoners (Burma).[139]

On the contemporary period more broadly, a first-time visitor to Myanmar could profitably begin by browsing through David Steinberg's essential primer, *Burma/Myanmar: What Everyone Needs to Know*.[140] A different kind of starting point is *The Disorder in Order: The Army–State in Burma since* 1962 by Donald Seekins, which describes in straightforward terms the development of the military regime up to the turn of the century.[141] The story is picked up by Hans-Bernd Zollner in *The Beast and the Beauty: The History of the Conflict between the Military and Aung San Suu Kyi in Myanmar, 1988–2011, Set in a Global Context*.[142] At a different level, Ian Holliday's *Burma Redux: Global Justice and the Quest for Political Reform in Myanmar* surveys Myanmar's problems to that date and thoughtfully canvasses a range of possible solutions.[143] The military government's point of view is given in Hla Min's *Political Situation of Myanmar and Its Role in the Region*.[144] For many years, successive editions of this work summarized the regime's policies and responses to its critics.

The advent of President Thein Sein's "reformist" quasi-civilian government in 2011 prompted a flood of new publications, both inside and outside the country. The election of Aung San Suu Kyi and the National League for Democracy in 2015 was the trigger for another wave of histories, analyses and commentaries.

Over the past decade a host of authors has written about such matters as Myanmar's governance, economic growth, internal security, civil society and human rights, from particular points of view. Not all the works produced can be described as accurate or objective. However, a newcomer to the field can get a good overview of the country's many daunting challenges by dipping into edited collections of papers written by acknowledged experts, such as *Myanmar: The Dynamics of an Evolving Polity*, edited by D.I. Steinberg.[145] The 2018 *Routledge Handbook of Contemporary Myanmar* is a comprehensive reference, although inevitably it has been overtaken by events.[146] Andrew Selth's *Interpreting Myanmar*, a collection of ninety-seven articles posted on the Lowy Institute's *Interpreter* blog between 2008 and 2019, covers a wide range of current issues.[147] For informative and insightful pieces on several subjects of enduring interest, see also *Unraveling Myanmar's Transition* by Pavin Chachavalpongpun and others.[148] The Australian National University's biennial Myanmar Update conferences have yielded several works that discuss a range of contemporary issues. Good examples include *Debating Democratization in Myanmar* and *Living with Myanmar*.[149]

In turn, prisoner of conscience, Nobel Peace Prize winner, NLD party leader and (until February 2021) de facto prime minister of Myanmar, Aung San Suu Kyi, is named as the author of several books. These include *Freedom from Fear, Letters from Burma* and *The Voice of Hope*.[150] She has also written two short biographies of her father, General Aung San.[151] Some speeches and informal comments to her followers have been collected by Hans-Bernd Zollner and published as *Talks over the Gate: Aung San Suu Kyi's Dialogues with the People, 1995 and 1996*.[152] Aung San Suu Kyi's official policy positions, assumed also to represent her personal views, were presented to the public in the 43rd Singapore Lecture, given in 2018 under the title *Democratic Transition in Myanmar: Challenges and the Way Forward*.[153] Important as contributions to the public record, but not for the faint-hearted, are the four weighty volumes of documents, speeches and interviews published in 2020 by Alan Clements and Fergus Harlow under the title *Burma's Voices of Freedom*.[154] They include the transcripts of a number of interviews with Aung San Suu Kyi.

Aung San Suu Kyi has been the subject of several biographies. These include *The Daughter* by Hans-Bernd Zollner and Rodion Ebbighausen, *Perfect Hostage: A Life of Aung San Suu Kyi* by Justin Wintle, and *The Lady and the Peacock: The Life of Aung San Suu Kyi* by Peter Popham.[155] Another contribution to this genre is *The Lady: Aung San Suu Kyi: Nobel Laureate and Burma's Prisoner* by Barbara Victor. It was reportedly based on "exclusive interviews" arranged with the help of Myanmar's military intelligence service. Most of these books are easy to read, but few take a critical approach to their main subject. Indeed, to a greater or lesser extent, all fail rigorously to interrogate the available evidence regarding Aung San Suu Kyi's character and performance, both as a human rights icon and as a practising politician.[156] Myths and rumours are sometimes interpreted as facts. As Kyaw Yin Hlaing pointed out in an excellent review article in 2007, for many years readers faced a choice between excessively sympathetic accounts of Aung San Suu Kyi's life and work, and diatribes against her by supporters of the military regime, among others.[157]

Until her reputation collapsed in 2016, at least in the eyes of the international community, the most critical work about the Nobel Peace laureate was Bertil Lintner's *Aung San Suu Kyi and Burma's Struggle for Democracy*.[158] In 2017, her dramatic fall from grace was examined in Andrew Selth's *Aung San Suu Kyi and the Politics of Personality*.[159] Even before then, Shwe Lu Maung had dared to ask the question *Is Suu Kyi a Racist?*[160] He looked at the Rohingya clearances, the Kachin war and the dominance of the ethnic Bamar in

Myanmar's politics, economy and society. The world is still waiting for a detailed and objective analysis of Aung San Suu Kyi's political thinking and place in modern Burmese politics, but a start has been made by Michal Lubina in *The Moral Democracy: The Political Thought of Aung San Suu Kyi* and his later study *A Political Biography of Aung San Suu Kyi*.[161] In the meantime, she continues to mesmerize her followers and remains a highly marketable commodity. This is perhaps best demonstrated by a collection of fashion photographs and quotations titled *Images of Mother Loved by the People*.[162] Even Aung San Suu Kyi's former cook has published a memoir about his two decades working for her.[163] Since the February 2021 coup, her public defence of the atrocities perpetrated against the Rohingyas has faded into the background and she is once again being described as a champion of democracy.[164]

Myanmar is connected to a number of other notable individuals who have been the subject of biographies and autobiographies. Several of these works have already been mentioned, but others worth reading include Ronald Lewin's biography of William Slim, which is still considered one of the best works about that remarkable soldier.[165] Trevor Royle's controversial biography of the eccentric general Orde Wingate, founder of the Chindits, is also worth a look.[166] Another book set in the Second World War is the compelling account by Stephen Brookes of his trek from Myanmar to India in 1942, *Through the Jungle of Death: A Boy's Escape from Wartime Burma*.[167] Bilal Raschid's book *The Invisible Patriot* is noteworthy not only for the account of his own life but also for the observations about his father, the Muslim nationalist and politician U Raschid.[168] As Benedict Rogers admits, his biography *Than Shwe* draws heavily on "rumour and reported anecdote", but it is the only study to date of Myanmar's military leader from 1992 to 2011.[169] There are also some fascinating memoirs by European and Burmese women caught up in Myanmar's wartime and post-independence struggles, including *Twilight over Burma* by Inge Sargent and *A Journey in Time* by Wai Wai Myaing.[170]

For insights into daily life in Myanmar under the generals, particularly after the 1988 uprising, the best source is Christina Fink's *Living Silence: Burma under Military Rule*.[171] If a copy can be found, it is also worth dipping into *Nowhere to Be Home: Narratives from Survivors of Burma's Military Regime*, edited by Maggie Lemere and Zoe West.[172] Similar themes are pursued in *Burmese Lives: Ordinary Life Stories under the Burmese Regime*, edited by

Wen-Chin Chang and Eric Tagliacozzo.[173] For a unique local perspective, see *Little Daughter: A Memoir of Survival in Burma and the West* by Zoya Phan and Damien Lewis.[174] Everyday life in modern Myanmar is also the subject of Matthew Mullen's interesting and thoughtful book *Pathways That Changed Myanmar*.[175] Phil Thornton provides a trenchant but entertaining account of life on the Myanmar-Thailand border in *Restless Souls*.[176] A first-rate description of Myanmar under military rule by a well-informed foreign observer is Emma Larkin's *Secret Histories: Finding George Orwell in a Burmese Teashop*.[177] Equally informative and readable is Larkin's later book *Everything is Broken: The Untold Story of Disaster under Burma's Military Rule*.[178]

One notable aspect of the struggle for democracy and human rights in Myanmar since 1988 is the extent to which activists from both Myanmar and foreign countries have used modern communications technology and information-sharing techniques to promote their causes. This has included the publication of a large number of English language reports, booklets, briefings and pamphlets. Most have been posted online, through readily identifiable websites. However, many have also been published in hard copy, albeit often in small print runs meant for select audiences. Anyone wishing to become familiar with the scope and content of such publications could start by looking at the reports released over the past thirty years by organizations like Amnesty International, Human Rights Watch and Fortify Rights. Although they are a little harder to find, a range of other works were issued by ethnic minority organizations such as the Karen Human Rights Group and specific interest groups, including the Assistance Association for Political Prisoners (Burma). A selection of reports by these organizations has been listed in this and past editions of the bibliography.

Access to the internet in Myanmar has long been the subject of close interest by human rights campaigners. A useful introduction to the subject, with a section on the implications for Myanmar, is *Open Networks, Closed Regimes: The Impact of the Internet on Authoritarian Rule* by Shanthi Kalathil and T.C. Boas.[179] A more focused study was *Internet Filtering in Burma in 2006-2007: A Country Study*, initially published by the Open Net Initiative in 2007 and updated in 2012.[180] In 2014, Reporters Without Borders issued a report entitled *Enemies of the Internet*, which included a section critical of the situation in Myanmar.[181] Also relevant is "The State of Internet Censorship in Myanmar" by the Open Observatory of Network

Interference.[182] Censorship was also a major theme of Carolyn Wakeman and San San Tin in *No Time for Dreams*.[183] On the news media and communications in Myanmar more generally, a good foundation is provided by the works of Lisa Brooten, including "'Media as our Mirror': Indigenous Media in Burma (Myanmar)" in *Global Indigenous Media: Cultures, Poetics and Politics* edited by Pamela Wilson and Michelle Stewart.[184] Brooten also co-edited *Myanmar Media in Transition*, which provided an excellent overview of the country's media landscape before the February 2021 coup.[185]

For an invaluable overview of legal issues in Myanmar, and the way they have been approached by Western (and other) scholars over the years, see Melissa Crouch's "Rediscovering 'Law' in Myanmar: A Review of Scholarship on the Legal System in Myanmar" in the *Pacific Rim Law and Policy Review*.[186] Andrew Huxley offers a different kind of introduction to these issues in "Precolonial Burmese Law: Conical Hat and Shoulder Bag".[187] For a collection of papers relating to contemporary legal questions, it is hard to go past *Law, Society and Transition in Myanmar*, edited by Melissa Crouch and Tim Lindsey.[188] Although it is aimed more at specialists, also recommended is Nick Cheesman's *Opposing the Rule of Law: How Myanmar's Courts Make Law and Order*.[189] Myanmar's 2008 constitution and its impact, at least until February 2021, is expertly discussed by Melissa Crouch in *The Constitution of Myanmar: A Contextual Analysis*.[190] Also useful in this regard is *Constitutionalism and Legal Change in Myanmar*, edited by Andrew Harding.[191] Both should be read in conjunction with the *Constitution of the Republic of the Union of Myanmar*.[192] For an amusing and instructive treatment of legal issues set in a colonial Burmese context, see *The Brothel Boy and Other Parables of the Law* by Norval Morris.[193]

Perhaps reflecting the breadth and complexity of Myanmar's economic problems, and their changing character over the decades, there are few books or reports that offer a comprehensive overview of these issues for non-specialists. However, a good historical introduction is Ian Brown's *A Colonial Economy in Crisis*.[194] This helps put into context the seminal 1974 study by Michael Adas, *The Burma Delta*.[195] Should anyone wish to explore these subjects more deeply, a good start would be P.J. Perry's *Myanmar (Burma) since 1962: The Failure of Development*, published in 2007.[196] More comprehensive and up to date is Ian Brown's *Burma's Economy in the Twentieth Century*.[197] A later publication that was written with the general reader in mind is the Open Society's *Opportunities and Pitfalls: Preparing for Burma's Economic Transition*.[198] However, that too was left behind by developments under the NLD government. On the evolution of Myanmar's financial system, the best source is Sean Turnell's *Fiery Dragons: Banks, Moneylenders and Microfinance in Burma*.[199] It is now over twenty years old, but Teruko Saito and Lee Kin Kiong's *Statistics on the Burmese Economy* is still a valuable reference tool.[200]

On economic developments since 1988, a good source is *The Economic Transition in Myanmar after 1988: Market Economy versus State Control*, edited by Koichi Fujita, Fumihara Mieno and Ikuko Okamoto.[201] Lex Rieffel's USIP report about Myanmar's economy on the eve of the 2010 elections provides a useful snapshot of that period.[202] Konosuke Odaka takes the story forward to 2016 in *The Myanmar Economy: Its Past, Present and Prospects*.[203] Also worth consulting for its astute observations on Myanmar's economy and a number of related subjects is *The Business of Transition: Law Reform, Development and Economics in Myanmar*, edited by Melissa Crouch.[204] It remains to be seen what eventuates, but following the February 2021 coup economic sanctions appear once again to be on the table. Lee Jones made an important contribution to this vexed debate in *Societies Under Siege: Exploring How International Economic Sanctions (Do Not) Work*.[205] Also important in this regard is the extended article "Feeling Good or Doing Good" by Thihan Myo Nyun.[206] US sanctions in place before the coup were summarized by Michael Martin in *US Restrictions on Relations with Burma*.[207]

Given their place in Myanmar's history and economy, it is worth mentioning a few works on the country's jade and gemstone industries. An easy introduction to the former is an article by Richard Hughes and others on the *Lotus* website, but also of interest is S.K. Samuel's more specialized *Imperial Jade of Burma and Mutton-Fat Jade of India*.[208] The iniquities of Myanmar's modern jade mining industry are spelt out in *Jade: Myanmar's "Big State Secret"*, a 2015 report by Global Witness.[209] On gemstones, a good start is Joseph Kessel's classic *Mogok*, about Myanmar's famous ruby mining district in 1960.[210] There are also a few interesting White Lotus reprints about the area.[211] Another work of note is the version edited by Richard Hughes of *The Book of Ruby and Sapphire*, written in the 1930s by J.F. Halford-Watkins, who lived in Mogok for over twenty years.[212] More up to date is an article on Mogok written by Robert

Kane and Robert Kammerling for the journal *Gems and Gemology*.[213] A colourful (in all senses of the word) description of Myanmar's gems and gem trade is *Burma Gems* by Vladislav Yavorskyy.[214] Carol Clark provides an overview of the ruby trade in *Seeing Red*.[215]

While brief, an excellent introduction to Myanmar's ethnic minorities and their troubled relationships with the central government is Martin Smith's *State of Strife: The Dynamics of Ethnic Conflict in Burma*.[216] Smith is also a contributor to a sumptuous photographic survey by R.K. Diran titled *The Vanishing Tribes of Burma*.[217] Another worthwhile study is Ashley South's *Ethnic Politics in Burma: States of Conflict*.[218] A more personal perspective on ethnic issues can be gained from Pascal Khoo Thwe's *From the Land of Green Ghosts: A Burmese Odyssey*.[219] Although it was written thirty years ago, Jonathan Falla's *True Love and Bartholomew: Rebels on the Burmese Border* is still worth reading for its eloquent description of the plight of the Karens along the Myanmar-Thai border.[220] An important counterweight to this book is Ardeth Maung Thawnghmung's *The "Other" Karen in Myanmar: Ethnic Minorities and the Struggle without Arms*.[221] While a rather weighty tome, in several respects, Mandy Sadan's *Being and Becoming Kachin* is a comprehensive and scholarly study of the Kachin peoples.[222] Sadan has also edited an excellent study of the Kachins and the 1994–2011 ceasefire.[223]

On other ethnic minorities, Chao Tzang Yawnghwe's memoir offers a personal perspective on the complexities of Shan history and politics.[224] Ashley South has written incisively about Mon nationalism and its modern manifestations.[225] On the Wa, Bertil Lintner demonstrates rare access and knowledge in a research monograph and a book.[226] Often overlooked in discussions of Myanmar's ethnic groups are the long-established, if still not entirely accepted, Indian and Chinese communities. While now dated, useful background to the former is provided by N.R. Chakravati in *The Indian Minority in Burma*.[227] Its more recent circumstances are discussed by Renaud Egreteau in "Burmese Indians in Contemporary Burma: Heritage, Influence and Perceptions since 1988", published in the journal *Asian Ethnicity*.[228] A couple of good histories of Myanmar's Chinese community have been published over the past few years, including *Mapping Chinese Rangoon: Place and Nation among the Sino-Burmese* by Jade Roberts.[229] On a more idiosyncratic note, Hillel Halkin's *Across the Sabbath River* describes his investigation of the claim that one of Israel's "lost tribes" can be found on the Myanmar-India border.²³⁰

Thanks to the 2016–17 pogroms in Rakhine State, there are now a large number of books and reports that claim to answer the many questions surrounding the ethnic minority known as the Rohingyas. Some are not worth reading, and several others need to be treated with caution. A few are blatantly racist. For the background to current tensions, see Moshe Yegar's *Between Integration and Secession: The Muslim Communities of the Southern Philippines, Southern Thailand, and Western Burma*.²³¹ Another good introduction is Jacques Leider's "Competing Identities and the Hybridized History of Rohingyas" in *Metamorphosis: Studies in Social and Political Change in Myanmar*, edited by Renaud Egreteau and François Robinne.²³² Leider also published an article on Rohingya identity in the *Oxford Research Encyclopaedia of Asian History* that has sparked considerable interest.²³³ Also recommended is Derek Tonkin's well-researched and well-argued chapter in *Citizenship in Myanmar*, edited by Ashley South and Marie Lall.²³⁴ Nick Cheesman has edited a collection of thoughtful articles on Muslims and communal violence in Myanmar.²³⁵ Carlos Galache's history of the "Rohingya tragedy" provides newcomers with an excellent introduction to a very complex subject.²³⁶ The role of Myanmar's security forces in the latest Rohingya crisis was examined by Andrew Selth in a 2018 USIP Peaceworks report.²³⁷

On all these matters, as on so many other issues to do with Myanmar, it is always worth reading the reports issued periodically by the International Crisis Group, notably those written by its senior adviser, Richard Horsey.²³⁸ Another good source are the reports occasionally published by the US Congressional Research Service, particularly those authored by its specialist in Asian affairs, Michael F. Martin.

There are few major works that examine Myanmar's security environment, the study of which suffers from some major gaps.²³⁹ The subject was introduced in 2001 by Andrew Selth in *Burma: A Strategic Perspective*.²⁴⁰ Thant Myint U discussed Myanmar's current geostrategic significance in *Where China Meets India*.²⁴¹ Selth also provided a detailed analysis of the Tatmadaw in *Burma's Armed Forces: Power without Glory*.²⁴² For a similar but later Burmese treatment of this subject, see Maung Aung Myoe's *Building the Tatmadaw: Myanmar Armed Forces since 1948*.²⁴³ Maung Aung Myoe is also the author of a well-informed study of Myanmar's defence expenditure and the Tatmadaw's commercial interests, in *Praetorians, Profiteers or Professionals?*, edited by Michael Montesano and others.[244] John Buchanan's 2016 study *Militias in Myanmar* is another important source.[245] For a thoughtful examination of wider issues, see Kim Jolliffe's *Democratising Myanmar's Security Sector*.[246] The challenges faced by all those writing about Myanmar's security forces are discussed in Andrew Selth's 2009 article "Knowns and Unknowns: Measuring Myanmar's Military Capabilities", in the journal *Contemporary Southeast Asia*.[247]

Very little has been written in English about Myanmar's national police forces, but for the colonial period a good introduction is Lalita Hingkanonta Hanwong's *Policing in Colonial Burma*.[248] Book six of William Boyd Sinclair's ten-volume history *Confusion beyond Imagination* looks at questions of policing in the China-Burma-India theatre during World War II.[249] For the later period, Andrew Selth has published two working papers through the Griffith Asia Institute that examine aspects of the modern police force, including *Police Reform in Burma (Myanmar): Aims, Obstacles and Outcomes*.[250] Selth has also published a short article for *The Interpreter* titled "Burma: Police Reforms Expand Women's Roles".[251] The prison system in Myanmar has also been neglected by foreign scholars despite its prominent role in the country's colonial and post-colonial histories. However, a good entry point to the subject is Ian Brown's 2007 article in the *Journal of Southeast Asian Studies*, "A Commissioner Calls: Alexander Paterson and Colonial Burma's Prisons".[252] For a sobering look at more modern institutions, see Lu Nan's photographic survey, *Prisons of North Burma*.[253]

Despite being the subject of a great deal of comment and speculation over the years, Myanmar's intelligence agencies are even more opaque. There are few serious studies on this subject, but some works are helpful in understanding key capabilities, events and personalities. One is Des Ball's detailed study of Myanmar's signals intelligence operations, titled *Burma's Military Secrets*.[254] Others include Andrew Selth's chapter on Myanmar in Bob de Graaff's edited volume *Intelligence Communities and Cultures in Asia and the Middle East*.[255] The most recent major work in English is *Secrets and Power in Myanmar: Intelligence and the Fall of Khin Nyunt*, also by Selth.[256] This study reprises and takes the story forward from an academic article published in 1998 under the title "Burma's Intelligence Apparatus".[257] Rhys Thompson has looked closely at the history of the Myanmar Police Force's Special Branch, which functions as an integral part of the intelligence community.²⁵⁸ All these works attempt to provide objective, evidence-based analyses, free of the moralizing and political bias that often characterizes discussions of intelligence issues, particularly by members of the activist community.

The difficulty of obtaining accurate data about Myanmar's strategic environment, security forces and defence policies has not deterred some commentators from repeating inaccurate, and at times quite outlandish, rumours on these subjects. Such cases famously include claims that in 1948 the departing British armed forces left behind up to twenty Spitfire fighter aircraft, buried in crates around the country. There was also a period around 2006 when some journalists and other observers asserted that China had established military bases in Myanmar, radically changing the strategic outlook of the entire Indo-Pacific region. Also, from about 2000 to around 2015, various exile and activist groups argued that Myanmar's military regime was developing, or had even developed, nuclear, chemical and biological weapons. Despite the lack of hard evidence, such claims were given a prominence in the news media that they did not deserve. For correctives to such flights of fancy, see for example Andy Brockman and Tracy Spaight's *The Buried Spitfires of Burma*, Andrew Selth's *Chinese Military Bases in Burma: The Explosion of a Myth* and the chapter on Myanmar in the 2009 strategic dossier by the International Institute for Strategic Studies, *Preventing Nuclear Dangers*.²⁵⁹

There are surprisingly few major studies of Myanmar's international relations. A good summary of the situation up to 2006 is Jurgen Haacke's *Myanmar's Foreign Policy: Domestic Influences and International Implications*.²⁶⁰ A more recent overview is provided by Renaud Egreteau and Larry Jagan, *Soldiers and Diplomacy in Burma: Understanding the Foreign Relations of the Burmese Praetorian State*.²⁶¹ On regional connections, a good start is Stephen McCarthy's chapter on Myanmar and ASEAN in Lowell Dittmer's edited volume, *Burma or Myanmar? The Struggle for National Identity*.²⁶² A slim study of Myanmar's relationship with the European Union was released in 2020.²⁶³ On bilateral relationships, see for example *Modern China-Myanmar Relations: Dilemmas of Mutual Dependence* by D.I. Steinberg and Hongwei Fan, *Wooing the Generals: India's New Burma Policy* by Renaud Egreteau and *Burma and Japan since 1940: From "Co-Prosperity" to "Quiet Dialogue"* by D.M. Seekins.²⁶⁴ Kenton Clymer filled a major gap in the literature in

2015 when he published *A Delicate Relationship: The United States and Burma/Myanmar since 1945*.[265] There is still no detailed study of Myanmar's controversial relationship with North Korea, but Andray Abrahamian compares and contrasts the two countries in *North Korea and Myanmar: Divergent Paths*.[266]

The face of insurgency in Myanmar is changing so quickly that anything recommended here would soon be out of date. That said, a useful introduction is Paul Keenan's *By Force of Arms: Armed Ethnic Groups in Burma*.[267] Another dated but more nuanced overview is Martin Smith's "Ethnic Conflicts in Burma: From Separatism to Federalism", in *A Handbook on Terrorism and Insurgency in Southeast Asia*, edited by A.T.H. Tan.[268] See also the Asia Foundation's valuable survey *The Contested Areas of Myanmar: Subnational Conflict, Aid, and Development*.[269] The reconciliation process and related peace negotiations are also constantly shifting. It is now out of date, but Zaw Oo and Win Min's *Assessing Burma's Ceasefire Accords* is worth a quick look.[270] The same can be said for Kyaw Yin Hlaing's edited volume *Prisms on the Golden Pagoda: Perspectives on National Reconciliation in Myanmar*.[271] An overview by a close observer is Min Zaw Oo's *Understanding Myanmar's Peace Process: Ceasefire Agreements*.[272] A rare personal perspective is provided by Aung Naing Oo in *Lessons Learned from Myanmar's Peace Process*.[273] There are a number of good book chapters on this subject, among them Ashley South's "Update on the Peace Process" in *Burma/Myanmar – Where Now?*, edited by Mikael Gravers and Flemming Ytzen.[274] For a sobering assessment of the peace process, see Bertil Lintner's *Why Burma's Peace Efforts Have Failed to End Its Internal Wars*.[275] The advent of a new military regime will doubtless leave some of these works behind.

Myanmar is the world's second-largest producer of opium, after Afghanistan. It is also a major exporter of methamphetamines. The origins of the drug trade in the Golden Triangle (of northern Myanmar, Thailand and Laos) are described in Alfred McCoy's groundbreaking study *The Politics of Heroin: CIA Complicity in the Global Drug Trade*.[276] This account is complemented well by Richard Gibson and Wenhua Chen in *The Secret Army: Chiang Kai-shek and the Drug Warlords of the Golden Triangle*.[277] The issue is also examined, albeit from quite different viewpoints, in *A Failing Grade: Burma's Drug Eradication Efforts* and Martin Jelsma et al., *Trouble in the Triangle: Opium and Conflict in Burma*.[278] The methamphetamine problem is explored in Bertil Lintner and Michael Black's

Merchants of Madness: The Methamphetamine Explosion in the Golden Triangle.[279] For recent discussions of these and related issues, see Tom Kramer's *The Current State of Counternarcotics Policy and Drug Reform Debates in Myanmar* and Vanda Felbab-Brown's *Myanmar Maneuvers: How to Break Political-Criminal Alliances in Contexts of Transition.*[280] The UN Office on Drugs and Crime (UNODC) has posted a range of useful publications relating to Myanmar on its website.

Books by foreigners describing their experiences and emotions in Myanmar are proliferating as more people visit the country and take up temporary residence there. Needless to say, some of these works are better than others. Indeed, as David Scott Mathieson has noted, Myanmar has produced "a minor canon of self-promotional reportage".[281] Unsurprisingly, given their mixed quality, several of these books are self-published. However, there have been some travelogues published over the past century that must be considered essential reading.

One early visitor was Somerset Maugham, who gave his impressions of Myanmar in 1923 in *The Gentleman in the Parlour.*[282] A later but equally celebrated effort was by Norman Lewis, who described his 1951 visit there in *Golden Earth.*[283] Another notable work in this genre is Bertil Lintner's *Land of Jade* about his extraordinary journey across Myanmar from India to China in 1985–87.[284] In a similar vein is Shelby Tucker's *Among Insurgents.*[285] Not quite as adventurous, but no less entertaining, is Andrew Marshall's *The Trouser People.*[286] A Western-style travel book by a contemporary Burmese writer is Ma Thanegi's *The Native Tourist: A Holiday Pilgrimage in Myanmar.*[287] As already noted, memoirs by tourists and temporary residents are often eminently forgettable, but there are some notable exceptions. Pico Iyer makes astute and often amusing observations about Myanmar during the Ne Win era in *Video Night in Kathmandu.*[288] Rory MacLean's *Under the Dragon* is worth reading, as is Timothy Syrota's *Welcome to Burma.*[289] David Eimer's book *A Savage Dreamland: Journeys in Burma* rates as one of the better recent contributions to this genre.[290] As an aside, it is a delight to compare Paul Theroux's impressions of Myanmar, as brilliantly recorded in *The Great Railway Bazaar* in 1975, with those in his *Ghost Train to the Eastern Star*, written more than thirty years later.[291]

The best known description in English of classical Burmese culture and customs is J.G. Scott's *The Burman: His Life and Notions*, first published under the pseudonym "Shway Yoe" in 1882.²⁹² Another standard work, still useful for its description of traditional Burmese life, is Mi Mi Khaing's *Burmese Family*.²⁹³ Khin Myo Chit's book *Festivals and Flowers*, charmingly illustrated by Paw Oo Thet, is a good guide for foreigners not familiar with Myanmar's many public holidays and celebrations.²⁹⁴ An unusual but illuminating study of social mores is Georg Noack's *Local Traditions, Global Modernities: Dress, Identity and the Creation of Public Self-Images in Contemporary Urban Myanmar*.²⁹⁵ Another book that appeals on several levels is Dawn Rooney's *The Thiri Rama: Finding Ramayana in Myanmar*.²⁹⁶ A major gap in the study of Myanmar's culture and society was filled by the publication in 2019 of *The Politics of Love in Myanmar* by Lynette Chua.²⁹⁷ It was the first scholarly examination (in English) of local lesbian, gay, bisexual and transgender (LGBT) issues.

There have been a number of good books written over the past decade about the prominent place of women in Burmese society and their important role as agents of change. However, the best introduction to the subject probably remains Mi Mi Khaing's *The World of Burmese Women*.²⁹⁸ This classic work is put into a wider context by Chie Ikeya's excellent *Refiguring Women, Colonialism, and Modernity in Burma*.²⁹⁹ Bringing the story up to date is *The Female Voice of Myanmar* by Nilanjana Sengupta.³⁰⁰ Other modern treatments of gender issues include Jessica Harriden's *The Authority of Influence: Women and Power in Burmese History* and Tharapi Than's *Women in Modern Burma*.³⁰¹ For those interested in such issues, it is worth consulting two other works that examine the often unrecognized influence of women on Myanmar's politics, economy and society. These are *The Other Ladies of Myanmar* by Jennifer Rigby and *Women, Peace and Security in Myanmar: Between Feminism and Ethnopolitics* edited by Ashid Kolas.³⁰²

There are few major studies of Myanmar's performing arts in the English language. The subject is briefly introduced in Noel Singer's *Burmese Dance and Theatre*.³⁰³ A more recent production worth consulting is Daniel Ehrlich's photographic tribute to the world of traditional theatre and folk festivals, titled *Backstage Mandalay: The Netherworld of Burmese Performing Arts*.³⁰⁴ Gavin Douglas provides an erudite introduction to traditional Burmese music in his chapter "Myanmar (Burma)" in *Encyclopaedia of Popular Music of the World*, edited by John Shepherd et al.³⁰⁵ Modern Western-style music in Myanmar is examined by Heather Maclachlan in *Burma's Pop Music Industry: Creators, Distributors, Censors*.³⁰⁶ Myanmar's traditional puppet theatre has attracted considerable interest over the years. There are more recent books on the subject, but Ma Thanegi's work *The Illusion of Life* provides an eminently readable introduction.[307] In 2016, David Eimer wrote a useful overview of the Burmese film industry in the *South China Morning Post*'s magazine.[308] In 2020, the industry celebrated its hundredth anniversary, prompting several interesting articles in the local news media.[309]

It is not possible to visit Myanmar without being struck by the central role Buddhism plays in daily life. A good introduction to this subject is still Htin Aung's *Folk Elements in Burmese Buddhism*.[310] A more scholarly work is Juliane Schober's *Modern Buddhist Conjunctures in Myanmar: Cultural Narratives, Colonial Legacies, and Civil Society*.[311] Also worth consulting, mainly for its insights into the clash of cultures and religious traditions, is Alicia Turner's *Saving Buddhism: The Impermanence of Religion in Colonial Burma*.[312] Its findings are relevant to modern Myanmar as the country embraces the worlds of international capitalism and global mass culture. For Buddhism's role in modern Burmese politics, see Matthew Walton and Susan Hayward's *Contesting Buddhist Narratives: Democratization, Nationalism, and Communal Violence in Myanmar*.[313] Walton followed this work with a scholarly study of *Buddhism, Politics and Political Thought in Myanmar*.[314] To consider religious extremism in Myanmar in a wider context, see Peter Lehr's far-ranging study *Militant Buddhism*.[315] For the historical and religious significance of the Shwedagon Pagoda in Yangon, a good start is Elizabeth Moore, Hansjorg Mayer and U Win Pe's *Shwedagon: Golden Pagoda of Myanmar*.[316]

Despite being written over fifty years ago, Ernest Shattock's memoir *An Experiment in Mindfulness* is still of interest as an autobiographical account by a Westerner studying Buddhist meditation in a Burmese monastery.[317] Another book in this vein is Sande Pulley's *A Yankee in the Yellow Robe: An American Buddhist Monk's Role in East-West Cultural Interchange*.[318] Equally enjoyable to read is *Journey into Burmese Silence* by Marie Byles.[319] The *satipatthana vipassana* method practised by Shattock, Pulley and Byles was explained by one of Myanmar's most eminent practitioners in Mahasi Sayadaw's *The Fundamentals of Insight: Discourse on Meditation Practice*.[320] The historical roots of this school, and its place in modern Burmese history, are examined in Erik Braun's *The Birth of Insight: Meditation, Modern Buddhism, and the Burmese Monk Ledi Sayadaw*.[321] The role of meditation in secular, as well as religious, life in the country is discussed by Ingrid Jordt in her well-researched book *Burma's Mass Lay Meditation Movement: Buddhism and the Cultural Construction of Power*.[322] A memorable recent addition to the literature is *The Irish Buddhist: The Forgotten Monk who Faced Down the British Empire* by Alicia Turner, Lawrence Cox and Brian Bocking.[323]

For those wishing to learn about other faiths in Myanmar, Islam's position was summarized by Curtis Lambrecht in *Voices of Islam in Southeast Asia: A Contemporary Sourcebook*, edited by Greg Fealy and Virginia Hooker.[324] However, that chapter needs to be read in conjunction with more up-to-date works that examine Myanmar's Muslim communities and the "Rohingya question", such as John Holt's recent collection of interviews.[325] Ruth Cernea's *Almost Englishmen: Baghdadi Jews in British Burma* covers the decline of the local Jewish community from its heyday under the British colonial administration.[326] In addition to those works about Christianity already cited, a revealing description of missionary life in Upper Burma before the Second World War can be found in Anne Carter's *Bewitched by Burma: A Unique Insight into Burma's Complex Past*.[327] A fascinating account of the adventures of a missionary family in northern Myanmar following the country's independence is *Exodus to a Hidden Valley* by Eugene Morse.[328] A study of the Anglican Church in Myanmar is in the publishing pipeline.[329] No survey of religious beliefs in Myanmar would be complete without mention of the nats, as simply described in *Nats: Spirits of Fortune and Fear* by Ma Thanegi and Barry Broman.[330] On religious monuments, it is hard to go past Donald Stadtner's invaluable survey *Sacred Sites of Burma: Myth and Folklore in an Evolving Spiritual Realm*.[331]

Kyi May Kaung wrote in 2007 that "Burma has become a favourite choice of novelists looking for an exotic locale with a hint of danger".[332] That was true, but Myanmar had figured in fictional works long before then. Some were by Burmese authors.[333] Ma Ma Lay's *Not Out of Hate*, for example, is a classic.[334] Patricia Milne's translations of Thein Pe Myint's *Selected Short Stories* are a delight to read.[335] More recent offerings are Ludu U Hla's *The Caged Ones*, Wendy Law-Yone's *The Road to Wanting* and Nu Nu Yi's *Smile as They Bow*.[336] An important recent contribution to this field is the edited volume by Lucas Stewart and Alfred Birnbaum *Hidden Words, Hidden Worlds: Contemporary Short Stories from Myanmar*, published by the British Council.[337] The best collection of Burmese folk tales is Gerry Abbott and Khin Thant Han's *The Folk-Tales of*

*Burma: An Introduction.*³³⁸ There are others, but, as Kyi May Kaung has also pointed out, some very good Burmese novels have never been translated into English (or any other language).³³⁹ That has left the field largely to foreign authors, but their output has been very mixed. Some novels written in recent years are simply not worth reading, including several that take the 2016–17 Rohingya crisis as their central theme.³⁴⁰ However, there are some works of fiction set in Myanmar and written by foreigners that repay the time spent reading them.

It is now a little outdated, but, for a concise guide to Myanmar as portrayed in popular English literature, a good beginning is the chapter by Anna Allott in *Traveller's Literary Companion to Southeast Asia*, edited by Alastair Dingwall.³⁴¹ This survey covers some books that have already been mentioned, but it prompts a closer look at a few classic novels. These include *The Lacquer Lady* by F. Tennyson Jesse, *She Was a Queen* by Maurice Collis, *Burmese Days* by George Orwell, *Burmese Silver* by Edward Thompson, *The Purple Plain* by H.E. Bates and *Forests of the Night* by Jon Cleary.³⁴² Other well-received foreign novels about Myanmar include Karel Van Loon's *The Invisible Ones*, Karen Connelly's *The Lizard Cage*, Daniel Mason's *The Piano Tuner* and Amitav Ghosh's *The Glass Palace*.³⁴³ Best-selling author Amy Tan takes her readers to Myanmar in *Saving Fish from Drowning*.³⁴⁴ A different approach is taken by Charmaine Craig in her historical novel *Miss Burma*.³⁴⁵ Myanmar's modern literary scene is helpfully described in *Saffron Shadows and Salvaged Scripts* by Ellen Wiles.³⁴⁶

Over the years, Myanmar does not seem to have been of much interest to foreign playwrights and poets, either as a setting or as a subject in its own right. However, that does not mean that there are no published works of interest. One celebrated example is *For Love of the King: A Burmese Masque*, published in 1922.³⁴⁷ Ostensibly a lost work by Oscar Wilde, it was in fact written by an eccentric Irish woman named Mabel Cosgrove. A more recent play was *The Lady of Burma* by Richard Shannon, which capitalized on the global appeal of then opposition leader Aung San Suu Kyi.³⁴⁸ The thought-provoking *Eastern Star*, published in 2018 by Guy Slater, also enjoyed a measure of critical success on the British stage.³⁴⁹ Looking at the theatre scene from a local point of view, Htin Aung's 1937 study of *Burmese Drama* remains a classic, if only for its novel comparison of Burmese plays with those of William Shakespeare.³⁵⁰

Rudyard Kipling wrote several poems that referred to Myanmar, notably "Mandalay".[351] Other collections of poetry with a Myanmar connection range from the truly dreadful to a number that deserve more sympathetic consideration. An example of the former is *Fluttering Leaves* by the self-proclaimed Buddhist Archbishop of Latvia, Friedrich V. Lustig.[352] An example of the latter is *When at Nights I Try to Sleep* by Maung Myint Thein.[353] Two other charming works by Myint Thein are *Burmese Proverbs Explained in Verse* and *Burmese Folk-Songs*.[354] Highly recommended is *Burma Storybook* by Petr Lom and others, which showcased the work of several contemporary Burmese poets.[355] Also worth a look is *Monsoon Diary* by the award-winning Irish poet Joseph Woods, who was inspired by his time spent in Myanmar.[356]

One interesting development in Western publishing circles over the past thirty years has been the growing popularity of graphic novels. About two dozen have been set in Myanmar. Most take a historical approach, such as *Burma Banshees* by Romain Hugault and Yann, and *Mandalay* by Philippe Thirault.[357] A number, however, like *Burmese Moons* by Sophie Ansell and Sam Garcia, have focused on more recent developments.[358] Aung San Suu Kyi has been the subject of several graphic novels, such as Chantal Van den Heuvelal and Michel Pierret's rather reverential 2013 work *Aung San Suu Kyi: The Lady of Rangoon*.[359] Most of these works were initially published in French, but English language versions of many are now available, including Guy Delisle's delightful *Burma Chronicles*.[360] The field was surveyed by Andrew Selth in the *Nikkei Asian Review* in 2018.[361] For those interested in looking at Myanmar through the eyes of its cartoonists, two works are recommended. The first is Harn Lay's *Defiant Humour: The Best of Harn Lay's Political Cartoons from The Irrawaddy*.[362] The second is Lisa Brooten's chapter on Burmese political cartoons in John Lent's *Southeast Asian Cartoon Art*.[363]

There are not many children's books in English with a specific Myanmar theme, but the number is growing. It is possible to see how the genre has developed over the past 150 years by dipping into it at different stages. A typical early work is G.A. Henty's jingoistic adventure novel *On the Irrawaddy: A Story of the First Burmese War*.[364] A later contribution (also set in the colonial period) was *Drummer Boy of Burma* by W.O. Stevens.[365] Between the 1930s and 1950s, "Captain" W.E. Johns set seven of his "Biggles" juvenile adventure stories in Myanmar.[366] Some twenty years later, the Asia Society in the United States helped to publish a more culturally sensitive story by P.W. Garlan and Maryjane Dunstan titled *Orange-Robed Boy*.[367] It was illustrated by the noted Burmese artist Paw Oo Thet. One children's book that can usually be found in Western bookshops these days is Jean Merrill's retelling of a Burmese folk tale in *Shan's Lucky Knife*.[368] A more recent multilingual effort is *I See the Sun in Myanmar (Burma)* by Dedie King and Judith Inglese.[369] There have also been several books for children about Aung San Suu Kyi, including a graphic novel entitled *The Caged Bird*, referring to a song about the Nobel Peace laureate by the Irish rock band U2.[370]

The most impressive English language survey of Burmese arts and crafts is Sylvia Fraser-Lu's *Burmese Crafts, Past and Present*.[371] By the same author is *Splendour in Wood: The Buddhist Monasteries of Burma*.[372] Fraser-Lu also collaborated with Donald Stadtner to edit the impressive *Buddhist Art of Myanmar*.[373] For more specialized studies, see *Burmese Painting: A Linear and Lateral History* by Andrew Ranard, *Textiles from Burma* edited by Elizabeth Dell and Sandra Dudley, and *Lacquerware Journeys: The Untold Story of Burmese Lacquer* by Than Htun.[374] The best source on Burmese "opium" weights is a new book by Rick Willis and Greg Herman.[375] There is a chapter on Myanmar in Mick Shippen's *The Traditional Ceramics of South East Asia*, and the country is covered in Anne Richter's *The Jewelry of Southeast Asia*.[376] Myanmar also features in M.A. Stanislaw's *Kalagas: The Wall Hangings of Southeast Asia*.[377] Often, however, the best sources of learned and well-illustrated articles on Myanmar's arts and crafts are publications like the bimonthly *Arts of Asia*, produced in Hong Kong. Sylvia Fraser-Lu has published several excellent pieces in that journal, as have other Myanmar afficionados and collectors. See, for example, "Collecting Burmese Textiles" by Thweep Rittinaphakorn, "Survivors from a Burmese Palace" by Noel Singer and "Burmese Silver from the Colonial Period" by Wynyard Wilkinson and others.[378]

For those with an interest in Myanmar's increasingly threatened flora and fauna, a readable introduction (to the former, at least) is Charles Lyte's *Frank Kingdon-Ward: The Last of the Great Plant Hunters*.[379] Also worth buying is E.C. Nelson's delightful *Shadow among Splendours: Lady Charlotte Wheeler-Cuffe's Adventures among the Flowers of Burma, 1897–1921*.[380] Another beautifully presented book on this subject is Dudley Clayton's *Charles Parish – Plant Hunter and Botanical Artist in Burma*.[381] A much-loved book about Burmese elephants, written by a real "jungle wallah", is *Bandoola* by J.H. Williams.[382] For ornithologists, nothing can beat the monumental work of B.E. Smythies, *The Birds of Burma*, but a more convenient reference for travellers is Kyaw Nyunt Lwin and Khin Ma Ma Thwin's *Birds of Myanmar*.[383] Two books that are both informative and entertaining are *Beyond the Last Village: A Journey of Discovery in Asia's Forbidden Wilderness* by Alan Rabinowitz and *The Weeping Goldsmith: Discoveries in the Secret Land of Myanmar* by W.J. Kress.[384] A more scholarly treatment of Burma's environmental problems can be found in Adam Simpson's *Energy, Governance and Security in Thailand and Myanmar (Burma): A Critical Approach to Environmental Politics in the South*.[385]

Once upon a time, few people knew anything about Myanmar's culinary traditions, which, if not dismissed out of hand, tended to be overwhelmed by those of its better-known neighbours, India, China and Thailand. However, there is now a growing number of books about Myanmar's cuisine containing a wide variety of recipes, old and new. A good introduction is Bridget and Stephen Anderson's beautifully presented *Burma: Food, Family and Conflict*, which sets particular dishes in their historical, cultural and social contexts.[386] Another rich source of inspiration, highlighting regional variations, is Bryan Koh's hefty tome, *0451 Mornings Are for Mont Hin Gar: Burmese Food Stories*.[387] If that is not available, an alternative source is Mohana Gill's *Myanmar: Cuisine, Culture and Customs*.[388] For the novice chef, Ma Thanegi has provided an excellent description of the most common (and popular) dishes in *An Introduction to Myanmar Cuisine*.[389] There is also a chapter on Myanmar in Charmaine Solomon's classic (and frequently updated) work, *The Complete Asian Cookbook*.[390] For an example of the fusion starting to occur between Burmese and Western styles, see *The Modern Salad: Innovative New American and International Recipes Inspired by Burma's Iconic Tea Leaf Salad* by Elizabeth Howes.[391]

For the non-specialist stamp collector, a simple introduction to Burmese philately is Min Sun Min's *Stamps of Burma: A Historical Record through 1988*.[392] A much more comprehensive guide to the subject is Edward Proud's *The Postal History of Burma*.[393] A truly monumental work designed for the specialist, but also of interest to the generalist, is James Song's study of the postage stamps produced during the British colonial period.[394] If copies can be found, an informative and entertaining source of information for Myanmar philatelists is *The Burma Fantail*, the newsletter and journal of the UK-based Burma (Myanmar) Philatelic Study Circle. In 2005, under its editor Richard Warren, it replaced *The Burma Peacock*, which was produced in Canada from 1979 to 2000 and ran to seventy-seven issues.[395] Although now over thirty years old, the best and most detailed guide to Burmese numismatics is M. Robinson and L.A. Shaw's *The Coins and Banknotes of Burma*.[396] A more recent but specialized work is *Auspicious Symbols and Ancient Coins of Myanmar* by Than Htun (Dedaye).[397] Also helpful in this regard are two online sources, *The Banknote Book: Burma* and *The Banknote Book: Myanmar*, by Owen W. Linzmayer.[398]

Another way of looking at Myanmar is from the outside, through books written by former colonials, migrants, expatriates and exiles. One work that springs to mind in that regard is the Britain-Burma Society's delightful collection *Lines from a Shining Land*, which records the anecdotes and memories of thirty-three former residents between 1910 and 1980.[399] Also worth reading in this regard are Sue Arnold's *A Burmese Legacy* and Wendy Law-Yone's *Golden Parasol*.[400] Harriet O'Brien, whose father was the British ambassador to Myanmar from 1974 to 1978, skilfully blends history and personal recollections of the country in *Forgotten Land: A Rediscovery of Burma*.[401] Constance Allmark has written three books about her life in Myanmar and continuing links to the country after she took up residence in Australia in 1964.[402] Another Burmese to migrate to Australia was Sao Khemawadee Mangrai, who later published *Burma My Mother – And Why I Had to Leave*.[403] A more recent contribution to this genre is Alex Wagner's *Futureface*, about an American woman's quest to trace her Burmese roots and learn what it means to be of mixed race.[404] In a different vein, Michael Spurlock's *All Saints* tells the uplifting story of how a group of Karen refugees saved a small Christian community in the United States.[405]

Myanmar's place in popular Western culture has long been neglected, but this situation is gradually changing. In 2020, the subject was surveyed in Andrew Selth's research paper for the Griffith Asia Institute, *Making Myanmar: Colonial Burma and Popular Western Culture*.[406] For a more specialized discussion of Myanmar in pulp fiction magazines, see Selth's "Colonial-Era Pulp Fiction Portrays 'Technicolor' Myanmar".[407] For an examination of Myanmar's depiction in comic books, see the same author's "Burma and the Comics", a two-part article posted on the Australian National University's *New Mandala* blog.[408] The subject of Myanmar and matchbox labels was briefly examined in "Colonial Burma, history and phillumeny", also found on *New Mandala*.[409] Similarly, a look at Myanmar's place in the world of cigarette and trading cards can be found in Andrew Selth's "Colonial Burma, as Seen through Collectible Cards", published in the *Nikkei Asian Review* in May 2016.[410] For a description of Myanmar as seen through old postcards, a good start is Noel Singer's *Burmah: A Photographic Journey, 1855–1925*.[411] Also of interest is Edith Mirante's "Escapist Entertainment: Hollywood Movies of Burma", published in *The Irrawaddy*, and Selth's article "Burma, Hollywood and the Politics of Entertainment" in the journal *Continuum*.[412]

Finally, to take a further step backwards, studies of Myanmar have expanded dramatically since the 1988 pro-democracy uprising thrust the country into the world's headlines and sparked a surge in popular interest. As noted in the introduction and prefaces to this bibliography, the flow of new and reprinted works since then has gathered momentum. For a survey of these trends, a reader is referred initially to Andrew Selth's article "Modern Burma Studies: A Survey of the Field".[413] The same author followed up this work with two occasional papers on aspects of Myanmar-watching, both published by the GAI.[414] They should be read in conjunction with the impressive collection of articles edited by Matrii Aung Thwin in a special 2008 issue of the *Journal of Southeast Asian Studies* on the theme, "Communities of Interpretation and the Construction of Modern Myanmar".[415] There are also a number of articles and blogs written by academics, postgraduate students and journalists that give a flavour of what it has been like to research, observe and write about Burma over the past forty years.[416] One recent piece of interest in this regard is Reshmi Banerjee's interview with Li Yi about the latter's book on the Chinese migrant community in colonial Burma.[417]

At a personal level, such works help round out the picture for newcomers to the field and give a sense of what it has been like for scholars and others to produce the works cited in this appendix.

Notes

1. An earlier version of this essay has been published separately as Andrew Selth, *Myanmar (Burma): A Reading Guide*, Research Paper (Brisbane: Griffith Asia Institute, Griffith University, 2021).
2. On the Rohingya question, for example, see the comprehensive list of sources compiled by Network Myanmar, at http://www.networkmyanmar.org/Arakan.html.

3. Such lists are briefly discussed in Andrew Selth, "Myanmar: Bibliographies and Booklists", *New Mandala*, 25 November 2016, at http://www.newmandala.org/myanmar-bibliographies-booklists/. Also, see for example "The Best Books on Burma", recommended by Bertil Lintner, *Five Books*, n.d., at https://fivebooks.com/best-z books/bertil-lintner-on-burma/; Keith Rice, "Dispatches from Burma: 8 Best Books on Myanmar", *Signature*, 15 November 2017, at http://www.signature-reads.com/2017/11/dispatches-burma-8-best-books-myanmar/; and "Peter", "15 Best Books about Myanmar", *Atlas and Boots Outdoor Travel Blog*, 19 July 2017, at https://www.atlasandboots.com/best-books-about-myanmar-burma/.
4. For example, not mentioned but still worthy of inclusion is the idiosyncratic and delightful Moe Myint, *List of Books from the Library of U Moe Myint, 2008, with Pictures and Descriptions* (Yangon: The author, 2008).
5. *Myanmar: Land of the Spirit* (Bangkok: Asia Books, 1996).
6. John Falconer et al., *7 Days in Myanmar: A Portrait of Burma by 30 Great Photographers* (Singapore: Editions Didier Millet, 2014).
7. David Lazar, *Myanmar: A Luminous Journey* (Bangkok: The author, 2016). Another Australian contribution to this genre is Anna Swain, *Burma: Tiffin, Nuns and Tumeric* (Byron Bay: Shutter Books, 2016).
8. Ma Thanegi and Barry Broman, *Myanmar Architecture: Cities of Gold* (Singapore: Times Editions, 2005).
9. Nic Dunlop, *Brave New Burma* (Stockport: Dewi Lewis, 2013).
10. Elizabeth Rush, *Still Lifes from a Vanishing City: Essays and Photographs from Yangon*, foreword by Emma Larkin and afterword by Thant Thaw Kaung (San Francisco: Things Asian Press, 2015).
11. P.J. Heijmans, *Relics of Rangoon* (Yangon: Inya Media, 2016).
12. Roger Taylor et al., *Captain Linnaeus Tripe: Photographer of India and Burma, 1852–1860* (Washington DC and New York: National Gallery of Art and the Metropolitan Museum of Art, 2014); N.F. Singer, *Burmah: A Photographic Journey, 1855–1925* (Gartmore: Paul Strachan/Kiscadale, 1993); and Elizabeth Dell (ed.), *Burma: Frontier Photographs 1918–1935* (London: Merrell, 2000).
13. See, for example, Lukas Birk, *Burmese Photographers* (Yangon: Goethe Institute, Myanmar, and the author, 2018).
14. Caroline Courtauld, *Myanmar: Burma in Style: An Illustrated History and Guide* (Hong Kong: Odyssey, 2013).
15. Caroline Courtauld, *The Irrawaddy: Burma's Kingly Stream* (London: Sanctuary Retreats, 2014).
16. Simon Richmond et al., *Myanmar (Burma)* (Melbourne: Lonely Planet, 2017).
17. *Myanmar (Burma)* (London: Apa Publications, 2019).
18. Gavin Thomas, Stuart Butler and Tom Deas, *The Rough Guide to Myanmar (Burma)*, 2nd edition (London: Rough Guides, 2017).

19. Morgan Edwardson, *To Myanmar with Love: A Travel Guide for the Connoisseur* (San Francisco: ThingsAsian Press, 2009).
20. D.M. Seekins, *Historical Dictionary of Burma (Myanmar)* (Lanham: Rowman and Littlefield, 2017). The publishers are currently planning a new edition that brings the book up to date.
21. Win Pe, *Dos and Don'ts in Myanmar* (Bangkok: Book Promotion and Service Ltd., 1996).
22. Saw Myat Yin, *Culture Shock! Myanmar: A Survival Guide to Customs and Etiquette* (Singapore: Marshall Cavendish, 2013).
23. H.C.M. Sim, *Myanmar on My Mind: A Guide to Living and Doing Business in Myanmar* (Singapore: Times Books International, 2001).
24. Michael O'Kane, *Doing Business in Myanmar* (Santa Monica: Andalus Publishing, 2018).
25. Bui, Hana, *When Global Meets Local: How Expatriates Can Succeed in Myanmar: A First-Time Guidebook* (Yangon: The author, 2019).
26. *Burmese Phrasebook and Dictionary* (Melbourne: Lonely Planet, 2014).
27. John Okell, *Burmese (Myanmar)*, 4 volumes, including *An Introduction to the Spoken Language, Book 1*; *An Introduction to the Spoken Language, Book 2*; *An Introduction to the Script*; and *An Introduction to the Literary Style* (De Kalb: Centre for Southeast Asian Studies, Northern Illinois University, 1994).
28. Mary Callahan, "Language Policy in Modern Burma", in M.E. Brown and Sumit Ganguly (eds.), *Fighting Words: Language Policy and Ethnic Relations in Asia* (Cambridge: MIT Press, 2003).
29. Kyaw Yin Hlaing, "The Politics of Language Policy in Myanmar: Imagining Togetherness, Practising Difference", in Lee Hock Guan and Leo Suryadinata (eds.), *Language, Nation and Development in Southeast Asia* (Singapore: Institute of Southeast Asian Studies, 2008).
30. Jacques Dumarcay and Michael Smithies, *Cultural Sites of Burma, Thailand and Cambodia* (Kuala Lumpur: Oxford University Press, 1995).
31. E.H. Moore, *Early Landscapes of Myanmar* (Bangkok: River Books, 2007).
32. D.M. Stadtner, *Ancient Pagan: Buddhist Plain of Merit* (Bangkok: River Books, 2005).
33. Claudine Bautze-Picron, *The Buddhist Murals of Pagan: Timeless Vistas of the Cosmos* (Bangkok: Orchid Press, 2003).
34. Pamela Gutman, *Burma's Lost Kingdoms: Splendours of Arakan*, photographs by Zaw Min Yu (Bangkok: Orchid Press, 2001).
35. Myint Aung, *Revealing Myanmar's Past: An Anthology of Archaeological Articles* (Yangon: Tun Foundation Bank Literary Committee, 2012).
36. Gustaaf Houtman, "Remaking Myanmar and Human Origins", *Anthropology Today* 15, no. 4 (August 1999), pp. 13–19.
37. E.C. Cangi, *Faded Splendour, Golden Past: Urban Images of Burma* (Kuala Lumpur: Oxford University Press, 1997).

38. Sarah Rooney, *30 Heritage Buildings of Yangon: Inside the City that Captured Time* (Chicago: Association of Myanmar Architects and Serindia Publications, 2012).
39. Virginia Henderson and Tim Webster, *Yangon Echoes: Inside Heritage Homes* (Bangkok: River Books, 2015). See also Bary Broman, "Relics of the Raj: Colonial Architecture in Myanmar", *Arts of Asia* 27, no. 6 (November–December 1997), pp. 88–97.
40. Bob Percival, *Walking the Streets of Yangon: The People, Stories & Hidden Treasures of Downtown Cosmopolitan Yangon (Rangoon)* (Yangon: U Thein Myint, 2016).
41. Dhida Saraya, *Mandalay: The Capital City, The Centre of the Universe* (Bangkok: Muang Boran, 1995).
42. Michael Aung-Thwin, *Pagan: The Origins of Modern Burma* (Honolulu: University of Hawai'i Press, 1985).
43. Uta Gartner, "Nay Pyi Taw – The Reality and Myths of Capitals in Myanmar", in Volker Grabowsky (ed.), *Southeast Asian Historiography: Unravelling the Myths* (Bangkok: River Books, 2011), pp. 258–67.
44. Michael Charney, *A History of Modern Burma* (Cambridge: Cambridge University Press, 2009).
45. Thant Myint U, *The Making of Modern Burma* (Cambridge: Cambridge University Press, 2001).
46. Thant Myint U, *The Hidden History of Burma: Race, Capitalism, and the Crisis of Democracy in the 21st Century* (New York: W.W. Norton, 2020).
47. Richard Cockett, *Blood, Dreams and Gold: The Changing Face of Burma* (New Haven: Yale University Press, 2015).
48. Michael Aung Thwin and Matrii Aung Thwin, *A History of Myanmar since Ancient Times: Traditions and Transformations* (London: Reaktion Books, 2013).
49. Victor Lieberman, *Strange Parallels: Southeast Asia in Global Context, c.800–1830, Volume 1: Integration on the Mainland* (Cambridge: Cambridge University Press, 2003), pp. 85–211.
50. Michael Aung Thwin, *Myth and History in the Historiography of Early Burma: Paradigms, Primary Sources, and Prejudices* (Athens: Ohio Centre for International Studies, Ohio University, 1998).
51. Jame Dibiasio, *Who Killed the King of Bagan?* (Singapore: Penguin, 2021).
52. "Research", *SOAS Bulletin of Burma Research* 2, no. 2 (Autumn 2004), pp. 1–200, https://www.soas.ac.uk/sbbr/editions/soas-bulletin-of-burma-research-volume-2-issue-2.html.
53. D.G.E. Hall, *Europe and Burma* (London: Oxford University Press, 1945). Hall also produced a more detailed study of *Early English Intercourse with Burma, 1587–1743* (London: Frank Cass, 1968).
54. W.O. Dijk, *Seventeenth-Century Burma and the Dutch East India Company, 1643–1680* (Copenhagen: NIAS Press, 2006).

55. Arash Khazeni, *The City and the Wilderness: Indo-Persian Encounters in Southeast Asia* (Oakland: University of California Press, 2020).
56. Michael Symes, *An Account of an Embassy to the Kingdom of Ava in the Year 1795* (New Delhi: Asian Educational Service, 1995); Michael Symes, *Journal of his Second Embassy to the Court of Ava in 1802* (London: George Allen and Unwin, 1955); John Crawfurd, *Journal of An Embassy from the Governor General of India to the Court of Ava in the Year 1827* (Cambridge: Cambridge University Press, 2012); and Henry Yule, *Narrative of the Mission to the Court of Ava in 1855* (Kuala Lumpur: Oxford University Press, 1968).
57. Charles Crosthwaite, *The Pacification of Burma*, 2nd edition (London: Frank Cass, 1968).
58. Ni Ni Myint, *Burma's Struggle against British Imperialism (1885–1895)* (Rangoon: The Universities Press, 1983).
59. Maung Maung, *Burmese Nationalist Movements, 1940–1948* (Edinburgh: Kiscadale, 1989).
60. Tekkatho Sein Tin, with Kan Nyunt Sein, *Thakin Ba Sein and Burma's Struggle for Independence* (Saarbrucken: VDM Verlag Dr Müller, 2011).
61. Khin Yi, *The Dobama Movement in Burma (1930–1938)*, 2 volumes (Ithaca: Southeast Asia Program, Cornell University, 1988).
62. Aye Kyaw, *The Voice of Young Burma*, Southeast Asia Program Series no. 12 (Ithaca: Southeast Asia Program, Cornell University, 1993).
63. Angeline Naw, *Aung San and the Struggle for Burmese Independence* (Chiang Mai: Silkworm Books, 2001).
64. Paul Webb, *The Peacock's Children: The Struggle for Freedom in Burma, 1885–Present* (Bangkok: Orchid Press, 2009).
65. Gerry Abbott (ed.), *Inroads into Burma: A Travellers' Anthology* (Kuala Lumpur: Oxford University Press, 1997).
66. H.G. Trager, *Burma through Alien Eyes: Missionary Views of the Burmese in the Nineteenth Century* (Bombay: Asia Publishing House, 1966).
67. V.C.S. O'Connor, *The Silken East: A Record of Life and Travel in Burma* (London: Hutchinson, 1928).
68. G.W. Bird, *Wanderings in Burma*, introduction by Guy Lubeigt, reprint of 1897 edition (Bangkok: White Lotus, 2003), p. ii.
69. Mrs Ernest Hart, *Picturesque Burma: Past and Present* (London: J.M. Dent, 1897).
70. G.E. Mitton, *A Bachelor Girl in Burma* (London: Adam and Charles Black, 1907).
71. Barbara Cossette, *The Great Hill Stations of Asia* (Boulder: Westview, 1998).
72. Rudyard Kipling, *Barrack-Room Ballads and Other Verses* (London: Methuen, 1892).
73. Rudyard Kipling, *From Sea to Sea and Other Sketches: Letters of Travel* (New York: Doubleday, Page, 1927), pp. 196–213. See also Andrew

Lycett (ed.), *Kipling Abroad: Traffics and Discoveries: From Burma to Brazil* (London: I.B. Taurus, 2010), pp. 81–7.

74. "Kipling's Burma", *The Kipling Journal*, no. 219 (September 1981), pp. 12–31.

75. G.H. Webb, "Kipling's Burma: A Literary and Historical Review", *Asian Affairs* 15, no. 2 (1984), pp. 163–178. This article was republished as George Webb, "Kipling's Burma: A Literary and Historical Review, Part 1", *Kipling Journal*, no. 301 (March 2002), pp. 25–32; and George Webb, "Kipling's Burma: A Literary and Historical Review, Part 2", *Kipling Journal*, no. 302 (June 2002), pp. 10–19.

76. Andrew Selth, *Kipling, "Mandalay" and Burma in the Popular Imagination*, Working Paper no. 161 (Southeast Asia Research Centre, City University of Hong Kong, Hong Kong SAR, 2015), http://www.cityu.edu.hk/searc/Resources/Paper/15011914_161%20-%20WP%20-%20Dr%20Andrew%20Selth.pdf.

77. Andrew Selth, *Burma, Kipling and Western Music: The Riff from Mandalay* (New York: Routledge, 2017).

78. H.T. White, *A Civil Servant in Burma* (London: Edward Arnold, 1913).

79. M.S. Collis, *Trials in Burma* (London: Faber and Faber, 1938); M.S. Collis, *Lords of the Sunset: A Tour in the Shan States* (London: Faber and Faber, 1938); and M.S. Collis, *Into Hidden Burma: An Autobiography* (London: Faber and Faber, 1953).

80. Leslie Glass, *The Changing of Kings: Memories of Burma, 1934–1949* (London: Peter Owen, 1985).

81. Damrong Rajanubhab, *Journey through Burma in 1936* (Bangkok: River Books, 1991).

82. C.A. Boshier, *Mapping Cultural Nationalism: The Scholars of the Burma Research Society, 1910–1935* (Copenhagen: NIAS Press, 2017).

83. David Donnison, *Last of the Guardians: A Story of Burma, Britain and a Family* (Newtown: Superscript, 2005); and C.H. Campagnac, *The Autobiography of a Wanderer in England and Burma* (Raleigh: Sandra Campagnac-Carney and Lulu Enterprises, 2011).

84. J.H. Williams, *Elephant Bill* (London: Rupert Hart-Davis, 1950); and V.C. Croke, *Elephant Company* (New York: Random House, 2014).

85. W.C.B. Purser, *Christian Missions in Burma* (London: Society for the Propagation of the Gospel in Foreign Parts, 1911); and P.A. Bigandet, *An Outline of the History of the Catholic Burmese Mission from the year 1720 to 1887* (Bangkok: White Orchid Press, 1996).

86. M.D. Leigh, *Conflict, Politics and Proselytism: Methodist Missionaries in Colonial and Postcolonial Upper Burma, 1887–1966* (Manchester: Manchester University Press, 2011); and J.G. Duesing (ed.), *Adoniram Judson: A Bicentennial Appreciation of the Pioneer American Missionary* (Nashville: B&H Publishing, 2012).

87. J.R. Case, *An Unpredictable Gospel: American Evangelicals and World Christianity, 1812–1920* (Oxford: Oxford University Press, 2012), pp. 19–102.
88. Wim Vervest, *The Lost Dictionary: A History of the Chin People, the Newland Family and the American Baptist Chin Mission*, edited by C.M. Jordan (Fremantle: Vivid Publishing, 2014).
89. Jon Latimer, *Burma: The Forgotten War* (London: John Murray, 2004); and Frank McLynn, *The Burma Campaign: Disaster into Triumph, 1942–45* (London: The Bodley Head, 2010).
90. Julian Thompson, *Forgotten Voices of Burma* (London: Ebury Press, in association with the Imperial War Museum, 2009).
91. Louis Allen, *Burma: The Longest War, 1941–45* (London: Dent, 1984).
92. William Slim, *Defeat into Victory* (London: Cassell, 1956).
93. George MacDonald Fraser, *Quartered Safe Out Here: A Recollection of the War in Burma* (London: HarperCollins, 2000).
94. Philip Davies, *Lost Warriors: Seagrim and Pagani of Burma, The Last Great Untold Story of WWII* (Croxley Green: Atlantic, 2017); and Richard Duckett, *The Special Operations Executive in Burma: Jungle Warfare and Intelligence Gathering in World War II* (London: I.B. Taurus, 2018).
95. Michael Pearson, *The Burma Air Campaign, December 1941 – August 1945* (Barnsley: Pen and Sword, 2006).
96. Andrew Boyd, *The Royal Navy in Eastern Waters: Linchpin of Victory, 1935–1942* (Singapore: NUS Press, 2017).
97. Robert Lyman, *Among the Headhunters: An Extraordinary World War II Story of Survival in the Burmese Jungle* (Boston: Da Capo Press, 2016); and Brendan Koerner, *Now the Hell Will Start: One Soldier's Flight from the Greatest Manhunt of World War II* (New York: Penguin, 2008).
98. Izumiya Tatsuro, *The Minami Organ*, translated by U Tun Aung Chain (Rangoon: Universities Press, 1985).
99. Won Z. Yoon, *Japan's Scheme for the Liberation of Burma: The Role of the Minami Kikan and the "Thirty Comrades"* (Athens: Ohio University Centre for International Studies, Ohio University, 1973).
100. John Nunneley and Kazuo Tamayama, *Tales by Japanese Soldiers of the Burma Campaign, 1942–1945* (London: Cassell, 2000).
101. Kohei Morirama, Kobayashi and Yukata Kurisaki, *Victory into Defeat: Japan's Disastrous Road to Burma (Myanmar) and India*, translated by Myanma Athan Kyaw Oo, Hasio Tanabe and Tin Hlaing (Yangon: Thu Ri Ya Publishing House, 2007).
102. Yuji Aida, *Prisoner of the British: A Japanese Soldier's Experiences in Burma* (London: Cresset Press, 1966).
103. T.R. Sareen, *Japanese Prisoners of War in India, 1942–46: Bushido and Barbed Wire* (Folkestone: Global Oriental, 2006).
104. Michio Takeyama, *Harp of Burma*, translated by Howard Hibbett (Rutland: Charles E. Tuttle, 1972).

105. Ba Maw, *Breakthrough in Burma: Memoirs of a Revolution, 1939–1946* (New Haven: Yale University Press, 1968).
106. Khin Myo Chit, *Three Years under the Japs* (Sanchaung: The author, 1945); and Nu, *Burma under the Japanese* (London: Macmillan, 1954).
107. *Marxism and Resistance in Burma, 1942–1945: Thein Pe Myint's "Wartime Traveller"*, translated and edited by Robert H. Taylor (Athens: Ohio University Press, 1984).
108. Theippan Maung Wa (U Sein Tin), *Wartime in Burma: A Diary, January to June 1942* (Athens: Ohio University Press, 2009).
109. Kyaw Ma Ma Lay, *A Man Like Him: Portrait of the Burmese Journalist, Journal Kyaw U Chit Maung*, translated by Ma Thanegi (Ithaca: Cornell Southeast Asia Program, Cornell University, 2008).
110. This issue is discussed in Christopher Thorne, *Allies of a Kind: The United States, Britain and the War against Japan, 1941–1945* (London: Oxford University Press, 1978).
111. Rowley Richards, *A Doctor's War* (Sydney: HarperCollins, 2005); and Kazuo Tamayama, *Railwaymen in the War: Tales by Japanese Railway Soldiers in Burma and Thailand 1941–47* (London: Palgrave Macmillan, 2005).
112. S.A. Eldredge, *Captive Audiences/Captive Performers: Music and Theatre as Strategies for Survival on the Thailand–Burma Railway, 1942–1945* (St Paul: Macalester College, 2014), http://digitalcommons.macalester.edu/thdabooks/1/. This book should be read in conjunction with Norman Carter, *G-String Jesters* (Sydney: Currawong, 1966).
113. P.H. Kratoska (ed.), *The Thailand–Burma Railway, 1942–1946: Documents and Selected Writings*, 6 volumes (London: Routledge, 2006).
114. P.H. Kratoska (ed.), *Asian Labour in the Wartime Japanese Empire: Unknown Histories* (London: Routledge, 2005).
115. Lionel Hudson, *The Rats of Rangoon* (London: Leo Cooper, 1987).
116. Jean Newland, *Guests of the Emperor: Allied POWs of WWII in Rangoon Burma* (Bloomington: AuthorHouse, 2012).
117. U Nu, *U Nu – Saturday's Son* (New Haven: Yale University Press, 1975).
118. M.D. Leigh, *The Collapse of British Rule in Burma: The Civilian Evacuation and Independence* (London: Bloomsbury, 2018).
119. Kin Oung, *Who Killed Aung San?*, 2nd edition (Bangkok: White Lotus, 1996). A revised edition was published as Kin Oung, *Eliminate the Elite: Assassination of Burma's General Aung San and His Six Cabinet Colleagues* (Sydney: The author, 2011).
120. R.H. Taylor, "Politics in Late Colonial Burma: The Case of U Saw", *Modern Asian Studies* 10, no. 2 (1976), pp. 161–93.
121. U Ba U, *My Burma: The Autobiography of a President* (New York: Taplinger, 1959).
122. Mary Callahan, *Making Enemies: War and State Building in Burma* (Ithaca: Cornell University Press, 2003).

123. R.G.A. Campagnac and S.L. Campagnac-Carney, *Burma's Son* (Raleigh: Blue Mist Publications, 2020).
124. Hugh Tinker (ed.), *Burma: The Struggle for Independence, 1944–1948*, 2 volumes (London: Her Majesty's Stationery Office, 1983 [vol.1] and 1984 [vol.2]).
125. L.W. Pye, *Politics, Personality and Nation Building* (New Haven: Yale University Press, 1962).
126. Andrew Selth, "Geoffrey Gorer and the Study of Burma's 'Personality'", *Journal of Burma Studies* 25, no. 1 (2021), pp. 29–67.
127. E.F. Schumacher, *Small is Beautiful: Economics as if People Mattered* (New York: Harper and Row, 1975).
128. Thant Myint U, *The River of Lost Footsteps: Histories of Burma* (New York: Farrer, Straus and Giroux, 2006).
129. R.H. Taylor, *General Ne Win: A Political Biography* (Singapore: Institute of Southeast Asian Studies, 2015).
130. R.H. Taylor, *The State in Myanmar* (London: Hurst, 2009).
131. Kyi Win Sein (Malcolm), *Me and the Generals of the Revolutionary Council: Memoirs of Turbulent Times in Myanmar* (Whitley Bay: Consilience Media, 2015).
132. Josef Silverstein, *Burma: Military Rule and the Politics of Stagnation* (Ithaca: Cornell University Press, 1977); and David I. Steinberg, *Burma's Road toward Development: Growth and Ideology under Military Rule* (Boulder: Westview Press, 1981).
133. Yoshihiro Nakanishi, *Strong Soldiers, Failed Revolution: The State and Military in Burma, 1962–88* (Singapore: NUS Press, 2013).
134. Martin Smith, *Burma: Insurgency and the Politics of Ethnicity* (London: Zed Books, 1999); and Bertil Lintner, *Burma in Revolt: Opium and Insurgency since 1948* (Chiang Mai: Silkworm Books, 1999).
135. Bertil Lintner, *Outrage: Burma's Struggle for Democracy* (Bangkok: White Lotus, 1990).
136. Maung Maung, *The 1988 Uprising in Burma*, Yale Southeast Asia Studies, Monograph no. 49 (New Haven: Yale University, 1999).
137. Hans-Bernd Zollner, "Behind the Smoke of 'Myth' and 'Counter-Myth': Contours of What Happened in Burma in 1988", in Grabowsky (ed.), *Southeast Asian Historiography: Unravelling the Myths* (Bangkok: River Books, 2011), pp. 248–57.
138. Ma Thanegi, *Nor Iron Bars a Cage* (San Francisco: ThingsAsian Press, 2013); and Ma Thida, *Prisoner of Conscience: My Steps through Insein* (Chiang Mai: Silkworm Books, 2016).
139. *The Darkness We See: Torture in Burma's Interrogation Centres and Prisons* (Mae Sot: Assistance Association for Political Prisoners [Burma], 2005).
140. D.I. Steinberg, *Burma/Myanmar: What Everyone Needs to Know*, 2nd edition (Oxford: Oxford University Press, 2013).

141. D.M. Seekins, *The Disorder in Order: The Army-State in Burma since 1962* (Bangkok: White Lotus, 2002).
142. Hans-Bernd Zollner, *The Beast and the Beauty: The History of the Conflict between the Military and Aung San Suu Kyi in Myanmar, 1988–2011, Set in a Global Context* (Berlin: Regiospectra, 2012).
143. Ian Holliday, *Burma Redux: Global Justice and the Quest for Political Reform in Myanmar* (Hong Kong: University of Hong Kong Press, 2011).
144. Hla Min, *Political Situation of Myanmar and Its Role in the Region*, 26th edition (Yangon: Office of Strategic Studies, Ministry of Defence, 2000).
145. D.I. Steinberg (ed.), *Myanmar: The Dynamics of an Evolving Polity* (Boulder: Lynne Rienner, 2014).
146. Adam Simpson, Nicholas Farrelly and Ian Holliday (eds.), *Routledge Handbook of Contemporary Myanmar* (London: Routledge, 2018). This was followed by a shorter but updated volume covering a similar range of subjects. See Adam Simpson and Nicholas Farrelly (eds.), *Myanmar: Politics, Economy and Society* (London: Routledge, 2021).
147. Andrew Selth, *Interpreting Myanmar: A Decade of Analysis* (Canberra: Australian National University Press, 2020).
148. Pavin Chachavalpongpun, Elliott Prasse-Freeman and Patrick Strefford (eds.), *Unraveling Myanmar's Transition: Progress, Retrenchment, and Ambiguity amidst Liberalization* (Singapore and Kyoto: NUS Press and Kyoto University Press, 2020).
149. Nick Cheesman, Nicholas Farrelly and Trevor Wilson (eds.), *Debating Democratization in Myanmar* (Singapore: Institute of Southeast Asian Studies, 2014); and Justin Chambers, Charlotte Galloway and Jonathan Liljeblad (eds.), *Living with Myanmar* (Singapore: ISEAS – Yusof Ishak Institute, 2020).
150. Aung San Suu Kyi, *Freedom from Fear* (Harmondsworth: Penguin, 1995); Aung San Suu Kyi, *Letters from Burma* (London: Penguin, 1997); and Aung San Suu Kyi, *The Voice of Hope: Conversations with Alan Clements, with Contributions by U Kyi Maung and U Tin U* (New York: Seven Stories, 2008).
151. See, for example, Aung San Suu Kyi, *Aung San of Burma* (Edinburgh: Kiscadale Publications, 1991).
152. Hans-Bernd Zollner (ed.), *Talks over the Gate: Aung San Suu Kyi's Dialogues with the People, 1995 and 1996* (Hamburg: Abera, 2014).
153. Aung San Suu Kyi, *Democratic Transition in Myanmar: Challenges and the Way Forward*, the 43rd Singapore Lecture (Singapore: ISEAS – Yusof Ishak Institute, 2018).
154. Alan Clements and Fergus Harlow, *Burma's Voices of Freedom: In Conversation with Alan Clements: An Ongoing Struggle for Democracy*, 4 volumes (Vancouver: World Dharma Publications, 2020).

155. Hans-Bernd Zollner and Rodion Ebbighausen, *The Daughter: A Political Biography of Aung San Suu Kyi* (Chiang Mai: Silkworm Books, 2018); Justin Wintle, *Perfect Hostage: A Life of Aung San Suu Kyi* (London: Hutchinson, 2007); and Peter Popham, *The Lady and the Peacock: The Life of Aung San Suu Kyi* (London: Rider Books, 2011).
156. See Andrew Selth, "Book Review: *The Daughter: A Political Biography of Aung San Suu Kyi*", *Journal of Current Southeast Asian Affairs* 37, no. 3 (25 March 2019), pp. 193–99, https://journals.sagepub.com/doi/full/10.1177/1868103418037000309.
157. Kyaw Yin Hlaing, "Aung San Suu Kyi of Myanmar: A Review of the Lady's Biographies", *Contemporary Southeast Asia* 29, no. 2 (2007), pp. 359–76.
158. Bertil Lintner, *Aung San Suu Kyi and Burma's Struggle for Democracy* (Chiang Mai: Silkworm Books, 2011).
159. Andrew Selth, *Aung San Suu Kyi and the Politics of Personality*, Regional Outlook no. 55 (Brisbane: Griffith Asia Institute, Griffith University, 2017).
160. Shwe Lu Maung, *Is Suu Kyi a Racist?* (US: Shahnawaz Khan, 2014).
161. Michal Lubina, *The Moral Democracy: The Political Thought of Aung San Suu Kyi* (Warsaw: Scholar Press, 2019); and Michal Lubina, *A Political Biography of Aung San Suu Kyi: A Hybrid Politician* (London: Routledge, 2021).
162. *Images of Mother Loved by the People: Daw Aung San Suu Kyi's World Famous Speeches and Historic Words*, translated by Nay Win San, photographs by Kyaw Soe Naing (Yangon: Book Street, 2003).
163. Moe Linn [Pho Lay], *Up Close: Two Decades of Close Encounters with Aung San Suu Kyi*, translated by Khin Aung et al. (Yangon: MCM Books, 2013).
164. Gwen Robinson, "The West Needs to Talk to Myanmar's Generals", *Financial Times*, 4 February 2021, https://www.ft.com/content/9eac3854-e2d9-4b60-84ff-e5773343562b.
165. Ronald Lewin, *Slim: The Standardbearer* (London: Leo Cooper, 1976).
166. Trevor Royle, *Orde Wingate: Irregular Soldier* (London: Weidenfeld and Nicolson, 1995).
167. Stephen Brookes, *Through the Jungle of Death: A Boy's Escape from Wartime Burma* (London: John Murray, 2000).
168. B.M. Raschid, *The Invisible Patriot: Reminiscences of Burma's Freedom Movement* (Charleston: The author and CreateSpace, 2015).
169. Benedict Rogers, *Than Shwe: Unmasking Burma's Tyrant* (Chiang Mai: Silkworm Books, 2010).
170. Inge Sargent, *Twilight over Burma: My Life as a Shan Princess* (Honolulu: University of Hawai'i Press, 1994); and Wai Wai Myaing, *A Journey in Time: Family Memoirs (Burma, 1914–1948)* (New York: iUniverse, 2005).

171. Christina Fink, *Living Silence: Burma under Military Rule*, 2nd edition (London: Zed Books, 2009).
172. Maggie Lemere and Zoe West (eds.), *Nowhere to Be Home: Narratives from Survivors of Burma's Military Regime* (San Francisco: McSweeney, 2011).
173. Wen-Chin Chang and Eric Tagliacozzo (eds.), *Burmese Lives: Ordinary Life Stories under the Burmese Regime* (Oxford: Oxford University Press, 2014).
174. Zoya Phan and Damien Lewis, *Little Daughter: A Memoir of Survival in Burma and the West* (London: Simon and Schuster, 2009).
175. Matthew Mullen, *Pathways That Changed Myanmar* (London: Zed Books, 2016).
176. Phil Thornton, *Restless Souls: Rebels, Refugees, Medics and Misfits on the Thai-Burma Border* (Bangkok: Asia Books, 2006).
177. Emma Larkin, *Secret Histories: Finding George Orwell in a Burmese Teashop* (London: John Murray, 2004).
178. Emma Larkin, *Everything is Broken: The Untold Story of Disaster under Burma's Military Rule* (London: Granta, 2010).
179. Shanthi Kalathil and T.C. Boas, *Open Networks, Closed Regimes: The Impact of the Internet on Authoritarian Rule* (Washington: Carnegie Endowment for International Peace, 2003).
180. "Burma (Myanmar)", *Open Net Initiative*, 6 August 2012, https://opennet.net/research/profiles/burma.
181. Reporters Without Borders, *Enemies of the Internet 2014*, https://rsf.org/sites/default/files/2014-rsf-rapport-enemies-of-the-internet.pdf.
182. Open Observatory of Network Interference, "The State of Internet Censorship in Myanmar", 29 March 2017, https://ooni.org/post/myanmar-report/.
183. Carolyn Wakeman and San San Tin, *No Time for Dreams: Living in Burma under Military Rule*, introduction by Emma Larkin (Lanham: Rowman and Littlefield, 2009).
184. Lisa Brooten, "'Media as our Mirror': Indigenous Media in Burma (Myanmar)", in Pamela Wilson and Michelle Stewart (eds.), *Global Indigenous Media: Cultures, Poetics and Politics* (Durham: Duke University Press, 2008).
185. Lisa Brooten, J.L. McElhone and Gayathry Venkiteswaran (eds.), *Myanmar Media in Transition: Legacies, Challenges and Change* (Singapore: ISEAS – Yusof Ishak Institute, 2019).
186. Melissa Crouch, "Rediscovering 'Law' in Myanmar: A Review of Scholarship on the Legal System in Myanmar", *Pacific Rim Law and Policy Review* 23, no. 3 (June 2014), pp. 543–75.
187. Andrew Huxley "Precolonial Burmese Law: Conical Hat and Shoulder Bag", International Institute of Asian Studies *Newsletter*, no. 25 (2001), https://iias.asia/iiasn/25/theme/25T7.html.

188. Melissa Crouch and Tim Lindsey (eds.), *Law, Society and Transition in Myanmar* (Oxford: Hart, 2014).
189. Nick Cheesman, *Opposing the Rule of Law: How Myanmar's Courts Make Law and Order* (Cambridge: Cambridge University Press, 2015).
190. Melissa Crouch, *The Constitution of Myanmar: A Contextual Analysis* (Oxford: Hart, 2019).
191. Andrew Harding (ed.), *Constitutionalism and Legal Change in Myanmar* (Oxford: Hart, 2017).
192. *Constitution of the Republic of the Union of Myanmar (2008)*.
193. Norval Morris, *The Brothel Boy and Other Parables of the Law* (New York: Oxford University Press, 1994).
194. Ian Brown, *A Colonial Economy in Crisis: Burma's Rice Cultivators and the World Depression of the 1930s* (London: RoutledgeCurzon, 2005).
195. Michael Adas, *The Burma Delta: Economic Development and Social Change on an Asian Rice Frontier, 1852–1941* (Madison: University of Wisconsin Press, 1974).
196. P.J. Perry, *Myanmar (Burma) since 1962: The Failure of Development* (Aldershot: Ashgate, 2007).
197. Ian Brown, *Burma's Economy in the Twentieth Century* (Cambridge: Cambridge University Press, 2013).
198. *Opportunities and Pitfalls: Preparing for Burma's Economic Transition* (New York: Open Society Institute, 2006).
199. Sean Turnell, *Fiery Dragons: Banks, Moneylenders and Microfinance in Burma* (Copenhagen: NIAS Press, 2009).
200. Teruko Saito and Lee Kin Kiong, *Statistics on the Burmese Economy*, Data Paper Series, Sources for the Economic History of Southeast Asia, no. 7 (Singapore: Institute of Southeast Asian Studies, 1999).
201. Koichi Fujita, Fumihara Mieno and Ikuko Okamoto (eds.), *The Economic Transition in Myanmar after 1988: Market Economy versus State Control* (Singapore: NUS Press, 2009).
202. Lex Rieffel, *The Economy of Burma/Myanmar on the Eve of the 2010 Elections*, Special Report (Washington DC: United States Institute of Peace, 28 May 2010).
203. Konosuke Odaka (ed.), *The Myanmar Economy: Its Past, Present and Prospects* (Tokyo: Springer, 2016).
204. Melissa Crouch (ed.), *The Business of Transition: Law Reform, Development and Economics in Myanmar* (Cambridge: Cambridge University Press, 2017).
205. Lee Jones, *Societies Under Siege: Exploring How International Economic Sanctions (Do Not) Work* (Oxford: Oxford University Press, 2015).
206. Thihan Myo Nyun, "Feeling Good or Doing Good: Inefficacy of the US Unilateral Sanctions against the Military Government of Burma/Myanmar", *Washington University Global Studies Law Review* 7, no. 3 (2008), pp. 455–518.

207. Michael Martin, *US Restrictions on Relations with Burma* (Washington DC: Congressional Research Service, 18 March 2020).
208. R.W. Hughes et al., "Burmese Jade: The Inscrutable Gem", *Lotus*, http://lotusgemology.com/index.php/library/articles/267-burmese-jade-inscrutable-gem?showall=1; and S.K. Samuels, *Imperial Jade of Burma and Mutton-Fat Jade of India: Mining, Trade and Use from Antiquity to the Present* (Tucson: SKS Enterprises, 2014).
209. *Jade: Myanmar's "Big State Secret"* (London: Global Witness, 2015).
210. Joseph Kessel, *Mogok: The Valley of Rubies*, translated by Stella Rodway (London: Macgibbon and Kee, 1960).
211. See, for example, V.C.S. O'Connor, *Rubies of Mogok: Thabeit-Kyin, Capelan, Mogok*, reprints of 1904 and 1888 publications (Bangkok: White Lotus, 2008); and E.C.S. George, *Ruby Mines District*, reprint of 1962 edition (Bangkok: White Lotus, 2007).
212. J.F. Halford-Watkins, with R.W. Hughes, *The Book of Ruby and Sapphire* (US: RWH Publishing, 1997). Halford-Watkins died in 1938 before he could publish his book. It was rediscovered and published sixty years later by the noted gemologist Richard Hughes.
213. R.E. Kane and R.C. Kammerling, "Status of Ruby and Sapphire Mining in the Mogok Stone Tract", *Gems and Gemology* 28, no. 3 (Fall 1992), pp. 152–74. Also of interest is R.C. Kammerling et al., "Myanmar and Its Gems – An Update", *Journal of Gemmology* 24, no. 1 (January 1994), pp. 3–40.
214. V.Y. Yavorskyy, *Burma Gems* (Hong Kong: The author and Gemforest, 2018).
215. Carol Clark, *Seeing Red: A View from inside the Ruby Trade* (Bangkok: White Lotus, 1999).
216. Martin Smith, *State of Strife: The Dynamics of Ethnic Conflict in Burma* (Washington DC: East-West Centre, 2007).
217. R.K. Diran, *The Vanishing Tribes of Burma* (London: Weidenfeld and Nicolson, 1997).
218. Ashley South, *Ethnic Politics in Burma: States of Conflict*, 2nd edition (London: Routledge, 2010).
219. Pascal Khoo Thwe, *From the Land of Green Ghosts: A Burmese Odyssey* (London: HarperCollins, 2002).
220. Jonathan Falla, *True Love and Bartholomew: Rebels on the Burmese Border* (Cambridge: Cambridge University Press, 1991).
221. Ardeth Maung Thawnghmung, *The "Other" Karen in Myanmar: Ethnic Minorities and the Struggle without Arms* (Lanham: Lexington Books, 2012).
222. Mandy Sadan, *Being and Becoming Kachin: Histories beyond the State in the Borderworlds of Burma* (London: The British Academy, 2013).
223. Mandy Sadan (ed.), *War and Peace in the Borderlands of Myanmar: The Kachin Ceasefire, 1994–2011* (Copenhagen: NIAS Press, 2016).

224. Chao Tzang Yawnghwe, *The Shan of Burma: Memoirs of a Shan Exile* (Singapore: Institute of Southeast Asian Studies, 2010).
225. See, for example, Ashley South, *Mon Nationalism and Civil War in Burma: The Golden Sheldrake* (London: RoutledgeCurzon, 2003).
226. Bertil Lintner, *The United Wa State Army and Burma's Peace Process*, Peaceworks no. 147 (Washington DC: United States Institute of Peace, April 2019); and Bertil Lintner, *The Wa of Burma and China's Quest for Global Dominance* (Chiang Mai: Silkworm Books, 2021).
227. N.R. Chakravati, *The Indian Minority in Burma: The Rise and Decline of an Immigrant Community* (London: Oxford University Press, 1971).
228. Renaud Egreteau, "Burmese Indians in Contemporary Burma: Heritage, Influence and Perceptions since 1988", *Asian Ethnicity* 12, no. 1 (2011), pp. 33–54.
229. Jade Roberts, *Mapping Chinese Rangoon: Place and Nation among the Sino-Burmese* (Seattle: University of Washington Press, 2016).
230. Hillel Halkin, *Across the Sabbath River: In Search of a Lost Tribe of Israel* (Boston: Houghton Mifflin Company, 2002).
231. Moshe Yegar, *Between Integration and Secession: The Muslim Communities of the Southern Philippines, Southern Thailand, and Western Burma* (Lanham: Lexington Books, 2002).
232. Jacques Leider, "Competing Identities and the Hybridized History of the Rohingyas", in Renaud Egreteau and François Robinne (eds.), *Metamorphosis: Studies in Social and Political Change in Myanmar* (Singapore: NUS Press and IRASEC, 2016), pp. 151–78.
233. Jacques Leider, "Rohingya: The History of a Muslim Identity in Myanmar", *Oxford Research Encyclopedia of Asian History*, May 2018, http://asianhistory.oxfordre.com/view/10.1093/acrefore/9780190277727.001.0001/acrefore–9780190277727-e–115.
234. Derek Tonkin, "Exploring the Issue of Citizenship in Rakhine State", in Ashley South and Marie Lall (eds.), *Citizenship in Myanmar: Ways of Being in and from Burma* (Singapore: ISEAS – Yusof Ishak Institute and Chiang Mai University Press, 2017), pp. 222–63.
235. Nick Cheesman (ed.), *Interpreting Communal Violence in Myanmar* (London: Routledge, 2018).
236. C.S. Galache, *The Burmese Labyrinth: A History of the Rohingya Tragedy* (London: Verso, 2020).
237. Andrew Selth, *Myanmar's Armed Forces and the Rohingya Crisis*, Peaceworks no. 140 (Washington DC: United States Institute of Peace, August 2018).
238. See, for example, *The Long Haul ahead for Myanmar's Rohingya Refugee Crisis*, Asia Report no. 296 (Yangon/Brussels: International Crisis Group, 16 May 2018).
239. David Mathieson, "Bridging the 'Burma Gap' in Conflict Studies", *Tea Circle*, 7 May 2018, https://teacircleoxford.com/2018/05/07/bridging-the-burma-gap-in-conflict-studies/.

240. Andrew Selth, *Burma: A Strategic Perspective* (San Francisco: Asia Foundation, 2001).
241. Thant Myint U, *Where China Meets India: Burma and the New Crossroads of Asia* (London: Faber and Faber, 2011).
242. Andrew Selth, *Burma's Armed Forces: Power without Glory* (Norwalk: EastBridge, 2002).
243. Maung Aung Myoe, *Building the Tatmadaw: Myanmar Armed Forces since 1948* (Singapore: Institute of Southeast Asian Studies, 2009).
244. Maung Aung Myoe, "The Defence Expenditures and Commercial Interests of the Tatmadaw", in M.J. Montesano, Terence Chong and Prajak Kongkirati (eds.), *Praetorians, Profiteers or Professionals? Studies on the Militaries of Myanmar and Thailand* (Singapore: ISEAS – Yusof Ishak Institute, 2020).
245. John Buchanan, *Militias in Myanmar* (Yangon: Asia Foundation, July 2016).
246. Kim Jolliffe, *Democratising Myanmar's Security Sector: Enduring Legacies and a Long Road Ahead* (London: Saferworld, November 2019).
247. Andrew Selth, "Known Knowns and Known Unknowns: Measuring Myanmar's Military Capabilities", *Contemporary Southeast Asia* 31, no. 2 (2009), pp. 272–95.
248. Lalita Hingkanonta Hanwong, *Policing in Colonial Burma* (Chiang Mai: Centre for ASEAN Studies, Chiang Mai University, 2015).
249. W.B. Sinclair, *Confusion beyond Imagination: Book 6, Police, Pleaders, and Prisoners : Too Few for Too Many* (Coeur d'Alene: Joe F. Whitley, 1989).
250. Andrew Selth, *Police Reform in Burma (Myanmar): Aims, Obstacles and Outcomes*, Regional Outlook Paper no. 44 (Brisbane: Griffith Asia Institute, Griffith University, 2013). See also Andrew Selth, *Burma's Police Forces: Continuities and Contradictions*, Regional Outlook Paper no. 32 (Brisbane: Griffith Asia Institute, Griffith University, 2011).
251. Andrew Selth, "Burma: Police Reforms Expand Women's Roles", *The Interpreter*, 1 May 2015, https://www.lowyinstitute.org/the-interpreter/burma-police-reforms-expand-womens-roles.
252. Ian Brown, "A Commissioner Calls: Alexander Paterson and Colonial Burma's Prisons", *Journal of Southeast Asian Studies* 38, no. 2 (June 2007), pp. 293–308.
253. Lu Nan, *Prisons of North Burma* (Beijing? China National Art Photograph Publishing House, 2015).
254. Desmond Ball, *Burma's Military Secrets: Signals Intelligence (SIGINT) from the Second World War to Civil War and Cyber Warfare* (Bangkok: White Lotus, 1998).
255. Andrew Selth, "Myanmar", in Bob de Graaff (ed.), *Intelligence Communities and Cultures in Asia and the Middle East: A Comprehensive Reference* (Boulder: Lynne Rienner, 2020).

256. Andrew Selth, *Secrets and Power in Myanmar: Intelligence and the Fall of Khin Nyunt* (Singapore: ISEAS – Yusof Ishak Institute, 2019).
257. Andrew Selth, "Burma's Intelligence Apparatus", *Intelligence and National Security* 13, no. 4 (Winter 1998), pp. 33–70.
258. Rhys Thompson, "Securing the Colony: The Burma Police Special Branch (1896–1942)", *Intelligence and National Security* 35, no. 1 (2020), pp. 35–53.
259. Andy Brockman and Tracy Spaight, *The Buried Spitfires of Burma: A "Fake" History* (Cheltenham: The History Press, 2020); Andrew Selth, *Chinese Bases in Burma: The Explosion of a Myth*, Regional Outlook no. 10 (Brisbane: Griffith Asia Institute, Griffith University, 2007); and *Preventing Nuclear Dangers in Southeast Asia and Australasia* (London: International Institute for Strategic Studies, 2009), pp. 101–18.
260. Jurgen Haacke, *Myanmar's Foreign Policy: Domestic Influences and International Implications* (London: International Institute for Strategic Studies, 2006).
261. Renaud Egreteau and Larry Jagan, *Soldiers and Diplomacy in Burma: Understanding the Foreign Relations of the Burmese Praetorian State* (Singapore: NUS Press, 2013).
262. Stephen McCarthy, "Burma and ASEAN: A Marriage of Inconvenience", in Lowell Dittmer (ed.), *Burma or Myanmar? The Struggle for National Identity* (Singapore: World Scientific, 2010), pp. 327–62.
263. Ludovica Marchi (ed.), *The European Union and Myanmar: Interactions via ASEAN* (London: Routledge, 2020).
264. D.I. Steinberg and Hongwei Fan, *Modern China-Myanmar Relations: Dilemmas of Mutual Dependence* (Copenhagen: NIAS Press, 2012); Renaud Egreteau, *Wooing the Generals: India's New Burma Policy* (New Delhi: Authors Press, 2003); and D.M. Seekins, *Burma and Japan since 1940: From "Co-Prosperity" to "Quiet Dialogue"* (Copenhagen: NIAS Press, 2007).
265. Kenton Clymer, *A Delicate Relationship: The United States and Burma/Myanmar since 1945* (Ithaca: Cornell University Press, 2015).
266. Andray Abrahamian, *North Korea and Myanmar: Divergent Paths* (Jefferson: McFarland, 2018).
267. Paul Keenan, *By Force of Arms: Armed Ethnic Groups in Burma* (New Delhi: Vij Books India, 2013).
268. Martin Smith, "Ethnic Conflicts in Burma: From Separatism to Federalism", in A.T.H. Tan (ed.), *A Handbook on Terrorism and Insurgency in Southeast Asia* (Cheltenham: Edward Elgar, 2007).
269. Adam Burke et al., *The Contested Areas of Myanmar: Subnational Conflict, Aid, and Development* (Yangon: Asia Foundation, 2017).
270. Zaw Oo and Win Min, *Assessing Burma's Ceasefire Accords*, Policy Studies 39 (Washington DC: East-West Centre, 2007).

271. Kyaw Yin Hlaing (ed.), *Prisms on the Golden Pagoda: Perspectives on National Reconciliation in Myanmar* (Singapore: NUS Press, 2014).
272. Min Zaw Oo, *Understanding Myanmar's Peace Process: Ceasefire Agreements* (Bern: Swisspeace, 2014).
273. Aung Naing Oo, *Lessons Learned from Myanmar's Peace Process* (Siem Reap: Centre for Peace and Conflict Studies, 2018).
274. Ashley South, "Update on the Peace Process", in Mikael Gravers and Flemming Ytzen (eds.), *Burma/Myanmar – Where Now?* (Copenhagen: NIAS Press, 2014).
275. Bertil Lintner, *Why Burma's Peace Efforts Have Failed to End Its Internal Wars*, Peaceworks no. 169 (Washington DC: United States Institute of Peace, October 2020).
276. A.W. McCoy, *The Politics of Heroin: CIA Complicity in the Global Drug Trade*, 3rd edition (Chicago: Lawrence Hill, 2003).
277. R.M. Gibson and Wenhua Chen, *The Secret Army: Chiang Kai-shek and the Drug Warlords of the Golden Triangle* (Singapore: John Wiley and Sons, 2011).
278. *A Failing Grade: Burma's Drug Eradication Efforts* (Bangkok: ALTSEAN Burma, 2004); and Martin Jelsma et al., *Trouble in the Triangle: Opium and Conflict in Burma* (Chiang Mai: Silkworm Books, 2005).
279. Bertil Lintner and Michael Black, *Merchants of Madness: The Methamphetamine Explosion in the Golden Triangle* (Chiang Mai: Silkworm, 2009).
280. Tom Kramer, *The Current State of Counternarcotics Policy and Drug Reform Debates in Myanmar* (Washington: Brookings Institution, 2015); and Vanda Felbab-Brown, *Myanmar Maneuvers: How to Break Political-Criminal Alliances in Contexts of Transition*, Crime-Conflict Nexus Series no. 9 (Tokyo: United Nations Centre for Policy Research, United Nations University, April 2017).
281. Mathieson described "a slew of terrible books by faux adventurers" in "One Flew Over the Pigeon's Nest", *The Irrawaddy*, 11 May 2020, https://www.irrawaddy.com/culture/books/one-flew-pigeons-nest.html.
282. Somerset Maugham, *The Gentleman in the Parlour* (New York: Marlowe, 1989).
283. Norman Lewis, *Golden Earth: Travels in Burma* (London: Eland Books, 1984).
284. Bertil Lintner, *Land of Jade* (Bangkok: White Orchid, 1996).
285. Shelby Tucker, *Among Insurgents: Walking through Burma* (London: Radcliffe Press, 2000).
286. Andrew Marshall, *The Trouser People: Burma in the Shadow of the Empire* (Bangkok: River Books, 2012).
287. Ma Thanegi, *The Native Tourist: A Holiday Pilgrimage in Myanmar* (Chiang Mai: Silkworm Books, 2004).

288. Pico Iyer, *Video Night in Kathmandu and Other Reports from the Not-So-Far East* (London: Bloomsbury, 1988); and Rory MacLean, *Under the Dragon: Travels in a Betrayed Land* (London: HarperCollins, 1998).
289. Timothy Syrota, *Welcome to Burma and Enjoy the Totalitarian Experience* (Bangkok: Orchid Press, 2001).
290. David Eimer, *A Savage Dreamland: Journeys in Burma* (London: Bloomsbury, 2019).
291. Paul Theroux, *The Great Railway Bazaar* (London: Hamish Hamilton, 1975), pp. 179–206; and Paul Theroux, *Ghost Train to the Eastern Star* (London: Hamish Hamilton, 2008), pp. 258–94.
292. Shway Yoe [J.G. Scott], *The Burman: His Life and Notions* (Whiting Bay: Kiscadale, 1989).
293. Mi Mi Khaing, *Burmese Family* (Bombay: Longmans, Green, 1946).
294. Khin Myo Chit and Paw Oo Thet, *Festivals and Flowers of the Twelve Burmese Seasons* (Bangkok: White Orchid, 2002).
295. Georg Noack, *Local Traditions, Global Modernities: Dress, Identity and the Creation of Public Self-Images in Contemporary Urban Myanmar* (Berlin: RegioSpectra, 2011).
296. D.F. Rooney, *The Thiri Rama: Finding Ramayana in Myanmar* (London: Routledge, 2017).
297. Lynette Chua, *The Politics of Love in Myanmar: LGBT Mobilisation and Human Rights as a Way of Life* (Stanford: Stanford University Press, 2019).
298. Mi Mi Khaing, *The World of Burmese Women* (Singapore: Times Books International, 1984).
299. Chie Ikeya, *Refiguring Women, Colonialism, and Modernity in Burma* (Honolulu: University of Hawai'i Press, 2011).
300. Nilanjana Sengupta, *The Female Voice of Myanmar: Khin Myo Chit to Aung San Suu Kyi* (New Delhi: Cambridge University Press, 2015).
301. Jessica Harriden, *The Authority of Influence: Women and Power in Burmese History* (Copenhagen: NIAS Press, 2012); and Tharapi Than, *Women in Modern Burma* (London: Routledge, 2014).
302. Jennifer Rigby, *The Other Ladies of Myanmar* (Singapore: ISEAS – Yusof Ishak Institute, 2018); and Ashid Kolas, *Women, Peace and Security in Myanmar: Between Feminism and Ethnopolitics* (London: Routledge, 2019).
303. Noel Singer, *Burmese Dance and Theatre* (Kuala Lumpur: Oxford University Press, 1995).
304. Daniel Ehrlich, *Backstage Mandalay: The Netherworld of Burmese Performing Arts* (Bangkok: River Books, 2012).
305. Gavin Douglas, "Myanmar (Burma)", in John Shepherd et al. (eds.), *Encyclopaedia of Popular Music of the World*, vol. 5 (London: Continuum, 2005), pp. 196–202.

306. Heather Maclachlan, *Burma's Pop Music Industry: Creators, Distributors, Censors* (Rochester: University of Rochester Press, 2011).
307. Ma Thanegi, *The Illusion of Life* (Bangkok: White Orchid, 1994).
308. David Eimer, "Myanmar's Once-Booming Film Industry Gears Up for Act Two", *South China Morning Post*, 16 January 2016, http://www.scmp.com/magazines/post-magazine/film-tv/article/1900617/myanmars-once-booming-film-industry-gears-act-two.
309. See, for example, Phoe Wa, "A Flick Back to Myanmar's Film Industry", *Myanmar Times*, 27 March 2020, https://www.mmtimes.com/news/flick-back-myanmars-film-industry.html.
310. Htin Aung, *Folk Elements in Burmese Buddhism* (London: Oxford University Press, 1962).
311. Juliane Schober, *Modern Buddhist Conjunctures in Myanmar: Cultural Narratives, Colonial Legacies, and Civil Society* (Honolulu: University of Hawai'i Press, 2011).
312. Alicia Turner, *Saving Buddhism: The Impermanence of Religion in Colonial Burma* (Honolulu: University of Hawai'i Press, 2014).
313. Matthew Walton and Susan Hayward, *Contesting Buddhist Narratives: Democratization, Nationalism, and Communal Violence in Myanmar* (Honolulu: East-West Centre, 2014).
314. M.J. Walton, *Buddhism, Politics and Political Thought in Myanmar* (Cambridge: Cambridge University Press, 2017).
315. Peter Lehr, *Militant Buddhism: The Rise of Religious Violence in Sri Lanka, Myanmar and Thailand* (Cham: Springer Nature Switzerland, 2019).
316. Elizabeth Moore, Hansjorg Mayer and U Win Pe, *Shwedagon: Golden Pagoda of Myanmar* (London: Thames and Hudson, 1999).
317. E.H. Shattock, *An Experiment in Mindfulness* (London: Rider, 1958).
318. Sande Pulley, *A Yankee in the Yellow Robe: An American Buddhist Monk's Role in East-West Cultural Interchange* (New York: Exposition Press, 1967).
319. Marie Byles, *Journey into Burmese Silence* (London: George Allen and Unwin, 1962).
320. Mahasi Sayadaw, *The Fundamentals of Insight: Discourse on Meditation Practice* (Bangkok: Buddhadhamma Foundation, 2001).
321. Erik Braun, *The Birth of Insight: Meditation, Modern Buddhism, and the Burmese Monk Ledi Sayadaw* (Chicago: University of Chicago Press, 2013).
322. Ingrid Jordt, *Burma's Mass Lay Meditation Movement: Buddhism and the Cultural Construction of Power* (Athens: Ohio University Press, 2007).
323. Alicia Turner, Lawrence Fox and Brian Bocking, *The Irish Buddhist: The Forgotten Monk Who Faced Down the British Empire* (New York: Oxford University Press, 2020).

324. Curtis Lambrecht, "Burma (Myanmar)", in Greg Fealy and Virginia Hooker (eds.), *Voices of Islam in Southeast Asia: A Contemporary Sourcebook* (Singapore: Institute of Southeast Asian Studies, 2006), pp. 23–30.
325. J.C. Holt, *Myanmar's Buddhist-Muslim Crisis: Rohingya, Arakanese, and Burmese Narratives of Siege and Fear* (Honolulu: University of Hawai'i Press, 2019).
326. R.F. Cernea, *Almost Englishmen: Baghdadi Jews in British Burma* (Lanham: Lexington Books, 2007).
327. Anne Carter, *Bewitched by Burma: A Unique Insight into Burma's Complex Past* (Kibworth Beauchamp: Matador, 2012).
328. Eugene Morse, *Exodus to a Hidden Valley* (London: Collins, 1975).
329. Edward Jarvis, *The Anglican Church in Burma: From Colonial Past to Global Future* (University Park: Pennsylvania State University Press, forthcoming).
330. Ma Thanegi, *Nats: Spirits of Fortune and Fear*, photographs by Barry Broman (Bangkok: Ava Books, 2011).
331. D.M. Stadtner, *Sacred Sites of Burma: Myth and Folklore in an Evolving Spiritual Realm* (Bangkok: River Books, 2011).
332. John Feffer and Kyi May Kaung, "Out of Burma", *Foreign Policy in Focus*, 11 July 2007, https://fpif.org/out_of_burma/.
333. See, for example, U On Pe, "Modern Burmese Literature", *The Atlantic*, February 1958, https://www.theatlantic.com/magazine/archive/1958/02/modern-burmese-literature/306830/.
334. Ma Ma Lay, *Not Out of Hate*, translated by Margaret Aung-Thwin (Athens: Ohio University, 1991).
335. *Selected Short Stories of Thein Pe Myint*, translated and with an introduction by Patricia M. Milne, Data Paper no. 91 (Ithaca: Southeast Asia Program, Cornell University Press, June 1973).
336. Ludu U Hla, *The Caged Ones*, illustrated by U Wa Thone (London: Orchid Press, 2006); Wendy Law-Yone, *The Road to Wanting* (London: Chatto and Windus, 2010); and Nu Nu Yi, *Smile as They Bow*, translated by Alfred Birnbaum and Thi Thi Aye (New York: Hyperion, 2008).
337. Lucas Stewart and Alfred Birnbaum (eds.), *Hidden Words, Hidden Worlds: Contemporary Short Stories from Myanmar* (London: British Council, 2017).
338. Gerry Abbott and Khin Thant Han, *The Folk-Tales of Burma: An Introduction* (Leiden: Brill, 2000).
339. See "Best Burmese Novels", *First Rangoon Corporation*, 9 March 2019, https://firstrangoon.wordpress.com/2019/03/09/best-burmese-novels/.
340. See, for example, Lucas Stewart, "14 Novels on the Rohingya Crisis", *Lucas Stewart*, 4 February 2020, https://sadaik.com/2020/02/04/14-novels-on-the-rohingya-crisis/. Also relevant is "Rohingya in Modern

Fiction", *Lucas Stewart*, 12 July 2018, https://sadaik.com/2018/07/12/rohingya-in-modern-fiction/.

341. Anna Allott, "Burma", in Alastair Dingwall (ed.), *Traveller's Literary Companion to Southeast Asia* (Brighton: In Print Publishing, 1994), pp. 1–54.

342. F. Tennyson Jesse, *The Lacquer Lady* (London: Virago, 1979); Maurice Collis, *She Was a Queen* (London: Penguin, 1943); George Orwell, *Burmese Days*, reprint of the 1934 edition, with an introduction by Emma Larkin (London: Penguin, 2009); Edward Thompson, *Burmese Silver* (London: Faber and Faber, 1937); H.E. Bates, *The Purple Plain* (London: Michael Joseph, 1947); and Jon Cleary, *Forests of the Night* (Sydney: Collins, 1963).

343. Karel Van Loon, *The Invisible Ones* (London: Maia Press, 2006); Karen Connelly, *The Lizard Cage* (London: Harvill Secker, 2007); Daniel Mason, *The Piano Tuner* (New York: Alfred A. Knopf, 2002); and Amitav Ghosh, *The Glass Palace* (London: HarperCollins, 2000).

344. Amy Tan, *Saving Fish from Drowning* (New York: Random House, 2006).

345. Charmaine Craig, *Miss Burma* (New York: Grove Press, 2017).

346. Ellen Wiles, *Saffron Shadows and Salvaged Scripts: Literary Life in Myanmar under Censorship and in Transition* (New York: Columbia University Press, 2015).

347. Oscar Wilde [Mabel Cosgrove], *For Love of the King: A Burmese Masque* (London: Methuen, 1922).

348. Richard Shannon, *The Lady of Burma* (London: Oberon, 2008).

349. Guy Slater, *Eastern Star* (London: Oberon, 2018).

350. Maung Htin Aung, *Burmese Drama: A Study, with Translations of Burmese Plays* (Calcutta: Oxford University Press, 1937).

351. Rudyard Kipling, "Mandalay", in *Rudyard Kipling's Verse: Definitive Edition* (London: Hodder and Stoughton, 1940), pp. 418–20.

352. Friedrich V. Lustig, *Fluttering Leaves* (Rangoon: The author, 1970). Lustig also published his own translations of Burmese poems. See, for example, *Ashin Ananda: Burmese Poems through the Ages. A Selection Translated by Friedrich V Lustig, Buddhist Archbishop of Latvia, Lilac Laureate Poet* (Lakehead: M.M. Kardell, 1969).

353. Maung Myint Thein, *When at Nights I Try to Sleep: A Book of Verse* (Oxford: The Asoka Society, 1971). Myint Thein was the Chief Justice of Myanmar from 1957 to 1962.

354. Maung Myint Thein, *Burmese Proverbs Explained in Verse* (Singapore: The author, 1984); and Maung Myint Thein, *Burmese Folk-Songs: Collected and Translated by Maung Myint Thein* (Oxford: The Asoka Society, 1970).

355. Petr Lom et al. (eds.), *Burma Storybook*, introduction by Emma Larkin, translations by Maung Tha Noe, Maung Day, Zeyar Lynn, Pandora,

Kenneth Wong, ZawTun and Khun Cho, photographs by Dana Lixenberg (Amsterdam: ZINdoc: 2017).

356. Joseph Woods, *Monsoon Diary* (Dublin: Dedalus, 2018).
357. Romain Hugault and Yann, *Burma Banshees*, volume 1 of *Angel Wings* (6 volumes) (Geneva: Paquet, 2014). See also Philippe Thirault et al., *Mandalay* (Los Angeles: Humanoids Inc., 2015).
358. Sophie Ansell and Sam Garcia, *Burmese Moons* (San Diego: Idea and Design Works, 2019).
359. Chantal van den Heuvelal and Michel Pierret, *Aung San Suu Kyi: La Dame de Rangoon* (Durbuy: Coccinelle BD, 2013).
360. Guy Delisle, *Burma Chronicles* (Montreal: Drawn and Quarterly, 2008).
361. Andrew Selth, "Graphic Novels Chart Myanmar's History", *Nikkei Asian Review*, 1 April 2018, https://asia.nikkei.com/Life-Arts/Arts/Graphic-novels-chart-Myanmar-s-history. Also of interest in this regard is Jean-Marc Rastorfer, "La Birmanie dans la bande dessinee occidentale", *Bulletin du Cedok*, vol. 39 (2017), published by the Centre d'Etudes et de Documentation sur le Karenni, Lausanne.
362. Harn Lay, *Defiant Humour: The Best of Harn Lay's Political Cartoons from The Irrawaddy*, 2nd edition (Yangon: U Thaung Win, 2016).
363. Lisa Brooten, "Political Cartoons and Burma's Transnational Public Sphere", in J.A. Lent (ed.), *Southeast Asian Cartoon Art: History, Trends and Problems* (Jefferson: MacFarland, 2014), pp. 178–204.
364. G.A. Henty, *On the Irrawaddy: A Story of the First Burmese War* (London: Blackie, 1897).
365. W.O. Stevens, *Drummer Boy of Burma* (London: Collins, 1946).
366. Andrew Selth, "Biggles in Burma: Giving Boys What They Want", *Griffith Review*, March 2018, https://griffithreview.atavist.com/biggles-in-burma.
367. P.W. Garlan and Maryjane Dunstan, *Orange-Robed Boy* (New York: The Viking Press, 1967).
368. Jean Merrill, *Shan's Lucky Knife* (New York: W.R. Scott, 1960).
369. Dedie King and Judith Inglese, *I See the Sun in Myanmar (Burma)* (Hardwick: Satya House, 2013).
370. Claire Kelly, *The Caged Bird*, illustrations by Mike Rooth (Oxford: Oxford University Press, 2009).
371. Sylvia Fraser-Lu, *Burmese Crafts, Past and Present* (Oxford: Oxford University Press, 1994).
372. Sylvia Fraser-Lu, *Splendour in Wood: The Buddhist Monasteries of Burma* (Bangkok: Orchid Press, 2001).
373. Donald Stadtner and Sylvia Fraser-Lu (eds.), *Buddhist Art of Myanmar* (New Haven: Asia Society Museum and Yale University Press, 2015).
374. Andrew Ranard, *Burmese Painting: A Linear and Lateral History* (Chiang Mai: Silkworm Books, 2009); Elizabeth Dell and Sandra

Dudley (eds.), *Textiles from Burma* (London: Philip Wilson, 2003); and Than Htun (Dedaye), *Lacquerware Journeys: The Untold Story of Burmese Lacquer* (Bangkok: River Books, 2013).

375. R.J. Willis and Greg Herman, *Burmese Weights and Other Animal-Shaped Weights* (Melbourne: Hintha Books, 2019).

376. Mick Shippen, *The Traditional Ceramics of South East Asia* (London: A&C Black, 2005); and Anne Richter, *The Jewelry of Southeast Asia* (London: Thames and Hudson, 2000).

377. M.A. Stanislaw, *Kalagas: The Wall Hangings of Southeast Asia* (Singapore: Ainslie's, 1987).

378. Thweep Rittinaphakorn, "Collecting Burmese Textiles", *Arts of Asia* 47, no. 2 (March–April 2017), pp. 138–50; Noel Singer, "Survivors from a Burmese Palace", *Arts of Asia* 18, no. 1 (January–February 1988), pp. 94–102; and Wynyard Wilkinson, Mary-Louise Wilkinson and Barbara Harding, "Burmese Silver from the Colonial Period", *Arts of Asia* 43, no. 3 (May–June 2013), pp. 69–81.

379. Charles Lyte, *Frank Kingdon-Ward: The Last of the Great Plant Hunters* (London: John Murray, 1989). See also F. Kingdon-Ward, *Return to the Irrawaddy* (London: Andrew Melrose, 1956).

380. E.C. Nelson, *Shadow among Splendours: Lady Charlotte Wheeler-Cuffe's Adventures among the Flowers of Burma, 1897–1921* (Dublin: National Botanic Gardens of Ireland, 2013).

381. Dudley Clayton, *Charles Parish – Plant Hunter and Botanical Artist in Burma* (London: Ray Society, 2017).

382. J.H. Williams, *Bandoola* (London: Rupert Hart-Davis, 1953).

383. B.E. Smythies, *The Birds of Burma* (Edinburgh: Oliver and Boyd, 1940); and Kyaw Nyunt Lwin and Khin Ma Ma Thwin, *Birds of Myanmar* (Chiang Mai: Silkworm, 2003).

384. Alan Rabinowitz, *Beyond the Last Village: A Journey of Discovery in Asia's Forbidden Wilderness* (Washington DC: Shearwater Books, 2001); and W.J. Kress, *The Weeping Goldsmith: Discoveries in the Secret Land of Myanmar* (New York: Abbeville Press, 2009).

385. Adam Simpson, *Energy, Governance and Security in Thailand and Myanmar (Burma): A Critical Approach to Environmental Politics in the South* (Farnham: Ashgate, 2014).

386. Bridget Anderson and Stephen Anderson, *Burma: Food, Family and Conflict* (Valencia: Makhin Markets SL, 2020).

387. Bryan Koh, *0451 Mornings Are for Mont Hin Gar: Burmese Food Stories* (Singapore: Xochpilli Press, 2015).

388. Mohana Gill, *Myanmar: Cuisine, Culture and Customs* (Singapore: Marshall Cavendish International [Asia], 2014).

389. Ma Thanegi, *An Introduction to Myanmar Cuisine* (Yangon: Yone Kyi Chet Sarpay, 2004).

390. Charmaine Solomon, *The Complete Asian Cookbook* (Sydney: Paul Hamlyn, 1976). Solomon was born in Colombo, but her mother was from Myanmar.
391. Elizabeth Howes, *The Modern Salad: Innovative New American and International Recipes Inspired by Burma's Iconic Tea Leaf Salad* (Berkeley: Ulysses Press, 2016).
392. Min Sun Min, *Stamps of Burma: A Historical Record through 1988* (Chiang Mai: Mekong Press, 2007).
393. E.B. Proud, *The Postal History of Burma* (Heathfield: Proud-Bailey, 2002).
394. James Song, *Burma: The Stamps and Postal History under the Reign of the Three British Kings 1901–1947, Part 1 and Part 2, Airmail in Burma* (Singapore: James Song Philatelics, 2020).
395. *The Burma Peacock*, edited by Alan Meech, vol. 1, no. 1 (Fall 1979) to vol. 20, no. 3 (Fall 2000).
396. M. Robinson and L.A. Shaw, *The Coins and Banknotes of Burma* (Manchester: The authors, 1980).
397. Than Htun (Dedaye), *Auspicious Symbols and Ancient Coins of Myanmar* (Selangor: Ava House, 2007).
398. Owen W. Linzmayer, *The Banknote Book: Burma*, https://banknotebook.contentshelf.com/shop#!cs/store=S12121100000000A&action=product&product=I140403000002B6D; and Owen W. Linzmayer, *The Banknote Book: Myanmar*, https://banknotebook.contentshelf.com/shop#!cs/store=S12121100000000A&action=product&product=I13010200000048D.
399. Derek Brooke-Wavell (ed.), *Lines from a Shining Land* (Caversham: Britain-Burma Society, 1998).
400. Sue Arnold, *A Burmese Legacy: Rediscovering My Family* (London: Hodder and Stoughton, 1996); and Wendy Law-Yone, *Golden Parasol: A Daughter's Memoir of Burma* (London: Chatto and Windus, 2013).
401. Harriet O'Brien, *Forgotten Land: A Rediscovery of Burma* (London: Michael Joseph, 1991).
402. See, for example, C.V. Allmark, *Rebel of Burma* (Lynwood: UsForOz, 2004).
403. Sao Khemawadee Mangrai, *Burma My Mother – And Why I Had to Leave* (Sydney: Sydney School of Arts and Humanities, 2014).
404. Alex Wagner, *Futureface: A Family Mystery, An Epic Quest, and the Secret to Belonging* (New York: One World, 2018).
405. Michael Spurlock, *All Saints* (Minneapolis: Bethany House, 2017). This book was later made into a feature film. See *All Saints*, directed by Steve Gomer (Affirm Films, 2017), International Movie Database (IMDb), https://www.imdb.com/title/tt4663548/.
406. Andrew Selth, *Making Myanmar: Colonial Burma and Popular Western Culture* (revised version), Research Paper (Brisbane: Griffith Asia Institute, Griffith University, 2020), https://www.griffith.edu.au/__

data/assets/pdf_file/0027/1075338/Making-Myanmar-Colonial-Burma-and-popular-Western-culture.pdf.
407. Andrew Selth, "Colonial-Era Pulp Fiction Portrays 'Technicolor' Myanmar", *Nikkei Asian Review*, 11 July 2016, http://asia.nikkei.com/Life-Arts/Arts/Colonial-era-pulp-fiction-portrays-technicolor-Myanmar?page=1.
408. Andrew Selth, "Burma and the Comics, Part 1: Wars and Rumours of Wars", *New Mandala*, 9 August 2016, http://www.newmandala.org/burma-comics-wars-rumors-wars/; and "Burma and the Comics, Part 2: Heroines, Heroes and Villains", *New Mandala*, 10 August 2016, http://www.newmandala.org/heroines-heroes-villains/.
409. Andrew Selth, "Colonial Burma, History and Phillumeny", *NewMandala*, 24 May 2016, http://asiapacific.anu.edu.au/newmandala/2016/05/24/colonial-burma-history-and-phillumeny/.
410. Andrew Selth, "Colonial Burma, as Seen through Collectible Cards", *Nikkei Asian Review*, 11 May 2016, http://asia.nikkei.com/Viewpoints/Viewpoints/Andrew-Selth-Colonial-Burma-as-seen-through-collectible-cards.
411. Singer, *Burmah: A Photographic Journey, 1855–1925*.
412. Edith Mirante, "Escapist Entertainment: Hollywood Movies of Burma", *The Irrawaddy*, March 2004, https://www2.irrawaddy.com/article.php?art_id=932&page=1; and Andrew Selth, "Burma, Hollywood and the Politics of Entertainment", *Continuum: Journal of Media and Cultural Studies* 23, no. 3 (June 2009), pp. 321–34.
413. Andrew Selth, "Modern Burma Studies: A Survey of the Field", *Modern Asian Studies* 44, no. 2 (March 2010), pp. 401–40.
414. Andrew Selth, *Burma Watching: A Retrospective*, Regional Outlook no. 39 (Brisbane: Griffith Asia Institute, Griffith University, 2012); and Andrew Selth, *Myanmar-Watching: Problems and Perspectives*, Regional Outlook no. 58 (Brisbane: Griffith Asia Institute, Griffith University, 2018).
415. See, for example, Matrii Aung-Thwin, "Introduction", pp. 187–92.
416. See, for example, Mary Callahan, "Burmese Research Days or, A Day in the Life of a Nearly Extinct Life-Form: A Foreign Researcher in Burma", *Southeast Asia Program Bulletin*, Cornell University, Spring 1994, pp. 1–4; and Bertil Lintner, "Reporting Isn't Easy: The Foreign Correspondent in Rangoon", *Nieman Reports*, Winter 1996, pp. 69–70. In a similar vein is Andrew Selth, "Burma after Forty Years: Still Unlike Any Land You Know", *Griffith Review*, 26 April 2016, https://griffithreview.com/wp-content/uploads/Selth.Burma_.Essay_.Final_.set_.pdf.
417. Reshmi Banerjee, "A Candid Conversation with a Fellow Researcher", *Tea Circle*, 28 April 2017, https://teacircleoxford.com/2017/04/28/a-candid-conversation-with-a-fellow-researcher/. See also Li Yi, *Chinese in Colonial Burma: A Migrant Community in a Multiethnic State* (New York: Palgrave Macmillan, 2017).

APPENDIX 2
Maps and Charts of Myanmar

The twelfth-century Chinese historian Zheng Qiao once wrote of the benefits of mingling textual and pictorial descriptions of landscape, describing the images as the warp threads and the written words as the weft.[1] This prompts the thought that any list of books about a relatively unknown country like Myanmar would benefit from a short accompanying list of maps that can be consulted by readers should they wish to find a particular place, orient themselves or seek what has become known as "ground truth". In this regard, Myanmar-watchers have not always been well served, but the picture is gradually changing as more and more people travel to Myanmar or read books about it.[2]

Maps and charts of Myanmar (or Burma, Burmah, Pegu, Ava or Aracan, depending on the date and source), its near neighbours and surrounding seas have a long history. In European terms alone, they can be traced back at least to the sixteenth century. In this regard, an excellent resource is the monumental *Comprehensive Atlas of the Dutch East India Company*, published between 2006 and 2010.[3] The final volume includes several maps of the Burmese coastline and river ports like Syriam and Pegu. Anyone interested in looking closer at this early period is also referred to Kay Shelton's article on the maps of Myanmar made by European cartographers and currently held in the special collections of Northern Illinois University. The article was published in the *Bulletin of the Burma Studies Group* in 2003.[4] Shelton compiled a bibliography of maps for the same issue.[5] Another important reference is Tin Naing Win's study of early Burmese maps, with its focus on folding paper *parabaik* and old cloth maps, most dating from the eighteenth and nineteenth centuries.[6] Ten beautiful old maps of Myanmar, most dating from the eighteenth century, have been posted on the website of the Burma Boating Company.[7]

After the British began their three-stage conquest of Myanmar in 1824, first the Honourable East India Company and then the British government made a major effort to map the country, the better to bring it under their control, administer it and, it must be said, to exploit its natural resources. As the years passed, these works were updated and expanded using data, drawings and photographs provided by assorted officials, soldiers, explorers, missionaries and adventurers.[8] A local pundit was employed to help find the source of the Irrawaddy River.[9] These contributions were complemented by expedition reports, route guides and gazetteers, which usually contained detailed descriptions of the country, as observed by their authors.[10] The production of maps was assisted by technological advances, notably the development of lithographic printing techniques. Early guide books often included small scale maps of the region, or the country, and by the turn of the century coloured maps of Myanmar and its two main population centres were routinely included in publications designed for tourists and other visitors.[11]

During the Second World War, the Allies produced a wide range of high-quality maps of Burma (as it was then called), in English and at different scales. Many of these maps, such as the 1:63,360 (one inch to the mile) topographic series produced by the Survey of India, continued to be used well after the war's end, including by the new Burmese government (with over-printed Burmese language annotations). Gazetteers produced during the war also retained their value, at least for a period, because of General Ne Win's isolationist policies.[12] From 1945 to the 1990s, however, the Myanmar-watching public was poorly served in cartographic terms. The best maps were those produced by the major powers for strategic planning purposes, including plastic-moulded raised relief topographic maps. However, outside official circles such maps were difficult to obtain. Also, after the coup in 1962 the military government in Myanmar restricted the availability of local maps for security reasons. As late as 2006, an American academic visiting Naypyidaw was told by a senior Burmese official that there were no maps of the new capital city as ethnic armed groups could use them to plan an attack.[13] It was a couple more years before maps of the new national capital became readily available.

Ironically, given the regime's nervousness about external threats, good paper maps of Myanmar's peripheral regions could be obtained through its neighbours. Thailand and India, for example, produced 1:50,000 (one centimetre to half a kilometre) scale survey maps of their border provinces, which also showed parts of Myanmar. Also useful were the navigation charts periodically produced by the British Admiralty and the International Civil Aviation Organisation (ICAO). However, sales of some Thai and Indian maps were restricted and the charts were not intended for members of the general public touring Myanmar on land. They usually had to rely on small-scale wall maps and guides like *Motor Roads of Burma*, produced by the Burmah Oil Company, which only contained rudimentary route maps.[14] This situation changed in 1996, which was officially declared "Visit Myanmar Year". The Ministry of Hotels and Tourism authorized the production of several basic maps to cater to the expected influx of tourists.[15] This did not occur, largely because of campaigns led by foreign activists on behalf of detained opposition leader Aung San Suu Kyi. However, after President Thein Sein's election in 2011, and the easing of both official and unofficial travel restrictions, there was a heightened interest in Myanmar and a flood of foreign visitors. Many sought to acquire maps to help guide their sightseeing and for other reasons.

There is now a plethora of paper maps for sale, both in Myanmar and overseas. For example, several European and Asian firms offer colourful topographical maps for tourists ranging in scale from 1:2,150,000 to 1:1,000,000. There are also a number of larger scale maps that focus on specific areas of interest, such as Caroline Courtauld's *Bagan and Upper Myanmar* and her map of *Myanmar Featuring Myeik*. Myanmar's three largest cities, Rangoon, Mandalay and Naypyidaw, are now covered by good quality maps and there are even a few street directories available. The latter can be found in local bookstores, and it is possible to buy large wall maps of Myanmar in Yangon's street markets.[16] There is also a growing demand for specialist maps. For example, in 2003, Rod Beattie of the Thailand–Burma Railway Centre in Thailand produced the first comprehensive *Map of the Thai–Burma Rail Link*. A 2007 map titled *The British Raj in India* also covered colonial Myanmar (which did not become a separate colony until 1937). In 2010, the Myanmar Heritage Trust sponsored a map titled *Historical Walks in Yangon*. A wide range of official publications, including some high-grade military maps, are now available for purchase online.[17]

A selection of the more easily acquired paper maps is given below. They are listed alphabetically by subject. The scale of each map is provided, where known. It should be noted, however, that the quality of these maps is variable. Many are pleasing to the eye and sufficiently comprehensive to be used by tourists and armchair travellers, but lack important details.[18] For example, several earlier editions are based on unverified data and are not always very accurate.[19] Even some of the more recent maps, including the otherwise excellent 1:50,000 scale maps of Myanmar produced by East View Geospatial of Minneapolis, are based largely on satellite imagery and have not been field-checked. This means that they cannot be considered completely reliable or used for detailed analyses.[20] Not included in the list below are the "City Maps" produced by James McFee in 2017 and advertised widely on the internet. They are so rudimentary and of such a scale as to be virtually useless as practical guides to anyone trying to find particular streets or major landmarks in the population centres covered.

Also listed below are some older maps chosen mainly because they can be useful when reading histories and some specialized works. They include a few maps produced by Western intelligence agencies and the armed forces of various countries. Most are now hard to find, but it is sometimes possible to track down copies through online suppliers and on sites like Ebay. They are included simply to give potential visitors to Myanmar an idea of what resources are available if they wish to go beyond the usual commercial products that are found in bookshops, travel shops and online sites. Some are of considerable historical interest, such as the silk "escape and evasion" maps (numbers 44 and 49 in the list below) produced by the Allied forces during the Second World War.[21] As the Myanmar-watcher and author Edith Mirante demonstrated some years ago, they can still be useful for those wishing to visit less travelled parts of the country.[22] A range of other maps can be found on the internet, including many useful US and Soviet maps of Myanmar produced during the Cold War. There is also a lengthy list of maps, of all kinds, on the Online Burma/Myanmar Library website.[23]

As Kay Shelton pointed out in her article for the *Bulletin of the Burma Studies Group*, nautical charts of Myanmar have an even longer history than topographical maps, dating back to the very first foreign visitors to the country, almost all of whom arrived in ships (Marco Polo's reported visit in the late thirteenth century stands out as a possible exception to that rule). Some British charts predate the colonial period. In any case, the British Admiralty has been producing charts since 1795, and since 1821 has been selling them to the general public. Always a fundamental component of military and commercial operations, such charts are now being used to support an increasing range of tourist activities around Myanmar such as cruising, diving and exploring. A selection of charts covering Myanmar's coast and territorial waters has been listed below. A full catalogue of Admiralty maps can be found online at the UK Hydrographic Office website. They should be read in conjunction with *Admiralty Sailing Directions: Bay of Bengal Pilot*.[24]

General

1. *Asia, South-East*, scale 1:5,800,000 (Edinburgh: John Bartholomew and Son, 1994)
2. *Bagan and Upper Myanmar*, scale 1:2,150,000, text by Caroline Courtauld (Hong Kong: Odyssey Publications, 2015)
3. *Burma*, scale 1:1,500,000 (Hong Kong: APA Press, 1986)
4. *Burma*, scale 1:3,990,000 (Washington DC: Central Intelligence Agency, 1972)
5. *Burma: Administrative Divisions*, scale approx.1:2,000,000 (Langley: Central Intelligence Agency, 2007)
6. *Burma: Physiography*, scale approx.1:2,000,000 (Langley: Central Intelligence Agency, 2007)
7. *Burma: Transportation*, scale approx.1:2,000,000 (Langley: Central Intelligence Agency, 2007)
8. *India and Burma*, scale 1:6,000,000 (Washington DC: National Geographic Magazine, 1946)
9. *Myanmar*, Globetrotter Travel Maps, scale 1:1,700,000 (Bielefeld: Reise Know-How Verlag, 2015)
10. *Myanmar*, scale 1:3,000,000 (Ottawa: MapSherpa, 2018)
11. *Myanmar*, scale 1:2,150,000, text by Louise Taylor (Hong Kong: Odyssey Publications, 2012)
12. *Myanmar, Yangon, Bagan, Mandalay*, Map 'N' Guide, keyhole maps at different scales, text by Aaron Frankel (Bangkok: Groovy Map, 2013)

13. *Myanmar: Political*, scale 1:2,200,000 (New Delhi: V.C. Prakashan, 2014)
14. *Myanmar (Burma)*, scale 1:1,500,000 (Bielefeld: Reise Know-How Verlag Peter Rump, 2017)
15. *Myanmar (Burma)*, scale 1:1,500,000 (Munich: Nelles, 2016)
16. *Myanmar (Burma)*, scale 1:1,350,000 (Richmond: International Travel Maps and Books, 2016)
17. *Myanmar (Burma)*, Periplus Travel Maps, 4th edition, scale 1:2,000,000 (Hong Kong: Periplus Editions [HK], 2014)
18. *Myanmar (Burma) Adventure Travel Map*, scale 1:1,480,000 (Washington DC: National Geographic Maps, 2015)
19. *Myanmar (Burma) Road Map*, scale 1:1,000,000 (Vienna: Freytag and Berndt, 2019)
20. *Myanmar Featuring Myeik*, scale 1:625,000, text by Caroline Courtauld (Hong Kong: Odyssey Publications, 2015)
21. *Myanmar, Featuring the Irrawaddy*, scale 1:2,150,000 (Hong Kong: Airphoto, 2012)
22. *Myanmar Featuring Yangon*, scale 1:2,150,000, text by Caroline Courtauld and Sarah Rooney (Hong Kong: Odyssey Publications, 2016)
23. *Myanmar Guide Map*, scale unknown (Yangon: Design Printing Services, 2005)
24. *South Asia, with Afghanistan and Myanmar*, scale 1:7,345,000 (Washington DC: National Geographic, 1997)
25. *Southern China*, scale 1:1,500,000 (Munich: Nelles, 2005)
26. *Thailand, Malaysia, Myanmar, Singapore*, scale 1:2,800,000 (Frankfurt: Karto and Grafik Hildebrand Maps, 2016)
27. *Thailand, Vietnam, Laos and Burma*, Insight Travel Map, scale 1:4,000,000 (Singapore: APA Publications, 2013)
28. *Tourist Maps of Myanmar*, keyhole maps at different scales (Yangon: Design Printing Services, 2016)

City Maps

29. *Mandalay: Gateway to Myanmar*, scale 1:2,150,000 (city map scale 1:1,700), text by Caroline Courtauld (Hong Kong: Odyssey Publications, 2014)
30. *Mandalay Tourist Map* (Yangon: Business Pocket Guide, 1996)

31. *Nay Pyi Taw: Green Hub City*, scale 1:60,000, text by Caroline Courtauld (Hong Kong: Odyssey Publications, 2015)
32. *Nay Pyi Taw and Yangon*, scale 1:60,000 (Nay Pyi Taw) and 1:27,500 (Yangon), text by Caroline Courtauld (Hong Kong: Odyssey Publications, 2014)
33. *Illustrated Map of Yangon and Nay Pyi Taw*, scale 1:60,000 (Nay Pyi Taw) and 1:27,500 (Yangon) (Yangon: Myanmar Book Centre, 2013)
34. *The Map of Naypyitaw, Myanmar*, Various scales (Naypyidaw: Naypyitaw Development Committee, 2007)[25]
35. *The Map of Yangon* (Yangon: Yangon City Development Committee, 1998)
36. *The Map of Yangon: Street Directory*, 3rd edition (Yangon: Design Printing Services, for the Yangon City Development Committee, 2001)[26]
37. *Travel Like a Local – Map of Yangon: The Most Essential Yangon (Myanmar) Travel Map for Every Adventure*, text by Maxwell Fox (US: CreateSpace, 2018)
38. *Yangon City Map* (Yangon: Printing and Publishing Enterprise, 1993)
39. *Yangon City Map* (Yangon: Design Printing Services, 2016)
40. *Yangon Tourist Map*, Various scales (Yangon: Design Printing Services, 1996?)

Historical and Specialist Maps

41. *AAF Aeronautical Chart: Gulf of Martaban (677)*, scale 1:1,000,000 (Washington DC: US Army Map Service, 1945)[27]
42. *AAF Aeronautical Chart: Cheduba Island (676)*, scale 1:1,000,000 (Washington DC: US Army Map Service, 1944)
43. *Bagan Tourist Map* (Yangon: Business Pocket Guide, 1996)
44. *Burma (South), Siam (Thailand) (West Central), French Indochina (Part of)*, Map 44C, and *Burma (Extreme South), Siam (Thailand) (South)*, Map 44D, scale 1:1,000,000 (New Delhi?: Royal Air Force?, 1944).[28]
45. *Burma: Land Cover – Land Use Associations*, scale 1:1,000,000 (Washington DC: World Bank, 1976)
46. *Geological Map of the Socialist Republic of the Union of Burma*, scale 1:1,000,000 (Rangoon: Department of Geological Survey and Exploration, 1977)

47. *Great Coco Island*, scale 1:50,000 (Minneapolis: East View Geospatial, 2021)
48. *Historical Walks in Yangon*, A Myanmar Heritage Trust Guide Map (Chiang Mai: Silkworm Books, 2010)
49. *India (Part of), Burma (North West)*, Map 44A, and *Burma (North East), Siam (Thailand) (North)*, Map 44B, scale 1:1,000,000 (New Delhi?: Royal Air Force?, 1944).[29]
50. *Inle Lake*, scale 1:40,000 (Hong Kong: Odyssey Publications, 2015)
51. *Map of the Shwedagon Pagoda* (Yangon: Board of Trustees Shwedagon Pagoda, 2014?)
52. *Map of the Thai–Burma Rail Link*, reprint of 2003 edition, scale 1:250,000, compiled by Rod Beattie (Kanchanaburi: Thailand–Burma Railway Centre, 2008)
53. *Operational Navigation Chart ONC-J10: Bangladesh, Burma, China, India, Laos, Thailand, Vietnam*, scale 1:1,000,000 (St Louis: US Defence Mapping Agency, 1989)
54. *The British Raj in India*, scale approx. 1:6,060,606 (London: New Holland Publishers [UK], 2007)
55. *The Mekong River: Source to Sea*, scale 1:3,150,000 (Hong Kong: Odyssey Publications, 2012)
56. *The Map of Bagan* (Yangon: Design Printing Services, 1998)
57. *World Aeronautical Chart: Irrawaddy River (468)*, scale 1:1,000,000 (Washington DC: Aeronautical Chart Service, US Air Force, 1954)

Nautical Charts

58. *Approaches to Myeik (Mergui) Harbour*, British Admiralty Chart 1075, scale 1:75,000 (Taunton: United Kingdom Hydrographic Office, 2006)
59. *Bay of Bengal*, British Admiralty Chart 4706, scale 1:3,500,000 (Taunton: United Kingdom Hydrographic Office, 1977)
60. *Bay of Bengal*, National Geospatial-Intelligence Agency Nautical Chart 706, scale 1:3,500,000 (Springfield: National Geospatial-Intelligence Agency, 1986)
61. *Coco Channel and Northern Approaches to Port Blair*, British Admiralty Chart 1419, scale 1:150,000 (Taunton: United Kingdom Hydrographic Office, 1988)

62. *Elephant Pt/Mun Aung*, British Admiralty Chart 817, scale 1:350,000 (Taunton: United Kingdom Hydrogaphic Office, 2019)
63. *Heinze Islands to Myeik (Mergui)*, British Admiralty Chart 824, scale 1:300,000 (Taunton: United Kingdom Hydrogaphic Office, 2009)
64. *Kalingapatam to Goyagyi Kyun*, National Geospatial-Intelligence Agency Nautical Chart 63020, scale 1:900,000 (Springfield: National Geospatial-Intelligence Agency, 1993)
65. *Manaung (Cheduba) Island to Pathein River*, British Admiralty Chart 818, scale 1:350,000 (Taunton: United Kingdom Hydrographic Office, 2009)
66. *Mawlamyine (Moulmein) River and Approaches*, British Admiralty Chart 1845, scale 1:60,000 (Taunton: United Kingdom Hydrographic Office, 2009)
67. *Myeik Archipelago*, British Admiralty Chart 216, scale 1:300,000 (Taunton: United Kingdom Hydrographic Office, 2010)
68. *Pathein River and Approaches*, British Admiralty Chart 834, scale 1:75,000 (Taunton: United Kingdom Hydrographic Office, 2009)
69. *Pathein River to Yangon (Rangoon) River*, British Admiralty Chart 823, scale 1:300,000 (Taunton: United Kingdom Hydrographic Office, 2017)
70. *Sittwe*, British Admiralty Chart 1885, scale 1:25,000 (Taunton: United Kingdom Hydrographic Office, 2009)
71. *White Point to Mergui*, British Admiralty Chart 824, scale 1:300,000 (Taunton: United Kingdom Hydrographic Office, 2009)
72. *Yangon (Rangoon) River to Heinze Islands*, British Admiralty Chart 826, scale 1:300,000 (Taunton: United Kingdom Hydrographic Office, 2017)
73. *Yangon River (Rangoon River) and Approaches*, British Admiralty Chart 833, scale 1:60,000 (Taunton: United Kingdom Hydrographic Office, 2017

Notes

1. Cited in Gavin Francis, *Island Dreams: Mapping an Obsession* (Edinburgh: Canongate, 2020), p. 8.
2. For more information on this subject, see Andrew Selth, "Journeys without Maps in Myanmar", *New Mandala*, 12 September 2016, http://www.newmandala.org/journeys-without-maps-myanmar/.
3. *Comprehensive Atlas of the Dutch East India Company* (*Grote atlas van deVerenigde Oost-Indische Compagnie*), edited by G. Schilder et al., 7 volumes (Voorborg: Asia Maior, i.s.m. KNAG, Nationaal Archief en Explokart/Fac. Geowettenschappen, 2006–10).
4. Kay Shelton, "Maps of Burma by European Cartographers in NIU Special Collections", *Bulletin of the Burma Studies Group*, no. 71 (March 2003), pp. 11–16.
5. Kay Shelton, "Bibliography of Maps of Burma", *Bulletin of the Burma Studies Group*, no. 71 (March 2003), pp. 17–29.
6. Tin Naing Win, *Myanmar Historical Cartography: Parabaik Maps and Other Map Sources: A Post-doctoral Research Work Done by the Support of the Korea Foundation for Advanced Studies, Seoul, Korea* (Saarbrucken: LAP Lambert Academic, 2018).
7. "10 Beautiful Ancient Maps and Charts of Myanmar", *Burma Boating*, 9 August 2015, https://www.burmaboating.com/blog/best-of/10-beautiful-ancient-maps-and-charts-of-myanmar/.
8. John Crawfurd's mission to the Burmese court in 1826, for example, resulted in a map described as "the first accurate map of Burma". See *A Map of the Burman Dominions and Adjacent Countries* (London: John Walker, 1829). Another notable example, produced in 1886 after the fall of Mandalay, was *A Map of Burmah and Surrounding Countries* (London: James Wyld, 1886).
9. In Anglo-Indian use, a pundit was a native of India who was trained and employed to survey inaccessible regions, usually beyond the British frontier. See, for example, *The Journey of Pandit Alaga: Sources of Irawadi River*, map illustrating the paper of Major J.E. Sandeman, Bengal Staff Corps, 1882.
10. See, for example, *Routes in Upper Burma, Including the Shan States, to which are Added a Number of Routes Leading from Lower Burma and Siam into Those Districts, compiled for the Quartermaster-General of the Madras Army by Major A.B. Fenton* (Madras: Superintendent, Government Press, 1894).
11. See, for example, *The Modern Traveller: A Popular Description, Geographical, Historical, and Topographical, of the Various Countries of the Globe: Birmah, Siam and Anam* (London: James Duncan, 1826); and *A Handbook for Travellers in India, Burma and Ceylon* (London: John Murray, 1918).

12. See, for example, *Gazetteer to Maps of Burma, Compiled by the United States Board on Geographical Names* (Washington: Army Map Service, War Department, April 1944).
13. The academic told the Burmese official that he had used Google Earth to find his way around the city and assumed that insurgents could do the same. Personal communication, September 2016.
14. *Motor Roads of Burma* (Rangoon: The Burmah Oil Company, 1948).
15. Copies of these maps were widely available, often being left in hotel rooms for the use of guests.
16. Both Burmese and English language versions are available. Personal observation, January 2017.
17. For example, a wide range of maps produced by the former Soviet Union can be ordered from East View Geospatial, at https://shop.geospatial.com/. Various US Air Force charts can be ordered from firms like Internationales Landkartenhaus in Stuutgart, at https://www.ilh-geocenter.de/.
18. For example, during his momentous trek from India to China (across northern Myanmar) from October 1985 to April 1987, the journalist Bertil Lintner found his 1:1,000,000 scale US Operational Navigation Charts were inadequate, forcing him at times to make his own maps. He also drew on detailed maps provided to the Communist Party of Burma (CPB) by the Chinese, that appeared to be based on old British maps. Personal communication, 20 March 2021.
19. See, for example, Bertil Lintner, "On Track, Off Track", *Far Eastern Economic Review*, 16 October 1997, p. 53.
20. The accuracy of such maps became particularly important in the mid-2000s, when Myanmar was accused of hosting secret Chinese military bases and of launching a secret nuclear weapons programme.
21. Many of the "silk" maps produced for the Pacific theatre by the US Army Map Service were in fact made from rayon acetate. While designed mainly for air crews, these maps were sometimes issued to special forces units like (the US) Detachment 101 and the (British) Chindits.
22. Edith Mirante used one of these maps when travelling in southern Myanmar, prior to publication of her book *Burmese Looking Glass: A Human Rights Adventure and a Jungle Revolution* (New York: Grove Press, 1993), pp. 78–79.
23. "Maps and Satellite Imagery", Online Burma/Myanmar Library, 5 December 2019, https://www.burmalibrary.org/en/category/maps-and-satellite-imagery.
24. *Admiralty Sailing Directions: Bay of Bengal Pilot, NP21*, 12th edition (Taunton: United Kingdom Hydrographic Office, 2013).
25. This book contains 54 "sectional maps", at scales ranging from 1:3700 to 1:200,000.

26. This book contains 180 "sectional maps", at scales ranging from 1:5,000 to 1:40,000.
27. This map, and AAF (Army Air Force) aeronautical chart 676 immediately following, have LORAN (Long Range Navigation) maps on the reverse side.
28. This is a cloth map.
29. This is a cloth map. The US Army Map Service also produced two cloth maps of Burma in 1944, at a scale of 1:2,000,000.

APPENDIX 3
English Language Films about Myanmar (Burma)

The following is a selection of English language films made about Myanmar or set in Myanmar (in whole or in part) that give a flavour of the country, help illustrate how it has been portrayed by film-makers over the years, or comment on contemporary developments. Within two sections, covering full-length feature films and shorter documentaries, these works are listed chronologically by the formal date of production or first release. Several of the more recent feature films were joint ventures, but in those cases only the first listed production credit is cited. For more details on specific films (where available), it is suggested that the online International Movie Database (IMDb) be consulted.[1] Also of interest is Andrew Selth's "Burma, Hollywood and the Politics of Entertainment", in *Continuum: Journal of Media and Cultural Studies*, and Edith Mirante's earlier article "Escapist Entertainment: Hollywood Movies of Burma", in *The Irrawaddy*.[2] For a brief discussion of documentary films about Myanmar, see also Selth's "Burma-Watching on film", posted on *The Interpreter*, the blog of the Sydney-based Lowy Institute in 2010.[3]

Although there are a few exceptions, this list does not include feature movies that make only passing references to Myanmar or have scenes set in Myanmar that are not central to the plot, such as *The Wind Cannot Read*, directed by Ralph Thomas (Rank Organisation, 1958), or the American action movie *Stealth*, directed by Rob Cohen (Columbia Tristar, 2005). Nor does it include movies made in languages other than English. In addition to those made in Burmese, such as the internationally recognized *Return to Burma* (2011) and *Golden Kingdom* (2015), this category includes a few well-known movies such as *Crossing Salween*, a Karen language film directed by Brian O'Malley (Irish Film Board, 2010), *Rangoon Rowdy*, a Telugu language movie directed by Narayana Rao Dasari (Vijaya Madhavi, 1979), and the Hindi language feature *Rangoon* (Viacom 18, 2017) directed by Vishal Bhardwaj.[4] Also omitted from the list are several Thai language films with Burma-related themes such as *Bang Rajan* (BEC-TERO Entertainment, 2000) and *Suriyothai* (American Zoetrope, 2001).[5]

Nor, as a general rule, does the list below include short films made primarily for television, and which are not usually treated as stand-alone documentaries, for example by being released separately on DVD. Notable examples in this category include Adrian Cowell's groundbreaking reports on the guerrilla conflicts and opium trade in northern Myanmar, starting with *The Unknown War* in 1966 and ending with *The Heroin Wars* (in three parts) in 1996.[6] Martin Smith's *Burma – Dying for Democracy*, screened by the UK's Channel Four television station on 15 March 1989 as a programme in the "Dispatches" series, has been described by some observers as the best documentary made about the 1988 pro-democracy uprising.[7] Another notable practitioner in this field is the Australian film-maker Evan Williams, who has been reporting on Myanmar for more than fifteen years. His latest production is the BAFTA prize-winning documentary *Myanmar's Killing Fields*, about the Rohingya refugee exodus in 2016–17.[8]

Feature Films

1. *A Maid of Mandalay*, directed by Maurice Costello (Vitagraph Company of America, 1913)
2. *The Road to Mandalay*, directed by Tod Browning (Metro-Goldwyn-Mayer, 1926)
3. *The Road to Mandalay*, directed by E.M. Newman (Vitaphone Corporation, 1931)
4. *Mandalay*, directed by Michael Curtiz (Warner Brothers, 1934)
5. *The Girl from Mandalay*, directed by Howard Bretherton (Republic Pictures, 1936)

6. *Moon over Burma*, directed by Louis King (Paramount Pictures, 1940)
7. *Burma Convoy*, directed by Noel M. Smith (Universal Pictures, 1941)
8. *A Yank on the Burma Road*, directed by George B. Seitz (Metro-Goldwyn-Mayer, 1942)
9. *Bombs over Burma*, directed by Joseph H. Lewis (Alexander-Stern Productions, 1942)
10. *China Girl*, directed by Henry Hathaway (20th Century Fox, 1942)
11. *Rookies in Burma*, directed by Leslie Goodwins (RKO Radio Pictures, 1943)
12. *Objective Burma*, directed by Raoul Walsh (Warner Brothers, 1945)
13. *The Hasty Heart*, directed by Vincent Sherman (Associated British Picture Corporation, 1949)
14. *The Purple Plain*, directed by Robert Parrish (Two Cities Films, 1954)
15. *Escape to Burma*, directed by Allan Dwan (Benedict Bogeaus Production, 1955)
16. *Never So Few*, directed by John Sturges (Metro-Goldwyn-Mayer, 1959)
17. *Yesterday's Enemy*, directed by Val Guest (Hammer Films, 1959)
18. *Operation Bottleneck*, directed by Edward L. Cahn (Robert E. Kent Productions, 1961)
19. *The Long and the Short and the Tall*, directed by Leslie Norman (Associated British Picture Corporation, 1961)
20. *Merrill's Marauders*, directed by Samuel Fuller (Warner Brothers, 1962)
21. *Beyond Rangoon*, directed by John Boorman (Castle Rock Entertainment, 1995)
22. *To End All Wars*, directed by David L. Cunningham (Argyll Film Partners, 2001)
23. *Rambo*, directed by Sylvester Stallone (Lionsgate, 2008)
24. *Largo Winch II: The Burma Conspiracy*, directed by Jerome Salle (Pan Europeenne, 2011)
25. *The Lady*, directed by Luc Besson (Europa Corporation, 2011)

26. *Ninja: Shadow of a Tear*, directed by Isaac Florentine (Millennium Films, 2013)
27. *Twilight over Burma*, directed by Sabine Derflinger (Dor Film Produktionsgesellschaft, 2015)
28. *Shooting an Elephant*, directed by Juan Pablo Rothie (TUSK Pictures, 2016)
29. *The Road to Mandalay*, directed by Midi Z (Bombay Berlin Film Productions and CMC Entertainment, 2016)
30. *Hard Target 2*, directed by Roel Raine (Universal 1440 Entertainment, 2016)
31. *All Saints*, directed by Steve Gomer (Affirm Films and Provident Films, 2017)
32. *Mudras Calling*, directed by Christina Kyi (Business Alliance Hub Entertainment, 2018)
33. *Escape and Evasion*, directed by Storm Ashwood (Bronte Pictures, 2019)

Short Films and Documentaries

34. *Burma Victory*, directed by Roy Boulting (British Army Film Unit, 1945)
35. *The Stilwell Road*, (US Office of War Information, 1945)
36. *Lines of Fire*, directed by Brian Beker (First Run Features, 1990)
37. *Barefoot Student Army*, directed by Catherine Marciniak (Open Channel in association with Lyndal Barry and Sophie Barry, 1992)
38. *Royal Air Force Burma* (Imperial War Museum, 1995)
39. *Inside Burma: Land of Fear*, directed by David Munro (Central Independent Television, 1996)
40. *Portrait of Courage: Aung San Suu Kyi in Conversation with John Pilger*, directed by David Munro (Carlton UK Productions, 1996)
41. *Our Burmese Days*, directed by Lindsey Merrison (Westdeutscher Rundfunk, 1996)
42. *Sir Peter Ustinov in Burma: The Road to Mandalay*, directed by John McGreevy (Primetime, 1996)
43. *Lost over Burma: Search for Closure*, directed by Garth Pritchard (National Film Board of Canada, 1997)
44. *Burma Diary*, directed by Jeanne Hallacy (Documentary Educational Resources, 1997)

45. *Best of the Best Jokes of Zar Ga Na* (Maung Sein Tun, 1997?)
46. *Birth: Voices from the 1988 Uprising in Burma*, directed by Shwe Htee? (Non-Violence Empowerment Organisation, 1998)
47. *History Undercover: Jungle Battle Burma*, directed by Patrick King (Flashback Television, 1998)
48. *Fei Hu: The Story of the Flying Tigers*, directed by Frank Christopher (1999)
49. *Sacrifice: The Story of Child Prostitutes from Burma*, directed by Ellen Bruno (1999)
50. *Anonymously Yours*, directed by Gayle Ferraro (Aerial Productions, 2002)
51. *Burma Railway of Death* (Delta Entertainment, 2002)
52. *Burma Bridge Busters*, directed by James Moll (National D-Day Museum, 2003)
53. *Burma: Anatomy of Terror*, directed by Isabel Hegner (Burma Jade Films, 2003)
54. *British Campaigns Burma, 1941–1945* (Simply Media, 2004)
55. *Don't Fence Me In*, directed by Ruth Gumnit (Documentary Educational Resources, 2005)
56. *On the Road to Bagan*, directed by Francesco Uboldi (2005)
57. *Burma's Secret War*, directed by Sarah MacDonald (Australian Broadcasting Corporation, 2006)
58. *Burmese Nights*, directed by Sarah Sandring (2006)
59. *Total Denial*, directed by Malena Kineva (MK Productions, 2006)
60. *Mystic Ball*, directed by Greg Hamilton (Black Rice Productions, 2006)
61. *Ancient Burma, Clashing with Modern Myanmar*, directed by Cynthia Bassett (Am Tech Video, 2006)
62. *Prayer of Peace: Relief and Resistance in Burma's War Zones*, directed by Matt Blauer (Front Films, 2007)
63. *Burma* (Siren Visual Entertainment, 2007)
64. *Tortured in Myanmar*, directed by Grace Baek (2007)
65. *Burma's Open Road: An Insight into Myanmar*, directed by David Adams (Pegasus Entertainment, 2007)
66. *Burma's Saffron Revolution*, directed by Ashin Yevata (2008)
67. *Burma VJ*, directed by Anders Ostergaard (Kamoli Films, 2008)

68. *Freedom House*, directed by Benjamin Schultz (Sons of Thunder Productions, 2008)
69. *Burma All Inclusive: 16 Days of Truth*, directed by Roland Wehap (Rowe Productions, 2008)
70. *Burma: A Forgotten War*, directed by Lea Rekow (Lea Rekow, 2008)
71. *Myanmar beneath the Surface* (Wilderness Productions, 2009)
72. *Karma Trekkers: Myanmar* (Resource Media Inc., 2009)
73. *Shoot on Sight: The Ongoing SPDC Offensive on Civilians in Eastern Burma*, directed by Burma Issues (Witness, 2009)
74. *Burma's Medics*, directed by Grace Baek (2009)
75. *Breaking the Silence: Inside Burma's Resistance*, directed by Helene Magny and Pierre Mignault (InformAction Films Inc., 2009)
76. *Myanmar: In My Father's Footsteps*, directed by Pauline Hayton (Pauline Hayton, 2009)
77. *Burma: An Indictment*, directed by Jeremy Taylor (2009)
78. *Burma Soldier*, directed by Nic Dunlop, Ricki Stern and Anne Sundberg (LeBrocquy Fraser Productions, 2010)
79. *Freedom from Fear*, directed by Eric Torres (The Freedom Campaign, 2010)
80. *Burmese Dreaming*, directed by Timothy Syrota (Ostrow and Company, 2010)
81. *Aung San Suu Kyi: Lady of No Fear*, directed by Anne Gyrithe Bonne (Kamoli Films, 2010)
82. *Burma Displaced*, directed by Roland Wehap (Syndicado, 2010)
83. *The Genocidal Generals: Their Corporate Cronies, The Lady and Our Three Sons of Burma*, directed by Michael John Chahine (The Sun Maker Movies and Documentaries, 2010)
84. *Under the Radar: Burma*, directed by Neil Hollander (Adventure Film Productions, 2010)
85. *For Your Tomorrow*, directed by Don Clark (For Your Tomorrow, 2011)
86. *Burmese Butterfly*, directed by Lindsey Merrison (2011)
87. *Burma: A Human Tragedy*, directed by Neil Hollander (Adventure Film Productions, 2011)
88. *Breaking Open Burma*, directed by Patricia W. Elliott and Susan Risk (Live Wire Video Productions, 2012)

89. *They Call it Myanmar: Lifting the Curtain*, directed by Robert H. Lieberman (PhotoSynthesis Productions, 2012)
90. *Burmese Refugee*, directed by Michael Tacca (Speedafix Productions, 2012)
91. *How Can a Boy*, directed by Ed Kucerak (Kublacom Pictures, 2012)
92. *Return to Burma*, directed by Midi Z (Terracotta Media, 2012)
93. *Into the Current: Burma's Political Prisoners*, directed by Jeanne Hallacy (Democratic Voice of Burma and Assistance Association for Political Prisoners [Burma], 2012)
94. *Miss Nikki and the Tiger Girls*, directed by Julie Lamont (Titan View, 2012)
95. *Electric Burma*, directed by Natalie Johns (Bill Shipley Presents, 2012)
96. *Father Clemente Vismara: One Life is Not Enough*, directed by Paolo Pellegrini (Vision Video, 2013)
97. *Myanmar Emerges: Promise and Peril*, directed by Jonah Kessel (Global Post, 2013)
98. *Myanmar Goes Democrazy*, directed by Daniel Grendel and Silvana Santamaria (2014)
99. *Top Gear: The Burma Special*, directed by Kit Lynch-Robinson (BBC, 2014)
100. *Expedition Burma* (*Wild Burma: Nature's Lost Kingdom*), produced by Susanna Handslip (BBC Earth, 2014)
101. *Myanmar: Bridges to Change*, directed by Eric Daft and Mark Fisher (Fisher Creative, 2014)
102. *Siam Burma Death Railway*, directed by Kurinji Vendan (Nadodigal Productions, 2014)
103. *Building Burma's Death Railway: Moving Half the Mountain*, directed by Helen Langridge (HLA+/BBC, 2014)
104. *Buried in Burma*, directed by Mark Mannucci (Room 608, 2014)
105. *Myanmar Year Zero*, directed by Michael Henry Wilson (2015)
106. *Sailing a Sinking Sea*, directed by Olivia Wyatt (Daniel 13 Productions, 2015)
107. *The Black Zone*, directed by Grace Baek (Madrone Films, 2015)
108. *The Last King of Burma*, directed by Aditya Thayi (Mahic Hour Films, 2015)

109. *The Buddhist bin Laden*, directed by Emily Lee Gibson (Berkeley Film Foundation, 2015)
110. *13 Burmese Days*, directed by Garlen Lo (2016)
111. *The Burma Campaign*, directed by David Tennyson Thompson (2016)
112. *Get Lost in Myanmar*, directed by Melanie de Klerk (2016)
113. *Messages Home: Lost Films of the British Army*, directed by Paul Berczeller (Oxford Scientific Films, 2016)
114. *We Were Kings: Burma's Lost Royal Family*, directed by Alex Bescoby (Grammar Productions, 2017)
115. *Burma Storybook*, directed by Petr Lom (ZINdoc and JabFilm, 2017)
116. *The Venerable W*, directed by Barbet Schroeder (Les Films de Losange, 2017)
117. *Adoniram and Anne Judson: Spent for God*, directed by Robert Fernandez (Vision Video, 2018)
118. *Myanmar's Killing Fields*, directed by Patrick Wells (US Public Broadcasting System, 2018)
119. *Forgotten Allies: The Search for Burma's Lost Heroes*, directed by Alex Bescoby (Grammar Productions, 2019)
120. *Free Burma Rangers*, directed by Brent Gudgel and Chris Sinclair (Deidox Films, 2020)
121. *The Ladies Diary*, directed by Sara Trevisan (Walking Cat Productions, 2020)

Notes

1. International Movie Database (IMDb), at https://www.imdb.com/.
2. Andrew Selth, "Burma, Hollywood and the Politics of Entertainment", *Continuum: Journal of Media and Cultural Studies* 23, no. 3 (June 2009), pp. 321–34. See also Edith Mirante, "Escapist Entertainment: Hollywood Movies of Burma", *The Irrawaddy*, March 2004, https://www2.irrawaddy.com/article.php?art_id=932&page=1.
3. Andrew Selth, "Burma-Watching on Film", *The Interpreter*, Weblog of the Lowy Institute for International Policy, Sydney, 30 November 2010, http://www.lowyinterpreter.org/post/2010/11/30/Burma-watching-on-film.aspx.
4. The latter is not to be confused with the lesser-known Tamil language film *Rangoon*, directed by Rajkumar Periasamy (Murugadoss Productions, 2017).

5. For more on these Thai films, and their portrayal of Burma, see Glen Lewis, "The Thai Movie Revival and Thai National Identity", *Continuum: Journal of Media and Cultural Studies* 17, no. 1 (March 2003), pp. 69–78.
6. See, for example, "The Heroin Wars", Adrian Cowell Films, http://www.adriancowellfilms.com/#/the-heroin-wars/4574347436.
7. *Burma – Dying for Democracy*, directed by Christopher Mould, written and narrated by Martin Smith, Channel Four, "Dispatches", season 3, episode 11, 15 March 1989.
8. *Myanmar's Killing Fields*, reported by Evan Williams, directed by Patrick Wells, produced by Evan Williams, Eve Lucas and Patrick Wells. It was first aired on the US Public Broadcasting System's *Frontline* programme on 8 May 2018. The transcript is available at https://www.pbs.org/wgbh/frontline/film/myanmars-killing-fields/transcript/.

APPENDIX 4
Western Music with Burmese Themes, 1824–1948

Compiling a list of songs and tunes with Myanmar-related titles and themes is no easy task, even if it is confined to the colonial period (1824–1948).[1] Some compositions were so ephemeral that they appear never to have been published or recorded. Some were only produced in small numbers. Most of them soon passed from the musical scene and a number appear to have been lost forever. Others, like the musical settings inspired by Kipling's ballad "Mandalay", were so popular that they themselves spawned a wide range of melodies, arrangements and lyrics. Many had the same or similar titles, usually involving signature words like "Burma" (or "Burmah"), "Mandalay" and, to a lesser extent, "Rangoon". Copyright lists, collections of sheet music and old recordings held by libraries and sound archives are helpful in identifying such works, but until an authoritative list can be compiled, the following must be considered provisional only.[2]

The following list does not include works that only refer to Myanmar (or related places like Rangoon or Mandalay) in passing; for example, as a brief mention in a song about something else. Nor does this list include different arrangements of the same tune or song unless it differs significantly from other versions; for example, the various musical settings of the poem "Mandalay". Also absent are the different arrangements of particular songs and tunes recorded by bands and singers after the development of gramophone records. Most hymns and soldiers' songs have been left out on the grounds that, despite their wide use in Myanmar for certain periods, they were not 'popular' in the usual sense of the word, and often did not refer specifically to the country. In any case, only works that have a direct connection to Myanmar have been included.

All musical compositions have been listed in chronological order by first publication or original recording. Where those details are not known, they are listed according to the date of their first mention in published sources. Songs and tunes that appear never to have been published have been listed according to the date on which copyright was first granted as shown in the annual catalogue of copyright entries for musical compositions by the US Library of Congress.[3] Where any information is not available or is unreliable, this is shown by the use of question marks in the appropriate place. All these general rules have been broken, however, if a work does not meet any of the above criteria but is considered in some way important for an understanding of Myanmar's musical history.

The Early Period (1824–89)

1. "The Parting Scene: Lines Written on the Sailing of Messrs Wheelock and Colman for India, from Boston, Nov. 16, 1817", words by Thomas Baldwin, in Daniel Chessman, *Memoir of Rev. Thomas Baldwin DD* (Boston: True and Greene, 1826)
2. "General Campbell" (broadsheet) (Durham: Walker, Printer, 1827?)
3. "Parting Hymn of Missionaries to Burmah", by L.H. Sigourney, in L.H. Sigourney, *Zinzendorff: And Other Poems* (New York: Leavitt, Lord, 1836)
4. "Burman Mission Hymn: Dedicated to American Baptist Board of Foreign Missions", words by "W.C.R.", music by Lowell Mason (New York: Hewitt and Jaques, 1836)
5. "The Burman Lover", words and music by John C. Baker, in *First Set of Songs and Glees: The Bakers of New Hampshire* (Boston: Keith's Music, 1845)
6. "The Burial of Mrs Judson at St Helena, Sep. 1, 1845", words by H.S. Washburn and music by Lyman Heath (Boston: Oliver Ditson, 1846)

7. "Farewell to the Missionaries", by A.M.O. Edmund, in John Dowling (ed.), *The Judson Offering, Intended as a Token of Christian Sympathy with the Living and a Memento of Christian Perfection for the Dead* (New York: L. Colby, 1847)
8. "A Mound Is in the Graveyard, or the Missionary-Mother's Lament, Written by Mrs Judson Addressed to a Missionary Friend in Burmah, on the Death of Her Little Boy Thirteen Months Old, in Which Allusion Is Made to the Previous Death of His Little Brother", words by E.C. Judson and music by I.B. Woodbury (Boston: G.P. Reed, 1851)
9. "The Burman Lover", music by John C. Baker, arranged by Louis Tripp (Louisville: G.W. Brainard, 1853)
10. "The Mounted Infantry"? (1887?), words by B. May, in Lewis Winstock, *Songs & Music of the Redcoats: A History of the War Music of the British Army, 1642–1902* (London: Leo Cooper, 1970)
11. "*Kayah Than* (Sound of the Trumpet)", music recorded by W.G. St Clair (London: Boosey, 1887)
12. "Christian Brethren O'er the Main", words by F.J. Crosby and music by W.H. Doane, in *Songs of the Kingdom Prepared for the Use of Young People's Societies and Adapted for Prayer Meetings, Sunday Schools and the Home* (Philadelphia: American Baptist Publication Society, 1896)
13. "The Maid of Mandalay; or Nam Le Voo", in John MacGregor, *Through the Buffer State: A Record of Recent Travels through Borneo, Siam and Cambodia* (London: F.V. White, 1896)
14. "The 1st Burma Rifles' Quickstep" (1890?), music by A. McLeod, in David Glen (ed.), *David Glen's Collection of Highland Bagpipe Music*, book 11 (Edinburgh: David Glen and Sons, 1906?)

Kipling's 'Mandalay' and After (1890–1939)

15. "'Mandalay': No. 2 of a Set of Barrack Room Ballads", words by Rudyard Kipling and music by Gerard F. Cobb (London: Herman Darewski Music, 1892)
16. "'Mandalay', Musical Kindergarten Sketch No. 20", music by Gerard F. Cobb, arranged by Theo Bonheur [Charles Rawlings] (London: Charles Sheard, 1892)
17. "Mandalay", words by Rudyard Kipling and music by A.W. Thayer (Philadelphia: Theodore Presser, 1892)

18. "Mandalay Waltz", music by Bewicke Beverley (London: Charles Sheard, 1893)
19. "Memories of Burma: Waltz", music by Amy E. Warde (London: Weekes, 1894)
20. "On the Road to Mandalay", words by Rudyard Kipling and music by Henry Trevannion (Joseph Flanner: Milwaukee, 1898)
21. "Mandalay", words by Rudyard Kipling and music by Walter J. Damrosch (Cincinnati: John Church, 1898)
22. "Mandalay", music by Percy Grainger (unpublished, 1898)
23. "The Mandalay: Two Step", music by Henry Trevannion (Joseph Flanner: Milwaukee, 1899)
24. "On the Road to Mandalay: Rudyard Kipling's Celebrated 'Barrack-Room Ballad'", music by Walter Hedgcock (London: Charles Sheard, incorporating Herman Darewski Music, 1899)
25. "Mandy, from Mandalay: 'A Black Man's Burden', A Long Way after Kipling", words by W.H. Ford, music by J.W. Bratton (New York: M. Witmark and Sons, 1899)
26. "Under the British Flag: Fantasia on Songs and Dances of Great Britain and Her Colonies", music by J.A. Kappey (London: Boosey, 1900?)
27. "'Mandalay', in 'Rudyard Kipling's Barrack-Room Ballads Set to Music'", music by Arthur Whiting (New York: G. Schirmer, 1900)
28. "Rangoon", words by Arnold Brooks and music by Charles Wood (Edinburgh: *Foreign Mission Chronicle*, 1900)
29. "On the Road to Mandalay", words by Rudyard Kipling and music by Dyneley Prince (New York: G. Schirmer, 1903)
30. "You'd Better Come to Burmah", words and music by Paul A. Rubens, in *The Blue Moon*, by Howard Talbot and P.A. Rubens (New York: Chappell, 1905)
31. "Burmah Girl", words and music by Paul A. Rubens, in *The Blue Moon*, by Howard Talbot and P.A. Rubens (New York: Chappell, 1905)
32. "Little Blue Moon", words by Percy Greenbank, music by Howard Talbot, in *The Blue Moon*, by Howard Talbot and P.A. Rubens (New York: Chappell, 1905)
33. "My Maid of Mandalay", words by Roderic Penfield and music by Hans Scherber (New York: Maurice Shapiro, 1907)

34. "On the Road to Mandalay", words by Rudyard Kipling and music by Oley Speaks (Cincinnati: John Church, 1907)
35. *The Pagoda of Flowers: A Burmese Story in Song*, words by Frederick J. Fraser and music by Amy Woodforde-Findon, arranged by Sydney Baynes (London: Boosey, 1907)
36. "Mandalay", words by Rudyard Kipling and music by Henry Handel Richardson [Ethel Richardson] (1908), in Bruce Steele and Richard Divall (eds.), *Songs by Henry Handel Richardson for Voice and Piano* (Sydney: Currency Press, 2000)
37. "Love Scene from *The Pagoda of Flowers: A Burmese Story in Song*", words by Frederick J. Fraser and music by Amy Woodforde-Findon (London: Boosey, 1909)
38. "In Far Off Mandalay", words by Alex Rogers and music by Al Johns (Chicago: Will Rossiter, 1909)
39. "Burma L.M." (1909?), words by Philip Doddridge and music by T.B. Mosley, in W.L. Higgins (ed.), *Crimson Glory: Our 1939 Book for Church, Sunday Schools and Conventions* (Dalton: A.J. Showalter, 1938)
40. "The Maid of Mandalay", words by Joseph Blethen with music composed by Harry Girard (also known as Victor Kemp) (from *The Maid of Mandalay* (San Francisco, 1910?)
41. *Four Songs of Burma*, words by R.C.J. Swinhoe and music by J.W.J. Alves (London: Boosey, 1910) (includes "The Cold Weather", "The Well", "The River" and "Ma Lay Lay")
42. "Danse Birmane: Piano solo", music by Maurice Yvain (Paris: Max Eschig, 1911)
43. "Mandalay", words by Rudyard Kipling and music by Charles Willeby (Cincinnati: John Church, 1911)
44. "The Golden Land of Burma", words by R.C.J. Swinhoe and music by J.W.J. Alves (Rangoon: Misquith, 1911)
45. *The Cat's Eye: A Burmese Operetta*, words by R.C.J. Swinhoe and music by J.W.J. Alves (Rangoon, 1911?)
46. *Songs of Burma (Second Set)*, words by R.C.J. Swinhoe and music by J.W.J. Alves (London: Boosey, 1912) (includes "Lullaby", "The Loom", "Rubies", "Sunrise" and "The Maiden and the Buddh")
47. "The Bells of Burmah", words by Ed Teschemacher and music by Herbert Oliver, in *Songs of the Orient* (London: J.H. Larway, 1912)
48. "Burma Maid: Dance Intermezzo", music by Charles W. Ancliffe (London: Hawkes and Son, 1913)

49. *A Palace Plot, or The Maiden Aunt's Revenge*, words by R.C.J. Swinhoe and music by J.W.J. Alves (Mandalay: Upper Burma Advertiser Press, 1913)

50. *The Moon Maiden: A Burmese Operetta*, book and lyrics by George L. Stoddard, music by Charles Berton (New York: M. Witmark and Sons, 1913) (includes "Maiden Fair", "Cupid Holds the Key", "Hope On, Dear Heart", "Just for You", "Pansies and Poppies", "Say You'll Be My Own, Dear", "Until the End I'll Love but You", "Forever" and "Childhood Days")

51. "I'm on My Way to Mandalay", words by Alfred L. Bryan and music by Fred Fisher [Fred Fischer] (New York: Leo Feist, 1913)

52. "I'm on My Way to Mandalay (Including Patriotic Version)", words by A.L. Bryan and music by Fred Fisher [Fred Fischer] (New York: Leo Feist, 1914?)

53. "I'm on My Way to Mandalay: Medley Overture" (Feist's Song Medley No. 2), arranged by Lee Orean Smith (New York: Leo Feist, 1914)

54. "Mandalay", words by Rudyard Kipling and music by Gerard F. Cobb, in *Jack and Tommy's Favourite Patriotic Tunes*, arrangements by Stanley Gordon (London: Charles Sheard, 1914)

55. "Mandalay (March Song), dedicated to S.S. Mandalay", words and music by Mabel Besthoff (New York: Delaware-Hudson Steamship Company, 1914)

56. "Mandalay", words by Rudyard Kipling and music by Arthur Foote (Boston: Arthur P. Schmidt, 1915)

57. "When the Mission Bells Were Ringing (Down in Burma by the Sea)", words by Al Dubin and music by Gustav Benkhart (Philadelphia: Emmett J. Welch, 1916)

58. "There's a Burmah Girl a-Calling' (in Burmah by the Sea)", words by Harry Flanagan and music by Earl Burtnett (New York: A.J. Stasny Music, 1916)

59. *The Road to Mandalay: A Comic Opera in Two Acts*, book by W.H. Post, words by William McKenna and music by Oreste Vesella (New York: M. Whitmark and Sons, 1916) (includes "Road to Mandalay", "Alone", "Firefly", "Love That's Never Been Told" and "Shadows")

60. "A Burmese Ballet", words by Harold Atteridge and music by Sigmund Romberg, Otto Motzan and Herman Timberg, in *The Show of Wonders* (New York, 1916)

61. "Mandalay", words by J.E. Hazzard and Percival Knight, music by A.B. Sloane, in *Dew Drop Inn* (New York: Leo Feist, 1917)

62. "Mandalay", music and words by C.B. Weston (unpublished, 1917)
63. "In Mandalay", words by Clifford Gray and music by N.D. Ayer, in *The Bing Boys on Broadway* (London: B. Feldman, 1918)
64. "A Burmese Boat", music by C. Gilbert (New York?, 1918?)
65. "Burmah Moon", words and music by Gitz Rice (New York: Henry Burr Music, 1919)
66. "Burmese Belles", music by Patricia Platzman, recorded by Art Hickman and his Orchestra (New York: Columbia Gramophone, 1919)
67. "Burmese Bells: One Step", music by Eugene Platzman (New York: Shapiro, Bernstein, 1919)
68. "My Rose of Mandalay", words by Harold G. Frost and music by F. Henri Klickman (Chicago: McKinley Music, 1919)
69. "Rose of Mandalay", words by Ballard MacDonald and music by Herbert Claar (New York: Shapiro, Bernstein, 1919)
70. "Hindu Moon", words by Lucille Palmer, music by Frank Magine and H.R. Cohen (Chicago: Will Rossiter, 1919)
71. "Dancing on the Mandalay", words and music by Lee David (New York: Delaware-Hudson Steamship Company, 1919)
72. "'In Mandalay', part of 'Suite, Op. 85'", music by Joseph Holbrooke (London?, 1920s?)
73. "In Old Rangoon", words and music by Gitz Rice (New York: G. Ricordi, 1920)
74. "Moonlight in Mandalay", words by Jack Yellen and music by Abe Olman (Chicago: Forster Music, 1920)
75. "Burmah Bells", words and music by Zo Elliott (London: Keith, Prowse, 1920)
76. "Mandalay", words by Neville Fleeson and music by Albert Von Tilzer (New York: Broadway Music, 1920)
77. "When I'm Back in Mandalay Again", words by Allan Flynn and music by Jack Egan (New York: Irving Berlin, 1920)
78. "Mandalay", words by H.M. Lockwood and music by L.W. Lockwood (unpublished, 1920)
79. "Maid of Mandalay", words and music by John Finke (unpublished, 1920)
80. "My Burmah Girl" (unpublished?, 1920)

81. "My Song of India", words and music by Harley Rosso and H.L. Alford (St. Paul: McClure Music, 1921)
82. "Schuetz Burmah Air", music by H.W. Yost (unpublished, 1921)
83. "Mandalay", words and music by F.W. Thomas (unpublished, 1921)
84. "Twenty Miles from Mandalay", words by Henry Creamer and music by Joe Jordan (New York: Irving Berlin, 1922)
85. "Burmah Bells", words by Olga Yardley and music by Paul Michelin (Sydney: W.H. Paling, 1922)
86. "Burmah Bells", words and music by D.G. Owens (Vancouver: Weaver Music Supply, 1922).
87. "Rangoon", words and music by Toni Farrell (New York: Enoch and Sons, 1922)
88. "Burma Nights", words by Ray Valentine and music by Louis St Clair (London: Chappell, 1922)
89. "Mandalay", words and music by Lew Brown and Carey Morgan (New York: Leo Feist, 1922)
90. "Burma", music by Richard Cherkasky and Lucien Schmit, arranged by Dave Kaplan (unpublished, 1922)
91. "In Dreamy Burma", music by F.B. Winegar, arranged by L.S. Montgomery (unpublished, 1922)
92. "Meet Me in Mandalay", words and music by Albert Schiller (unpublished, 1922)
93. "Rose of Mandalay", music by Lynn Stroud (unpublished, 1922)
94. "Rangoon", words and music by J.H. Flynn (unpublished, 1922)
95. "Down in Old Rangoon", words by Wyn Ewart and music by Charles Prentice (London: Chappell, 1923)
96. *Burmah Rubies: A Cycle of Four Eastern Songs*, words by Percy Edgar and music by Mark Strong [J.L. Harris] (London: Boosey, 1923) (includes "Burmah Rubies", "The Forest Temple", "My Bamboo Flower" and "The Dacoit's Song")
97. "Maid O' Mandalay", words and music by Tom King and Jack Fewster (Adelaide: Saturday Journal, 1923)
98. "Rose of Burmah", words by Percy Edgar and music by Lawrence Emlyn, in *Shuffle Along* (London: St Giles, 1923)
99. "Chant Birman", words and music by Andre Messager, in *L'Amour Masque* (Paris: Francis Salabert, 1923)

100. "From Mandalay to Hudson Bay, as Long as I'm with You", words by Owen Murphy and music by Al Sherman (New York: Clarke and Leslie Songs, 1924)
101. "Little Mandalay Princess: Oriental Idyll", music by Cedric Lamont (London: Keith Prowse, 1924)
102. "Mandalay: Fox Trot Ballad", words and music by Earl Burtnett, Abe Lyman and Gus Arnheim (New York: Jerome H. Remick, 1924)
103. "Mandalay", words by Rudyard Kipling and music by Frederic Ayres (New York: G. Schirmer, 1924)
104. "Mandalay Moon", words and music by Tom King and W.J. Munday [Jack Fewster] (London: West's, 1924)
105. "I'm Going to Jazz My Way to Mandalay" (also known as "I'm Jazzin' My Way to Mandalay"), words and music by J.G. Gilbert (London: Lawrence Wright Music, 1925)
106. "Moonlight in Mandalay", words by Marty Fay, music by Lou Herscher and Elmer Naylor (New York: Jack Mills, 1925)
107. "On the Road to Mandalay, Poem from *Barrack-Room Ballads* by Rudyard Kipling", musical setting by George Gilder (New York: F.B. Haviland, 1925)
108. "Burma Rifles March Past" (Maymyo?: Queen's Own Highlanders, 1925)
109. "Beneath the Burmese Moon", music by Herschel Henlere (London: ACO Records, 1925)
110. "A Burmese Pwe: An Impression of Burma", music by Henry Eichheim (New York: Neighbourhood Playhouse, 1926)
111. "A Burmese Yein Pwe", music by Clifford Vaughan (Singapore?: Denishawn Dancers, 1926)
112. "Mandalay: 'The Isle of a Thousand Palms'", words and music by F.W. Salley (Tampa: Booster Record and Publishing, 1926)
113. "The Pagoda of Flowers: Burmese Suite", music by Sydney Herbert (London: Boosey and Hawkes, 1926)
114. "Rangoon Wedding", words and music by Gitz Rice (?), in *Nic Nax of 1926* (New York, 1926)
115. "Burma – Orchestra Suite", music by Henry Eichheim (Chicago, 1927)
116. "Burma: Oriental Fox-trot", words by Rudy Bertram and music by Ben Evers (London: Rexborough Music, 1927)

117. "In Mandalay with My Fair Lady", words by Sidney Holden and music by Otto Motzan (New York: Otto Motzan, 1927)
118. "Mandalay: 'From the Barrack-Room Ballads': Song", lyrics by Rudyard Kipling, music by Harold Dixon (New York: Mills Music, 1927)
119. "Mandalay Lady", words by Eric Valentine and music by Rob Katscher, banjo and ukulele arrangement by A.D. Keech (London: B. Feldman, 1927)
120. "Mandalay", words by Rudyard Kipling and music by A.M. Baldwin (unpublished?, 1927)
121. "Burmese Dance", in "Piano Concerto No. 2, L'Orient, Op. 100", music by Joseph Holbrooke (London, 1928?)
122. "Rose of Mandalay: Fox Trot Song", words and music by Ted Koehler and Frank Magine (New York: Leo Feist, 1928)
123. "Burma Girl: Foxtrot", words and music by Anthony Picton, banjo and ukulele arrangement by A.D. Keech (London: Billy Thorburn Music, 1928)
124. "A Lagoon in Rangoon: A Burmese Barcarolle", words and music by Val Valentine, banjo and ukulele arrangement by A.D. Keech (London: B. Feldman, 1928)
125. "Burmese Chant", music by Evan Marsden (London: Joseph Henry Larway, 1928)
126. "Yearning for Mandalay", music by Sheik Taylor (Chicago: Chicago Music, 1928)
127. "Song of Mandalay", in *Happy End*, book by Elisabeth Hauptman, words by Bertolt Brecht and music by Kurt Weill (Berlin, 1929)
128. "Festival of Empire: Grand Patriotic Fantasia", music by John Mackenzie-Rogan (London: Boosey, 1929)
129. "Rangoon", composer unknown, vocals (in Urdu) by Habloo Quawal (Dum Dum: Columbia Records, 1920s?)
130. "Rangoon Rice Carriers", music by Joseph Holbrooke (London: Piccadilly Records, 1930?)
131. "Burma Girl", music by Charlie Lawrence, recorded by Paul Howard and the Quality Serenaders (Hollywood: Victor Records, 1930)
132. "Mandalay, Moonlight and You", music by Lee David (New York: Delaware-Hudson Steamship Company, 1930)

133. "In Old Mandalay", words by Haven Gillespie, music by De Witt Parker and Harriett Bevson (Chicago: Milton Weil Music, 1931)
134. "On the Road to Mandalay: Song", words by Rudyard Kipling and music by Charles H. Maskell (Philadelphia: Morris Music, 1932)
135. "Calling Me Home Again", words by Perceval Graves and music by Vera Buck (London: Boosey, 1935)
136. "Mandalay", words by Rudyard Kipling and music by Erling Winkel (Copenhagen: Musikk-Husets, 1936)
137. "Six Melodies of Burma for Pianoforte", arranged by Ma Hla Phroo (Cambridge: Heffer and Sons, 1937)
138. "By an Old Pagoda", words by Jimmy Kennedy and music by Hugh Williams (London: Peter Maurice Music, 1938)

The War Years and After (1940–48)

139. "Moon over Burma", words by Dick McIntyre and L.L. Redman, music by Will Livernash (New York: Whitney Blake Music, 1940)
140. "Moon over Burma: As Sung by Dorothy Lamour in the Paramount Picture *Moon over Burma*", words by Frank Loesser and music by Frederick Hollander (New York: Paramount Music, 1940)
141. "Burma Convoy: End Title", music by Heinz Roemheld and Frank Skinner (New York: Universal Music, 1941)
142. "Burma Road", words and music by Gene Burdette? (unpublished, 1941)
143. "A Burmese Ballet", music by Sid Phillips, recorded by Bert Ambrose and his Orchestra (New York: Decca, 1942)
144. "Burma Patrol", music by Karl L. King, arranged by James Swearingen (Oskaloosa: C.L. Barnhouse, 1942, reprinted 2009)
145. "Mandalay", words by Rudyard Kipling and music by Erling Winkel, lyrics translated into Danish by Kai Fris Moller (Copenhagen: Skandinavisk og Borups Musikforlag, 1942)
146. "Burma Bomber", music by William Bauer, with Abe Lyman and his California Orchestra (n.p., 1942)
147. "Burma Girl", music by W.P. Burnett (St. Louis: Porter Burnett, 1942)

148. "I'm on My Way to Mandalay: Medley Overture", arranged by L.O. Smith (New York: Leo Feist, 1942)
149. "Bombers over Burma", music by Bob Carleton (unpublished, 1942)
150. "Burma Road", music by M.E. Kreger (unpublished, 1942)
151. "Air Raid over Burma", words and music by J.A. Burton (unpublished, 1942)
152. "Temple Bells of Mandalay", words and music by E.M. Curtis (unpublished, 1942)
153. "We're on Our Way to Mandalay", words and music by L.L. Schroeder (unpublished, 1942)
154. "From Tokio to Mandalay", words by Joan Haudenschield and music by C.A. Grimm (Chicago: General Music Sales, 1942)
155. "Greater Mandalay", words and music by E.A. Nunez (unpublished, 1942)
156. "Love from Mandalay", words by J.L. Guiu (unpublished, 1942)
157. "The Moon Was Shining Bright on Burma Valley", words and music by J.N. Lenz (Detroit: Golden Tune, 1943)
158. "Bee-line for Burma", music by Harold Grant (New York: Colonial Music, 1943)
159. "Mandalay Moon", music by Robert Pollack (unpublished, 1943)
160. "I'm Dreaming of Burma Road", words and music by H.A. Campbell (unpublished, 1943)
161. "Yellow Rose of Burma" (1943?), words by Anonymous, in W.R. Peers and Dean Brelis, *Behind the Burma Road* (London: Robert Hale, 1964)
162. "Burma Bounce", music by Frankie Masters and Al Hecker (New York: Embassy Music, 1944)
163. "Song of the Chindits", words by 'Frolik' (John Hollington) (Colombo: *SEAC*, 1944)
164. "Over the Chindwin", music by Evan Macrae (1944), in *The Cabar Feidh Collection: Pipe Music of the Queen's Own Highlanders (Seaforth and Camerons)* (London: Paterson's Publications, 2004)
165. Suite from the film *Burma Victory* (1944), music by Alan Rawsthorne (London: Ministry of Information, 1945) (includes "Dropping Supplies", "Dawn and Jungle Advance", "Building Boats" and "Mandalay")

166. "Burma Flyer", music by E.V. Bonnemere (unpublished, 1944)
167. "Irma from Burma", music by A.W. Halgerson (unpublished, 1944)
168. "Irma from Burma", words and music by Lew (Louis) Tobin (unpublished, 1944)
169. "Irma from Burma", words and music by Fred Fensterer (unpublished, 1944)
170. "9th Battalion Gordon Highlanders Crossing the Irrawaddy", music by A.A. Sim (1945), in *The Cabar Feidh Collection: Pipe Music of the Queen's Own Highlanders (Seaforth and Camerons)* (London: Paterson's Publications, 2004)
171. "South of Meiktila", words by Tommy Wren (1945), in Martin Page, *"Kiss Me Goodnight, Sergeant Major": The Songs and Ballads of World War II* (London: Hart-Davis, MacGibbon, 1973)
172. Score from the film *Objective, Burma!*, music by Franz Waxman (Los Angeles: Warner Brothers, 1945) (includes "Briefing in an Hour", "Taking Off", "Jumping", "Killing the Sentry", "Stop Firing", "Andante", "Two Came Back", "Burmese Village", "Resting", "Missing the Plane", "At Night", "Invasion" and "The Camp")
173. "Burma Road", music by Ray Terry and Nat Temple (London: Campbell Connelly, 1945)
174. "Burma Road Blues, Parts 1 and 2", words by Lionel Hampton, performed by Roy Milton's Sextet (Los Angeles: Hamp-Tone 104, 1945).
175. "Burma Bound", words and music by Johnny Uphill (Calcutta: Bernstein & Hills, 1945)
176. "Down by Mandalay", words by Anonymous, in Martin Page, *"Kiss Me Goodnight, Sergeant Major": The Songs and Ballads of World War II* (London: Hart-Davis, MacGibbon, 1973)
177. "Bury Me out in the Jungle", words by Anonymous, in Martin Page, *"Kiss Me Goodnight, Sergeant Major": The Songs and Ballads of World War II* (London: Hart-Davis, MacGibbon, 1973)
178. "Spud Spedding's Broken Boys", words by Anonymous, in Martin Page, *"Kiss Me Goodnight, Sergeant Major": The Songs and Ballads of World War II* (London: Hart-Davis, MacGibbon, 1973)
179. "The Minden Dandies", words by Anonymous, in Roy Palmer, *"What a Lovely War!" British Soldiers' Songs from the Boer War to the Present Day* (London: Michael Joseph, 1990)

180. "Sweetheart out in Burma", music by Nat Vincent or D.M. Shelby (unpublished 1945)
181. "Lookin' at the Burma Moon", music by Leo Richard and Hector Richard (unpublished 1945)
182. "The Temple Bells of Mandalay", words and music by E.M. Curtis (unpublished, 1945)
183. "Burma Moon", words and music by E.J. Roth (unpublished, 1945)
184. "On the Burma Road", music by B.L. Allaire (unpublished, 1945)

Notes

1. An earlier version of this list can be found in Andrew Selth, *Burma, Kipling and Western Music: The Riff from Mandalay* (London: Routledge, 2017), pp. 229–39.
2. Worth mentioning in this regard is Jason Gibbs et al. (eds.), *Longing for the Past: The 78 rpm Era in Southeast Asia* (Atlanta: Dust-To-Digital, 2013). This is a rich collection of erudite comment, illustrations and musical recordings. Myanmar (called Burma) is well represented in all three categories.
3. US Library of Congress, *Catalogue of Copyright Entries, Musical Compositions* (Washington: US Government Printing Office, various years).

Index of Names

The numbers given below are those used to refer to the specific works listed in this bibliography. Names appear as they have been given, although entries have been consolidated in cases where both first names and initials have been used. Joint authors, editors, translators, photographers and illustrators have been listed individually, as have those who have contributed introductions, forewords and afterwords. Other people named in the prefaces, foreword, introduction, appendices and notes of this bibliography have not been listed. Diacritical marks, where relevant, have not been included.

A
A Tatmadaw Researcher, 2109
A Zun Mo, 1161
Abbott, Gerry, 311, 312, 779, 780, 2368
Abe, Masato, 2196, 2245, 2253, 2297
Abhayasundara, Praneeth, 1979
Abonyi, David, 2196, 2245
Abrahamian, Andray, 1978
Abrahamson, K.L., 2427, 2428, 2429
Abram, David, 50
Abreu, Robert, 314

Adams, Nel, 667
Adams, Simon, 1078
Adas, Michael, 2197
Adirex, Paul, 2430
Aebi, Ernst, 2431
Ahmed, Intiaz, 1079
Ahmed, Kawser, 1080
Ahmed, Sabbir, 1090
Ai Pun, 2369
Ainsworth, Leopold, 668
Akimoto, Yuki, 222
Alexander, J.E., 315
Allan, David, 2634
Allardice, Rory, 343

346 Index of Names

Allden, Kathleen, 1377
Allen, M.P., 1308
Allmark, C.V., 781, 782
Allott, Anna, 428, 775, 1173, 2348
Allsebrook, Annie, 950
Alvin, Johan, 1716, 1937
Amakawa, Naoko, 2198
Ampika Rattanapitak, 2349
Amporn, Jirattikorn, 1499
An Officer, 316
Anderson, Bridget, 2671
Anderson, John, 317
Anderson, Joseph, 669
Anderson, Liz, 2432
Anderson, Stephen, 2671
Anderson, Vincent, 2618
Andrews-Speed, Philip, 2240
Andrieux, Aurelie, 1681
Anguelov, Nikolay, 1926
Ansel, Sophie, 1084, 1101, 2528
Aosenba, 1027
Apple, Betsy, 1395, 1396
Archer, Geoffrey, 2433
Aris, Michael, 858, 861
Armour-Hileman, Victoria, 819
Armstrong, R.M., 980
Arnold, Matthew, 1805, 1865
Aron, Gabriel, 1085
Artist Hla Myint Swe, 957, 958, 2539, 2572, 2595
Arunatilaka, Ahungalle, 1979
Ashforth, Tom, 74
Ashin Jagaralankara, 1212
Ashin Yevata, 2370
Ashon Nyanuttara, 1213
Astor, Gerald, 546
Atcherley, Harold, 645
Augustin, Andreas, 2268
Augustin, F.X., 135
Aung Aung, 1826
Aung Aung Taik, 783, 2672
Aung Chin Win Aung, 484, 1682, 2508
Aung Hein, 1382
Aung Htoo, 867
Aung Khine, 400
Aung Kyaing, 116
Aung Min, 2573
Aung Myint, 2573

Aung Myo Min, 2386
Aung Naing Oo, 2035, 2036
Aung San Suu Kyi, 855, 856, 857, 858, 859, 860, 861, 862
Aung Than Batu, 1378
Aung Than Tun, 2159
Aung Thein, 2687
Aung Thin, Michelle, 2372, 2434
Aung Thwin, Margaret, 2398
Aung Thwin, Matrii, 384, 433
Aung Thwin, M.A., 384, 429, 430, 431, 432, 459
Aung Tun Thet, 2199
Aung Zaw, 868
Aungkana Kamonpech, 1540
Ausland, J.C., 730
Ausland, J.E., 730
Avicenna, Milo, 2698
Aye Aye Myint, 14
Aye Chan, 1128
Aye, Henri-Andre, 993
Aye Kyaw, 485, 1392, 1683, 2160
Aye Myint, 1777, 2574, 2593
Aye Myint, Oscar, 1777
Aye Saung, 784

B

Ba Han, 1162
Bachoe, Ralph, 1962
Bader, Michael, 131
Badgley, J.H., 1683, 1980
Bagan Maung Maung, 184
Bagshawe, L.E., 434, 775
Bahadur, Mutua, 1045
Bahar, Abid, 1086
Bailey, Philip, 2642
Baillie, Allan, 2435
Bainbridge, John, 2054
Baines, Frank, 731
Baird-Murray, Maureen, 670
Baker, Chris, 479, 1011
Baker, E.C.S., 244
Baker, Richard, 671
Bakshi, Akhil, 344
Ball, Desmond, 1455, 2037, 2096, 2110, 2148
Ball, Joseph, 820
Bamforth, Vicky, 1541
Bandele, Biyi, 2436, 2437

Banerjee, Dipankar, 1981
Banerjee, Reshmi, 1982
Banks, Arthur, 633
Bannert, Dietrich, 199
Bansal, Ben, 93
Barber, A.J., 200
Barden, Stanley, 2438, 2439
Bari, M.A., 1088
Barnett, L.D., 2699
Barrett, Kenneth, 52
Barron, Sandy, 1517, 1518
Barua, S.N., 1046
Bastian, Adolf, 318
Basu, Rimli, 1927
Batcheler, Richard, 1778
Bates, A.B., 672
Bates, Paul, 239
Bates, R.F., 732
Bauer, Andrew, 2200
Bautze-Picron, Claudine, 117, 282, 1214
Bayly, Christopher, 94
Bayne, Nicholas, 673
Bechert, Heinz, 2373
Becka, Jan, 385
Becker, Reinhard, 132
Belcher, J.J., 2667
Bello, Walden, 1318, 2201
Belton, Suzanne, 1491
Benegal, R.S., 733
Benfield, Andy, 345
Benge, Geoff, 1285
Benge, Janet, 1285
Bengtsson, Jesper, 869
Berchiolly, Carmin, 140
Berg, Erika, 1519
Bergeron, R.A., 527
Berlatsky, Noah, 1089
Berlie, J.A., 1274
Bezbaruah, M.P., 2269
Bhasin, Balbir, 2270
Bhatia, R.K., 1983
Bhatia, Rajiv, 1984
Bhattacharya, A.K., 2540
Bhattacharya, Andindya, 2202
Bhattacharya, Swapna, 386, 1985
Bhattacharya, Tania, 2202
Bhattacharyya, Harihar, 1827
Bhone Tint Kyaw, 435

Bhui, Sudip, 962
Bi Bi, Noorjahan, 1170
Bickersteth, Jane, 66
Bieber, Joey, 133
Bierman, John, 674
Bigandet, P.A., 436, 1215
Bigg, P.J., 134
Bimal, Samridhi, 1976, 2299
Bin Ali, Asif, 1090
Bingham, Page, 2673
Bird, G.W., 319
Birk, Lukas, 135, 136, 137, 138, 139, 140
Birnbaum, Alfred, 2417
Bischoff, Roger, 1216, 2716
Bissinger, Jared, 2203
Bjorklund, Ruth, 870
Black, Michael, 1474
Blackburn, T.R., 437, 438, 439, 440, 441, 442, 443, 444, 445, 2541
Blank, Jonah, 2204
Bleming, T.J., 960
Blickman, Tom, 1471
Block, Lawrence, 2240
Blum, Franziska, 1684, 1779
Blurton, T.R., 284, 2606
Bo Bo Zaw, 141
Bocking, Brian, 722
Bogle, J.E., 1217
Bollepally, Sudhakshana, 1047
Bon, Olk, 1028
Bond, Brian, 515
Bose, S.C., 486
Bose, S.K., 486
Boshier, C.A., 487
Boucaud, Andre, 1456
Boucaud, Louis, 1456
Boundy, Anthony, 2674
Bourdier, Frederic, 2205
Bowen, C.G., 547
Bower, Robin, 2441
Bowers, Alexander, 446
Bowman, Vicky, 1163, 1164
Boyd, Andrew, 634
Boyd, John, 646
Brac de la Perriere, Benedicte, 95, 1218, 1309
Brackenbury, Wade, 142
Brackin, A.L., 911

Bradley, David, 1145, 1163
Bradley, John, 2635
Brancati, Emanuele, 1379
Brandon, J.J., 1685
Brandsma, David, 2442
Branfoot, Crispin, 192
Braun, Erik, 1219
Braun, Heinz, 2373
Bray, John, 1928
Breazeale, Kennon, 349
Breen, M.G., 1828, 1829
Brenner, David, 2038, 2039
Briels, Edwin, 143
Brinham, Natalie, 1113
Brockman, Andy, 488
Broman, Barry, 86, 118, 144, 145, 146, 147, 821, 1031, 1313, 1345, 2559
Brooke-Wavell, Derek, 785
Brookes, Stephen, 734
Brooten, Lisa, 1437
Broughton, M.D., 786
Brown, A.S., 600
Brown, Ian, 2206, 2333
Browne, Peter, 2443
Brunner, Jake, 2334
Bruns, A.R.H., 73, 2619
Bryant, R.L., 2335
Buchanan, John, 2040, 2041, 2207
Buddee, Kim, 148
Bugher, Matthew, 1554
Bui, Hana, 53
Bunker, Alonzo, 961
Burke, Adam, 2042
Burling, Alexis, 871
Burney, Henry, 320
Butler, John, 675
Butler, Stuart, 89
Button, Christopher, 1146
Byar Bowh Si, Oliver, 1286, 1321
Byrne, James, 2509, 2510

C

Caballero-Anthony, Mely, 1929
Caldicott, Alistair, 346
Callahan, M.P., 928, 1830, 2043
Callahan, R.A., 516
Campagnac, C.H., 676
Campagnac, R.G.A., 2044
Campagnac-Carney, S.L., 735, 2044
Campbell, Ivan, 2054
Cangi, E.C., 55
Cannon, J.W., 1831
Caouette, T.M., 1403, 1500
Carbine, J.A., 1220
Carey, Peter, 861, 1691, 1692
Carmack, Robert, 2676
Carpenter, E.A., 1322
Carpenter, J.W., 2520
Carr, Thomas, 1895
Carruthers, Bob, 548
Carson, L.H., 1288
Carstensen, Nils, 2107
Carter, Anne, 787
Carter, Nick [Canon, Jack], 2444
Casino, E.S, 1
Cassacia, Jimi, 173
Cemmell, James, 1556
Cernea, R.F., 1310
Chaichuen Khamdaengyodtai, 2419
Chaikin, R.B., 736
Chalk, Peter, 1780
Chalker, Jack, 647
Cham, M.R., 2325
Chambers, Justine, 1832, 1833
Chambers, Paul, 2301
Chan, Susan, 2677
Chan Chao, 149, 150
Chandra, Puran, 2
Chang, Wen-Chin, 1323, 1501
Chaney, E.N., 1290
Chao Tzang Yawnghwe, 788, 1694, 1695
Chapman, Alison, 2445
Chapman, Dean, 1035
Charney, M.W., 387, 447, 2311
Chase, D.Y., 1044
Chase, Jackie, 2542
Chattopadhyay, Basudeb, 448
Chaudhury, S.B.R., 1092
Chaudoir, Georges, 321
Chaw Chaw Sein, 1947
Cheesman, Nick, 1696, 1781, 1782, 1783, 1834, 1835, 2162
Chen, Fu Hua, 789
Chen, Kai, 2131
Chen, Wenhua, 1463
Chevrillon, Andre, 347

Chew, Anne-May, 1221
Chhor, Heang, 2208
Child, Kenneth, 2511
Childers, J.S., 348
Chin, Ko-lin, 1457, 1458, 1459
Chinnery, Philip, 549
Chit Win, 1833
Cho, Ara, 2591
Cho, Violet, 2519
Chong, Terence, 2064
Chopra, P.N., 56
Chopra, Prabha, 56
Chouvy, P.A., 1460
Christel, Pascal, 1222
Christensen, Russ, 1048
Chu, Winston, 790
Chua, L.J., 1324
Chung, Amy, 2678
Chung, Emily, 2678
Chuu Wai Nyein, 354
Clancy, John, 635
Clancy, Tomas, 3
Clapp, Priscilla, 1365, 1697, 1784, 1785, 1786, 1787, 1836, 2211
Clark, Carol, 209
Clarke, S.L., 929, 2045
Clayton, Dudley, 265
Clements, Alan, 1223, 1698, 1699, 1837
Clymer, Kenton, 1990
Cobden, Richard, 449
Cochrane, W.W., 994
Cockett, Richard, 388
Coe, Debbie, 2664
Coe, Randy, 2664
Coggan, Philip, 96
Cole, B.E., 1991
Cole, Frank, 2703
Coleman, Eli, 1308
Collett, Henry, 266
Collins, Robert, 57
Colmer, David, 2501
Colvin, John, 550
Combs, Daniel, 2271
Conant, Jennet, 637
Connelly, Karen, 822, 2446
Connew, Bruce, 823
Constantine, Greg, 151
Conway, Susan, 995, 1311

Cooler, R.M., 2596
Coomar, P.C., 962
Cordingly, Arthur, 2512
Corey, Daniel, 2529
Corfield, Justin, 2701
Corley, T.A.B., 2272
Corpuz, M.I., 2312
Coubrough, C.R.L., 648
Courtauld, Caroline, 58, 59, 60, 61, 62
Cox, H.C.M., 322
Cox, Hiram, 322
Cox, Lawrence, 722
Craig, Charmaine, 2447
Crain, Carolyn, 677
Crawfurd, John, 323
Cribbs, Gillian, 4
Croke, V.C., 737
Crouch, Melissa, 1275, 2153, 2164, 2165
Crow, M.J., 200
Crozier, L.A., 791
Cruickshanks, Lucy, 2448
Cull, Brian, 624
Cung Lian Hup, 1292
Cunningham, Nancy, 1167, 2401
Currie, Kelley, 1896
Cushing, J.N., 1184
Czarnecki, Amanda, 996

D

D'Hubert, Thibaut, 2350
D'Souza, Trophy, 771
Dada, Feroze, 824
Dahlberg, Keith, 2449
Dale, J.G., 1788
Damrong Rajanubhab, 349, 450
Dana, L.P., 2212
Daniel, Malcolm, 192
Danitz, Tiffany, 1438
Dapice, David, 1094
Das, Asha, 1224
Das, D.K., 1976, 2299
Das, Gurudas, 2273, 2274
Daughery, L.J., 601
Davey, Jessica, 1952
Davey, Mary, 649
David, Roman, 1838
Davidson, Toni, 2450

Davidson-Shaddox, Brenda, 63
Davies, P.N., 651
Davies, Philip, 551
Davis, Bill, 1380
Davis, Gerald, 2643
Davison, Geoffrey, 259
Davison, Peter, 2483
Daw Ena Win, 2679
Daw Khin Hnin Oo, 825
Daw Khin Khin Su, 2373
Daw Khin Thein, 1248
Daw Than Han, 1963
Daw Than Than Nu, 405
Daw Tin Tin Myint, 2373
Day, Francis, 245, 2336
De, Prabir, 2275
De Bont, Hein, 1312
De Hetrick, A.F.V., 2451
De La Cour Venning, Alicia, 1098, 1099
De Lajonquiere, Lunet, 350
De Terra, Hellmut, 283
De Thabrew, W.V., 1225
De Vosjoli, Philippe, 246
De Vries, Clare, 351
Dean, Karin, 981
Deas, Tom, 89
Decobert, Anne, 1897
DeFilipps, R.A., 268
Delang, C.O., 963, 1560
Delesgues, Lorenzo, 2200
Delisle, Guy, 2530
Dell, Elizabeth, 152, 2597
Delphin, Tin Tin, 391
Demartini, Liliana, 1361
Denaro, Jason, 2452
Denham, A.V., 2453
Denis, Gavin, 650
Desaine, Lois, 1789
Devereux, Brian, 738
Devi, T.N., 1964
Dey, Amrita, 1840
Dey, Babul, 1932
Di Crocco, V.M., 1226
Diamond, Jon, 153, 552, 553
Dibiasio, Jame, 451
Dickinson, Tony, 1432
Diebold, William, 602
Diecidue, Anthony, 2529

Dijk, W.O., 452
Dilipkumar, Sapam, 1328
DiMaggio, Suzanne, 1786, 1787
Diran, R.K., 930
Dittmer, Lowell, 1702
Dixon, Leonard, 1997
Doherty, Faith, 1563
Doja, Shehzar, 2510
Dolan, Theo, 1439
Donkers, Jan, 1703
Donnison, David, 678
Doveton, F.B., 679
Dowling, H.G., 247
Downie, Don, 603
Draguet, Michel, 1029
Drouyer, I.A., 1030
Drouyer, Rene, 1030
Drucker, Zachary, 1308
Drummond, Allan, 872
Duckett, Richard, 638
Dudley, Ronald, 739
Dudley, S.H., 1521, 2597
Duesing, J.G., 1293
Duffield, Mark, 1542
Duguid, Naomi, 2680
Dukalskis, Alexander, 1841
Dumarcay, Jacques, 2543
Dunlop, Graham, 517
Dunlop, Nic, 154
Dunlop, Richard, 639
Duroiselle, Charles, 111, 201
Durrenberger, E.P., 2337
Dutta, Abhijit, 352

E

East, E.H., 1012
Easton, D.S., 680
Eather, C.E.J., 792
Ebashi, Masahiko, 1704
Ebbighausen, Rodion, 905
Eberhardt, Nancy, 997
Eckert, Detlef, 1202
Edwardson, Morgan, 65
Efron, Shira, 2204
Egerton, Wilbraham, 392
Egreteau, Renaud, 1791, 1842, 1843, 1844, 1845, 1933, 1934, 1994
Ehlers, O.E., 324
Ehrlich, Daniel, 2620

Eimer, David, 353
Einspruch, Andrew, 5
Eliot, Joshua, 66
Elkin, Chantal, 2334
Elliott, Patricia, 793
Ellis, Beth, 681
Ellis, Jean, 740
Enriquez, C.M., 119, 538, 741, 982
Erikson, Brian, 1564
Escritt, Ewart, 651
Esderts, Hans-Joachim, 1950
Ethell, Jeff, 603
Evans, Bryn, 604
Evans, Charles, 554
Evans, E.P., 682, 683, 1294, 1296
Everarda, Ellis, 155
Ezdani, Y.V., 742

F

Fable, James, 354
Falconer, John, 156, 2544, 2545
Falla, Jonathan, 964
Falise, Thierry, 157
Fan, Hongwei, 2025
Farquarson, R.H., 555
Farr, Ellen, 268
Farrelly, Nicholas, 38, 39, 1049, 1782, 1833, 1835, 1849
Farzana, K.F., 1096
Felbab-Brown, Vanda, 2168, 2169
Felber, Ron, 1461
Fenton, James, 744
Ferdinand, Peter, 1792
Ferguson, J.M., 998
Fergusson, Bernard, 556
Ferrars, Max, 6
Ferrars, Bertha, 6
Fetherling, George, 355
Fielding-Hall, H., 2375
Findon, Angus, 605
Finger, H.W., 1227
Fink, Christina, 1326
Fink, Jella, 2598
Fischer, Edward, 518
Fitzpatrick, Gerald, 557, 558
Fleischmann, Klaus, 1705
Florento, Hector, 2312
Flotats, Roser, 2626
Foley, Matthew, 1935

Fong, Jack, 965
Foran, Tira, 2213
Forbes, Andrew, 1050
Forbes, C.J.F.S., 393
Forchhammer, Emil, 2170
Ford, Daniel, 606
Forsyth, Patrick, 356
Fortescue, J.W., 453
Foucar, E.C.V., 539
Fowells, Gavin, 684
Fowler, William, 559
Fox, Elliott, 93
Fox, J.W., 1909
Francis, C.M., 248
Francq, Philippe, 2531
Frankovic, K.A., 1793
Franks, Norman, 607, 608, 609
Fraser, B.G., 2599
Fraser, D.W., 2599
Fraser, G.M., 745
Fraser, J.O., 1185
Fraser-Lu, Sylvia, 2546, 2547, 2575, 2600, 2601
Fredholm, Michael, 2046
Freeman, J.H., 685
Freeman, Michael, 123
Freeman, N.J., 2277
Freer, A.F., 560, 2454
Froese, Deborah, 2376
Frost, Frank, 1936
Fryer, Frederic, 933
Fujita, Koichi, 2214, 2338
Fung, Wai-Ming Terry, 2047
Furnivall, J.S., 455
Futamatsu, Yoshihiko, 651

G

Gabbett, Michael, 561
Gaese, Hartmut, 100
Galache, C.S., 1097
Gallardo, Juan, 2681
Galloway, Charlotte, 1832
Ganesan, N., 1706
Gansser, Gabriella, 360
Gansser, Luca, 360
Ganz, Nicholas, 71
Garcia, Sam, 2528
Garth, Gary, 646
Gartner, Uta, 7

Gaynor, Maurice, 2455
Gear, Donald, 2548, 2549
Gear, Joan, 2548, 2549
Gearon, Liam, 873
Geary, Grattan, 456
Geok, A.C., 874
George, E.C.S., 210
Germaine, E.T., 159, 540, 686, 687
Ghosh, Amitav, 357, 2456
Ghosh, Lipi, 394, 1996
Ghosh, Parumal, 395
Ghosh, S.K., 1013
Giannini, Tyler, 1566, 1717
Gibson, R.M., 1463
Gilbert, David, 2519
Gilhodes, A., 983
Gill, Geoff, 652
Gill, Mohanna, 2682
Gilmore, Scott, 747
Gin Khan Thang, T., 1014
Godwin, Henry, 457
Goff, S. Le M., 688
Goh, Geok Yian, 458, 459
Golden, Steve, 97
Goldston, J.A., 1565
Gommans, Jos, 396
Gonzales, Jessy, 1168
Goodall, Felicity, 541
Goodden, Christian, 318, 358
Goode, F.C., 748
Goodman, Jim, 1051
Gordon, C.A., 325
Gordon, J.F., 1997
Gordon, J.W., 610
Gotoh, Masaharu, 160
Gotu, Masaru, 1517
Goudeau, Jessica, 1523
Gouger, Henry, 326
Grabowsky, Volker, 460
Graham, Gordon, 2703
Grandjean, Jean-Pierre, 1228
Grant, Colesworthy, 327
Grant, I.L., 542, 562
Gravers, Mikael, 934, 1707, 1794
Gray, James, 2377
Gray, Stephen, 1439
Gregory-Smith, Judyth, 826
Green, Alexandra, 284, 2551
Green, Penny, 1098, 1099

Greenberg, Cynthia, 2457
Greenlaw, Olga, 611
Greenough, Sarah, 192
Greenwood, Nicholas, 69, 397
Greer, Jed, 1566
Grehan, John, 543, 563
Grierson, G.A., 1147
Griffiths, M.P., 1327
Griggs, W.C., 2414
Grover, Verinder, 1708
Guillon, Emmanuel, 1008
Gumaer, Oddny, 1524
Guo, Xiaolin, 1937, 2048
Gurung, Madhu, 2378
Gutman, Pamela, 8
Gutter, P., 2171
Guzel, M.S., 1485
Gwynne-Timothy, J.R.W., 612

H

Haacke, Jurgen, 1938, 1939, 1998
Habib, Mohshin, 1100
Habiburahman, 1101
Hackett, J.L., 1256
Hadden, R.L., 2705
Haining, Peter, 636
Haksar, Nandita, 1999
Haldhar, S.M., 1229
Halford-Watkins, J.F., 211
Halili, P.R., 2325
Hall, L.G., 653
Halliday, Robert, 1009, 1010
Halton, Elaine, 461
Hamid, Naved, 2246
Hamilton, J.A.L., 564
Han, Y.M.V., 719
Hanjabam, S.S., 1328, 2000
Hanson, Ola, 984
Hantover, Jeffrey, 2458
Hantzis, S.J., 519
Hanwong, L.H., 2143
Haque, M.M., 1120
Har Si Yone, 135
Harding, Andrew, 2155
Hare, W.F., 689
Hargrave, Karen, 1102
Harkins, Benjamin, 1545
Harlow, Fergus, 1223, 1837
Harn Lay, 2532, 2533, 2534

Harriden, Jessica, 1409
Harris, Mike, 1440
Harvey, Caroline [Joanna Trollope], 2459
Hasday, J.L., 875
Haseman, John, 2049
Hasinoff, E.L., 359
Hasson, Haskia, 2576
Haupeur, J.H., 2535
Haws, Duncan, 2313
Hayami, Yoko, 966
Hayward, Susan, 1273
Hazra, K.L., 1230
Head, W.R., 1015
Heagney, Brenda, 654
Heath, David, 161
Heath, Ian, 2112
Hedley, J.D.H., 749
Heidel, Brian, 1329
Heijmans, P.J., 98
Heimburger, D.J., 2315
Heinemann, T.S., 2001
Heinold, P.A., 1942
Helfrich, P.Z., 794
Hellings, David, 690
Hemsley, W.B., 266
Henderson, Virginia, 99
Hendrickson, Dylan, 2050
Hengshoon, Harry, 520
Henley, David, 1050
Herbert, P.M., 1231, 2351, 2706
Herman, Greg, 2571
Herman, H.S., 2644
Hertz, H.F., 1186
Hibbett, Howard, 2497
Hickey, Michael, 565
Hidalgo, C.P., 795
Hiebert, Murray, 2002
Higgs, Colin, 566
Hill, Cameron, 1657
Hill, N.W., 1148
Hill, John, 567, 568
Hillier, Geoffrey, 162
Hillier, Mark, 605
Hilsman, Roger, 750
Hinchey, Jane, 9
Hinton, Elizabeth, 967
Hirono, Ryokichi, 1920
Hla Gyaw, James, 2379

Hla Ko, 2188
Hla Min, 1659, 1940
Hla Myint Swe, 1232
Hla Oo, 490, 796
Hla Shain, 1803
Hla Thamein, 2380
Hla Thein, 462
Hla Tin Htun, 2577
Hla Tun Aung, 10, 202
Ho, Juh Lee, 163
Ho, T.C., 1410
Hoey Middleton, S.E., 2665
Hoffmeister, Wilhelm, 1720
Hohmeyer, Ursula, 1795
Holland, James, 569
Holliday, Ian, 39, 1796, 1838
Holt, J.C., 1103
Hon, Ah Fah, 806
Honda, Hiromu, 2602
Hook, David, 1797
Hopkins, J.E.T., 570
Hornig, Laura, 1330
Horsey, Richard, 1631
Horstmann, Ingrid, 11
Horton, Guy, 1567
Hough, G.H., 1169
Houghton, A.T., 1295
Houtman, Gustaaf, 1709, 1710
Howard, David, 935
Howard, M.C., 2603, 2604
Howes, E.B., 2683
Hpone Thant, 946, 1052
Hsu, Douglas, 827
Htet Aung Kyaw, 828
Htike, M.T., 1965
Htoo Kyaw Win, 1781
Htun Shaung, 271
Htun Tin Htun, 1233
Htun Yee, 463
Htwe Htwe Win, 310
Huang, R.L., 1846
Hudson, Lionel, 655
Hudson-Rodd, Nancy, 1331, 1332
Hug, Felix, 96
Hughes, R.W., 211
Hughes, Robert, 2460
Huguet, J.W., 1503
Hume, Allan, 249
Humphreys, Roy, 751

Humphries, Richard, 1486
Hurlimann, Martin, 164
Hutton, J.S., 909
Huxley, Andrew, 2172

I
Ibrahim, Azeem, 1104
Idd Idd Shwe Zin, 228
Igbino, John, 571
Ikeya, Chie, 1411
Inglese, Judith, 2463
Inoue, Sayuri, 2621
Isaac, A.H., 572
Isaacs, Ralph, 2606
Isawa, Yasuho, 624
Isby, David, 613
Ishizawa, Yoshiaki, 286
Ismail, Benjamin, 1443
Ismara, Clemente, 1296
Ito, Yu, 277
Ivanoff, Jacques, 360, 1053, 2381
Iyer, L.A.N., 212
Iyer, Venkat, 1444

J
Jacob, Cecilia, 1335
Jacobson, A.S., 1445
Jackson, Jack, 2636
Jaffe, Lucy, 521
Jaffe, Sally, 521
Jagan, Larry, 1933, 1934
Jagoi, Ngathingkhui, 1034
James, Helen, 1336, 1941
James, Jamie, 229
James, R.R., 752
James, Sharon, 691
Jantori, Wutinun, 1084
Jelsma, Martin, 1464, 1465, 1466, 1471
Jenner, J.V., 247
Jenny, Mathias, 1011, 1149, 1187
Jensema, Ernestien, 1467
Jeynes, Jacqueline, 656
Jhala, A.D., 1054
Joelene, Cindy, 2290
Johnson, Amy, 876
Johnson, B.K., 829
Johnson, Pamela, 1487
Johnson, R.G., 692, 1297

Johnston, Nathalie, 135, 2573
Johnston, R.F., 361
Jolliffe, Kim, 937, 938, 941, 968, 1371, 1380, 1488, 1497, 2050, 2053, 2054
Jolliffe, Pia, 969
Jones, Lee, 1943
Jordan, C.M., 1025
Jordt, Ingrid, 1234
Joshi, K.D., 522
Josi, C.V., 1188
Jotow, Elena, 71
Jottrand, Emile, 321
Journal Kyaw Ma Ma Lay (Ma Ma Lay), 2382
Jowett, Philip, 523, 524
Judson, Adoniram, 1189

K
K, 797, 2552
Kan Nyunt Sein, 718
Kanayama, Hisahiro, 2219
Kanbawza Win, 877, 1711, 1944, 2003
Kantar, Sally, 999, 2383
Kanwar, Amar, 2353
Karim, Abdul, 1105
Karim, M.A., 1106
Karnath, Lorie, 2553
Kasai, Yasuyuki, 2461
Kasamatsu, S., 2717
Katherine (Sister), 328
Katoch, H.S., 573, 574
Katsiaficas, George, 1798
Kawanami, Hiroko, 1235, 1337
Kayalar, Jim, 165
Kean, Leslie, 1699
Keane, Fergal, 575, 859
Keay, John, 180
Keck, S.L., 491
Keeler, Ward, 1236, 1257, 1712
Keenan, Paul, 2055
Kelly Claire, 2536
Kelly, Desmond, 753
Kelly, R.G.T., 12
Kelsey-Wood, Dennis, 250
Kemp, Hans, 166
Kenmore, F.J., 2462
Khammai Dhammasami, 1237

Khan, M.A., 2175
Khan, Omar, 2668
Khanidtha Kanthavichai, 1002
Khaw Tailo, 1298
Khazeni, Arash, 329
Khet Mar, 2384
Khiangte, Laltluangliana, 1016
Khin Hnin Yu, 2385
Khin Khin Oo, 2155
Khin Khin Si, 2622
Khin Let Ya, 492, 2578
Khin Ma Ma Thwin, 251
Khin Mar Mar, 2707
Khin Maung, M.I., 910, 2220
Khin Maung Kyi, 2221
Khin Maung Nyunt, 13, 72, 116, 287, 398, 399, 1338, 1901, 2280, 2354, 2554, 2555
Khin Maung Phone Ko, 1299
Khin Maung Saw, 1107, 1108
Khin Maung Soe, 2340, 2341
Khin Maung Win, 727
Khin Maung Yee Khawsiama, 1203
Khin Mya Swe, 1195, 1196, 1197, 1198
Khin Mya Zin, 2579
Khin Myo Chit, 1339, 2556, 2557
Khin Oo, 1730
Khin Soe Kyi, 1504
Khin Swe Oo, 2386
Khin Thant Han, 2368
Khin Win, 2342
Khin Yi, 493
Khin Zaw, 200
Khin Zaw Latt, 2580
Khng, Pauline, 47
Khoo Thwe, Pascal, 830
Khun Cho, 2516
Khundrakpam, Padmabati, 2281
Khup Chin Pau, S., 1017
Khup Za Go, 1018
Kilvington, Maude, 754
Kim, Dalchoong, 2300
Kin Oung, 494, 495
Kin Thida Oung, 693, 694
King, Dedie, 2463
King, W.C., 614
King, W.L., 1238
King-Clark, Rex, 755

Kingdon-Ward, Frank, 362, 363, 364
Kinvig, Clifford, 657
Kipgen, Nehginpao, 1799, 1847, 1848
Kirby, S.W., 525
Kirichenko, Alexey, 1239
Kirkness, Bill, 615
Kirkpatrick, Robert, 1150
Kironska, Kristina, 1800
Kiryu, Minoru, 2282
Kitley, Alan, 616
Kleiner, S.M., 617
Kline, O.A., 2464
Klingenberg, Roger, 246
Knight, Si, 2213
Ko Ko, 1381
Ko Ko Thett, 865, 866, 2387, 2509
Ko Lwin, 1902
Ko Myo (Arimaddana), 288
Ko Tun Shaung, 130
Koenig, W.J., 464
Koerner, B.I., 756
Koh, Bryan, 2684
Koh Kim Seng, 1801
Kolas, Ashild, 1412
Kollner, Helmut, 73
Kono, Yasushi, 286
Koretsky, Donna, 2607
Koretsky, Elaine, 2607
Kosem, Samak, 1340
Kozlovsky, J., 618
Kraas, Frauke, 14, 74, 100, 1341
Kraft, Heinrich, 15
Kraft, M.M., 15
Krajanek, S.I., 2388
Kramer, Tom, 1038, 1041, 1464, 1465, 1466, 1468, 1469, 1470, 1471, 1802, 2056, 2207
Kratoska, P.H., 658
Kratz, E.U., 2708
Kress, W.J., 267, 268
Krishnan, M.S., 203
Kubo, Koji, 2283
Kudo, Toshihiro, 2222
Kumagai, Satoru, 2222
Kumar, Manish, 1446
Kunlabutr, Punvasa, 2608
Kuok, Lynn, 2004

Kurisaki, Kobayashi, 585
Kurisaki, Yukata, 585
Kurz, Sulpiz (Sulpice), 269
Kurzweil, Hubert, 270
Kusakabe, Kyoko, 1509
Kushnir, Ivan, 2223
Kwoh, Henry, 163
Kyaw Kyaw Hlaing, 465
Kyaw Kyaw Win, 1052
Kyaw Lat, 120
Kyaw Lwin, 1381
Kyaw Ma Ma Lay, 695
Kyaw Maung Maung Nyunt, 2389
Kyaw Myint Maung, 2645
Kyaw Nyunt Lwin, 251
Kyaw Sein, 1849
Kyaw Soe, 271
Kyaw Soe Naing, 863
Kyaw Swe, 2595
Kyaw Thu, 1447
Kyaw Win, 831, 1803
Kyaw Yin Hlaing, 1706, 1713, 1714, 1804
Kyaw Zwa Moe, 832
Kyawt Maung Maung Nyunt, 2390, 2391
Kyed, H.M., 2176, 2177
Kyi Kyi Hla, 16, 375
Kyi Kyi May, 75
Kyi Maung, 860
Kyi May Kaung, 798, 799, 1109
Kyi Pyar Chit Saw, 1805
Kyi Thein, 1961
Kyi Win Sein, Malcolm, 800, 801

L

La Bella, Laura, 878
La Forte, R.S., 659
La Ring, 1342
Lagerkvist, Johan, 1945
Lahkdhir, Linda, 1570, 1571
Lahpai Shawng Htoi, 911
Lall, Marie, 1343, 1362, 1372, 1373, 1375, 1806, 1850
Lall, Vikram, 1240
Lamb, Vanessa, 232
Lammerts, D.C., 2178
Landis, Taylor, 1132
Lang, Derek, 2646
Lang, H.J., 1525, 1526, 2037
Lanjouw, Steven, 1541
Laoutides, Costas, 1142
LaPolla, R.J., 1151
Lark, 196
Larkin, Emma, 106, 151, 179, 365, 851, 1715, 2483, 2516
Larkin, Stuart, 2224, 2225
Larrabee, Eric, 772
Lasi Bawk Naw, 230
Laskin, P.M., 2465
Lat Swan Htan, 2420
Latimer, Jon, 576
Latter, Thomas, 1190
Laube, Lydia, 366
Laurie, W.F.B., 466, 467
Law, David, 2514
Law-Yone, Wendy, 802, 2392, 2393, 2394
Lawrence, Eugene, 2466
Lazar, David, 167
Lazarus, Leo, 367
Le Roy, Patricia, 2467
Leach, E.R., 986
Leahy, Kate, 2695
Leake, J.E., 1903
Lederberger, R.A., 168
Ledgard, Edna, 2395
Ledi Sayadaw, 1241, 1242
Lee, Kin Kiong, 2251
Lee, Ronan, 1110
Lee, Tang Lay, 1505
Lefevre-Pontalis, Pierre, 330
Lehane, Leigh, 1506
Lehr, Peter, 1243
Leider, Jacques, 396
Leigh, M.D., 496, 544, 1300
Leitich, K.A., 420
Lejard, Thierry, 360
Lemere, Maggie, 1489
Len, Christopher, 1716
Lenarcik, Marek, 833
Leonard, Raymond, 2468
Leonard, T.M., 169
Leone, Faye, 1717
Levenstein, S.L., 1719
Lewin, Ronald, 757
Lewis, Damien, 842
Lewis, P.W., 2369

Lewis, S.D.W., 2666
Lewis, Su Lin, 1946
Li, Chenyang, 1720, 1947
Liang, Chi-shad, 1948
Liddell, Zunetta, 1573
Liesener, Lisa, 2359
Liljeblad, Jonathan, 1832
Lin Htet Aung, 1851
Lindsey, Tim, 2165
Ling, Bettina, 879
Ling, S.N., 1204
Lintner, Bertil, 368, 880, 881, 987, 1042, 1472, 1473, 1474, 1721, 1722, 1723, 2005, 2057, 2099
Listowel, Earl of, 696
Lisupha, 1055
Lixenberg, Dana, 2516
Lockerbie, Jeannie, 1290
Lockhart-Mure, E.J., 758
Loffler, L.G., 1056
Lokethar, 2515
Lom, Petr, 2516
Longmuir, M.V., 2284, 2285
Looker, Bob, 759
Lopes Cardozo, M.T.A., 1374
Lorenz, Jens, 7
Lovett, Anne, 2469
Loviny, Christophe, 135, 882
Lu, Nan, 170
Lu Zoe [San Lwin], 2396
Lubeigt, Guy, 319
Lubina, Michal, 883, 884
Luce, G.H., 480
Ludu U Hla, 2397
Luto, James, 577
Lutter, H.M., 2181
Luzoe, 1152
Lyall, E.E., 1949
Lycett, Andrew, 331
Lydekker, Richard, 252
Lyen, A.S., 199
Lyman, Robert, 526, 578, 579
Lyons, Keith, 76, 107, 834

M

Ma Ma Lay, 2398
Ma Ma Naing, 2623
Ma Ohmer, 184
Ma Thanegi [Thanegi], 17, 77, 78, 121, 369, 370, 695, 835, 1031, 1244, 1313, 1345, 2385, 2413, 2558, 2559, 2581, 2582, 2583, 2609, 2624, 2685, 2686, 2690
Ma Thida, 836
Ma Tin Cho Mar, 1170
Ma Tint Sein, 1346
Maber, E.J.T., 1374
Macallister, John, 2709
Macdonald, A.St.J., 2637
Macdonald, Denise, 697
Macdonald, Martin, 2100
Mace, Martin, 543, 563
MacGregor, John, 332
Mackay, James, 171
Mackenzie, K.R.H., 18
MacLachlan, Heather, 2625
MacLean, Joanna, 172, 837
MacLean, Rory, 371
MacManus, Thomas, 1098, 1099
Magnusson, Anna, 1966
Mahasi Sayadaw, 1245
Mahe de la Bourdonnais, A., 468
Mahlo, Dietrich, 2660
Mahmood, Rohana, 1950
Mains, A.A., 640
Malcolm, Donald, 2647
Malcolm, Howard, 333
Malik, Preet, 2006
Malindog, A.R., 2132
Man-kri Mahasirijajeya-su, 1246
Manieri, R.A., 2470
Manson, Ken, 2710
Manwaring, Randle, 580
Marcello, R.E., 659
Marchi, Ludovica [Balossi-Restelli, L.M.], 1967
Margesson, Rhoda, 1071
Marks, Copeland, 2687
Marsh, Tim, 1012
Marshall, Andrew, 372
Marshall, C.H.T., 249
Marshall, H.I., 970
Marston, D.P., 516, 581
Martin, Andrew, 760
Martin, Michael, 1071, 1575, 1608, 1609, 1807, 1808, 2007, 2008
Martin, Veronika, 1395

Mason, David, 2471
Mason, E.B., 1413
Mason, Francis, 1301
Mason, H.A., 527
Mason, Jana, 1547
Mason, Mark, 79
Massieu, Isabelle, 334
Mat, Bakri, 1120
Mate, Rituraj, 1527
Mathieson, D.S., 1610, 1725, 2101
Matsugi, Takashi, 1603
Matthews, Bruce, 940, 1247
Maudy, Jacques, 173
Maung, Cynthia, 1491
Maung Aung Myoe, 125, 2009, 2010, 2060, 2113, 2114, 2115, 2116
Maung Bo, Charles, 845
Maung Day, 2516, 2573
Maung Htin Aung, 2399
Maung Khine Zaw, 101
Maung Kyaa Nyo, 19
Maung Maung, 497, 698, 1726
Maung Maung Lin, 2648
Maung Maung Lwin [Sit-Tu-Yin], 2669
Maung Maung Myint, 2384
Maung Maung Ta, 1276
Maung Swe Thet, 2011
Maung Swe Tint, 2400
Maung Tha Hla, 1057, 1112
Maung Tha Noe, 1245, 2516
Maung Zarni, 1113, 1852
Mawdsley, James, 838
May, R.J., 1725, 1732
Mayer, Hansjorg, 2149
Mayerchak, P.M., 2711
Mayo, I.F., 2355
McCartan, Brian, 941
McCarthy, Gerard, 1833, 2061
McCarthy, Stephen, 1347, 1348, 1727, 1728, 1729, 1968, 1969
McClelland, Mac, 2102
McConnachie, Kirsten, 1528
McCormick, Patrick, 1011, 1200
McCoy, A.W., 1475
McCoy, Cliff, 231
McDevitt, Michael, 1949
McElhone, J.M., 1437

McElroy, Jack, 1306
McGill, Forrest, 2560
McGonagle, John, 261
McIntyre-Brown, Arabella, 2317
McKay, Melyn, 1205
McPhedran, Colin, 761
McLynn, Frank, 582
McVee, M.B., 1535
Mears, E.S., 1371
Meech, Alan, 2643, 2712
Meech-Pekarik, Julia, 1252
Mehner, Martin, 80
Meissonnier, Joel, 1460
Melloul, Jeremy, 2528
Merchant, J.T., 81
Metraux, D.A., 1730
Metro, Rosalie, 400, 2472
Mi Mi Aye, 2688
Mi Mi Kyi, 100, 1341
Middleborg, Jorn, 2584
Middleton, Carl, 232
Midwood, Jimmy, 401, 699
Mieno, Fumiharu, 2214
Migacheva, Katya, 2204
Miksic, J.N., 459
Miller, Russell, 762
Milligan, Chris, 1952
Milne, Leslie, 1000, 1058
Mimic, 2517
Min Maung Maung, 1663
Min Naing, 946
Min Sun Min, 2649
Min Thu, Z., 988
Min Wae Aung, 2585
Min Yu Wai, 1248
Min Zaw Oo, 2063
Min Zin, 1809
Minamida, M.I., 886
Minbu Aung Kyaing, 1239
Minoletti, Paul, 1382, 1415
Minye Kaungbon, 1664
Mirante, Edith, 373, 374
Mitchell, Andrew, 204
Mitchell, Derek, 1952
Mitchiner, Michael, 2661
Miyake, Marc, 1153
Mizuha, Akazu, 2517
Moe, Julien, 2401
Moe Aye, 839

Moe Lin [Pho Lay], 885
Moe Min, 174
Moe Myint, 2713
Moe Thuzar, 1907
Mohiudden, Helal, 1080
Moilanen, Irene, 2561
Mole, Robert, 700
Molloy, Sylvia, 701
Mon Mon Myat, 2402
Montesano, M.J., 2064
Mooney, Brian, 731
Moore, C.G., 2473
Moore, E.H., 289, 310, 469
Moore, Elizabeth, 112, 2149
Moore, H.C., 2474
Moreman, Tim, 583
Moremon, John, 584, 660
Morgan, Francis, 102
Mori, Takato, 528
Mornin, Edward, 2562
Mornin, Lorna, 2562
Mororama, Kohei, 585
Morris, D.G., 529
Morris, Norval, 2182
Morris, M.S., 680
Morrison, Cameron, 205
Morrison, G.E., 335
Morrison, Gary, 1084
Morrissey, Di, 2475
Morse, Gertrude, 702
Mortimer, Graham, 1541
Moser, Claus, 861
Movius, H.L., 283
Mrat Lunn Htwann, 2573
Mu Mu Aung, 277
Muecke, James, 175
Mullen, Matthew, 1349
Munier, Christophe, 2586
Munier-Gaillard, Cristophe, 1239, 1309
Murakami, Nancy, 1377
Murkett, Marvin, 253
Murphy, S.A., 2563
Mya Doung Nyo, 498
Mya Han, 1803, 1810
Mya Maung, 2226, 2227, 2228, 2229
Mya Nandar Thin, 1366
Mya Than, 1970, 2230, 2286, 2287

Mya Than Tint, 1350
Mya Win, 1665
Myanma Athan Kyaw Oo, 585
Myat Min Hlaing, 2564
Myat Thein, 2236, 2287
Myint Aung, 290, 1250, 2586
Myint Kyi, 1667, 1670
Myint Myint Kyu, 1059
Myint Myint Soe, 2689
Myint Swe, James, 2403
Myint Zan, 2356
Mylne, B.H., 586
Myo Myint, 403, 470
Myo Nyunt, 1331
Myo Thant, 2357
Myo Zaw Oo, 1830
Myoma Lwin (Myomalwin), 499, 2119

N

Nai Pan Hla, 291, 1191
Naidu, S.K., 1251
Naing Thit, 2638
Naing Ye Kyaw, 2623
Nair, Deepak, 1954
Nair, Veena, 2139
Nakaji Nay Win, 1192
Nakanishi, Yoshihiro, 500
Nam, Kee-Yung, 2325
Nan Hlaing, 292
Nan San San Aye, 2690
Nang Pann Ei Kham, 1467
Nang Zing La, 840
Naono, Atsuko, 1385
Narayanan, Usha, 2420
Naw, Angelene, 501
Naw, Angiline, 1667
Naw Ja, C.C., 982
Naw May Oo, 1386
Naw Sheera, 975
Nawrahta, 1668
Nay Myo Aung, 2343
Nay Win San, 863
Naziree, Shireen, 2587
Ndegwa, David, 1508
Nee, P.W., 24
Neiser, Birgit, 176, 182
Nelson, E.C., 273
Nemoto, Kei, 587, 886

Nesbit, R.C., 588
Newland, A.G.E., 471
Newland, Jean, 661
Ni Ni Myint, 404, 1416
Nichols, Alan, 1302, 2426
Nichols, J.P., 2289
Nicolle, Francine, 2381
Nijhuis, Minka, 1703
Nijman, Vincent, 255, 256
Niksch, L.A., 2012
Ninh, K.N.B., 1797
Nixon, Hamish, 1812, 2290
Noack, Georg, 1357
Noah, 887
Noetling [Notling], Fritz, 206
Nolan, Stephen, 1172
Noonan, William, 589
Novak, Tibor, 2610
Nu Nu Yi, 2405
Nugent, Nicholas, 75
Nugent-Smith, Jerome, 2476, 2477
Nunneley, John, 530, 590
Nurhasim, Moch., 2237
Nyan Htun, 278, 279
Nyan Thin, 214
Nyan Tin, 274
Nyein Han, 1563
Nyein Set Lin, 2344
Nyein, Sonny, 2582
Nyi Nyi Kyaw, 1206, 1207
Nyi Nyi Lwin, 1172
Nyunt, Peter, 1246, 2714

O

O'Brien, Alex, 2478
O'Brien, Harriet, 803
O'Brien, Terence, 641
O'Connor, V.C.S., 113, 215, 336
O'Doherty, Mark, 1853, 1872
O'Hara, Randolph, 804, 2479, 2480, 2481, 2482
O'Kane, Mary, 1418
O'Kane, Michael, 2292
O'Keefe, Sherry, 888
O'Shannassy, Teresa, 1419
Odaka, Konosuke, 2238
Oertel, F.O., 337
Oh, Su-Ann, 25, 1855, 2139, 2240
Ohnmar Nyunt, 1449

Oishi, Mikio, 889
Oka, Manuel, 93
Okamoto, Ikuko, 2214, 2241, 2338
Okell, John, 1173, 1193, 1194, 1195, 1196, 1197, 1198
Okudaira, Ryuji, 2186
Oldham, R.D., 2715
Olinga-Shannon, Stephanie, 975, 1049
Olszewski, Peter, 841
On Kin, 1813
Onishi, Shingo, 234
Oolay, [M.C. Poole], 2518
Orwell, George [Eric Blair], 703, 2483
Othman, Zarina, 1120
Ott, M.C., 2069
Otto, Silke-Susann, 2243
Ounsted, Rosie, 263
Ousaka, Y., 2717
Overland, Indra, 1863
Owens, D.C., 2611
Oye, Mari, 2260
Ozhegov, S.S., 2561

P

P-B, E.M., 704
Pack, M.E., 1500
Pagan U Khin Maung Gyi, 2293
Pal, Pratapaditya, 1252
Pandora, 2516
Pann Hmone Wai, 2579
Paragu, 375
Parenteau, John, 890
Parker, E.H., 2013
Parkes, Meg, 652
Parkitny, J.U., 177
Paske, C.T., 705
Pattaratorn Chirapravati, M.L., 2560
Patton, T.N., 1253
Pavin Chachavalpongpun, 1856, 1907, 2014
Paw Family, 1179
Paw Oo Thet, 2557
Paxman, Jeremy, 703
Pe Kin, 502
Pe Maung Tin, 480
Pearson, Michael, 591, 619

Pearson, Ruth, 1509
Pedersen, Daniel, 971
Pedersen, M.B., 1731, 1732, 1955, 1966
Pederson, Rena, 891
Peek, I.D., 763
Pekin Pyan Win Ko, 2638
Peng, Nian, 2015
Percival, Bob, 103
Perhult, Malin, 2107
Perkins, Mitali, 2484
Perry, P.J., 2244
Peters, Anne, 2373
Phan, Zoya, 842
Phayre, A.P., 472
Phillips, Barnaby, 764
Pho Shoke, 1477
Phone Kyaw, 126
Pichard, Pierre, 26, 293, 294, 295, 296, 297, 298, 299, 300, 301
Pickford, S.C., 765
Pickrem, Paul, 843
Pim Koetsawang, 1510
Poa, Dory, 1151
Polillo, Roberto, 178
Polkinghorne, Morrison, 2676
Pollock, F.T., 2639, 2640
Poncar, Jaroslav, 179, 180
Poole, Matt, 615
Popham, Peter, 892, 893
Powell, M.D., 2016
Prabhakar, C.P., 2406
Pradhan, M.V., 405
Pradhan, S.K., 2017
Prajak Kongkirati, 2064
Prakai Nonthawasi, 1001
Prasse-Freeman, Elliott, 1856
Pratt, H.S., 2612
Preecharushh, Dulyapak, 127
Prefer, N.N., 592
Premjai Vungsiriphisal, 1921
Preston-Hough, Peter, 620
Price, E.H., 2485
Pritchard, Ashley, 956
Pritchard, Bill, 1359
Proud, E.B., 2652
Pruitt, W., 2407, 2716, 2717
Pu Loi Hom, 2408
Puangsuwan, Yeshua, 1681
Pum Khan Pau, 1019
Pun, Angela, 2369
Purkayastha, R.K., 2273
Puusaag, Kamile, 2245
Pyone Mjinzu Lwin, 1387

R

Rabinowitz, Alan, 237, 238
Racey, Andrew, 207
Raghavan, V.R., 2071
Raha, M.K., 962
Rahman, R.R., 2409
Rajah, Ananda, 972
Rajkumar, Brajananda, 1588
Rajshekar, 503
Raju, P.K., 1961
Rameshchandra, Ningthoujam, 1328
Rana, P.B., 2246
Ranard, Andrew, 2589
Randle, John, 593
Ranjan, Vikash, 1983
Rao, V.K., 2590
Raschid, B.M., 805
Rasor, E.L., 2718
Rastorfer, Jean-Marc, 1040, 2326, 2719
Rato, Montira, 1002
Rawson, Philip, 2565
Ray, Niharranjan, 1254, 1255, 1314
Ray, Valeria, 2691
Ray Chaudhury, A.B., 2018
Raychaudhuri, Ajitava, 2275
Rebac, Zoran, 2641
Redding, Tony, 594
Reece, Andrea, 1101
Reeman, Douglas, 2486
Regan, Lilith, 864
Reiss, S.W., 746
Renard, R.D., 1478
Renaut, Thomas, 95
Renfrow, J.A., 527
Renner, Zsuzsanna, 2610
Rhoden, T.F., 104, 1175, 1199, 1534
Rhoden, T.L.S., 1534
Richards, Rowley, 766
Richell, J.L., 473
Richmond, Simon, 83
Richter, Jill, 2487

Ridd, M.F., 207
Rieffel, Lex, 1734, 1909, 2249
Rigby, Jennifer, 1421
Ripley, H.J., 1301
Ritter, J.T., 531
Rizvi, S.H.M., 1020
Robert, Claudia Saw Lwin, 2692
Roberts, Christopher, 1974
Roberts, J.L., 1060
Robertson, Joan, 706
Robertson, P.S., 1511
Robinette, M.A., 844
Robinne, Francois, 26, 989, 1845
Robinson, H.R., 707
Rodger, Ellen, 1124, 1125
Rodrigues, Yves, 2626
Rogers, Benedict, 845, 846, 973, 1814
Rollason, Russell, 1914
Romeo, Nicoletta, 1155
Roof, Lisa, 1535
Rooney, David, 767, 768
Rooney, D.F., 2358, 2602
Rooney, Sarah, 105
Rooth, Mike, 2536
Rorke, Grace, 708
Rose, Simon, 894
Rotberg, R.I., 1735
Rotkin, K.A., 1857
Roux, Emile, 338
Roy, Shibani, 1020
Roycee, A.T., 1956
Royle, Trevor, 709
Rozenburg, Guillaume, 1218, 1256, 1257
Rudland, Emily, 1732
Rush, Elizabeth, 106
Russel, D.R., 1068
Russell, Oliver, 1038
Russell, Rosalind, 847
Rustam, M.S., 806
Ryley, J.H., 474

S

Sabido, E.H., 57
Sacquety, T.J., 642
Sadan, Mandy, 989, 990, 991, 2720
Saddiqui, Habib, 1126
Saha, Jonathan, 475
Saha, S.R., 1915
Sai Aung Tun, 1003
Sai Kam Mong, 1004, 2415
Sai Kham Mong, 1061
Sai Seng Sai, 2295
Sai Wai Lwin Moe, 2410
Sai Wansai, 1858
Saibaba, V.V.S., 1258
Saikia, Pahi, 2018
Saitner, Gerard, 28
Saito, Teruko, 2251
Sakhong, L.H., 947, 1021, 1022, 1695
Sakhong, Run Pen, 1736
Sakhuja, Vijay, 1983
Salerno, Carin, 1422
Samaddar, Ranabir, 1092
Samaranayake, J.F., 710
Samuels, S.K., 216, 2488
San C. Po, 974
San Lin Tun, 107, 2411, 2638
San San Hnin Tun, 1187, 1200
San San Khine, 1923
San San Tin, 851
San Shwe Baw, 2412
San Thein, 2345
San Yein, 1670
Sanchez-Cacicedo, Amaia, 1975
Sanda Khin, 122
Sandamuni, U., 1156
Sann Kyaw, 1048
Sansome, R.S., 621
Santoro, David, 2073
Sao Htun Hmat Win, 1259
Sao Khemawadee Mangrai, 711
Sao Sanda, 807
Sao Saimong Mangrai, 482
Saraya, Dhida, 114
Sareen, T.R., 662
Sargent, Inge, 808
Sarosi, Diana, 1681
Satoko, Hiwa, 2520
Saul, J.D., 1032
Saw Lwin, 270
Saw Maung Doe, 1303
Saw Myat Sandy [Sandy Minsat], 1737
Saw Myat Yin, 29, 84
Saw Ralph, 975

Saw Tun, 1195, 1196, 1197, 1198
Sayar Mya (MOFA) [Mya Tun], 895, 1859
Scalea, N.S., 181
Scherman, Christine, 182, 2566
Scherman, Lucian, 2566
Schink, Hans-Christian, 183
Schneebaum, S.M., 1738
Schober, Juliane, 1260
Schram-Evans, Zoe, 376
Schrank, Delphine, 1815
Schwertner, S.M., 2721
Scott, J.G. [Shway Yoe], 85
Sechler, R.P., 2328
Seekins, D.M., 30, 406, 1368, 1739, 2019
Sein Htay, 1332
Sein Myo Myint, 184
Sein Tu, 254
Sell, Julie, 31
Selth, Andrew, 32, 33, 34, 407, 408, 409, 505, 506, 896, 1127, 1279, 1860, 1861, 2020, 2021, 2022, 2023, 2074, 2075, 2076, 2077, 2078, 2079, 2080, 2081, 2082, 2083, 2084, 2085, 2120, 2121, 2122, 2123, 2124, 2125, 2126, 2127, 2128, 2140, 2145, 2146, 2149, 2150, 2723, 2724
Semwal, D.K., 275
Sen, B.K., 2171
Sendker, Jan-Philipp, 2359, 2489, 2490
Seng Aung Sein Myint, 929
Sengupta, Nilanjana, 1423
Shah, Sudha, 507
Shanle, Leland, 2491
Shannon, Richard, 2521
Sharma, Prem, 2492, 2493
Sharp, Gene, 1740
Sharpe, Philip, 769
Sharples, Rachel, 1493
Shaw, J.C., 2613
Shaw, Scott, 185, 186
Shaw Zan, 1128
Shephard, Alastair, 595
Shepherd, C.R., 255, 256
Shepherd, Elizabeth, 2522
Sherman, Patrice, 897
Shimazu, Noriki, 2602
Shippen, Mick, 36
Shirr, Ohnmar, 2693
Shores, C.F., 623, 624
Shortell, Paul, 2200
Shrestha, H.L., 2024
Shway Yoe [J.G. Scott], 37
Shwe Lu Maung, 898, 1129, 1130, 1262, 1280, 1741
Shwe Shwe Sein Latt, 1425
Shwe Sin Aye, 2591
Shwe Zan, 128
Si Si Hla Bu, 239
Sidasathian, Chutima, 1131
Silverstein, Josef, 508, 1742, 1743
Sim, H.C.M., 2296
Simion, Kristina, 2187
Simpson, Adam, 38, 39, 240
Sims, Matt, 377
Sinclair, W.B., 532
Singer, N.F., 108, 187, 476, 477, 2627, 2628
Singer, Peter, 2653
Singh, Balwant, 509
Singh, K.B.N., 510
Singh, K.S., 909
Singh, L.S., 1744
Singh, M.P., 1957
Singh, N.B., 2274
Singh, T.H., 2086
Singh, T.S., 511
Skaggs, Jeremy, 2634
Skidmore, Monique, 40, 1696, 1745, 1746, 1747, 1783
Slater, Guy, 2523
Slater, R.L., 1263
Sloggett, Diane, 712
Smith, Colin, 674
Smith, J.S.F., 478
Smith, Martin, 948, 949, 950, 975, 1038, 1388, 1450, 1591, 1748, 2104
Smith, Matthew, 1132
Smith, Roland, 2494
Smith, Vivienne, 257
Smithies, Michael, 2543
Smyth, David, 2360
Snodgrass, J.J., 713
So-Hartmann, Helga, 1201

Soans, Aaron, 2253, 2297
Sochaczewski, P.S., 41
Soe, Meiji, 2567
Soe Lynn Htwe, 1451
Soe Marlar Lwin, 2361
Soe Myint, 1749
Soe Saing, 1916
Soe Thane, 1862
Soe Thuzar Myint, 479
Solnit, David, 1157
Solomon, Charmaine, 2694
Somkiart Lopetcharat, 1264
Song, James, 2654
Soni, Sujata, 1265
South, Ashley, 951, 1361, 1362, 1375, 1488, 1495, 1496, 1497, 1750, 1816, 1817, 2105, 2106, 2107
Spaight, Tracy, 488
Spain, Jack, 313
Spencer, Lynette, 714, 2416
Spill, G.H., 770
Spill, Nick, 770
Spiro, Melford, 693
Spohner, Regine, 14, 74
Sprague, Sydney, 1315
Spurlock, Michael, 1537
Stadelbauer, Jorg, 74
Stadtner, D.M., 123, 1208, 1309, 2575, 2592
Stahr, Erica, 1512
Stanaway, John, 625
Stanford, M.P., 538
Stanley, Les, 378
Stanley, Tracy, 378
Stargardt, Janice, 303, 304, 1266
Stasinopoulou, Dimitra, 188
Stein, P.T., 2087
Stein, Wolfgang, 2566
Steinberg, D.I., 42, 1751, 1752, 1753, 1754, 1755, 1756, 1818, 1949, 2025, 2088, 2254, 2723
Steinemann, Gabriela, 2141
Stepan, Alfred, 952
Stephenson, Charles, 771
Sterken, R.E., 848
Stevens, Jake, 2188
Stevens, S.W., 715
Stevenson, John, 86

Stewart, J.A., 2629
Stewart, Lucas, 2362, 2417
Stewart, Whitney, 899
Stibbe, P.G., 663
Stilwell, J.W., 772
Stirn, Aglaja, 1033
Stokke, Kristian, 1863
Stokle, Tony, 1538
Stothard, Debbie, 1962
Strachan, Paul, 87, 124, 379, 380, 2329, 2626
Strait, C.U., 1023
Strait, F.T., 2495
Strefford, Patrick, 1856
Street, Robert, 773
Streissguth, Thomas, 208
Streit, Cornelius, 2089
Strettell, G.W., 276
Stromberg, B.E., 2026
Stuart, A.W., 716
Stuart, John, 411
Stulberg, Scott, 189
Su Mon Thant, 1864
Su Mon Thazin Aung, 1865
Suantak, Joseph, 1024
Suantak, Paoneikhai, 1014
Sudo, Sueo, 1603
Suga, Hiroshi, 190
Sulistiyanto, Priyambudi, 2255
Sumitr Pitiphat, 2614
Sun Thit Aung, 465
Sunait Chutintaranond, 479, 2027
Supang Chantavanich, 1540, 1545
Suragamika, 2418
Sureeporn Punpuing, 1503
Sutcliffe, D.H., 626
Suthep Kritsanavarin, 1084
Swain, Anna, 191
Swan Tha Khin, 1777
Swazo, N.K., 1133
Sweeney, John, 2496
Swift, J.W., 717
Symes, William, 339
Symns, J.M., 2524
Syrota, Timothy, 381

T

Tachikawa, Kyoichi, 515
Tagliocozzo, Eric, 1323

Tainturier, Francois, 115
Takano, Hideyuki, 1479
Takeda, Makiko, 1368, 1428
Takeyama, Michio, 2497
Talbot, George, 258
Talbott, Kirk, 2334
Tamayama, Kazuo, 542, 590, 664
Tan, Amy, 2498
Tan, Desmond, 2695
Tan, J.L.H., 2230
Tan, Teck Meng, 2298
Tan, Terence, 306
Tanabe, Hasio, 585
Tanaka, Nobuyuki, 277
Tanaka, Norio, 277
Tanaka, Yoshitaka, 278, 279, 280
Taneja, Nisha, 1976, 2299
Tannenbaum, Nicola, 1005, 2337
Tanner, D.A., 774
Tanner, R.E.S., 774
Taranov, Andrey, 1177, 1178
Tarling, Nicholas, 320
Tate, William, 665
Taw Sein Ko, 307
Tay, S.S.C., 2258
Taylor, R.H., 173, 809, 810, 953, 1714, 1757, 1758, 1820, 1866
Taylor, Roger, 192
Tea, Billy, 2028, 2029
Team, Ben, 253
Teasdale, Malcolm, 1209
Teich, Anne, 1267
Tekkatho Sein Tin, 718
Tekkatho Maung Thu Hlaing, 2630
Temple, R.C., 1316
Ten Veen, R.C., 1281
Tenberg, Esther, 45
Terwiel, B.J., 2419
Tet Soe, 126
Tett, David, 2657
Thaing Htun, 2189
Than Nyun, 2300
Than Htay, 199
Than Htun (Dedaye), 2615, 2662
Than Htun (Shwebo), 2568
Than Than Win, 2382
Than Tun, 43, 129, 282, 308, 413, 414, 1268, 2027, 2593
Than Win, 309

Thanegi [Ma Thanegi], 126
Thanoe, 2574
Thant Myint U, 415, 416, 1867, 1959
Thant Thaw Kaung, 106
Tharapi Than, 1429
Thaung, 811
Thaw Kaung, 88, 417, 418, 2363
Thawnghmung, A.M., 954, 976, 977, 1759, 2259
Thein Hlaing, 1269, 1803, 1810
Thein Nyunt, Peter, 1305
Thein Pe Myint, 2421
Thein Swe, 2301
Thein Win, 310
Theippan Maung Wa [Sein Tin], 775
Themelis, Ted, 218, 219
Thet Aung Lynn, 2260
Thet Tun, 419, 812, 2422
Thet Zaw Naing, 259
Thi Thi Aye, 2405
Thirault, Philippe, 2537
Thitiwut Boonyawongwiwat, 1006
Thom, W.S., 2640
Thomann, Th.H., 2594
Thomas, Andrew, 627
Thomas, C.J., 2274
Thomas, Craig, 2499
Thomas, G.J., 643
Thomas, Gavin, 89
Thomas, William, 900
Thompson, Julian, 534
Thorell, Tord, 260
Thorn, Philip, 2642
Thornton, Phil, 955
Thu Ra Myint Maung, 44
Thura Aung, 2147
Thura U Shwe Mann, 1868
Thuzar Winn, 1202
Timmons, W.V., 2500
Tin, 483
Tin Cho Chaw, 2696
Tin Hlaing, 585
Tin Htut Oo, 2346
Tin Maung, 2344
Tin Maung Aye, 813
Tin Maung Maung Than, 1714, 1765, 2261, 2262

Tin Maung Than, 1797
Tin Myaing Thein, 2616
Tin Myo Ngwe, 271
Tin Naing Win, 2725
Tin Tin Aye, 1306
Tin Tin Yee, 278, 279, 280
Tin U, 860
Tin Yee, 1043
Tinsa Maw-Naing, 719
Tinsley, Terence, 776
Tinzar Lwyn, 1430
Tips, W.E.J., 164, 318, 321, 324, 330, 332, 334, 338, 347, 468, 2566, 2594
Titcomb, J.H., 720
Tiwari, A.K., 1961
Tizard, Robert, 259
Todd, Ann, 644
Todd, David, 1597
Toe Zaw Latt, 1766
Tomar, Ravi, 1767
Tooze, G.H., 721
Topich, W.J., 420
Toru, Ohno, 2569, 2570
Tower, Jason, 1365
Towill, Bill, 596
Tran, Jason, 2634
Trivedi, Sonu, 1822, 1869
Trotier, Friederike, 1684
Troughton, Joanna, 2423
Tucker, Mike, 978
Tucker, Shelby, 512, 849
Tun, Frankie, 865, 866
Tun Aung Chain, 422, 423, 424, 1269, 2379
Tun Shwe Khine, 130, 1270
Tun Thwin, 1431
Tun Tin, Frankie, 193
Tun Tin, J.K., 814
Turnell, Sean, 2303, 2304, 2305, 2306, 2307, 2308
Turner, Alicia, 722, 1218, 1271
Turton, Andrew, 460
Tyn Myint-U, 2264

U
U Sein, 1248
U Thaung, 1381
U Wa Thone, 2397

Uddin, Nasir, 1141
Ullathorne, Feraya, 850
Umezaki, So, 2222
Underbrink, Robert, 628
Upfill, M.S.D., 724
Urbano, Mia, 1432

V
Vakulchuk, Roman, 1863
Valentine, W.H., 2663
Van Breugel, Seino, 1180
Van de Paverd, P.J., 1703
Van Ham, Peter, 1033
Van Hamme, Jean, 2531
Van Loon, Karel, 2501
Van Schendel, Willem, 2265
Van Tibes, Ken, 382
Vater, Tom, 166
Vaughn, Bruce, 1071
Vaughn, Dennis, 2502
Vella, Carolyn, 261
Venkiteswaran, Gayathry, 1437
Verlander, Harry, 777
Vervest, Pietje, 1465, 1466
Vervest, Wim, 1025
Vickery, Alison, 2309
Victor, Barbara, 901
Visser, L.J., 992
Von Hauff, Michael, 2266
Voss, Peter, 194
Vroman, B.F., 2503

W
Wade, Francis, 162, 1211
Wagner, Alex, 1513
Wagner, John, 2538
Wai Wai Myaing, 725, 815
Wai, Wing-Kun Henry, 2347
Wakeman, Carolyn, 851
Walaiporn Tantikanangkul, 956
Walker, Andrew, 425
Walsh, Stephen, 523
Walton, M.J., 1272, 1273
Wan, Tiffany, 2686
Ware, Anthony, 1142, 1910
Warner, Jeffrey, 195
Warren, Alan, 535
Warren, Richard, 2658
Warwick, N.W.M., 629

Watanabe, Chika, 1925
Watkins, Gary, 1391
Watkins, Justin, 1158, 1159, 1181
Watkins, R.A., 630
Watson, Nigel, 2330
Wax, Andrew, 597
Webb, M.J., 2610
Webb, Paul, 426, 1498
Webster, Donovan, 536
Webster, Tim, 99
Weerwag, Nola, 1623
Welch, Larry, 852
Weller, Marc, 1770
Welman, Frans, 1034
Wells, Tamas, 1873
Welsh, Bridget, 1870
Wessendorf, Larah, 513
West, Zoe, 1489
Western, Mike, 2538
Wheeler, J.T., 340
White, Lyn, 2372
White, Theodore, 772
Whitehead, John, 726
Whiting, Charles [Leo Kessler], 2504
Wiggins, Marianne, 2505
Wijeyewardene, Gehan, 455
Wilasinee, Sittisomboon, 2030
Wiles, Ellen, 2364
Wiliarty, Kevin, 2359, 2489, 2490
Wilkins, Robert, 2665
Wilkinson, W.R.T., 2617
Willaschek, Wolfgang, 11
Willat, Felice, 196
Williams, Gavin, 305
Williams, H.E., 2525
Williamson, M.C., 2631
Willis, Michael, 1266
Willis, R.J., 2571
Wilson, Trevor, 853, 1696, 1746, 1747, 1771, 1782, 1783
Win, Junior, 727
Win Aung, 1392
Win Ko Ko, 262
Win Maung, 262, 1331
Win May, 1435
Win Min, 1775
Win Naing Oo, 1624, 1625
Win Pe, 91, 2149

Win Tint, 2726, 2727
Win Win May, 2147
Windon, Deanna, 728
Windsor, Neville, 729
Winter, Michael, 1366
Winterberger, Georg, 45
Winterfield, Bettina, 28
Winther, Barbara, 2526
Wintle, Justin, 902
Winward, John, 1823
Wolleng, Angelee, 1063
Wong, Kenneth, 816, 1182, 2516
Wong, Yvonne, 2310
Woodier, J.R., 1871
Woods, Joseph, 2527
Woods, K.M., 2267
Woods, Kevin, 1470, 2207
Woods, Philip, 545
Woodard, C.G., 2031
Wray, M.R., 2506
Wright, Arnold, 46
Wright, Ashley, 1482
Wrisley, Betsy, 1179
Wunna Kyaw Tin, 957, 958, 2595
Wunna Kyaw Tin Dr Myint Swe, 778
Wurlitzer, Rudolph, 383
Wyler, L.S., 1367

Y

Y'Blood, W.T., 537
Yamahata, Chosein, 1368, 1603
Yan Nan Aye, 1680
Yang, Bo, 2425
Yang, Li, 817
Yates, Timothy, 1307
Yavorskyy, V.Y., 220
Yawnghwe, Samara, 1007
Ye Dway, 2632, 2633
Ye Htut, 1824
Yee, Jaffee, 197
Yegar, Moshe, 1283
Yerande, V.L., 903
Yhome, K., 1772
Yi, Li, 1064
Yin Yin Kyi, 268
Yip, Dora, 47
Young, E.M., 598, 599, 632
Young, Gordon, 2507

Young, H.M., 1044
Young, J.L., 2451
Young, M.G., 2670
Younghusband, G.J., 341, 342
Ytzen, Flemming, 1794
Yu, Defen, 1160
Yu, J.J., 2424
Yun Sun, 2032, 2033
Yunus, Mohammed, 427
Yusuf, C.F., 1284

Z

Zabra Yu Siwa, 929
Zack, Michele, 1065
Zafari, N.M.K., 1183
Zahler, Diane, 48
Zai Chi Oo, 1823
Zakreski, Ron, 854
Zali Win, 1813
Zan, Saw Spencer, 818
Zarny Tun, 778
Zaw Gyi, 2426
Zaw Min Htut, 1144
Zaw Min Yu, 8
Zaw Oo, 1773, 1774, 1775
Zaw Tun, 2516
Zeiger, Stacy, 904
Zeyar Lynn, 2516
Zhang, S.X., 1458, 1459
Zhu, Xianghui, 1947
Zin Mar Than, 243
Zollner, Hans-Bernd, 514, 865, 866, 905, 1684, 1776, 2365, 2366, 2367
Zuo, D.L., 263
Zwillinger, Steven, 2659

About the Author

Andrew Selth is an Adjunct Professor at the Griffith Asia Institute, Griffith University, in Brisbane, Australia. He has been studying international security issues and Asian affairs for more than forty-five years, as a diplomat, strategic intelligence analyst and research scholar. Between 1974 and 1986 he was assigned to the Australian missions in Rangoon, Seoul and Wellington, and later held senior positions in both the Defence Intelligence Organisation and Office of National Assessments. He has been an Adjunct Associate Professor in the Coral Bell School of Asia Pacific Affairs at the Australian National University (ANU), a Visiting Fellow at the ANU's Strategic and Defence Studies Centre, a Chevening Scholar at St Antony's College, Oxford University, an Australian Research Council Fellow at Griffith University and a Harold White Fellow at the National Library of Australia. Dr Selth has published ten books, twenty-five research papers and more than fifty other peer-reviewed works, most of them about Myanmar (Burma) and related subjects. He has also contributed to the public debate on Myanmar through numerous articles, commentaries and reviews in magazines, newspapers and online fora.

Books by the Author

1986 *The Terrorist Threat to Diplomacy: An Australian Perspective*
1988 *Against Every Human Law: The Terrorist Threat to Diplomacy*
1996 *Transforming the Tatmadaw: The Burmese Armed Forces since 1988*
2002 *Burma's Armed Forces: Power without Glory*
2012 *Burma (Myanmar) since the 1988 Uprising: A Select Bibliography*

2015 *Burma (Myanmar) since the 1988 Uprising: A Select Bibliography* (2nd edition)
2017 *Burma, Kipling and Western Music: The Riff from Mandalay*
2018 *Burma (Myanmar) since the 1988 Uprising: A Select Bibliography* (3rd edition)
2019 *Secrets and Power in Myanmar: Intelligence and the Fall of General Khin Nyunt*
2020 *Interpreting Myanmar: A Decade of Analysis*

www.ingramcontent.com/pod-product-compliance
Lightning Source LLC
Chambersburg PA
CBHW071228290426
44108CB00013B/1323